MW00817672

THE AGE OF INSURRECTION

ALSO BY DAVID NEIWERT

Red Pill, Blue Pill:
How to Counteract the Conspiracy Theories That Are Killing Us

Alt-America:
The Rise of the Radical Right in the Age of Trump

Of Orcas and Men:
What Killer Whales Can Teach Us

And Hell Followed With Her:
Crossing the Dark Side of the American Border

Over the Cliff:
How Obama's Election Drove the American Right Insane (with John Amato)

The Eliminationists:
How Hate Talk Radicalized the American Right

Strawberry Days:
How Internment Destroyed a Japanese American Community

Death on the Fourth of July:
The Story of a Killing, a Trial, and Hate Crimes in America

In God's Country:
The Patriot Movement and the Pacific Northwest

THE AGE OF INSURRECTION

THE RADICAL RIGHT'S ASSAULT
ON AMERICAN DEMOCRACY

DAVID NEIWERT

MELVILLE HOUSE
BROOKLYN • LONDON

The Age of Insurrection: The Radical Right's Assault on American Democracy

First published in 2023 by Melville House
Copyright © David Neiwert, 2022
All rights reserved
First Melville House Printing: April 2023

Melville House Publishing
46 John Street
Brooklyn, NY 11201
and
Melville House UK
Suite 2000
16/18 Woodford Road
London E7 0HA

mhpbooks.com
@melvillehouse

ISBN: 978-1-68589-036-0
ISBN: 978-1-68589-037-7 (eBook)

Library of Congress Control Number: 2023933288

Designed by Patrice Sheridan

Printed in the United States of America
1 3 5 7 9 10 8 6 4 2

A catalog record for this book is available from the Library of Congress

Contents

THE AGE OF
INSURRECTION

PREFACE

The Road to Sedition

ON JANUARY 10, 49 B.C.E., Gaius Julius Caesar, then governor of Cisalpine Gaul but on the cusp of being stripped of all power, ordered one of his legions to cross the Rubicon River, explicitly in defiance of the Roman Senate, which had ordered him to disband his army, which by law was not permitted within the borders of the Roman Republic. His action set off four years of civil war in Italy, culminating with the demise of the republic as Caesar assumed complete dictatorial control of the empire.

On January 6, 2021, Donald Trump—on the verge of being officially unseated from the presidency—heeded the urgings of his most rabid supporters and crossed his own Rubicon. Speaking that day to a crowd of tens of thousands of supporters who had turned out to "Stop the Steal" of the 2020 presidential election, he falsely claimed that he had been cheated out of the presidency and urged them to march to the Capitol to protest the outcome.[1]

Now, it is up to Congress to confront this egregious assault on our democracy. And after this, we're going to walk down, and I'll be there with you, we're going to walk down, we're going to walk down . . .

Because you'll never take back our country with weakness. You have to show strength and you have to be strong. We have come to demand that Congress do the right thing and only count the electors who have been lawfully slated, lawfully slated.

I know that everyone here will soon be marching over to the Capitol building to peacefully and patriotically make your voices heard.

As he said these words, people in the crowd could be heard shouting: "Storm the Capitol!" "Invade the Capitol building!" "Let's take the Capitol!" "Let's take it!" "Take the Capitol!"

As Trump wrapped things up, he concluded:

And we fight. We fight like hell. And if you don't fight like hell, you're not going to have a country anymore.

So we're going to, we're going to walk down Pennsylvania Avenue. I love Pennsylvania Avenue. And we're going to the Capitol, and we're going to try and give.

The Democrats are hopeless—they never vote for anything. Not even one vote. But we're going to try and give our Republicans, the weak ones because the strong ones don't need any of our help. We're going to try and give them the kind of pride and boldness that they need to take back our country.

So let's walk down Pennsylvania Avenue.

Many of his supporters, in fact, were already at the Capitol at that moment, tussling with Capitol Police at the barricades. Thousands more surged in that direction. Trump, despite saying he would, did not join the march.

He tried. As he entered the presidential limousine, he told his Secret Service detail to take him to the Capitol. (He later told *The Washington Post* he tried to go there: "Secret Service said I couldn't go. I would have gone there in a minute.")[2] The agents refused, saying the security risk was too great. According to several witnesses, he attempted to take control of the steering wheel. In the end, he conceded to his security detail, retreating to the White House and watching the drama unfold from there.

Like Caesar or any other commanding general, he knew they would follow his orders, even if that part about being "peaceful" slipped their minds. As it did.

———————

THE MOB THAT DONALD Trump unleashed that day was not, as its Republican apologists would later claim, simply an aggregation of angry conservatives who "got out of hand" while protesting his defeat in the 2020 election. The siege of the Capitol had been carefully planned, orchestrated by paramilitary claques who spearheaded the attack, and supported by an army of true believers of various stripes: conspiracy theorists, Christian nationalists, and far-right street brawlers. Trump's MAGA army.

The January 6 insurrection was an attack on the hallmark of American democracy: the peaceful transfer of power. No American president in the nation's history had refused to acknowledge and participate in this tradition, which is often credited with being the foundation of the stability of its core democratic institution—namely, elections, the final reckoning of the public will. Well before the 2020 election, Trump had made his contempt for this institution plain, and after he lost, he made it manifest by claiming without any evidence he had been cheated, cultivating an army of people ready to use violence to prevent his dethronement and then marshalling them into an attack on Congress, eagerly crossing the Rubicon on his behalf.

Preventing the certification of the Electoral College votes, however, was only the temporal objective of Trump's army. In a larger sense, the insurrection's intent was to overthrow democracy itself and replace it with an authoritarian autocracy. The intended outcome was to install Trump as the nation's permanent president for life: a dictator in the mold of Russia's Vladimir Putin, Hungary's Viktor Orban, or Turkey's Recep Tayyip Erdogan.

In this respect, the tide of authoritarianism that swept over Washington, D.C., on January 6 was in fact only a manifestation of a much larger phenomenon: the global ascent of right-wing authoritarian rule.[3] In addition to major players where authoritarianism has been in place for a generation or longer like China and Russia, in nations around the world—from the Philippines to Italy to Brazil and numerous places in between—autocratic regimes not only have secured political power, but have worked to enact its spread globally.

This spread has been enabled by a media, internet, and social media environment in which misinformation and disinformation that readily disrupts democratic discourse have become the ordinary state of things. It's manifested in the rise of far-right political groups, many of them engaging in intimidation and street violence, while others work assiduously to insinuate themselves within the democratic electorate even as they undermine democracy itself.

Around the globe, democracies have faced sustained campaigns—fomented both by interior forces and those from outside—in which far-right operatives and leaders undermine the rule of law, pervert elections, attack media freedom, and inflame discrimination against minorities and mistreatment of migrants. Nowhere have these attacks had as significant an effect on pluralistic institutions than in the United States, long considered the world's leading exponent of democracy.

There have been several powerful indicators of American decline: a surge in political domination, embodied in the saturation of intimidation and violence in its discourse; the worsening of long-standing discrimination against racial and ethnic minority groups as well as recent policies on asylum and immigration, eroding their equal treatment under the law; and most particularly the sudden and sharp decline in confidence in its elections, toxified by Trump and his fellow Republicans both before and after his defeat in 2020.

But the United States is only one of the many democracies under siege. In Hungary and Turkey, democratic institutions have already been replaced by autocratic rule.[4] In other nations like India, a theocratic and intolerant majority has despoiled the principles of pluralism and equal citizenship.[5] In European nations like Germany, Sweden, and Italy, far-right political parties are ascendant and acquiring power and influence.[6]

In the latter case, the far right's rise to power was led by a longtime neo-fascist named Giorgia Meloni, who won the prime minister's seat in Italy's September 2022 elections. For many observers, it was the final manifestation of the long process by which right-wing extremism has been mainstreamed in the West—and, for that matter, the world.[7]

This has been the realization of a long-term project to spread right-wing "populist" politics around the world by well-financed political operatives, most recently Stephen Bannon, the onetime Trump adviser who spent much of 2018–2020 traveling Europe, Australia, and dozens of other locales to coach politicians on how to spread their bigoted brand of politics. Among his protégés was Meloni.[8]

However, the most important figure in the spread of the global radical right is unquestionably Vladimir Putin. His authoritarian regime in Russia has been extraordinarily active in the past decade in spreading its influence throughout the world, primarily by undermining democratic rule in other countries—particularly in Europe and the United States—and encouraging and sponsoring right-wing extremist groups and politics. Russia has mounted massive disinformation campaigns that disrupt the democratic process, especially around elections, while empowering far-right parties such as Meloni's with offers of loans, cooperation, and propaganda that provides political cover.[9]

The disinformation machine being financed by Russian oligarchs is able to distribute its wares throughout Europe, particularly via identitarian and other far-right nationalist groups.[10] In Sweden, the most powerful of these is the party that gained 18 percent of the vote in recent elections, Sweden Democrats—whose history is deeply rooted in swastika-bearing neo-Nazi groups from the 1980s.

Putin and his oligarchs have been busy financing far-right nationalists throughout Europe and elsewhere. Among the beneficiaries of Russian largesse, besides Sweden Democrats, have been France's Marine Le Pen, chair of the far-right National Rally (formerly National Front); Greece's nationalist Golden Dawn party; Austria's far-right Freedom Party; and the German AfD (Alternative for Germany) party—one AfD parliamentarian is believed to be completely in Russia's pocket. Putin is notably close with Hungary's far-right prime minister, Viktor Orban, whose anti-Semitism and rabid nationalism are cornerstones for his administration. Italy's far-right Lega party was revealed to have discussed how to funnel Russian funds into its own coffers, while Meloni's Brothers of Italy party is also believed to have received Russian financing. All told, Russia is believed to have spent over $300 million since 2014 on the covert campaign.[11]

Perhaps just as important, European far-right radicals unanimously voice their support for Putin and the Russian regime. Similar fan-like support can also be found among American white nationalists (at one time, chants of "Russia is our friend" were commonly heard at alt-right street events), particularly alt-right godfather Richard Spencer and noted neo-Nazi Andrew Anglin (who called Putin a "great white savior, a being of immense power").[12]

Likewise, Putin and his regime have cultivated ties with a wide range of American Christian nationalist groups, embodied by the World Congress of Families (WCF), an Illinois-based group that began developing a relationship with Russia and its oil oligarchs in 2014 and eventually grew from an obscure fundamentalist organization to a global operation holding Christian nationalist conferences in locations around the world.[13] The nexus of this coalescence has been fundamentalists' ongoing campaign not only to demonize the LGBTQ community, but to render homosexual behavior illegal outright; WCF leaders openly praise the Russian regime, particularly for its protofascist 2013 laws that banned gay people from the public square, as the center of what they call "traditional values."[14] "I think Russia is the hope for the world right now," pronounced WCF managing director Larry Jacobs in 2014.

Russian operations began financing disinformation campaigns designed to sow chaos and conflict in American and European politics around the same time, focusing particularly on social media platforms that allowed them to reach huge audiences with relatively little interference. These efforts reached a kind of climax in the 2016 elections, when Russian trolling operations set up hundreds of Facebook and other social media accounts that used a two-pronged approach for spreading disinformation: Rile up conservative voters with ads, fake stories, and distorted memes that amplified their distrust and dislike of minorities into undiluted fear and loathing while depressing Democratic turnout by targeting minority communities with memes and false or distorted information designed to feed their distrust of white liberals.[15] These efforts had the secondary effect of inspiring a wave of hate crimes that further spread the sense of minority disenfranchisement.[16]

"These ads broadly sought to pit one American against another by exploiting faults in our society or race, ethnicity, sexual orientation, and other deeply cynical thoughts," observed Rep. Adam Schiff, chair of the House Intelligence Committee. "Americans should take away that the Russians perceive these divisions as vulnerabilities and to a degree can be exploited by a sophisticated campaign."

So while the significance of the ongoing Russian disinformation assault on American democracy should not be understated or ignored, and is in fact probably worthy of a book-length investigation, this is not that book. The fault lines and cracks in our democracy that are being exploited by Russia and its allied autocracies existed long before any of them began doing so, and had been deepening and widening for many years before 2014. If Putin's regime and his sphere of influence were to collapse overnight, those fissures and the resulting threat to American democracy would remain intact. Identifying and understanding those fissures in their current state is the necessary first step in being able to overcome them, to eventually defend and repair our democracy successfully. That is what this book intends.

THE FIRST AND MOST important step in that understanding entails coming to grips with the essence of the phenomenon with which the world—and the United States especially—now grapples: neofascism—that is, the revivified twenty-first-century form of the authoritarian pathology that nearly destroyed the world a hundred years ago. It is manifest on nearly every front now: in Russia's empowerment of explicitly fascist elements in its war on Ukraine;[17] in the thinly disguised anti-Semitism embedded in the governments of his autocratic allies like Hungary;[18] in the fascist roots of ascendant right-wing elements in Europe, including the Sweden Democrats, Germany's AfD, and Brothers of Italy; and the spread of explicitly ethnonationalist paramilitary street-fighting gangs like the Proud Boys and Patriot Front, as well as generically nationalist "Patriot" militia groups, both in the United States and elsewhere.

President Biden attempted to name this phenomenon in an August 2022 speech to the nation—"It's not just Trump, it's the entire philosophy that underpins the—I'm going to say something—it's like semi-fascism," he said, in a speech that mainstream networks refused to broadcast live because they feared it was "too political."[19] Right-wing politicians and pundits leaped to defend their audiences, claiming Biden was demonizing half the nation, while libertarians and centrist liberals insisted that the characterization was a gross exaggeration.

Historians of fascism, however, came to Biden's defense, saying that the behavior of Trump's MAGA army very neatly fits into how the pathology has historically manifested itself. Fascism, as Federico Finchelstein explained, has always had a specific set of identifiable traits:

> In historical terms, it was an ultranationalist, anti-liberal and anti-Marxist politics. Its primary aim was to destroy democracy from within to create a modern dictatorship from above. The state silenced the basic tenets of civil society, while eliminating the distinctions between the public and the private—or between the state and its citizens. Fascist regimes shut down the independent press and destroyed the rule of law.[20]

Columbia University historian Robert O. Paxton, in his 2004 book *The Anatomy of Fascism*, defined fascism as "a form of political behavior marked by obsessive preoccupation with community decline, humiliation, or victimhood and by compensatory cults of unity, energy, and purity, in which a mass-based party of committed nationalist militants, working in uneasy but effective collaboration with traditional elites, abandons democratic liberties and pursues with redemptive violence and without ethical or legal constraints goals of internal cleansing and external expansion."[21] Paxton identified nine "mobilizing passions" of fascism:

> A sense of overwhelming crisis beyond the reach of any traditional solutions;
>
> The primacy of the group, toward which one has duties superior to every right, whether universal or individual, and the subordination of the individual to it;
>
> The belief that one's group is a victim, a sentiment which justifies any action, without legal or moral limits, against the group's enemies, both internal and external;

Dread of the group's decline under the corrosive effect of individualistic liberalism, class conflict, and alien influences;

The need for closer integration of a purer community, by consent if possible, or by exclusionary violence if necessary;

The need for authority by natural leaders (always male), culminating in a national chief who alone is capable of incarnating the group's destiny;

The superiority of the leader's instincts over abstract and universal reason;

The beauty of violence and the efficacy of will, when they are devoted to the group's success;

The right of the chosen people to dominate others without restraint from any kind of human or divine law, right being decided by the sole criterion of the group's prowess in a Darwinian struggle.

The shock of recognition from the hard reality that all these traits are now plainly manifest in the MAGA army assembled by Trump has set off multiple waves of denial from the remnants of the Republican Party who are loath to acknowledge that their politics have become infected with this pathology. After Biden's speech, some angrily accused Democrats of projecting their own supposedly authoritarian traits onto their political opponents. (Many compared it to Hillary Clinton's infamously distorted 2016 remarks calling the same people a "basket of deplorables," again mischaracterizing the speech's content to claim that Biden was describing all Republicans thus.)

Others claimed that even using the term "fascism" was inappropriate, contending that the word really only describes a phenomenon that arose in early twentieth-century Europe in certain nations. *Washington Post* columnist Henry Olsen complained that Biden's "calumny is nonetheless inaccurate and inflammatory," claiming without evidence: "MAGA politicians usually argue that America's liberal tradition is under attack and needs to be saved, not that it is the root of all evil."[22] (Olsen clearly slept through the previous decade in which right-wing pundits regularly penned bestsellers denouncing liberals as innately evil, and in which far-right MAGA pundits like Alex Jones routinely described Democrats as "demonic.")[23]

In reality, scholars of fascism have long recognized that it is a highly adaptive and mutative phenomenon that can arise in any nation where democratic institutions have been attacked and degraded—and that, indeed, it has only arisen in nations that had been previously democratic. Just as Italian and German forms of fascism had aspects that made them distinct despite the underlying shared political impulses, an American form of fascism would manifest itself in its own distinct way: swaddled in red, white, and blue bunting, demanding fidelity to "Christian" principles, and pronouncing its innately seditionist politics "patriotism."

Those same historians moreover point out that not only have fascist impulses been a relentless presence on the American political landscape, but earlier American forms of protofascism were woven into the fabric of their European counterparts. Hitler's anti-Semitic Nuremberg Laws were modeled on the Jim Crow laws that had been in place in the US South since the 1880s, and his vision of creating "Lebensraum" for the "Aryan race" was inspired by the genocide of Native Americans in the 1800s.[24]

Paxton describes the US-based Ku Klux Klan (particularly its resurrected post-1915 version) as one of the earliest of all protofascist groups.[25] And the presence of such organizations in the United States has never stopped, even if they were pushed to the political fringes after World War II and the Holocaust, when the world saw for itself the horrifying end result of their politics. In addition to the atomized but still-extant KKK, groups like George Lincoln Rockwell's American Nazi Party, William Potter Gale's Posse Comitatus, and Richard Butler's Aryan Nations have been marching across our political landscape in a constant stream over the many decades since the war.

I HAVE BEEN A witness to this march for over forty years. As a young newspaper reporter and editor working in the northern Idaho Panhandle in the
1970s and '80s, I was present when the Aryan Nations moved its operations from Southern California to a small town just a little south of where I
worked called Hayden Lake, and then proceeded to both terrorize the local
population with waves of violent hate crimes perpetrated by the neo-Nazis
who moved there with them, as well as to slowly alter the local demographics by attracting scores of fellow far-right extremists to the region, where
they spread their politics of hate and division to their new neighbors.

What made the spread of these toxic extremists into the host community so seamless, I came to realize, was their seeming normalcy. There were
always the expected Hitler devotees who donned brown shirts and swastika armbands, as well as tattooed skinheads with threatening demeanors,
among the participants at the annual Aryan Congresses in Hayden Lake.
But the large majority of the people I would interview at these gatherings
looked and dressed like anyone else in Idaho at the time. More importantly, I came to recognize that their views were only extreme variations of
ideas and beliefs—about the federal government or education or minority
and women's rights or homosexuality—that I knew were already common
among my conservative Idaho neighbors, particularly among those already
immersed in the far-right John Birch Society, which had long been a significant political presence in the state. They were only a few turns of the
paranoia ratchet away from being the same.

The beliefs practiced at the Aryan Nations—whose official name was the
Church of Jesus Christ Christian—are those of a racist sect called Christian
Identity. It teaches that white people are the true Israelites, and that Jews are
literally the descendants of Satan. Non-whites, in their belief system, are soulless "mud people." And its adherents preach that America, including its government, is in the grip of a satanic cabal that uses abortion as a kind of sacrifice
to the devil. But in the context of recruitment, believers frequently muted their
more bigoted beliefs and emphasized their hatred of modern secular society.

A number of people were attracted to the Aryan Nations less for their open bigotry than for their shared white-hot hatred of "decadent" liberal democracy and the US government. Some of these were adherents to Gale's Posse Comitatus ideology, which preached a kind of radical localism based on a twisted (as well as both anti-Semitic and racist) interpretation of the Constitution, claiming that the federal government's powers—especially regarding civil rights laws—were extremely limited, that county sheriffs were the supreme law of the land, and that the FBI and other federal departments were illegitimate entities.

Others were people who had deeply held apocalyptic religious beliefs, and considered the government a tool of the devil. Randy Weaver and his family, hyper-religious transplants from Iowa who sought refuge in the deep-forested hills of the Idaho Panhandle, were just such eventual converts. Weaver subsequently became embroiled in a criminal investigation into the gun-running activities of another family they met at Hayden Lake, and ended up in 1992 engaging the FBI in an armed standoff at his home on Ruby Ridge in which his wife, Vicki, and son, Sammy, were killed. It fit the long tradition I had witnessed in which converts' absolute devotion to extremist beliefs only ended in tragedy and misery for everyone involved.[26]

That incident inflamed the radical right and spurred its leaders to action. Less than two months later in Colorado, a collection of white supremacists, gun-rights extremists, neo-Nazis, and Klansmen convened to discuss setting aside doctrinal differences and focusing on creating an armed response to federal "tyranny." The end result was what became broadly known as the "militia movement," although its own adherents (some of whom didn't join militias but instead pursued "constitutionalist" legal theories, declaring themselves "sovereign citizens" immune from federal and state laws) called it the "Patriot movement." After the misbegotten 1993 federal standoff at the Branch Davidian church near Waco, Texas, in which seventy-six people were killed when the cult leader set the building afire, the idea began to spread like wildfire.

I began reporting on their organizing activities in the Pacific and inland Northwest as a subject for my nascent freelance work. I chose to begin writing about them partly as a practical matter: my experience told me that if I wanted to tackle a subject that would produce a steady stream of news stories, right-wing extremism was an excellent bet, since over my years reporting and editing, it was an endless wellspring of human misery, social disruption, and frightening violence—the kind of behavior that always makes news.

After a young "Patriot" named Timothy McVeigh, out for revenge for the Ruby Ridge and Waco incidents, set off a truck bomb outside the federal building in Oklahoma City in April 1995, killing 168 and maiming hundreds more, it became clear to me that the movement was toxically dangerous: an existential threat not just to innocent people in its vicinity, but to democracy itself. The fascist beliefs and attitudes that informed the founding of the Patriot movement were not merely strands woven into its mainstream-friendly facade, but the foundational blocks hiding beneath their jingoistic enterprise. What was striking even at the time was how frequently their rhetoric waded into open sedition, calling for the overthrow of the "New World Order" government—even while claiming the mantle of "true" patriotism. It never went away.

So in the aftermath of the bombing, I decided to make right-wing extremism my primary beat, the focus of my work, and the subject of extensive research in the years that followed, which included conducting as much on-the-ground coverage and in-person interviews as possible. Mostly, I ended up monitoring and tracking the extremists' relentless activities over the ensuing years, leading me to realize eventually one core truth about them: They never, ever give up. They may go into hiding or keep lower profiles, but they are relentless in finding new ways to insinuate their toxic beliefs within the mainstream of American politics.

There was a brief downturn in the Patriot movement that began in 2000, when the "Y2K apocalypse" that many of them had furiously hyped in the years prior failed to materialize as promised on January 1 of the new millennium. The election of a Republican president later that year also seemed to lower their fervor, which initially had centered heavily around gun rights. But by 2003, a number of them had found a new cause célèbre around which to organize: immigration.

So along the southern US border, "Patriot" militia groups spouting far-right nativist rhetoric began forming, running vigilante "border watches" in sparsely populated desert lands, hoping to intercept "illegals" as they entered the country. The best known of these outfits called itself the Minutemen, and an April 2005 "border watch" intended to attract participants from around the country was heavily promoted on national networks like Fox News and covered by every major mainstream outlet, which treated their claims—including their insistence that they were only "patriotic citizens" out to defend the country from a perceived threat (of brown people)—credulously. However, within a few years, much of the energy around these new border militias began to trail off, especially as groups like the Minutemen crumbled apart in a wave of criminality (including the murders of a family living in a border town, a tragedy that I covered extensively) and financial malfeasance.

By 2008, however, these protofascist elements had found a new focus: the election of a Black president. Suddenly, the hysterical fears about gun rights, fueled by a raft of fresh conspiracy theories, and paranoid claims about "government tyranny" were being circulated widely—and a fresh wave of militia organizing began. In the first year of Barack Obama's presidency, the numbers of militia groups had nearly quadrupled from their 2007 numbers, from 131 to 512; by 2011, they had peaked at 1,360.

Much of this organizing revolved around the Tea Party movement, which had arisen early in Obama's tenure as a mobilizing reaction against his presidency—particularly any of his policy initiatives, such as healthcare reform—but which in short order became a conduit for reviving Patriot movement ideology and giving it fresh life within the conservative mainstream. It only took a few twists of the paranoia ratchet to get there: within short order, the Tea Party was overwhelmed with "constitutionalists" and militia advocates like the Oath Keepers, fueled with fresh new conspiracy theories ranging from claims about Obama's birth certificate to suggestions that normal Army exercises were preparations to round up conservatives into concentration camps. Far-right ideology bubbled up along with it: At one Tea Party event I covered in Montana, one of the exhibitors was selling copies of Hitler's *Mein Kampf.*

Simultaneously, the emergence of wide-open internet platforms, particularly social media and chat room sites, presented a fresh opportunity for dedicated white supremacists to spread their ideology into the mainstream, primarily by recruiting vulnerable and impressionable young white males simmering with resentments, particularly against women, LGBTQ folk, and ethnic/racial minorities. The emerging movement called itself "the alt-right," and, like the Tea Party, its alternative universe was a seething cauldron of conspiracism—especially the anti-Semitic kind—and venomous hatred.

All of these protofascist elements finally found their long-missing key ingredient—their authoritarian need for a "glorious leader" around whom they could realize their dream of returning to national power—in 2015 with the ascendance of Donald Trump to the top of the Republican presidential ticket. The broad range of elements of the American protofascist right—the Patriots, the white nationalists, the conspiracists, and their mainstream enablers—all congealed in unrequited support for Trump and played a powerful role in his ultimate election to the presidency. I detailed all of these events in my 2017 book, *Alt-America.*

I knew on the night that Trump was elected that life in America would never be the same—and particularly not for someone in my line of work. I knew that he had already begun prying the lid off the Pandora's box that is our national id—the chest full of our darkest impulses—and that his ascendance to the White House would remove the lid altogether, and all the demons held therein would come flying out into our midst. I was not shocked when, in the first two months after his election, hate crimes spiked to previously unseen levels.[27]

In the succeeding years, Trump would unleash a politics of menace and intimidation on the national landscape unlike anything seen since the Klan years. As a correspondent for the Southern Poverty Law Center, I was there to report on much of it. On the night of Trump's inauguration, I witnessed an anti-fascist being shot by alt-right fans of Milo Yiannopoulos on the University of Washington campus.[28] Over the course of the ensuing weeks and months, I was present as gangs of street brawlers who gave themselves names like Patriot Prayer and the Proud Boys organized riots in West Coast urban centers like Berkeley, Portland, and Seattle, using the pretext of defending "free speech" to deliberately create scenes of violence for which they came fully prepared. The trend spread to other locations, and culminated in the lethal Unite the Right march in Charlottesville, Virginia, in August 2017, at the end of which a neo-Nazi rammed into a crowd of counterprotesters, killing one and maiming dozens.

Even after that tragedy, the neofascist Proud Boys and their like-minded thugs continued to organize marches, ranging from their epicenter in Portland to Providence, Rhode Island, and dozens of points in between. I covered nearly two dozen of these events over three years, and observed their unfolding strategy for simultaneously intimidating the general public while generating a phony narrative blaming leftists—particularly anti-fascists and Black Lives Matter—for the brutality they themselves inflicted on these cities. Even more disturbing was how I witnessed their politics seeping into the mainstream, drawing Republican Trump fans and police officers alike into their web of extremism.

I paid close attention to their rhetoric: the mounting eliminationism directed not just at "Antifa" and BLM but anyone they deemed "Communist"—a term of demonization so flexible that it included mainstream liberals like Joe Biden and Kamala Harris. I paid attention to their willingness to bring violence against peaceful liberal politicians on the campaign trail. And I listened as they gobbled up Donald Trump's claims about looming election fraud in the 2020 election and were heartened by his refusal in his sole debate with Biden to say whether he would hand over the presidency peacefully. I especially noticed how they were positively electrified by his shout-out to the Proud Boys in that same debate, telling them: "Stand back and stand by."

So when Trump in fact lost, I knew that at some point he would gather these forces in Washington, D.C., to prevent his removal from office. And by late December, it had become plain that January 6, 2021, would be the day. Reporting for the progressive news website *Daily Kos*, I warned readers that extreme violence directed at officials in Washington was coming, as did other journalists who could see the same black clouds taking shape.[29] Unfortunately, those warnings did not reach the higher echelons of the national media, nor the law-enforcement sectors that would nonetheless wind up saving democracy on that day despite being overwhelmed.

There was a brief moment, in the days immediately following the insurrection, when there was an opportunity by Republicans to bring the nation back from the brink—to recoil in horror at the violent attack on the backbone of our democracy, the peaceful transfer of power; to renounce the extremism that had overwhelmed their party both before and during the Trump years, to embrace their longtime role as a viable partner in democracy. But within a matter of days—especially when confronted with the painfully obvious need to impeach Trump for inciting the mob and attempting a coup, which should have been understood as a duty—they promptly regressed into the cultish authoritarianism of Trumpism, refusing his impeachment and dismissing the insurrection as a mere protest that had "gotten out of hand."

So rather than breaking the fever of right-wing extremism, January 6 became a starting point for a new age of American politics: an age in which insurrection is celebrated, seditionists are defended as "patriots," and the politics of menace and violence are woven into our everyday discourse and interactions. It will be an age in which smaller insurrections—directed at state legislatures, school boards, city councils, even public libraries—conducted by gangs of threatening Proud Boys, Patriots, and Christian nationalists will become common and even ordinary. It will be an age when random terroristic violence will strike with frightening regularity. Most of all, it will be an age when the forces of the radical right work feverishly to impose their radical antidemocratic agenda on the nation, and impose a system of plutocratic authoritarianism that will rob citizens of their rights and, if their eliminationist rhetoric is to be believed, their lives.

The Age of Insurrection is intended to help ordinary Americans—the ones who still believe that our democratic system is the best guarantor of our rights and freedoms and well-being—understand the nature of what it is we're up against: the ideologies and motivations and strategies of the ongoing far-right insurgency. January 6 demonstrated that the threat to democracy by these forces is very real, and its aftermath has manifested that the problem is not going away, but rather redoubling its forces in preparation for a culminating victory. Herein, I hope, you will find a toolbox containing the knowledge we all will need to deny them that.

PART I

The American Rubicon

1

An Uncivil War

ON MAY 14, 2022, a young man from Conklin—a rural New York town near the Pennsylvania border—drove over two hundred miles west to a Tops grocery store in a Black neighborhood in Buffalo that he had already scoped out. Live streaming the whole thing, he pulled into the parking lot, briefly bucked himself up—"Just got to go for it"—then got out of the car with his AR-15 in hand and promptly shot the first person he encountered outside the store, an elderly woman, in the head. He then went on a rampage, killing others in the parking lot as well before continuing inside the store, shooting the security guard who tried to confront him and then moving on to customers trapped inside the store. By the time he surrendered to police, ten people were dead and three were wounded.[1]

The brutal act of terrorism that unfolded that day was the act of a dedicated white nationalist who had specifically targeted a predominantly Black community. It was not an "isolated incident" committed by a "lone wolf." Rather the opposite.[2]

The violence, in fact, was only one entry in a long catalog of lethal attacks in the mounting radical-right insurgency against American democracy.

The white-nationalist ideology behind it—laid bare in the shooter's 181-page manifesto—had been widely adopted not just by young radicals like Payton Gendron, the alleged shooter that day, but at the highest reaches of the Republican Party, led by the most popular cable talk show host in the country, Tucker Carlson.

Before he opened fire on customers at the store, the eighteen-year-old Gendron posted a lengthy, rambling document riddled with classic fascistic white nationalism: hatred of Blacks, the belief that Jews are secretly manipulating government and culture, the fear of the demographic displacement of white people, the loathing of feminists and misogynistic demands for eugenicist birth rates, and the eager embrace of genocidal violence—they're all laced throughout the manifesto.

Gendron specifically targeted that store, he said, because he wanted to find a soft target filled with African Americans. He chose Buffalo, he said, because it "has the highest black population percentage and isn't that far away." He chose Blacks as his primary victims—eight of the ten victims were African American—because "they are an obvious, visible, and large group of replacers."

He was referring to replacement theory, the ideology that fueled his actions. Much of his manifesto was devoted to exploring various aspects of the "Great Replacement," the belief that Western society is being flooded with brown-skinned minorities as part of a long-running plot to replace white people—a plot overseen by Jewish "globalists."

It's an ideology that has its roots in the white-nationalist claims of "white genocide" and "cultural Marxism" that movement ideologues generated in the 1990s and early 2000s.[3] Replacement theory has been identified as a major ideological wellspring of domestic-terrorist violence: In addition to inspiring the chant at Charlottesville in August 2017—"You will not replace us!" soon morphing into "Jews will not replace us!"—it fueled mass killings in Christchurch, New Zealand; Pittsburgh, Pennsylvania; and El Paso, Texas.[4]

The theory, as a study from the Institute for Strategic Dialogue has explored, was a source of inspiration for a number of violent acts, in particular the massacre in March 2019 at two mosques in Christchurch.[5] The theory, the study found, has significant potential "to drive extreme-right mobilization and terrorist acts," in large part because it "lends itself to calls for radical action against minority communities—including ethnic cleansing, violence and terrorism."

The "Great Replacement" takes inspiration from the title of a 2011 novel by a French white nationalist that described a dystopian future Europe overwhelmed by Muslims and non-white cultures, a book that has become a white-nationalist bible. It's a worldview that has inspired calls for extreme action, ranging from nonviolent ethnic cleansing through "remigration" to genocide. The crisis narratives central to the theory often inspire a sense of apocalyptic urgency in its adherents.

The report observes that a sense of disempowerment helps drive these terrorists to violence, noting that the Christchurch shooter referenced the defeat of National Front leader Marine Le Pen in the 2017 French elections as a "turning point."

The Buffalo shooter described his radicalization in his manifesto, saying that nearly every step in the process took place online—particularly on far-right-friendly platforms like the message board 4chan and on Gab. He claimed he was inspired by the Christchurch shooter, as well as others, including the man who opened fire in an El Paso, Texas, Walmart in 2020: "These men fought for me and had the same goals I did. It was there I asked myself: Why don't I do something?"

Gendron was like most far-right terrorists, who typically don't believe their single act will change the world, but that there will be an accumulating record of violence that will gradually convince the public that their governmental institutions can no longer keep them safe and secure: "To add momentum to the pendulum swings of history, further destabilizing and polarizing Western society in order to eventually destroy the nihilistic, hedonistic, individualistic insanity that has taken control of Western thought," he wrote.

This is called "accelerationism," a belief system predicated on the idea that modern human civilization (and especially its multicultural features) is a blight, and that the only solution is to encourage its destruction through acts of terroristic violence.

Gendron embraced accelerationism, saying that "fascism is one of the only political ideologies that will unite Whites against the replacers. Since that is what I seek, calling me a fascist would be accurate."

This kind of radicalization has been openly encouraged by Republican officeholders including Congress members like Arizona's Paul Gosar and Georgia's Marjorie Taylor Greene, and a broad array of right-wing pundits (particularly Tucker Carlson of Fox News). These figures have transmitted white-nationalist and other far-right conspiracy theories into the mainstream of public discourse, ranging from the "Great Replacement" to the contradictory claims that "leftists" and "Antifa" were actually responsible for the January 6 violence and that the rioters, simultaneously righteous "patriots," sought to defend the nation from a Communist takeover.

Indeed, further data shows that "replacement theory" was a major ideological nexus for the Capitol insurrection. A University of Chicago Project on Security and Threats report found that about 63 percent of the participants in the insurrection believed in the Great Replacement narrative, while 54 percent subscribed to far-right QAnon conspiracism.[6]

Trump's insurrectionist army hasn't gone away. It's still focused on winning, on avenging his 2020 defeat, dismantling liberal democracy, displacing majority rule with minority rule, and imposing a right-wing authoritarian government—either in the person of Trump or someone very like him. After Jan. 6, however, it sharply redirected the focus of its attacks on democratic institutions from the top federal level to the local and state level, where its various factions already hold considerable sway, particularly in rural areas. This became clear when Patriot militiamen, Proud Boys, and neofascist white supremacists began showing up to disrupt school boards, city councils, state legislative bodies, and a broad range of mostly local-level institutions—not to mention a range of minority communities, such as Buffalo's Black populace or LGBTQ folk—to threaten and intimidate them over concocted controversies such as "critical race theory" and false smears accusing them of pedophilic "grooming" of children. It happened seemingly everywhere: From Texas to Idaho to California to Florida to Michigan. The same conspiracist, insurrection-prone "Patriots" who attacked the Capitol and applauded the siege afterward began threatening local institutions with violent rhetoric and behavior, with the intent of overthrowing liberal democracy from the bottom up.

This ongoing insurrection is the manifestation of the deluge of right-wing extremism that has overwhelmed American political discourse, both nationally and locally: conspiracist, unreasoning, threatening, bellicose, and authoritarian. The central thread running through it all—other than reflecting various aspects of mainstream right-wing discourse—is the inherent eliminationism: the crude demonization of their enemies (i.e., liberals and leftists, minorities, and the like) as existential threats to be crushed, mere objects fit only for extermination and expulsion.

There are always fresh targets for this kind of scapegoating. One year it's immigrants. Another it's "Antifa." Yet another it's Black Lives Matter. Or people teaching critical race theory. Or "baby killers." Or "groomers." It's always a menu.

This had been building for more than a decade—and almost entirely ignored by the media, by authorities, and by the public, who summarily dismissed the slow-rising floodwaters as merely a fringe phenomenon of little consequence. This is why, on January 6, the nation's democratic institutions came perilously close to being swamped entirely—and why, in the years following that open declaration of war on democracy, the peril persists.

The incoming tide hasn't subsided—and has, if anything, worsened in intensity.

———————

TUCKER CARLSON WAS ONLY the most prominent of the many Republican ideologues who had been promoting replacement theory and radicalizing their audiences and constituents prior to the Buffalo massacre. Carlson's partisan-reductionist version of this theory is that Democrats are secretly plotting "to replace the current electorate" with "more obedient voters from the Third World."[7] He repeatedly promoted it on his nightly talk show—and when the Anti-Defamation League demanded he resign afterward, Fox executives rushed to his defense, claiming disingenuously that he had actually denounced the theory. Carlson simply doubled down.[8]

Carlson already had a remarkable record of dabbling increasingly in white-supremacist rhetoric dating back to 2006, including recordings unearthed in 2019 of his earlier ramblings on radio.[9] His subsequent bigoted outbursts—the kind that made him a sensation with white-nationalist audiences—included a regurgitation of neo-Nazi propaganda about "white genocide" in Africa, not to mention his mutual promotion of the white-nationalist website *VDARE*.[10] There is a reason white supremacists love Carlson's show, and why they assiduously watch it in hopes of picking up pointers.[11]

Perhaps most egregiously, Carlson had repeatedly claimed that white-nationalist domestic terrorism is a "hoax." The very act of calling out white nationalism, according to Carlson, is a racist attack on white people: "You could live your entire life here without running into a white nationalist. No matter what they tell you, this is a remarkably kind and decent country," he claimed. "Attacking people for their race is exactly how you destroy a country. That's what Democrats are doing. They know that they are doing it, it's obvious they just don't care."[12]

Carlson's response to the January 6 insurrection (replete with a faux documentary series peddling the theory) followed the same logic even further: after a few brief attempts at other counters, he settled on a narrative claiming that in fact the whole affair was orchestrated by the FBI as part of a Biden administration conspiracy to persecute white conservatives.[13]

Naturally, this same narrative formed the core of Carlson's (and, more broadly, Fox News's) response to the Buffalo violence and his own culpability for promoting the same "replacement theory" narrative that had inspired the killer: it was all further evidence of Democrats' eagerness to begin rounding up Republicans.

He and his Fox News colleagues spent the Monday after the massacre furiously gaslighting their audience about whatever role they might have played. ("It's so weak," complained Laura Ingraham about the suggestion that Republican radicalization might have played a role. "I didn't even want to talk about it because it's so predictable. It's so lame. Because the real accomplices are in the media.") Like clockwork, they resorted to their time-tested rhetorical trope of accusing anyone connecting their rhetoric to the Buffalo violence of "waving the bloody shirt": engaging in cheap demagoguery over the corpses of victims just to score political points.

American conservatives have been refining this particular schtick since Reconstruction, when the "bloody shirt" trope was invented and then constantly waved by Confederacy apologists to whitewash the Southern campaign of anti-Black terror being waged by the Ku Klux Klan and Red Shirts and other violent white organizations.[14] It's become reflexive on the right, in fact, to deal with violence against minorities by sublimating it as a lesser issue, contending that the real problem isn't so much the violence itself but rather the supposed exploitation of it as a political matter.

That was the theme all day, it seemed, at Fox News, with not only Carlson weighing in at the top of his show but bringing in his regular sidekick Glenn Greenwald to loudly complain that Democrats were indulging in cheap, power-grabbing politics. Meanwhile, fellow Fox hosts Sean Hannity and Ingraham resorted to basic whataboutism to erase the terrorism from Saturday's horror and claim, once again, that the real problem was Democrats making political hay.

The responses were uniformly curious in one regard, however: None of them—not one—mentioned the Great Replacement or the fact that it had become a regular talking point for both Carlson and other Fox News pundits. Nor did any of them acknowledge that the so-called replacement theory had become a commonplace trope among Republican voters and party leaders. Carlson instead set out a narrative in which Democrats were ignoring violent crime in urban jurisdictions but launched a "coordinated campaign within minutes" to blame Republicans for the Buffalo killings. Their intention, he claimed, was to "suspend the First Amendment."

Carlson closed out the segment by bringing on Greenwald, who earlier in the day had called the people demanding a response from Carlson "ghoulish, soulless, and sick." On his show, they launched into a variation of this, with Carlson decrying "the immediate mobilization of a political party, using the pretext of a killing to make baldly political points. I don't think I've ever seen anything like it."

"They didn't care what the facts were," Greenwald said. "They saw an opportunity in those corpses laying on the ground, and the opportunity was political and exploitative and they seized on it together and quickly. And that made clear that their concern or sadness for the victims was a complete pretense. They instantly weaponized it before anything was known."

The essence of Carlson's and Greenwald's response is shock that people would try to hold them and their fellow Republicans to account for helping inspire an act of violent terrorism, when one of the primary reasons people have criticized Carlson for thoughtlessly peddling replacement theory is that it has in fact inspired multiple acts of violent domestic terrorism.

After all, when the Anti-Defamation League had demanded Tucker step down from his position at Fox News for peddling hate, it called out the danger clearly:

Make no mistake: this is dangerous stuff. The "great replacement theory" is a classic white supremacist trope that undergirds the modern white supremacist movement in America. It is a concept that is discussed almost daily in online racist fever swamps. It is a notion that fueled the hateful chants of "Jews will not replace us!" in Charlottesville in 2017. And it has lit the fuse in explosive hate crimes, most notably the hate-motivated mass shooting attacks in Pittsburgh, Poway and El Paso, as well as in Christchurch, New Zealand.[15]

Fox CEO Lachlan Murdoch defended Carlson, disingenuously claiming he had "decried and rejected replacement theory" when he said during the Thursday evening segment, "White replacement theory? No, no, this is a voting rights question."[16]

White nationalists were exultant. "This week Tucker redpilled 4 million people and there's nothing liberals can do about it," tweeted Nick Fuentes, leader of the white-nationalist "Groyper Army" and its associated "America First" movement. Fuentes later crowed again: "Daily reminder that replacement theory is now politically mainstream and there is nothing the ADL and SPLC can do about it."[17]

———————

FOR MOST OF SATURDAY, June 11, 2022, a crowd of several hundred people joyously celebrated Coeur d'Alene's annual Pride festival—music and dancing, food, and display booths, with a rainbow of colors and children romping amid blown bubbles.

Rain threatened, and there was a brief cloudburst. But festivalgoers were undaunted and went out parading in the downpour. They were determined to have a good day celebrating this northern Idaho town's vibrant LGBTQ community, as they had for years.

But there was a dark cloud over the whole affair, hovering around the fringes. In the weeks leading up to the festival, its organizers had been subject to a clamorous campaign of vicious rhetoric by far-right extremists depicting the organizers as "groomers," pedophiles, and satanists. And on the day of the event, a motley crew of white supremacists, "Patriots," Christian nationalists, and hate preachers circulated around the lakeside city park where the event was held.[18]

Their intentions weren't entirely clear until late in the day, when police, a block away from the park entrance, pulled over a U-Haul van about which they had received a tip. Sure enough, inside the van were thirty-one men, nearly all of them clad in white face coverings, blue shirts, and beige pants and ball caps. The uniforms and banners they carried identified them as members of the neofascist Patriot Front organization.

Police swarmed the van and ordered the men into custody, binding them with flex cuffs with their hands behind their backs and ordering them to sit or kneel on a grassy swath next to Northwest Boulevard just above a skate park. Then they processed all of them in public view, unmasking them as they did so.

"They came to riot downtown," Coeur d'Alene police chief Lee White told reporters a day later at a press conference. He said evidence collected and other documents demonstrated that they intended to begin the riot among the Pride crowd, but then fan out to other parts of downtown.

Among the men arrested was twenty-three-year-old Thomas Rousseau of Grapevine, Texas, the youthful founder of Patriot Front, which itself is the offspring of the neo-Nazi group Vanguard America, whose contingent Rousseau helped organize for the August 2017 Unite the Right march in Charlottesville, Virginia. Among the men he admitted to the group, and marched alongside that day, was James Alex Fields, who subsequently plowed his car into a crowd of counterprotesters, killing thirty-two-year-old Heather Heyer and maiming dozens. (Patriot Front denied admitting him as a member.)

Only two of the thirty-one men arrested were from Idaho, though a number were from the Pacific Northwest, including five from the nearby Spokane area. Men from as far away as Alabama, Texas, and Illinois came out to Idaho to participate.

A local resident saw them piling into a van near the intersection of Interstate 90 and Northwest Boulevard, about two miles from the park. He alerted Kootenai County sheriff Bob Norris, but it was Coeur d'Alene police—who had been out in force all weekend—who provided the bulk of the response, intercepting the van about five hundred yards from the park entrance.

"And they were all dressed like a small army," Norris said. "We had units in their area, and we were able to intercept them pretty quickly."

The Coeur d'Alene event, called Pride in the Park, had been targeted by right-wing extremists for several weeks, thanks to a campaign of intimidation first organized by a number of Christian nationalists in the Idaho Panhandle, but then spearheaded by a regional far-right bikers club, the Panhandle Patriots. The club announced it was holding an event called Gun d'Alene at a park less than a mile from the lakeside City Park. Spouting "groomer" rhetoric accusing the LGBTQ community of fostering pedophilia, two members of the club promised there would be a confrontation.[19]

"We are having an event the very same day," Jeff White, the club's sergeant at arms, told a gathering at a small church organized by an area Republican legislator, Heather Scott, who had introduced the men. "That very same day we actually intend to go head-to-head with these people. A line has to be drawn in the sand. Good people need to stand up. And she [Scott] was talking about the repercussions. We say, Damn the repercussions. Stand up, take it to the head. Go to the fight."

Gun d'Alene in fact had been billed as an anniversary of the day in 2020 that armed "Patriots" flooded the streets of Coeur d'Alene in response to hoax rumors of the impending arrival of buses full of black-clad "Antifa" vandals who, not so mysteriously, never showed up anywhere they were rumored to be going.[20] Dozens of people had shown up on armed patrol, toting AR-15s and wearing body armor, at a downtown shopping strip mall, while pickups with Gadsden "Don't Tread On Me" and Trump flags waving behind them prowled the streets.[21]

Once their plans for Gun d'Alene on June 11 were made public in the local press, the Panhandle Patriots retreated a step: "It is the media's goal to instigate a conflict, take photos of that conflict, and then produce media stories labeling our group and everyone associated with us as violent, racist, and hateful while ignoring the antics of Antifa, Black Lives Matter, and LGBT extremists," read a statement it issued in mid-May. It claimed that "Antifa members from across the country are planning on coming to Coeur d'Alene" for the event.

As a result, it changed the name of the event to the North Idaho Day of Prayer, adding: "The event popularly known as Gun d'Alene will be moved to a later date that is yet to be determined."[22]

White nationalist Dave Reilly of Post Falls began writing about Pride in the Park in his propaganda outlet, the *Idaho Tribune*. Notably, he happened to notice that one of the sponsors listed for the event was the Satanic Temple of Idaho, which became fodder for the national far-right ecosystem. This included the mega-popular Libs of TikTok account on Twitter, which began swiftly retweeting Reilly's posts to its 1.3 million followers.

The Satanic Temple—a harmless "pagan" sect whose real focus is civil liberties—dropped out of the event after Reilly's posts began circulating widely. But the damage was done, and the Coeur d'Alene Pride gathering became a national far-right lightning rod. By rebranding their event a "day of prayer" march, the Panhandle Patriots's gathering in a nearby park meant that it attracted a variety of Christian nationalist groups.

For nearly the entire day, the Pride gathering went uninterrupted, other than the brief rainstorm. Drag performers danced and sang onstage, and the crowd joined with them on the grass. People milled about the booths and gathered information, bought food and jewelry items, and generally conversed as they would have any other year.

At the same time, the threatening presence of the far right hovered nearby. One large man with camouflage gear, body armor, and a mask wandered around on the eastern side of the park while toting an AR-15. Another man with a cowboy hat stalked through the crowd several times while toting not just an AR-15 but a revolver stuck in his body armor and a large hunting knife. Christian nationalists wearing shirts denouncing homosexuality and "Patriots" wearing shirts with threatening slogans and depictions of guns firing mingled. A couple of men held signs on the edge of the event citing the Leviticus verse that recommends homosexuals be put to death.

To cap it all off, Matt Shea, the former Washington State Republican legislator who is deeply connected to the secessionist American Redoubt movement in the interior Northwest and currently leads a Christian nationalist church in the Spokane Valley, showed up at the competing "prayer" event nearby. He then led a march down Northwest Boulevard past City Park and the Pride gathering.

A group of men—one wearing a neo-Nazi "skull" mask, another wearing Patriot Front colors with the trademark white mask pulled down around his neck—gathered at the walkway on the park's southern lakeshore edge and unfurled a banner: "Groomers Are Not Welcome in Idaho."

About an hour later, joined by the two men with AR-15s, they again displayed the banner on the lawn across the interior walkway from the Pride gathering.

The intent to menace was clear, but no one could see any particular strategy unfolding. Nonetheless, the presence of unmistakable neo-Nazis suggested that something else was afoot—which became much clearer at about 2:00 p.m., when Coeur d'Alene police intercepted the U-Haul van and stopped the Patriot Front would-be rioters in their tracks.

While police remained mum about any weaponry carried by Patriot Front—which was reported to only consist of shields and sticks—it's not difficult to envision how the scenario could have played out inside the park had they arrived unimpeded and created a scene of violence at the gathering while the men with AR-15s, who were clearly part of their camp, stood on the periphery.

Their strategy, reportedly laid out in a seven-page planning document police found inside the U-Haul van, included moving into downtown Coeur d'Alene after they were finished inside the park and wreaking havoc there as well.

This was a marked shift in tactics for Patriot Front, which had primarily attempted to troll the media and public officials by staging marches in Washington, D.C., at which they mainly paraded their fasces-bearing banners in scenes eerily reminiscent of Nazi Brownshirt marches in 1920s Germany.[23] But this kind of gradual escalation reflected the planning by white nationalists and other extremists for expanding their movements in the post-Trump era.

The Coeur d'Alene Pride event was a chance for them to step things up while grabbing some publicity for themselves. It didn't quite work out the way they had hoped. But because the Idaho charges were initially only misdemeanors, the men were all out on three-hundred-dollar bail the next day. Some of them went panhandling in downtown Coeur d'Alene to scrape up enough money to get out of town.

Three weeks later, masked Patriot Front marchers showed up in Boston for the city's annual July Fourth celebration and marched through its downtown.[24] Thomas Rousseau, going unmasked, led the phalanx, shouting into a bullhorn outside the city library. An African American man was assaulted, but the marchers did not encounter law enforcement. This time, they arrived via public transit, and departed in individual cars they had parked nearby. No U-Hauls were seen.

––––––––––––

THE ELIMINATIONIST RHETORIC LABELING all LGBTQ people "groomers"—essentially connecting homosexuality and nonbinary gender identification with pedophilia—arose in early 2022 amid the debate over Florida's passage of its notorious Parental Rights in Education Act—better known as the "Don't Say Gay" law—which forbade educators from providing instruction on sexual orientation or gender identity to elementary school students.[25]

Gov. Ron DeSantis's press secretary, Christina Pushaw, in an attempt to reframe the legislation, alternatively described it as "the Anti-Grooming Bill" in early March, tweeting that if you're against it, "you are probably a groomer or at least you don't denounce the grooming of 4-8 year old children."[26]

This was, in fact, language directly inspired by the hysterical QAnon conspiracy cult, which is convinced that a range of Democrats, "globalists," and liberals (including many from Hollywood) are part of a massive worldwide pedophilia ring. For the most part, this rhetoric had circulated on the fringes of the conspiracist right, but in no time at all, Pushaw's tweets made "grooming" a mainstream right-wing talking point.

In March and April Fox News became obsessed with pedophilia. Pundits lined up to accuse those who allowed children to express their transgender identity as "groomers." As Vox reported, one guest on Fox and Friends suggested that educators were "being ripened for grooming for sexual abuse." On another Fox show Charlie Hurt echoed this by claiming that affirmative support for trans kids went "beyond predatory grooming . . . [into] psychological torture."

The usage went truly viral after the Disney Corporation (which operates the massive Disney World theme park in Florida) ended its silence on the Florida law after facing criticism for doing so, and officially came out in opposition. DeSantis savaged the company and its CEO publicly. And right-wing social media was suddenly aflame with posts identifying supposedly "woke" content in Disney films and TV shows,

Marjorie Taylor Greene, the QAnon-loving Georgia congresswoman, accused Disney of wanting to "take your children, and they want to indoctrinate them into sexual immoral filth." She added in an April 6 tweet that the Democrats were the party of "grooming and transitioning children, and pro-pedophile politics."

Donald Trump Jr. posted a meme on Instagram showing the Disney castle logo with the word "Groomers" written in the iconic Walt Disney style.

Pedophilia accusations also came up during confirmation hearings for new Supreme Court justice Ketanji Brown Jackson in March 2022, when Republican Missouri senator Josh Hawley accused Jackson of giving child pornographers unusually lenient sentences and "soft" treatment—claims that were quickly disproven.[27] Nonetheless, other right-wing figures like Greene and *Federalist* pundit Mollie Hemingway promoted the idea that Jackson was sympathetic to pedophilia, and so was anyone who supported her confirmation.[28]

It was not difficult to predict that this rhetoric would play out on the ground. Threats and actual violence soon followed. Far-right websites like Patriots.win went to work, trying to publicize the address of a school superintendent who placed a school nurse on leave for allegedly making inappropriate statements on Facebook about a student who may have been receiving gender-affirming care. The superintendent was accused of "grooming" children.[29]

Ultimately, this rhetoric led to scenes like those in Coeur d'Alene and elsewhere. Some of the most violent, in fact, began emanating from the Christian nationalist sphere.

Some fundamentalist preachers even called for genocide. Possibly the most strident of these preachers was "Brother" Dillon Awes, a member of Stedfast Baptist Church in Fort Worth, Texas, who spent over an hour, from the pulpit, denouncing homosexuality and demanding the systematic execution of any person found guilty of it:

> What does God say is the answer, is the solution for the homosexual, in 2022, here in the New Testament, here in the book of Romans—that they are worthy of death! These people should be put to death! Every single homosexual in our country should be charged with the crime, the abomination of homosexuality that they have, they should be convicted in a lawful trial, they should be sentenced with death, they should be lined up against the wall and shot in the back of the head! That's

what God teaches! That's what the Bible says. You don't like it, you don't like God's word.[30]

Awes used passages from the Bible to claim that LGBTQ people "are dangerous to society" and that "all homosexuals are pedophiles."

Meanwhile, Pastor Joe Jones of the Shield of Faith Baptist Church in Boise, Idaho, unleashed a similar tirade:

It's not God's fault! He told nations how to deal with that! He told the government of his own nation, the nation that he ruled, "Put them to death. Put all queers to death. They die." When they die, that stops the pedophilia. It's a very, very simple process.

Jones argued that "these people know they are worthy of death," which he claimed explained the high rate of suicide among trans people. "Why are the queers always blowing themselves up or whatever they do?" he added.

Awes's pastor at Stedfast Baptist Church, Jonathan Shelley, is known for his rabid anti-LGBTQ rhetoric. Originally based in the Fort Worth suburb of Hurst, Shelley's church was evicted from its building because Shelley's violent rhetoric violated the terms of his lease. Shelley subsequently relocated the church to another suburb, Watauga. The Southern Poverty Law Center designated Stedfast Baptist an anti-LGBTQ hate group in 2021.[31]

Shelley frequently calls for the death of members of the LGBTQ community, but he insists he's not calling for vigilante killings—he wants it done officially, at the hands of the state. In one sermon, he celebrated the death of a seventy-five-year-old gay man in Wilton Manors, Florida, after a vehicle accidentally ran him over during a Pride event: "And, you know, it's great when trucks accidentally go through those, you know, parades," he said. "I think only one person died. So hopefully we can hope for more in the future."

"You say, 'Well, that's mean.' Yeah, but the Bible says that they're worthy of death!" he continued. "They say, 'Are you sad when fags die?' No. I think it's great! I hope they all die! I would love it if every fag would die right now."

Shelley posted a video decrying his church's eviction and the negative publicity, claiming he was simply preaching within the Christian mainstream. At the end, he connected pedophilia with the LGBTQ community: "I believe that the Bible clearly teaches that those that are the LGBTQ are pedophiles in waiting and they would love to harm and hurt children. And so for the better interest of society, they should be punished according to God's word, no more or no less."

Awes's father-in-law, Pastor Aaron Thompson, oversees a fundamentalist church in Vancouver, Washington, where he preaches a similar message. Thompson tells his flock that teachers who encourage "the filth of sodomy" should be "shot in the back of the head." But like Shelley, he insists that he only wants the executions to occur at the hands of government officials. He clarifies that if any Christian acts on this outside the law, "they didn't get that idea from me."[32]

THE BARRAGE OF ELIMINATIONIST rhetoric directed at the LGBTQ community for 2022's Pride events shortly manifested itself in real-world threats in early June in Dallas, where a notorious white nationalist led a crew of protesters who attempted to invade a family-friendly drag show held as part of the city's Pride Week.[33]

Anti-fascist activists prevented them from storming the drag show, so the crowd of about forty protesters stood outside and hurled abuse at participants while carrying signs reading "Stop exploiting our kids" and "Confuse a child, abuse a child." It had been organized on Facebook by an anti-LGBTQ outfit called Protect Texas Kids, but the crowd's leader was John Doyle, a leading figure in the American Populist Union (APU) and a popular YouTuber who specializes in racist, misogynist, and homophobic rants. He marched up to the people gathering for the event, harassing them with snide remarks through a bullhorn, calling them groomers and pedophiles. One mother, who had accompanied children who fled in terror from Doyle and his posse of about a dozen MAGA-hatted Groypers, turned and berated the smirking young men: "Shame on you!"

Some of the protesters attempted to enter the venue through side doors and were prevented from doing so by anti-fascist counterprotesters.

Another man—an African American who told other protesters, "I'm not a Nazi, I'm a fascist"—attempted to follow a family with children who exited the venue but was likewise prevented from doing so by anti-fascist counterprotesters.

Doyle and his compatriots were undisguised provocateurs. One protester standing next to him and smirking told a rainbow-haired counterprotester, "It's going to be so kek [awesome] when we take away all your rights." Doyle chimed in: "Every one, every single one of them."

He later berated police officers who prevented them from tangling with anti-fascists, urging them to go inside and arrest the drag show's participants. "The sheriffs in Texas need to go in there and blow off all their heads," he told them. "That's what the badge is for."

Doyle is one of the white-nationalist radical right's fresh faces, unrepentantly bigoted and unapologetically neofascist in his politics. Thanks to his large YouTube following of over 300,000, he's one of the leading figures in the APU, which the ADL describes as "a Groyper-esque group that champions anti-immigration and anti-LGBTQ+ sentiments and regards the modern GOP as a corrupt, globalist conservative establishment."[34]

Doyle was a featured speaker at that year's America First PAC convention, held in Florida in February, organized by white nationalist Nick Fuentes and featuring an array of both Republican and extremist far-right speakers. Fuentes's America First organization is an alt-right-derived neofascist group that specializes in confrontational politics targeting other right-wing groups as well as promoting fanatical Trumpism and pro-Russian authoritarianism, with a growing "Groyper army" (a cartoon frog named Groyper is their mascot) that specializes in the politics of intimidation.

Arizona congressman Paul Gosar, the GOP's leading white nationalist in Congress, earlier in 2022 promoted his upcoming appearance at a "social mixer type event" sponsored by the APU featuring himself and Doyle, as well as Arizona Republican state senator Warren Petersen, to be held on April 20—Adolf Hitler's birthday (though the APU didn't mention that in its promotional material). When the event was publicized in the press, both Gosar and Petersen quickly retreated, claiming they had never agreed to appear.

Doyle's wildly popular YouTube channel, Heck Off, Commie!, is an amalgam of classic alt-right themes: racism, anti-Semitism, nativism, conspiracism, and heavy doses of insecurity-fueled misogyny. Doyle, just twenty one years old, offers to rescue his fellow young white men from emasculation and social alienation, urging them to revive their traditional roles as guardians of society. He also denounces pornography, claims the water supply is infused with estrogen, and fixates on IQ differences and physiognomy using pseudoscientific stereotypes. He commingles a hatred of the LGBTQ community with a reverence for what he and his cohorts call "an epic warrior masculinity," which they claim is "the strength that builds nations, slays giant beasts, and defends your city from an invading army."

Both Doyle and Fuentes have described themselves as "Christian fascists."[35] The event in Dallas, a week before the Pride event in Coeur d'Alene, was the first proof of how the young white Christian nationalist foot soldiers of the right were beginning to coalesce with the broader conservative mainstream—primarily when united around common enemies. And they now had a list of targets: "Groomers" and "Antifa" were just those now residing atop it. Enter the Proud Boys.

THE RIGHT-WING PANIC EQUATING the LGBTQ community with pedophilic "groomers" was tailor-made for neofascist attack dogs like the Proud Boys.

So it was hardly surprising that, after the initial wave of attacks on Pride events in 2022 were led by white nationalists and Christian nationalists, the white-nationalist street-brawling gang would swing into action. Aligning with their post-insurrection local-activism strategy, they began showing up at Pride events in small local venues, notably libraries where children were being read to during story hours.[36]

Proud Boys engaged in a number of attacks on Pride events, particularly those that were drag queen related. On June 11 in San Lorenzo, California—a Bay Area suburb—Proud Boys arrived at the local library during a drag queen story hour to shout homophobic slurs and threaten both the audience (which included children) and the person doing the reading.[37]

A day later in Arlington, Texas, a cluster of Proud Boys wearing polos and face masks from the Buc-ee's rest stop franchise (which have become the unofficial facial coverings of choice for Texas Proud Boys) showed up outside the Rangers stadium to protest a scheduled Pride Week brunch for drag queens—which was in fact a ticketed event exclusively for people twenty-one and older, so no children were nearby. Nonetheless, the Proud Boys and their Christian fascist cohorts not only continued to protest, but some invaded the event and harassed patrons, while others loudly threatened anti-fascists who had shown up.[38]

Nine days later in Wilmington, North Carolina, a group of Proud Boys showed up outside the library to support protesters who were decrying a Pride story hour reading going on inside. The men trooped into the building, flashing white-nationalist "OK" signs and heading down the hallways to the meeting room where the reading was being held, stopped outside the doorway, then shouted obscenities and epithets at the people inside. Eventually, the remaining families inside the event were escorted out a side door. The Proud Boys then reportedly began harassing regular library patrons. One of them scuffled with a patron outside who threatened to mace him, but police intervened.[39]

A few days later, at a library in South Bend, Indiana, seven Proud Boys shut down a similar Rainbow Storytime reading event.[40]

The ADL reported that it monitored seven in-person extremist actions targeting LGBTQ communities in one weekend alone, that of June 11 and 12. A number of these were organized by Christian nationalists, though other elements—notably militiamen, white nationalists, and neofascist paramilitary groups like the Proud Boys and Patriot Front, were also involved.[41] For the Proud Boys—which had developed a post-January 6 antidemocratic strategy of deploying their thuggery at primarily local events organized by others—it was an ideal fit.

"This is perversion and it can't be taught to children," one of the Proud Boys in South Bend could be heard telling the host in a video of the event. "What gives you the right to push a sexual question on a child?" demanded one of them to the librarian in charge. They later posted photos of themselves flashing the white-nationalist "OK" hand sign.

Kelly Neidert, the founder of Protect Texas Kids, was one of the primary generators of the hate campaign in Texas and elsewhere. She had been organizing protests outside Pride events, including the one in Dallas. Neidert—who also has described herself online as a Christian fascist—was eventually expelled from Twitter after she posted: "Let's start rounding up people who participate in Pride events."

It was Neidert who organized the failed protest involving Proud Boys at the Rangers stadium in Arlington. The same men showed up at a city council meeting in Frisco, Texas, where Neidert was testifying against the local Pride Week proclamation. Seated in front of them was Steph Gardella, who was running for local justice of the peace.

She told *Salon*'s Kathryn Joyce that she heard them call the LGBTQ community disgusting and pedophiles while implying that they should haul parents who brought their children to the event outside to beat them up.

"Bluster doesn't bother me. People being incredibly mouthy and saying hateful things doesn't bother me. But there was something about the energy of these guys that had the hackles on the back of my neck standing up," said Gardella. "What I saw in Frisco made me scared to open my door at home."[42]

The June 11 incident in San Lorenzo, California, was similarly frightening to local residents. Five Proud Boys disrupted the event, with children, parents, and other members of the community present.

They "began to shout homophobic and transphobic slurs" and were described as "extremely aggressive," deputies said, adding that they had a "threatening violent demeanor causing people to fear for their safety."

Drag queen Panda Dulce, who hosted the event, told *BuzzFeed News* that the attendees were singing a welcome song together—"as wholesome as you can imagine"—when the Proud Boys showed up.[43]

The men seated themselves in the second row, behind children and parents. One of them wore a T-shirt decorated with an AK-47 and the words, "Kill Your Local Pedophile." When Dulce stopped the song, the men yelled, "Who brought the tranny?" and hurled insults, calling her a pedophile and a groomer.[44]

Dulce warned that the LGBTQ community wouldn't be backing down: "They want us to disappear. They want us to not exist so they don't have to confront their own discomfort with the idea that there are people different from them in the world," she said. "But guess what? There are people different from you in the world. And we're going to stay here. And we're going to continue doing what we're doing. And we're going to be visible about it."

AS MORE MAINSTREAM REPUBLICANS participated in and condoned this campaign of hatred, it became clear that the long-running radicalization of the Republican Party, both at its highest reaches and among its rank-and-file membership, had sharply intensified since the January 6 insurrection. It was the kind of radicalization into an antidemocratic entity that raised serious doubts that the Republican Party could be a reliable partner in a viable democratic system.[45]

So the Southern Poverty Law Center set about to determine just how deeply this radicalization process had infected the party, as well as its effects on the larger body politic, by partnering with Tulchin Research to poll 1,500 Americans about their political beliefs and attitudes. The findings, published in June 2022, were disturbing: nearly 70 percent of Republicans believed in the Great Replacement theory—claiming that liberals are plotting to replace white Americans with brown immigrants—and even more of them believed that the 2020 election was "stolen."[46]

The GOP's radicalization manifested itself in numerous ways—notably, both in the numbers of far-right candidates seeking office in 2022 as well as in studies examining the spread of such belief systems among officials who already held public office. Whole state Republican parties were overwhelmed by extremists in places like Oregon and Florida.

Other studies have demonstrated the saturation of QAnon conspiracist-cult beliefs into the Republican power structure and its voting base. Most of all, the largest component of the growing Republican radicalization is the permeation of the far-right Patriot movement into its rhetoric and belief systems, the source of many of the extremist beliefs now common with the GOP mainstream.

Among the SPLC's findings in the poll:

- The seven out of ten Republicans who believe that America's ongoing demographic changes were being purposefully driven by liberal and progressive politicians intent on "replacing conservative voters" are just as likely to believe that the 2020 election was "stolen," and that the government was using the January 6 insurrection to persecute conservatives.

- While most Americans overall view the country's changing demographics positively, Republicans decidedly do not, with 67 percent viewing it as a threat to white people. In contrast, 64 percent of Democrats say they find the country's increasing diversity to be at least a somewhat positive development, while 25 percent say demographic changes represent a threat to white Americans.
- The majority of Republicans perceive the 2020 racial-justice protests as an attack on white people. When asked about the protests their preferred response was that they were a destructive "overreaction that has unfairly made white people the enemy in America."

The poll also found a growing consensus among right-wing Americans that transgender people and "gender ideology" constitute a threat to children and the larger society. While 52 percent of Americans overall agree that discrimination against transgender people is a serious problem, 39 percent of Republicans (and 23 percent of Democrats) agree that they are a threat to children. Some 63 percent of Republicans believe that transgender people "are trying to indoctrinate children into their lifestyle."

"Each side has radically different visions of America: On the right, a large faction is invested in pushing back against pluralism and equity, while the left largely embraces those values," the report observes.

There is also a stark difference in the two sides' views on the viability of democracy: Just over half of people polled agree that the government "has become tyrannical," including 70 percent of Republicans and 78 percent of those who consider themselves "very conservative." Only 29 percent of Republicans say they had even a fair amount of trust in the federal government, compared to 60 percent of Democrats. Significantly more Republicans have faith in their state and local governments—51 percent and 59 percent—while Democrats' level of confidence remains steady across those institutions.

Earlier in 2022, the SPLC's annual report on hate groups in America noted that, while the sheer numbers of such groups had been in decline in recent years, the underlying extremist beliefs that fuel them were spreading widely into the mainstream under the aegis of the Republican Party. There are fewer hate groups because their beliefs are no longer contained in hate groups. These numbers tell us not only how far these beliefs have spread, but are also an ample warning that democracy itself is nearing a crisis stage.[47]

Notably, the increasingly violent and threatening nature of right-wing extremism is instilling a like-minded response throughout the populace: "Across the political spectrum," the report warns, "we found substantial support for threatening or acting violently against perceived political opponents."

"When we asked respondents if they approved of threatening or assassinating a politician, for example, roughly one in five said they at least somewhat approved," it adds.

The polling found that Republicans more often agree that "some violence may be necessary to get the country back on track." Many Americans are increasingly pessimistic: 44 percent of the respondents—53 percent of Republicans and 39 percent of Democrats—say the "U.S. seems headed toward a civil war in the near future."

For many of the extremists on the radical right, that has been the intent all along.

2

"When Do We Get to Use the Guns?"

CHARLIE KIRK GOT A surprise question of sorts when he brought his Critical Racism Tour to Nampa, Idaho, in late October 2021. In front of a packed crowd at the Nampa Civic Center, Kirk—the leader of right-wing campus organization Turning Point USA (TPUSA)—regaled his audience with warnings of an "imminent cold war" being fomented by liberal provocateurs.[1]

During a Q&A session that followed, a bearded man in his early thirties asked Kirk pointedly: "At this point, we're living under a corporate and medical fascism. This is tyranny. When do we get to use the guns?"

When the crowd whooped, he insisted he wasn't joking: "How many elections are they gonna steal before we kill these people?" he asked.

The crowd seemed mostly supportive of this view, so Kirk tried to calm them down by distancing himself from the question, but he seemed to empathize with the underlying sentiment:

> No, uh, hold on. Stop, hold on. I'm gonna denounce that and I'm gonna tell you why. Because you're playing into their plans, and they're trying to make you do this . . . They are trying to provoke you and

everyone here. They are trying to make you do something that will be violent, that will justify a takeover of our freedoms and liberties the likes of which we have never seen. We are close to having momentum to get this country back on a trajectory using the peaceful means that we have at us.

So to answer your question—and I just think it's, you know, overly blunt—we have to be the ones that do not play into the violent aims and ambitions of the other side. They fear—let me say this very clearly—they fear us holding the line with self-control and discipline, taking over school board meetings. They're the ones that are willing to use federal force against us.

I know that people get fired up. We are living under fascism. We are living under this tyranny. But if you think for a second they're not wanting you to all of a sudden get to that next level, where all of a sudden they're going to say, "We need Patriot Act 2.0." If you think that Waco was bad, wait till you see what they want to do next.

His interlocutor responded: "I just want to know, where is the line?"
Kirk answered:

The line is when we exhaust every single one of our state ability to push back against what's happening. We haven't even started the process of having Idaho, or states like Idaho, get back to self-government as our founders envisioned. They gave us state sovereignty!

What is the line? Look, man, I think we're at the teetering edge of a regime that knows that good decent Americans are gonna get to the place where, like in the movie *Network*, 'I'm mad as hell and I'm not gonna take it anymore!' Right? Well guess what? Know that there's a deeper game at play. Understand the psychological warfare that's being played here. They're trying to animate you. They're trying to get you to do something that then justifies what they actually want to do.

So what's the solution? We need to start to demand Idaho to be Idaho, and the federal government can stay out of Idaho for just about everything.

Ultimately, Kirk's "denunciation" of the question amounted primarily to urging the audience to wait and hold on to that violence for the time being while proceeding to attack local and state governments when they fail to follow their extremist agenda.

When video of the exchange went briefly viral, most Idaho Republicans were silent—except for the local Republican legislator from Nampa, Rep. Ben Adams, who tweeted that it was a reasonable question:

> Our Republic would not exist without this kind of rhetoric. The question is fair, but Charlie Kirk probably isn't the person to ask.

Indeed, while the video caused a brief stir among mainstream liberals, this kind of discussion was already quite commonplace among right-wing circles online—particularly among the "Patriots" who were eager to defend the cause of the January 6 Capitol insurrection. After all, talk of a "civil war" had been circulating in militia-movement circles since their origins in the 1990s and had intensified as they became unleashed during Donald Trump's candidacy and tenure as president.

The impulse for eliminationist political violence, moreover, is latent in all of this (if not explicit, as Kirk's interlocutor was): even if Kirk's audience heeded his advice and bided their time, it was being told explicitly to overthrow local authorities if they failed to enact their extremist ideas and displace reality—such as Joe Biden's election as president—with their conspiracy theories and disinformation. No surprise that TPUSA was a major sponsor of the January 6 Stop the Steal rally that preceded the attack on the Capitol, providing seven buses carrying 350 people: this is how "conflict entrepreneurs" like Kirk operate.

The politics of eliminationism reached a fever pitch during Trump's tenure in the White House. In the post-Trump era, though, his rabid fans simply ripped off the mask of plausible deniability and began calling for killing liberals and Trump critics—which includes anyone who believes he lost the 2020 election to Joe Biden.

One way hard-core Trump fans expressed their eagerness to inflict lethal force on their political foes was by flying an American flag with the stars and stripes showing as varying shades of black. These flags, according to the people who promoted them on Facebook and other social media, were a way to declare "no quarter" against liberals in the "coming civil war."[2]

The black flags were promoted heavily on TikTok, where people posted videos of themselves or friends hanging the black flag from their front-porch flagpoles. The videos commonly used two different pieces of music as accompaniment: The first, "Hoist the Colours," is a gloomy sea shanty from *Pirates of the Caribbean: At World's End*, foretelling doom when the black flag is raised; the second, the song "God We Need You Now" by country rapper Struggle Jennings and cowriter Caitlynne Curtis, features QAnon-flavored lyrics that threaten retribution against the people who "desecrate" the "values of our country and our God."

Many of the same right-wing channels featuring black flag raisings were rife with "patriots" advising their cohorts to prepare for a civil war. Their primary grievance seemed to revolve around COVID-19 restrictions, with a number of military members talking about their imminent discharges for refusing to be vaccinated.

Curiously, these same extremists who accuse liberals of fomenting civil war discuss the idea of declaring or fighting a civil war with an intensity noticeably absent from liberal forums. Conversations about civil war, including discussions of strategies and weapons intended for use, proliferate almost entirely in right-wing social media circles.

On the first anniversary of the January 6 insurrection, a number of researchers from different organizations presented reports surveying the preceding year that were unanimous in several key findings: particularly that the conspiracist, insurrection-prone "Patriots" who attacked the Capitol and applauded the siege afterward had pivoted from organizing at the national level and were now focused primarily on asserting themselves within local right-wing Republican politics.[3] The intent was to overthrow liberal democracy from the bottom up.

Heidi Beirich, the longtime intelligence director at the Southern Poverty Law Center, now director of the Global Project Against Hate and Extremism, warned that the growing radicalization of the American right has pushed the United States to the brink of authoritarianism:

> The situation has become so serious that a member of the CIA's Political Instability Task Force warned in December that the U.S. is "closer to civil war" than most would ever believe. Professor Barbara Walter pointed out that, "if you were an analyst in a foreign country looking at events in America—the same way you'd look at events in Ukraine or Ivory Coast or Venezuela—you would go down a checklist, assessing each of the conditions that make civil war likely . . . And what you would find is that the United States, a democracy founded more than two centuries ago, has entered very dangerous territory." Walter believes that the U.S. has passed through stages of "pre-insurgency" and "incipient conflict" and may now be in "open conflict," beginning with the Capitol insurgency. Walter also says the U.S. has become an "anocracy"—"somewhere between a democracy and an autocratic state."[4]

The most troubling aspect of the radicalization, Beirich observed, was the spread of accelerationist beliefs that encouraged societal breakdown. She noted that while paramilitary groups like the Oath Keepers and Proud Boys played prominent roles in the insurrection, the "prosecutions of those involved . . . has failed to shut down these groups, as has the participation of active-duty military and veterans failed to inspire serious measures to weed out extremists and prevent troops from being radicalized."

The insurrectionist movement, in fact, is composed of people who not only are often heavily armed, but have been openly itching for a civil war—and have been doing so for a long time.

———

THE FIRST ITERATIONS OF right-wing agitation for a modern-day civil war came from the most vicious and extreme corners of the racist right that took root in the mid-1970s and came to life in the 1980s in places like northern Idaho, where the Aryan Nations (AN) operated for more than two decades, producing a wave of hate crimes and domestic terrorism that left a scar in the Pacific Northwest, the place where many of these racists dreamed of creating a "white homeland"—and where many still do.

Commingled with the separatism, and fueled by their racist Christian Identity belief system, the essence of the AN was a revolutionary fervor that was embodied by the novel *The Turner Diaries*, a badly written racial screed about a gang of fascist thugs whose terroristic acts spark a civil war that results in the mass hanging of white "race traitors" in America and the government's overthrow. Its author was William Pierce, the leader of the neo-Nazi hate group the National Alliance, for many years one of the favorite affiliations of skinhead thugs.

Pierce's book was popular among the people who participated in Aryan Nations events, particularly with a group of "action-oriented" racists who met there, led by a youthful militant named Robert Mathews. Following the blueprint in Pierce's book, they dubbed themselves the Order and set out to finance the racist right's "revolution" with robberies and counterfeiting, with an assassination agenda on the side. Their eight-month criminal rampage ended in December 1984, after the FBI tracked down its members—including Mathews, who died in a shootout with federal agents.

However, Pierce's novel continued to inspire mass murder. In 1995, a devotee of *The Turner Diaries* named Timothy McVeigh followed the recipe for making a truck bomb laid out in the book to blow up the Murrah Federal Building in Oklahoma City in retaliation for failed federal gun raids at Ruby Ridge, Idaho, and Waco, Texas.

McVeigh's terrorism was powered by the same far-right anger at the federal government that was intrinsic to the Patriot militia movement in whose meetings he sometimes participated. Even after the Oklahoma bombing, militias kept organizing, and domestic terrorists continued to strike. But the movement went into hiatus after 9/11 and remained on pause during most of the Bush years, manifesting mostly as border vigilante militias.

The Patriot militia movement and its attendant "civil war" rhetoric began to reemerge in late 2008 and early 2009, fueled primarily by right-wing backlash to the election of a liberal Black president. The so-called Tea Party movement—though usually portrayed in right-wing media as a wholesome collection of devoted, patriotic Americans—in short order became a major conduit for far-right extremists to promulgate their ideas and agendas within the mainstream of Republican discourse—including, of course, their revived warnings of a looming civil war, even as they were buying up guns and ammo by the Humvee-load.[5]

The conspiracist right-wing news website *WorldNetDaily* polled its readers in August 2009 on the question: "Is America on the verge of revolution?" Some 6,671 readers responded: 95 percent of them expressed eager assent. Some 49 percent of them agreed: "Yes, I'm overjoyed to finally see other Americans who feel like I do and who want to take our country back." Another 21 percent answered, "Yes, it's already started," while 18 percent responded, "Yes, the sleeping giant is finally waking up," and 7 percent said, "Yes, it makes me feel proud to be an American."

Pretty soon, Americans were seeing nutty conspiracy theories showing up on their mainstream cable television, particularly Glenn Beck's Fox News show, which warned that America would look like a *Mad Max* hellscape by 2014—run by "independent militias" and biker gangs.[6] Then there were people like ex-Marine Charles Dyer popping up on YouTube wearing death's-head masks and threatening civil war under Obama—that is, until he was arrested and imprisoned for molesting his own daughter.[7] And even more classically, there was Tyler Smith, the would-be "marauder" doomsday prepper who schemed about doing postapocalyptic home invasions, and was busted by authorities after appearing on the National Geographic TV program *Doomsday Preppers* toting numerous guns in spite of a felony conviction.[8]

As the Obama presidency continued and then wound down, the talk about civil war became louder, especially in the conspiracy-theory world led by *Infowars* host Alex Jones, who held forth on the idea of race war on his show during the height of the racial unrest in Ferguson, Missouri.[9] Meanwhile, Klansmen in West Virginia were telling their recruits that returning military veterans would be prime recruits for their white-nationalist cause.[10]

In between, there were rabid-right talk radio hosts like Michael Savage, an early supporter of the idea of a Donald Trump presidency (dating back to 2011). Savage published a book titled *Stop the Coming Civil War*. It was less about preventing one than preparing to engage in one.[11]

"The United States," Savage wrote, "may well be in the midst of a military, economic, and cultural collapse that is turning us into a country in danger of catastrophic failure and leading to the nightmarish scenario of a civil war."

Savage claimed that the entire Obama presidency was the product of a massive conspiracy: "The financial crash of 2008 was engineered by an elite group of financial professionals in order to help ensure the election of Barack Obama and guarantee the continued complicity of the U.S. government and its cadre of economic advisors," he wrote.

The Savage Truth of the matter is that our government is preparing for nothing less than the next civil war. It's marshaling forces to be used against the American people, but the very divisions that the government is creating are causing many Americans to think about what we must do to resist this government takeover.

While promoting the book, Savage was more explicit about just who the government will be waging this civil war against: white Americans. "It's very important to understand this. This entire federal government is geared up to fight a war against white people," Savage told his listeners. He also warned them that the administration is "planning to mow down all you white crackers."

His answer to stopping the looming conflict: Elect far-right Republicans to every office. Otherwise, you might as well get your guns ready.

The civil war talk came home to roost late in the Obama administration, when far-right militiamen held extended armed standoffs, led by Cliven Bundy and his sons, in Nevada in 2014 and then in Oregon in 2016, claiming the federal government had no right to ownership of public lands. Bundy claimed afterward to his fellow "Patriots" that the Lord told him that he needed to face down the agents, or the nation would need to "face these arms in a civil war" with the federal government.[12] A speaker at Bundy's ranch, militia figure Mike Vanderboegh, ranted that "we are still staring a civil war in its bloody face." The government eventually brought federal charges against the Bundys for both standoffs, but while some participants ended up with long prison terms, the cases against the primary instigators failed in court—setting a precedent that in many ways green-lighted the "Patriots" in ramping up seditionist resistance to the government.

Then, as Donald Trump's campaign for election to the presidency—and, with it, most of the far right's most fervent hopes and dreams—wound down to its final stages, the militiamen became active, warning that they were preparing for armed resistance to a Hillary Clinton administration.

And Trump's supporters at campaign events were just as explicit, warning that if Clinton won, they would not accept the results.[13]

"No, I don't care, because we are gonna take this country back no matter what," one Trump fan told a TV interviewer in October 2016. "She's going to prison. Even if they pull off the fake campaign with all the voter fraud, and she wins . . . We're going to rebellion. We're overthrowing this country. We're getting rid of this clown act. It's over. Clinton, the Marxists, it's over."[14]

WE'LL NEVER KNOW FOR certain whether accused domestic-terrorist-in-the-making Christopher Hasson would have ever acted on his desire to spark a racial civil war by committing the assassinations and mass killings for which he had so thoroughly prepared and about which he endlessly fantasized. We do know, however, exactly what might have been the spark to send the forty-nine-year-old Coast Guardsman from Baltimore off on a killing rampage, though: the impeachment of President Trump.

Hasson was arrested in February 2019 after an investigation into his illicit drug transactions on a Coast Guard base uncovered evidence that he had been plotting a massive domestic-terrorist attack, including a series of planned assassinations. Foremost among his targets were leading media and Democratic Party figures, including MSNBC's Joe Scarborough, Ari Melber, and Chris Hayes; CNN's Van Jones and Don Lemon; House Speaker Nancy Pelosi; Rep. Alexandria Ocasio-Cortez; and Sens. Kamala Harris, Elizabeth Warren, and Cory Booker.[15]

To carry out these assassinations, Hasson had amassed an armory in his basement, including fifteen weapons and one thousand rounds of ammunition. In his deleted emails, investigators found Hasson musing about carrying out a "two-pronged attack" using bioterror weapons and a sniper attack. Inspired in large part by Norwegian terrorist Anders Breivik—and in particular by Breivik's ardent belief in the white-nationalist hoax theory called cultural Marxism—Hasson wrote: "I am dreaming of a way to kill almost every last person on earth."

He also was a fanatical white nationalist. In addition to his admiration for Breivik, Hasson corresponded with other neo-Nazis. He was particularly keen on the work of white supremacist Harold Covington, who promoted creating a "white homeland" in the Pacific Northwest, but who died in 2018.

"How long can we hold out there and prevent niggerization of the Northwest until whites wake up on their own or are forcibly made to make a decision whether to roll over and die or wake up on their own remains to be seen," Hasson wrote Covington in a 2017 draft letter.[16]

Buried in Hasson's deleted emails were his working notes for events around which he was planning actions, notably: "what if trump illegally impeached" and "civil war if trump impeached."

It's not hard to find the source of Hasson's belief that civil war would erupt if President Trump were to face impeachment: By early 2019, civil war had become an endemic talking point and source of speculation among right-wing pundits. The same week as Hasson's arrest, longtime Republican operative Joseph diGenova went on Laura Ingraham's Fox News show and warned:

> We are in a civil war in this country. There's two standards of justice, one for Democrats, one for Republicans. The press is all Democrat, all liberal, all progressive, all left—they hate Republicans, they hate Trump. So the suggestion that there's ever going to be civil discourse in this country for the foreseeable future in this country is over. It's not going to be. It's going to be total war. And as I say to my friends, I do two things—I vote and I buy guns.[17]

This was now a commonplace among right-wing pundits and political figures. Longtime Trump aide Roger Stone was fond of warning that civil war lay around the corner if any attempt were made to remove Donald Trump from office.[18] Televangelist and Trump ally Jim Bakker made similar warnings only a few months into the presidency: "If it happens, there will be a civil war in the United States of America. The Christians will finally come out of the shadows because we are going to be shut up permanently if we're not careful."[19]

Far-right pundits like Kurt Schlichter have pondered what a civil war might look like—concluding, naturally, that the right will kick the left's asses:

> There are two Civil War II scenarios, and the left is poorly positioned to prevail in either one. The first scenario is that the Democrats take power and violate the Constitution in order to use the apparatus of the federal government to suppress and oppress Normal Americans. In that scenario, red Americans are the insurgents. In the second scenario, which we can even now see the stirrings of in California's campaign to nullify federal immigration law, it is the blue states that are the insurgents.
>
> The Democrats lose both wars. Big time.[20]

Even before Trump's election, talk of civil war was bubbling up with great frequency among far-right militiamen who believed a Hillary Clinton presidency would bring about a fresh kind of "tyranny," many of whom prepared for armed resistance in the event she won. Indeed, the talk cropped up in domestic-terrorism incidents: three Kansas militiamen arrested in October 2016 for plotting the truck bombing of a rural community of Somali refugees were acting under the assumption that Clinton would win, and were planning to attack the day after the November election as an opening act of resistance to her administration.[21]

But the prospect of Trump's premature removal from office had always sent his supporters on the extremist right into rhetorical frenzies and fueled their frequently violent action in street protests. That particularly became the case once Trump had, in fact, been impeached by the House in December 2019 for abuse of power involving his attempts to withhold aid from Ukraine as a means to pressure the nation's president into opening an investigation into Joe Biden.

After the House voted to impeach him on December 18, the fanatical MAGA supporters became even more unhinged.[22]

"He's not gonna be removed. He's not gonna be removed. He's not gonna be removed," one attendee at a Trump rally told a CBS reporter. When the reporter asked, "Do you feel confident in that?" he responded, "My .357 Magnum is comfortable with that. End of story."

Texas representative Louie Gohmert—who had talked up civil war on several previous occasions—went ballistic on the floor of the House, warning that impeachment meant the end of America: "This is a travesty. We're in big trouble," Gohmert huffed, adding, "Now it's lowered even further, the bar. [Impeachment] will be used for political battles and this country's end is now in sight. I hope I don't live to see it. This is an outrage."

Louisiana congressman Clay Higgins was even more unhinged: "They fear the true will of we the people. They are deep established D.C. They fear, they call this Republican map flyover country. They call us deplorables. They fear our faith, they fear our strength, they fear our unity, they fear our vote, and they fear our president. We will never surrender our nation to career establishment D.C. politicians and bureaucrats. Our republic shall survive this threat from within. American patriots shall prevail."

The real action, however, was on social media, where Facebook and Twitter posts eagerly anticipating the violent uprising to preserve Trump's presidency became as common as houseflies.

Ex–Navy SEAL Jonathan Gilliam, for instance, used Gohmert's comments as a springboard on Twitter for open discussion of a shooting civil war in which conservatives begin killing liberals for attempting to remove Trump: "Like so many, I see exactly what he sees. Therefor [sic] it is time we begin considering the possibility of civil war."

A fairly typical response among far-right extremists was to pledge utter fealty to Trump, even unto death. Rene Hollan, a Monroe, Washington, man who was a regular participant in far-right street events organized by Patriot Prayer and the Proud Boys in the Pacific Northwest, posted a screed (later removed by Facebook) vowing that he would even detonate a nuclear bomb in a major liberal city:

> As a naturalized U.S. citizen who swore the Oath of Allegiance, if President Trump orders me to drive a truck with a nuke into a city with Facebook offices or an illegal sanctuary city, and detonate it, killing myself, everyone in the city, and rendering it a sheet of glass, it would be my honor to comply.

Social scientist Caroline Orr collected a large tranche of these kinds of comments on Twitter, noting, "It's easy to laugh at the keyboard warriors in the mix, but there are definitely extremists using this opportunity to try to bring about social and political upheaval by issuing calls for violence."

"Lock N Load, PATRIOTS, the demonrats just told us what they want for Christmas: #CivilWar2," wrote one. "Let's make the demon rats live on the streets of their own districts!"

"ALERT!! If the Democrats impeach OUR PRESIDENT WE NEED TO HAVE A CIVIL WAR," tweeted another. "America as we have known it will be gone and the squad will be in charge of us. I shiver thinking of it. A civil war will be the only way to get America back as we remember it."

This kind of rhetoric isn't being introduced to the discourse by mere accident. The "civil war" talking point, in fact, has been deliberately promoted by Russian intelligence agencies as part of their campaign to undermine American democracy. A Justice Department affidavit released in 2018 noted that the "civil war" meme is being directly encouraged by Internet Research Agency (IRA), the Russian-financed disinformation agency that purchased 3,500 ads on Facebook during the 2016 campaign with the intent of undermining American political consensus. The affidavit describes directions given to IRA's writers:

> Forcefully support Michael Savage's point of view with competence and honesty. Savage made it clear that any attempt to remove Trump is a direct path to a civil war in the United States. Name those who oppose the president and those who impede his efforts to implement his pre-election promises. Focus on the fact that the Anti-Trump Republicans: a) drag their feet with regard to financing the construction of the border wall; b) are not lowering taxes; c) slander Trump and harm his reputation (bring up McCain); d) do not want to cancel Obamacare; e) are not in a hurry to adopt laws that oppose the refugees coming from Middle Eastern countries entering this country. Summarize that in case Republicans will not stop acting as traitors, they will bring upon themselves forces of civil retribution during the 2018 elections.[23]

Over at Trump-friendly *Russia Today*, op-ed writer Robert Bridge bolstered the civil war talk with a piece headlined "Democrats' Push to Impeach Trump Is Just the Latest Chapter of US Civil War 2.0," in which he concluded, "What is happening now in Washington DC between the Republicans and Democrats is just mere dress rehearsal for far more disasters down the road. I just hope the costumes don't end up being blue and gray, once again."[24]

THE FAR-RIGHT EAGERNESS FOR civil war eventually took on a life of its own, particularly on white-nationalist-friendly chat forums like 4chan, 8chan, and Reddit, where discussions of extraordinary violence were frequently cloaked in cartoonish jocularity and black irony. That was where they came up with a name for their new-age conflict: the Boogaloo.

It appears to have been coined in a June 2018 Reddit thread titled "Civil

War 2: Electric Boogaloo"—an ironic reference to a cheesy 1984 breakdanc-ing film, *Breakin' 2; Electric Boogalo*—devoted to a discussion of the belief that liberal government officials were "coming for their guns."[25] The usage spread among gun owners throughout 2019 in their online chats about how they would respond to any government attempt to confiscate their weapons.

One Twitter user urged readers to obtain whatever guns and ammo they might need for the future because their ability to do so would soon be "se-verely curtailed," adding, "Button up for the #boogaloo. Now." There were a range of Boogaloo-related hashtags—#Boogaloo2020, #BoogalooBois, and #Boojahideen—as well as popular phrases: "boogaloo ready," "bring on the boogaloo," "showing up for the boogaloo," and "when the boogaloo hits." One tweet with the Boogaloo hashtag warned about one hundred million "active shooter" situations "when the cops try to do nationwide gun confiscations."[26]

As the name became familiar, the people promoting it began to fear that using the term would eventually result in their removal by the larger so-cial media platforms—particularly Facebook and Twitter—where Boogaloo talk gained wider traction, largely because the violence underlying the dis-cussions clearly violated their terms of service. (This was, in fact, eventu-ally the case, though both platforms were initially sluggish in responding to the matter.) Anticipating the crackdown, they began devising alterna-tive phrases to refer to the same thing, mainly mnemonic variations on Boogaloo, such as Big Igloo and Big Luau.

Soon enough, there were not only hashtags and memes using the terms spreading on social media, but even concrete uses of the alternative names in their imagery: a logo featuring a large igloo soon became the official ban-ner of the movement. At the same time, Boogaloo adherents began showing up at public demonstrations wearing Hawaiian shirts (referencing the "Big Luau") along with their body armor and, frequently, their weapons.[27]

The Boogaloo concept reached a kind of early zenith in January 2020, when thousands of gun owners descended on Richmond, Virginia, to protest the imminent passage of a raft of mostly moderate gun-control measures advocated by then-governor Ralph Northam.[28] In the month preceding the rally organized by the Virginia Citizens Defense League, "Patriot" militia groups angrily organized an effort to bring their followers to the Virginia Capitol to protest; they called it the Boogaloo.

A favorite component of the social media chatter was a New World Order conspiracy theory claiming that Northam intended to call in blue-helmeted troops from the United Nations to quell the uprising. One Twitter account featured a photo of a UN vehicle transport on Interstate 81 in western Virginia, declaiming: "As predicted! UN vehicles in Virginia to assist with shock-troop gun control! Are you ready! Photo captured yesterday! Foreign troops!"

Another account urged participants: "Buy a gripful of pistols and rifles. Train Train Train. Aim for the blue helmets and black hoodies."

The conspiracy theory spread like kudzu among militiamen. The leader of Washington state's Three Percent militia organization posted on Facebook an extension of the theory: namely, that a job posting on the United Nations website suggested a plan to incarcerate protesters. He titled it "Boogaloo is coming."

Northam announced a "state of emergency" less than a week before the planned gun protest, ordering the area around the Capitol shut down, and banning any kind of weapons in the area. "No weapons will be allowed on Capitol grounds," said Northam at a press conference. "Everything from sticks and bats to chains and projectiles. ... The list also includes firearms. It makes no sense to ban every other weapon but allow firearms when intelligence shows that armed militia groups plan to storm the Capitol."

Many of the would-be participants and their supporters remained defiant after Northam's announcement. "Carry your weapons anyway. Northam is trying to suppress turnout," one posted on Twitter. "I encourage all brothers and sisters to BRING THEIR WEAPONS and DEFY Gov. Blackface this week!" posted another.[29]

The Richmond rally four days later—rife with men wearing Hawaiian Boogaloo shirts, as well as a full complement of Three Percent militiamen and Oath Keepers—was raucous but generally nonviolent. However, its organizers made clear that their frequently seditionist rhetoric was not going away. Oath Keepers founder Stewart Rhodes—who eventually played a key role in the Capitol insurrection—told protest supporters that the momentum was building for a civil war:

> So yes, it could come down to a standoff. That's why it's important for, like I said, we want to reach out to the state police and National Guard as part of our mission when we go to Virginia, is reach out to them and encourage them to stand down because if they do act under the command of the governor, they come into a county, and they're resisted by the local militia or the sheriff and his posse, it will kick off a civil war in this country. That's what will happen. There will be a civil war between the left and the right and we'd prefer to see that not happen. That's where it's going to go.[30]

Nothing, it seems, quite inflames conspiracist paranoia like the onset of a global pandemic of mysterious origin, followed shortly by mass civil unrest among the African American populace over racist policing by American law enforcement.

The COVID-19 pandemic, which erupted globally within a month after the Richmond protest, became a virtual petri dish for cultivating the fear of societal collapse essential to the Boogaloo worldview, as well as that of the various "Patriots" drawn to it. The conditions created by federal, state, and local governments' attempts to contain the deadly illness—shutting down businesses and schools, requiring masks, encouraging residents to remain indoors and to practice social distancing in public—while businesses switched to creating remote spaces where their employees could work from home online, all resulted in large swaths of society being trapped indoors for entire months with plenty of time to explore the Internet.

A report from the research firm Moonshot found that online engagement time by people living in states with local "stay at home" directives lasting more than ten days increased 21 percent. Overall, there was a 13 percent increase in engagement in white-supremacist content on Google nationwide. This increase began around late March 2020, aligning with the imposition of these stay-at-home measures.[31]

The states experiencing the greatest increase in this engagement were Connecticut with 66 percent, followed by Idaho (56 percent) and Kentucky (48 percent). It decreased in a number of states, including Rhode Island (-38 percent) and Iowa (-30 percent), and the District of Columbia (-42 percent).

All too often, increased screen time meant more exposure to conspiracy theories, which were far more readily consumed than they were before, thanks largely to the chaotic and apocalyptic atmosphere of the disease's outbreak. The cultic QAnon phenomenon, for instance, grew phenomenally during the first six months of the COVID pandemic, attaining global influence.[32] Other far-right entities, particularly accelerationists and eco-fascists, worked hard to exploit the turmoil on social media. Similarly, the Boogaloo concept began to spread, particularly among armed "Patriots" of the militiaman variety.

The lockdown measures provided ample evidence for the Boogaloo conspiracists—in their minds, at least—of their long-running contention that "globalists" are seeking ways to enslave the world. Various conspiracy theories popular on the far right claimed that the virus was created so that nefarious globalist conspirators like Bill Gates and George Soros could implant chips in people receiving the necessary vaccines.

Signs referencing the Boogaloo began popping up at a number of the far-right-led protests against the lockdown measures. One marcher at the Reopen rally in Topeka, Kansas, on April 23 carried a large black "Big Igloo" flag.

In a relatively short span of time, the COVID-19 pandemic sharpened the interest in a civil war. An April 2020 study by the Tech Transparency Project (TTP) found that most of the 125 Facebook groups devoted to the Boogaloo—some 60 percent—had been created just as the states began declaring lockdowns and social distancing measures. Perhaps more worryingly, "they have attracted tens of thousands of members in the [previous] 30 days."[33]

In several private Boogaloo Facebook groups that TTP was able to access, members discussed tactical strategies, combat medicine, and various types of weapons, including how to develop explosives and the merits of using flamethrowers. Some members appeared to take inspiration from Donald Trump's tweets calling on people to "liberate" states where governors imposed stay-at-home orders.

Daniel E. Stevens, executive director of Campaign for Accountability, the umbrella organization under which TTP operates, remarked: "There is nothing subtle about how these extremist groups are using Facebook's platform to advance their cause. Boogaloo proponents are not simply discussing ideas or political views; they are directly advocating for violent action and tactically planning how to defeat government entities."

Boogaloo enthusiasts laid out detailed plans for how to achieve their goals, both militarily and through propaganda. Moreover, government and law enforcement were not the only targets that Boogaloo memes discussed. A subcurrent in a number of the violent fantasies expressed in their memes was the idea of committing home-invasion robberies targeting their relatively hapless and untrained neighbors as a means of thriving during the civil war—or a pandemic.[34]

One popular meme among Facebook "Boogaloo" followers showed a SWAT-style armed raid team in military gear massing outside a door, with the script: "Me and my boys going for a grocery run at my asshole neighbor's house." Another featured a grid of graphics demonstrating military hand signals during a raid, all of which are interpreted in the language of a home invasion: "Shoot that dog." "Cover up the evidence." "I found cocaine. It's pretty good." "Wrong house. Let's boogie!"

Another featured a photo of an angry Joaquin Phoenix in the film *Joker* with the script: "When you dispatch the normie with ease to raid their stash because they stocked up on TP and not ammunition"—with a subscript across the bottom reading: "You get what you fucking deserve."

One of the more commonly shared of these memes actually makes fun of other "preppers," particularly those who are suddenly new to the business amid the pandemic. It shows a "Virgin Prepper" who is "always scared, can't sleep at night," and "has no fun," then contrasts him with an obviously fun-loving "Chad Raider" who "Takes your good shit and burns all the rest so no one else can have it," and is seen holding up a bag marked "All Your Shit." He's also "not scared of death or coronavirus."

Soon enough, the Boogaloo movement began taking shape in the real world. In late April 2020, hundreds of camo-clad, gun-toting militia "Patriots" from around Michigan descended on the state Capitol in Lansing and occupied it for several hours, brandishing their weapons and threateningly demanding an end to Gov. Gretchen Whitmer's lockdown orders. The terrorism worked: the Republican-led Michigan House readily acquiesced (mainly because they agreed with the protesters), choosing not to extend the lockdown for another twenty-eight days, as Whitmer had requested.[35]

Jammed into the rotunda, the protesters attempted to march onto the House floor, but were prevented from doing so by the sergeant at arms and state police. Some chanted, "Let us in!" and, "This is the people's house, you cannot lock us out."

In addition to the weapons and body armor, a number of the protesters wore Hawaiian shirts, indicating they were participating in the Boogaloo. Some legislators felt so threatened that they also wore body armor to the session. "Some of my colleagues who own bullet proof vests are wearing

them. I have never appreciated our Sergeants-at-Arms more than today,"
tweeted Sen. Dayna Polehanki.

One of the many signs held by protesters threatening violence read:
"Tyrants get the rope."

Donald Trump urged Whitmer to talk to the protesters: "The Governor
of Michigan should give a little, and put out the fire," Trump tweeted.
"These are very good people, but they are angry."

He added: "They want their lives back again, safely! See them, talk
to them."

Michigan was hit particularly hard by the novel coronavirus pandemic.
Through April, the state had had 41,379 cases of the coronavirus, with
3,789 deaths.

Jim Ananich, Michigan's Democratic state senate minority leader said:
"This protest wasn't about the stay-at-home order, it was an opportunity
for a small group of folks—very few of whom were engaging in social distancing or wearing masks—to show off their swastika posters, Confederate
flags, nooses hanging from cars and signs calling for murder."

The Hawaiian shirts began showing up everywhere. At a large late-April
anti-lockdown protest in Olympia, Washington, a number of "Patriots" wearing Hawaiian shirts underneath their body armor were in the crowd. The
chief organizer of the Boogaloo motif there was Matt Marshall, the leader of
the Three Percent of Washington, based in Eatonville, Washington.[36]

The Boogaloo movement soon took on a life of its own, as a systematic study of its spread through social media found in 2020. Conducted by
the independent Network Contagion Research Institute (NCRI), the study
explored, according to its subtitle, "how domestic militants organize on
memes to incite violent insurrection and terror against government and
law enforcement."

The NCRI study found not only that the discussion of the Boogaloo on
social media had surged, but that discrete groups were coalescing around
the discussion and creating the nascent forms of a movement. It warned:

Boogaloo, a joke for some, acts as a violent meme that circulates instructions for a distributed, viral insurgency for others. The topic network for boogaloo describes a coherent, multi-component and detailed conspiracy to launch an inevitable, violent, sudden, and apocalyptic war across the homeland. The conspiracy, replete with suggestions to stockpile ammunition, may itself set the stage for massive real-world violence and sensitize enthusiasts to mobilize in mass for confrontations or charged political events.[37]

One of the Boogaloo groups featured in the study, calling itself Patriot Wave, illustrated perfectly how the lines between militia "Patriots" and alt-right white nationalists were completely blurred and submerged in the larger project of fomenting a violent civil war. Its members wore alt-right Pepe the Frog patches with the title "Boogaloo Boys," while others wore the skull balaclava generally associated with members of the fascist Atomwaffen Division.

The study also pointed to a particular area of concern: namely, the ability of these extremists to simply blend into existing power structures, including law enforcement and the military. Christopher Hasson, the coastguardsman arrested in 2019 with a full arms cache and a plan to assassinate liberal political leaders, was also a Boogaloo advocate. A Patriot Wave member is quoted in the study: "Some of the guys we were with aren't exactly out of the military yet, so they had to keep their faces covered."

This kind of informational conflict—or what the study calls "memetic warfare"—has evolved, the study said, "from mere lone-wolf threats to the threat of an entire meme-based insurgency."

THEN CAME THE PROTESTS against police brutality that followed the late-May murder of a Black man named George Floyd by a Minneapolis police officer, which erupted across the nation in cities both large and small. In a number of large cities—notably Minneapolis, New York, Chicago, Portland, and Seattle—the protests became violent, particularly as marchers clashed in the streets with police.

It became a prime moment for the Boogaloo movement to exploit. Some adherents dispersed among the marching crowds with their guns, claiming to be sympathetic to Black Lives Matter in their shared hatred of police. As a result, some analysts suggested that the Boogaloo movement was essentially apolitical—which couldn't have been further from reality.

Like many conspiracist and paranoiac movements, the Boogaloo proved to have a powerful tendency to produce real-life violence. This violence, in fact, demonstrated the movement's fundamentally far-right foundation.

The anti-police protests also drew Boogaloo Bois (as they styled themselves) intent on exploiting the events in an entirely different fashion—namely, as an opportunity to amplify the violence, targeting police while shifting the blame to the BLM and "Antifa" activists they despised equally—intensifying the public's fear of the "violent left." And it largely worked.

Steven Carrillo, a thirty-two-year-old Air Force sergeant with special combat training tried to make the Boogaloo a reality in June 2020 in Santa Cruz, California, when he embarked on a killing rampage targeting law-enforcement officers.[38]

Carrillo had an accomplice in Oakland: a thirty-year-old man from Millbrae named Robert Justus. According to prosecutors, the two men met in a Facebook Boogaloo group and discussed using the ongoing protests against the killing of George Floyd as a pretext for fueling their hoped-for conflagration.

The morning of May 29, 2020, Carrillo and Justus had an exchange: "It's on our coast now, this needs to be nationwide. It's a great opportunity to target the specialty group soup bois [a Boogaloo reference to federal law-enforcement agents]," Carrillo wrote.

"Let's boogie," answered Justus.

"Go to the riots and support our own cause. Show them the real targets,"

Carrillo wrote in another post. "Use their anger to fuel our fire. Think outside the box. We have mobs of angry people to use to our advantage."

That evening, the two men met in downtown Oakland and drove past the scene of the Black Lives Matter protest, with Carrillo in the passenger seat with a sniper rifle. Several blocks away from the protest, Carrillo opened fire on two federal security officers manning a guard booth at a downtown federal office building, killing one of them—David Patrick Underwood, fifty-three, an African American who lived in Pinole—and wounding Underwood's partner.

Carrillo and Justus remained at large for another week. Following reports of a van seen in the Santa Cruz mountains matching the description of one that witnesses identified at the scene in Oakland, deputies arrived at what turned out to be Carrillo's mountain compound stocked with guns, bombs, and ammunition. As they arrived Carrillo's van pulled away. Carrillo fled to a home in Ben Lomond. When deputies went to arrest him, he unleashed a torrent of gunfire and pipe bombs, killing one deputy and wounding another.

Carrillo, now wounded, left the scene in a white sedan. He was found an hour later back at his compound. As soon as he saw the deputies, he ran through his backyard, jumped onto a neighbor's property, and entered his home, demanding his car keys. His neighbor obeyed, but seeing an opportunity, tackled Carrillo from behind, knocking away his AR-15 and then knocking away both a pipe bomb and Carrillo's handgun when he tried to reach for them while on the ground. The neighbor held him there until deputies arrived and took Carrillo away.

On the hood of his car, Carrillo had scrawled a series of messages: "I became unreasonable," "Boog," and "Stop the duopoly." He was also heard to shout the latter slogan during the firefight.[39]

Carrillo's crime spree was not the act of a single "lone wolf" and his accomplice, but rather part of a larger plot by a group of far-right extremists who called themselves the Grizzly Scouts and planned a series of deadly attacks on law-enforcement officers with the intent of making it appear to be the work of the "violent left."

The Grizzly Scouts, according to a grand jury indictment handed down in April 2021, plotted a variety of lethal actions targeting law enforcement in the months and weeks before Carrillo embarked on his rampage. Carrillo was a key member of the group, which, in addition to planning attacks on police, engaged in paramilitary training exercises at the home of a member near Turlock, California.[40]

The four men named in the indictment—Jessie Alexander Rush, twenty-nine, of Turlock; Robert Jesus Blancas, thirty-three, of Castro Valley; Simon Sage Ybarra, twenty-three, of Los Gatos; and Kenny Matthew Miksch, twenty-one, of San Lorenzo—and Carrillo used a WhatsApp chat group for the Grizzly Scouts labeled "209 Goon HQ" to plan their attacks.

They formed a so-called "Quick Reaction Force" intended to perpetrate acts of violence, and sent one member to scout a protest in Sacramento. They also cooked up an "Operations Order" document describing police officers as "enemy forces," and described kidnapping one: "POWs will be searched for intel and gear, interrogated, stripped naked, blindfolded, driven away and released into the wilderness blindfolded with hands bound."

On May 26, three days before he shot Underwood, Carrillo messaged Ybarra that he wanted to conduct a "cartel style" attack on police, and the two men met in person in Ybarra's van to discuss the idea. Before leaving his home in Ben Lomond for Oakland on May 29, Carrillo had texted Ybarra that he was heading out to "snipe some you know what's."

During the week following the shootings, the Grizzly Scouts discussed their hopes that Trump would invoke the Insurrection Act as a response to the violence at the protests.

"[T]hat ^^^ will be our sign," Rush—who had himself previously served in the military—texted the others. "That effectively means the federal gov has declared war on things they're afraid of." He added that "the gov spent 100s of thousands of dollars on training me, im gonna use that shit."

The Grizzly Scouts also plotted to concoct violence between leftist anti-fascist groups and police. Blancas told the others that he was "totally down" with the idea of disguising himself as an anti-fascist while stirring up violence.

"It's the tactically sound option," Blancas wrote. "Them f—ing each other up only helps us."

Carrillo's path of radicalization was the subject of a *ProPublica* investigative piece that detailed how social media and internet conspiracy sites led him to join the Grizzly Scouts and plan acts of terrorist violence in the name of a far-right-fueled civil war. The report uncovered documents showing how the Grizzly Scouts went about organizing for those acts:

> The documents also make clear that Carrillo's military background, in particular his advanced combat and weapons training, provided exactly the qualities the Grizzly Scouts wanted in its recruits. The Grizzly Scouts' members—law enforcement officials say the group had attracted 27 recruits—were given military ranks and roles based on their level of military training and prior combat experience. Some Grizzly Scouts were designated "snipers," others were assigned to "clandestine operations," and some were medics or drivers. Whatever their role, all were expected to maintain go kits that included "combat gauze" and both a "primary" and "secondary" weapon.[41]

"This group was different," Jim Hart, the sheriff of Santa Cruz County, where Ben Lomond is located, told *ProPublica*. "There was a definite chain of command and a line of leadership within this group."

Ironically, Carrillo's lethal violence succeeded in spreading the right-wing narrative that the "violent left" was primarily responsible for the mayhem around anti-police-brutality protests. The very killings he perpetrated, in fact, were trotted out by Republican senator Ted Cruz as evidence of "antifa violence" during a Senate hearing, and by then-vice president Mike Pence in his GOP convention acceptance speech.[42]

Carrillo was only one of several Boogaloo Bois who set out to make their online fantasies real. A Texas man named Ivan Harrison Hunter who had been in contact with Carrillo decided to deploy similar tactics by traveling from San Antonio to Minneapolis to join in the anti-police protests there. He ended up unleashing a fusillade of semiautomatic-weapons fire on a Minneapolis police substation and assisting in setting it afire.[43]

The FBI arrested Hunter in October. Though Hunter had sworn he would "go down shooting," agents arrested him in San Antonio without incident.

According to the affidavit, Hunter traveled from Texas to Minneapolis on May 27 at the behest of other Boogaloo activists in the state, who put out a national call for help on Facebook. Hunter was in contact with another Boogaloo Boi, Ryan Teeter of North Carolina, who also traveled from his home state to Minnesota. That day, Teeter posted to Facebook: "Lock and load boys. Boog flags are in the air, and the national network is going off."

The FBI says that on the evening of May 28, Hunter fired off multiple rounds from a rifle resembling an AK-47, then ran away shouting: "Justice for Floyd!"

The next day, he boasted on Facebook that he had participated in setting the building on fire. "I helped the community burn down that police station," he wrote, later adding: "I didn't protest peacefully dude . . . Want something to change? Start risking felonies for what is good."

"The BLM protesters in Minneapolis loved me [sic] fireteam and I," he wrote on June 11.

Hunter and Carrillo had previously formed the so-called "fire team"— an action squad designed to respond with violence in the event of police attempting to take people's guns away. They exchanged texts on May 29, a day after the police station had been set on fire—and mere hours after Carrillo had shot two federal protection officers in Oakland.

"Boog," Hunter texted Carrillo, an apparent call for action.

"Did," Carrillo answered.

"Luv," Hunter replied.

"Currently in hide mode," Carrillo said.

"Target police stations," Hunter answered.

"I did better lol," Carrillo texted back. Hunter later hit Carrillo up for money because he planned to "be in the woods for a bit." Carrillo sent him $200.

Hunter was planning even further violence on June 4 around Floyd-inspired protests in Austin, according to the affidavit: Austin police pulled him over in a truck with two other men, fully decked out in body armor and gear with multiple loaded semiautomatic magazines, along with three rifles and two pistols. Hunter denied owning any of the guns, which were confiscated by the police, and the men were released.

The domestic terror attacks by Carrillo and Hunter were far from the only incidents of actual or planned violence by Boogaloo adherents in 2020. The tally included:

Two others involved in the Minneapolis protests, Michael Robert Solomon and Ryan Teeter—the latter of whom traveled in conjunction with Hunter—were indicted in September for conspiring to provide material support for a foreign terrorist organization. The men had hoped to join the forces of the "Boojihadeen" with the radical Islamists, though the man with the Middle Eastern accent with whom they shared the plans was in fact a federal informant.[44]

Three Las Vegas–area Boogaloo Bois were arrested for building Molotov cocktails as part of a larger campaign to wreak havoc around the ongoing Black Lives Matter protests. They sought to use the BLM protests to target police officers and power infrastructure as a way of ramping up the violence around the protests.[45]

A Texarkana, Texas, man who intended to spark the Boogaloo by ambushing police officers was caught by officers who were alerted by his attempt to live stream his planned killing spree. He was arrested shortly thereafter.[46]

A Boogaloo enthusiast who posted comments on Facebook about bringing his rifle to a protest against stay-at-home orders in Denver attracted
the interest of FBI agents, who upon visiting him at his home discovered a
cache of homemade pipe bombs. The man openly expressed his intent to use
them to kill any federal agents who tried to invade his home.[47]

Another Boogaloo Boi planned to live stream his ambush on police officers at an Ohio national park, but was arrested by FBI agents before he
could pull off the plan.[48]

Some Boogaloo activists attempted to claim that their movement was
"about peace" and supported Black Lives Matter and other protesters. It
is, like many far-right enterprises, deliberately confusing about its politics.
After all, its recruitment strategy is focused on attracting mainly disen-
chanted and disenfranchised people who are so fed up with the status quo
that they want to blow it all up. That includes a very broad range of political
worldviews, both right and left.

But there can be no mistaking the reality of the Boogaloo movement established by its actions over time: It is a fundamentally far-right movement,
devoted to the destruction of liberal democracy, primarily by promoting
violent chaos directed at its institutions, beginning with law enforcement but extending to federal civil rights, environmental, and other wide-
reaching statutes. Like most far-right movements it seeks to recruit nearly
anyone susceptible to its beliefs, including people of color and those on
the far left; inevitably, however, its politics, agenda, and real-life behavior
are both authoritarian and fundamentally right-wing, if not protofascist
and accelerationist.[49]

———

AFTER A BUSY DAY harassing people in downtown Portland—roaring up
and down city streets in their pickups, flags waving, with men in the rear
shooting paintball guns at anyone they suspected of being "Antifa," or anyone they felt like splattering, for that matter—members of Patriot Prayer

and their associates in the Proud Boys settled in for the evening of August 30, 2020, with the prospect of creating some old-fashioned street violence. Parking the pickups, they began roaming the city on foot.[50]

It all went sideways late in the evening when a Patriot Prayer militiaman named Aaron Danielson, along with his companion Chandler Pappas, were confronted on the street by an anti-fascist they may have been tailing named Michael Reinoehl. When Danielson reached for his bear spray and unleashed it, Reinoehl pulled out a handgun and shot him dead, then fled into the night.

Immediately, right-wing media and chat rooms were filled with outrage and talk of revenge. "Looks like hunting season just opened up early this year MAGA," tweeted a follower responding to *Gateway Pundit* founder Jim Hoft describing Antifa as "pure evil."[51]

Right-wing actor James Woods tweeted: "This is civil war now. Democrats are fine with conservatives being murdered for wearing a hat they don't like. They are going to keep attacking law-abiding Americans in frenzied mobs, until they are dealt with the same way all bullies finally are."

Many of them, especially the people predisposed to such rhetoric, saw it as a call to civil war. Leading that parade was Stewart Rhodes of the Oath Keepers.

"The first shot has been fired brother," he tweeted the day after the shooting. "Civil war is here, right now. We'll give Trump one last chance to declare this a Marxist insurrection & suppress it as his duty demands. If he fails to do HIS duty, we will do OURS."

Rhodes demanded that Donald Trump declare a national emergency and an insurrection in the city, send in troops, and arrest anyone they identify as "Antifa." And if he failed to do that, the Oath Keepers would organize "constitutional" militias to go there and do it themselves.

Trump, Rhodes insisted, has "both the power and the duty to call the militia into federal service to suppress this rebellion/insurrection." And he made it clear that he was not just talking about the National Guard: "And, he further has the power to call US, the American military veterans, into federal service as well, as militia. And we will answer his call."

For his part, Trump seemed receptive to the idea in a Sunday night tweet: "Our great National Guard could solve these problems in less than 1 hour."

Federal marshals tracked down Michael Reinoehl four days later at an apartment complex near the Olympia suburb of Lacey, Washington, and gunned him down in short order. Trump later boasted at a rally: "We sent in the U.S. Marshals, it took 15 minutes and it was over, 15 minutes and it was over . . . They knew who he was, they didn't want to arrest him, and 15 minutes that ended."[52]

However, the idea that Trump could use the Insurrection Act gained real traction as the November 3 election approached and it looked like Trump would lose. And then, after he did lose, it swept through "Patriot" and other pro-Trump discussions, with Rhodes leading the charge.

Two days after the election, as Trump's defeat appeared inevitable and imminent, Rhodes sent a message to his leadership on the encrypted Signal platform, warning them: "We aren't getting through this without a civil war. Too late for that. Prepare your mind, body, spirit." He offered the overthrow of former Serbian president Slobodan Milosevic in 2000 as the model for a "step-by-step" plan to resist Trump's removal from office, including "complete civil disobedience," the storming of police barricades, and the capture of the Capitol.[53]

Rhodes was interviewed by Alex Jones on his *Infowars* program on November 10 and again raised the martial-law option: "And then he needs to use the Insurrection Act and use the military. In the past I've been opposed to using the military, but for this purpose he needs to use it."

He claimed that Oath Keepers would "have men already stationed outside D.C. as a nuclear option. In case they attempt to remove the President illegally, we will step in and stop it. We will be on the outside of D.C., armed, if the President calls us up."

Rhodes continued in the same vein while promoting the November 14 Million MAGA March in Washington, D.C., that served as a warm-up for successive pro-Trump protests: "We must refuse to EVER recognize this as a legitimate election, and refuse to recognize Biden as a legitimate winner, and refuse to ever recognize him as the president of the United States."[54]

Rhodes urged Trump to refuse to concede: "President Trump must refuse to recognize it as legitimate because it is not legitimate," he wrote, adding that "by President Trump refusing to concede, he is stopping a coup rather than engaging in one."

At least one member of Congress apparently supported this view: Republican Paul Gosar of Arizona. In November, he met with a group of Yavapai County Oath Keepers. Their leader Jim Arroyo said of this exchange: "We asked [Gosar] flat-out, at that time, do you think we're heading into a civil war?" group leader Jim Arroyo said of his exchange with Gosar. "And his response to the group was just flat-out, 'We're in it, we just haven't started shooting yet.'"

At the first Stop the Steal rally on Dec. 12, Rhodes was a featured speaker, wearing a black cowboy hat with an Oath Keepers insignia, exhorting the crowd: "He needs to use that now, he needs to invoke the Insurrection Act and suppress this insurrection." He also urged Trump to release what he and Alex Jones called secret intelligence files on "Deep State" actors like Hillary Clinton and Barack Obama, to "show the world who the traitors are, and then use the Insurrection Act to drop the hammer on them."

He added, "If he does not do it now, while he is commander in chief, we are going to have to do it ourselves later, in a much more desperate, much more bloody war."

Rhodes's foot soldiers in the Oath Keepers paid close attention, especially as they geared up for the big Stop the Steal rally planned for January 6.[55]

"If Trump activates the Insurrection Act, I'd hate to miss it," Oath Keeper Jessica Watkins of Ohio wrote a week before the Capitol attack. Kelly Meggs, the head of the Florida chapter of Oath Keepers, predicted in a separate conversation that Trump would stay in power and "claim the Insurrection Act."

When January 6 arrived, all of them gathered to hear Trump speak at the Ellipse, and then joined the angry mob that marched to the Capitol. After Vice President Mike Pence had refused to stop the counting of the Electoral College ballots—which both Trump and the marching "Patriots" saw as the essential step to preventing his loss—a discouraged Rhodes messaged his Oath Keepers leadership group that Trump was only complaining and not taking action: "So the patriots are taking it in their own hands. They've had enough."

Another "Patriot" marching with them, thirty-year-old Ryan Nichols of Longview, Texas, recorded a video en route to the Capitol, expressing his intentions that day.

I'm hearing reports that Pence caved. I'm telling you, if Pence caved, we're gonna drag motherfuckers through the streets. You fuckin' politicians are gonna get dragged through the streets. Because we're not gonna have our fuckin' shit stolen . . . If we find out you politicians voted for it, we're gonna drag your fuckin' ass through the street. Because this is the second fuckin' revolution! And we're fuckin' done! I'm tellin' you right now, Ryan Nichols said it: If you voted for fucking treason, we're gonna drag your fuckin' ass through the street![56]

Nichols was not alone.

3

Over the Rubicon

THE JANUARY 6 ATTACK on the US Capitol, like Caesar's crossing of the Rubicon, was both the culmination of long-building trends and a beginning, the opening salvo in an insurrectionist attack on American democracy: a declaration of their civil war.

The army of insurrectionists who followed Donald Trump's bidding on January 6 had been cultivated and gradually assembled by Trump during his four years in office—and it has remained fanatically committed to his grand goal of displacing liberal democracy with authoritarian one-party rule since.

Trump's army had five major components:

- The "Patriot" movement—its primary nexus—with its Oath Keepers and its Three Percent militias;
- The Proud Boys and their associated neofascist street brawlers;
- White nationalists, Christian nationalists, and accelerationists, all fueled by a shared militant bigotry;

- The conspiracists, particularly the authoritarian QAnon conspiracy cult and Alex Jones's far-right *Infowars* operation;
- Their mainstream Republican enablers, notably key members of Congress who encouraged Trump's schemes, amplified them, and inflamed the angry paranoia of the mob that attacked the Capitol, as well as the myriad right-wing pundits and media operations who normalized the far-right extremists and then, after the insurrection, defended, deflected, and excused the violence that day, eventually gaslighting the public by insisting that the insurrectionists had been gulled into committing crimes by the "Deep State," or alternatively that it was all "legitimate political discourse."

There is a significant crossover among these components—nearly all Patriots, Proud Boys, and white nationalists subscribe to the conspiracy theories peddled by Jones and others, for instance—but they are all united in their authoritarian devotion to Trump.

All five of these components were present January 6. All five have continued since then to wage their war not just in defense of Trump but on a broad range of American democratic institutions—from voting rights to public education to women's privacy rights—as well as on the health and well-being of the nation generally—including its struggle to recover from the COVID-19 pandemic, worsened exponentially by the American right's conspiracism-fueled refusal to vaccinate or accept requirements to do so, as well as through outright attacks on the ability of its economy to function through far-right truckers' protests that briefly shut down the nation's supply chains.

Trump cultivated this army carefully even before his first day in office: his policy proposals, along with the unrepentant bigotry with which he promoted them (particularly on immigration), and his open embrace of a conspiracist politics that reveled in violent rhetoric attracted right-wing extremists to his campaign beginning in 2015, and that support not only continued throughout his presidency but expanded and metastacized, so that formerly ordinary conservative Republicans became radicalized MAGA fanatics and QAnon cultists—in massive numbers.

Most voluminously, Trump—who was interviewed by Jones on his *Infowars* program, showering the conspiracism maestro with fulsome praise, during the 2015–16 campaign—trafficked in a broad array of right-wing conspiracy theories, many of them concocted by Jones.[1] His political career was built on his promotion of the racist theory that Barack Obama's Hawaiian birth certificate was illegitimate, which he had embraced in 2011.[2] He kept going avidly even after he won election, from promoting the suggestion that climate change was a "Chinese hoax" to the belief that vaccinations cause autism in children to his insistence that "voter fraud" cost him the popular vote in the 2016 election—all theories that gained fresh life in slightly revised forms in 2020.

As Philip Bump observed in *The Washington Post:* "Trump is the first president in modern history to make the embrace and propagation of conspiracy theories a central component of his administration."[3]

Similarly, at every turn throughout his presidency, Trump winked and nodded at white nationalists and other extremists. His most infamous moment in this regard occurred in August 2017, when he normalized the chanting alt-right marchers at the "Unite the Right" rally in Charlottesville, Virginia—at which a neo-Nazi murdered an anti-fascist and injured over a dozen more by ramming his car into a crowd of them—by describing "some of them" as "very fine people."

Asked to condemn far-right street brawlers like the Proud Boys during his only debate with Joe Biden in 2020, he instead proudly encouraged them: "Proud Boys—stand back and stand by," he said, as though he were delivering them orders. And as things turned out, he was.

Throughout his tenure, he insisted that the "tough" element among his supporters would come to his defense—seemingly in violent ways. At one rally in September 2018, amid the investigations that ultimately led to his first impeachment, Trump told the crowd that his opponents were "lucky that we're peaceful," adding: "Law enforcement, military, construction workers, Bikers for Trump . . . They travel all over the country . . . They've been great. But these are tough people . . . But they're peaceful people, and Antifa and all—they'd better hope they stay that way."[4]

As the House was debating his impeachment, Trump quoted far-right pastor Robert Jeffress in a tweet, who said on Fox News: "If the Democrats are successful in removing the President from office (which they will never be), it will cause a Civil War like fracture in this Nation from which our Country will never heal." Over the next several days, he continued in the same vein, calling the looming impeachment a "coup."[5]

Trump's tweet set the "Patriot" world aflame. "Civil War 2" trended on Twitter. Oath Keepers founder Stewart Rhodes chimed in: "This is the truth. This is where we are. We ARE on the verge of a HOT civil war. Like in 1859. That's where we are."

This was resurrected after Trump lost in 2020, when he claimed without evidence that Democrats had committed fraud to win. On December 19, he tweeted: "Big protest in D.C. on January 6th. Be there, will be wild!"[6]

Here was the green light to the would-be civil warriors. "On January 6, we find out whether we still have a constitutional republic," one MAGA fanatic tweeted on New Year's Eve. "If not, the revolution begins. I'd rather fight and die than live in a socialist society. Pretty sure 80 million Americans feel the same way."[7]

Kelly Meggs, the leader of the Oath Keeper's Florida chapter, boasted in mid-December:

> Well we are ready for the rioters, this week I organized an alliance between Oath Keepers, Florida 3%ers, and Proud Boys. We have decided to work together to shut this shit down.

On December 26, Meggs messaged his cohorts that they were targeting January 6 for an "insurrection": "Trumps staying in, he's Gonna use the emergency broadcast system on cell phones to broadcast to the American people. Then he will claim the insurrection act."

"That's awesome," someone replied. "Any idea when?"

"Next week," Meggs answered, adding: "Then wait for the 6th when we are all in DC to insurrection."[8]

A woman planning to attend posted a dramatic farewell on the pro-Trump message board TheDonald, shared widely on other social media platforms:

> I told my Mom goodbye today. I said I had a good life and I have no kids, no husband. I told her I want it to be peaceful but if our "leaders" do the wrong thing and we have to storm the Capitol, I am going to do it . . . See you there, pedes, it will be the honor of my life to fight alongside you![9]

When the day itself arrived, they were ready. Some of them wore sweatshirts to the Stop the Steal rally spelling it out: "MAGA Civil War January 6, 2021." When reporter Tess Owen of *Vice* asked a group of men wearing them if civil war was what they wanted, they answered firmly: "Yes!"[10]

On the right-wing platform Parler, "civil war" was already a hot topic—and as Trump spoke, it intensified. Mentions of the phrase "civil war" surged to nearly four times the level before it: "civil war" was used forty times in the hour before 12:15 p.m., when he began speaking; in the hour following, "civil war" mentions jumped to 156.[11]

When he told the crowd that "you'll never take back our country with weakness," a Parler user responded: "Time to fight. Civil war is upon us." Another wrote: "We are going to have a civil war. Get ready!!"

———

THE PATRIOT MOVEMENT COMPRISED the largest singular movement-oriented bloc of people who besieged the Capitol on January 6, in part because it consists of a broad range of participants: independent survivalists, "constitutionalists," and "sovereign citizens"; members of small, unaffiliated militia groups, as well as militias that identified with the Three Percent and Boogaloo; and members of the Oath Keepers, some of whom also were affiliated with other militia groups.

Two key things united the Patriots: first, the shared belief that a nefarious cabal of ultra-wealthy (and mostly Jewish) "globalists" secretly control America's political system, its government, and its media; and on January 6, they believed this cabal had conspired to manipulate the 2020 election to dethrone Trump and install a "Communist" puppet in the person of Joe Biden.

The majority of the crowd that day—a classified estimate reported by *Newsweek* indicated that it may have been as large as 120,000 (while Trump and his followers subsequently claimed—without evidence, as always—that there were a million people in the crowd)—were simply devoted "Make America Great Again" fanatics who had turned out to listen to Trump speak at the Stop the Steal rally and then perhaps to join the protest at the Capitol.[12] But nearly all of the over seven hundred people later arrested for entering the Capitol (authorities estimate that as many as 1,200 people got inside) identified themselves in one form or another as "Patriots."

Three days earlier, a collection of militia groups from various mid-Atlantic states met in the town of Quarryville, Pennsylvania, to prepare for the upcoming event. Its organizer, a New Jersey man named James Breheny, invited Stewart Rhodes via email, and gave him a briefing about their plans.[13]

"This will be the day we get our comms on point with multiple other patriot groups, share rally points etc. This one is important and I believe this is our last chance to organize before the show," Breheny wrote. "This meeting will be for leaders only." However, Rhodes did not attend.

Breheny—who later insisted that the meeting did not involve any plans to invade the Capitol—presented a PowerPoint slideshow to the group on "4th and 5th Generation Warfare." It explained: "A resistance force to a larger, well equipped military force needs to be light and agile. We are likely not going to be able to compete with money, technology, numbers of troops." The bulk of the presentation was focused on the technical aspects of communications for various kinds of users, recommending "radios for everyone." It also noted: "In order to train for possibilities, we need to stay under the radar of enforcement."

In the meantime, Rhodes posted a callout on the Oath Keepers website on January 4: "It is CRITICAL that all patriots who can be in DC get to DC to stand tall in support of President Trump's fight to defeat the enemies foreign and domestic who are attempting a coup, through the massive vote fraud and related attacks on our Republic. We Oath Keepers are both honor-bound and eager to be there in strength to do our part."[14]

Rhodes also had a brief meeting on January 5 with the then–national chairman of the Proud Boys, Enrique Tarrio, who had been arrested the day before on charges related to his participation in the burning of a Black Lives Matter banner in Washington during the December 12 Stop the Steal protests. They met in the parking garage of the Phoenix Park Hotel, though, according to an Oath Keepers attorney, they only exchanged pleasantries and engaged in no planning.[15]

Another Patriot group involved in both the preplanning for January 6 and with coordinating action on the ground that day was 1st Amendment Praetorian (1AP). The group first drew attention in the summer of 2020 by providing "security" for various far-right pro-Trump events.[16]

The organization, founded in September 2020 by a former US Army staff sergeant named Robert Patrick Lewis, takes its name from the Roman imperial guard—notorious for its violent role in ancient authoritarian politics. Like the Oath Keepers, it has recruited veterans from the ranks of the military and law enforcement, calling itself a "volunteer force of military, Law Enforcement & intel agency community professionals standing up to protect the 1st Amendment and those who use it."

Lewis tweeted that 1AP would protect Trump supporters from

harassment at his rallies, claiming they would safeguard free speech rights from "tyrannical, Marxist subversive groups."

The group's members appear to have been stationed outside the Capitol on January 6, while its core members—including Lewis—were huddled with Trump's "command center" inside the Willard Hotel, coordinating with administration insiders such as Michael Flynn and other Stop the Steal figures. These meetings had been in session since at least January 4, the day that 1AP's Twitter account posted: "There may be some young National Guard captains facing some very, very tough choices in the next 48 hours."

Lewis had also spoken the night before the insurrection at the pro-Trump Rally to Revival at Freedom Plaza, where he told the crowd they should not be "intimidated" by the "enemy at the gates."

On January 6, he was inside the Willard while the siege was under-way. Shortly after the Capitol was breached, he tweeted: "Today is the day the true battles begin." Two hours later, while the mob was still inside, he added: "The cost of Truth is Pain. The greater the Truth, the greater the potential for pain."[17]

The Oath Keepers, meanwhile, were preoccupied with a different kind of logistics: the paramilitary kind. Central to Rhodes's scheme was the quick reaction force (QRF) he had mentioned on *Infowars*—teams of armed men prepared to come to the city to back up their fellow Oath Keepers in the event of violence. Rhodes had chosen the Comfort Inn Ballston in Arlington, Virginia—a fifteen-minute drive to the US Capitol—as their "base of operations."[18]

So, on the eve of the insurrection, Oath Keepers were seen at the hotel trundling guns and ammunition stored inside crates and other contain-ers into designated storage rooms on luggage carts. The plan was to have men ready to transport the weapons and ammo cache into D.C. when they received a signal. The crates included a thirty-day supply of food in the event their plans went sideways and they found themselves in an armed standoff. The QRF plan even included having boats on the Virginia side of the Potomac River ready to transport guns to the Capitol in a pinch.

The next morning, the Oath Keepers rose early and headed into Washington to attend the Stop the Steal rally at the Ellipse and hear Trump speak. Several of them, including Rhodes, were backstage. Six Oath Keepers had been assigned as the personal security detail for longtime Trump adviser Roger Stone. Stone, who was part of the group of schemers in Trump's "War Room" in the Willard Hotel—one block away from the White House and the Ellipse—was captured on video with the men outside the Willard that morning. He had promised his followers on social media that he would make a speech near the Capitol, but he never appeared, and claimed he had remained at the hotel the entire time.[19]

His security detail, however, did not.

At about 12:50 p.m., while Trump was still speaking, a cluster of angry MAGA fanatics—led by a claque of Proud Boys—showed up at one of the barricades on the perimeter of the Capitol grounds on its west side, which faces toward the National Mall. They attacked the five Capitol police officers manning the barricade and broke it down, forcing the police to retreat, leaving an opening for the gathering mob to rush into. The other entrance to the area was similarly attacked and opened.

Soon, the large sloping lawn leading from the perimeter to the Capitol itself was full of red-hatted, flag-waving Trump fans, all surging toward the barricades that had been erected around the building. The mob featured a hodgepodge of far-right extremists: white nationalists waving Pepe the Frog and Kekistan banners, Christian nationalists waving their "An Appeal to Heaven" banners, and QAnon cultists ranting about pedophiles—but most of all, hundreds of Patriots bearing their Gadsden "Don't Tread On Me" flags and wearing Three Percent militia and Boogaloo patches.

Stewart Rhodes appears to have been among them, but mostly seems to have been hanging back and observing. As hundreds of people began battling police on those lines, hitting them with poles and baseball bats and spraying them with mace, Rhodes texted with his team back at the Ellipse. His attorneys later claimed that he was waiting outside, communicating with a contact from the White House, waiting for Trump to invoke the Insurrection Act and give them the green light to proceed as the president's own militia.

A rumor quickly popped up on the Oath Keepers' leadership chat channel on Signal that "Antifa" had penetrated the Capitol. Rhodes nixed the rumor: "Nope. I'm right here. These are Patriots." A little later, he added: "Pence is doing nothing. As I predicted . . . All I see Trump doing is complaining. I see no intent by him to do anything. So the patriots are taking it into their own hands. They've had enough."

Another participant wondered: "Are they actually Patriots—not those who were going to go in disguise as Patriots and cause trouble[?]" Rhodes answered: "Actual Patriots. Pissed off patriots[.] Like the Sons of Liberty were pissed off patriots."[20]

A team of Oath Keepers headed on the double toward the Capitol, including Meggs and Ohio-based militia leader Jessica Watkins, who had equipped themselves with communication devices and reinforced vests, helmets, goggles, and other tactical gear. This team had practiced creating a paramilitary stack formation for crowd situations. They planned to meet up with Rhodes on the Capitol's eastern side, where the mob had broken down the barricades around the concrete plaza and similarly began pushing violently against police lines that had formed around the building's entrances.

Back at the Willard, the team of six men guarding Roger Stone, led by Roberto Minuta and Joshua James, realized that they were missing out on the action. "Now we're talking, that's what I came up here for!" Minuta exclaimed. James directed the team to grab their gear to head to the Capitol. And they did so, at high speed—in golf carts. It was 2:00 p.m.[21]

The carts they had been using to escort Stone now became their high-speed transport from the Willard to the Capitol, careening down Pennsylvania, dodging pedestrians and police cars on the way. Minuta live streamed the whole thing on Facebook, commenting as he did so:

Patriots are storming the Capitol building; there's violence against patriots by the D.C. police; so we're en route in a grand theft auto golf-cart to the Capitol building right now . . . It's going down, guys; it's literally going down right now Patriots storming the Capitol building . . . Fucking war in the streets right now . . . Word is they got in the building . . . Let's go.

Rhodes remained on the northeast side of the building, trying to get some kind of word from his White House contact. But the team led by Meggs, already in the east plaza, stopped and exchanged a ninety-seven-second phone call with him. The call took place at 2:32 p.m., prosecutors say, "as, Meggs, Watkins, and the rest of the stack embedded themselves at east side Capitol building double doors."

Shortly afterward, at 2:41 p.m., the Oath Keepers stack led by Meggs and Watkins moved in disciplined formation up the steps of the Capitol through the mob, and then began leading efforts to team up and force their way past police. They forcibly entered the Capitol, pushing past police and causing severe damage to the Capitol doors. Rhodes posted a photograph of them, as well as a comment: "Trump better do his damn duty."

The team, dubbed "Stack One," then walked into the Rotunda—remaining in their formation the whole time—and exploring the building. They attempted to enter the Senate's chambers, but were driven back by pepper spray. So then they shifted their focus to the House, and headed down the hallways in search of House Speaker Nancy Pelosi's offices.

The second team—Stack Two—led by Minuta and James, had arrived near the Capitol at about 2:30 on its western side, then moved through the mob in formation, hands on one anothers' shoulders, until they reached the east-side entrances at about 3:00 p.m. They began menacing and taunting the remaining police. James spotted an entry point on the central steps and ordered the team: "They're going in over there, let's go!" They eventually forced their way in through the Rotunda doors and began scrumming with police who were trying to guard the adjacent lobby.

Minuta screamed: "This is what's bound to happen, just get out! Get out! Get these cops out! It's our fuckin' building! Get 'em out, get out!" James grabbed a Metropolitan police officer and screamed at him: "Get out of my Capitol! Get out! Get out of my Capitol!" He fell backward and then jumped back, yelling: "This is my fucking building! This is not yours! This is my Capitol!"

Afterward, when police descended on the building in large enough numbers to force out the intruders, the Oath Keepers team that had been inside the Capitol met up back in the east plaza with Rhodes. The green light had never come. The group then retreated back to their hotel rooms and continued chatting on Signal.

Rhodes texted the group: "Thousands of ticked off patriots spontaneously marched on the Capitol . . . You ain't seen nothing yet."

Oath Keeper Ed Vallejo of Arizona, who had been left in charge of the QRF operation back in Arlington, answered: "We'll be back to 6am to do it again. We got food for 30 days," adding, "We have only [begun] to fight!"

Meggs chimed in, too: "We aren't quitting!! We are reloading!!"

Rhodes added: "Patriots entering their own Capitol to send a message to the traitors is NOTHING compared to what's coming."

Later that evening, Rhodes continued to embrace his members' actions in another social media post: "The founding generation Sons of Liberty stormed the mansion of the corrupt Royal Governor of Massachusetts, and trashed the place . . . We are actually in a far more deadly situation given the FACT that enemies foreign and domestic have subverted, infiltrated, and taken over near every single office and level of power in this nation," he wrote. He did not call the siege an aberration from the Oath Keepers's "mission" on January 6 until the next day.

THE PROUD BOYS WERE the first organized group of Trump supporters to attack the police barricades, and its members were among the first to breach the Capitol an hour or so later. They just weren't quite as recognizable.

Eschewing their well-known uniforms—black Fred Perry polo shirts with yellow embroidery, bright red MAGA hats—the Proud Boys leadership had determined ahead of January 6 to show up "incognito" to avoid easy identification. National chairman Enrique Tarrio, posting on Parler, called on his cohorts to "turn out in record numbers" in D.C., but this time "with a twist": "We will not be wearing our traditional Black and Yellow. We will be incognito and we will be spread across downtown DC in smaller teams."[22]

Joe Biggs, a national board member from Florida, also took to Parler to stress the necessity of "blending in": "You won't see us," he wrote. "We are going to smell like you, move like you, and look like you. The only thing we'll do that's us is think like us! Jan 6th is gonna be epic."

The men agreed to all wear bright hunter-orange caps or similarly colored armbands as a way of being able to mutually identify one another.

As the date approached, the Proud Boys' preparations primarily unfolded on the encrypted platform Telegram, where the men used two channels for organizing their insurrection: a larger "Boots on the Ground" channel involving over sixty Proud Boys members present in Washington that day, and a smaller "New MOSD [Ministry of Self Defense]" channel evidently reserved for top leadership.

Their plans hit an obstacle when Tarrio was arrested by D.C. police when he landed at the airport on January 4 and charged with lighting the BLM banner afire during the December 12 protests. The Proud Boys' leadership roles were promptly assumed by Biggs and two other national-board members: Ethan Nordean, a thirty-year-old street brawler from Auburn, Washington, and Zach Rehl, the thirty-five-year-old leader of the Proud Boys' Philadelphia chapter. Nordean was given "war powers" to lead the men on the ground on January 6.

Shortly after the "Boots on the Ground" channel's creation, Biggs posted a message to it that read: "We are trying to avoid getting into any shit tonight. Tomorrow's the day," and then, "I'm here with rufio [Nordean] and a good group," according to the affidavit.

A group of about three dozen Proud Boys assembled at 10:00 a.m. the morning of January 6 near the base of the Washington Monument. After conversing a bit, they proceeded to walk up the National Mall toward the Capitol and then around to its eastern side, gathering on the lawn across from the building's eastern entrance.

Biggs and Nordean conversed with the men, with Biggs pointing out key locations around the Capitol and discussing how they could defend against attackers hitting them from behind. They milled about, seemingly waiting for the right moment.

In a video shot by a supporter, Proud Boy Dan "Milkshake" Scott could be heard shouting: "Let's take the fucking Capitol!" as he ordered his cohorts: "Tighten up!"

Someone admonished him: "Let's not fucking yell that, all right?"

Nordean, sounding disgusted, said into the bullhorn he was carrying: "It was Milkshake, man, you know. Idiot!"

Another man chimed in: "Don't yell it. Do it."

As Trump was still speaking, the Proud Boys began marching together around the northern perimeter of the Capitol, chanting: "Whose streets? Our streets!" and "USA! USA!" and "Fuck Antifa!" while heading toward the western side up Constitution Avenue. They turned left at First Street Northwest, straight toward the fenced-off lawn west of the Capitol where police had set up barricades at two entrances.

A sizable crowd of MAGA protesters had already gathered at the northwestern entrance, where only five Capitol police officers were stationed, supported by a couple dozen more closer to the Capitol. The crowd chanted: "We love Trump!"

Biggs was seen on video conferring briefly with Ryan Samsel, a Proud Boys organizer from Pennsylvania wearing a red MAGA cap and a jean jacket. Samsel later told the FBI that Biggs encouraged him to push on the barricades and challenge the police, and when he hesitated, Biggs flashed a gun and questioned his manhood, urging him again to attack the barricades (Biggs's attorneys would deny all this later).

Samsel was seen on video as the first man to approach the barricades and begin pushing on them and fighting police. Others joined in, toppling the metal barricades and knocking a police officer backward onto her head, causing a concussion. Meanwhile, the mob began pouring onto the lawn as the outnumbered police retreated to where their fellow officers had formed an interim line of resistance. Biggs, Rehl, and Nordean were among the first through, along with the rest of the Proud Boys who had marched with them.

One of these was Billy Chrestman, a Proud Boy from Olathe, Kansas, who took on the role of cheerleader for the crowd as it pushed against the barricades. "Whose House is it?" he shouted.

"Our House!" came the response.

"Do you want your House back?" Chrestman shouted.

"Yes!" the mob shouted.

"Take it!" he exhorted.

As the mob poured up the lawn, one man exulted: "D.C. is a fuckin' war zone!"[23]

The siege went on for more than an hour before the mob finally broke through police lines and into the Capitol. Again, Proud Boys played the central role, three of them in particular, all from upstate New York: Dominic Pezzola, a forty-three-year-old from Rochester; William Pepe, thirty-one, from Beacon; and Matthew Greene, thirty-four, of Syracuse. They knew one another through their regional Proud Boys chapter and had coordinated their travel plans to Washington.[24] They were part of the mob that first broke through the barricades. Pezzola was wearing an earpiece, indicating that he was in on the Proud Boys' communications (though he later claimed he was only listening to music).

All three were filmed participating in the violence on the west Capitol steps. When members of the mob discovered a path up some stairs to the Capitol plaza's second level covered by scaffolding—preparations for the coming inauguration on January 20—they were among the people who led the charge up them, battling police the whole way.

When they reached the second level and police fell back to form a new line at the center of the building, Pezzola and the others went left, heading straight toward a set of windows on one side of the second-level hall. Somewhere in the battle Pezzola had successfully snatched a riot shield away from a police officer, and he carried it over to the windows and began bashing at them with it. Soon a window gave way, and the men cleared out the glass and began jumping in. Pezzola was the second man to breach the Capitol, following Trump supporter Michael Sparks, who was the first to jump through the window at 2:13 p.m.

Pepe was right behind; dozens more followed. They flooded the Capitol hallways with shouting insurrectionists, toting Confederate flags and baseball bats, Biggs and Matthews among them. Their initial entry placed them near the Senate chambers; the Senate quickly suspended its certification process for the Electoral College ballots and evacuated the chambers to a protected area, Vice President Mike Pence first. As the mob rampaged through the halls above them, they could be heard chanting: "Hang Mike Pence!"

As the rest of the mob poured in, they shouted: "Where's the traitors?" "Bring them out!" "Get these fucking cocksucking Commies out!"[25]

Biggs went back outside and connected with Nordean. The two men and another cluster of Proud Boys then walked around the building to its east side, which they also found under siege by the mob. Joining eagerly, the Proud Boys forced open the Columbus Doors facing out onto the plaza, and Biggs, Nordean, and the others all rushed inside.

Someone recorded Biggs inside, still masked at the time. "Biggs, what have you got to say?" asked an enthusiastic fan who had been shouting an "Our House!" chant. Biggs pulled down his mask, smiled, and answered: "This is awesome!"

From there, the Proud Boys mostly dispersed. Many of them headed toward the House chambers, which had not been fully evacuated until well after the Capitol was breached. One Proud Boy, Gabriel Garcia of Miami, walked toward the offices of House Speaker Nancy Pelosi, calling: "Nancy! Come out and play!"[26]

Five Proud Boys helped disable crash barriers designed to descend from the ceiling even as police were trying to lower them. Eventually, they all exited the building when police reinforcements arrived at around 3:30. Biggs, Nordean, and others reconvened in the east plaza.

Pezzola bragged about breaking the windows to the Capitol and entering the building. Other members of the group, one witness said, boasted about their feats that day, saying anyone who they might have gotten their hands on would have been killed, particularly Pence and Pelosi.

The men vowed that they would return on Inauguration Day. The witness said they planned to kill "every single motherfucker" they could on that day.

They continued to boast on social media and in conversations. "I boxed a cop," said Chrestman in a phone call with some friends recorded by the FBI. "I got part of his fucking body armor, 'cause I thought he was attacking one of our boys. Turns out it wasn't one of our boys . . . Anyways, the cop was being kind of a dick . . . It was insane and you know what happened today? We stormed the Capitol Building and we took it over . . . We made the fucking House leave. Like, they couldn't finish their vote."[27]

He added, "And the first fence that was up there—bunch of people were standing against it, yelling at the cops, the cops started getting nervous and then—so I kicked the fence, I said, 'We wanna talk to the fucking House right now!' And all these people started yelling and I kicked the fucking fence again . . . I fucking started it. Yeah, I started a revolution. Because once everybody heard about this, and then we cleared out the House, they evacuated the House and everything, to stop those votes."

———————

WHITE NATIONALISTS WERE ALSO present in significant numbers among the January 6 mob, having planned for the event and promoted it heavily. However, they weren't nearly as organized as the Oath Keepers or Proud Boys—just, perhaps, more visible.[28]

Mostly, they made their presence known among the crowd with the banners they carried. Some carried Pepe the Frog banners celebrating the white-nationalist alt-right, while others carried the Kekistan flag—an alt-right variation on the Nazi war flag. Others toted the flag of the white-nationalist group VDARE, a red-white-and-blue banner with a lion logo at the center. One man wore a "Camp Auschwitz" sweatshirt.

The most common, however, were the America First banners representing Nick Fuentes's organization of the same name. Its participants are known less formally as the "Groyper army," and they use a cartoon-frog variation of Pepe as their main symbol. They had turned out in numbers on January 6, and several of their followers invaded the Capitol.

Fuentes, for that matter, had been one of the most avid promoters of the post-election pro-Trump protests, speaking at both the November 14 and December 12 events in Washington, as well as at election-result protests in places like Michigan, where he warned that "we're not remaining in our homes. We're on the streets now."[29]

On his popular podcast on January 4, Fuentes had flippantly suggested killing state legislators who were unwilling to overturn the 2020 election results. "What can you and I do to a state legislator—besides kill them?" he wondered rhetorically, then hastily added: "We should not do that. I'm not advising that, but I mean, what else can you do, right?"

An early alt-right figure named Tim Gionet—nicknamed Baked Alaska—who had attached himself to the Groyper army in 2020 by doing live streams at their events, was out doing his thing on the streets of Washington the night of January 5, interviewing MAGA protesters ginned up on violent rhetoric.[30]

One man he interviewed—later identified as an Arizona Oath Keeper named Ray Epps—told Gionet that "we're far beyond" the tax revolt that inspired the original American Revolution, adding: "In fact, tomorrow—I don't even like to say it because I'll be arrested—we need to go into the Capitol."

"Let's gooooo!!!" Gionet shouted enthusiastically in response.

The next day, after Trump's speech, Fuentes spoke to a crowd of supporters at Freedom Plaza: "It is us and our ancestors that created everything good that you see in this country. All these people that have taken over our country—we do not need them . . . It is the American people, and our leader, Donald Trump, against everybody else in this country and this world . . . Our Founding Fathers would get in the streets, and they would take this country back by force if necessary. And that is what we must be prepared to do."[31]

Shortly afterward, as the crowd at the Ellipse began making its way to the Capitol, Fuentes got on a bullhorn and addressed his followers:

> We have just got word that they have stopped the vote of the Electoral College in Congress! I say that we should not leave this Capitol until Donald Trump is inaugurated president! We the American people will not let this fraudulent election go forward one more step!

Fuentes himself never went inside the Capitol. But a number of his followers did. Several men later charged with trespass and obstruction were seen carrying America First banners inside the Capitol and wearing the organization's T-shirts and hats—in particular, the insurrectionists who entered Pelosi's office and trashed the place. "Nancy, I'm hoooome!!!" one crowed, in the manner of Jack Nicholson in *The Shining*.[32]

One America Firster was Riley Williams, a twenty-two-year-old woman from Pennsylvania who had a predilection for donning neo-Nazi gear and making TikTok videos of herself saluting the camera Nazi style, posting on social media as a white-nationalist Groyper and participating in a popular neo-Nazi Telegram channel and other far-right accelerationist online spaces. When she got into Pelosi's office, she live streamed herself rifling through papers and examining a Hewlett-Packard laptop computer—which she then apparently stole.[33]

Williams's ex-boyfriend showed investigators the videos from her live stream, and told them that Williams intended to sell the laptop to a Russian agent, but the deal had fallen through. The laptop was never located, and Williams's attorney adamantly denied she stole the computer.

Gionet was one of the ringleaders of the Groypers inside Pelosi's office, and he had of course also been live streaming the whole thing from its beginnings. The video—later collected by investigators—showed him entering the Capitol, chanting: "Patriots are in control!" Whose house? Our house!" and "Traitors, traitors, traitors!" He told the audience, after showing his face: "We are in the Capitol Building, 1776 will commence again." A little later he added: "Unleash the Kraken, let's go."[34]

Eventually, when Gionet reached Pelosi's office, he became especially antic, picking up a phone and acting out a call with members of the Senate. "Let's call Trump!" he said. "Dude! Dude! Let's tell Trump what's up. He'll be happy, whaddya mean? We're fighting for Trump. We need to get our boy Donald J. Trump into office."

A little later, he added: "Occupy the Capitol let's go. We ain't leaving this bitch." But when he finally was convinced to leave the building, it wasn't without a conflict: His live stream showed him heading toward the exits and accusing a police officer of shoving him, though the video showed no physical contact. Nonetheless, Gionet verbally attacked the officer: "You're a fucking oath breaker, you piece of shit!" he told the man, then shouted "Fuck you!" four times, concluding: "You broke your oath to the Constitution."

Afterward, Gionet, Williams, and a number of other Groypers (ten of them altogether) who entered the Capitol were arrested by the FBI and charged with various felonies for their actions that day—though Fuentes, who remained on the outside, was not. Fuentes did, however, advise all of his followers who were present during the insurrection to simply destroy their cell phones and SIM cards to erase any evidence (which itself would be a federal obstruction-of-justice crime).[35]

Fuentes also complained that he had to be more careful after January 6: "Everything is gay now. The feds are watching me. I can't say anything cool anymore, because the government is watching me," Fuentes said.

Six months later, while lamenting Gionet's arrest and prosecution, Fuentes told his podcast audience about how much fun January 6 had been.

"I am unapologetic. I thought the Capitol [riot] was awesome; it was awesome! And so was Trump. And Trump was awesome because he was racist. Trump was awesome because he was sexist," Fuentes stated. "The only thing Trump wasn't awesome for was being anti-Semitic; he wasn't anti-Semitic."

"But the rest was awesome. And people have got to get racist," he added.[36]

Derek Black, a former white supremacist who grew up in the movement, told The Washington Post's Jonathan Capehart that the presence of white nationalists was a natural outgrowth of the preceding four years:

> Because there were definitely plenty of people in that crowd who were white supremacists. There were people in that crowd who were present at Charlottesville. You could see them livestreaming from the House Chamber, and if you go back through the old Charlottesville videos, you'll see a lot of the same faces. And I think that's something that we need to reckon with. I think there was a belief that I encountered every

now and then between when the Charlottesville march happened in 2017 and now that that had been defeated or driven out of the public eye, and the reality was, it was much harder to organize after Charlottesville. But these people were still around. They were still present. They were still organizing. And to see them showing up at the Capitol is exactly what you should expect. [37]

Black also warned an interviewer that white nationalism was gathering steam nationally and was unlikely to be requited by the insurrection: "Unless we go through the act of confronting it, it's going to continue and to be a dangerous force in what the country is."[38]

———

CONSPIRACISTS COMPRISED THE LARGEST portion of the January 6 mob. In most regards, everyone who besieged and invaded the Capitol was a believer in conspiracy theories, and one in particular: that a sinister cabal of "globalists" had colluded to commit large-scale voter fraud to eject Donald Trump from the White House.

This is in no small part a reflection of the reality that all the far-right movements that played central roles in the insurrection—the Patriots, the Proud Boys, the white nationalists, as well as their mainstream Republican enablers—are profoundly conspiracist in nature. They all fundamentally dwell in the same alternative universe—a semi-functioning epistemological bubble composed of misinformation and disinformation and fabulist conspiracy theories leavened with a few grossly distorted facts, which I have elsewhere named Alt-America. They occupy varying zones of this universe, meaning that they differ at times on the details and emphasis, but are united in the essential view that the world—its politics, its media, its cultures—are being deviously manipulated by the same cabal that brought down Trump to impose their "New World Order" enslavement on us all.

Despite its attachment to these movements, there exists an even larger bloc of people who do not necessarily affiliate with them—though they often sympathize with and encourage them—but rather for whom the conspiracy theories themselves form the basis for their politics, and for whom, on January 6, these fake narratives provided all the fuel they needed to besiege a Capitol they had come to believe had been corrupted by sinister Marxists and possibly satanists.

There were two main nexuses of this component of Trump's army: Alex Jones and his *Infowars* operation, and the authoritarian QAnon conspiracy cult.

Jones is the most famous conspiracy-monger in America and, for that matter, the world. He also has identified consistently on-air with the Patriot movement dating back to at least 2009, and realistically back to 1995, when he first began airing militia-movement "FEMA concentration camp" and "New World Order" conspiracy theories.[39] Stewart Rhodes was a frequent guest, and Joe Biggs had been a regular Infowars host before he became a Proud Boys leader.[40] Before Jones was removed from YouTube in 2018 for his hate-mongering and disinformation, his channel had millions of subscribers. He adjusted his strategy by continuing his Infowars operation, replete with videos and podcasts, on the independent hosting service Epik, and though his audience now is more limited—and his future in doubt, thanks to losing major lawsuits to the victims of his bogus claims—he remains enormously popular.[41]

Moreover, Jones also is one of Donald Trump's most perfervid supporters, dating back to 2015, when Jones hosted Trump on his program and was lathered with praise by the then-candidate. The connection only deepened during Trump's presidential tenure, and it reached meltdown levels after Trump lost the 2020 election.[42]

Jones played a leading role in promoting the earliest pro-Trump Stop the Steal events in Washington on November 14 and December 12. For the January 6 event, Jones personally ponied up $50,000 of his own money, and moreover arranged for Publix heiress Julie Jenkins Fancelli to donate $300,000, which was the lion's share of the funding needed for the half-million-dollar rally.[43]

As the date approached, Jones's rhetoric became more strident and violent. Three days before the rally, he ripped into Trump supporters hesitant to travel to D.C. "I've seen people making a lot of excuses. 'Oh, Antifa is dangerous.' It's a lot more dangerous walking across the street. There's hardly no Antifa. They are a bunch of cowards," he said.[44]

Jones and *Infowars* host Owen Shroyer traveled to Washington, along with an Infowars video editor named Samuel Montoya. As part of the March to Save America rally in Freedom Plaza near the White House on January 5, both Jones and Shroyer spoke.

Shroyer's language was typically militant: "Thomas Jefferson once said when the government fears the people, there is freedom. But for too long now the people have feared the government," he said. "I can tell you that the crooked politicians that occupy our Capitol are in fear right now. Do you know how I know this? Because they are scurrying around in secret tunnels to avoid 'we the people.' Right now as we speak they're scurrying around like the little rats that they are to try to avoid you."[45]

Jones spoke the familiar language of "civil war." He told the crowd that "we have only begun to resist the globalists" and that "they have tried to steal this election in front of everyone."

"I don't know how all this is going to end, but if they want a fight, they better believe they've got one," he went on. "This will be their Waterloo. This will be their destruction." He then led the crowd in a "1776" chant.[46]

The morning of January 6, Jones organized a rally near the Ellipse, and again both he and Shroyer spoke, amping up the violent rhetoric. Shroyer told the crowd: "They said you lost this election in a landslide to Biden. We said, 'No, we don't buy your bullshit.' But, guess what? You want to feed us bullshit? We're going to bring it right to your front door and you can eat it yourselves."

Jones was again predictably over the top: "We declare 1776 against the New World Order," he said. "We need to understand we're under attack, and we need to understand this is twenty-first-century warfare and get on a war footing!"

The men marched to the Capitol, but once there, Jones was able to assess the violence unfolding, and he changed his tone. "We're not Antifa; we're not BLM," he told the mob through a bullhorn. "You're amazing. I love you. Let's march around the other side, and let's not fight the police and give the system what they want. We are peaceful, and we won this election. And as much as I love seeing the Trump flags flying over this, we need to not have the confrontation with the police. They're gonna make that the story. I'm going to march to the other side, where we have a stage, where we can speak and occupy peacefully."

Jones continued: "Trump is going to speak over here. Trump is coming."

Trump, of course, never came. Neither did the dark forces of Antifa to which they had devoted so much preparation.

Neither Jones nor Shroyer ever entered the Capitol, though they did enter a restricted area by walking up on the west-side lawn; they retreated to a "secure location" instead.[47] However, Samuel Montoya was among the mob that got in from the east side, recording video the whole time, reporting to the audience as "your boy Sam with Infowars.com."[48] (Shroyer and Montoya were both later charged and arrested.) After crossing the threshold, Montoya shouted jubilantly: "Guess what? We are in the Capitol, baby!" He joined the mob that then besieged the House and tried to get in through the Speaker's entrance. He was standing near a woman named Ashli Babbitt when she was shot there by a security guard.

———————

IN MANY WAYS, ASHLI Babbitt was the living embodiment of the QAnon cult. Sucked down its conspiracy-theory rabbit hole, she had become alienated from friends and workmates, and over the several years in which she lived in that alternative universe, she became so radicalized and so full of anger that she flew across the country on a mission to save Donald Trump.

Raised in Southern California, Babbitt enlisted in the US Air Force in 2006 and became an Air National Guard member in 2010, ultimately serving seven overseas deployments before leaving in 2016 as a senior airman. She set herself up in a swimming-pool-maintenance business in the San Diego area that struggled.[49]

And she became a devoted Trump fan, despite having voted twice for Barack Obama, or so she claimed. On her Twitter account—where she posted more than eighty-six thousand tweets—she regularly described her belief that Trump was destined to save America, and that Hillary Clinton belonged in prison.

During the 2016 campaign, her adoration of Trump was unbridled; one October tweet featured a meme with Trump's name above three signs nailed to a tree: "Make America Great Again," "H FOR PRISON," and "CHRISTIAN DEPLORABLES LIVE HERE." Babbitt added the hashtag #Love.

When Trump won the election, she cried, and wrote an encomium declaring that "today we save America from the tyranny, collusion and corruption."

The first QAnon posts began appearing shortly after the election, and by early 2017 were spreading widely among pro-Trump conspiracists—including Babbitt. Like the rest of the cult's true believers, she ardently promoted the claims that a coterie of "globalists" was operating a secretive, worldwide pedophilia/child-trafficking ring that kidnapped children and harvested their blood, headed by Hillary Clinton, Barack Obama, and others—and that their hero, Donald Trump, was gathering a "Storm" in which all these evildoers would be arrested, tried, and executed. By 2020, she was regularly spouting their cryptic jargon and hashtags.

"The best is yet to come," she tweeted in February. A month later, she quoted "Q drop": "What is dark will come to light!" At other times, she adopted QAnon-borne hashtags and "causes": "We have to #SaveTheChildren," she wrote.

She also believed that the COVID-19 pandemic was blown out of proportion, that the disease (the "controla virus") was a hoax ("a FUCKING JOKE"), designed by the same nefarious globalists in a scheme to enslave everyone: "We are being hoodwinked," she tweeted in July 2020. "The sheep need to wake up."

After Trump lost the election in November, Babbitt's account was wild with fury, repeating #StopTheSteal and #TheStormIsComing hashtags amid angry claims that Democrats had committed massive voter fraud—as well as the belief that Trump would still emerge triumphant in the end.

When Kamala Harris, who was then the vice president-elect, promised on Twitter "to ensure Americans mask up, distribute 100M shots, and get students safely back to school," Babbitt replied furiously: "No the fuck you will not! No masks, no you, no Biden the kid raper, no vaccines . . . sit your fraudulent ass down . . . we the ppl bitch!"

When Trump announced the January 6 rally in D.C., Babbitt was ecstatic, and began eagerly retweeting posts—from figures ranging from Secretary of State Mike Pompeo and Donald Trump Jr. to white nationalist Jack Posobiec—encouraging Trump supporters to turn out en masse to overturn the election.

The entire QAnon cult was raging with similar claims. Top QAnon influencers on social media like the pseudonymous Joe M, JuliansRum, and Pepe Lives Matter led the parade:

It's a bad crime to attempt to cheat in an election. It's a worse crime to actually cheat in an election. It's the worst crime of all to actually steal an election, certify fraudulent votes and get to the finish line. Maximum penalties are now on the table, and we caught them all. Buckle up.

Patriots have exercised more patience than I ever thought possible. But we've reached the point where patience is no longer a realistic expectation. People are fucking PISSED. And it's 100% justified. Trump and his allies must take action soon.

The Storm was always gonna be ugly. Remember this my frens: The alternative timelines were much much uglier. We are the calm before and during the storm.[50]

One of QAnon's leading promoters, Ron Watkins—whose close ties to the cult's origins on the fringe 8kun message board have led to suggestions that he actually might be Q himself—concocted a claim, shortly after the election was called for Biden—that employees of Dominion Voting Systems, one of the major software providers for voting machines, had managed to switch votes for Trump to Biden votes in key battleground states. He appeared as a guest on the pro-Trump One America News Network to explain the theory on November 12.[51]

The next day, Trump himself eagerly promoted the Dominion theory on Twitter, telling his millions of followers that Dominion had deleted more than a million votes, citing OAN. The race was on: On Twitter, Trump supporters went wild, tweeting the #Dominion hashtag 35,700 times a day. One study found that one in seven of these tweets came from self-identified QAnon accounts.[52]

In the leadup to January 6, QAnon accounts grew excited. More than half of the 20,800 QAnon-identified accounts on Twitter mentioned the date and the rally, though only a minority called for violence. Rather, most of them posted their typically outlandish claims intended to outrage and inflame readers.[53]

"No wonder the President said January 6 in DC was going to be wild. @LLinWood just told us many of our politicians are raping and killing children. They won't be able to walk down the street," one QAnon account on Parler posted.[54]

Ashli Babbitt believed the protest was a pivotal moment that would fulfill several key QAnon "prophecies" regarding "the Storm": "Nothing will stop us," she tweeted on January 5. "They can try and try and try but the storm is here and it is descending upon DC in less than 24 hours . . . dark to light!"[55]

She flew out from San Diego the day before the rally, seated next to *USA Today* staff writer Will Carless, who (unknown to Babbitt) had written frequently about QAnon. They did not talk politics much, but instead spent most of their conversation on the subject of favorite beach towns.

When the crowd gathered at the Ellipse to hear Trump's speech, it was thick with signs of QAnon's presence: T-shirts, sweatshirts, signs, and banners with QAnon symbols and slogans: "Where We Go One We Go All" (also shortened to the hashtag #WWG1WGA), "Trust the Plan," "The Storm is Here," "Q Sent Me," and the like—and they remained with the mob that marched up the National Mall to the Capitol and besieged the building. Babbitt was among them.[56]

They were mixed among the Proud Boys and Oath Keepers who entered at the first breach. One of them, Douglas Jensen, forty-one, of Des Moines, Iowa—wearing a sweatshirt with a large Q symbol and the words "Trust the Plan"—was at the forefront of the mob that first attempted to enter the Senate chambers, and was drawn away from the entrance and up a flight of stairs by a quick-thinking Capitol police officer, Eugene Goodman. Jensen later told FBI investigators that he "wanted to have his T-shirt seen on video so that 'Q' could 'get the credit.'"[57]

The most eye grabbing of the QAnon figures was Jacob Chansley, nicknamed "the QAnon Shaman" for his buffalo-horn fur hat, flag-painted face, and bare torso adorned with multiple conspiracist tattoos: eventually, he would become the symbolic face of the insurrection. Chansley, a thirty-four-year-old from Arizona, had previously donned his outlandish garb for Stop the Steal protests outside polling centers.[58]

Chansley was among the rioters who had stormed into the Capitol from the upper west terrace after the Proud Boys had breached the building there. First seen strolling the halls of the Capitol, he entered the Senate chambers, announcing as he entered: "Time's up, motherfuckers!" Proceeding to the Senate floor, he greeted his fellow insurrectionists: "Heyyyy, glad to see you, man. Look at you guys, you guys are fuckin' Patriots!"

Mounting the dais with others, Chansley led a group prayer with fellow rioters—which a prosecutor later read aloud prior to his sentencing:

> Thank you, Heavenly Father, for gracing us with this opportunity . . .to allow us to send a message to all the tyrants, the Communists, and the globalists, that this is our nation, not theirs. That we will not allow America, the American way of the United States of America to go down . . . Thank you for filling this chamber with Patriots that love you . . . Thank you for allowing the United States of America to be reborn. Thank you for allowing us to get rid of the Communists, the globalists, and the traitors within our government.[59]

Chansley also left an ominous note on the dais in the Senate, apparently directed at Vice President Mike Pence: "It's only a matter of time. Justice is coming!"[60]

Working mainstream journalists in the crowd remarked on the influence of QAnon among the mob, even for those who did not necessarily identify as followers of the cult. *The New York Times*'s Matthew Rosenberg remarked afterward that "it was remarkable how many other people in the crowd who would say they did not buy into QAnon repeated many of the conspiracy theory's main ideas about powerful pedophiles and vaccines filled with nanobots and all kinds of other nonsense."[61]

Ashli Babbitt was among the mob that breached the Capitol a little later, on the east side of the building, and was at the forefront of the rioters who scrambled to get inside the House chambers, intent not only on stopping the vote but on taking out their fury on members of Congress. Blunted in their first attempt to get in through the main entrance, she joined the group that peeled off and rushed to find another route to the rear of the chambers—which they did, at an entrance to the Speakers Lobby.[62]

The door was locked and guarded by only three Capitol officers, who attempted to stand stoically in the way as the mob banged on the glass.

Babbitt, wearing an American-flag backpack, was one of the people who harangued the officers. As it happened, the evacuation of House members from the chambers had begun only a few minutes beforehand, their exit route within the line of sight of the lobby.

Then, through the windows on the doors, Babbitt and others spotted the last of the House members making their escape, and she went ballistic. "There they are!" she shouted. "What the fuck!!!??" Members of the mob began punching the windows with their fists, cracking them.

Then, a heavily armed SWAT unit arrived to the rear, and so the three police officers moved up to meet them. That created an opening for the rioters to begin inflicting serious damage on the doors and glass, and they finally punched out a window on the right side of the doors. At about this time, a security officer on the inside of the chambers, positioned just inside a facade near the door, shoved out his weapon and pointed it so that everyone could see it.

"There is a gun! He's got a gun!" people began shouting. "Hey! He's got a gun!"

Babbitt, however, was undeterred. She leaped up onto the panel where the pane had been smashed out and prepared to jump inside to pursue the escaping members of Congress. Instead, the guard fired his gun once, hitting her in the upper chest and knocking her back into the hallway outside.

A medical team was promptly called and the halls cleared to make way for them. Babbitt was semiconscious as she was taken out on a gurney, and died in the ambulance en route to the hospital.

Babbitt became an instant martyr for the insurrectionists and particularly for the QAnon faithful. The siege itself was broadly celebrated both among its participants and those who watched from a distance. It had, after all, played out in real life just like a QAnon fantasy: summoned to Washington by their beloved leader, they had risen up by the thousands and seized the seat of democracy while its denizens, cowering under desks, finally learned to fear the people.

When the dust had settled and the Capitol finally cleared, they congratulated themselves, firm in their belief that Trump would emerge triumphant. "Time for rest. I had to stay up to watch the conclusion of the greatest attempted theft in history. Now it is a completed crime," tweeted Lin Wood, the QAnon-loving lawyer who had served for a while as one of Trump's attorneys in his ill-fated attempts to challenge the election results in court. "Many traitors will be arrested & jailed over the next several days. President Donald J. Trump will serve 4 more years!!!"[63]

"QAnon Shaman" Chansley was not just unrepentant in press interviews but exultant. He told NBC News: "The fact that we had a bunch of our traitors in office hunker down, put on their gas masks and retreat into their underground bunker, I consider that a win."[64]

BESIDES THE INSURRECTIONISTS THEMSELVES, the mob violence on January 6 was set into motion by a large number of people who operate within the mainstream of American politics, particularly Republican politicians and media figures who were close within Donald Trump's political orbit. They ranged from the president's advisers and attorneys to members of Congress to Trumpist pundits in the right-wing media—none of whom actually participated in the siege themselves.

The idea for a Stop the Steal campaign actually originated with longtime Trump adviser Roger Stone—in 2016. Stone devised the slogan during that year's Republican primaries, claiming the GOP establishment was attempting to rig the vote to defeat Trump—accusing a "Bush-Cruz-Kasich-Romney-Ryan-McConnell faction" of plotting to stop their primary foe. He set up a website at StopTheSteal.org and fundraised with requests for $10,000, warning Trump supporters: "If this election is close, THEY WILL STEAL IT."[65]

After Trump won the nomination, he repurposed the site for the general election and kept raising money. "Donald Trump thinks Hillary Clinton and the Democrats are going to steal the next election," his website said that October. It's unclear what became of the money he raised after Trump won in November.

Stone—a longtime Republican political operative, dating back to his work in 1972 as dirty trickster for Richard Nixon's reelection campaign, as well as his involvement in the 2000 "Brooks Brothers riot" in Palm Beach, Florida, that affected the course of the decisive recount in that year's presidential election—was part of Trump's inner circle of friends for years, and was an adviser to Trump's campaign for its first two months in 2015 until he was fired when the two men argued over strategy.[66] Stone nonetheless remained an ardent Trump supporter, and kept an informal relationship with the president—which turned out to be helpful when Stone was convicted in 2019 on seven felony counts of obstruction and lying to investigators about his relationship with the WikiLeaks operatives who leaked emails hacked from the Clinton campaign, and was sentenced to forty months' prison time: Trump shortly afterward commuted the sentence, and ultimately issued a full pardon (in mid-December 2020, after he had lost the election). [67]

Just as in 2016, Stone repurposed the Stop the Steal slogan for the 2020 general election, especially as the campaign wound down and it became apparent that Trump was likely to lose. He set some of his far-right protégés to work reviving it. One of these was Ali Alexander, a right-wing activist of mixed African American and Arab descent who had gained notoriety for, among other things, orchestrating the false claim that Joe Biden was suffering from a debilitating disease. Alexander also had been briefly banned from Twitter in 2019 for a post warning Rep. Alexandria Ocasio-Cortez: "I would *literally* put you down if you came near me, Marxist. I would call 911 to come retrieve your body. Have a Good Friday!"[68]

In mid-September, Alexander posted a video announcing, "I'm thinking about bringing Stop the Steal out of retirement . . . In the next coming days we are going to build the infrastructure to stop the steal." On social media, he began using the hashtag #StopTheSteal—and created a Stop the Steal website that guided Trump supporters to locations around the country where election-count protests were being held, in states such as Arizona and Michigan, where Trumpist conspiracy theorists claimed votes had been stolen.

Other players in Trump's inner circle also became involved, particularly Steve Bannon, the campaign-manager-turned-presidential-adviser who had also been subjected to an unceremonious firing but remained loyal. On November 4, the day after the election, a group of people associated with Bannon and Stone, led by right-wing activist Amy Kremer, started up a Stop The Steal group on Facebook devoted to organizing pro-Trump protests.[69]

Kremer was a veteran of the Tea Party movement who ran a pro-Trump outfit called Women for America First. She had previously operated a super PAC called Women Vote Trump in partnership with Stone's ex-wife, Ann Stone. The group page's administrators included Dustin Stockton and Jennifer Lawrence, both of whom had previously written for Bannon's *Breitbart News* operation, and had been part of his core team for We Build the Wall, the fraud-riddled crowdfunding campaign for Trump's border wall that ultimately caused Bannon to be charged with misappropriating funds.[70]

Their "Stop the Steal" Facebook group was an immediate sensation, drawing over 300,000 followers in its first twenty-four hours. It also inspired dozens of knockoffs employing variations of the slogan. Commenters at these groups used "threatening rhetoric anticipating a civil war, or talk from members about how they are locked and loaded," said Ciaran O'Connor, a disinformation analyst with the Institute for Strategic Dialogue.[71]

Violent rhetoric was a common feature of the group, encouraged by its leaders. "Clean your guns," said Stockton on a live stream video. "Things are going to get worse before they get better." (Stockton later dismissed critics by saying the remarks were just "common political hyperbole.")

Facebook shut the page down on November 5, citing its spread of election disinformation, but other groups using the name and concept continued to operate. Bannon himself started up a Stop the Steal page on Facebook on November 5, but then promptly changed it to "Own Your Vote," after Facebook took down Kremer's original page; it remained up on Facebook until January 6.

The associated Stop the Steal groups altogether amassed 2.5 million followers, according to an analysis by the activist group Avaaz.[72] Another analysis by *Just Security* found that the 8,200 online news articles featuring "Stop the Steal" published between the election and the insurrection garnered some seventy million engagements across a variety of platforms, with more than 43.5 million of them occurring in December 2020. On YouTube, Stop the Steal videos attracted 21,267,165 views, 863,151 likes, and 34,091 dislikes. Mentions of Stop the Steal on Facebook, Twitter, and Google spiked in the days associated with their largest protests—on November 14 and December 12 in Washington—and immediately preceding January 6.[73]

The December 12 Stop the Steal protest in Washington was primarily an Ali Alexander production.[74] He created a trailer for what appeared to be a film project about the campaign that he published three days before, featuring appearances from Stone and other far-right figures, notably America First's Nick Fuentes and longtime nativist pundit Michelle Malkin, fondly dubbed by Fuentes's followers "Groyper Mom" due to her close association with and support for Fuentes.[75] Both Fuentes and Malkin heavily promoted the #StopTheSteal hashtag.

A week later, at an Arizona Stop the Steal event, Alexander boasted that he had been "on the phone" with "people from the White House" while indulging in the violent metaphors that had become the movement's forte:

> To all these weak-kneed Republicans I say, what would you do if somebody broke into your house and stole something and they were— well, I don't want to say still in your front yard because I know what we'd do. Let's say they made it out to the road. I don't want to be accused

of anything yet. Yet. Let them hear that. Yet. What if somebody stole something from your house, and they'd made it out in the street. Would you pursue? Hell yeah. We have a moral obligation to pursue them, don't we?[76]

A December 27 email from StopTheSteal.us, headlined "TRUMP JUST TWEETED JAN 6TH EVENT! AGAIN!" encouraged followers to attend, directing them to the website Alexander had created for the event, dubbed "Wild Protest." "PRESIDENT TRUMP WANTS YOU IN DC JANUARY 6," it emphasized, adding that the organization was working to secure the votes of Republican senators to oppose Biden's certification: "We've identified six (seven including Senator-elect Tommy Tuberville) that could join our cause. StopTheSteal.us is working closely, whipping the vote up, with patriots in the Congress."[77]

Trump himself referenced the slogan in a January 1 tweet: "The BIG Protest Rally in Washington, D.C., will take place at 11:00 AM on January 6th. Location details to follow. StopTheSteal!" Other Republicans joined in: Texas senator Ted Cruz spoke at a January 3 Stop the Steal rally, telling the crowd, "We will not go quietly into the night. We will defend liberty."

Charlie Kirk's Turning Point USA got in on the action, too. On Twitter, Kirk claimed that TPUSA was "sending 80+ buses full of patriots to DC to fight for this president." He added that the rally "will likely be one of the largest and most consequential in American history."[78]

Roger Stone, meanwhile, worked assiduously to promote turnout for the event. He appeared on Alex Jones's *Infowars* program, pronouncing the Biden victory a "hoax": "I think our headline is Join the Patriots in Washington, D.C. this weekend to protest the hoax that is the theft of this election and demand that we Stop the Steal," he said, hastily adding a promotional note: "Hashtag Stop the Steal."[79]

He appeared at the Rally to Revival event in Freedom Plaza on January

5, telling the crowd that the president's enemies sought "nothing less than the heist of the 2020 election and we say, No way!" Furthermore: "We will win this fight or America will step off into a thousand years of darkness. We dare not fail. I will be with you tomorrow shoulder to shoulder." (Of course, as it turned out, he was not; according to his own account, he stayed at the Willard Hotel all day.)

Likewise, Bannon pounded the Stop the Steal war drum incessantly, including on his Own Your Vote Facebook page, which promoted Trump's "Big Lie" that the election had been stolen, intermingled with QAnon conspiracy theories. But his podcast, *Steve Bannon's War Room*, was particularly influential in pushing the same disinformation and promotion for January 6 in the podcasting space.[80]

The *War Room* podcast led what a study by Brookings Institute called "a massive and sustained post-election increase in episodes that endorsed unsubstantiated allegations of voter fraud and related narratives." After November 3, the study found, just over 50 percent of the popular US political podcasts sampled were trafficking in false or misleading claims. Moreover, Bannon was, in his own formulation, "flooding the zone with shit": His podcast, along with others that specialized in the false narrative, like Sean Hannity's and Rush Limbaugh's, "produced the largest total number of post-election episodes."

On January 5, Bannon made a prediction:

I'll tell you this. It's not going to happen like you think it's going to happen. OK, it's going to be quite extraordinarily different. And all I can say is, strap in.

All hell is going to break loose tomorrow. Just understand this. All hell is going to break loose tomorrow. It's gonna be moving. It's gonna be quick . . . We're on the point of attack. You have made this happen and tomorrow it's game day. So strap in. Let's get ready.[81]

At least one senior Trump adviser later confirmed that Bannon and Trump had been in close communication in the weeks leading up to January 6, revolving mainly around Trump's election conspiracy theories and his strategy for staying in office.[82]

———

THE STOP THE STEAL organizers and their allies created multiple rallies for January 5 and 6. On Tuesday the fifth, there was an early-afternoon Save the Republic rally created by Moms for America at Area 9 across from the Russell Senate Office Building; a One Nation Under God rally with Christian nationalist themes near the US Supreme Court Building; and the main Rally to Revival at Freedom Plaza featuring Alex Jones, Roger Stone, and others. Ali Alexander led the crowd in a "Victory or death!" chant.[83]

The big event on January 6 was the March to Save America at the White House Ellipse, at which Trump was to speak. There were other rallies scheduled to follow: Ali Alexander's Wild Protest, scheduled to take place northeast of the Capitol; and three variations on Stop the Steal rallies at Freedom Plaza, just east of the White House. These later events were largely shortcircuited by the insurrection.

When the big event at the Ellipse began at 9:00 a.m., the audience was treated to a series of warmup speakers, interspersed with propaganda videos. One of these, a collage of images and snippets from Trump's speeches, portrayed America as descending into chaos due to the corruption and greed of elites, both corporate and government. The clear message: the only way to save the American way of life was to keep Trump in the White House.[84]

The speeches were uniformly tailored to whipping the audience into a frenzy. Well-known figures in Trump's inner circle stepped up to the podium and offered incendiary rhetoric: Donald Trump Jr. thanked the "redblooded, patriotic Americans" in the crowd "for standing up to the bullshit," and attacked congressional Republicans: "The people who did nothing to stop the steal, this gathering should send a message to them: This isn't their Republican party anymore. This is Donald Trump's." He added, "If you're gonna be the zero and not the hero, we're coming for you and we're going to have a good time doing it!"

Trump's personal attorney Rudy Giuliani was also among the speakers. "Over the next ten days, we get to see the machines that are crooked, the ballots that are fraudulent. If we're wrong, we will be made fools of," he said. "But if we're right, a lot of them will go to jail. So let's have trial by combat."[85]

And then there were the members of Congress—namely, the ones who had schemed to help set the whole thing in motion.

One of the first speakers was Rep. Mo Brooks of Alabama—in body armor—who told the crowd: "I want you to take to your heart, and take back home, and along the way, stop at the Capitol!"

That day, he told them, is "the day American patriots start taking down names and kicking ass." As he wrapped up, he demanded to know: "Are you willing to do what it takes to fight for America? Louder! Will you fight for America?"[86]

Rep. Madison Cawthorn of North Carolina—freshly elected and sworn in for the first time—came out in his wheelchair and pumped up the audience: "Wow, this crowd has some fight," he began. He painted Trump supporters like themselves as victims: "The Democrats, with all the fraud they have done in this election, the Republicans, hiding and not fighting, they are trying to silence your voice."[87]

Brooks and Cawthorn, as a *Rolling Stone* investigation later revealed, were two of the seven Republican House members who coordinated closely with the Stop the Steal organizers in forming a strategy to pressure Congress into delaying the Electoral College ballot certification. The others were Marjorie Taylor Greene of Georgia, Lauren Boebert of Colorado, Louie Gohmert of Texas, and Andy Biggs and Paul Gosar of Arizona.[88]

Gosar had been particularly strident leading up to the insurrection. At a December Stop the Steal rally in Arizona, he had told the crowd: "Once we conquer the Hill, Donald Trump is returned to being the president." He announced on Twitter that he would be in D.C. for the protests with "the rest of America," adding that he would "fight back against the leftists who have engaged in sedition to run a Technology Coup."[89]

The morning of the rally, Gosar tweeted: "Biden should concede. I want his concession on my desk tomorrow morning. Don't make me come over there. #StopTheSteal2021 @ali."[90]

Gosar was one of the House Republicans, along with Brooks and Biggs, identified by Alexander in an earlier interview as one of the key members who had helped organize the January 6 protests. "I was the person who came up with the January 6 idea with Congressman Gosar, Congressman Mo Brooks, and Congressman Andy Biggs," Alexander said in December. "We four schemed up on putting maximum pressure on Congress while they were voting so that—who we couldn't lobby—we could change the hearts and the minds of Republicans who were in that body hearing our loud roar from outside."[91]

An investigation by *The New York Times* found at least two other key House Republicans—Rep. Scott Perry of Pennsylvania and Rep. Jim Jordan of Ohio—also played key roles in coordinating the attempt to overturn the election, mainly inside the realm of congressional action (or inaction, in this case), with Trump's chief of staff, Mark Meadows, who was the primary liaison between the president and his cohorts in Congress.[92]

Trump met with members of the so-called Freedom Caucus—namely, Gosar, Jordan, Biggs, and Brooks—on December 21 to discuss their plans. Afterward, Gosar tweeted about the meeting: "President is resolute," he wrote. "We will not accept disenfranchisement of 80 million who cast a vote for @POTUS . . . This sedition will be stopped."[93]

At least two members of the Senate also participated in the campaign to derail the certification of Joe Biden's victory: Ted Cruz of Texas and Josh Hawley of Missouri. Cruz spoke at Stop the Steal rallies, and both had announced beforehand that they intended to vote to object to the certification. "Somebody has to stand up. 74 million Americans are not going to be told their voices don't matter," Hawley had tweeted.[94] Cruz announced that he was joining him on December 2, and claimed that at least ten other Republicans would join them.[95]

While most GOP members of Congress were content to regurgitate claims of voter fraud, this core circle of Trumpists went well beyond that. They used their offices to bombard the Department of Justice with anecdotal claims of voter fraud that turned out to be groundless, and participated in efforts to pressure members of state legislatures, as well as secretaries of state, to conduct audits that would delay the count and cast a shadow over the election's viability. Most of all, they schemed up ways to disrupt the January 6 ceremonial certification of the Electoral College ballots that favored Biden over Trump 306–232.

So when Congress convened in a joint session to certify the ballots at 1:00 p.m. on January 6, the mob led by Proud Boys had already broken through the perimeter on the west side of the Capitol and was streaming onto the lawn below the steps and the entrances. At 1:13, Gosar filed the first objection to the Electoral College certification, with Cruz serving as his senatorial sponsor, claiming that there was fraud in Arizona's election. With a two-hour limit on debate, each man set about arguing against certifying the vote in their respective chambers.[96]

Shortly after the Proud Boys first breached the Capitol at 2:07, Cruz's speech was cut short as the Senate went into recess and Secret Service agents evacuated Vice President Mike Pence to a safe location, with senators filing out quickly afterward. But in the House, the proceedings continued with Gosar droning on about hypothetical and anecdotal reasons to audit Arizona's elections, even as the mob broke through on the east side of the Capitol a little after 2:30 and began pouring through the halls in the direction of the House.

The House only narrowly escaped the mob. Because of Gosar's delay,

many of them were still making their way out of the lobby when the insurrectionists reached the Speakers Lobby doors and went berserk at the sight
of their escaping targets. Other key House members, including Democratic
Progressive Caucus leader Rep. Pramila Jayapal of Seattle, were on the upper
balcony at the time of the evacuation and were forced to shelter there until a
SWAT team was able to rescue them—drawing guns on the insurrectionists
outside the balcony doors who were attempting to get in and forcing them to
lie prone on the floor. They were still lying there when the House members
and their staffs trapped there were finally evacuated, filing past them.[97]

———————

TERRORIZING MEMBERS OF CONGRESS was always part of the plan to overturn
the election. So was battling Antifa in the street. The latter, however, never
materialized—and so neither did the intended outcome. Either way, it came
perilously close to succeeding, as the fleeing congress members and senators and staffers could readily attest.[98]

Although the January 6 insurrection was the epitome of chaos, that was
largely by design. Donald Trump did not cross the Rubicon with his army
on January 6 without a carefully mapped strategy in place. His entire tenure
as president, for that matter, was a ceaseless litany of ways to unleash chaos
for authoritarian goals, and its ending was its apotheosis.

The January 6 scheme was a classic inside-outside strategy, wherein you
can achieve institutional change by operating on the inside to create the
conditions for transformation, and then applying pressure from the outside to make it reach fruition, both operations achieving a kind of syn-
ergy in the process. For Trump, his minions in Congress and the White
House provided the inside game, while the assembled army of right-wing
extremists and conspiracist authoritarians were always intended to bring
the outside game.

Trump's inside game had both legal and political components. The legal
strategy was based on a pair of memoranda by Claremont Institute fellow

John Eastman, who ascended within Trump's inner circle during his last months in office on the basis of a proposed plan to overturn the election results and keep him in office.[99] Eastman dubiously contended in the memos that the Constitution designates the vice president as the "ultimate arbiter" of the election with the power to determine and declare the victor.

Eastman proposed that members of Congress from six battleground states where Trump's team was attempting to contest the outcome in court—Arizona, Georgia, Michigan, Nevada, Pennsylvania, and Wisconsin—could object to the certification of the Electoral College ballot from their state on the basis of the legal challenges, which would draw out the debate long enough for the Republican legislatures in those states to declare alternate slates of electors. This would give Vice President Mike Pence the opportunity to assert that he had competing slates from these states, forcing him to exclude their votes, thus giving Trump a 232–222 Electoral College victory.

The plan proceeded well enough that Republican activists in each of those states filed bogus slates of electors who submitted false certificates declaring the election for Trump. (The National Archives refused to accept the unsanctioned documents.) On January 6, Eastman—who also spoke that morning at the Ellipse rally—was one of the political operators in Trump's "War Room" at the Willard Hotel, rubbing shoulders with Roger Stone and his Oath Keepers crew and others.[100]

This fraudulent legal scheme required a political strategy to enact it, and its main architect was Steve Bannon, who called the inside-game move he planned "the Green Bay Sweep," after the legendary football team's Vince Lombardi–era play that had the running back or quarterback following behind a massive phalanx of blockers to score touchdowns. What that meant in Trump's circle was sending waves of cohorts in Congress to block the certification long enough for their "quarterback"—the vice president—to push the ball over the goal line for Trump.

Trump adviser Peter Navarro later boasted that it was "a perfect plan," noting: "We had over 100 congressmen committed to it."[101]

This put Mike Pence at the center of their schemes, and Trump and his cohorts began applying massive pressure on him. Pence, however, consistently refused to play along. At a meeting with both Trump and Eastman, Pence had asked the lawyer: "Do you think I have such a power?"

When Eastman demurred that, while he might have such authority, it would be foolish to exercise it before the battleground states certified alternate slates of electors, Pence turned to Trump and said: "Did you hear that, Mr. President?" Trump did not respond, as if it had gone in one ear and out the other.[102]

The inside game was not going to be enough to achieve Trump's goals. That's where the outside game and Stop the Steal came in.

Trump had developed an interest in his ability to trigger the Insurrection Act—which essentially establishes martial law in emergency situations—over the course of the summer of 2020, during national protests over police brutality inspired by the murder of an African American man, George Floyd, by Minneapolis police in May.[103] He had even prepared a draft version to sign in order to call out the National Guard in Washington during protests there in early June, but was ultimately persuaded not to take the action, despite public support from Republican senator Tom Cotton of Arkansas, who penned a *New York Times* op-ed calling on Trump to use the act.[104]

The idea remained an active option in Trump's mind. Later that summer he declared that he was still considering invoking it: "Our country's going to change," Trump said. "We're not supposed to go in, unless we call it an insurrection. But you know what we're going to do? We're going to have to look at it."

This discussion excited the Patriot element, particularly Oath Keepers leader Stewart Rhodes, who, as we have seen, began urging Trump to use the Insurrection Act to stop Antifa through October, and then began suggesting it as a solution to Trump's loss after the election. Most of the Oath Keepers came to Washington fully expecting the president to pull the trigger.[105]

Trump himself was indeed preparing to use the Insurrection Act around January 6.[106] He ordered attorneys to prepare a draft version of a national emergency declaration, one in which the military would be permitted to seize election-related "assets"—such as voting machines and ballot boxes. The order would have authorized the Pentagon to seize election machinery in designated states.[107] Just a few days after Biden's election victory, Trump also fired his defense secretary, Mark Esper, and a number of key Pentagon officials and replaced them with Trump loyalists like Christopher Miller, the new acting defense chief.[108]

A PowerPoint presentation shared among the team working to overturn the election also called for Trump to declare a national emergency based on the pretext that "the Chinese systematically gained control over our election system constituting a national security emergency." Among its recommendations was that members of Congress be briefed on "foreign interference" and that a "national security emergency" be declared. "Declare electronic voting in all states invalid," it suggested.[109]

Generals in the Pentagon feared that Trump was about to try to use military forces to retain power, including the chairman of the Joint Chiefs of Staff, Gen. Mark Milley.[110] He foresaw a "nightmare scenario" in which Trump would attempt "to use the military on the streets of America to prevent the legitimate, peaceful transfer of power." They were not alone: On January 3, all ten then-living ex-secretaries of defense published an extraordinary letter in *The Washington Post*, warning: "Efforts to involve the U.S. armed forces in resolving election disputes would take us into dangerous, unlawful and unconstitutional territory."[111]

Trump knew that he would have a massive mob at his disposal on January 6. But he would not activate the Insurrection Act in order to use the military against his own supporters. That was where Antifa came in.

For four years, Trump had hyped the supposed existential threat of the anti-fascist movement, describing them as terrorists and evildoers. When he had told the Proud Boys to "stand back and stand by" during his October

2020 debate with Biden, Trump had added: "But I'll tell you what, I'll tell you what, somebody's got to do something about Antifa and the left because this is not a right-wing problem."

He began beating this drumbeat even more loudly after he lost the election. When the November 14 March for Trump devolved into evening violence—primarily involving Proud Boys assaulting random protesters on the streets—Trump blamed it all on Antifa, tweeting:

> Antifa SCUM ran for the hills today when they tried attacking the people at the Trump Rally, because those people aggressively fought back. Antifa waited until tonight, when 99% were gone, to attack innocent #MAGA people. DC Police, get going—do your job and don't hold back!!![112]

In the minds of Trump and his rabid supporters, Antifa and the Black Lives Matter movement had become inextricably intertwined, gradually becoming the same "violent left" threat. When Trump's supporters gathered in D.C. for another Stop the Steal rally on December 12, they again engaged in random street violence with counterprotesters—and then attacked two African American churches that bore BLM banners, vandalizing the buildings and then tearing the banners and setting them aflame.[113] (Among the Proud Boys who were seen on video lighting the banners was national chairman Enrique Tarrio, who was arrested for the act when he returned to D.C. to participate in the January 6 events.)

On January 5, Trump signed a resolution urging Secretary of State Mike Pompeo to designate Antifa a "terrorist organization." "The violence spurred on by Antifa—such as hurling projectiles and incendiary devices at police, burning vehicles, and violently confronting police in defiance of local curfews—is dangerous to human life and to the fabric of our Nation," the memorandum read. "These violent acts undermine the rights of peaceful protestors and destroy the lives, liberty, and property of the people of this Nation, especially those most vulnerable."[114]

Trump supporters eagerly prepared for their designated enemies to turn out in force, and shared "sightings" of them in the days leading up to January 6. On Parler, a prominent QAnon account posted a photo of two black tour buses featuring the Black Lives Matter slogan on their sides, warning:

> To all the Patriots in Washington DC, Virginia, MD. Let us know where BLM and Antifa buses are staying, give us addresses and pictures. We will send to Proudboys. We need to get them before they go out to the streets, this will make all patriots safer at the March . . . January 6, 2021.

There was just one flaw with all these plans. Anti-fascists were able to see through Trump's scheme and encouraged all their colleagues to avoid the capital city on January 6. On social media, they shared hashtags like #DontTakeTheBait and #January6TrumpTrap that spread the word.

One widely shared meme showed a bear trap, with the text: "On January 6th in Washington DC the Proud Boys are cordially inviting you to be part of Donald Trump and Roger Stone's plan to destroy American democracy." Moreover, anti-fascists in reality (quite unlike the figments of right-wing imaginations) comprise an almost entirely reactive movement that organizes to oppose far-right extremism when it manifests in their communities. They're not particularly aligned with any political party and have no active affiliations with any mainstream party, including Joe Biden's Democrats.

So when the mob gathered on the National Mall on January 6 and headed toward the Capitol, they encountered no resistance from any counterprotesters, much to their surprise. Oath Keepers and Proud Boys alike had been warning one another for weeks to prepare for Antifa or BLM violence. Instead, the only resistance they encountered came from Capitol Police.

The first key step in Trump's plan—for Pence to play along and decline to accept the ballots from the key battleground states—fell apart when Pence did his constitutional duty and certified the Electoral College vote in the Senate. Then Trump's plans to use what he fully expected to happen—that is, violence between his army of "Patriots" and Antifa—as the pretext for invoking the Insurrection Act were dismantled by the reality that "Antifa" was a concocted bogeyman, and vanished back into the mists of their imaginations.

The pro-Trump right-wing media and his defenders on social media were prepared to trot out the presence of violent anti-fascists on January 6 as justification for whatever Trump did. On Rush Limbaugh's radio talk show, guest host Todd Herman said as the scenes from the insurrection unfolded: "It's probably not Trump supporters who would do that. Antifa, BLM, that's what they do. Right?" The right-wing *Washington Times* ran a story falsely claiming that a facial-recognition firm had identified activists in the crowd at the Capitol as Antifa (it was corrected about twenty-four hours later). Fox News talk show hosts like Laura Ingraham and Sean Hannity suggested on national TV that night that Antifa might somehow be to blame, and the claim was made all day on Fox.[115]

"We did have some warning that there might be Antifa elements masquerading as Trump supporters in advance of the attack on the Capitol," Mo Brooks told Fox Business host Lou Dobbs.

When it became clear, however, that he couldn't blame Antifa for the violence, Trump's options for overturning the election had shrunk down to a simple and clear one: for the insurrectionists to successfully stop the Electoral College ballot count—and to do it in a way that could forestall the proceeding indefinitely. In other words, for them to succeed in their frenzied desire to not merely terrorize Congress, but to get their hands on members and lynch them.

This played a decisive role in the failure of the D.C. National Guard—which Trump commands, and had placed on standby—to show up to resist the insurrection until over three hours after the Capitol had first been breached and Capitol Police had requested their deployment. Throughout the afternoon, the departing president resisted pleas from his staff, his confidants, and his congressional allies to stand up and stop the violence.

Many of them texted his chief of staff, Mark Meadows. Donald Trump Jr. was especially agitated: "He's got to condemn this [shit] ASAP," he wrote. "I'm pushing it hard. I agree," Meadows responded.[116]

"Mark, the president needs to tell people in the Capitol to go home," popular Fox News host Laura Ingraham texted Meadows. "This is hurting all of us. He is destroying his legacy."

One of Trump's favorite Fox cohosts, Brian Kilmeade, urged Meadows to "please get him on TV," warning the violence was "destroying everything you have accomplished." Trump's close confidant at Fox, Sean Hannity, asked Meadows whether Trump could "make a statement" and "ask people to leave the Capitol." Still, nothing happened.[117]

House Republican Minority Leader Kevin McCarthy, one of Trump's closest allies in Congress, kept trying to reach the president by phone, and eventually did. Rep. Jaime Herrera-Buetler of Washington state was privy to the exchange.[118]

"When McCarthy finally reached the president on Jan. 6 and asked him to publicly and forcefully call off the riot, the president initially repeated the falsehood that it was antifa that had breached the Capitol," Herrera-Buetler later explained. "McCarthy refuted that and told the president that these were Trump supporters. That's when, according to McCarthy, the president said, 'Well, Kevin, I guess these people are more upset about the election than you are.'"

Finally, after it became clear that members of Congress had been safely evacuated and were planning to return later that evening to complete the certification of the vote, and a combined force of Capitol Police and D.C. Metropolitan officers had successfully shut down the violence and begun clearing the Capitol, the word came down for the National Guard to deploy.

A little while later, Trump finally made his public plea to the mob: He tweeted a video downplaying the events of day and sympathizing with his followers: "I know your pain. I know your hurt." He added, "But you have to go home now. We have to have peace. We have to have law and order. We don't want anybody hurt."

An hour later, he tweeted out a justification for the violence he had unleashed:

> These are the things and events that happen when a sacred landslide election victory is so unceremoniously & viciously stripped away from great patriots who have been badly & unfairly treated for so long. Go home with love & in peace. Remember this day forever![119]

———————

AUTHORITIES ESTIMATE THAT MORE than two thousand people illegally entered the Capitol that day, and several thousand had trespassed on the grounds outside as well.[120] Four protesters, including Ashli Babbitt, died in the violence, primarily from personal health issues; one Capitol police officer, Brian Sicknick, died that evening at home from a stroke almost certainly induced by the stress of the day's events. More than 140 officers were injured. The cost of the cleanup and repairs was more than $1.5 million, perhaps as much as $30 million.[121]

Some of the arrested insurrectionists were immediately regretful and contrite. Douglas Jensen, the QAnon fan who had followed Officer Goodman up the stairs near the Senate entrance, was initially apologetic and claimed he no longer believed in QAnon: "Jensen became a victim of numerous conspiracy theories that were being fed to him over the internet by a number of very clever people," his attorney explained in a court filing. "Six months later, languishing in a DC Jail cell, locked down most of the time, he feels deceived, recognizing that he bought into a pack of lies."[122] (Jensen was later returned to jail for violating his release conditions by watching a conference online dedicated to proving that Trump won the election.) Similarly, "QAnon Shaman" Jacob Chansley's attorney caustically blamed Trump for not issuing a pardon to the insurrectionists and claimed that Chansley had been "duped by the president."[123]

Others, notably Proud Boys like Ethan Nordean, felt abandoned by Trump and were angry about it. Nordean vented in a Proud Boys chat on Telegram:

> Alright I'm gunna say it. FUCK TRUMP! Fuck him more than Biden. I've followed the guy for 4 years and given everything and lost it all. Yes he woke us up, but he led us to believe some great justice was upon us . . . and it never happened, now I've got some of my good friends and myself facing jail time cuz we followed this guys lead and never questioned it.[124]

Nordean, however, still believed in the underlying cause—namely, the long-anticipated civil war he and his fellow Proud Boys believed they were now engaged in.

"This is a very fragile time for the club, but we must be more vigilant than ever, not just for those that look up to us in the club," Nordean wrote. "We are on the brink of absolute war."

PART II

The MAGA Army

4

Patriots of the Seditionist Kind

YOU'LL OFTEN HEAR HARD-CORE right-wing Trumpists refer to themselves as "patriots." Repeatedly. Donald Trump himself regularly refers to his devoted followers the same way. And because the word has a common, generic meaning, most of us glance over its use without giving it much attention.

We shouldn't, because the word is a kind of code, a signal of team membership. Certainly, its use has an obvious propaganda purpose: if Trump's supporters are "patriots," then his opponents by right-wing logic must be unpatriotic and un-American. But more importantly, identifying as one signals to others your affiliation with the far-right Patriot movement—better known to some as the militia movement or "constitutionalists." And understanding this is central to understanding that this movement is the nexus of the right's insurgent war on democracy.

"Patriot" has become the word that far-right ideologues, including various pundits and politicians, and their army of followers use to identify one another. "Ladies and gentlemen, it is time for us as patriots to stand up," admonished Republican Senate candidate J. D. Vance in calling for support for the young shooter who had killed two protesters in Wisconsin.[1] Tucker Carlson titled his pseudo-documentary promoting a conspiracy theory that "the left" is now persecuting conservatives "Patriot Purge."[2] The January 6 insurrectionists arrested called the section in the D.C. detention facility where they were held the "Patriot Wing."[3]

The insurrectionists' use of the name "Patriots," however, is not simply the generic one suggesting people with a deep love of American democracy. In reality, you've never met a more seditionist lot; well before the attack on the Capitol, it was common for them to speak among themselves of overthrowing the government and "the globalists" and preparing for civil war. Their notions of patriotism revolve around enforcing authoritarian adherence to "legitimate" leadership figures and not around the democratic values of our historical traditions.

In psychological terms, it's an expression of a deep need to see oneself, and to be seen by others, as heroic. The dynamics of achieving that heroic status inform everything they do and say, particularly their constant reification of concocted enemies against which they set out to do battle. In the 1990s, the threat was the "New World Order" and its black helicopters; in the 2000s, it became an invading horde of immigrants, combined with the threat of Islamist terror; under Trump, it became "Antifa" and Black Lives Matter and critical race theory.

In practical terms, it is also an identification with the far-right conspiracist "Patriot" movement that, for the past thirty years, has been organizing so-called "citizen militias," as well as violent "sovereign citizen" extremists, border-watching Minutemen vigilantes, armed Three Percent gun fanatics, and, more recently, street-brawling Proud Boys—all of them built around an alternative far-right universe composed of conspiracy theories.

While the "Patriot" movement has been typically described over the decades since it began organizing in the 1990s by researchers who have monitored it as "antigovernment," that term may not give the most accurate sense of their ideology. Given that many of them deny they are opposed to government—they in fact believe government would be just fine if they were in charge, as they believed they were under Donald Trump; they simply oppose any kind of liberal democratic government—and that many of them are unmistakable in their hostility to democratic principles and democracy itself, it is more fundamentally an antidemocratic movement.

Their hostility to democracy is reflected in one of the movement's embedded truisms: "America is a republic, not a democracy"—which is, as historian George Thomas explained in detail in *The Atlantic*, not just an ahistorically wrong claim, it's dangerously toxic:

> When founding thinkers such as James Madison spoke of democracy, they were usually referring to direct democracy, what Madison frequently labeled "pure" democracy. Madison made the distinction between a republic and a direct democracy exquisitely clear in "Federalist No. 14": "In a democracy, the people meet and exercise the government in person; in a republic, they assemble and administer it by their representatives and agents. A democracy, consequently, will be confined to a small spot. A republic may be extended over a large region." Both a democracy and a republic were popular forms of government: Each drew its legitimacy from the people and depended on rule by the people. The crucial difference was that a republic relied on representation, while in a "pure" democracy, the people represented themselves . . .
>
> American constitutional design can best be understood as an effort to establish a sober form of democracy. It did so by embracing representation, the separation of powers, checks and balances, and the protection of individual rights—all concepts that were unknown in the ancient world where democracy had earned its poor reputation.[4]

As Thomas notes, no less an authority than Alexander Hamilton, one of the Federalist Papers' chief coauthors, argued for popular government and called it democracy: "A representative democracy, where the right of election is well secured and regulated & the exercise of the legislative, executive and judiciary authorities, is vested in select persons, chosen really and not nominally by the people, will in my opinion be most likely to be happy, regular and durable."

None of this matters to "constitutionalist" Patriots, particularly not the people who turned out to protest the outcome of the 2020 election. The trope—which was popularized by the far-right conspiracist John Birch Society in the 1960s—is deeply embedded in their belief system, which is founded on a narrative that the current American government has been overthrown by a nefarious cabal. Birch Society founder Robert Welch set the table in a 1961 speech in which he claimed that in a democracy, "there is a centralization of governmental power in a simple majority. And that, visibly, is the system of government which the enemies of our republic are seeking to impose on us today."[5]

That narrative has remained a cornerstone of the far right in the succeeding decades, particularly among the constitutionalist crowd. In a 2020 interview, "constitutional" police chief Loren Culp—the long-shot Republican nominee for the governor's seat in Washington state—asserted that "democracy is mob rule" and that "famous Chinese leaders like Mao Zedong and Mikhail Gorbachev loved democracy because democracy is a step toward socialism, which is a step towards communism."[6]

Similarly, Utah Senator Mike Lee, a devoted Trumpist, insisted in 2020 that "we're not a democracy," adding that "democracy isn't the objective; liberty, peace, and prosperity are." As Zack Beauchamp explained at *Vox*:

The idea that majority rule is intrinsically oppressive is necessarily an embrace of anti-democracy: an argument that an enlightened few, meaning Republican supporters, should be able to make decisions for the rest of us. If the election is close, and Trump makes a serious play to steal it, Lee's "we're not a democracy" argument provides a ready-made justification for tactics that amount to a kind of legal coup.[7]

Which is exactly what proceeded to happen on January 6.

WHILE THE PATRIOT MOVEMENT has often been considered synonymous with the militia movement of the 1990s, it really is more of an umbrella term encompassing a range of far-right extremists. In the post-alt-right era, it has been adopted for identification by an even broader range of ideological warriors, including the Alex Jones *Infowars* crowd and the Proud Boys.

The Anti-Defamation League defines the Patriot movement thus: "A collective term used to describe a set of related extremist movements and groups in the United States whose ideologies center on anti-government conspiracy theories. The most important segments of the 'Patriot' movement include the militia movement, the sovereign citizen movement and the tax protest movement. Though each submovement has its own beliefs and concerns, they share a conviction that part or all of the government has been infiltrated and subverted by a malignant conspiracy and is no longer legitimate."[8]

The use of the name originated with right-wing extremists in the mid-1980s who called themselves Christian Patriots, and were unabashedly racist—many of its participants could be found at annual Aryan congresses assembled by the Christian Identity Aryan Nations near Hayden Lake, Idaho. This movement was studied in depth by sociologist James Aho in his 1990 book, *The Politics of Righteousness: Idaho Christian Patriotism*.[9] Derived in many regards from the openly racist and anti-Semitic Posse Comitatus belief system, Christian Patriots also claimed that ordinary people could declare themselves "sovereign citizens" to free themselves from rule by the federal government (including paying taxes), and that the county sheriff was the supreme law of the land, able to countermand federal law if they deemed it unconstitutional. Civil rights laws, public land ownership, a federal education department—these were all considered null and void in their world of radical anti-federalism.

Following the tragic outcomes of the armed federal standoffs at Ruby Ridge, Idaho, in 1992 and at the Branch Davidian compound near Waco, Texas, in 1993, an idea that had been circulating in far-right circles for several years—a strategy called "leaderless resistance" that called for forming small, action-directed "cells," along with violent acts of "lone wolf" domestic terrorism—became the consensus response among Christian Patriots.[10] They called them militias—a reference intended to invoke the wording of the Second Amendment to justify their existence.

Moreover, to broaden their appeal to more secular-minded recruits, the movement dropped "Christian" and began calling itself simply the "Patriot movement." The name stuck permanently.

At the time he blew up the Murrah Federal Building in Oklahoma City in 1995, Timothy McVeigh self-identified as a "Patriot," as did Eric Rudolph, the 1996 Atlanta Olympics backpack bomber. The Montana Freemen—purveyors of "sovereign citizen" pseudo-legal scams and major figures in the Patriot movement—engaged the FBI in an eighty-one-day armed standoff near Jordan, Montana, in 1996.

Despite the connection to public violence, however, the Patriot movement—as I explained in my 1999 book *In God's Country: The Patriot Movement and the Pacific Northwest*—decisively repackaged their ideas and agendas.[11] The general idea was to strip their overt bigotry (especially the innate anti-Semitism and racism) from their radical localist and nativist politics and to present them wrapped in American-flag bunting and lofty-sounding "constitutionalist" rhetoric that disguised its utterly nonsensical nature with heavy doses of jingoist jargon.

Throughout the 1990s, the Patriots continually organized their vigilante paramilitaries as militia groups and preached the "constitutionalist" approach to government to anyone who would listen, along with their never-ending web of "New World Order" conspiracy theories, peddling maps of "FEMA concentration camps" and sightings of "UN black helicopters." The conspiracism reached a fever pitch in 1999 over the supposed looming "Y2K apocalypse," but after that proved to be a non-event, it then receded into a low-level hiatus during most of the early 2000s, with conspiracists mostly devoted to the massive speculation industry that sprang out of the terrorist attacks of September 11, 2001.

Among the leaders of that industry was radio host Alex Jones, a onetime John Birch Society member who began his career in Texas regurgitating conspiracy theories originally concocted by the Militia of Montana and other "Patriots," then packaging them for mass consumption.[12] Shortly after the embarrassment of having hysterically hyped the Y2K apocalypse, Jones seized on the 9/11 attacks as a fresh, and wildly promotable, avenue for drawing listeners into his web of fantasies. Over the years, Jones increasingly identified on-air with "the Patriots" in their "war against the globalists." It was Jones, in fact, who broadly popularized the use of "Patriot" to describe himself and his fellow conspiracists.

In the early 2000s, much of the radical right, including white nationalists, began organizing around immigration as an issue because of what they saw as an unwelcome tide of nonwhites permanently altering the American cultural landscape. Among Patriots, vigilante border-watch militias were formed; they took it upon themselves to detain and threaten border crossers, motivated by a far-right conspiracy theory that immigration from Latin America was part of a New World Order plot to turn the American Southwest back over to Mexico in a "Reconquista."

The most successful of these was the 2005 Minuteman Project. Patriots from around the country participated in a large vigilante patrol on the

Mexico border that drew massive media coverage. Within five years, however, the Minutemen had crumbled apart amid internal bickering and the increasing criminality of its participants, culminating in the 2009 murders of an Arivaca, Arizona, man and his nine-year-old daughter in a botched home invasion by a Minuteman leader named Shawna Forde and her henchmen.[13] Minuteman cofounder Chris Simcox is now in prison for a child-molestation conviction.[14]

Around the time of the election of Barack Obama to the presidency, the Patriot movement suddenly came roaring back to life. While the numbers of militia groups had declined to a mere 131 groups in 2007, they revived sharply over the next two years, to 512. By 2012, there were a record 1,360 militia groups.[15]

The revival of the Patriot movement during the Obama years primarily revolved around the Tea Party movement. By mid-2010, it had become clear that the Tea Party—first promoted by mainstream media as a kind of normalized right-wing populist revolt against liberal Democratic rule in the Obama era—had swiftly transformed into a massive conduit for conspiracy theories, ideas, and agendas directly from the Patriot movement. Attending a Tea Party gathering after that year, particularly in places like rural Montana, was indistinguishable from the scene one could have found fifteen years before at a militia gathering: the same speakers, the same books, the same rhetoric, the same plenitude of paramilitary and survivalist gear for sale.[16]

The ultimate emblem of this ideological takeover by the Patriots was the ascendance of the Gadsden flag ("Don't Tread On Me") as the Tea Party's most prominent symbol. The flag had originally been revived in the 1990s by the Patriot movement and was prominently displayed at their gatherings, as well as available through the Militia of Montana mail-order catalog. It was prominently used by Minutemen groups while organizing vigilante patrols on both the Mexican and Canadian US borders.

But soon after the Tea Party began organizing rallies in the spring and

summer of 2009 the banner became the best-known symbol of that movement—reflective of the flood of Patriot movement ideologues who seized
control of the Tea Party agenda.[17]

The yellow Gadsden flag and its coiled rattlesnake appeared during two
armed standoffs with federal law enforcement in the West led by Nevada
rancher Cliven Bundy and his family, first in Nevada in 2014, and then
in the Malheur National Wildlife Refuge in Oregon in 2016.[18] Two of the
participants in the Nevada standoff, Jerad and Amanda Miller, went on a
murder spree two months afterward in Las Vegas; after shooting two police
officers to death in a pizza parlor, they covered the slain officers' bodies with
a Gadsden flag.[19]

The same flag was waved by many of the mob that invaded the Capitol
on January 6; one of the five people who died that day in the crowd, a thirty-
four-year-old Georgia woman named Rosanne Boyland, had carried her own
Gadsden flag to the rally (it was later determined she had died of an acciden-
tal amphetamine overdose).[20] One insurrectionist left their flag, still attached
to its pole, sticking out of a large waste can for crews to clean up afterward.[21]

It now appears everywhere there is a right-wing protest, including
Proud Boys marches. It flaps prominently from the back ends of jacked-
up pickups that cruise with "Trump Trains" and anti–Joe Biden protests, alongside "Blue Lives Matter," "Trump Is My President," and "Fuck
Biden" flags.

The seep of the Patriot movement's most recognizable emblem into
mainstream right-wing politics is symbolic of the movement's gradual, and
now seemingly complete, absorption into American conservative politics
and, by extension, the Republican Party.

BACK IN 2009, WHEN the Tea Party was first gaining national recognition,
one of the leading new faces among its increasingly dominant Patriot
faction was an organization tailored to appeal to military veterans and

law-enforcement officers, but also anyone with an inclination to paranoid right-wing conspiracy theories. They called themselves the Oath Keepers.

The brainchild of Stewart Rhodes, a Yale graduate and onetime staffer for Rep. Ron Paul of Texas, the Oath Keepers portrayed themselves as a kind of citizens' defense against looming government tyranny by the people entrusted with enforcing its laws.[22] The core idea was that members would adopt their creed, detailing "ten orders" they "will not obey," all supposedly involving commonsensical rights that everyone naturally would stand up for. However, none of the orders it lists pertain to any real threatened authoritarian commands; rather, they are a list of commands fevered right-wing conspiracy theorists claimed that New World Order conspirators were plotting to unleash:

> We will NOT obey any order to disarm the American people.
>
> We will NOT obey orders to conduct warrantless searches of the American people.
>
> We will NOT obey orders to detain American citizens as "unlawful enemy combatants" or to subject them to military tribunal.
>
> We will NOT obey orders to impose martial law or a "state of emergency" on a state.
>
> We will NOT obey orders to invade and subjugate any state that asserts its sovereignty.
>
> We will NOT obey any order to blockade American cities, thus turning them into giant concentration camps.
>
> We will NOT obey any order to force American citizens into any form of detention camps under any pretext.
>
> We will NOT obey orders to assist or support the use of any foreign troops on U.S. soil against the American people to "keep the peace" or to "maintain control."
>
> We will NOT obey any orders to confiscate the property of the American people, including food and other essential supplies.

We will NOT obey any orders which infringe on the right of the people to free speech, to peaceably assemble, and to petition their government for a redress of grievances.[23]

In a 2009 interview, Rhodes pledged to "prevent a dictatorship in the United States" with his organization: "The whole point of Oath Keepers is to stop a dictatorship from ever happening here," Rhodes said. "My focus is on the guys with the guns, because they can't do it without them.

"We say if the American people decide it's time for a revolution, we'll fight with you."[24]

Rhodes insisted he wanted nothing to do with white supremacists and distanced himself from the militia label: "We're not a militia," he said. "And we're not part and parcel of the white supremacist movement. I loathe white supremacists."

In reality, the Oath Keepers were associated with violent, threatening extremists from the very outset, and Rhodes later proved very tolerant indeed of white supremacists. One of the first prominent members of the group was a man named Charles Dyer, whose online nom de plume was July4Patriot.[25] He represented the Oath Keepers at early Tea Party events when he wasn't producing ominous videos urging his fellow "Patriots" to prepare themselves for armed resistance to the newly elected Obama administration.

About a year later, in 2010, Dyer was arrested for raping his daughter and eventually convicted. Police found a missile launcher in his personal armory.[26] Stewart Rhodes and the Oath Keepers claimed he was never really a member and distanced themselves from Dyer as fast as they could.[27] (Rhodes's ex-wife, Tasha Adams, later told me in an interview that Rhodes had taken Dyer under his wing, and Dyer had been sleeping on their couch around the time of his arrest.)[28]

By 2010, Patriot groups like the Oath Keepers had become the primary face of the Tea Party. Rhodes boasted of his prominent role in the movement to Fox News's Bill O'Reilly: "We like the Tea Party movement a lot, we think it's great. It's a revitalization of our core Americanism and core constitutionalism."

Rhodes structured the Oath Keepers as a nonprofit led by a board of directors. He served as the organization's president, with a vice president and other elected or appointed national leaders. The national Oath Keepers emphasizes organizing around state and county militias at the local level. These county-level units are their action arm.[29]

According to a "warning order" issued by Rhodes, these units are "made up of willing patriots in a county, who are from that county, under leadership who are also from that county, elected by the men of that county." Rhodes made it clear that the movement's power came from communities, not from existing associations: "It's not about our groups, whether we are Oath Keepers, Three Percenters, or self-organized local or state level militia groups . . . It's about our communities . . . Form your community up and let the men elect their officers."

The "warning order" described how each county unit would be comprised of two divisions: A quick reaction force (QRF), intended to be constituted of prepared-to-act and fit "patriots"; and a "Home Guard or Family Safe Unit" who would protect the QRF members' families, homes, and communities.[30]

Rhodes always attempted to present Oath Keepers as a mainstream organization intent on "defending the Constitution" (and particularly gun rights), with an emphasis on protecting ordinary citizens from federal "tyranny," but the facade was thoroughly exposed in 2009 by Justine Sharrock at *Mother Jones*, whose in-depth report revealed a cadre of armed and angry extremists with paranoid ideas and unstable dispositions behind the claims of normalcy and civic-mindedness, with the patina of authority that having military and law-enforcement veterans on your membership rolls can provide.[31]

The Oath Keepers played a prominent role in the 2014 Bundy ranch armed standoff with the Bureau of Land Management in Nevada, among them Stewart Rhodes.[32] The contingent of Patriot militiamen, many of them in Oath Keepers gear, grew large, and they played a key role in the April 14 conflict when weapons were drawn and the scene very nearly exploded into violence.[33]

Afterward, Oath Keepers organized the continuing presence of armed Patriots at the Bundy ranch to ensure that federal officers didn't attempt any rear-guard actions. Things nearly devolved into a lethal mess later that month, though, when tensions between independent Patriot militiamen and the Oath Keepers boiled over.[34]

A paranoid rumor of an imminent drone strike on the encampment began circulating. The team spreading the drone-strike rumor—namely, Rhodes's Oath Keepers—urged people to pull out, which sparked the wrath of militiamen. The militiamen accused the Oath Keepers of being "deserters" and voted to oust the Oath Keepers, and a couple even spoke of shooting Rhodes and his men in the back, which they deemed the proper battlefield treatment of runaways. The situation slowly defused as more participants became disillusioned and left.

The closing fiasco notwithstanding, the Bundy ranch standoff became a boon for the Oath Keepers. Rhodes realized that the key to recruiting new members entailed taking part in headline-grabbing news stunts involving concocted confrontations with government officials.

Rhodes's version of accountability came into sharp focus when the Oath Keepers organized "vigils" outside military recruiting stations after right-wing media claimed that the Obama administration was leaving such stations vulnerable to terrorist attack by insisting that recruiters be unarmed. At one of these vigils, a would-be "protector" mishandled his rifle and dropped it, discharging a round that narrowly missed bystanders.[35]

Rhodes quickly waved off any responsibility, claiming that the man wasn't a member: "Thankfully, not one of ours," he said in an article posted to the group's website. "Good intentions on the part of volunteers are not enough, because we all know where the road paved with them leads," the article mused.

They were next seen in Oregon in April 2015, attempting to reenact the Bundy ranch standoff, this time at the remote Sugar Pine Mine near Grants Pass, where they claimed two longtime miners were being persecuted by the Bureau of Land Management—which, as in Nevada, was simply trying to enforce long-standing regulations by ordering the miners to clear away equipment and a cabin, both of which had been illegal for generations, from the claim they were working.[36] The standoff fizzled, however—mainly because no federal law enforcement attempted to engage them—and the Oath Keepers wandered away from the scene.[37] Many of its participants, however, soon after joined Cliven Bundy's son Ammon in Burns, Oregon, during a monthlong armed standoff at the Malheur National Wildlife Refuge intended to protest the imprisonment of a pair of local ranchers, Dwight and Steven Hammond, for a federal public-lands arson conviction.

At the national level, the Oath Keepers voiced unhappiness with the occupation at the refuge's operations center, not so much because it was illegal but, as Rhodes wrote, "specifically because it is not being done with the consent of the locals or at their request, without the request of the Hammond family . . . and because it is not in direct defense of anyone." [38]

Rhodes attempted to play dealmaker by writing an open letter to Ammon Bundy, asking him "to submit yourself to the authority of the Committee of Safety and the people of Harney County at large, and let them know, in no uncertain terms, that they are now in charge, and you will comply with whatever they decide must be done, whether you agree with it or not." Bundy declined.[39]

By mid-January, the Oath Keepers vigorously supported the armed occupation. Rhodes said it was "essentially a civil disobedience sit-in like the left has been doing for decades . . . People need to get over it and chill out." On their website, the Oath Keepers called on their members to come to Harney County, much as it had done in Nevada in 2014.

Rhodes also appeared on the radio with LaVoy Finicum, a rancher from Utah who had joined the occupation, whose colorful personality had drawn a lot of media attention. The Oath Keepers leader advised Finicum to leave the refuge and seek the protection of a "constitutional" county sheriff. Two days later, Finicum was killed by state police troopers at an FBI roadblock en route to a meeting with Grant County's "constitutional" sheriff, Glenn Palmer.[40] Though a few holdouts back at the refuge lingered for a couple of weeks, the arrests that day effectively ended the standoff.[41]

Many Patriots never forgave Rhodes or the Oath Keepers for their waffling at Malheur. Among them was Joseph Rice, who had led the Oath Keepers chapter in Josephine County involved in the would-be Sugar Pine Mine standoff, and then had served as chief liaison between the occupiers and federal officials at the Malheur. He left the organization afterward, disillusioned.

Rhodes, Rice said, was attracted to conflict as the centerpiece of the Oath Keepers's business model: conflict brings media attention, which spurs income from donations, merchandise sales, and fifty-dollar-a-year membership dues.[42]

"Like a moth to the flame," said Rice. "He flies in, throws up a PayPal, and then disappears."

———————

THE OATH KEEPERS, LIKE most Patriot groups, angrily reject charges that they are a racist or white-supremacist organization, and frequently point to members who are people of color as proof that they are not. However, the presence of such members, as well as the organization's occasional rhetorical embrace of civil rights ideals, is a facade (along the lines of "my best friend is Black") for a movement founded on a core of white-supremacist beliefs, reflected by their origins in the racist Posse Comitatus movement of the 1970s.

When you follow the conversations local activists have among themselves, however, openly racist ideas and sentiments come tumbling out. Responding to a Facebook post in a Patriot group proclaiming, "I've yet to meet a white supremacist," Oregon Oath Keeper Sally Telford replied, "I am a proud white/Caucasian and I support and stand with all other white/Caucasians," and elaborated that, "I stand with free white people."[43]

It's common for Patriot movement adherents to deny the existence of structural or interpersonal racism. They typically define it narrowly as hatred of individuals purely for their race, a "conscious, vocalized action." The Oath Keepers, for instance, instructed readers at their now-defunct website to: "Realize there is no such thing as white privilege or male privilege: In reality, there is only institutionalized 'privilege' for victim-status groups. There is no privilege for whites, males, white males or straight white males."

Even more acutely, the Patriot movement has long been antagonistic to a number of non-white ethnic groups and organizations:[44]

- Latino immigrants. One of its major subgroups that kept the Patriot movement alive in the early 2000s was the Minutemen vigilante border-watch movement of 2005–10, which organized public rallies that denigrated Hispanics and encouraged violence against them.
- Native Americans. Patriot movement conspiracists—many of them operating in states with Indian reservations and, consequently, conflicts between tribes and nontribal residents and fishermen over land and water rights—have been highly active in organizing campaigns, built primarily on "New World Order" conspiracy theories, to attack tribal treaty rights and even decertify certain tribes.
- Muslim refugees. A number of more recent Patriot groups have been highly active in promoting Islamophobic campaigns against Muslims generally and refugees in particular. In 2015–16, Three Percenter militia groups organized multiple protests in Idaho against the presence of a refugee-relocation program based in the city of Twin Falls, claiming it was part of a globalist conspiracy to eventually replace the white population there.
- Black Lives Matter. Most Patriot groups are unapologetic in their disdain and hatred for the Black Lives Matter movement. The Oath

Keepers in particular have prominently attacked BLM activists as innately violent Marxists and a threat to the nation, as have Three Percenter militia groups and the Northwest-based Patriot Prayer street-brawling group, at whose events participants carried signs declaring, "BLM is a hate group." When Proud Boys marched violently through the streets of Washington, D.C., on December 14, 2020, their primary targets became African American churches adorned with Black Lives Matter banners and signs, which they tore down and burned.

The underlying racism of the Patriot movement, however, is only one feature of the danger it poses to American democracy. The greater threat, indeed, lies in its conspiracism-fueled propensity for violence, embodied in its embrace of seditionist rhetoric about overthrowing the "globalist" government, and its fetish-like obsession with civil war.

GIVEN THEIR GROUNDING IN conspiracism, it was inevitable that, once the groundless conspiracy theories about Obama's supposedly "fake" or "incomplete" birth certificate, known as the Birther theories, began circulating as early as 2008, the Patriot movement (and the Tea Party) would avidly embrace them. That's also where Donald Trump first entered the picture.

Trump built the foundations of his political career in 2011 by promoting the Birther theories, creating such a broad media sensation that eventually, after two years of distractions created by the spread of this crackpottery into mainstream politics, Obama conceded and ordered Hawaii officials to publicly produce his "long-form" birth certificate in an attempt to satisfy the conspiracists. Of course, it signally failed to do so; encouraged by Trump's public ambivalence over whether he accepted the evidence as legitimate, the conspiracists in no time produced a fresh round of theories claiming that the new certificate was fake.[45]

Around the same time, Trump claimed the mantle of leader for the Tea Party, telling a Fox interviewer: "I think the people of the Tea Party like me, because I represent a lot of the ingredients of the Tea Party. What I represent very much, I think, represents the Tea Party."[46]

Beginning in mid-2015, Trump enjoyed substantial support for his 2016 presidential campaign from an array of radical-right organizations, notably a solid phalanx composed of the Patriot movement. His ascension to the presidency was widely hailed by various Patriots, not to mention Alex Jones, who had hosted Trump on his *Infowars* program.

The radical right's subsequent focus on defending Trump became immediately apparent at his inauguration in 2017 when they turned out in numbers to combat what they described as an insidious, evil force known as "Antifa"—ostensibly the face of a Communist plot to prevent him from being sworn in. Even though that threat never materialized, the bogeyman they had concocted continued to play a central role in the conspiracist narrative that followed, including a brief panic in October and November of 2017, when Jones and other conspiracists claimed Antifa intended to attempt a coup against Trump.

No such coup ever materialized. But the ensuing narrative—depicting a "violent left" that needed to be violently confronted by "patriots"—was repeated throughout the 2020 election campaign, and ardently adopted by the Oath Keepers and Proud Boys.

The Oath Keepers's alignment with Trump came early and often in his tenure, and in typically paranoiac ways: The group was among the more belligerent promoters of far-right conspiracy theories, theories that eventually metastasized into the current mainstream-right narrative depicting Antifa and leftists as violent Marxists intent on destroying America. Early on they claimed "Marxist coups" against Trump were in the offing.[47]

At Trump events, Oath Keepers showed up to provide "security" intended to deal with protesters and "Antifa."[48] When Trump tweeted out the suggestion that America was on the brink of a civil war should he be removed from office via impeachment, Rhodes responded with his tweet claiming that Americans "ARE on the verge of a HOT civil war."[49]

The Oath Keepers were also present at some of the earliest far-right rallies on the West Coast in 2017, notably the ultraviolent riots in Berkeley, California, in April, as well as the large Patriot Prayer rally in Portland, Oregon, that followed the murder of two commuters on a MAX train by a far-right extremist. At the Berkeley event, Rhodes spoke to the crowd in front of an alt-right "Kekistan" banner, and he was followed on the dais by notorious white nationalist Brittany Pettibone.

Rhodes's reputation among his far-right cohorts waxed and waned though, particularly as the Oath Keepers increasingly backed out of participation in various events. They failed to appear, for instance, at a protest against Democratic representative Maxine Waters that they themselves had organized.[50] Before a Proud Boys march in Portland on August 2019, Rhodes raised hackles by loudly announcing he was pulling Oath Keepers out of the event because of the likely presence of racist bigots among the Proud Boys and their allies, notably the American Guard.

"We do not, and cannot, knowingly associate with known or suspected white nationalists," he claimed then.[51]

Rhodes's vision for the Oath Keepers appears to have changed during the Trump years, his quest for legitimizing their paranoid worldview realized by becoming increasingly associated with the Trump campaign. The endpoint of this vision was for Oath Keepers to become an unofficial adjunct paramilitary force that could be deployed by President Trump at his own discretion—say, if he were to be impeached. Rhodes was explicit about this when he announced plans to provide a kind of specialized "Spartan" training program to prepare Oath Keepers for combat with "Antifa" and whatever other leftists might be lurking out there.

> We're going to have our most experienced law enforcement and military veterans, as well as firefighters, EMTs, Search and Rescue . . . so that

they are available for the sheriff as a posse, under a Constitutional governor to be a state militia, or if it was called out by the President of the
United States to serve as a militia of the United States . . . to execute our
laws, repel invasions, and to suppress insurrections, which we're seeing
from the left right now.[52]

A key point frequently lost in Rhodes's pseudo-legal babble is that the
Oath Keepers are not only well outside the realm of any kind of au-
thoritative law-enforcement entity, but they are also a private army that
has no accountability to anyone. If anyone is injured or harmed by any
Oath Keepers at these events, their history indicates that Rhodes and
his group would simply disavow whatever member has been involved in
the transgression.

The Oath Keepers' belief in their own heroism, however, obscured any
such niceties. What mattered to them was their belief that real Patriots
backed Trump to the hilt, and would go to war for him. Even civil war.

A shooting in Portland, Oregon, was the final straw for Rhodes. In late
August 2020, a marcher with the Proud Boy–esque Patriot Prayer street-
brawling group was shot and killed one night by a self-described anti-fascist
during a brief confrontation downtown (federal marshals shortly tracked
down and killed the shooter). Rhodes declared "civil war" and urged Trump
to declare martial law.

Rhodes went ballistic on Twitter and on the Oath Keepers website, prof-
fering what he considered the appropriate response: Donald Trump needed
to declare a national emergency and an insurrection in the city, send in
troops, and arrest anyone they identify as "Antifa." He vowed that should
Trump fail to do that, Oath Keepers would organize "constitutional" militias to go there and do it themselves.[53]

The Oath Keepers were only one of many voices vowing revenge for the
shooting death of Aaron Danielson, thirty-nine, of Portland. But Rhodes
was much more specific: "This was a terror attack, on US soil, by a member

of an international terrorist organization—Antifa," he wrote. "And the terrorist gunman's Antifa comrades celebrated the murder and continue to plan more of the same. President Trump must declare there to be a Marxist insurrection. And he needs to declare that Marxist insurrection to be nationwide, carried out by both Antifa and BLM, with the goal of terrorizing Americans into submission in furtherance of their attempt to overthrow our Constitution, as they plainly state is their goal."

———————

TRUMP HAD CALLED HIS followers "patriots" for a very long time, including in his fundraising emails. What's noteworthy is that he often applied it to a specific bandwidth of his supporters—namely, those engaging in acts of intimidation and thuggery against leftists and liberals.

It served as a neat rhetorical trick for Trump: playing on neutral observers' propensity to interpret the use of the word generically, while acting as a direct dogwhistle to his followers who identified with the Patriot movement. Even more Machiavellian was the effect its use had on nonextremist supporters by encouraging them to identify indirectly with a far-right movement.

Throughout his tenure, Trump made regular references to "patriots" in his speeches. In his September 2019 speech to the United Nations he declared: "The future belongs to patriots." He used the word to describe backers of his attempt at shutting down the government in 2019, and for farmers who had been devastated by his trade war with China. He also described members of his administration as "great patriots," as well as Republican candidates he endorsed.

Trump's campaign emails also regularly used the word, encouraging donations by describing recipients as patriots, and particularly for supporters who attended his rallies and purchased his MAGA merchandise. Notably, in 2020 and afterward, these emails regularly capitalized "Patriot" to describe would-be donors.

On the same August 2020 evening when Danielson was shot, a "Trump caravan"—with the usual Trump, Gadsden "Don't Tread On Me," "Blue Lives Matter," and ordinary American flags streaming from their pickups—drove through downtown Portland, Oregon, engendering images of his Proud Boys supporters firing paint and pellet guns at protesters. Trump tweeted out a video of the caravan on the move, hailing its participants as "GREAT PATRIOTS!"

The violent rhetoric intensified after Trump lost the election. Oath Keepers began discussing what a civil war would entail. "It's time to start killing the news media live on air," one of them opined in an Oath Keepers channel.

Rhodes spoke at a December 12, 2020, pro-Trump rally in Washington and urged him to invoke the Insurrection Act and declare martial law. On the Oath Keepers website, he had pleaded with Trump in a December 23 open letter: "Do your duty, and do it now. Recognize you are already in a war, and you must act as a wartime president, and there is not a minute to lose."

THE CORE ANIMATING BELIEFS of the Patriot Movement today are either direct descendants of their original worldview from the old far-right white-supremacist movements (in particular, the Posse Comitatus) in which they are rooted; permutations of long-held cultural values; or modern-day adaptations of those values to fit their narratives about current events and politics:

- The world is secretly controlled by an elite cabal of "globalists" who seek to enslave the world under a single, tyrannical world government (long known, and still referred to at times, as the New World Order).
- The "unpatriotic" Americans they oppose—variously liberal Democrats, civil rights and immigrant-rights leaders, environmentalists, mainstream journalists—are the willing tools of socialists,

who are Marxists, who are Communists, who are actually the real fascists. All are worthy of elimination.

- In addition to the government, media and educational institutions are under the control of the cabal, and are dedicated to brainwashing American children with Marxist propaganda.

- All of these coconspirators are encouraging non-white immigration into America so that the traditional white demographic base of the country will be permanently altered with more "obedient" races.

- America is not a democracy; it is a republic. "Democracy" is a socialist lie.

- The Second Amendment not only forbids gun-safety restrictions, it also enshrines the formation of private armies accountable to no one because they are "militias."

- The same amendment exists to enable ordinary citizens to obtain any kind of armament they desire so that they can rise up and prevent any kind of "Communist takeover" by taking up arms against a "tyrannical" world government. (This is known as the insurrectionary theory of the Second Amendment.)

- The globalist cabal knows that the resulting heavily armed populace is the chief obstacle for their nefarious schemes, which is why they work so relentlessly to undermine the Second Amendment—and why Patriots must defend it with their blood and their arms.

- The Constitution severely limits the power of the federal government, which should not be permitted to own federal lands, enforce civil rights or environmental laws, engage in overseeing public education, or any other traditional function outside of providing a national defense.

- The extraordinary extremism now exhibited by their enemies— endorsing "socialist" government-funding schemes, supporting same-sex marriage and abortion rights, embracing a movement to end racist policing—means they have been overwhelmed by Marxist ideology and are an existential threat to their Republic.

This means that any kind of force, especially lethal force, is a reasonable response to this threat.

- Donald Trump's presidency came under relentless attack from the globalist conspiracy even before he won election, because he is a real American Patriot who espouses and defends real American values. The 2020 election was stolen from him by the cabal using election fraud, and the January 6 riot in Washington, D.C., was a justifiable attempt by ordinary Patriots to prevent the theft of his presidency.
- Joe Biden is not only being controlled by the elite cabal, he is also in the pocket of the Chinese Communist Party, and his administration is now engaged in a program of destroying America to pave the way for a Communist takeover.

These beliefs, all of them fundamentally extremist, form the cornerstones of the Patriot movement's worldview and how it organizes and recruits. And as we can see, a number of them are being voiced steadily and regularly by ostensibly mainstream right-wing figures, particularly Fox News pundits, social media trolls, and Republican politicians.

This is how extremism has crept into the mainstream, like the Gadsden flag: unremarked upon, quietly, and with only a few raised eyebrows within mainstream political discourse. In the same way, the Patriot movement has silently insinuated itself at the center of that discourse and radicalized an entire political party along the way.

The Patriot movement is the nexus of the insurgent war on democracy that is currently well underway. And January 6 was their open declaration of that war.

AS THE EVIDENCE PILED up and the federal indictments from the January 6 insurrection mounted, a clearer picture of what happened that day began to emerge. At the center of that picture was the Oath Keepers and the Proud

Boys, who, as we have seen, played key roles in overwhelming Capitol Police barricades that day and leading the mob inside the building.

Ominously, the response to one of the indictments raised the possibility that these groups may have been coordinating with official law-enforcement authorities: Ohio militia leader Jessica Watkins's attorneys claimed in a filing that she had been organizing "security" at the Donald Trump rally at the Ellipse prior to the Capitol siege and had been communicating with members of Trump's Secret Service. The court filing said:

> On January 5 and 6, Ms. Watkins was present not as an insurrectionist, but to provide security to the speakers at the rally, to provide escort for the legislators and others to march to the Capitol as directed by the then-President, and to safely escort protestors away from the Capitol to their vehicles and cars at the conclusion of the protest . . . She was given a VIP pass to the rally. She met with Secret Service agents. She was within 50 feet of the stage during the rally to provide security for the speakers. At the time the Capitol was breached, she was still at the site of the initial rally where she had provided security.[54]

The Secret Service adamantly denied that it had employed any Oath Keepers: "To carry out its protective functions on January 6th, the U.S. Secret Service relied on the assistance of various government partners. Any assertion that the Secret Service employed private citizens to perform those functions is false," a spokesperson said in a statement to CNN.

The indictments themselves also pointed to the Oath Keepers playing a central role in the coordinated attack that opened the doors of the Capitol to the mob.[55] Conspiracy charges against six people—including Watkins—detailed how they formed a stack (typically a maneuver requiring military training) to move their phalanx of body-armored members up the east steps of the Capitol and into the front, where they were able to overpower the police.

The court documents said that Oath Keepers considered bringing "heavy weapons" to Washington after the election. Some members indicated plans to bring mace, gas masks, batons, and armor to the Capitol—however, they were in agreement not to bring guns to Washington because of local anti-gun laws. Instead, they chose to create a quick reaction force with weapons several minutes away, stashed in vehicles and hotel rooms.

Watkins and coconspirator Bennie Parker communicated their plans via text messages over several months. In a November conversation, Parker wrote: "Unfortunately, we can't take weapons." Watkins replied: "Not into the city, no. Just mace, tasers and nightsticks."[56]

It was obvious the prosecutors were circling around Rhodes's organization as well as Rhodes himself. Filings in Watkins's case showed Rhodes had used the encrypted platform Signal to chat with her and Kelly Meggs. The filing said he directed them to rally during the siege to the Capitol's southeast steps, following which members forcibly entered the east side of the building.

Prosecutors said the chat recovered on Signal called "DC OP: Jan 6 21" showed "that individuals, including those alleged to have conspired with [others], were actively planning to use force and violence." They asserted that Rhodes, Watkins, Meggs, and "regional Oath Keeper leaders" discussed plans to "provide security to speakers and VIPs" at events on January 5 and 6 in Washington with members and affiliates.

The messages, combined with Rhodes's previous statements, "all show that the co-conspirators joined together to stop Congress's certification of the Electoral College vote, and they were prepared to use violence, if necessary, to effect this purpose," prosecutors said. "They were plotting to use violence to support the unlawful obstruction of a Congressional proceeding."

Rhodes claimed the new allegations were "total nonsense." In a text to *The Washington Post*, he said the government was trying to "bootstrap" a few Oath Keepers' actions into a conspiracy in order to depict his organization as the "boogeyman."[57]

"They are trying to manufacture a nonexistent conspiracy," Rhodes said, "I didn't say 'don't enter the Capitol,' I never figured they would do that." He added of federal investigators, "They got nothing, they got a message from me saying, 'Meet here.'"

In a lengthy interview with the *Post* Rhodes denied that he had any advance knowledge of any Oath Keepers' plans to invade the Capitol. He instead blamed members who "went off the reservation."

"Just so we're clear on this: We had no plan to enter the Capitol, zero plan to do that, zero instructions to do that, and we also had zero knowledge that anyone had done that until after they had done that—afterwards," Rhodes said.

He added: "They went totally off mission. They didn't coordinate with us at all while they were there. They did their own damned thing." He also claimed that Thomas Caldwell, who led the Oath Keepers' "Stack One" into the Capitol, was not actually a dues-paying member of Oath Keepers.

Nonetheless, Rhodes anticipated being arrested. "I want to say a few things before they send me off to a gulag," he told the audience at a right-wing anti-immigration rally in Texas in March 2021.[58]

"I may go to jail soon," Rhodes said. "Not for anything I actually did, but for made-up crimes. There are some Oath Keepers right now along with Proud Boys and other patriots who are in D.C. who are sitting in jail denied bail despite the supposed right to a jury trial before you're found guilty and presumption of innocence, were denied bail because the powers that be don't like their political views."

He also claimed his members were innocent. "If we actually intended to take over the Capitol, we'd have taken it, and we'd have brought guns," Rhodes said. "That's not why we were there that day. We were there to protect Trump supporters from Antifa."

Finally, in mid-January 2022, more than a year after the insurrection, the Justice Department closed the circle by charging Rhodes and ten other Oath Keepers—most of them already in detention—for seditionist conspiracy. They arrested him at a home in Texas where he had been hiding out.[59]

The indictment charged Rhodes and his fellow Oath Keepers with organizing a wide-ranging plot to storm the Capitol to prevent the certification of Biden's victory. His attorneys later tried to assert that Rhodes and his Oath Keepers were awaiting word from Trump that day giving them the green light to act on his behalf as his personal militia. Nonetheless, the attorneys said, "To date, we are unaware of any direct communications that ever took place between the Oath Keepers and Trump, or anyone in his inner circle."

Rhodes's indictment revealed more than a mountain of evidence that the Justice Department had acquired in the prosecutions of key players in the insurrection. It also made clear the DOJ's larger strategy of moving up the food chain of players in the historic attack—with Donald Trump and his inner circle now only steps away.

––––––––––

THE TRIAL OF STEWART Rhodes and four other Oath Keepers who participated in the Capitol siege—Kelly Meggs, Kenneth Harrelson, Jessica Watkins, and Thomas Caldwell—on charges of seditionist conspiracy, obstructing the congressional affirmation of Biden's victory, and impeding lawmakers on January 6 finally got under way in early October 2022.[60] From the outset, prosecutors emphasized the threat to American democracy their actions manifested.

"That was their goal — to stop by whatever means necessary the lawful transfer of presidential power, including by taking up arms against the United States government," Assistant U.S. Attorney Jeffrey Nestler said during opening statements in federal court. The conspirators descended on Washington "to attack not just the Capitol, not just Congress, not just our government—but our country itself."

Throughout the trial, jurors were shown evidence demonstrating the procession of steps that Rhodes and his cohorts took to prepare for "the insurrection" on January 6: how Rhodes spent thousands of dollars on a rifle, firearm accessories, and paramilitary gear; how the Oath Keepers cached firearms at a Virginia hotel the day before for a "quick reaction force" standing by in the event that Trump called on them.

Private communications between Rhodes and others he presumed to be Trump confidants showed how he demanded they pressure the defeated president to make that call, both before and after January 6. In the days following the insurrection, Rhodes used the phone of a man he believed to be in contact with Trump to send the then-president a message: "You must use the Insurrection Act and use the power of presidency to stop him. All us veterans will support you," Rhodes wrote.[61]

Their attorneys tried various strategies to assert the defendants' innocence. Caldwell's attorneys attempted to blame the FBI for allegedly manipulating them into breaking the law, while Rhodes's attorneys claimed that all of his invocations of the Insurrection Act and his "constitutionalist" conspiracy theories were simply matters of free speech.

None of it worked. On November 29, after two days of deliberation, the jury returned a mixed but unmistakable verdict: Rhodes and Meggs were guilty of seditious conspiracy, obstructing an official proceeding, and destroying evidence. Caldwell, Watkins, and Harrelson also were convicted of the latter charges, while Meggs and Watkins were also convicted of conspiring to stop the congressional proceeding and (along with Harrelson) interfering with members of Congress in the attack.

While awaiting sentencing, Rhodes testified via cell phone in the December 2022 trial of an Alaska lawmaker accused of violating the state's disloyalty clause by virtue of his membership in the Oath Keepers. When attorneys queried him about whether the Oath Keepers's behavior on January 6 was an act of sedition, he insisted that it was the opposite.[62]

"My perspective is that we're preserving the Constitution, and it's—I wouldn't even call it insurrection, I would call it a counter-revolution against an insurrection," Rhodes answered. "It's my opinion that the left was engaged in open insurrection throughout 2020."

5

Proud of Your Boys

A SINGLE PUNCH MADE Ethan Nordean a legend among the Proud Boys.

It happened during one of the Proud Boys' multiple incursions into downtown Portland, Oregon—on June 30, 2018, during a march organized by their regular partners in violence, another street-brawling group called Patriot Prayer.[1] In a video Nordean can be seen aiming a hard right hook at a black-clad anti-fascist swinging a baton at him and simply flattening the man onto the section of Main Street where brutal street fighting had become concentrated.

The clip of Nordean became a viral sensation with the far-right set.[2] Gavin McInnes, the Proud Boys founder, replayed it on a loop for the audience of his popular video podcast, and Proud Boys began sharing it widely as a GIF. McInnes considered the moment definitive in shaping the violent identity of the Proud Boys: "I honestly think that that knockout is a pivot in the movement, it marks the beginning of the end of Antifa, and the beginning of being safe and proud to be Trump."[3]

Nordean was arrested by Portland Police and then released a short while later with no charges. The next week, he was named "Proud Boy of the

Week" on the group's Facebook pages and made an appearance on Alex Jones's *Infowars* broadcast, which he used to recruit new members.[4]

Jones, like McInnes, reveled in the violence. "I just love how your giant roundhouse right hook and then shove him down so his head hits the pavement," he said. "That probably hurt him worse. Gawd, I love it. I gotta tell ya, it's better than a fake Rocky movie."

Nordean had been a pivotal figure in the Northwest Proud Boys scene. A resident of Auburn, a Seattle suburb, he made a living selling vitamin supplements and working for his father's chowder house in nearby Des Moines. Like a number of Proud Boys, he was a weightlifter who exulted in his ability to wreak havoc on anti-fascist counterprotesters.

He was nicknamed "Rufio Panman" (a moniker Nordean had taken from a character in the 1991 movie *Hook*) and became known for the extraordinary levels of thuggish violence he brought to these events—as well as clearly playing a command role among his cohorts. He frequently wore communications gear to planned protests, and was regularly seen in the company of white nationalists, such as Jake Von Ott of Identity Evropa and a man known only as Germany, a member of the Portland-based Stormers, a neo-Nazi group.[5]

The punch on Main Street made Nordean a hero among the Proud Boys and right-wing extremists generally, and eventually elevated him to a position in their national organization on its board of Elders. So when the board's chairman, Enrique Tarrio, was arrested two days before the planned siege of the US Capitol on January 6, Nordean was handed "war powers" to serve as their field general that day.

Nordean is a moderately intelligent man with a steady demeanor, so it is not surprising that the Proud Boys gladly deferred to him and readily followed his commands that day. Before he joined the Proud Boys, he was a less-than-successful businessman with modest accomplishments; but he became a superstar in the charged realm of right-wing street-brawling gangs.[6]

His fellow Proud Boys looked up to him not because of any natural leadership skills, but because of what he stood for. Nordean embodies what the Proud Boys are ultimately all about because of what made him famous: violence. Visceral, vicious, eliminationist, redemptive violence.

———————

THE PROUD BOYS' CELEBRATION of the aesthetic of violence is what makes them tick, and their most obviously fascist trait: most scholars of fascism have found this aesthetic essential to the fascist phenomenon. Neofascism—that is, fascism in modernized form, with new aspects and attributes but driven by the same core pathology—was baked into the Proud Boys, both as an idea and an organization, from the very start, by their founder, Gavin McInnes.[7]

McInnes is a wealthy Canadian immigrant who cofounded *Vice* magazine in the early 1990s and moved the operation to New York City late in the decade. Much of McInnes's early "hipster" branding involved his disdain for "political correctness." He boasted of converting *Vice* readers to conservatism.

"I love being white and I think it's something to be very proud of," he told *The New York Times* in 2003, revealing an ideology that would become the foundation of the Proud Boys.[8] "I don't want our culture diluted. We need to close the borders now and let everyone assimilate to a Western, white, English-speaking way of life." The *Times* described his views as "closer to a white supremacist."

He parted ways with *Vice* in 2008 and cofounded an advertising agency named Rooster, where he was the creative director. He continued to burnish his credentials as a gadfly who fought political correctness by embracing the ideas and rhetoric of white nationalists and other bigots. He wrote for white-nationalist magazines like *VDARE* and *American Renaissance*. In 2014, he wrote a hate-filled piece for *Thought Catalog* titled "Transphobia Is Perfectly Natural": "They are mentally ill gays who need help, and that help doesn't include being maimed by physicians," he wrote. "These aren't women trapped in a man's body. They are nuts trapped in a crazy person's body."[9]

Rooster parted ways with McInnes after the piece. Soon afterward he was offered the opportunity to host a show on Anthony Cumia's Compound Media, a subscription-based streaming media platform dedicated to "free speech" and combating "political correctness." *The Gavin McInnes Show* premiered in June 2015, and promptly attracted a large online audience. The show became a rallying space for frustrated young white men. McInnes and his guests explored his recurring themes: that racism is a myth created by guilty white liberals, that feminism "is about de-masculinizing men," that Western culture is superior to all others, and that Islam is a radical culture of violence.[10]

He and his circle of male friends from Compound Media began hanging out in New York City dive bars, and McInnes began spreading the idea for others in his audience. These gatherings gave birth to the concept of the Proud Boys.

McInnes officially announced the group in the far-right *Taki's Magazine* in September 2016, saying they took their name from their fondness for ironically singing a tune from the Broadway musical *Aladdin* called "Proud of Your Boy," which McInnes and his cohorts deeply loathed as the mewlings of an emasculated man. McInnes wrote that "the meetings usually consist of drinking, fighting, and reading aloud from Patrick Buchanan's Death of the West."[11]

This wasn't just a minor detail. Buchanan, the former presidential candidate who in 1992 had originally issued a call for a "culture war" at the Republican National Convention, had fully embraced white nationalism when he published *The Death of the West: How Dying Populations and Immigrant Invasions Imperil Our Country and Civilization* in 2001, particularly the conspiracy theory generated by right-wing extremists in the

1990s that all of the world's ills could be laid at the feet of something called cultural Marxism.[12]

The general outline of this conspiracy, according to the progenitors of the theory, is fairly simple: A group of Jewish academics, all Marxists with a base of operations at the Institute for Social Research in Frankfurt am Main—known as the Frankfurt School—were responsible for concocting the ideas behind multiculturalism and "critical theory," which they saw as a means for translating Marxist ideals into cultural values. During the 1930s, the story goes, they moved from Frankfurt to New York and Columbia University, and their influence became so profound that it now dominates both academia and modern popular culture. Indeed, as they tell it, nearly all modern expressions of liberal democratic culture—feminism, the civil rights movement, the '60s counterculture movement, the antiwar movement, rock and roll, and the gay rights movement—are products of the scheming of this cabal of Jewish elites.

While the influence of the Frankfurt School has made some inroads in art theory, cultural studies, political theory, philosophy, sociology, and literary studies, it is far from being hegemonic in the academy and is, in some respects, antithetical to poststructuralism and postmodernism, which its critics often conflate it with—indeed, these are often identified by right-wing ideologues as leading examples of "cultural Marxism." Nor were its members leaders of any kind of international conspiracy to destroy Western civilization.[13] Contrary to the characterizations of the conspiracy theorists, most of the "cultural Marxists" of the Frankfurt School were refugees from Nazism who were sharply critical of the modern entertainment industry, which they saw not as a tool for their own ideology but as a kind of modern "opiate of the masses" that was inimical to their values.[14]

Buchanan's book picked up the bastardized version of history from the theory's proponents (primarily 1990s right-wing "thought leaders" like William Lind of the Free Congress Foundation) and ran with it, describing "cultural Marxism" as a "regime to punish dissent and to stig-matize social heresy as the Inquisition punished religious heresy. Its trade-mark is intolerance."

Death of the West ascribes nearly superhuman powers to critical theory. "Using Critical Theory, for example, the cultural Marxist repeats and re-peats the charge that the West is guilty of genocidal crimes against every civilization and culture it has encountered," Buchanan averred. It "repeats and repeats that Western societies are history's greatest repositories of rac-ism, sexism, nativism, xenophobia, homophobia, anti-Semitism, fascism and Nazism. [That] the crimes of the West flow from the character of the West, as shaped by Christianity . . . Under the impact of Critical Theory, many of the sixties generation, the most privileged in history, convinced themselves that they were living in an intolerable hell."[15]

Buchanan also regurgitated the longtime far-right claim—dating back to the eugenicists of the 1920s, and more recently to the white-nationalist agitation of David Duke and his fellow neo-Nazis—that the "white race" is about to be swamped by a horde of "colored people." But McInnes's gift, such as it was, lay in his ability to launder these ideas into a mainstream twenty-first-century setting by using slightly different words to say the same things. He claimed to reject white nationalism while embracing and amplifying its tropes.

Thus, McInnes's opening description of the Proud Boys—that they are "Western chauvinists who refuse to apologize for creating the modern world"—was something he and others repeated often in interviews. But it was essentially a different formulation of the same ideas—namely, that white "civilization" faced a relentless assault from an array of nefarious forces—contained in the infamous credo of neo-Nazis known as "the 14 Words": "We must secure the existence of our people and a future for white children."[16]

McInnes was aware of this. On one episode of his video podcast, a guest named Emily Youcis—a vocal supporter of white nationalism—implored him to say "the 14 Words" to prove he was at the crux of "this movement." McInnes responded by simply reciting them, but replacing the word "white" with "Western."[17]

McInnes and his show became a major gateway for young men who eventually became hard-core white nationalists: a 2018 Southern Poverty Law Center study of white nationalists conversing in a popular alt-right on-line forum found that McInnes was one of the most frequently cited figures who had introduced them to white-nationalist ideas and hard-core veterans of the movement.[18]

"All his jokes, all his content when I first started listening to him was all freakin' alt-right stuff and racial issues and funny, comedic ways to like try to point out that white civilization has been superior," a white nationalist and former Proud Boy told a far-right podcast regarding McInnes.[19]

McInnes was the creator of the Proud Boys uniform—black Fred Perry polo shirts with yellow striping, and bright red MAGA hats. He denied that the fashion choice was an homage to the 1980s racist skinheads, some of whom wore Perry polos (as did the supporters of the multiracial Two Tone music movement during this period); rather, he told an interviewer, the idea was "to align his group with the working-class toughness of the late '60s hard mods."[20]

The Proud Boys had bizarre initiation rituals and rules that were all about their twisted conceptions of masculinity. Their first rule of the organization—and the primary means of entrée—was a requirement for all initiates to state that they identify as Proud Boys who "refuse to apologize for creating the modern world." But that was only the first step in the initiation.

The next step involved getting encircled by a group of Proud Boys who lightly hit you with their fists until you can name five kinds of breakfast, after which you take a vow to stop masturbating or viewing porn any more than once a month (sealed with the hashtag #NoWanks). Getting a Proud Boy tattoo is the next. And the final step that seals your membership as a "fourth degree" member of the organization is to engage in physical combat with members of Antifa and other leftist movements.

"We will kill you," McInnes said on his Compound Media show in mid-2016. "That's the Proud Boys in a nutshell. We will kill you."[21]

THE PROUD BOYS QUICKLY graduated from being a forum for men to drink and bitch after Donald Trump was elected to becoming a paramilitary street-fighting force dedicated to violence. This happened in early 2017, primarily in response to the left-wing protests occurring around public-speaking appearances by key alt-right figures, particularly Milo Yiannopoulos, the erstwhile *Breitbart News* editor who enjoyed brief popularity in 2015–17 as a fascism-friendly cultural and political gadfly.[22]

At a Milo Yiannopoulos appearance in Seattle on Trump's Inauguration Day in 2017, a large group of counterprotesters blocked ticket holders from entering the venue, setting off numerous scuffles, at the culmination of which a woman, whose alt-right husband had been engaged in the fighting, shot and nearly killed an anti-fascist who had been trying to keep the man from pepper-spraying people.[23]

So when Yiannopoulos tried to bring his speaking tour to Berkeley, California, for a February 1 appearance, a massive crowd of protesters shut down the event and forced Milo to flee the campus under police protection and wearing body armor. Right-wing extremists responded by organizing a kind of counter-event scheduled for March 4 that was initially planned as a protest in defense of "free speech."[24] However, Milo's career tanked suddenly and with finality that same month after he made remarks defending pedophilia that made him radioactive to every political camp.[25]

Organizers shifted gears and changed it to a march for Trump—with the Proud Boys prominently mentioned on flyers as participants—correctly figuring it would attract a similarly hostile reaction from anti-fascists. And it did; when about five hundred Trump supporters—nearly all of them from out of town—showed up at Berkeley's downtown city park, they were met by an even larger crowd of local counterprotesters. Brawls and arrests ensued.[26]

Among them was a Bay Area commercial diver named Kyle Chapman, who arrived at the event prepared for battle with a shield adorned with an American flag, football-style padding and helmet, and a long wooden signpost he wielded like a baseball bat. A video of Chapman breaking the post over the head of an anti-fascist protester went viral and gave birth to his nickname, "Based Stickman." Chapman was charged with multiple counts of felony assault, which he eventually plea-bargained down to a single charge and five years' probation.

His next big moment, however, was also the Proud Boys' inaugural event: the April 15, 2017, "free speech" rally they dubbed the Next Battle of Berkeley and which proved to be a seminal moment for white-nationalist groups such as Identity Evropa and the Rise Above Movement, the leaders of which were all present. A broad swath of right-wing extremists participated, ranging from white nationalist Brittany Pettibone (who eventually married German Identitarian leader Martin Sellner) to Oath Keepers founder Stewart Rhodes, both of whom addressed the crowd that day.[27]

Nathan Damigo, a founder of the student-oriented white-nationalist Identity Evropa organization, acted as a provocateur throughout the day, egging on protesters and leading a group of young white men with "fashy" haircuts in confrontations on the street. Damigo was videotaped sucker-punching a young woman in black who was embroiled in the street brawls.

Afterward, the alt-right was exultant, claiming "victory": Chapman claimed that "Berkeley got sacked." The Proud Boys boasted: "Today was an enormous victory! I could not be more proud or grateful for every one who attended the event! This was the turning point!"[28]

McInnes was so impressed that he anointed Chapman a leader of the Proud Boys and placed him in charge of organizing what he considered the group's "tactical defensive arm," dubbed the Fraternal Order of Alt-Knights (FOAK). Chapman described FOAK as a "fraternal organization," a Proud Boys affiliate chapter, "with its own bylaws, constitution, rituals and vetting processes."

However, over the ensuing months and years, nothing ever came of the FOAK project, mainly because Chapman wound up facing multiple charges arising from a variety of violent incidents: for hitting a Texas man over the head with a barstool, for fighting a person in Berkeley while filming a promotional video, and for operating a vehicle off-road. He also did relatively little to organize FOAK cells.

Thanks to their growing profile on social media, though, the Proud Boys kept gathering members and chapters around the country. Their primary recruitment pitch—preparing to fight Antifa in the streets—had one drawback, however: Antifa rarely turned out for its own events, but rather reacted to the presence of right-wing extremists. So if they wanted to fight them, they needed to create events to serve as a pretext for violence.

On the West Coast, this was where Patriot Prayer came in.

————————

AMONG THE CROWD IN Berkeley on April 15 was a thirty-three-year-old Japanese American man named Joey Gibson, wearing a Trump T-shirt and shades, who wound up participating in that day's street violence. Returning to his home in Vancouver, Washington—a suburb of Portland situated across the Columbia River—he decided to bring his own street-fighting organization into the fray.

As Gibson would tell his audiences later, he had originally been deeply immersed in survivalist "prepper" culture, believing himself "mostly apolitical" but nonetheless an avid consumer of the conspiracist beliefs that fueled much of that movement—and gradually became more "politically aware" through his absorption of Patriot movement "constitutionalist" beliefs. He also socialized with bikers from the American Freedom Motorcycle Association in Vancouver. These bikers formed a kind of "Bikers for Trump" political wing that called itself American Freedom Keepers.[29]

Gibson called his group Patriot Prayer, reflecting both its militia-movement and Christian nationalist orientations. He later claimed he had gotten the idea to form the group after watching violence break out at a June 2016 Trump event in California, saying his goal was to "liberate the conservatives on the West Coast."[30] At the group's first official event—on April 29, 2017, in southeastern Portland, protesting Portland officials' cancellation of an annual parade out of fear that it would attract violence—AFK members comprised the event's security, such as it was, even as marchers clashed with anti-fascist protesters.

One of those marchers, Jeremy Christian, wrapped himself in an American flag, complained about the police separating the two sides, and loudly called one of the anti-fascists a "white nigger"—which brought a quick shutdown from the bikers who were acting as security for the march. Eventually, they ejected Christian from the march for being too far right-wing.[31]

Three weeks later, Christian was riding a Portland MAX commuter train when he began verbally assaulting two women of color; when three men tried to intervene, he slashed their throats with a knife. Two of the men died; the third, a young man named Micah Fletcher, had been one of the anti-fascists who had confronted him in April.

At his arraignment, Christian shouted the kinds of slogans used by his fellow far-right marchers: "Free speech or die, Portland! You got no safe place. This is America! Get out if you don't like free speech! Death to the enemies of America! Leave this country if you hate our freedom. Death to Antifa! You call it terrorism, I call it patriotism!"

Patriot Prayer, as it happened, had scheduled a large "free speech" rally to take place the following Sunday, June 4, in downtown Portland.[32] Ignoring the pleas of local officials to delay the event until things had cooled down after the MAX murders, Gibson (who denied any connection to Jeremy Christian) and a group of several hundred alt-right figures—including Kyle Chapman and white nationalist Tim "Baked Alaska" Gionet, as well as the ubiquitous Stewart Rhodes—held their rally but were outnumbered by a massive crowd of several thousand counterprotesters, most of them local Portlanders. It, like most future Patriot Prayer events, eventually devolved into violence. Leading the fray in the streets were a number of Proud Boys immediately identifiable by their black Fred Perrys and red MAGA hats.[33]

The two organizations became street-fighting partners. By early August 2017, Proud Boys were playing the role of "security" for Patriot Prayer, with Ethan Nordean playing a leading role. The most striking figure at the earlier Patriot Prayer rallies was Gibson's then-right-hand man, a large Samoan named Tusitala "Tiny" Toese, who had a knack for being in the middle of violent brawls, often instigating them. Toese and Gibson, in fact, seemed nearly inseparable, with the hulking sidekick setting the tone for most of the group's street confrontations with anti-fascists. Toese also had a propensity for getting charged with assault—which eventually led to him fleeing the country. But by then, Gibson had already discarded him.[34]

Gibson's rallies continued to tout variations of the "free speech" cause as he continued to organize his street-theater events, though he also showed how flexible Patriot Prayer's organizing philosophy could be when large numbers of his group showed up in Seattle later in June for a March Against Sharia organized by the anti-Muslim hate group ACT for America.[35] Another June rally entailed bringing his motley crew to the campus of Evergreen State College in Olympia after a national controversy erupted—primarily on Fox News and other right-wing outlets—over a planned campus exercise in race consciousness that was portrayed instead as an exercise in anti-white bigotry.[36] Again, violence was the course of the day at the protest, sparked by an assault on an anti-fascist by a mob of Patriot Prayer members. A rally on August 6, 2017, in Portland, also publicizing free speech as the cause, was again clearly an attempt to troll leftists into violence.[37]

The right-wing appetite for violence reached its apex on August 11–12 in Charlottesville, Virginia, at the infamous Unite the Right rally that brought white nationalists of various factions from around the country together, ostensibly to protest the removal of a Confederate monument but, once again, intended as an opportunity to create mayhem and promote their ideology. It climaxed in the tragic murder of an anti-fascist protester named Heather Heyer, who was among multiple victims mowed down by a Dodge Challenger driven by a neo-Nazi.[38]

McInnes had warned his Proud Boys to stay away from the event, and for the most part they did, but not all of them. Among the brawlers in the crowd that day was Enrique Tarrio, who had just begun to climb in the organization's ranks, already trotted out as proof that the group included non-whites. The event's primary organizer, Jason Kessler, was also a Proud Boy, though McInnes gave him the boot shortly afterward.[39]

The next day in Seattle, Joey Gibson held a comparatively subdued rally in which he tried to sound like a peacemaker.[40]

"Listen, what happened yesterday, if you believe in your heart that what happened yesterday is not what you stand for, if you are against what happened yesterday, do not ever let these people make you feel bad!" he told the rallygoers. "Because we weren't there, and we had nothing to do with that! Patriot Prayer has always preached peace, and has always preached love, a hundred percent of the time!"

Later, as the rally wound down, he became more explicit.

"Fuck white supremacists! Fuck neo-Nazis!" Gibson told the crowd, reminding them that he himself is a person of color, "and I have no use for that kind of thinking. It's wrong." It was one of Gibson's many attempts to distance himself from the extremists his rallies attracted—and as it turned out, it was a relatively short-lived sentiment.

After that, Patriot Prayer events became increasingly generic, with the violence remaining a constant: Gibson organized a "free speech" rally for San Francisco that turned out to be mostly a bust, but he and his cohorts were able to spark violence the next day in Berkeley.[41] A September Peaceful March for Freedom held across the Columbia River from Portland in Vancouver, Washington, was largely uneventful, except for the Patriot Prayer members who cruised the city's downtown afterward and assaulted several counterprotesters, nearly running over a couple with their pickups.[42] And a February 2018 rally in Seattle again championed free speech on college campuses, and again attracted a substantial contingent of white nationalists and neo-Nazis, while also devolving into violence at the end.[43]

The organizing cause for these events began to vary widely, signaling clearly what had already become obvious to observers: namely, the designated cause was just a beard for right-wing outsiders to wear while planning street violence in the urban centers they loathed, like Seattle and Portland. One rally was organized in Seattle to protest that city's strict gun ordinances. Another was organized in Portland to defend men's rights; they called it a #HimToo rally.[44] The June 30, 2018, rally that produced some of the most vicious violence—including Nordean's infamous punch—was organized as a protest against Portland's "sanctuary city" immigration policies.[45]

As the tension ratcheted upward, so did the street brawlers' vicious and bloodthirsty rhetoric. In a video he made with a YouTube QAnon conspiracy theorist named Tiny Mercado, Toese brandished his fist and promised "Antifa" that they would learn "the hard way" if they kept fighting him.[46]

Mercado shouted: "We have guns, niggas! We will never, we will never submit to you motherfuckers. We will never submit to you. You all gonna get hurt." Toese mentioned that "they're threatening me with five years"— an apparent reference to an ongoing investigation by Portland police into his activities, which included a number of assaults at various venues—and promised: "I ain't goin' down."

Another social media video posted by Patriot Prayer leader Reggie Axtell was filled with similarly murderous intent, voiced by an anonymous off-camera person referred to as Steve, while Axtell counseled against murdering anti-fascists.

"Yeah, but killing 'em ain't the fucking point, dude," Axtell said at one point.

"Well, you ain't gotta kill all of 'em," replied "Steve."

"What, you're just gonna kill a couple of 'em? That's it?"

"That's it. They will get the point."

"Well, how many of them do you think you need to kill before they get the point?"

"Ohhhhh . . . a hundred seventy-five."

"You're gonna kill a hundred seventy-five . . ."

"Well, not me myself."

Two other Patriot Prayer and Proud Boy stalwarts, Russell Schultz and Haley Adams, posted a video boasting that Schultz had nearly run over an anti-fascist protester while leaving a Portland parking garage. A few weeks later, Schultz talked further about running people over in a December video in which he announced his intent to kill any anti-fascist who flings human waste at him. "At the last rally, I nearly ran you over with a car, and I don't feel bad about it one bit. You're lucky I didn't kill you, because I wouldn't feel any remorse," he said, warning them against flinging feces at him: "I am going to shoot you. And here's what the best part of the odds is. I still have a chance to fight for my freedom in court. You don't have a chance to fight for your freedom, 'cause you're fucking dead."

The continuing violence in Portland from Patriot Prayer and the Proud Boys took its next natural step when the groups began organizing smaller incursions into what they considered enemy territory, such as a May 2019 brawl at the Antifa-friendly Cider Riot pub.[47] The ensuing violence resulted in multiple criminal charges against the right-wing participants, including Gibson himself.

Along the way, an internecine war broke out between Patriot Prayer members and the local Proud Boys, leading to Toese announcing he was leaving his old cohorts and embracing the black-and-yellow uniform.

What precipitated Toese's falling-out with Patriot Prayer is unclear, but it appears to revolve around Haley Adams, who had become an increasingly visible presence at the organization's events over the previous year, notably by being the chief organizer of the #HimToo event.

Social media conversations suggested that Adams, who may have been playing manipulative power games within the group, was planning to "dox" some of the Proud Boy participants, which led Toese to denounce Adams. According to one account, Adams was denounced by the Proud Boys' national board of "Elders."

In response, Adams's most fervent defenders in Patriot Prayer—namely Reggie Axtell and Russell Schultz—took to social media to make the split with Proud Boys clear and unequivocal. "Haley Adams has my full approval to say whatever she wants to say," Schultz said in his video. "If the Proud Boys want to attack her, that just tells me they are getting triggered and beat by a little girl."

Calling the Proud Boys "beta," Schultz went on to promise he would "kill" any Proud Boys who wanted to fight him over the dispute. "This shit cannot happen," he said. "You are a psycho, you need to get out of the fucking movement. If you're afraid of being doxxed, get out of the fucking movement, you don't need to be here, you're a cancer. You have a problem with me, want to come at me, I'm gonna fucking waste you. You have no chance against me. I may even come looking for you one day."

Joey Gibson, who had been touring the state to promote the idea of individual counties declaring themselves "gun sanctuaries" free of the strictures of recently enacted gun-safety legislation, remained conspicuously absent from the discussion.[48] Eventually, he was able to get the warring factions to settle down, so that by early 2019 Proud Boys and Patriot Prayer were back to marching together.

The brawlers found their political intimidation tactics were transferable to other causes beyond free speech. Patriot Prayer and Proud Boys members turned up in significant numbers at a Salem rally in June 2019 to protest an attempt by the Oregon legislature to pass cap-and-trade legislation.[49] They also were a primary presence at a Seattle rally organized by Three Percent militiamen (who hailed, as always, from rural and exurban areas) to protest the "domestic terrorism" of anti-fascists being enabled by Seattle politicians—as well as to defend far-right Republican legislator Matt Shea from charges he had been involved with domestic terrorists.[50]

Joey Gibson once explained on Facebook, prior to a Seattle event, the ideology behind the protests:

> The West Coast has slowly been infected with communist ideologies throughout our entire culture. It is a belief that the individual is weak and that we are all victims. This is the lie of the century. No matter who you are, we are all amazing people with the ability to do anything that we put our minds to. These liberal strongholds run off of hatred and negativity. Patriot Prayer will bring in a positive message to Seattle that the people are starving for. With light we will change the hearts and minds of those who are surrounded by darkness.[51]

Thus Patriot Prayer's tactics settled into an established strategy that became a national blueprint: organizing right-wing activists primarily from rural and exurban areas to invade liberal urban centers and intimidate them with thuggish behavior. These tactics proved flexible enough to apply across a range of right-wing issues, succeeding in creating a violent Antifa/leftist bogeyman narrative that could translate readily on friendly right-wing media such as Fox News. It began showing up nationally in the context of other scenes of right-wing conflict across the nation.

AS JOEY GIBSON BECAME more of a celebrity—Alex Jones interviewed him on *Infowars*, he was given an oddly congenial interview on MSNBC, and he showed up on multiple podcasts—he traveled widely: to Austin, Texas, and San Diego, California, notably.[52] Along the way, he expanded his reach among both the Proud Boys and other street-brawling groups. Predictably some of these were explicit white nationalists—including the East Coast–based American Guard (AG), which was founded by a longtime skinhead organizer named Brien James.

After being initially skittish about American Guard, in October 2018, Gibson traveled to Providence, Rhode Island, where he connected with AG members (taking a selfie with John Camden, another leading AG figure) who had organized a far-right rally there. Toese had also flown out. He stirred up violence at the rally, which ended with the Proud Boys and AG members mostly fleeing the scene.[53]

When confronted as he was leaving the rally by anti-fascist Daryle Lamont Jenkins about how easily he rubbed shoulders with white supremacists, Gibson shrugged.

"You've got straight-up Nazis out there, and they're here with you," Jenkins said.

"That's just fine. They can hang with us. I don't care," Gibson replied. "As long as they're not causing problems, they're fine."

Toese expressed a similar lack of concern. He went on a far-right podcast and explained that he didn't really have any problems with white supremacists. "I don't give a fuck if real racists come to the rallies, real alt-right," he said.[54]

"We've been trying to beat these people up for a long time, it ain't gonna work. The only thing that we can do to solve this whole fucking problem with Nazis and all this shit is to have a civil conversation. And both sides understanding what the other side wants."

When it was all over and the tear gas had cleared from the Providence rally, the collected warriors for the radical right—Proud Boys, Patriots, and American Guardsmen alike—all gave one another manly hugs and went their separate ways, bonded by the day's battle. Their previous differences were all washed away, it seemed.

As always, the violence was the point. Proud Boys began showing up to street events wearing black T-shirts proclaiming, "Pinochet Did Nothing Wrong," with a simple diagram of a helicopter and people falling out of it on the backside of the shirt—referring to the late Chilean dictator Augusto Pinochet's history of executing leftists by hurling them out of aircraft. Toese wore one to several Portland protests; when *HuffPost* reporter Christopher Mathias asked him, "Didn't Pinochet kill like 35,000 people?" Toese replied: "Aren't they all communists?"[55]

The eliminationist rhetoric, unsurprisingly, also attracted unstable personalities in the Jeremy Christian mold. One of these was Shane Kohfield, a thirty-two-year-old Iraq war veteran who, as his father later told reporters, was undergoing treatment for mental illness. Kohfield drew the attention of the FBI's Joint Terrorism Task Forces in July when he joined a protest outside the home of Portland mayor Ted Wheeler organized by Patriot Prayer and Haley Adams. Handed the group's bullhorn, he had proceeded to tell them that he had a plan for wiping out anti-fascists on a national scale. "If Antifa gets to the point where they start killing us, I'm going to kill them next," Kohfield, said. "I'd slaughter them and I have a detailed plan on how I would wipe out Antifa."[56]

Right-wing Portland radio host Lars Larson invited Kohfield onto his popular daily talk program and asked Kohfield to describe the plan for his listeners. Kohfield obliged by reading from a proposal he had already published online:

> Veterans join Antifa's social media pages and groups and get names of most active members on social media along with getting the arrest records from rallies and record the names of all previous and future offenders.
>
> The Veterans will use background check programs to find home addresses of all the members of Antifa.
>
> The Veterans will take a map of cities with members of Antifa that live there.

Grid overlays will be placed over those maps of the cities.

The Veterans will be broken down into squads. Each squad will be assigned its own Grid and given a list of names and addresses in their assigned grid square.

He then described how he planned to use a phone app used by delivery truck drivers to "hunt down the most violent members of Antifa in their beds at night until every one of them was gone in every city in America, if need be, in a single well-coordinated night." He predicted "catastrophic" effects for the anti-fascist movement.

In response, the FBI invoked Oregon's "red flag" law that allows for seizure of weapons from people deemed a threat to the public, and confiscated five weapons, including an AR-15 semiautomatic rifle, from Kohfield. He was not charged, however.

———————

IN THE COURSE OF the first month after Nordean's watershed punch, membership in private Facebook "vetting pages" for the Proud Boys spiked nearly 70 percent. One recruit's Facebook comment typified the sentiment there: "Seeing that soy boy antifa scum get knocked the fuck out has been the highlight of my year. Ive [sic] watched it over and over."[57]

The appeal to angry young white men for a chance to indulge in some consequence-free violence against the people they hate was all too effective. Recruitment was rolling along, and McInnes reveled in the Proud Boys' swelling ranks and rising profile.

Then it all began going sideways—thanks, unsurprisingly, to the violence.

The pushback began in earnest in February 2018, when the Southern Poverty Law Center officially designated the Proud Boys a hate group in its annual listings under the category "general hate"—groups that "peddle a combination of well-known hate and conspiracy theories, in addition to unique bigotries that are not easily categorized."[58] The SPLC's definition of a hate group is "an organization that—based on its official statements or principles, the statements of its leaders, or its activities—has beliefs or practices that attack or malign an entire class of people, typically for their immutable characteristics."

The organization's growing recruitment success over the summer of 2018 gave McInnes the latitude to dismiss his critics as inconsequential. McInnes claimed repeatedly that "fighting solves everything," and told his podcast audience: "You're not a man until you've had the crap beaten out of you [and] beaten the crap out of someone."

When *Guardian* reporter Jason Wilson asked McInnes whether sharing video of Nordean's punch amounted to the promotion of violence, McInnes responded by calling him a "fucking weak human being," a "vile little pussy," and a "tepid cunt." Launching into a rant about "the media class," McInnes complained that journalists "sit there picking fights, call everyone a Nazi, and then when someone dares defend themselves, and someone else says 'Yay,' you say: 'Well you're promoting violence.'"[59]

Then came his speech at New York City's Metropolitan Republican Club the night of October 12, and, most of all, its aftermath.

The topic, as always, was a glorification of eliminationist violence against leftists: in this case, McInnes commemorated the assassination of a Japanese socialist leader on television by a young ultranationalist named Otoya Yamaguchi in 1960 by reenacting the horrifying event. The day after the speech, McInnes on his podcast explained his inspiration for the speech, calling Yamaguchi a "fucking badass": "He didn't get him in his scope on a grassy knoll, he charged him on stage with a samurai sword. And his mugshot looks really cool . . . I just thought 'What a great icon, what a great hero!'"[60]

That night at the speech, after the reenactment, McInnes exhorted his audience: "We need to get back to the era where you could insult someone's religion, you could insult their ethnicity, you could insult everything about them."

The Proud Boys' appetite for violence was whetted to a full roar. "I'm ready to swing right," one of the Proud Boys exiting the venue said within earshot of a journalist. "No one better fuck with us tonight." As they exited, they spotted protesters in black. "You ready? Go boys!" one of them yelled.

The Proud Boys charged, beating the protesters down and kicking at them as they lay on the sidewalk. One of them screamed "Faggot!" at his victim. Another later boasted about kicking a protester "right in the fucking head," adding: "He was a fucking foreigner."

Unlike what happened regularly with similar attacks in Portland, prosecutors in New York promptly charged ten Proud Boys with riot and attempted assault. (Eventually, two of them—Maxwell Hare and John Kinsman—were found guilty on charges of attempted gang assault, attempted assault, and riot, and sentenced to four years in prison, while seven others entered guilty pleas and received lesser sentences.)[61] Suddenly, the news coverage surrounding the Proud Boys had become decidedly negative, with the SPLC's hate-group designation mentioned with increasing prominence.

A month later, in November 2018, Wilson of *The Guardian* uncovered an internal FBI memo describing the Proud Boys as an "extremist group with ties to white nationalism." The memo, obtained through Washington state law enforcement, also said: "The FBI has warned local law enforcement agencies that the Proud Boys are actively recruiting in the Pacific northwest," and: "Proud Boys members have contributed to the recent escalation of violence at political rallies held on college campuses, and in cities like Charlottesville, Virginia, Portland, Oregon, and Seattle, Washington."[62]

Two days later, McInnes announced that he was leaving the organization in order to insulate the group from his critics both in the press and in the courtroom. "As of today . . . I am officially disassociating myself from the Proud Boys," he said, and then launched into a rambling defense of the group he founded.[63]

"We are not an extremist group and we do not have ties with white nationalists," he said, later claiming that "such people don't exist." He also attacked the SPLC and claimed that his New York Proud Boys were only being prosecuted because of "lazy journalism." His various exhortations to violence, he said, had been taken out of context.

It was unclear, though, just how far he was removing himself, describing the announcement as a "stepping down gesture, in quotation marks." A couple of months later, he announced that he was filing a lawsuit against the SPLC for defamation; the civil rights organization responded that "the fact that he's upset with SPLC tells us that we're doing our job exposing hate and extremism."[64]

McInnes's departure set off an internecine scramble for organizational control and cooled off the Proud Boys' organizing efforts for a while. Other would-be leaders emerged claiming they were McInnes's successor. A Texan named Jason Van Dyke, who held the organization's legal paperwork, announced himself as the new chairman. Van Dyke was notorious for threatening journalists who wrote about the Proud Boys as a designated hate group or labeled them white nationalists, sending them cease-and-desist letters insisting they "do not now, nor have they ever, espoused white nationalist, white supremacist, anti-Semitic, or alt-right views."[65]

Not that Van Dyke had a great deal of credibility in this area: As a college student at Michigan State, he had been affiliated with the leader of a notorious white-nationalist campus group there; according to the SPLC, when campus police searched his dorm, they found neo-Nazi literature, including *The Turner Diaries* and *The Protocols of the Elders of Zion*. He was also arrested in 2000 for domestic violence.

The nasty streak continued well into his adulthood in Dallas–Fort Worth, Texas. On his Twitter page in 2014, he threatened another user, a Black man, with a photo of a noose and text reading, "Look good and hard at this picture you fucking nigger. It's where I am going to put your neck."

Van Dyke's tenure, however, was short-lived. In late November, the Proud Boys announced that Van Dyke "is no longer a member of the Proud Boys fraternity, and will no longer be representing the fraternity in any legal capacity." (A few weeks later, he was arrested after failing to show up for a bond hearing on a threat he had made.)

The new leadership, the organization announced, would be in the hands of a select group of members called "the Elder Chapter," whose identities initially were to be kept secret, except for that of the new chairman, Enrique Tarrio.

However, within a week, the identities of the Elder Chapter were unveiled, thanks to their decision to publish their new bylaws publicly—with the Elders' names (Harry Fox, Heath Hair, Patrick William Roberts, Joshua Hall, Timothy Kelly, Luke Rohlfing, and Rufio Panman, aka Ethan Nordean) embedded and unredacted at the top for everyone to read.[66]

———

UNLIKE THE NEW YORK Proud Boys, Ethan Nordean never faced any consequences for his infamous punch. Police did arrest Nordean that day—but then released him thirty minutes later. He was never charged; instead, prosecutors charged his victim, who suffered a "severe concussion," with assault.

Over time, the police's kid-glove handling of Proud Boys, Patriot Prayer, and other street-brawling thugs helped feed these men's beliefs that their violent tactics had the tacit support of law enforcement and other authorities. Nordean and his cohorts, as *The New York Times* later explored in depth, had been let off the hook by local police in Portland and Seattle on numerous occasions, notably on the day Nordean delivered his infamous punch.[67]

A pattern evolved, particularly with the Portland Police Bureau (PPB): Proud Boys would bus in men armed for street combat from out of town, sometimes even driving their pickup trucks through the downtown and shooting pedestrians with paintball guns, while police stood by and did nothing. When a man hurled a pipe bomb at Black Lives Matter demonstrators in the summer of 2020 and he was identified on social media, police chose not to investigate because no witnesses came forward to place the man there.[68]

In February 2019, reporters revealed text exchanges between Portland police officers and Joey Gibson displaying a startling chumminess with the far-right activists and clear sympathy for their views.[69]

Many of the texts—only released after journalists filed a records request with the Portland Police Bureau, which had originally denied they existed when officials from the Council on American-Islamic Relations sought them—showed PPB lieutenant Jeff Niiya expressing sympathy for Gibson's activism, including his quixotic campaign for the US Senate in Washington state. Other exchanges show Niiya being protective of Gibson's group in the middle of rallies.

"Heads up just told 4-5 black Bloch [Antifa] heading your way. One carrying a flag," Niiya texted Gibson during a December 2017 protest. "We will have officers nearby but you may want to think about moving soon if more come." Niiya also coached Gibson before Patriot Prayer's August 2018 rally: "As you march we move to keep you both separated. No patriots going to them no Antifa to you. If they get close we will be in between."

"I want you to know you can trust me. Don't want to burn that," Niiya told Gibson in a September 2017 message. Later, Gibson apologized to Niiya for making a public announcement that "Portland police has our back."

This pattern continued and deepened. Prior to their August 2019 End Domestic Terrorism rally, Proud Boys leader Joe Biggs openly encouraged violence. Biggs urged his Twitter followers: "Get a gun. Get ammo. Get your gun license. Get training. Practice as much as you can and be ready because the left isn't playing anymore and neither should we." He followed that with a "Death to Antifa" meme featuring an image of a corpse in a plastic body bag.[70]

Supporters chimed in with memes depicting ISIS-style beheadings of anti-fascists, along with comments expressing their unquenched desire to "exterminate" far-left activists. "I fully expect [an] armed conflict to break out on Aug. 17," one commenter said. "People may die this is the real deal."

Police provided some of the Proud Boys marchers that day with an escort. Toward the end, they turned their attention to anti-fascist demonstrators in downtown Portland and arrested thirteen of them. A September 2020 Proud Boys rally in Portland had essentially the same outcome, though with many fewer demonstrators involved.[71]

It later emerged, after Biggs was arrested for working with Nordean to besiege the US Capitol, that he had developed a cozy relationship with law enforcement in Oregon, including the FBI. The revelation was contained in a court filing by his attorney, John Hull, who claimed that Biggs spoke with local and federal law enforcement officials in Portland about rallies he was organizing there in 2019 and 2020, and sometimes received "cautionary" phone calls from FBI agents.[72]

"The FBI has known about his political commentary and role in planning events and counter-protests in Portland and other cities since at least July 2020 and arguably benefitted from that knowledge in efforts to gather intelligence about Antifa in Florida and Antifa networks operating across the United States," Hull's filing reads.

After an FBI agent contacted Biggs in late July 2020 and he met with two agents at a restaurant, the filing claims, Biggs agreed to feed the agency information about anti-fascist activists, both in Florida and elsewhere. Hull said the agents wanted to know what he was "seeing on the ground." Afterward, an agent asked follow-up questions in a series of phone calls, and Biggs answered them.

"They spoke often," added Hull.

On the day of the August 17 march, Portland police coordinated with Proud Boys organizers to keep counterprotesters from interfering and provided escorts for separate marching contingents. At the time, Biggs was observed shaking hands and joking with Portland police officers who helped escort the group across the Hawthorne Bridge after the demonstration ended. Afterward, police began arresting leftist counterprotesters in large numbers in downtown Portland.

A year later, according to Hull, police had a similar arrangement with the Proud Boys when Biggs organized another march in Portland—one where attendance was markedly down. Nonetheless, predictably, police reserved their aggressive tactics for leftist protesters in downtown Portland later that evening.[73]

Biggs was also present in Washington on December 12, 2020, when the Proud Boys rampaged through the city's downtown at the culmination of the day's Stop the Steal rally. At the peak of the violence, a group of Proud Boys led by Enrique Tarrio tore down a Black Lives Matter banner from a local African American church and attempted to set it afire.[74]

The violence had been heightened by Proud Boys' mounting confrontations with police in D.C., causing the street brawlers to turn on Metropolitan police officers and accuse them of betrayal for intervening in their attempts to assault alleged "Antifa" (who appear to have been mostly hecklers) among the people on the street. Biggs was among them, angry at police for not only intervening between Proud Boys and protesters, but also frequently placing the former under arrest. Biggs was outraged when two Proud Boys were stabbed by a man they had surrounded and were attempting to beat, and police arrested the black-shirted instigators.

"We are the ones that back you!" he yelled at riot officers through a bullhorn. "That thin blue line is getting thinner and thinner."

The same disillusionment with the police began bubbling up elsewhere among the far right. Nick DeCarlo, a far-right media personality, told a live stream host that the pro-Trump crowd no longer had faith in police: "No, absolutely not. In fact, there were much more people today shouting, 'Fuck these guys, they're traitors to us, they don't protect us. Look at what they're doing.'"

At a Mass Civil Disobedience rally and march—protesting both Trump's election defeat and COVID-19 restrictions—in Salem, Oregon, on January 2, Proud Boys and militiamen began verbally attacking Salem riot police who were attempting to keep the pro-Trump crowd separate from counterprotesters.[75]

"No more backing the blue!" the pro-Trump crowd screamed at riot officers. "Fuck the blue!"[76]

They became fully unhinged later that day when Tarrio was arrested by D.C. police as he arrived at Washington National Airport to prepare for the January 6 event, charged with burning the BLM banner on December 12. They also found two high-capacity firearms magazines in his luggage.

This inflamed the Proud Boys: "Burn D.C. to the ground. Start with metro police HQ," one of them posted on Parler. "Once a cop violates the oath he took, he loses any protections that oath provided. Fair game."[77]

———————

THE PROUD BOYS WERE always about bringing the violence, and that was what they did on January 6. From the assault on the police barricades to the first breach of the Capitol to the search for members of Congress to "bring to justice," they played their role to a T—that role being a paramilitary street-fighting force like their predecessors, the Brownshirts and Blackshirts.

The centrality of their ethos of eliminationist violence—its celebration and cultivation, the training and preparation for it, the essential role it played in organizing events designed to provide opportunities for it directed against their concocted enemies—is what not only distinguishes the Proud Boys from ordinary street gangs and brawlers, but defines them unmistakably as neofascists—that is, a modern iteration of fascist organizing replicating its essential elements. As historian Robert O. Paxton puts it, a central "mobilizing passion" of fascism is "the beauty of violence and the efficacy of will, when they are devoted to the group's success."[78]

There are other components to the Proud Boys culture that confirm this identity, all reflecting the essential aspects of fascism as it has been identified by scholars and analysts over the past century, when the phenomenon first emerged:

- Its palingenetic agenda: The belief that their violence will bring about a phoenix-like rebirth of the nation harkening back to a mythological golden era. The primary symbol of this mythological core is the red Make America Great Again ball caps that are part of the Proud Boy uniform, and the centrality of the Donald Trump slogan to their belief system. It's also embedded in the organization's initiation oath as "Western chauvinists" to "refuse to apologize for creating the modern world."[79]

- Their contempt for weakness. Paxton describes this as another key "mobilizing passion," namely, "the right of the chosen people to dominate others without restraint from any kind of human or divine law, right being decided by the sole criterion of the group's prowess in a Darwinian struggle."

- Its misogynistic treatment of women and hatred of feminism, coupled with a twisted version of male sexuality. Hitler and Mussolini both were ardent in their sexism: "The Nazi Revolution will be an entirely male event" was one of Hitler's most repeated phrases. The Proud Boys' insistence on male-only camaraderie combined with a puritanical approach to masturbation and pornography and a bizarre quasi-mystical approach to sex replicate the original fascist ethos.

- Its authoritarianism, or what Stanley Payne calls fascism's "specific tendency toward an authoritarian, charismatic, personal style of command, whether or not the command is to some degree initially elective."[80] For the Proud Boys, Donald Trump constitutes this "glorious leader," and their fealty to him is unqualified—or at least it was in the years leading up to January 6.

- Its cult of heroism. As Umberto Eco says, in fascist society, "everybody is educated to be a hero."[81] Proud Boys, like all far-right extremists, conceive of themselves as heroes dedicated to saving the world—the kind of heroism that consequently justifies any kind of action, particularly the violent kind. Moreover, because one cannot be a hero without having an identifiable enemy, and these enemies in fact define what kind of hero one is, they set about reifying and concocting their enemies out of whatever cultural strands serve their purpose: for the Proud Boys, this is Antifa, Black Lives Matter, and other supposedly "Marxist" elements.

Ultimately, the purpose of fascism is to overthrow liberal democracy by turning its own liberalities into weapons—using free speech to advocate an agenda of authoritarian suppression of opposing views, for instance—and threatening its cooperative ethos with violence and intimidation, all in order to displace it with autocratic right-wing rule by a strongman dictator. In this regard, the Proud Boys now play a role functionally identical to the historical paramilitary street-fighting forces that played central roles in the rise of fascists to power, particularly in Germany and Italy.

In Germany, they were called Sturmabteilung ("Storm Detachment"), or SA, but were better known as the Brownshirts. In Italy, they wore black clothing and thus were known as Blackshirts or Squadristi. These thugs historically have served multiple functions: intimidating and threatening leftists with violence; creating public propaganda depicting those leftists as the sources of the violence; and establishing a common cause with the mainstream elements (primarily businesses, corporate owners, and landowners) threatened by leftist causes.

German propaganda was especially adroit at promoting images of brave Brownshirts being victimized by violent leftists. The Nazi marching song— "Horst Wessel Lied"—was a celebration of a young Brownshirt who had been killed by leftists. This appeal was central to the Nazis' ongoing campaign to portray themselves as the sole effective defenders of mainstream society against the threat of an evil, nefarious left that was part of a global Communist conspiracy.

The Proud Boys likewise have made much of the violence directed at them by local anti-fascists, demonizing those who turn up to protest their urban incursions by hyping their existence into a national threat. And in identical fashion, they have responded by depicting them as nonhumans— "Communists" or "Marxists" or "pedophiles" or "groomers" or numerous other epithets that elicit eliminationist disgust—fit only for hurling from helicopters.

The self-righteous belief in their own heroic mythology led them to besiege the Capitol on January 6 and assault even the police officers they previously saw as their allies. And even though they failed in their attempt to prevent the peaceful transfer of power that had long been the hallmark of American democratic stability, their fervent belief in this mythos ensured that they would not stop. They would never give up.

———————

IN THE IMMEDIATE AFTERMATH of the failure of the insurrection to prevent Joe Biden's certification as the winner of the 2020 election, the Proud Boys started thinking about their next steps and their most potent strategy going forward. Ethan Nordean, who was not arrested until early February 2021, was helping lead these internal discussions.[82]

His messages also directed the dismayed invective of a betrayed follower at Donald Trump, notably an extended rant from January 20, the one in which he angrily spat, "FUCK TRUMP!":

> We are now and always have been on our own. So glad he was able to pardon a bunch of degenerates as his last move and shit on us on the way out. Fuck you trump you left us on [t]he battle field bloody and alone.

It was clear that, rather than retrench and lower their profile, they had no intention of slowing things down, but rather planned to ratchet up the violence.

In a January 20 message on Telegram, Nordean laid out the agenda for the February 2 meeting of Washington state Proud Boys officers in the central Washington town of Leavenworth, which included "Secure Vetting," "Communications," "SHTF [Shit Hits The Fan] safe locations," "Bulk armor deals," and "Bugout bags."

The national organization's initial response was to order a short-term "stand down" for Proud Boy–led rallies ("Almost none of my guys want to do rallies now," one message read) intended to last until May 1. And indeed, the Proud Boys' activities remained muted until that date, when they held an intimidating rally at a city park in Salem, Oregon.

However, Nordean vociferously disagreed with suggestions that they cease activity altogether in the interim. "They're coming for you no matter what you [guys]," he wrote. "Wake the hell up. I'm not gunna be sitting on my ass waiting for the end."

In an exchange with another Proud Boy later charged in the conspiracy, Nordean wrote: "Yeah, this is just to organize and prepare for when we do decide to get active again. At the very least there's lots of good excuses to just get out and do meet n greets with the public, raise money, community service, security for events etc . . . but we can work on an effective process so we look more organized and have properly vetted members who are representing the club."

Nordean was arrested by the FBI on February 3 and charged with four federal felonies, including obstruction of Congress; eventually he would be charged, along with Biggs and other Proud Boys, with seditionist conspiracy. However, the Proud Boys simply kept on organizing without him, following the blueprint he had laid out: namely, scale down their operations and spread their recruitment by focusing on local issues, mainly by attaching themselves to local right-wing organizers and providing "security" for their events. In Miami, for instance, Proud Boys leader Enrique Tarrio turned up uninvited with several cohorts, offering "support" for a protest by the Cuban American community backing dissidents in Cuba.[83]

This was consistent with their self-image as regular American guys, their belief right up to January 6 that the police were on their side, and their ongoing denials of being racist or extremist. The localized issues were often the same right-wing grievances being ginned up nightly on Fox News, as with critical race theory in New Hampshire schools. The common thread among the issues being hijacked by Proud Boys was that they were congenial to (if not fueled by) conspiracism, and primarily revolved around concocted enemies.

The first post-insurrection Proud Boys event of note was an early May rally at a city park in Salem, Oregon, at which journalists were threatened and ejected and guns were on broad display. The police were conspicuous by their absence.[84] However, another Proud Boys event held in Oregon City on June 15 was shut down by police when they declared it a riot.[85]

Proud Boys resurfaced over the ensuing month at a number of venues in locales around the country: At a July 4 parade in Buhl, Idaho, where they had entered a float; at a rally in Tallahassee, Florida, to demand the release of the January 6 "political prisoners"; at a protest outside a Planned Parenthood clinic in Salem, Oregon, that turned into a brawl; outside a Wi Spa gymnasium in Los Angeles, where they showed up at a right-wing protest revolving around a transgender gym worker, which again devolved into brawling; outside a court hearing for a tavern owner charged with assault in Red Bluff, California, flashing white-nationalist symbols; and at a COVID-denialist rally in Tampa, Florida.[86] Proud Boys also poked up their heads in towns like Helena, Montana, and Scotland, South Dakota, trying to organize ostensibly mainstream fundraising events, but quickly shut down when they were publicly exposed.[87]

The Proud Boys' strategy was insidious in the way it manipulated small-town environments to insinuate themselves within them, and once there, how it divided and created turmoil within those communities where little existed previously.

As it turned out, they were just getting started.

6

White Fright

WHEN FLYERS BEGAN APPEARING around Kitsap County—a mostly rural place in Washington's southwestern Puget Sound, centered around the midsize city of Bremerton and its US Navy shipyard—in the fall of 2017, officials quietly took them down. But then someone plastered them along a busy boulevard in Gig Harbor (located in neighboring Pierce County), forcing local police to peel them off lampposts, and attracting local news reporters.[1]

In large black letters, they read, variously: "Resurrection Through Insurrection," featuring a large fascist symbol, and "Conquered Not Stolen," accompanied by a map of the United States. They all directed readers to the Patriot Front website at bloodandsoil.org.

Residents were shocked and baffled at the prospect of neo-Nazis in their midst. "I didn't even know there were any in Gig Harbor, or anywhere else in this area," one woman told a KIRO-TV reporter.[2]

The flyers, and other auguries of white-supremacist organizing activity, were not just relegated to one small rural county in western Washington, however. All around the United States—in Texas, Maryland, Florida, California, South Carolina, Kansas, and Delaware—identical flyers were appearing, plastered onto light poles and windows, all of them touting the same Patriot Front and its website.

What people were seeing, in fact, was not just a tiny local faction of neo-Nazis, but the first manifestations of a new nationwide network. Although still relatively small, they were eager to band together as a white-nationalist army working to create "the new American nation state." As their website promised: "Democracy has failed in this once great nation, now the time for a new Caesar to revive the American spirit has dawned."

In those nascent phases, the bulk of that activism had revolved around guerrilla-plastering various public locales at nighttime, as well as setting up freeway banners on overpasses that advertised their website to drivers.

In Gig Harbor, police chief Kelly Busey wound up with a pile of about thirty crumpled flyers on his desk, which he told a Tacoma reporter he threw away. City officials said the flyers were taken down not because of their content, but because posters of any kind weren't permitted at those locations.

There had been other indications of neo-Nazi organizing in Kitsap County, as well as elsewhere in the Puget Sound region generally, notably the freeway overpass banners. One of those, reading "America is White," was reported to Busey, but had been taken down before an officer could arrive to remove it.

"I went on their website and read their manifesto," Busey said. "It's a bunch of blah, and towards the end it talks about minorities. This does not come to a free-speech issue for us. We did look to see if this was a hate crime, but the answer to that was no."

Wherever the flyers have appeared, authorities have wondered: Where are these neo-Nazis coming from? And just who and what is Patriot Front anyway?

The answers lay in Charlottesville.

———

THE ALT-RIGHT—THE MOSTLY ONLINE white-nationalist movement that arose amid the wide-open internet and social media environment of the early 2010s, festering and growing in chat rooms, on message boards, and on overtly racist websites—was feeling its oats in early 2017. It had played a key role in Donald Trump's ascension to the presidency, and there was a broad sense of empowerment within the movement.[3] It had its moment in the spotlight in 2016, when the alt-right claimed credit for Donald Trump's victory in the presidential election; alt-right godfather Richard Spencer infamously flashed a Nazi salute at a press conference, saying, "Hail Trump!"[4]

The core of the alt-right's recruitment process was essentially a process of online radicalization. Alt-righters called it "red-pilling," as though they were the Neos of *The Matrix* who had awakened to the reality of a world run by nefarious conspiracies. It's a conceit with a toxic double bind: once you believe you see this new reality, then reality itself becomes unmoored.

These theories tell the same larger narrative: that the world is secretly run by a cabal of globalists (who just happen to be Jewish), and that they employ an endless catalog of dirty tricks and "false flags" to ensure the world doesn't know about its manipulations, the whole purpose of which ultimately is the enslavement of mankind. Each day's news events can thus be interpreted through the up-is-down prism this worldview imposes, ensuring that every national tragedy or mass shooting is soon enmeshed in a web of theories about its real purpose.

The alt-right itself had little compunction about identifying its target demographic for red-pilling. Andrew Anglin, publisher and founder of the neo-Nazi site The Daily Stormer, asserted in 2017, "My site is mainly designed to target children."[5] At the annual white-nationalist American Renaissance conference in Tennessee in April 2018, longtime supremacists bragged about their demographic support: "American Renaissance attendees are now younger and more evenly divided among the sexes than in the past," one speaker noted, before gushing over the white-nationalist college campus group Identity Evropa.[6]

When authorities, both in the United States and abroad, have talked about online radicalization in the recent past, they tended to think of it in terms of radical Islamists from groups such as the Islamic State who have been known to leverage the technology to their advantage, particularly social media. A study by terrorism expert J. M. Berger published in 2016 found that white nationalists were far outstripping their Islamist counterparts, however: "On Twitter, ISIS's preferred social platform, American white nationalist movements have seen their followers grow by more than 600 percent since 2012. Today, they outperform ISIS in nearly every social metric, from follower counts to tweets per day."[7]

"Online radicalization seems to be speeding up, with young men, particularly white men, diving into extremist ideologies quicker and quicker," Berger said, adding that "the result seems to be more violence, as these examples indicate. It is a serious problem and we don't seem to have any real solutions for it. These cases also show that an era of violence brought on by the internet is indeed upon us, with no end in sight."

The radicalization process itself often begins with seemingly benign activity, such as spending hours in chat rooms or playing computer games, and these activities provide a kind of cover for the process as it accelerates. Eventually, recruits grow tired of playing rhetorical games online and start organizing ways to bring their ideas to life in the real world—preferably on the streets.

This was where alt-right-adjacent street-brawling groups like the Proud Boys came in. The violence around Proud Boys protests created the impetus for various kinds of street-fighting groups, including a number of explicitly white-nationalist groups such as Identity Evropa and the Rise Above Movement (RAM), both of which had played major roles in the violence around the first Proud Boys event in Berkeley in April 2017.[8]

RAM members were among the first people to cross the police barrier separating the attendees and protestors that day, and were seen viciously assaulting protestors. Afterward, they boasted on Twitter about how they instigated the violence at the event throughout the day, saying, "We were the first guys to jump over the barrier and engage [which] had a huge impact."[9]

Several were caught on camera engaging in some of the more extreme violence. One RAM leader named Michael Miselis had broken his hand by punching someone in the back of the head, and later casually stood by and watched other RAM members beat protesters, texting his cohorts that he "was about to jump into that but our guys were just wrecking them" and that there was "not even any room to get a hit in." Another RAM leader, Ben Daley, was seen pursuing other protestors down the street, one of whom he ran up to and kicked from behind.[10]

RAM's primary line of recruitment was a combination of the promise of street violence—their meetings were often just white-nationalist variations on "fight clubs" in which members battered each other in preparation—and explicit neo-Nazi-style racism, replete with anti-Semitic conspiracism and fantasies of engaging in race war. They were also explicitly acceleration-ist: cynically hoping to push humankind over the brink because they saw people as a foul infection on the planet.

"Contrary to many white supremacist groups, RAM's image and its membership were calculated to make their more incendiary racist and anti-Semitic views appeal to the mainstream right-wing and alt-right sym-pathizers with the goal of later indoctrinating new recruits," a later Justice Department memorandum explained. "RAM members also sought to in-filtrate traditional and mainstream conservative groups, conceal their ex-tremist views, and indoctrinate (or 'red-pill') them. For example, when an individual contacted Daley on whether any RAM groups were in his area, Daley told him that 'We are not branching out but we do heav[il]y encour-age our style of networking and activism . . . if the[y] have trump or maga events out where you are definitely go. Good place to meet people. Also can have guys get in with the college republicans.'"[11]

After Berkeley, a number of alt-right figures, particularly Spencer and several of his white-nationalist cohorts, decided to create an event that would draw white nationalists and their allies from around the country into a singular place. They settled on Charlottesville, Virginia.

A monument to Confederate general Robert E. Lee in the town's center had become the focus of a campaign to remove it and a countercampaign to keep it in place. After the city council voted in favor of removal, one of the local organizers of the latter—a Charlottesville white nationalist named Jason Kessler, who had been leading anti-removal protests since 2016, calling it an effort to "attack white history"—decided to create an event called Unite the Right on August 11–12 to protest the change.

It quickly attracted the attention and support of white nationalists around the nation, including Spencer, Anglin, and the growing cadre of alt-right online-media figures, all of whom joined in sponsoring the event. Longtime neo-Nazi David Duke announced that he planned to attend. They were joined by neo-Confederate groups like the League of the South and Identity Dixie, as well as various chapters of the Ku Klux Klan. Neo-Nazi groups like the Traditionalist Worker Party and National Socialist Movement also signed on, as did alt-right white nationalists like Identity Evropa, Vanguard America, and the Rise Above Movement. Only the Proud Boys—an organization Kessler belonged to—declined to participate, though it did not bar members from attending (as a number did).[12]

Like all of these groups, RAM members prepared to travel to Charlottesville knowing full well they intended to participate in acts of violence, so they worked hard to cover their paper trail—buying tickets through friends, disguising purchases of helmets and tiki torches. The latter were Richard Spencer's idea; he wanted all the participants to arrive prepared for a march on Friday night, August 11, with the torches and uniforms composed of white shirts and khakis.

As Spencer told participants both before and after the march, his idea was to create an event that would supersede the issue of Confederate monuments and instead announce the presence of the white-nationalist movement as a significant player in American politics. The march, he told them, would proceed to the University of Virginia (UVA) campus—rather than the Lee monument—with the statue of Thomas Jefferson there the destination.

So at about 8:45 p.m., some 250 men dressed in the prescribed uniform and carrying lit tiki torches began to gather at an area behind UVA's Memorial Gymnasium called Nameless Field. They marched in a two-by-two formation, heading to the university's rotunda, where the Jefferson statue stands. As they marched, they chanted "Blood and Soil!"—a translation of the Nazi slogan "Blud und Boden," extolling one's ties to their ethnic origins and homeland—and "You Will Not Replace Us!"—a reference to the white-nationalist conspiracy that white people are being deliberately replaced by immigrants imported by a nefarious Jewish cabal. It quickly morphed into "Jews Will Not Replace Us!"

At the base of the Jefferson statue, the marchers encountered about thirty students from the university who were attempting to defend the site with arms locked in a circle. The mob of marchers encircled them and began shouting, "White lives matter!" and making monkey sounds, before they began assaulting the students. Police intervened eventually, and there were injuries reported on both sides.

The men were exultant. On his GoPro, Michael Miselis could be heard yelling, "Total victory!" and "We beat you tonight, we'll beat you tomorrow too!"[13]

The next morning, both sides of the protest began gathering early in the area around the park at the Lee monument, well before the rally's scheduled noon starting time. The protesters grew restless, and at 10:30 a.m., a group of alt-right protesters with shields began advancing on a line of anti-fascists who were trying to prevent them from entering the park. They swung sticks at one another and sprayed mace; soon, bottles and rocks were thrown. The violence lasted for nearly an hour before police broke it up.

Members of RAM knocked protesters to the ground, kicking them so hard that Miselis broke his own toe. Daley infamously attacked a feminist and began strangling her, and then threw her to the pavement with such force that she suffered a concussion.

Afterward, online conversations made clear that their chief regret about their time in Charlottesville, as the DOJ put it, "was not having exacted enough violence."

The two sides retreated, with counterprotesters spreading out to the city streets, but followed by alt-right protesters, so brawls continued to break out. The main force of alt-righters retreated to a park a mile north of downtown. But others remained behind.

One of them was a twenty-year-old member of Vanguard America from Maumee, Ohio, named James Alex Fields, who had driven to Charlottesville in his beefed-up Dodge Challenger. At 1:42 p.m., Fields revved up his engine and tore off at high speed down Fourth Street, ramming his vehicle into a large crowd of counterprotesters, then putting his damaged car in reverse and heading back in the other direction.

He maimed twenty people, including a thirty-two-year-old Charlottesville woman named Heather Heyer, who was killed instantly. The other victims eventually recovered, but several suffered permanent injuries. Fields was arrested shortly afterward and charged with murder, malicious wounding, and, eventually, federal hate crimes law violations.[14]

The next day, Spencer was recorded ranting angrily to his cohorts:

We are coming back here like a hundred fucking times. I am so mad. I am so fucking mad at these people. They don't do this to fucking me. We are going to fucking ritualistically humiliate them. I am coming back here every fucking weekend if I have to. Like this is never over. I win! They fucking lose! That's how the world fucking works.

Little fucking kikes. They get ruled by people like me. Little fucking octoroons . . . I fucking . . . my ancestors fucking enslaved those little pieces of fucking shit.[15]

It didn't work out that way. Instead, the violence turned Charlottesville into the alt-right's Waterloo.

Spencer's think tank—the National Policy Institute (NPI), based in Virginia and Montana—was named a codefendant in the civil lawsuit against Unite the Right organizers filed in 2019 by the victims of the violence, largely for its key role in co-organizing the event. The man who filed the lawsuit, Bill Burke of Athens, Ohio, was among the twenty people injured by Fields's rampage. Burke suffered a crushed left arm and head and knee injuries, and is expected to require treatment for years, perhaps permanently.[16]

However, neither NPI nor Spencer ever responded to Burke's legal filings. Because no attorney ever entered a court appearance, filed any response to the lawsuit, or otherwise tried to defend the group, the court found NPI in default. Federal judge Michael Watson closed the lawsuit by handing down a $2.4 million judgment against NPI—including $217,613 for past and future medical expenses, $350,000 in punitive damages, $500,000 for pain and suffering, and $1 million for emotional distress.

Spencer's NPI gradually vanished from public view. In 2017, the Internal Revenue Service revoked its nonprofit status. Most of Spencer's former allies abandoned him. Since 2019, its website has been entirely silent, and the group ceased any kind of activism or organizing. Spencer, however, was not yet done facing culpability for Charlottesville.

Neither were the leaders of the RAM group that flew out to Charlottesville from California, who faced even more severe consequences—though it took a while. Over a year later, on October 2, 2018, the Justice Department charged four of them—Daley, twenty-six, of Hermosa Beach; Miselis, thirty, of Lawndale; Tom Gillen, twenty-five, of Torrance; and Cole Evan White, twenty-four, of Clayton—with multiple federal counts of conspiracy to riot and crossing state lines to riot. Four others—Robert Rundo, twenty-eight, of Huntington Beach; Robert Boman, twenty-five, of Torrance; Tyler

Laube, twenty-two, of Redondo Beach; and Aaron Eason, thirty-eight, of Anza—were charged three weeks later with traveling around California to participate in violence at street rallies.[17]

White cut a cooperative plea deal with prosecutors, providing key evidence in the case, and wound up serving seven months in prison. The rest of the group charged with traveling to Charlottesville—Daley, Gillen, and Miselis—pleaded guilty the following May and were given prison sentences of thirty-seven months, thirty-three months, and twenty-seven months, respectively.

Robert Rundo fled to Central America but was promptly arrested and extradited.[18] However, US district judge Cormac J. Carney dismissed the charges against Rundo, Boman, Laube, and Eason in June 2019, ruling that using the federal Anti-Riot Act was "unconstitutionally overbroad in violation of the First Amendment."[19] That ruling, however, was subsequently overturned by the US Court of Appeals for the Ninth Circuit in 2021, which found the challenged provisions of the Anti-Riot Act were, in fact, constitutional, and the charges were reinstated.[20]

The Ninth Circuit panel wrote that "the freedoms to speak and assemble which are enshrined in the First Amendment are of the utmost importance in maintaining a truly free society. Nevertheless, it would be cavalier to assert that the government and its citizens cannot act, but must sit quietly and wait until they are actually physically injured or have had their property destroyed by those who are trying to perpetrate, or cause the perpetration of, those violent outrages against them."[21]

Boman, Laube, and Eason currently are in limbo, having filed an appeal of the appeals court ruling to the US Supreme Court. Rundo again fled the country, reportedly hiding out in Serbia, Bosnia, and Herzegovina.[22]

The main effect Charlottesville had on the alt-right was a crushing one: Groups splintered and organizers sought cover from the legal and social consequences. A number of newer recruits peeled away, and most of the less radical groups—particularly any Patriot militiamen in the crowd—disavowed the whole affair. However, many of the radicalized white nationalists doubled down, more convinced of their righteousness than ever.

But no one wanted to be associated with the alt-right any longer. So the term—and, in most regards, the movement itself—was quickly discarded. No one identified as an alt-right group after Charlottesville.

That hardly meant the white nationalists and neofascist extremists went away; rather the opposite. Like a blob of mercury crushed under a thumb, they simply spread out into newer, smaller blobs—some of them more toxic and pernicious than ever.

AMONG THE PEOPLE MARCHING alongside James Fields that day with Vanguard America was the aforementioned Thomas Rousseau, just eighteen at the time. He managed to avoid any legal consequences for his participation in the day's violence, and upon returning home to Texas, set about to create a new organization that would avoid its predecessors' mistakes. He called it Patriot Front.[23]

Rousseau's idea originated in neo-Nazi organizing that began in 2015 at the messageboard IronMarch.org, itself an outgrowth of the community of dedicated fascists who commented at online forums such as 4chan and Stormfront, and allegedly founded by Russian nationalist Alexander Slavros. IronMarch in turn spun off the neo-Nazi activist group Atomwaffen (German for "Atomic Bomb") Division, whose members engaged in various far-right terrorist actions. Atomwaffen activists also favored plastering flyers advertising their organization.[24]

While Atomwaffen was explicit in its embrace of German-style Nazism, other fascists at IronMarch began discussing ways to broaden their reach in order to compete with alt-right and "white identitarian" groups such as Identity Evropa for young recruits. Out of these discussions they created a new group in 2015, first named Reaction America, then renamed in 2016 as American Vanguard (AV).

When one of that group's leaders was exposed for offering up information to an anti-fascist group and IronMarch users and administrators began doxing AV members, the group broke away from IronMarch. In early 2017, the organization once again rebranded as Vanguard America (VA). After an Atomwaffen member in Florida shot and killed two other members in May 2017, telling authorities the group was planning to blow up a nuclear plant, a number of Atomwaffen participants joined ranks with Vanguard America.

The leader of Vanguard America, a Marine Corps veteran from New Mexico named Dillon Irizarry (but better known by his *nom de plume* Dillon Hopper), began organizing rallies at which members openly carried firearms. At its website, VA claimed that America was built on the foundation of white Europeans, and demanded the nation recapture the glory of the Aryan nation, free of the influence of the international Jews.

VA had a significant presence in Charlottesville at the Unite the Right rally, particularly in the person of James Alex Fields. The organization later issued a statement claiming that Fields was not actually a member of VA. Yet photographed only two marchers away from Fields was Rousseau, who had been responsible for vetting the VA's roster that day. Rousseau noted in chats that VA's statement "never said that [Fields] did anything wrong." Soon after Charlottesville, he and other participants were recommending yet another name change.

On August 30, Rousseau split with Irizarry/Hopper, and announced that his new group would be known as Patriots Front (the "s" was dropped in short order). "The new name was carefully chosen, as it serves several purposes. It can help inspire sympathy among those more inclined to fence-sitting, and can easily be used to justify our worldview."

The mention of "fence-sitting" referred to the ongoing discussion within the online neo-Nazi community about recruiting young men sympathetic to their underlying cause but not yet fully radicalized. There have been similar discussions about drawing in "Patriots" from the far-right militia movement, which has traditionally (though not rigorously) drawn a line at participating in outright white-supremacist activity.

Rousseau's plan was to translate online discussion into real-world, concrete activism: "You will be expected to work, and work hard to meet the bar rising," he wrote. "Inactivity will get you expelled, unwillingness to work and contribute in any capacity will as well."[25]

The "work" has primarily comprised making their presence felt at rallies and protests, spreading the word with freeway banners, and plastering flyers in public locations, where they are often summarily removed. The group first made its presence felt in Houston in September 2017, about a month after the Unite the Right rally in Charlottesville, when about a dozen members appeared outside a book fair and demanded a fight with anti-fascist organizers who reportedly were inside giving a talk. (Rousseau later led a similar protest outside an Austin bookstore.)

Other members began taking their activism public. In Seattle's Fremont neighborhood in September 2017, a group of masked neo-Nazis briefly unfurled a swastika-laden banner advertising IronMarch.org; two months later, in suburban Bellevue, a similar group put up a banner advertising bloodandsoil.org on an Interstate 90 overpass, where it was shortly removed by Department of Transportation workers. In October, someone erected a Patriot Front "Resurrection Through Insurrection" banner on a freeway near Los Angeles. And in November, Patriot Front activists put up a banner in San Antonio, Texas, on the Texas–San Antonio campus.

Places like Gig Harbor and San Antonio were deluged with stark black-and-white posters—featuring a variety of slogans, including "We Have a Right to Exist," "Fascism: The Next Step for America," and "Will Your Speech Be Hate Speech?" as well as screeds urging "Patriots" to "reconquer your birthright," while others urged "all white Americans" to "report any and all illegal aliens"—that were glued to lampposts, telephone poles, windows, doors, bulletin boards, and anywhere else they could be seen by the public. They especially targeted college campuses.

Patriot Front was notable for its utterly undisguised and unrepentant fascism. It also lacked the often transgressive, juvenile humor, and use of pop culture and irony that were core to much of the appeal of the alt-right online. Instead, its dead-serious advocacy of white-supremacist ideology was intended to appeal to a more militant mindset. As the manifesto on its website explains:

> The American identity was something uniquely forged in the strug-
> gle that our ancestors waged to survive in this new continent. America
> is truly unique in this pan-European identity which forms the roots of
> our nationhood. To be an American is to realize this identity and take
> up the national struggle upon one's shoulders.

In its nascent stages, Patriot Front was mainly composed of small clusters of dedicated neo-Nazis intent on spreading their fascist gospel, especially to "fence-sitting" alt-righters potentially attracted to violent street action. What was noteworthy, even alarming, was the speed with which it spread to nearly every corner of the country, and the success of its open appeals to young white males—as well as the confidence with which they not only spread hateful ideologies but indulged in their real-world violence and criminality.

ANOTHER FACE IN THE alt-right crowd that August day in 2017 in Charlottesville was one that would become well-known by January 6, 2021: a fresh-faced eighteen-year-old from the Chicago suburbs named Nicholas Fuentes, who had promoted Unite the Right on Facebook the morning of August 12 by writing that "a tidal wave of white identity is coming." He did not partici-pate in the violence that day, but blamed James Fields's lethal car attack on the leftist counterprotesters: "I don't think it's a surprise that you're going to get a lunatic doing something like that," he said.[26]

Fuentes had made a minor reputation with his YouTube live stream channel called "America First With Nicholas J. Fuentes" during his freshman year at Boston University in 2016–17, but left the school because of what he called harassment directed at him for his views. These views included his open expressions of contempt for immigrants and non-whites, and his conspiracist eliminationism: "Who runs the media? Globalists. Time to kill the globalists," he said in April 2017, adding: "I want the people that run CNN to be arrested and deported because this is deliberate."[27]

"We can talk about black pride, Latino pride, and gay pride all day long, but talk about white pride, or pride in European heritage, and you're suddenly an apologist for Adolf Hitler and the Ku Klux Klan," he wrote on Facebook in August, shortly after the Charlottesville riots. "Enough is enough! I'm sick of being asked to condemn or apologize for racism every 15 minutes for being born white."[28]

The volume of criticism for his participation drove him to consider attending Auburn University in Alabama ("I think I will be happy there and I will be safe. It's solidly red territory") but he never followed through. However, his increasingly violent rhetoric finally convinced the network hosting his program, Auburn-based Right Side Broadcasting Network, to dump him: "Nick was just taking things a little too far into right field for us," its chagrined CEO told reporters.[29]

So he shifted gears and gave up on higher education altogether. He set up shop with another noted white nationalist named James Allsup, a Pacific Northwest agitator who had been present at the April 2017 Berkeley protest and Charlottesville as well. They ran a podcast titled *Nationalist Review*, which billed itself as a "weekly podcast about American nationalism, traditionalism, and alternative right-wing politics." However, that quickly fell apart due to egos and mutual accusations of laziness, ineptitude, and malfeasance, and they each turned to cultivating audiences at their personal YouTube channels.[30]

Fuentes returned to using "America First" as his primary brand name, creating live stream podcast talk shows almost daily. Though it took its name from Trump's campaign slogans and speeches, it began to veer sharply from Trump, even denouncing the White House for being too congenial to Israel, a nation that the profoundly anti-Semitic Fuentes openly loathes. And it largely worked, especially as he began cultivating his knack for saying outrageously hateful things.

The audience Fuentes attracted was the same alt-right crowd, brimming with social-media-ese and its ironic racism-as-humor detachment (their responses always seem to include at least one "LOL") and references to memes and 4chan trends like Pepe the Frog. Fuentes's followers adopted a variation on Pepe—with a broader mouth and eyes, longer fingers, and more sardonic smirk—named Groyper as their symbol and mascot, and began calling themselves the "Groyper army."[31]

Fuentes rejected the white-nationalist label as an annoying encumbrance, even as he embraced every aspect of white-nationalist ideology. He insisted that he was only an "American nationalist"—even though he and his group parroted hoary white-supremacist ideas like "white genocide," not to mention his unrepentant anti-Semitism and fanatical authoritarianism, eventually advocating for a dictatorship: "We need to take control of the media, take control of the government, and force the people to believe what we believe."[32]

As Ben Lorber explained at Political Research Associates: "Fuentes seeks to secure a place for white nationalist concerns within the shifting consensus that defines movement conservatism. His momentum both accelerates and reflects the mainstreaming of white nationalism in U.S. politics, and highlights the challenges posed to existing 'counter-extremism' strategies in the face of an increasingly normalized far right."[33]

Fuentes described this strategy on one of his podcasts:

My job, and the job of the Groypers and America First, is to keep
pushing further . . . We're gonna get called racist, sexist, anti-Semitic,
bigoted, whatever . . . and when the party is where we are two years
later, we're not gonna get the credit for the ideas that become popular . . . but that's OK. That's our job. We are the right-wing flank of the
Republican Party, and if we didn't exist, the Republican Party would be
falling backwards all the time, constantly falling backwards, receding
into the center and the left.

Fuentes strategically decided that this entailed a frontal assault on mainstream conservatives and timid Republicans, particularly those he decided
were competing for the demographic group he wanted to recruit—namely,
angry young white males, and young authoritarians like himself more generally. This put Charlie Kirk and his Turning Point USA organization directly in his line of fire.

Kirk, another product of the Chicago suburbs, had been building
TPUSA in a more traditional fashion—slowly obtaining financial support
from mainstream conservatives and cultivating ties to the Republican Party
while focusing its recruitment and messaging for college-age conservatives.
Founded in 2012, by 2016 it had raised $8.2 million and was surreptitiously
financing the campaigns of student conservatives in campus elections.

The Groypers, however, had little patience for his mainstream-friendly
approach; they soon began turning up at TPUSA events featuring Kirk and
his accompanying speakers, who they deemed insufficiently "red-pilled."
Groyper audience members would roil these events by asking Kirk and
other speakers openly anti-Semitic, racist, and homophobic questions.

In 2019, Kirk embarked on a national speaking tour to tell college students about how nasty leftists were to conservatives these days, but found
himself unprepared to deal with how much nastier far-right extremists can
be as well. Kirk and his speakers ran into a blizzard of white nationalist,
paleo-conservative, and homophobic trolls at a late October event on the

Ohio State University campus in Columbus. During a question-and-answer session featuring Kirk and Black gay conservative Rob Smith, trolls pelted them with relentless questions about immigration, gay rights, and white nationalism that clearly demonstrated that Kirk's attempts to separate his would-be youth movement from the alt-right were not working.[34]

One questioner asked: "How does anal sex help us win the culture war?" Another asked: "Can you prove that our white European ideals will be maintained if the country is no longer made up of white European descendants?"

One young man, wearing a red MAGA ball cap and a pro-Israel button, mocked Kirk in classic alt-right fashion by ironically speaking as though he were an ardent supporter of TPUSA's philo-Semitic positions, and then concluded by urging everyone to google a notoriously anti-Semitic white-nationalist meme about "dancing Israelis."

Kirk attempted to push back ("I find that to be a racist question," he responded at one point) but shouts of derision and boos could be heard throughout the affair. Afterward, Kirk and TPUSA denounced his alt-right interlocutors, and Kirk went on the syndicated radio show of former White House adviser Sebastian Gorka the next day to "reject the vile anti-Semites."

Kirk, of course, had no one to blame but himself for the company he has kept. TPUSA, in fact, first attracted an audience by making explicit appeals to the alt-right.

An organization that claimed to have chapters at more than one thousand colleges, TPUSA's ties to the alt-right date back to its earliest days organizing on campuses in 2014–16, thanks largely to Kirk's fondness for inflammatory far-right rhetoric friendly to white-nationalist sentiments, such as his insistence that white privilege is a myth: "They're trying to discredit good ideas and good arguments, just because you're white, and that's ridiculous," he liked to say.[35]

Bloomsburg University professor Wendy Lynne Lee collected a "bibliography" that documented, as the Southern Poverty Law Center described it, "connections between TPUSA, its funders, advisors and guest speakers and online expressions of anti-Semitism, anti-Muslim sentiment, racism, misogyny and anti-LGBT bias, as well as connections to prominent alt-right personalities." The publication of the piece resulted in Lee being viciously attacked by the alt-right on social media and elsewhere.

A *New Yorker* exposé similarly revealed that the organization was indulging in shady "dark money" operations on some campuses, and was looking the other way when it came to ugly expressions of racism within its ranks.[36]

After at least one campus chapter disbanded and several of TPUSA's most prominent figures—including gun activist Kaitlin Bennett and Black conservative Candace Owens—left the group, Kirk began working to distance the group from the alt-right. A chapter president from Las Vegas was prominently booted from TPUSA in 2019 after a viral video of him surfaced in which he screamed "White power!" at the camera.

Realizing the association had become a toxic one, Kirk and TPUSA began threatening activists and others who described the organization as "alt-right" with libel. He also promoted the work of Smith, whose presence angered many conservatives, even despite his rabidly far-right, pro-Trump pronouncements attacking liberals.

An internecine war broke out on the far right between the alt-right and the alt-lite. While more mainstream figures like ex–Trump adviser Sebastian Gorka supported Kirk, the unapologetically white-nationalist alt-right—including many TPUSA members who were radicalized into believing anti-Semitic and anti-immigrant conspiracy theories through the organization's community—began organizing to attack Kirk and other conservatives who were deemed too friendly to Jews, gays, and immigrants.

Donald Trump Jr. found himself confronted by Groypers during a TPUSA event in Los Angeles on the UCLA campus. They were trying to promote Trump Jr.'s ghost-written book, *Triggered: How the Left Thrives on*

Hate and Wants to Silence Us. They were silenced that day, it turned out, by right-wing extremists who heckled Trump Jr. off the stage after organizers—spotting a number of Groypers in the crowd—announced that there would be no question-and-answer session.[37]

The crowd grew so hostile that Trump Jr.'s fiancé, Kimberly Guilfoyle, chastised them: "Let me tell you something, I bet you engage and go on online dating because you're impressing no one here to get a date in person." That inflamed them even further, and Trump and Guilfoyle soon retreated backstage.

"Our problem is not with @DonaldJTrumpJr who is a patriot—We are supporters of his father!" Fuentes tweeted the next day. "Our problem is with Charlie Kirk's TPUSA organization that SHUTS DOWN and SMEARS socially conservative Christians and supporters of President Trump's agenda. We are AMERICA FIRST!"[38]

A similar TPUSA event in Tempe, Arizona, featuring Republican congressman Dan Crenshaw of Texas, also attracted the army of Groypers, and it similarly turned into a shouting match and was cut short.

Crenshaw asked the trolls: "What do you guys call yourselves? There's a name for your group, right?"

His interlocutors responded with a series of sarcastic names. Eventually they started chanting: "America First! America First!"[39]

That was the recipe: after the Ohio State outburst, Andrew Anglin, editor/publisher of the explicitly neo-Nazi website *The Daily Stormer*, had explained to his readers how deniability was built into all these public expressions of support for white-nationalist beliefs: "If you say any of the things said in OSU on Tuesday night, you can just say 'no of course I'm not an ALT-RIGHT NEO-NAZI RACIST WHITE SUPREMACIST, I'm just an America First nationalist and MAGA supporter.'"[40]

Some well-known right-wing figures were also caught in the crossfire, but quickly sided with the Groypers. Michelle Malkin, a Filipina American pundit whose involvement in white nationalism dates back to her appearances in 2002 in the white-nationalist webzine *VDARE*, was fired by the mainstream-conservative Young America's Foundation (YAF) (where she had been one of the organization's mainstays in its campus lecture program) due to her ongoing support for Fuentes, which included speeches at some of his events.[41]

"There is no room in mainstream conservatism or at YAF for holocaust deniers, white nationalists, street brawlers, or racists," the YAF tweeted as its official statement.

Malkin fired back that the "Keepers of the Gate" had spoken, adding: "My defense of unjustly prosecuted Proud Boys, patriotic young nationalists/groypers & demographic truth-tellers must not be tolerated. SPLC is cheering."

As the battle lines in the "Groyper War" were drawn, Malkin consistently supported Fuentes and the Groypers. Malkin praised both Fuentes and his fans as "New Right leaders," and called on establishment conservatives to engage with them. She labeled their critics "cringe." Malkin's stand earned her the deep affection of Fuentes's followers, who dubbed her the "Groyper Mommy."[42]

Fuentes continued to attract a large audience that, in truth, exhibited more fervency and energy than anything Charlie Kirk could concoct. Fuentes achieved near-viral status on Twitter with videos in which he defended racial segregation; called for the hanging of CNN reporters; and denied the Holocaust.

"Enough with the Jim Crow stuff," he told his audience in one video. "Who cares? 'Oh, I had to drink out of a different water fountain.' Big fucking deal . . . Oh no, they had to go to a different school . . . And even if it was bad, who cares? . . . It was better for them, it's better for us."[43]

Eventually, in January 2020, YouTube demonetized his videos—one of his primary sources of income—and then terminated his account a month later for violating its policies on hate speech. He promptly switched to an alternative hosting service, and continued to attract large numbers of followers and subscribers, quickly becoming the most-viewed live streamer on the DLive platform—which eventually banned him more than a year later.[44]

Not that that was going to stop him.

———————

AS DONALD TRUMP'S FIRST term as president wound down and his imminent reelection defeat in 2020 began appearing more clearly on the horizon, white nationalists began preparing for life when their "Glorious Leader" (alt-right leader Andrew Anglin's name for him) was no longer in charge. What would their movement look like after the man who had empowered them was gone from office?

For the openly fascist Patriot Front, it was seen as simply the next natural step in their political evolution. Thanks to group chats that were exposed in early 2022, we know they were already looking ahead by then. Indeed, Trump himself is often discussed in those pre-election 2020 chats with a kind of derisive contempt by many Patriot Front members, much as they see rival far-right groups as simply not radical enough.[45]

Even the election was irrelevant to Patriot Front. "It does not matter what people personally believe about it," Thomas Rousseau wrote in a group chat on the encrypted forum Rocket.Chat. "Casting a ballot is a submissive gesture to legitimize tyranny. It is fundamentally amoral. It is done as an insult to the nation's cause and the organization."

"In many ways, a lot of people in the white power movement are not fans of Trump, but they do see him as useful to their movement, introducing some of their ideas and carrying out some of the policies that they favor," said Cassie Miller, an analyst at the SPLC. "But in some ways, they see him as buying them time."

They sneered at rival far-right organizations. "Proud Boys are a bunch of cucks," wrote one Patriot Front member from Texas. "They call themselves 'Western Chauvinists' which means they are a bunch of liberals who don't like PC culture and 'snowflakes' yet they are too scared to actually stand up to these things in a meaningful way lest they be called RACISTS!!!!"

Though they share similar goals, the "Boogaloo" civil-war movement is viewed similarly. "The whole 'Boogaloo' thing is a reminder that if you joke about anything long enough, you'll stop joking," Rousseau told another member online. "An offhand forum slapstick joke could become something that someone shoots someone over if its left to fester and rot like the mold-like idea it is."

Nick Fuentes was similarly clear that overthrowing mainstream conservatism had to be the primary objective of white nationalists, but he was more focused on the pragmatic politics, which he saw as fundamental to his movement building. He promoted a strategy to overtake the Republican Party, primarily by driving out old-style conservatives, reflected in his oft-repeated catchphrase "destroy the GOP." He told his podcast audience: "We needed to redefine the right wing by solidifying the political realignment that Donald Trump initiated in 2016, under the banner, and under the slogan, and under the principles of America First."[46]

Fuentes emphasized that what he called the "civil war" between the "conservative establishment and the America First pro-Trump base" is "now playing out" in national electoral politics. Fuentes nonetheless saw Trump's reelection as essential to white-nationalist interests, even if he too took a longer view of how their movement should evolve. He ardently supported Trump during the 2020 campaign, and became a fanatical supporter of the Stop the Steal campaign, showing up at events around the country to protest vote counts, and playing a leading role in the November 14 Million MAGA March protest in Washington, D.C., that served as a violent warmup for January 6—though with many fewer protesters.[47]

Throughout the November event, far-right extremists of all stripes announced their presence: Fuentes's Groyper army rushed to lead the procession from the White House to the Congress and Supreme Court Building, their blue "America First" banners held high. Oath Keepers and other militiamen, wearing body armor and prepared for battle—though unarmed, since Washington forbids open carry of guns within its city limits—joined eagerly in the procession.

At one point, Fuentes addressed the crowd with a bullhorn. "We're up against the media, and against the giant corporations, and against the swamp, and the government, and the CIA, and the FBI, and the intelligence community, and it is a pretty big path ahead of us," he said. "There are a lot of them, and they wield much power. But I think to myself this: I have much confidence in knowing that God is on our side!" The crowd roared.[48]

So Fuentes's presence outside the Capitol on January 6, exhorting the crowd to violence, as well as the presence of multiple Groypers inside the Capitol—a total of ten of them were charged afterward—was the next natural step.[49] After all, the worldview that Fuentes and the Groypers represented was considered conventional wisdom for much of the mob.

A post-insurrection survey of the participants in the January 6 attack by the University of Chicago Project on Security and Threats found that, in addition to Trump's lies about the election, white-nationalist beliefs formed much of the common ground among the mob that day. The survey showed that "the No. 1 belief among insurrectionists—shared by fully 75 percent of respondents—is the 'great replacement' of the electorate by the Democratic Party and that this idea is also the most important separator of people in the 21 million from the general population, where the theory doesn't hold much sway."[50]

Likewise, the key demographic characteristic of the insurrectionists was that they came from counties around the nation—particularly in urban areas—where the white share of the population is declining the fastest.

After the insurrection, Fuentes emphatically promoted the idea that the attempt to keep Trump in office was not merely justifiable, but the Capitol siege an event to be positively celebrated. That was the line he adopted the day after the siege on his podcast.

"At every step of the way, the Republican Party could have kept Trump in office," Fuentes claimed. "Whether it was the party apparatus—the Republican Party itself, the RNC—stopping the voter fraud on Election Day. You could've had Republican state legislatures take their own electors and appoint them and send them to D.C. You could've had Trump-appointed justices intervene and make this right.

"And ultimately tomorrow you could've had Republican senators and House representatives object to and throw out enough votes that we could've forced a contingent election and gotten President Trump inaugurated that way," he said.

"Frankly, I think it was completely justified," he added. "And, if I'm being totally honest, I loved what happened yesterday. And we will see what the consequences will be of yesterday, and we will deal with them, and we will adapt to them, and they're not gonna be good . . . But what I saw yesterday was beautiful. It was righteous. It was American. Our ancestors from our founding smiled upon us yesterday. And I have nothing to apologize for."[51]

————————

LIKE MOST LITERAL FASCISTS, the guys who run Patriot Front never miss a trick. Which is why they turned up in Washington, D.C., in late January 2021, a little over a week after Joe Biden's inauguration, staking a claim as the first far-right group to return to the city and march down the Capitol Mall since the insurrection.[52]

ProPublica journalist Lydia DePillis observed them the morning of January 29 marching in formation, about one hundred strong, masked and wielding their organization's banners—styled after the American flag, but featuring a fasces (an axe with a bundle of sticks, the traditional symbol of fascism) where the stars normally are—and then marching from the Jefferson Memorial up the Mall to the Capitol. They apparently dispersed afterward.

Founder Thomas Rousseau knew that marching down the National Mall so soon after the insurrection would attract a lot of attention. "[Rousseau] wants to really focus on spectacle, and he thinks that a performative show of strength is the most effective kind of propaganda that they can engage in," SPLC analyst Cassie Miller remarked.[53]

Rousseau spectacularly lost control of the narrative, though, when Patriot Front's Rocket.Chat data was leaked and published by the journalism collective Unicorn Riot in January 2022.[54] The leak did more than simply expose its members to public identification on social media—though that quickly began happening apace, much to the chagrin of the unmasked young fascists.

Most of all, it opened a window into the world of these young white male extremists, and how they are working to establish their organization within the American body politic. Besides revealing embarrassing personal details such as their porn habits and the amateurish combat "training" sessions for members, it also gave researchers a clear view of their recruitment methods and targets, as well as the breadth of their reach within the mainstream—including the military.

The leak featured thousands of pages of internal conversations within some four hundred gigabytes of data. This data originated on Patriot Front's internal Rocket.Chat boards for members and prospective recruits. The portrait that emerged is of an organization intensely focused on recruiting like-minded young white men: ardent nationalists, nativists, segregationists, misogynists, and Hitler-worshiping fascists who've grown tired of concealing their secret lives, and want to begin making their fantasies of enacting his Final Solution real.

One report examining the data from the Southern Poverty Law Center found that one in five of the young men applying to join Patriot Front have ties to the US military. Of the eighty-seven applicants on the chat, eighteen of them (21 percent) claimed to have current or former military experience; one of these, claiming to be an ex-Marine, told the chat that he is currently employed by the Department of Homeland Security.[55]

One of the primary dangers of commingling far-right extremism with military service is that people who by training and nature are skilled at handling weapons and materiel and are knowledgeable about engagement tactics are being radicalized into this seditionist extremism. The chats revealed this danger explicitly: one applicant who claimed to have served as an Army Ranger listed "great land-navigation, great physical fitness, able to clear rooms," as well as "basic medical training" as skills he would bring to Patriot Front.

Another applicant boasted of experience in "Marine martial arts," adding that he had been "trained in firearms." Others claimed they had worked in military intelligence, had backgrounds in computer networking and programming, and were conversant in signals intelligence. One who said he was an ex-Marine claimed to be a leader of a hate group, the Kansas Active Club.

Rousseau and senior members called "network directors" oversaw the chats, organized by region. They organized real-world "actions" in the chat rooms, which included several criminal acts of vandalism, such as defacing memorials, statues, and murals in highly public places. These included a memorial to George Floyd in New York City, as well as other works of public art that provoked their ire, such as a mural supporting Black Lives Matter in Olympia, Washington, and depictions of Black heroes such as Martin Luther King Jr. and Harriet Tubman.

They also clearly believed they could do so with impunity. "As our recent actions have shown we can walk down busy avenues at prime time in Seattle and deface the largest most well protected mural in shitlib Olympia without so much as being accosted once," one member who apparently participated in the Olympia vandalization wrote.[56]

Patriot Front again organized a January march in Washington, D.C., in 2022, timed in conjunction with the antiabortion March For Life.[57] About forty of them formed a phalanx that eventually was forced to separate from the main crowd by counterprotesters and police.

Unicorn Riot reported that Patriot Front secured a police escort for that march by placing a "false" 911 call about themselves. Rousseau directed a member to call police "from a burner [phone]" as Patriot Front left their nearby camp for D.C., pretending to be a concerned citizen, ostensibly to "soften the police up before our big visual contact on the bridge, and provide a little confusion and misinfo that's within the realm of honest dialogue."[58]

Rousseau and his lieutenants set quotas for members to engage in various "actions," including regional group quotas of at least "10 big actions a month." Acts of vandalism were recorded in a spreadsheet.

The group also monitored its roughly 220 members' personal lives in a fanatically controlling way. Members were required to regularly log their weight and fitness regimen, follow an apparently disordered diet obsessively, and update their superiors on their "bad habits," such as pornography and junk food. Leaders pointedly chastised members for failing to participate in enough chats or meetings or to file their mandatory fitness updates.

This kind of routine humiliation was evident in several of the "training" videos that were uncovered in the leak: Out-of-shape men forced to perform push-ups and pull-ups while their cohorts harass them; men trying to wrestle each other to the ground while groping various body parts; groups practicing the use of shields, linking arms in group cohesion exercises; being groped as "trainers" demonstrate how to pat a suspect down for a weapon; trying (and failing) to carry "fallen" teammates; practicing tactical retreats in which they all run backward while touching one another's shoulders.

WHILE THE YOUNG NEOFASCISTS in Patriot Front focused on training and other manly pursuits, the white-nationalist Groyper army got religion—specifically, Christian nationalism.[59]

Most of the far-right extremist movements that arose online and then in real life over the past decade—the alt-right, white nationalists, and other authoritarian protofascists—have been generally ecumenical and a-religious in their rhetorical appeals and organizing, other than their frequent expressions of anti-Semitism. But with Nick Fuentes leading the way, it became much more common to hear the America First Groypers and other white nationalists embracing Christian nationalism, a movement revolving around the idea of remaking the United States into a fundamentalist Christian theocratic state that dispenses with liberal democracy.

After the Capitol insurrection, Fuentes and his America First cohorts began employing Christian nationalist rhetoric: chanting "Christ is king" at the antiabortion March for Life in Washington and at anti-vaccine protests, using crucifixes as protest symbols, and similar rhetorical appeals. In a speech at the America First conference in Orlando in March at which he declared America "a Christian nation," Fuentes warned his audience that America will cease to be America "if it loses its white demographic core and if it loses its faith in Jesus Christ."

"Christian nationalism—and even the idea of separatism, with a subtext of White, Christian and conservative-leaning [influences]—took a more dominant role in the way that extremist groups talk to each other and try to propagandize in public," Jared Holt of the Atlantic Council's Digital Forensic Research Lab told *The Washington Post*.[60]

While many Christian nationalists are grounded in more traditional evangelical views, there is also a component who are cynically embracing religious fervor as a way of expanding their recruitment base.

The striking aspect of the surge of Christian nationalism has been its ability to unify sectors of the radical right, from militia-oriented Patriots to bigoted white nationalists to conspiracists like the authoritarian QAnon cult.

"This unification is pretty unprecedented," Alex Newhouse, deputy director of the Center on Terrorism, Extremism, and Counterterrorism at the Middlebury Institute of International Studies, told the *Post*. "The infusion of Christian nationalism throughout that unification process has been particularly interesting and, in my opinion, is going to end up being pretty dangerous."

Moreover, a number of these white nationalists appear to be pushing even further into a particularly ugly—and previously stagnant—brand of religious nationalism: Christian Identity, the bigoted theological movement claiming that white people are the true "Children of Israel," that Jews are the literal descendants of Satan, and that all non-white people are soulless "mud people."

Since 2019 Newhouse has noticed a sudden uptick of interest in Christian Identity, particularly the Aryan Nations operation in the northern Idaho Panhandle between 1978 and 2000, which was an Identity church.

One of the leading voices in this resurgence, Newhouse says, was Kyle Chapman, the cofounder of the Proud Boys–affiliated Fraternal Order of Alt-Knights, who later attempted to create an explicitly racist and anti-Semitic offshoot called Proud Goys.

Newhouse said Chapman had been interacting with Christian Identity influencers on the encrypted chat platform Telegram while "blasting out Christian Identity propaganda," the sort of propaganda like "two seedline theory"—which claims that Eve also mated with Satan in the Garden of Eden and thus gave birth to Jews.

"There's this gradual move toward a more revolutionary, burn-it-all-down posture, and I think Christian Identity for a lot of these people has become a way for them to organize their thoughts," he said.

Christian nationalist beliefs were not limited in their creeping influence only to far-right extremists. Perhaps even more pernicious and striking was their spread among mainstream conservatives in the media and especially within the MAGA wing of the Republican Party.

Christian nationalists heavily supported Trump in the 2020 election, bringing not only their conspiracist belief in their persecution but also that the government's legitimacy derives not from its democratic institutions but from its adherence to what they call a "traditional" cultural, ethnic, and religious heritage. Their innate authoritarian tendencies melded neatly with MAGA authoritarianism, which meant that their propensity for conspiracism quickly metastasized the further they became absorbed into Trump's alternative universe. On January 6, they could be seen and heard in the mob attacking the Capitol, linking arms with all the other factions present, repeating Trump's lies about being cheated out of the presidency.

And in the weeks following the insurrection, their embrace of those lies deepened. At Christian nationalist conferences, speakers regularly claimed that the 2020 election was fraudulent, and valorized the January 6 defendants as "political prisoners." Christian nationalist radio host Eric Metaxas told a Florida gathering, "The reason I think we are being so persecuted, why the January 6 folks are being persecuted—when you're over the target like that, oh my."[61]

Christian nationalist beliefs became conventional wisdom among MAGA Republicans. An October 2022 poll by Pew Research Center found that 67 percent of Republicans—and 45 percent of the nation—believe the United States should be a Christian nation, and 76 percent of them say that was the intention of the Founding Fathers. Among those who hold those views, 54 percent said that they believe the Bible should influence US laws and take precedence over the will of the people.[62]

This antidemocratic impulse was shared by the mainstream Republicans, white nationalists, Proud Boys, and conspiracy theorists with whom Christian nationalists coalesced in the months and years after the insurrection, amassing around a campaign of extreme election denialism. By the summer of 2022, evangelical churches had become the recruitment centers for building an army of Trump fans who believed the 2020 election was stolen through fraud, built on a series of carnival-like far-right roadshows that drew in the true believers like flies.

And while their anger revolved around Trump's defeat, they were only focused on 2020 insofar as they could "prove" that American elections were riddled with "voter fraud." Their chief focus, however, was the future.

7

Alt-America with a Q

OVER THE COURSE OF his political career, Donald Trump perfected a three-step tango with the radical right—a dance in which he'd pull them close in an embrace, spin away while staying connected, and then pull them back to close quarters. Acknowledge, deny, validate. Lather, rinse, repeat.[1]

It was a dance that enabled Trump to court and embrace the radical right with a wink and a nod while maintaining a plausible deniability that he supported them. All of them, Trump and extremists alike, were united in their shared reality: the alternative universe of right-wing conspiracism, founded on the essential belief that the world is being secretly controlled by a cabal of elite "globalists" whose agenda is to place the world, America particularly, under their totalitarian control. It's a universe woven together out of conspiracy theories, disinformation, distorted tidbits of fact, and a paranoid fearfulness that, ironically, all become components of their own authoritarian appeal.

Trump built his political career out of this universe, entering presidential politics in 2011 by promoting the Birther conspiracy theories claiming that Barack Obama had fabricated his birth certificate. He managed to largely mute his conspiracist politics during the 2016 campaign, but it lurked in the background of the ceaseless demands to "Lock her up!" in reference to Hillary Clinton on the basis of the false belief that she had committed egregious breaches of national security through her mishandling of her emails, and in his neverending demand to "Build the wall!" predicated on both nativist bigotry and the conspiracist belief that border-crossing immigrants represented a terrorist national-security threat.

Most of all, he continuously courted the conspiracist element in right-wing politics, appearing on Alex Jones's *Infowars* program and constantly referencing the sinister influence of "globalists," and he kept it going all during his presidency. The most constant of these claims entailed his continuous insistence that all the elections in which he was involved were "rigged" against him—including the Republican primary and general election of 2016. For the next year and longer, Trump claimed that he lost the popular vote to Clinton only because Democrats had engaged in massive fraud in states like California.

So when the 2020 election rolled around, Trump once again beat the "election fraud" drum, claiming that undocumented immigrants were illegally voting and fraudulently running up large numbers for Democrats. Just as he did in 2016, he refused to commit to a peaceful transfer of power in the event he lost, claiming the only way such an event was possible was if there was "massive fraud," and insisted (without evidence) that mail-in ballots were ripe for such fraud. He told reporters at a press conference: "We'll see what happens . . . Get rid of the ballots and you'll have a very peaceful—there won't be a transfer, frankly. There will be a continuation."[2]

As the 2020 campaign wound down, Trump's open embrace of conspiracy theories intensified. And his purposeful distance from the massive authoritarian cult that had grown up around him during his presidency known as QAnon vanished.

The QAnon cult was born in the early stages of Trump's presidency, the product of a Russian hacking operation that had exposed a tranche of emails on the computer accounts of the Democratic National Committee, particularly DNC chair John Podesta, which were exposed to the public by WikiLeaks in October 2016.[3] Though the emails contained very little of actual note content-wise, in the weeks and months following the election, conspiracy-theory mills went to work and began concocting a brand-new theory claiming that Clinton and other Democrats were secretly operating a pedophilia ring operating out of a Washington, D.C., pizza parlor.

It became known as Pizzagate, and attracted such a massive audience that one true believer drove to Washington, D.C., and entered the restaurant—Comet Ping Pong, a pizzeria in the Chevy Chase neighborhood—with a gun demanding entry to the dungeon where he believed children were being held, and shot up a door that turned out to be a broom closet.[4]

But rather than fade to ignominy like most discredited conspiracy theories, the underlying beliefs of the Pizzagate theories not only remained alive and well, but took on a life of their own in the form of QAnon and "the Storm," the politically apocalyptic event these cultists believed was in the works, one where all of these evildoers would be swept away into prison and/or executed at the hands of Donald Trump and his allies.

The origins of QAnon lie in Trump's cryptic remarks of October 6, 2017, saying that a gathering of military leaders represented "the calm before the storm." When asked what he meant, Trump responded: "You'll see."

Three weeks later, an anonymous poster at the online message board 4chan—one of the main organizing and recruitment forums for the alt-right—who claimed they had high-level "Q" national-security clearance began publishing a series of cryptic messages that they claimed were "intel drops" intended to start informing the public through such channels about what was really happening inside the White House, and what Trump really meant by his odd remarks.

According to QAnon, Trump's remark was a reference to the indictments handed down by Robert Mueller in late October, ostensibly related to his investigation of the Trump campaign and its alleged collusion with

Russian intelligence. Most news reports about those indictments, reported to number in the hundreds, presumed that they were related to criminal behavior around the campaign.

Not so, said QAnon, who claimed that Trump was never really under investigation. Instead, those indictments were all being directed at a massive conspiracy involving a global pedophilia ring operated by high-level Democrats and other "globalists" who were simultaneously part of a plot to overthrow Trump's presidency with a "Deep State" coup—the same human trafficking operation that was the focus of Pizzagate.

However, in the new, expanded version of the theory, the pedophilia ring had gone global, drawing in alleged participants from all around the nation, and occurring in locations ranging from Hollywood to Europe. (One version of the pedophilia theory entertained by Alex Jones claimed that the child victims were being secretly shipped to a colony on Mars.)

QAnon and the conspiracy theorists who piled on at 4chan, 8chan, and on YouTube and Twitter claimed that contrary to the running story in mainstream media, this pedophilia ring was the real focus of Mueller's investigation. The general conclusion, spread through the #QAnon hashtag on social media, was that a wave of arrests—including Clinton, Obama, Podesta, philanthropist George Soros, Sen. John McCain, and a number of leading Hollywood figures and Democrats—was about to happen.[5]

As with all such fantasy-based universes, the QAnon theories kept mutating and metastasizing, especially as more people piled on and joined in on the "research." Eventually, it became established truth in their world that not only were large numbers of children being abducted and trafficked, but that they were being secretly held in facilities where their blood could be drawn, from which scientists could then extract adrenochrome—a human hormone that they claim has life-extending "fountain of youth" properties—from it.[6]

Trump, however, was rarely asked about the QAnon cult, and typically pleaded ignorance, but he regularly retweeted some 129 QAnon accounts at least 216 times, sometimes multiple times a day.[7] Asked about the cult at an August 2020 press conference, he responded: "I don't know much about the movement, other than I understand they like me very much, which I appreciate."

A reporter then asked whether he supported the idea that he "is secretly saving the world from this satanic cult of pedophiles and cannibals," Trump responded: "Well, I haven't heard that, but is that supposed to be a bad thing or a good thing?"[8]

At a televised town hall event on NBC that he participated in on October 20, Trump performed his familiar three-step: He offered a perfunctory, pro-forma denunciation of white supremacists that (as usual) convinced no one but his followers—and least of all white supremacists. He then pivoted to a semi-embrace of far-right conspiracy theories, both of the QAnon cult and of the QAnon-related—and, as always, absurdly false—claims he had tweeted earlier in the week claiming President Obama had secretly ordered the deaths of the Navy SEAL team that killed Osama bin Laden.[9]

The whole routine was slathered with a heavy helping of the Republican right's favorite gaslighting narrative—the one about the violent radical leftists of Antifa posing an existential threat to America, which doubled as a smokescreen for the incipient extremism that was overwhelming the GOP and movement conservatism.

After nominally distancing himself from the far right, Trump deftly pivoted when panelist Savannah Guthrie asked him about whether he would denounce QAnon—which, as she explained to Trump, believes that Democratic leaders and liberal media figures are part of a global pedophilia conspiracy, and that he is the hero of the theory.

"I don't know anything about QAnon," Trump said. "I know nothing about it," he continued. "I do know they are very much against pedophilia, they fight it very hard. I'll tell you what I do know about, I know about Antifa and I know about the radical left and how violent and vicious they are, and I know how they're burning down cities run by Democrats, not run by Republicans."

He continued to express utter ignorance of the QAnon cult, despite the fact that he retweeted multiple posts from QAnon accounts on his Twitter page. "I just don't know about QAnon," he said.

"But you do!" Guthrie responded.

"I don't know. No, I don't know," Trump insisted, with the expression of a five-year-old near the scene of a broken vase.

Pressed on it further, he rambled—and then finally suggested he considered it a realistic possibility that there is indeed a satanic cult being run by Democrats: "Let me just tell you what I do hear about it, is they are very strongly against pedophilia and I agree with that. I do agree with that very strongly," Trump said.

"But there's not a satanic pedophile cult being run by—" Guthrie began.

"I don't know that," Trump interjected. "No, I don't know that. And neither do you know that."

A little later, Guthrie brought up another far-right conspiracy theory—this one promoted by a QAnon fan who claimed that not only did Obama's SEAL team accidentally kill bin Laden's body double and not the man himself, Obama then had all the team members assassinated to cover it up—that was retweeted by Trump.

"I know nothing about it . . . That was a retweet—that was an opinion of somebody," Trump answered. "I'll put it out there, people can decide for themselves, I don't take a position."

"I don't get that, you're the president, you're not like someone's crazy uncle who can just retweet whatever," Guthrie said.

"Frankly, because the media is so fake and so corrupt, if I didn't have social media . . . I wouldn't be able to get the word out," Trump said.

"The word is false," Guthrie said.

THE READY ABSORPTION OF the QAnon cult into the Republican Party reflected both how thoroughly Trump and his conspiracist base had taken control of the GOP by 2020 and how congenial the party had become over the preceding decade to extremist ideas. QAnon's authoritarianism wove neatly and easily into the existing Republican fabric. It also played an outsize role in the January 6 insurrection and the ongoing insurgency that followed.[10]

Trump himself regularly retweeted QAnoners' authoritarian paeans to his presidency and its attacks on his critics. His former national security adviser Michael Flynn posted video of himself and a group of friends taking the "QAnon oath."[11] Trump's son Eric tweeted out open support of the Q conspiracy theories.[12] Trump's favorite cable-news channel, *One America News*, featured reporters who openly embraced the theories.[13] Dozens of Republican candidates openly spouted QAnon claims and rhetoric, and GOP organizations used their Facebook accounts to promote QAnon theories.[14]

The fantastic aspects of this conspiracism—particularly the obdurate insistence by the growing hordes of true believers that "Q has always been right" in the face of the mounting reality that not one of the theories' predictions or claims has ever proven accurate—make it difficult in many ways to take it seriously. In an ordinary world, it would be dismissed as a joke.

But the up-is-down belief system inherent in conspiracist worldviews like QAnon has spread so far that it not only has infected democratic discourse with garbage disinformation, but its underlying nature is profoundly violent—which presents the very real threat of unhinged QAnon believers acting out and wreaking potentially significant levels of harm.

After all, there was a reason the FBI warned in 2019 that QAnon was a likely vector for fueling domestic terrorism: "The FBI assesses these conspiracy theories very likely will emerge, spread, and evolve in the modern information marketplace, occasionally driving both groups and individual extremists to carry out criminal or violent acts."[15]

Yet it continued to seep into mainstream Republican politics with almost nary a raised eyebrow in the face of open conspiracist nuttiness. Oregon's QAnon-loving GOP Senate nominee, Jo Rae Perkins, called for the imposition of martial law in her home state (to battle "Antifa") without any notable pushback from either the GOP or the mainstream press.[16] The Republican Party resolutely—and silently—refused to withdraw its support for a single one of the sixty-four GOP candidates in 2020 with QAnon connections.[17]

"They've done absolutely nothing to discourage QAnon followers from believing as they do," QAnon researcher Travis View told *Politico*, adding that this only stokes the community's fervor. "I mean, QAnon is premised on the idea that there is a secret plan to save the world, so they take the silence more as part of that secrecy."[18]

The White House and its allies were disingenuous when asked about the proximity of the president's inner circle to the cult. When Flynn posted his fifty-three-second clip to Twitter on the Fourth of July showing him saying the "QAnon oath"—which was in fact simply the same oath sworn by members of Congress—he was participating in a ritual already being shared widely that week as video posts by the QAnon community (Perkins among them) under the hashtag #TakeTheOath.[19] The trend was in fact inspired by a person using the Q identity on the message board 8kun to "symbolically take the oath on social media platforms."[20] At the video's end, Flynn recited the QAnon slogan: "Where we go one, we go all!"

Flynn lawyer Sidney Powell told *The Washington Examiner* that there was no intent on Flynn's part to embrace QAnon conspiracy theories—rather, she claimed, Flynn only "wanted to encourage people to think about being a citizen."[21] She claimed the phrase "Where we go one, we go all" was first engraved on a bell on one of President John F. Kennedy's sailboats—which in fact is a falsehood first propagated by the Q persona in a message board post. Powell also told CNN that "implying anything wrong with words long ago inscribed on a bell to encourage the unity of the human race is malevolent and just plain wrong. There is nothing more to the story."

Experts laughed at Flynn's denial. "This is absolutely pro-QAnon," researcher/author Mike Rothschild told CNN. Moreover, Flynn's public embrace was a major validation for the cult's true believers, he explained.[22]

"The Q community is really excited by all of this. Flynn is a hugely important figure to them, seen as a warrior who infiltrated the deep state by pretending to plead guilty," Rothschild said. "The video of Flynn actually taking the oath is, to them, total validation that they were right, that Flynn is a warrior who fights for them, and that they can be digital soldiers on his level."

This underlying vision—of being a heroic warrior for truth battling against the vilest of evils—is what attracts so many followers to QAnon, and simultaneously creates permission in their minds for committing the most atrocious acts of violence one can imagine. We've already seen this playing out in domestic-terrorism incidents that, fortunately, did not reach fruition. For instance, a QAnon fanatic armed with an AR-15 and an armored truck blocked traffic on the Hoover Dam and demanded the inspector general's report on the government investigation of Hillary Clinton's email practices in June 2018.[23] Six months later a California man who was arrested with bomb-making materials in his car told investigators he intended to use them to "blow up a satanic temple monument" in the Springfield, Illinois, capitol rotunda.[24] His larger intentions, he said, were to "make Americans aware of Pizzagate and the New World Order, who were dismantling society." Then there was the strange case of the young man who murdered acting Gambino mob boss Frank Cali in his home in Staten Island. He had gorged on QAnon theories online, telling investigators he committed the crime because he believed that Cali was part of the "Deep State" operation to sabotage Trump's presidency.[25]

The QAnon cult has always had this violent idea of heroism at its dark heart, even among the once-respectable Republicans who have been consumed by it. One of the most prominent of these is Michael Scheuer, the former CIA analyst, college lecturer, and onetime Fox News regular whose career as a pundit metastasized from virulent Islamophobia to unapologetic anti-Obama Birtherism.

By 2020, Scheuer could be found penning lengthy defenses of QAnon and its nonsense, claiming that dire consequences lay just around the corner for the usual laundry list of Trump critics and journalists who dared question the regime: "Maybe all of the following, gallows-headed traitors will write a Q on their palm and claim innocence by insanity?" he mused in December 2019 after Trump's impeachment.[26]

The supposed "Storm" arrests were only the beginnings of Scheuer's fantasies, however. Another essay, penned a year before the QAnon screed, laid out his vision of a citizens' uprising—replete with lynchings and domestic terrorism—in response to the "treason" of attacking Donald Trump:

> American patriots have so far, praise God, been remarkably disciplined in not responding to tyranny and violence with violence. For now they must remain so, armed but steady. But the time for such patience is fast slipping away; indeed, that patience is quickly becoming an obviously rank and self-destructive foolishness. If Trump does not act soon to erase the above noted tyranny and tyrants, the armed citizenry must step in and eliminate them.[27]

Eliminationism like this is the raison d'être of the QAnon cult: its ultimate agenda is the extirpation of liberal Democrats—many of them hanged in the mass executions that cultists envision—from the national body politic, punishment for the unbelievable levels of child molestation and trafficking they concoct in their conspiracy theories.

Whether any of these fantasies have even a faint basis in reality—something that might be discounted by the realization that all of Q's many predictions have never transpired—is inconsequential to the cult's true believers. What matters is believing they are heroic warriors battling nefarious forces of darkness to save the nation.

That became pronouncedly clear when the central fact of the QAnon belief system—that Trump would lead a wave of arrests that would expose the globalist cabal and free all the enslaved and abducted children—completely fell apart the first week of November 2020, when Trump lost the presidential election.

THE PEOPLE WHO WRITE zombie-apocalypse screenplays clearly missed out. In all the dozens of movies and TV shows about pandemic-fueled end-of-the-world scenarios, none of them managed to imagine whole subpopulations of characters who believed the zombie disease was actually a "Deep State" hoax, a pretense for government enslavement, and rushed out into the streets to join the infected zombies and attack efforts to combat the spread of the virus.

On March 13, 2020, Donald Trump officially designated the pandemic a national emergency, two days after the World Health Organization declared a global pandemic. But he had been strangely in denial about it in the weeks beforehand: "This is a flu. This is like a flu," he told reporters in late February. "It's going to disappear. One day, it's like a miracle, it will disappear," he said a little later. "You have to be calm. It'll go away."[28] On the day of the WHO's announcement, he gave a televised speech where he told the nation: "It goes away . . . It's going away. We want it to go away with very, very few deaths." He also claimed that for "the vast majority of Americans, the risk is very, very low."[29]

The first weeks and months of the pandemic were eerily apocalyptic. Entire urban downtowns closed. Streets became deserted as people huddled inside their homes and apartments. Schools shut their doors. Store shelves cleared out of basic supplies like toilet paper, and sterilizing hand cleaner became nearly impossible to find. The skies cleared out, like they did after the 9/11 terrorist attacks in 2001, with the same unsettling silence in urban airspace. Restaurants and movie houses and storefronts closed shop.

Sports leagues, including Major League Baseball, suspended all activities. The world fell disquietingly quiet.

As states began imposing strict restrictions on public gatherings, as well as requiring people to remain indoors with some exceptions, and as students around the nation suddenly found themselves taking their classes on Zoom, and workers around the globe began replacing their real-world workplaces with digital ones, the mass of ordinary people found themselves spending inordinate amounts of time online. In the context of the surreal reality of everyday life, it was a perfect environment for the spread of far-right conspiracism that had riddled much of the online world over the previous decade and longer.

Trump's reluctance to admit the magnitude of the pandemic—driven in large part by his fears that it could damage the nation's economy, and that public alarm might depress the stock markets—played a central role in this. Even after announcing the national emergency, he continued to play down the pandemic's severity and its effects on the national psyche.

When a reporter asked him: "What do you say to Americans who are watching you right now who are scared?" Trump answered angrily: "I say that you're a terrible reporter, that's what I say. I think it's a very nasty question, and I think it's a very bad signal that you're putting out to the American people."[30]

He kept insisting: "Stay calm, it will go away. You know it—you know it is going away, and it will go away, and we're going to have a great victory."[31] He also began suggesting dubious cures and treatments, claiming he was taking hydroxychloroquine because he believed it was an effective preventative.[32]

Trump's army of conspiracist followers promptly fell in line. Alex Jones started out mingling disinformation about the disease with pitches to his audience to buy his line of "herbal" tinctures and toothpaste, which he claimed could prevent and even cure the disease (Google banned the Infowars app from its services in response). He claimed on his program that the COVID-19 virus was a specially designed bioweapon produced by the Chinese government with the intention of bringing Trump down.[33]

Republicans seeking his approval and endorsement quickly joined the conspiracy chorus. Joanne Wright, a Trumpist candidate for a California congressional seat, tweeted out a conspiracy theory claiming that Microsoft cofounder Bill Gates was part of the "globalist" plot: "The Corona virus is a man made virus created in a Wuhan laboratory. Ask @BillGates who financed it." She added: "Doesn't @BillGates finance research at the Wuhan lab where the Corona virus was being created? Isn't @georgesoros a good friend of Gates?"[34]

This particular idea soon became a stock item on the American right's conspiracist shelf to explain away Trump's malfeasance in his handling of the pandemic, both before and after the outbreak. Like all core conspiracy theories, it soon produced a thousand theoretical offspring.

None of them, however, became as hyperactive or as unhinged in their response to the pandemic as the QAnon conspiracy cult. The surreality and end-of-the-world sense of the early months of the national emergency were a natural operating environment for a movement that claimed the world was being run and manipulated by a "globalist" cabal (comprised of people like Soros, a longtime bogeyman of the far right who just happens to be Jewish) that secretly operates a worldwide pedophilia ring and human trafficking operation that drains terrified children of their blood in order to harvest their life-lengthening adrenochrome—and that Trump was secretly preparing to arrest them all.[35]

Once QAnon dove into the COVID conspiracies, the unreality of their alternative universe expanded exponentially—and so did the reach of the theories and the deliberate disinformation they manifested. The twin viruses—one physical, one epistemological—developed a symbiotic relationship: The COVID-19 pandemic fueled the conspiracism, and the conspiracy theories helped magnify the lethal reach of the virus. It was catastrophic: Two years later, over a million Americans, and over six million people around the world, had died from the disease, and countless others were rendered indefinitely impaired.

The unholy marriage of a real and still-mysterious viral pandemic and the conspiracist resistance to health measures intended to combat it—replete with the usual scapegoating and demonization of leading figures speaking out on behalf of those measures, as Dr. Anthony Fauci and others discovered—produced bizarre scenes that could have come from horror films about the apocalypse.

Take the locomotive engineer in Los Angeles who, in late March 2020, intentionally derailed a train near the docking site of the US Naval Ship *Mercy*—which had been a major focus of the American response to the pandemic on the West Coast—in an attempt to damage the ship. The train engine smashed through concrete barriers at the track's end, through a chain-link fence, through a couple of empty lots, and then halted about eight hundred yards away from the ship.

As he was being arrested, the man who drove the engine—identified as Eduardo Moreno, forty-four, of San Pedro—told police: "You only get this chance once. The whole world is watching . . . I had to. People don't know what's going on here. Now they will."[36]

The Department of Justice released a statement saying Moreno believed the *Mercy* "had an alternate purpose related to COVID-19 or a government takeover." The conspiracy theory at work was one invented by QAnon activists—namely, that the Mercy was actually planning to take its shipful of COVID-19 victims to Guantanamo Bay in Cuba. Other QAnon theorists had begun claiming, like Jones, that the pandemic was a Chinese bioweapon.

Liz Crokin, a popular QAnon-loving pro-Trump conspiracy theorist, had been in the forefront of the theories about the *Mercy*. She posted a video on March 26—five days before the train attack—viewed over 7,200 times (though eventually deleted), featuring footage from the interior of the Mercy, speculating that the ship "could be used to treat rescued trafficking victims especially since they're only taking non-COVID-19 patients," as she wrote on Facebook.[37]

Those weren't the only "contrarian" right-wing conspiracy theorists spouting coronavirus-related nonsense, however. Far more common were claims that the pandemic was being "blown out of proportion" by the media, part of an attempt to impose "government control" over the American populace, often accompanied by outright resistance to social distancing measures.

James O'Keefe's scurrilous Project Veritas, a right-wing smear operation, led that particular parade. A video on its website featured O'Keefe conversing in a parking lot (through closed windows) with a worker at a Glen Island Park, New York, coronavirus site telling him the media had overblown the pandemic: "It's the flu! . . . I'm in the tents with them!"

Other COVID-19 conspiracy theorists took to recording videos of empty parking lots at New York–area hospitals, promoting a social media hashtag to connect the reports, #FilmYourHospital. It appeared heavily on Crokin's social media accounts.

On Facebook, Crokin posted videos in which she pulled into hospital lots and found them empty. In one posted March 29 from Scripps Hospital in San Diego, she worked hard to creep out her audience: "It is fucking creepy. It is a ghost town here. It is so weird, you guys. There's no one even walking around."

The theories received airtime on Fox News as well. Fox contributor Jason Chaffetz, a former Utah congressman, livened up a panel discussion on March 29 by remarking: "I would love to see statistics, for instance, on how full our hospitals really are. I mean, I see these passionate—you know, these people coming out of caring for these people, and it's hard to watch and I believe them from their heart—but I would love to know what those real numbers are."[38]

Other Fox News figures offered similar thoughts. Todd Starnes, a regular on Sean Hannity's show, tweeted a photo showing an empty Brooklyn hospital's parking lot: "This is the 'war zone' outside the hospital in my Brooklyn neighborhood," he commented.

After the attack on the *Mercy*, Crokin dismissed the locomotive engineer in a Facebook post: "The Deep State is activating their MKULTRA sleepers."

CONSPIRACY THEORISTS QUICKLY DEMONSTRATED their eagerness to parlay the novel coronavirus pandemic into various kinds of moneymaking scams. And as is always the case, the unhinged behavior they inspired began posing a threat to public safety, and not merely because it encouraged a defiance of health measures that helped spread COVID-19.

One form of dangerously violent behavior that erupted globally was spurred by a particularly goofy theory: namely, that incoming 5G cell phone technology was actually the source of COVID-19, and was causing its spread wherever it was being installed. In both the United Kingdom and in Nigeria, people who believed these claims began setting 5G towers ablaze.[39]

The #5GCoronavirus hashtag's spread on social media—particularly among the conspiracy-prone Infowars and QAnon vectors of the internet— reflected how quickly the claims gained credence, even without a scintilla of evidence (as is nearly always the case). And the ease of its spread manifested a predisposition among conspiracists to claim quasi-magical properties— often of a toxic or sinister nature—for ordinary technology, including high-power lines and cell phone radiation.

The theories originated with a single erroneous story in the regional edition of an obscure Belgian newspaper, *Het Laatste Nieuws*. The story, an interview with a physician named Kris Van Kerckhoven, focused on his view that 5G technology was bad for human health, and mentioned his view that it might be connected to the coronavirus, because a number of 5G towers had been constructed in Wuhan, the Chinese province where the virus is believed to have originated.

Van Kerckhoven added a caveat—"I have not done a fact check," he said—and the story was removed from the paper's website within hours. But by then, anti-5G activists in Europe had already picked up the story and run with the theory.

In short order, it spread throughout the conspiracy-theory world like wildfire. Celebrities such as actor Woody Harrelson and the singer M.I.A. picked it up and tweeted out their views supporting the theory.[40] Tabloid and other sensationalist media outlets regurgitated the claims. On a UK radio station, Uckfield FM, an interview with a woman identified as a "registered nurse" (it later emerged that her credentials were in "alternative" medicine) spread the theory further:

What we're seeing with these cases in Wuhan and we've all seen it on social media is these people suddenly just fall over and they have a dry cough. I have never seen a patient be walking along doing their own thing and suddenly fall over because they've got pneumonia, it just doesn't happen. However, it does happen with 5G . . .

What 5G actually does, it absorbs oxygen and that's really important to know. So, on your oxygen molecules, the little electrons, with 5G they start to, like, oscillate, so this 5G is absorbing the oxygen and then your hemoglobin can't take up the oxygen. So how long do you think it's going to take the human body to fall over because it suddenly cannot take up oxygen into the cells? Every cell in the body needs oxygen. It's not going to take very long, it's probably not even going to take a minute. It's going to take seconds.[41]

Uckfield FM was found in violation of national broadcasting rules by regulatory agency Ofcom for the interview.

Nonetheless, social media was soon filled with posts promoting the theory. Some displayed maps showing the similarity between 5G installation activity and the spread of the virus. Others featured videos shot by people who were finding dead animals—mostly birds—on the ground in the vicinity of 5G towers. One woman's video noted a new 5G tower going up in her neighborhood, leading her to pronounce: "Now we're fucking going to die."

Many began offering their own theories. "5g spins the oxygen molecules that then spin the electrons and this makes the hemoglobin unable to uptake the oxygen and get it to the rest of your body," tweeted one conspiracist, who included a QAnon hashtag with his post.

It began creeping into mainstream media. The cohost of a popular UK morning show, Eamonn Holmes, agreed with a guest who debunked the claims, but added the caveat that "what I don't accept is mainstream media immediately slapping that down as not true when they don't know it's not true. No one should attack or damage or do anything like that, but it's very easy to say it is not true because it suits the state narrative."[42]

Notorious conspiracy theorist David Icke—who also promotes the belief that the world is secretly run by alien lizards who disguise themselves as elite humans—jumped all over the claims and made them the centerpiece of his website. Even more appalling, a UK television channel, London Live, ran a lengthy interview in which Icke expounded on the claims, telling viewers that "5G poisons the cells."[43]

He also claimed that the nefarious intent of 5G was proven by the fact that work on tower construction was continuing even during the pandemic lockdown. Icke concluded: "If you look at the situation and if 5G continues and reaches where they want to take it, human life as we know it, it's over."

Then videos began appearing on social media featuring would-be citizen "investigators" harassing utility contractors performing installation work. One Facebook video showed a woman interrogating contractors installing 5G fiber-optic cable under a city street, suggesting they were part of a plot to kill off the British population.

"Do you realize what you're doing, you're laying 5G?" she says. "So do you know that kills people? You know when they turn this on, it's going to kill everyone. That's why they're building the hospitals." She also mentions that "they're building 25,000 concentration camps of death."

Broadband installation workers were threatened.[44] The incidents affected the ability of tech firms to maintain the networks providing critical connectivity both to emergency services and hospitals as well as the public that was then working at home, the industry lobby group Mobile UK noted.

All this was soon accompanied by arson attacks on 5G towers throughout the UK—over forty such attacks. People recorded themselves firing rockets at the towers. Others posted videos of towers going up in flames with approving comments, such as: "The resistance is just beginning," and, "5G is the real silent killer, not the 'Corona Virus'!!!" One tweet noted: "They're camouflaging 5G killtennas as trees now, but something tells me that plastic fake branches might be highly flammable."[45]

On Facebook, a group formed to organize arson attacks against the towers. After initially ruling that the group did not violate their terms of service, Facebook eventually blocked them.

The attacks spread to other nations as well. In the Netherlands, nine 5G tower arsons were reported.[46] In Nigeria—a nation that had no 5G towers yet—angry followers of a popular pastor, Chris Oyakhilome, opposed the construction of new towers because of their supposed connection to COVID-19, though he later recanted this charge. Nonetheless, Nigerian activists recorded themselves burning a cellular phone tower, and vowing to continue.[47]

In some instances, the harm was direct. A hospital in Birmingham in the UK lost all connectivity to the internet when a nearby 5G tower was torched, which meant that dying patients whose only contact with their families was through video platforms were disconnected.[48]

"It's heart-rending enough that families cannot be there at the bedside of loved ones who are critically ill," said Nick Jeffery, CEO of Vodafone UK, whose mast was the one destroyed. "It's even more upsetting that even the small solace of a phone or video call may now be denied them because of the selfish actions of a few deluded conspiracy theorists."

These theories were in many ways a product of a conspiracy-theory industry long wedded to bizarre, near-magical claims about technology and
its effects on humans. Even before the coronavirus, there were numerous
claims being made about 5G's supposed ill effects, all of which echoed previous claims about other cell phone technologies, as well as computers, mi-
crowaves, televisions, and high-power transmission lines.

And, naturally, the claims were not only utterly groundless as a scientific
matter, the scenarios the conspiracists proposed were actually physically
impossible, including the suggestions that they made the human immune
system uniquely vulnerable to the virus.

Several observers noted that the spread of the conspiracy theories bore
the appearance of a deliberate disinformation campaign aimed at harming
Chinese industrial interests, and that among the major vectors for the theories were Russian propaganda organs, notably the US-based RT America
operation.[49] In 2019, *The New York Times* published an investigation revealing how RT was at the forefront of promoting false anti-5G information.[50]
Additionally, a European Union report examined how Russian outlets specialized in spreading misinformation about COVID-19: "Among COVID-
19-related content published by RT and Sputnik, articles covering conspiracy
narratives such as that 'the virus was man-made' or intentionally spread,
typically received more social engagement than other stories," it reported.[51]

"The coronavirus has created the perfect environment for this message
to spread," Josh Smith, senior researcher at Demos, a think tank, told *Wired*.
"Like many conspiracy theories, the idea that 5G is to blame for the uncertain, frightening situation we find ourselves in is a comfort. It provides an
explanation, and a scapegoat, for the suffering caused by this pandemic; as
well as—cruelly—suggesting a way we might stop it: take down the masts
and the virus will go away."[52]

Only a handful of 5G towers were targeted in the United States. There,
the conspiracist discourse tended to focus on health-care facilities—as
did the consequent violence. One popular far-right theory that made the

rounds—spread, once again, by a viral video, this time on Instagram—was that hospitals were deliberately infecting people with the novel coronavirus upon their arrivals, which was why so many then ended up dying there.

In the video, a woman claiming to be a nurse practitioner says she got her information from a "nurse friend" who was working "on the front lines" of the pandemic in New York.

"In New York City right now, in some of the hospitals, this is what is going on. People are sick, but they don't have to stay sick. They are killing them; they are not helping them. She used the word 'murder'—coming from a nurse who went to New York City expecting to help. Patients are left to rot and die—her words. She has never seen so much neglect. No one cares. They are cold and they don't care anymore. It's the blind leading the blind."[53]

There was, of course, not a shred of truth to this smear. Unsurprisingly, as with the Mercy conspiracy theories, enough people came to believe this nonsense that some of the more unstable personalities began to act on them.

In Michigan, a seventy-year-old man named Jesse McFadden—reputed to be a member of the Michigan Militia—attempted to steal a Coast Guard helicopter May 17 in the hope that he could fly it to a local hospital and use its guns to attack the place, claiming he wanted to "free" victims of the novel coronavirus from their quarantines. He didn't make it far, and was arrested and charged.[54]

The incident at the Coast Guard station in Essexville began when a man later identified as McFadden called an Arenac County dispatcher and reported that he planned to steal a helicopter so that he could shoot up a local hospital. He said he "wanted to disrupt the power to the hospital, unlock the doors, and release patients under the COVID-19 quarantine," according to the criminal complaint.[55]

After he hung up, the dispatcher alerted Arenac County deputies and provided information about McFadden's previous criminal history. In the meantime, McFadden himself drove to the Coast Guard station in Essexville in a pickup truck, pulled up to the gate, and began punching buttons on the security keypad in an attempt to get the gate to open. He then called the command communications center via the phone line at the gate and demanded they open it, but the personnel there declined even as McFadden threatened to ram the gate with his truck before he drove off.

A Michigan state trooper found McFadden's truck about forty minutes later at an Essexville gas station while he was inside. The officer confronted McFadden when he came out. In the passenger seat of McFadden's pickup was a shotgun loaded with five shells. When the officer attempted to confiscate it, a struggle ensued in which McFadden hit the trooper, but he eventually was subdued with a Taser and taken into custody. (Some charges were dropped against McFadden; he was placed on probation and asked to address his mental health problems.)

———————

ALSO IN MICHIGAN, THE anti-COVID-measure protests eventually turned into a kind of dry run for the January 6 insurrection.

In mid-April 2020, a huge phalanx of cars, reportedly numbering in the thousands, flooded the streets of downtown Lansing, driven by people—mostly conservative Republicans, but featuring a healthy contingent of gun-wielding far-right extremists—protesting Gov. Gretchen Whitmer's lockdown orders for the Great Lakes state.[56]

Called Operation Gridlock, the protest—organized primarily by the Michigan Conservative Coalition, a group with connections both to far-right extremists and to Education Secretary Betsy DeVos—successfully shut down all traffic in and around Lansing. That included traffic to and from Sparrow Hospital, the city's main coronavirus treatment center, as well as in and out of the capitol building, whose entrance at one point was blocked by a truck bearing a large sign for the Michigan Proud Boys.

Most of the vehicles were pickup trucks, many of them adorned with signs and flags. Ordinary American flags, yellow "Don't Tread On Me" Gadsden flags, and deep-blue Trump flags dominated the scene. A couple of Confederate flags—including one modified to feature an AR-15 silhouette—were also in the crowd. The Michigan Militia also was present.

The majority of protesters remained in their cars. However, about 150 of them parked and got out to carry protest signs, along with guns, up the steps of the state capitol building. According to some reports, those protesters generally maintained social distancing rules, but not all of them. At least one group of protesters that gathered on the steps for a video was clustered fairly closely.

"I think every single person here is probably going to get coronavirus, we're all within six feet of each other," protester Nick Somber told WILX-FM.

Multiple photos posted on social media showed an ambulance stuck in the middle of the gridlocked traffic around the hospital. Another photo showed a pickup with a large "Michigan Proud Boys" banner blocking the entrance. Yet another photo showed a doctor out in the middle of the stopped traffic, pleading with drivers to clear a path for the ambulance.

Two weeks later, hundreds of camo-clad, gun-toting militia Patriots from around the state descended on the state capitol and occupied it for several hours, brandishing their weapons and threateningly demanding an end to Gov. Gretchen Whitmer's lockdown orders. The terrorism worked: with Trump's encouragement, the Republican-controlled Michigan House chose not to extend the lockdown for another twenty-eight days, as Whitmer had requested.[57]

It happened in Idaho, too. In late August, longtime Patriot movement leader Ammon Bundy led a mob of armed Patriots and anti-restriction activists into the statehouse in Boise to force the state legislature to accede to their demands to repeal the COVID restrictions. It was a scene that, in retrospect, also clearly foreshadowed the siege of the US Capitol a little over four months later.

Monday, August 24, marked the opening day of the special legislative session called by Gov. Brad Little to deal with complications created by the pandemic—mainly civil liability issues and concerns raised by county clerks about absentee ballots and a lack of polling workers. However, those were picayune affairs compared to the agenda of the protesters.[58]

After gathering on the capitol steps, the mob led by Bundy broke into the chambers of the statehouse, shoving their way past state troopers, pounding on doors, shouting and breaking doors and windows along the way, and then invading committee hearing rooms. Their chief demand: rescind Little's stay-home order and business closures.

Bundy led the crowd of entirely maskless protesters at the statehouse steps, who began chanting "Let us in!" after access to the gallery seating in both senate and house chambers was restricted to half-capacity and seats quickly filled up. First they shoved their way past Idaho State Police troopers standing guard, then they banged on doors and windows demanding entry past the gallery doors on the fourth floor. One of the men, according to the Associated Press, was carrying an assault-style rifle.

Rather than enforce the rules and eject the protesters, Republican house speaker Scott Bedke chose to allow the gallery to fully open. Lawmakers on the floor pleaded with the protesters to stop the chants and be respectful. Eventually, the crowd quieted down after all the seats had filled to capacity.

"I want to always try to avoid violence," Bedke told the Associated Press later. "My initial reaction of course was to clear the fourth floor. But we had room for at least some more."

That was hardly the end of it. The protesters eventually made their way into committee rooms, where they similarly ignored distancing rules and filled the rooms to capacity. They defaced signs designating empty seats, and mocked a Democratic legislator who chose to leave the meeting because of the violations.

No citations were issued by Idaho State Police, nor were any arrest warrants issued for the property destruction and vandalism. Little tweeted out his thanks to the state patrol, Boise Police, and capitol security forces afterward "for their efforts in preserving a safe and productive special legislative session."

Bundy boasted on Facebook afterward: "They would not let us in to attend the legislative session. So we did what all people must do. We pushed our way in!"

ALL THE TRUMP-LOVING, LIBERAL-HATING rhetoric and the yellow "Don't Tread on Me" flags and the signs denouncing "tyranny" and the belligerent behavior accompanying the anti-government protests that began hitting state capitals around the nation had an all-too-familiar look to them: the look of aggressive authoritarianism, wearing the guise of "freedom."

Trump himself openly encouraged the defiance, beginning with tweets encouraging people to follow the example of the Michigan protesters: "LIBERATE VIRGINIA, and save your great 2nd Amendment. It is under siege!"[59]

This tweet was an undisguised wink and nudge in the direction of the same far-right protesters who descended on Richmond in January to protest impending gun-control legislation, and who continued to whip up "constitutionalist" pro-gun hysteria in rural Virginia counties. Despite those protests, much of the legislation passed and was signed into law in April by Gov. Ralph Northam.

"The president has linked this stay-at-home issue to the Second Amendment," remarked former FBI assistant director Frank Figliuzzi on MSNBC, explaining that the nation had entered an extremely dangerous phase, primarily because Trump deliberately encouraged this aggression. "Remember that ['Liberate Virginia'] tweet? . . . That's going to motivate the crazies amongst us to do some very ugly things. And law enforcement's gotta hunker down for that."[60]

Washington governor Jay Inslee, a Democrat, also called out the behavior. "The president is fomenting domestic rebellion and spreading lies even while his own administration says the virus is real and is deadly, and that we have a long way to go before restrictions can be lifted," Inslee said.

"To have an American president to encourage people to violate the law, I can't remember any time in my time in America we have seen such a thing. It is dangerous, because it could inspire people to ignore things that could save their lives," Inslee told ABC's George Stephanopoulos later.

The people showing up at the COVID protests were many of the same people who had shown up for street brawls with anti-fascists and black bloc in places like Charlottesville, Berkeley, Portland, and Seattle. They all reveled in paranoid conspiracy theories, all were peculiarly immune to logic, facts, or reason, all of them eager consumers of far-right propaganda.

In mid-April, hundreds turned out in Olympia, Washington, to protest Inslee's stay-at-home directives. A typical tweet from a protester used all the classic Patriot movement tropes, including an absurd inflation of the crowd's size: "Fuck the tyrannical government action! Power hungry democrats in office have put us under a quasi martial law! So today we say fuck you to Inslee's stay at home order and social distancing! Three thousand strong today!"[61]

One of the speakers—a state legislator, Rep. Robert Sutherland of Granite Falls—made explicitly violent threats. "We're starting a rebellion in Washington, we're not listening to this governor, we're taking our state back," Sutherland told the crowd, with a pistol tucked into his pants.

"When we go fishing, they're going to send their guys with guns, and they're going to write us tickets," added Sutherland. "Governor, you send men with guns after us when we go fishing, we'll see what a revolution looks like."

A similar protest in Lancaster, Pennsylvania, had a similar tenor, with Republican state senator Doug Mastriano providing the verbal fireworks. "It heartens me to see my brothers and sisters across the state here, coming together here to fight this tyranny, this overreach," said Mastriano. "Never before in the history of this commonwealth has a governor exercised so much power . . . It's time to roll that back."[62]

In Texas, Alex Jones joined the crowd and shook hands with the participants. "Don't let them tell you, like the Nazis did, that you are not essential," Jones told protesters. "Whether you are old, whether you are young, whether you are Black, whether you are white, you are essential."[63]

Following Michigan's large protest, organizers elsewhere scrambled to create similar events around the country. But the day after a protest in Lexington, Kentucky, Governor Andy Beshear announced that the state had just experienced its largest single-day spike in COVID-19 infections.[64]

However, Trump denied that he was whipping up potentially violent responses to efforts by state governors to bring the pandemic under control.[65]

"Some governors have gone too far," Trump said during a press briefing. He defended the protesters, claiming they appeared to be adhering to social distancing measures.

"No, I am not," he responded to a question about whether he was inciting violence. "I've never seen so many American flags. These people love our country. They want to get back to work."

He added: "It was a very orderly group of people . . . They've got cabin fever. They want their lives back." Any similarity to his remarks defending the Charlottesville protesters in 2017 as "very fine people" was probably intentional.

As for whether he had any concern about the possibility that these rabid supporters might die as a result of expanding their exposure to COVID-19 at these rallies, Trump also gave a clear answer when NBC's Yamiche Alcindor asked him about one of his admirers whose entire family caught the virus after following his advice.

"A lot of people love Trump, right?" he said. "A lot of people love me. You see them all the time. I guess I'm here for a reason."[66]

IF CONSPIRACIST AUTHORITARIAN CULTS like QAnon were based on anything remotely resembling a rational or evidence-based worldview, the events around Election Day 2020 would have destroyed it utterly. After all, not only was the intrepid, all-controlling/all-seeing hero of their meta-theory—Donald Trump, who Q had predicted would be reelected in a landslide—roundly defeated at the polls, but the anonymous persona at the center of the cult had completely and permanently dropped from sight.[67]

Some believers, at least briefly, had their worldview rattled: "My faith is shaken" became a common refrain on Q message boards.

"We're losing," one tweeted. "Not sure I trust the plan anymore. Not sure there even is a plan."

Certainly, the notion of a legitimate defeat at the polls was inconceivable. Predictably, many Q believers chose to believe Trump's claims that he would prove he won the election in the courts, and that the media was lying. After all, he had already laid the groundwork for this narrative in the months before the election.[68]

"Biden will NEVER be president," wrote one QAnon adherent.

"Trump knows what he is doing," a QAnon forum participant assured his fellows. "He is letting the Dems, technocrats and media publicly hang themselves."

The silence from the anonymous figure known as Q, who only posted their cryptic messages at the anything-goes message board 8kun, after the election unsettled many followers.[69] Their penultimate post, early in the morning of Election Day, featured a massive American flag with a quote from Abraham Lincoln, and a vow: "together we win." Their final "drop" was on December 8: a YouTube video of the '80s hair band Twisted Sister performing their hit "We're Not Gonna Take It." And that was it for Q, thousands of cryptic and allusive posts and multiple whiteboards of con-spiracist connections later.

Even though Q's silence was not atypical—they had gone silent for several weeks at a time previously—it nonetheless left some followers in a frantic state: "HOW CAN I SPEAK TO Q????" one wrote. "MY FAITH IS SHAKEN. I FOLLOWED THE PLAN. TRUMP LOST!!!!!!!!!!! WHAT NOW?????? WHERE IS THE PLAN???"[70]

"Have we all been conned?" another user asked on 8kun.

Those concerns, however, were quickly assuaged by other leading influencers within the cult. The QAnon account Praying Medic, which had more than four hundred thousand Twitter followers, soothingly explained that Trump's strategy was still in motion to the many supporters who "had to be talked off the ledge" in the past. Praying Medic tweeted: "He's going to stick the knife in and twist it. He has no plans to leave office. Ever."

"Some QAnon followers are bewildered, but most are still trusting the plan," Travis View said. "Honestly, QAnon is so Trump-centric that there's little hope of followers accepting defeat until Trump does. And even then it's not a guarantee."[71]

The evidence-free theme around which QAnon platforms coalesced was one built to survive well into a Biden administration and beyond: Namely, that Biden was attempting to illegally steal the election, doing so with the assistance of the "Deep State" and the "liberal media." It was an idea promoted on Twitter by Trump himself, by leading Republican politicians, and by multiple other prominent right-wing figures.

After Trump had settled on this narrative, the QAnon world focused on building up an accompanying rationale. One of the biggest QAnon accounts, under the moniker Joe M (aka @StormIsUponUs), posted his own theory about the meaning of it all:

> Think again of the constants:
>
> 1) Biden will never be president.
>
> 2) The Left are celebrating his victory.
>
> 3) We have a 2 month hard deadline.
>
> Now, extrapolate. This means turbulent and destabilizing times are imminent. It will require the kind of smoking gun that leaves no room for interpretation. It means habbenings like we haven't yet experienced. There is no other way, shit's about to get real.[72]

For many major QAnon figures, Inauguration Day—January 20, 2021—initially loomed as a bright red line for the movement.

"A lot of the influencers are really establishing that as the final deadline, this is something we haven't really seen before," Fredrick Brennan, the founder of 8kun, told *Vice*.

"They were wrong a lot before but were always able to fall back on the complexity of the plan," Brennan said. However, "they're really marrying themselves to no inauguration. Certainly after Biden is inaugurated the Q landscape will change dramatically."[73]

Some believers, however, were saying the results were just more evidence that Q was right all along, and that the evil globalist Democrats and the "Deep State" secretly control society at all levels. Not that this deterred them or persuaded them to rethink their life choices.

Rather, as *Vice*'s David Gilbert reported, "there are dozens of reports from family members of QAnon supporters showcasing how the election result has not diminished their beliefs, but has in fact reinforced them."

"We knew the left was going to do everything they could to delay this," wrote a major QAnon Instagram influencer. "Trump won & they're trying to rely on fraudulent mail in ballots. it's not going to work. Trump knew they were going to do this, too. He is prepared."

"PATRIOTS ARE IN CONTROL," reminded other major Instagram accounts, which also urged followers to "trust the plan [and enjoy] the show."

On Twitter there was a similar shift in sentiment: "Trust Trump. He knew this was coming. He said so for months," one supporter tweeted. "In the coming days the REAL Patriots will be identified," wrote another. "Fight and win or die fighting."

Rita Katz, the executive director of SITE Intelligence Group, which monitors online extremism, told *The Washington Post* that she expected the QAnon following would continue to grow and metastasize online.[74]

"It's a dangerous movement that truly believes that Biden and other Democrats are killing kids," Katz said. "And now, with Biden's projected victory, the QAnon movement believes with the same zealous certainty that the whole thing is a sham. And that's a major problem, because . . . these aren't a bunch of harmless keyboard warriors—they're adherents of a movement that has resulted in real-life violence."

———————

THE CONSPIRACISTS WHO COMPRISED much of Trump's support—especially those who believed his lies about widespread voter fraud—at first adamantly protested his defeat and sought to overturn the outcome at polling places around the country.[75]

Wherever vote tallies were being contested in America—in Michigan, Pennsylvania, Arizona, and Nevada particularly—Trump supporters, fueled by his exhortations on Twitter and elsewhere to "Stop the Count!" began organizing protests intended to disrupt the vote-counting process. None succeeded.

Their message varied depending on the state counting votes and Trump's relative position in the count. Some, as in Philadelphia, began demanding that vote counting be stopped since Trump led in the state in early tabulations. But in Arizona, where Trump was trailing, a bellicose crowd—ginned up on a baseless conspiracy theory claiming Democrats had conspired to erase Republican votes using Sharpies—descended on a Phoenix ballot-counting center to demand they "count all the votes."[76]

In Detroit, a crowd of protesters pounded on the windows inside the city's vote-counting center, demanding to be allowed into the vote-counting area, which was at its capacity of 570 vote challengers already inside the room. The protesters, who chanted in support of a Trump lawsuit demanding the counting be stopped due to transparency claims, eventually were rebuffed—as was Trump's lawsuit.[77]

In Philadelphia, protesters from both pro-Trump and pro-Biden camps gathered outside the city's convention center, where ballot-counting operations were centered. The pro-Trump protesters, who included several

Proud Boys, were organized by FreedomWorks For America, the right-wing "astroturf" group credited with cocreating the Tea Party phenomenon. "CALLING ALL PATRIOTS! We cannot let the radical Left steal this election!" the group posted on Facebook. In another post it urged protesters to turn out to "make sure Joe Biden does not steal the election."[78]

Over the next few weeks, these protests amounted to nothing. Trump's attempts to contest the election results through the courts, resulting in some sixty lawsuits, all were dismissed in short order. By early December, it had become clear that he had no legal leg to stand on—just throngs of true believers.

Those throngs were thrilled, then, when on December 18, 2020 Trump announced the protest of January 6 on Twitter. The tweet became a call to arms for his army of uncivil warriors, telling them when and where to come to prevent his removal from office as a result of losing what he falsely claimed was a fraudulent election.[79]

The tweet cited a report by his minion Peter Navarro (later debunked) in the *Washington Examiner* claiming there was enough fraud in key battleground states to swing the election. "Statistically impossible to have lost the 2020 Election," he claimed, and exhorted his readers: "Big protest in D.C. on January 6th. Be there, will be wild!"

Many Trump supporters promptly leaped into action, preparing to come to Washington to prevent their "Glorious Leader" from being swept from office. And they not only heard Trump's call, they responded just as he had hoped they would—by putting Congress under physical siege and attempting an insurrection.[80]

Extremists began setting up encrypted communications channels, acquiring protective gear, and preparing heavily armed "quick reaction forces." And they began whipping up followers and cohorts with a drumbeat of bellicose, frequently violent language, their private chats dominated by an apocalypytic, end-of-the-world mood.

Some two dozen GOP officials and organizations in at least twelve states used Facebook as a platform to organize bus trips to the rally. The posts advertising the buses were unsparing in the use of incendiary rhetoric, too.

"This is a call to ALL patriots from Donald J Trump for a BIG protest in Washington DC! TAKE AMERICA BACK! BE THERE, WILL BE WILD!" wrote the New Hanover County GOP of North Carolina in a Facebook post advertising bus seats.

Trump himself kept tweeting. December 27: "See you in Washington, DC, on January 6th. Don't miss it. Information to follow."

December 30: "JANUARY SIXTH, SEE YOU IN DC!"[81]

When the day arrived, the thousands of QAnon believers drawn to D.C. were primed for action. Trump's tweet inspired a broad swath of conspiracists unconnected to the Oath Keepers or Proud Boys, usually involving only a handful of actors. In one such case, a trio of extremist Trump supporters from California traveled to Washington, in their own words, to "violently remove traitors" and "replace them with able bodied Patriots." [82]

The trio, Los Angelenos all—Gina Bisignano, Daniel Rodriguez, and Edward Badalian—knew one another online before January 6, met up at the Stop the Steal rally before the siege, and then traveled together to the Capitol, split apart somewhat while participating in the exterior attack, and then joined back up once inside the building. From there, the three of them ransacked at least one congressional office.

Bisignano owned a beauty salon in Beverly Hills. She took part in the Capitol siege wearing a Louis Vuitton sweater. (Her name was redacted from the indictment and remains under court seal because she has entered into a cooperation agreement with prosecutors, but it has been confirmed by multiple journalists.)[83] Both Rodriguez and Badalian lived in suburban Los Angeles, in the San Fernando Valley. Rodriguez's arrest in March 2021 primarily arose from his assaults on police officers at barricades, most notoriously his electroshock-device attack on Michael Fanone, the Capitol police officer. (Rodriguez has subsequently attempted to claim that his confession to the FBI upon his arrest was obtained under duress.)

Bisignano had already achieved viral notoriety even before the insurrection after a video released in December 2020 showed her spewing homophobic epithets and COVID denialism.[84] Her business subsequently experienced an appropriately harsh backlash on social media.[85]

The three of them apparently met on a Telegram channel called "Patriots 45 MAGA Gang," where they shared Trump-related conspiracy theories and agreed that action needed to be taken to prevent Trump from being unseated as president.[86]

"We gotta go handle this shit in DC so the crooked politicians don't have an army of thugs threatening violence to back their malevolent cabal ways," wrote Badalian in one thread.

"We are taking this shit back," Badalian wrote in another thread. "Yeah, absolutely, yes," Rodriguez replied.

In other conversations, Rodriguez told his cohorts that he would "assassinate Joe Biden" if he got the chance and "would rather die than live under a Biden administration." On December 29, Rodriguez posted: "Congress can hang. I'll do it. Please let us get these people dear God."

The trio gathered weapons and gear—a stun gun, pepper spray, gas masks, and walkie-talkies—in the weeks before January 6. Badalian and Rodriguez traveled together from California, and "joined a caravan" in Kentucky on January 5 headed to the Stop the Steal event, setting up communications with a radio app on cell phones.

When they arrived in Washington, Rodriguez texted his cohorts on Telegram: "There will be blood. Welcome to the revolution."

All three, the evidence shows, played leading roles in assaulting police at the Capitol barricades, as well as in assisting the mob's entry into the building through broken windows.

Curiously, two days after the Capitol siege, two of them went on the *Infowars* program *War Room with Owen Shroyer* and claimed that "Antifa" was responsible for heightening the violence and breaking windows.[87]

Badalian—using the nom de plume "Turbo"—and Bisignano, who just went by "Gina," both used Bisignano's video to show that members of the crowd had claimed that rioters wearing Trump gear and breaking windows were actually "Antifa" activists in disguise, and they had tried to prevent them from attacking the Capitol.

During the interview, Bisignano accidentally blew Badalian's cover by referring to him as "Ed." (Badalian and Rodriguez then went to Bisignano's home two days later, helped her destroy evidence, and warned her not to use their real names again.) That clue apparently helped investigators identify him eventually.

Badalian told Shroyer that the people smashing windows in the Capitol made him angry because "that's like a symbol of America to me." He thought their ranks had been "infiltrated." When he grabbed the man, others asked him why he had, and he said he told them: "We're not here to smash the building! We're not here to destroy the property! We're here for the traitors!"

He then claimed that it became "a wild situation after Antifa escalated—with the cops."

Bisignano claimed that she began taking footage from her perch on the same arched window then "so that we would have proof that they were breaking windows and being violent." She said "it was obvious they were not Trump supporters even though it said Trump on his helmet."

"To me, it was like, 'We don't want this. We don't want violence,'" Bisignano told Shroyer. "And they were like, 'No, we gotta break the window.' And I said, 'No, this is not a good look for us.'"

She also claimed she had urged everyone to go home. "I even said, 'Guys, we gotta go, Trump's said all Patriots need to go home.' And some of the people left, and some people are like, 'We don't believe it. We don't believe Trump really tweeted that.' I was just like, it's not worth risking your life. Violence isn't the answer. I was just begging them to stop."

The reality of the trio's vitriolic violence on January 6, however, was laid bare in their respective indictments. Bisignano in particular played a leading role in whipping the mob into a frenzy, her mindset evident in texts she sent—one, from the Ellipse, urging another person to "roll in force" to the Capitol, while another sent from the Capitol steps exulted that "the battle has begun."

She and Rodriguez battled with police at entryways, during which Rodriguez hurled a flagpole and discharged a fire extinguisher at officers.[88]

Bisignano told the police: "Liberty or death, gentlemen!"

Once on the window ledge, Bisignano can be seen encouraging another insurrectionist bashing the window that had been previously hammered by the man Badalian had pulled away in the *Infowars* video. She yelled encouragement to other rioters: "Hold the line, gentlemen! Don't surrender! Fight for Trump!" "Push forward, Patriots! If you are gonna die, let it be on Capitol Hill!"

After the window was broken, she climbed through the opening and into the Capitol, followed by Rodriguez and Badalian.

Badalian's claim that Antifa was responsible for the January 6 violence is also belied by a text he had sent earlier in the day, as they were marching toward the Capitol: "We don't want to fight antifa lol we want to arrest traitors," he said.

Their supposed reverence for the Capitol is similarly belied by the actions they took once inside. The trio found themselves in a congressional office suite, so after Rodriguez announced they should look for "intel," he and Bisignano began rifling through bags and papers. Rodriguez eventually made off with an emergency escape hood he found in the office.

Bisignano, of course, presented a very different picture of their role that day to Shroyer. "We were clearly there for a peaceful march," she told him. "And a lot of the people that infiltrated that crowd obviously were not there for that."

ALEX JONES DID HIS best to scramble away from any consequences for his role in the attack on the Capitol. Not only had Jones helped whip the mob into a frenzy that day and was present on the west lawn, but a guest *Infowars* host earlier that week had actually encouraged listeners to attack the building: "We're going to only be saved by millions of Americans moving to Washington, occupying the entire area, if necessary storming right into the Capitol," the host, Matt Bracken, had told the *Infowars* audience on December 29.[89]

On his *Infowars* show that week, Jones claimed he tried to discourage people from going inside the building, but described any attempts at containing the crowd as "mission impossible." Instead, he shouted fruitlessly into his bullhorn.

He later told congressional investigators that most people in the crowd—including himself—believed that Trump was going to join them in some capacity at the Capitol after his speech at the Ellipse.[90]

"We learned there were a bunch of people inside the Capitol," Jones later said. "And that was so stupid and so dumb. I didn't support it that day and I don't support it now."

"We got the hell out of there once we couldn't stop it," Jones added, calling January 6 a "horrible historic fiasco" and saying he wished it had "never happened."

On January 15, Jones unleashed his ire on a QAnon believer who called into his show.[91] Jones kept interrupting the man—as he often does when bullying people on-air—and when the man asked him why, Jones exploded: "Because you're lying! Because you're full of shit! That's why! Because every goddamned thing to come out of you people's mouths hasn't come true! And it's always—'Oh there's energy,' and 'Oh, now we're done with Trump.' You said he was the messiah! You said he was invincible!" He ended the rant with his hand over his eyes. "Get out of here, Q. I can't talk to you anymore. Jesus Lord help me."

In addition to his culpability for January 6, Jones already was looking down the barrel of a completely different financial and legal disaster—namely, the lawsuits filed by the parents of the murdered Sandy Hook Elementary students who were harassed by Jones's rabid followers afterward, when he had tried to claim that the 2012 mass shooting in Newtown, Connecticut, was a "false flag" hoax perpetrated by globalists.[92]

Jones had been attempting to derail the lawsuit in the courts, claiming that he was engaging in protected speech because he was addressing matters of public concern.

"The pursuit of so-called 'conspiracy theories' concerning controversial government activities has been a part and parcel of American political discourse since our Founding, and it is protected by the First Amendment," Jones's attorneys wrote. Their arguments failed in court, but each time, Jones kept appealing, all the way to the Texas Supreme Court. But on January 22, that court struck Jones's appeal and ruled that all the lawsuits could proceed.[93]

Jones has a long history of declaring any mass casualty event—from the 1995 Oklahoma City bombing to the 9/11 terrorist attacks to the 2017 Las Vegas massacre to the January 6 insurrection—"false flags" masterminded by "globalists" with the intention of taking Americans' freedoms away. He did so in the Sandy Hook case—the horrific December 14, 2012, massacre by a deranged lone gunman in Newtown that left twenty-six people dead, twenty of them young children—with particular zeal, claiming that the event was a "hoax," the victims were all "crisis actors" who did not really exist, and that the parents were all participants in a plot to take away Americans' gun rights.

The result was a flood of harassment directed at the grieving parents. One parent, Leonard Pozner, told reporters he had to go into hiding. "It turned into what seemed like Alex Jones had some sort of vendetta against me, because I was hurting his business. I was crippling his YouTube channel," he told PBS. Pozner said Jones kept repeating his and his son Noah's names, calling on his listeners to "investigate" Pozner.[94]

"Unimpeded conspiracy theories distort truth and erase history," Pozner told *The Washington Post*. "They dehumanize victims."

The lawsuits began arriving on Jones's doorstep in 2018, along with similar lawsuits brought against other "Sandy Hook hoaxers" with lesser reach than Jones's millions of followers. In all, nine families filed suits.

Jones attempted to engage in a delay game in the courts: refusing to turn over documents in discovery, failing to respond to court orders to do so, biding his time in hopes of stretching out the proceedings in a vain attempt to avoid the inevitable reckoning. The game finally came to a crashing halt in October 2021 when the judge overseeing the case, Maya Guerra Gamble of Texas's 459th District Court in Travis County, pulled the plug on Jones's obstruction tactics by declaring a default judgment in two of the central Sandy Hook lawsuits—meaning that the matter had been summarily decided and that Jones lost.[95]

A month later, another judge found Jones in default in another Sandy Hook lawsuit in Connecticut and ordered him to pay the families. A jury was called to settle the amounts he would owe in all three of the lawsuits. Finally, in August 2022, the Texas jury announced its finding that Jones owed the families $45.2 million in damages.[96]

That judgment, however, was dwarfed by the Connecticut jury, which found Jones owed the families $963 million in damages—more than four times his estimated worth. Jones claimed he was bankrupt and mocked the verdict: "This is hilarious," he said as the separate awards were listed. "Do these people actually think they're getting any money? . . . Ain't gonna be happening, ain't no money."[97]

Other Sandy Hook conspiracy theorists had already faced similar consequences in court. Pozner won an earlier lawsuit in Wisconsin against an author who published a book claiming that the massacre was a hoax, with the judge ordering $450,000 in damages.[98] Another "hoax" conspiracist, seventy-three-year-old Wolfgang Halbig of Lake County, Florida, was arrested in 2020 and charged with harassing the Pozners and other Sandy Hook families.[99]

One follower of Jones's *Infowars* program, fifty-seven-year-old Lucy Richards of Florida, was arrested and convicted in 2017 of threatening the Pozners. Richards left menacing voice mails and emails with Pozner, saying in one: "You gonna die . . . Death is coming to you real soon and there's nothing you can do about it." She received a five-month prison sentence.[100]

But while the Sandy Hook verdicts threatened to impoverish him, the shadow from January 6 loomed even larger for Jones. In August 2021, *Infowars*'s Owen Shroyer and Samuel Montoya were arrested and charged for their roles in the siege, having entered the building and participated in the mayhem.[101]

When Jones was subpoenaed by the House committee investigating the January 6 insurrection, he denounced the entire investigation as being McCarthy-like.[102]

"We talk about January 6, this is even worse than what Joseph McCarthy did. And I believe he went too far," Jones said. "This is the absolute declaration of war against the American people and against free speech. They don't even care in this committee that I was there at the Capitol trying to stop what happened?

"No, they want to basically put me on trial in the corporate media, showing selective information so that when people hear the name Alex Jones, they think we're talking about an insurrectionist criminal when I am the opposite."

THE QANON CONSPIRACY CULT kept spreading, like kudzu, to the nation's farthest reaches. And it kept mutating.

Sequim, Washington, is one of those classically quaint little seaside Pacific Northwest towns, located on the Strait of Juan de Fuca in Washington state's farthest northwestern corner: gorgeous scenery (near both the Dungeness Spit—native waters of the crab of the same name—and the Olympic Mountains), quirky (best known for both having low rainfall and a high retiree population), and a Native American name (pronounced "skwim"). In early 2021, it became known for something else: a town of seven thousand run by a QAnon-loving mayor who engineered a takeover with the help of a compliant city council.[103]

The mayor, a biker named Bill Armacost who runs a local hair salon, forced the resignation of Sequim city manager Charlie Bush in January through a series of closed-door executive sessions—apparently fueled by Armacost's ardent promotion of the QAnon conspiracy theories as well as his arch-conservative views that clashed with Bush's handling of the city during the COVID-19 pandemic.

At a city council meeting following Bush's ouster, a city resident named Josh—with the assault on the US Capitol evidently on his mind—ironically asked Armacost during a Zoom council session if he would kindly not join any new QAnon insurrections.

"At the very least, for the rest of this month, if you could promise not to commit any act of insurrection, that would be great," the man told the mayor. "Just as a citizen of Sequim, I don't like to be represented by terror-ists. So if we could promise to finish out this month without killing anyone, that would be great."[104]

Armacost was questioned about his QAnon beliefs from several audi-ence members. "Do you still stand behind your belief that QAnon is a truth movement?" asked Marsha Maguire, a frequent critic. He made no replies to any of these queries.

Sequim operates with a "weak mayor" system in which the day-to-day operations are run by a city manager who answers to the elected city coun-cil. The mayor is chosen from among council members, and in Sequim, the position has largely been ceremonial.

That tradition apparently ended when Armacost forced Bush's re-moval. Bush was widely well regarded both among city residents and his fellow local government officials in Clallam County, largely because the city has run smoothly on his seven-year watch, and more recently because he is believed to have been a highly effective administrator during the COVID-19 pandemic.

But he somehow got sideways with Armacost, and the mayor's ardent support of QAnon conspiracy theories played a leading role.

Armacost made a splash in late August when he began discussing QAnon theories on a regular city-sponsored radio show called *Coffee with the Mayor*.

"QAnon is a truth movement that encourages you to think for yourself," Armacost said. "If you remove Q from that equation, it's patriots from all over the world fighting for humanity, truth, freedom, and saving children and others from human trafficking."

The mayor then went on to urge listeners to check out a slick QAnon video on YouTube, and also urged them to check out both the videos and the (since-deleted) Twitter account of a prominent QAnon promoter named Joe M.

The episode created a local furor. "He believes that what he believes is the only truth, and he doesn't care that the majority of his citizens don't believe that," local resident Shenna Younger told *KING 5 TV*. "He doesn't represent us."[105]

Bush intervened, and he and Armacost issued a joint statement in which the mayor apologized for using a city-run radio show to platform his political views. Bush said Armacost had "commented on national politics that have nothing to do with the City of Sequim," adding that "any responses to questions reflecting the personal opinion of the mayor do not reflect policy positions of the Sequim City Council or the organization."

Armacost, who calls himself a "Warrior for Christ" on his Facebook page, is also an active biker who traveled to South Dakota during the pandemic in 2020 to attend the annual Sturgis Motorcycle Rally, a massive gathering that draws 500,000 and turned into a COVID-19 super-spreader event believed to have resulted in 260,000 nationwide infections afterward. When he returned, he immediately reopened his salon, ignoring recommendations for a two-week quarantine.

When Sequim residents began making it an issue, he responded with a letter to the editor of the local paper saying, "It is not required of me either by science, regulation, experience or custom," and dismissing critics as people "addicted" to fear:

> Love demands that I take reasonable personal precautions on behalf of my fellow citizens. In my shop, I have implemented common sense protocols for the protection of my customers and the community. Love also requires that I refuse to enable the addiction of others. The addict commands that others indulge his or her addiction in the name of caring or compassion. Love commands that I refuse the addict of the passion so craved.[106]

Bush also was at odds with Armacost over the placement of an opioid treatment center in downtown Sequim. A local hard-core conservative faction called Save Our Sequim, aligned with Armacost, were hysterical about plans for the medically assisted treatment (MAT) facility planned by the Jamestown S'Klallam Tribe, claiming it would "forever change the rural character of our town." Bush, however, did not oppose permits for the new facility, so Save Our Sequim demanded his resignation.

A gathering of about one hundred Sequim-area residents rallied in Bush's defense. Most of those protesting the forced resignation believed that the political engineering was similar to what they had seen from QAnon followers in the Capitol on January 6: a naked power grab.

"From everything I've read, he's done an exemplary job as city manager," resident Janine Bocciardi told the *Peninsula Daily News*.[107]

The rally organizers submitted a petition with 1,239 signatures urging the city council to retain Bush. Many thought Armacost's far-right political beliefs were fueling the purge. One sign read: "No QAnon Coup! Don't fire Bush!"

Armacost's embrace of QAnon dated back to at least 2019, when he began including the #WWG1WGA hashtag—a reference to the QAnon slogan "Where we go one, we go all"—on his Facebook page.

"He is QAnon completely," Maguire said. "He's not wavering, he's down the rabbit hole and all that."

The tide of support for Bush, however, fell on deaf ears: the council majority voted to accept Bush's severance package. Two of the five council members attempted to force a reconsideration, but Armacost and his two chief allies on the council outvoted them after yet another closed-door executive session.

———————

BACK WHEN IT WAS first gaining traction in the 1990s, the anti-vaccination movement—predicated on a hodgepodge of misinformation and conspiracy theories—was largely considered a far-left thing, attracting believers ranging from barter-fair hippies to New Age gurus and their followers to "holistic medicine" practitioners. And it largely remained that way . . . until 2020 and the arrival of the COVID-19 pandemic.[108]

Many anti-vaxxers were already engaged in protesting COVID-related public-health measures through the pandemic's first year. After the Food and Drug Administration approved the first major COVID vaccines for public use in December 2020, the connection metastasized and took on a life of its own.

Some began posting phony stories about people dying from the vaccine during tests.[109] Other conspiracy theorists tried to claim that the FDA hadn't actually approved the vaccines.[110]

One of the peculiar realities of conspiracism is that people who believe in conspiracy theories rarely ever believe just one; most conspiracy theories are interconnected by the nature of their afactual grounding, and often this forms a web of theories that lead to radicalization. This is why anti-vaxxers' conspiracies coalesced so seamlessly with far-right extremist movements in COVID denialism, and moreover why that commingling became a global phenomenon.

Indeed, the politics of the pandemic provided a new kind of breeding ground for the paranoid fantasies that comprise the denialists' conspiracy theories—one that openly intermingled old-fashioned anti-Semitism with New Age health-related conspiracies.[111]

"We're seeing something that we've probably never seen before in terms of how these ideologies work to feed off each other," extremism researcher Aoife Gallagher of the Institute for Strategic Dialogue said.

This kind of coalescence has always occurred to some extent, but the COVID-19 pandemic featured two conditions that shifted it onto a more intensive plane: 1) a high degree of official and media confusion and uncertainty about the nature of the disease and its spread, much of it engendered among highly placed sources; and 2) pandemic-response conditions that forced people to spend inordinate amounts of time online, where conspiracy theories spread like wildfire, and denialist organizing along with it, particularly on social media platforms like Facebook.

A prime example of this overlap was anti-vaxxer Piers Corbyn's appearance on a podcast with Nazi sympathizer Mark Collett, during which Collett remarked, "We obviously agree on a lot of things." At *Vice*, Nick Robins-Early delved into this and similar incidents of increasing ideological cross-pollination, which revealed that the politics of the pandemic had provided a new kind of breeding ground for the paranoid fantasies that comprise the denialists' conspiracy theories—one that openly intermingled old-fashioned anti-Semitism with New Age health-related conspiracism.

"As anti-vaccine activists continue to spread medical misinformation online and hold rallies targeting schools, hospitals, and government officials, pairings like Corbyn and Collett have become common," he wrote.

"White nationalists and QAnon influencers have become prolific sources for anti-vaccine propaganda, while far-right extremists march alongside anti-vaxxers at protests. In countries around the world, far-right and anti-vaccine movements are now deeply intertwined."

Street demonstrations in Italy and Australia featured openly fascist elements who turned out to support COVID denialists (particularly those opposing vaccine mandates). Some of these ended up engaging in insurrectionist violence. This phenomenon spread throughout Europe, notably in Germany.[112]

"We had big demonstrations in the streets in a lot of German cities, but also an evolving network of hate groups," Simone Rafael, a researcher at the German anti-racism group the Amadeu Antonio Foundation, said. "We could see the common thread throughout these groups was conspiracy ideologies and anti-Semitism."

One of the more prominent examples of the radicalization dynamic occurring within COVID-denialist organizing is the case of Attila Hildmann, a wildly popular vegan chef and cookbook author who in early 2020 began promoting pandemic-related conspiracy theories and organizing rallies. By June of that year, he had declared himself a "German nationalist" who admires Hitler and warned that Jews wanted to "exterminate the German race." Having fled Germany for his native Turkey to avoid prosecution, he now tells his followers that he is a "real Proud Nazi."[113]

A number of Stop the Steal organizers who promoted Donald Trump's conspiracist lie about losing the 2020 election suddenly shifted their focus toward opposing vaccines and government mandates. Trumpist and QAnon celebrities such as former national security adviser Michael Flynn and Simone Gold, founder of the far-right America's Frontline Doctors, both headlined anti-vaccine rallies. Some prominent anti-vaccine activists began jumping on the QAnon bandwagon, connecting vaccinations with their beliefs in broader conspiracies about global pedophile elites plotting to control the world.[114]

Along with far-right radicalization came the increasing presence of neofascist elements like the Proud Boys, who attached themselves to anti-pandemic-measure protests as "security." The result was a menacing air surrounding anti-vaccine-mandate marches and similar events.

"It's really grown in strength by becoming part of the whole far-right," Peter Hotez, codirector of the Center for Vaccine Development at Texas Children's Hospital, said. "As a consequence of that, people who want to show their allegiance to that movement do so by refusing vaccinations."

Far-right radicalization inevitably means that the underlying conspiracism is deeply anti-Semitic. This surfaced with the denialists' embrace of the term "pureblood" for people who have refused the vaccine—an obvious reference to fascist attempts to justify genocide as a matter of eugenics.

A January 2022 Defeat the Mandates march in Washington, D.C., however, demonstrated that there was no longer anything even remotely left-wing about the anti-vaxxer movement.[115] Populated with Proud Boys and "Patriot" militiamen, QAnoners and other Alex Jones–style conspiracists who blithely indulged in Holocaust relativism and other barely disguised anti-Semitism, and ex-hippies who now spouted right-wing propaganda—many of them, including speakers, encouraging and threatening violence—the crowd at the National Mall manifested the reality that "anti-vaxxers" now constitute a full-fledged far-right movement, and a potentially violent one at that.

The most prominent of these extremists was onetime progressive figure Robert F. Kennedy Jr., who had morphed over the past decade and longer, due to his obsession with the anti-vaccination cause, into a raving far-right conspiracy theorist. At the Defeat the Mandates rally—where the crowd was estimated to number several thousand—he was one of many who compared anti-pandemic measures such as masking and vaccine mandates to the Holocaust.

"Even in Hitler Germany [sic], you could, you could cross the Alps into

Switzerland. You could hide in an attic, like Anne Frank did," Kennedy said. "I visited, in 1962, East Germany with my father and met people who had climbed the wall and escaped, so it was possible. Many died, true, but it was possible."

Many of the rally attendees wore yellow replicas of the Star of David badges that were forced upon Jewish victims of the Holocaust, and many of them carried signs referencing both that horrific episode of history and the German Nazi regime that inflicted it. So did other speakers, such as Del Bigtree, CEO of the anti-vaccination group Informed Consent Action Network, who added a threatening tone directed at journalists.[116]

"Unlike the Nuremberg Trials that only tried those doctors that destroyed the lives of those human beings, we're going to come after the press," Bigtree told the crowd.

Violence was also an undercurrent in the audience, some members of which carried signs suggesting a lethal response: "Shoot those who try to kidnap and vaccinate your child." Another agreed with Bigtree, calling for "Nuremberg Trials 2.0."

The inherent anti-Semitism of the anti-vaxxers' conspiracism was also on full display: a large bus pulled up to the protest area blaring music with lyrics pronouncing "It's God Over Government," festooned on its side with mock "Wanted" posters featuring the anti-vaxxer bogeymen, notably Dr. Anthony Fauci, Microsoft founder Bill Gates, and attorney Jacob Rothschild—the latter of whom has no known connection to the vaccine or mandates whatsoever, but whose last name conjures up Hitler's anti-Semitic conspiracy theories that identified the family as one of the primary components of the Jewish cabal that Nazis believed secretly controlled the world.

The audience was a veritable showcase of far-right extremism. White nationalists from Nick Fuentes's Groyper army brought their "America First" banners. Proud Boys were also scattered throughout the crowd.

Just as inevitable as the coalescence of these conspiracist worldviews was the real-world violence that always accompanies far-right organizing—particularly death threats and other forms of intimidation directed at local officials and health-care institutions.[117] Hotez, who became a target of online hate and threats from anti-vaccine activists, told *Vice* that these threats increasingly expressed far-right views.

"Now when the threats come, it's of a different character," Hotez said. "It's about an army of patriots coming to take me down."

———————

TO SEE HOW RIGHT-WING conspiracists coalesced after 2020, you only had to go to gatherings like the Red Pill Festival.

Held in July 2021 in the small logging town of St. Regis, Montana, the two hundred or so people who drove from around the region to meet up in the town's little community park spent the day reveling in a familiar array of far-right conspiracy theories and disinformation: America is now under the control of a "Communist coup," Donald Trump was cheated out of the presidency, the COVID-19 pandemic is a "Deep State" operation intended to enslave the world, vaccines are "poison," public schools indoctrinate children into Marxist beliefs, and the United States is not a democracy, but simply a republic.[118]

The festival, intended to draw like-minded conspiracists from around the region—including Idaho, Washington, and Oregon—wasn't merely the usual gathering of dubious fringe characters. Mainstream Republican officials—including several currently serving lawmakers, as well as former Washington state legislator Matt Shea—were featured speakers, while the Mineral County GOP had a booth at the front of the event. It had the look and feel of a mainstream conservative Christian gathering—and given the radicalized state of the post-Trump Republican Party as an antidemocratic entity, that may have been the reality.

The event, which ran all day under smoke-filled skies and ninety-degree heat, offered a window into the alternative universe of far-right conspiracy theories. But these theories weren't merely being peddled by speakers and groups such as the John Birch Society from their festival booths—rather, it was clear that for the audience drawn to the gathering, they were already articles of faith among them.

"Do all of you believe or recognize that we are in a communist coup right now?" asked speaker René Holaday of the far-right secessionist group American Redoubt, one of the festival's primary organizers and promoters.

"Yes!" the audience replied unanimously.

Shea, the featured speaker, recognized that he was speaking to an audience that had already swallowed the far-right "red pill" the gathering was meant to promote.

"The technocrat global elitists are using communism and Islam to destroy the republic, OK?" Shea said. "You guys have heard all that. I don't need to talk to you about that today. What I want to talk to you about today is they are trying to destroy the republic. That operative word is trying, because they will not succeed.

"I don't care if the tyranny comes from London!" he continued. "We beat that tyranny twice. I don't care if the tyranny comes from Washington, D.C. Americans will not lose the fight for liberty. That's what makes us Americans!"

The spread-out, leisurely feel to the gathering helped emphasize the sense of normalcy. About twenty booths set up around the lawn hawked conspiracy theories; you could take a photo with a cardboard cutout of Donald Trump ("Our leader in exile" and "The real president") or buy T-shirts from the far-right street-brawling group Patriot Prayer, whose founder, Joey Gibson, was one of the day's featured speakers.

Another booth hawked an array of pro-Trump banners and flags (including the yellow "Don't Tread On Me" Gadsden flag), stickers ("2020 Was Rigged"), and ball caps (including an array of Trump 2020 ball caps stamped "Fraud," "Stolen," and "Rigged"). One Patriot entrepreneur from Yakima, Washington, brought a mobile kitchen trailer for his business,

Minutemen Coffee, from which he sold iced drinks that proved popular over the course of the long, hot day.

There was also a raffle. One of the more coveted prizes was a signed copy of G. Edward Griffin's conspiracy-theory tome, *The Creature from Jekyll Island*, a book that purports to expose the cadre of "globalist" elites who secretly control the world.

In addition to the long list of speakers, the day's entertainment included a couple of musical acts: an evangelical Christian rock band that favored songs about biblical characters, and "Patriot" songwriter Jordan Page, who performed songs about the Constitution and patriotism, as well as one dedicated to far-right martyr LaVoy Finicum.

The speakers all emphasized that they collectively represent the "real" America, and that their beliefs were shared by the majority of their communities. Accompanying that was a shared visceral contempt for their critics and the news media, which were regularly denounced as "propagandists" for the "Communists."

Montana legislator Derek Skees of Kalispell, that day's master of ceremonies, seemed particularly obsessed with the presence of a crew from *Vice News* led by reporter Vegas Tenold. Referring sneeringly to them as a pack of hapless New Yorkers, he told the audience that they planned to go back to their offices and paint a portrait of the festival as a gathering of violent racists—and then repeatedly asked the audience if a previous speaker had encouraged them to be violent or racist.

Later on, Shea made a point of encouraging people to confront journalists. "We need to ask these reporters. I want everybody, when we're done here, I want everybody to go up to those reporters, turn your phone on, and I want you to ask them that question," he said. "I want you to ask them, do you denounce Antifa? Will they denounce critical race theory? I want you to go down the list. Ask them. I've gotta tell you something, they're not reporters. They're propagandists. And they need to be held accountable for it."

The COVID-19 pandemic was very much on everyone's minds. Republican Idaho legislator Heather Scott theorized: "Was this all brought on by a virus with a 99.7 percent recovery rate?" she asked, to which the crowd emphatically responded: "No!" Scott shook her head and continued: "There's definitely something more going on. And you know, it appears that there's a plan that's been put into place to destroy our country piece by piece, transforming it into regions of a larger global world. We witness it daily.

"We're not fighting the COVID virus, but something way more sinister. And if we don't start diagnosing the right disease affecting our country, we're going to waste our time and energy with the wrong treatment."

Shea called the pandemic a "fake crisis," claiming: "We don't need face diapers and guidelines. We are Americans." He then took a deep breath and said: "I love breathing the free air, don't you?"

8

When Extremism Goes Mainstream

THE 2020 ELECTION WAS the turning point for America's epistemological crisis: the moment when the growing divide between people who believed in the old shared reality—based on reported facts and traditional authorities and institutions—and the people who believed in the new, alternative shared reality—the one concocted by Trump and the right-wing media ecosystem based on conspiracy theories, disinformation, wild conjecture, and flat-out falsehoods—became finally irreconcilable.

Trump had spent four years building his authoritarian army inside this realm. Whenever any Republican politician or media figure of any note had dared to step outside Trump's version of reality, he had called them out and humiliated them with his scorn—tweeting out derisive and juvenile nicknames, imitating them onstage at his rallies, calling reports "fake news," and trashing them publicly at press conferences.

Everyone remembered the example Trump had made of Reince Priebus, his first chief of staff, early in his administration.[1] The former Republican Party chairman had not been an early Trump supporter, but his presence in the White House in early 2017 was seen as a stabilizing influence. But

Trump chafed at Priebus's interference, and six months into the job hired a new communications director, Anthony Scaramucci, who Trump announced would report directly to him instead of to Priebus. Scaramucci then set about publicly trashing Priebus, implying he was responsible for leaks to the press and calling him "a fucking paranoid schizophrenic." Priebus resigned in short order, and was left sitting in a limousine on an airport tarmac while Trump's motorcade drove off.[2] He was out of politics after that.

So when Trump was impeached by House Democrats in 2019 over his withholding congressionally approved military aid to Ukraine while attempting, in a phone call, to extort President Volodymyr Zelensky into helping him gin up a fake scandal against Joe Biden, only one single Republican senator voted to convict him: Mitt Romney of Utah, the party's presidential nominee in 2012.[3]

Leading up to the November 2020 election, Trump persuaded many Republicans to support his contention that Democrats were engaging in massive election fraud, including senators like Romney's Utah colleague, Mike Lee.[4] Trump had cultivated this claim since the 2016 election, and became especially antic in the weeks leading up to Election Day in declaring that mail-in voting—which was already underway in states like Colorado, Utah, and Washington, where it had been the standard means of voting for years—was rife with fraud (made, as usual, without a whit of evidence).[5] He even told supporters at a North Carolina rally that they should vote by mail and then show up in person to cast another ballot—which would have, in fact, constituted voter fraud.[6]

"The ballots are out of control," he told reporters at a White House briefing. "We want to make sure the election is honest, and I'm not sure that it can be. I don't know that it can be with this whole situation—unsolicited ballots. They're unsolicited; millions being sent to everybody. And we'll see."[7]

But he wasn't alone in making the claim. Other Republicans, including Attorney General William Barr, echoed Trump's false claims to reporters: "There's so many occasions for fraud there that cannot be policed. I think it would be very bad."[8]

Everyone in the GOP played along until Election Day. And then came the final break with reality.

FOX NEWS SURPRISED EVERYONE—INCLUDING their own Donald Trump–loving viewers—on Election Night, November 3, 2020, by calling the race in Arizona for Joe Biden before the other networks, which waited several days to do the same. It seemed the longtime wellspring of right-wing disinformation might actually be displaying some journalistic integrity at last.[9]

It didn't last long. The Trump White House erupted in fury, as did millions of Trump fans, who popularized a #BoycottFoxNews hashtag on social media. Its ratings briefly plummeted. In the months that followed, the executives behind the decision were given the boot.

Moreover, as CNN's Brian Stelter revealed, Fox subsequently completed its utter radicalization as a Trumpian right-wing disinformation outlet: "We turned so far right we went crazy," one anonymous source told him.[10]

The slide from being a partisan news source into an outright wellspring of extremist disinformation came about, as Stelter suggested, because of pressure from the same authoritarian, fake-news-loving audience that Fox had created during Trump's tenure. The beast that they had created turned out to have an insatiable appetite for extremism.

"Fox is a really different place than it was pre-election," one of Stelter's Fox insiders told him after Biden was inaugurated.

"Fox News has always walked a fine line between trying to look like an independent news organization and supporting conservative politics," observed TV critic Eric Deggans. "There have to be moments where they act like an actual news organization in order to maintain their veneer of being an independent news organization."[11]

The wrath of Trump's followers descended on Fox immediately after its election-night call. Trump himself went on *Fox and Friends* and complained: "What's the biggest difference between this and four years ago," he asked rhetorically. "I say Fox. It's much different now."[12]

Outside Arizona's main election-counting center in Phoenix the day after the election, pro-Trump Stop the Steal protesters chanted, "Fox News sucks!"[13]

Fox's main problem was that it now had competition to its right in the form of the far-right Newsmax and One America News networks, which unabashedly feature right-wing conspiracy theories and false information about the election and other political topics.

Newsmax refused to initially call Biden the president-elect. One of its hosts, Greg Kelly, repeatedly claimed that Trump could remain in office another four years. "IT ISN'T OVER YET," Newsmax's website banners read.[14]

Fox's ratings sank. "We're bleeding eyeballs," one Fox producer told Stelter in December. "And we're scared."

On Facebook, the dismay among longtime Fox fans turned to fury. "Time to switch to Newsmax or One America News," one post read. "Fox News has officially joined the corrupt media."[15]

Fox executives decided to fix the problem, according to Stelter, by running "even further to the right." Fox News Media CEO Suzanne Scott decided to lure viewers back by giving them, as he noted, what they wanted: "False hope."

On Fox, Trump was treated as a political genius, not a lame duck who failed to win reelection. Some of the network's key shows waded deeper into the voter-fraud depths, eventually spurring massive defamation lawsuits by voting machine companies Dominion and Smartmatic.

"It's really emotionally taxing," a dissident Fox contributor told Stelter even as Trump's legal challenges imploded. "We denied the pandemic and now we're denying the election outcome."

Media Matters's Matt Gertz assembled a laundry list of Fox News's post-election embrace of Trumpian disinformation:

> Fox and its associates did everything they could to support Trump's autocratic maneuvers. In the two weeks after media outlets called the race for Biden, Fox personalities questioned the results of the election or pushed conspiracy theories about it nearly 800 times. They put the credibility of the network behind deranged lies about fraud plucked from the internet fever swamps, beaming batshit fantasies out to a huge national audience. It worked—polls following the election showed a majority of Republicans believed that the election was stolen from Trump.[16]

At the same time, Fox's descent began to include a more open embrace of right-wing extremist ideology, particularly the strange flavor of white nationalism that began getting more and more airtime on Tucker Carlson's evening program—Fox's top-rated show. Carlson promoted eco-fascist themes related to immigration; endorsed the idea that Republicans are being forced to abandon democracy and eventually embrace fascism because of liberal hegemony; defended the January 6 Capitol insurrectionists as being ordinary conservatives and decried their prosecutions; and spouted white-nationalist "replacement theory" in claiming that immigration is an attack on democracy itself.[17]

One of Carlson's most disturbing episodes, however, came when he attacked Biden's speech in Tulsa, Oklahoma, on the hundredth anniversary of the 1921 Tulsa Massacre, a "race riot" in which a white mob destroyed the city's Black business district and murdered hundreds of residents. Biden had decried the continuing existence of violent racist hatred, saying:

> I didn't realize hate is never defeated; it only hides. It hides. And given a little bit of oxygen—just a little bit of oxygen—by its leaders, it

comes out of there from under the rock like it was happening again, as if it never went away.

And so, folks, we can't—we must not give hate a safe harbor.

As I said in my address to the joint session of Congress: According to the intelligence community, terrorism from white supremacy is the most lethal threat to the homeland today. Not ISIS, not al Qaeda—white supremacists. (Applause.) That's not me; that's the intelligence community under both Trump and under my administration.[18]

This set off Carlson, who insisted on his program that evening that this meant Biden intended to target ordinary Republicans:

Yeah, you're not surprised. It's always the same people, isn't it? Those white Republican men—the very ones that just today Joe Biden warned us are more dangerous than ISIS. These are the people who have been beating up elderly Asian women in our cities, you've seen that plague unfold. These are the ones who don't believe in science, who have no decency, they're the problem.[19]

The next night, he insisted—despite abundant evidence to the contrary—that white-nationalist violence is not the most lethal threat to the American public: "There is no credible way to argue that white supremacy is the most lethal threat that we face. That's not an argument. It's its own form of racial attack."[20]

Carlson dove headfirst into this narrative with the blessing of Fox CEO Lachlan Murdoch, who even tried to claim that a review of Carlson's remarks show "that Mr. Carlson decried and rejected replacement theory."[21]

However, Carlson also let the curtain slip a bit in an interview with right-wing pundit Mollie Hemingway about election misinformation. While introducing Hemingway—whose book *Rigged* offers a wholly Trumpian take on his electoral defeat—the Fox host asserted that "so many people are lying at such high volume about the 2020 election, it's hard to know exactly what happened."[22]

That, in fact, is how the American right had come to deal with reality: just throw so much misinformation out there that the public becomes unable to discern fact from fiction—at which point right-wing authoritarians will naturally embrace their lying propaganda. Ex-Trump adviser Stephen Bannon calls it "flooding the zone with shit," creating so much uncertainty with a barrage of disinformation that many people default to the word of their preferred authority figures. "This is not about persuasion," observed Jonathan Rauch. "This is about disorientation."

As Deggans told *The Guardian*, Fox encouraged this kind of extremism for many years while working to maintain a veneer of journalistic credibility—and now was finally being dragged into the abyss, forced to abandon any such pretenses, by the monster it created.

"What's happening now is the Republican party is getting more strained, and there's more and more of a sense among Fox News viewership that anything that contradicts a worldview that is supportive of conservatives is wrong," Deggans said. "I think it's getting harder and harder for Fox News to ride that balance."[23]

ALL OF THE ABOVE is practically a functioning model of how authoritarianism works.

The 2020 election was hardly the first time Trump had attempted to assert that his version of reality is the only legitimate one, and that all others are "fake." It was a trademark of his 2016 election campaign and of his presidential tenure. Trump uses the gap between factual reality and the lies he proclaims as the truth as a wedge to drive his followers closer to him, where they form a mutual community of like-minded devotees.

The resulting chaos is by design, something Trump positively cultivated, following a pattern set by authoritarians throughout history: using the turmoil to create so much uncertainty that his unyielding, simultaneously reality-defying and reality-defining assertions eventually come to form the general consensus.

Anthony Scaramucci—who only lasted eleven days as Trump's communications director—called it Trump's "reality distortion field."[24]

"If you want me to say he's a liar, I'm happy to say he's a liar," said Scaramucci on CNN a year later. "He definitely has a reality distortion field around himself where he curves facts toward himself," he added. "He's living in that bubble."[25]

Trump's falsehoods serve a specific purpose: namely, to create an easily distinguished chasm between what he and his authoritarian followers believe and what people who live in a democratic reality believe. It's an assertion of his power—both to define reality as well as to rule as an authoritarian, with no constraints.

A classic example of this was his press conference of November 7, 2018, when CNN's Jim Acosta attempted to challenge Trump's characterization of a migrant caravan as an "invasion." He called Acosta "very rude," and told several reporters to "sit down." Acosta tried to follow up with another question, and Trump interrupted, telling him: "Put down the mic." Acosta, however, hung on to it even as an aide attempted to wrest it out of his hands.[26]

"CNN should be ashamed of itself, having you working for them," Trump said. "You are a rude, terrible person. You shouldn't be working for CNN." He went on, pointing at Acosta: "When you report fake news, which CNN does a lot, you are the enemy of the people."

Acosta wasn't the only reporter he berated that day. He chastised two African American women during the conference, telling April Ryan of American Urban Radio Networks to "sit down," and then berating Yamiche Alcindor of PBS when she asked Trump about his relationship to white nationalists, calling her question "racist": "What you said is so insulting to me," he told her.

The intended audience for these outbursts was less the journalists he was attacking and bullying as "the enemy of the people" than it was his voting base, which polls have found ardently agree with his disparaging view of the press. This is, in fact, how authoritarians throughout history have behaved: crush the credibility of objective journalism and assert the leader in its place as the arbiter of truth and reality. Because when you can define reality, you can lead people to do anything you say.

When most of us hear the term "authoritarianism" and picture its operations in our minds, we usually do so in the context of the leaders throughout history who have headed up authoritarian regimes—everyone from Napoleon to Hitler and Stalin to any number of petty banana-republic dictators. But that's not what makes authoritarianism work—or at least not the whole story. No authoritarian regime has ever existed without a substantial portion of the population it rules actively supporting and preferring it. They all have large armies of followers who sustain them in power.

So to understand authoritarianism, it's essential first to understand those followers, because they not only keep those figures in power, their version of reality takes on such a life of its own that they often wind up controlling the leading figure. There are distinctive personality types that are attracted to and support authoritarianism and understanding how they think helps us understand how and why they comprise the real threat to democracy itself.

As psychologists and political scientists such as Robert Altemeyer, Marc Hetherington, and Jonathan Weiler have explored in detail, most people have some level of authoritarian tendencies, but these are often leveled out by such factors as personal empathy and critical thinking skills, which tend to lead to a less black-and-white view of the world.[27] Nor is authoritarianism relegated just to the right side of the political aisle. There are also left-wing authoritarians, as any survivor of Stalinist Russia can attest.

Right-wing propaganda regarding "Antifa" and "critical race theory" notwithstanding, these authoritarian tendencies on the left remain comparatively muted. Most mainstream Democrats fall well into the zone of personality types that are resistant to authoritarianism, even if they underestimate it. The Republican Party, in stark contrast, is awash in a flood tide of right-wing authoritarianism that has been rising since at least the 1990s.

Are right-wing authoritarians born or made? Probably a combination of both, though it's clear that people's authoritarian tendencies increase the more fearful they are.[28] Identifying a threat and forming a focus on it are essential to shaping these personalities. This is why fearmongering—whether over Islamist radicals and terrorism after the 9/11 attacks or over border-crossing migrants or "Antifa" and Black Lives Matter—has been an essential component of Republican appeals for a generation and served as the centerpiece of Trump's ascension to the presidency and his tenure. Spreading fear is a surefire method of inducing an authoritarian response in the general public.

Some people, moreover, are wired this way from birth. Early theories on authoritarian personalities, now largely discredited, argued for a Freudian model in which harsh rearing environments and traumas produce people who insist on a world in which strong authorities produce order and peace. While this dynamic is still recognized, it's not the only recipe for authoritarianism. Most current models are flexible, finding that it usually depends on circumstances; but the one constant is that the subject finds his or her personal security—physical, financial, mental, and otherwise—endangered. Because it is innate to human personalities, it can remain latent during periods when people do not perceive a threat, and increase when they do.[29]

Periods of intense social change also can produce authoritarian backlash, as such changes are often perceived by some personalities as a kind of threat. This is why movements promoting palpable civil rights advances, such as Black Lives Matter, have so often been perceived as an attack on whites; authoritarian personalities are prone to seeing race as a zero-sum competition, in which any advance for one minority (racial or otherwise) necessarily entails a loss for the white heterosexual Christian majority.

Right-wing authoritarian personalities are built around three behavioral and attitudinal clusters:

- First: Authoritarian submission. This is the eager adherence to edicts, rulings, and opinions of the authorities and leaders who are deemed legitimate, built around the belief that a civil, ordered, and secure society requires such submission.[30]
- Next: Authoritarian aggression—the physical, verbal, and social aggression displayed toward anyone or any trend that runs counter to those authorities, or in the case of leadership, is deemed illegitimate.
- Finally: Conventionalism, the adamant embrace of what is perceived as the social norm and the "real" national identity, and the belief that one's immediate cultural community and self reflect that "real" identity.

These three clusters interact in myriad ways, and produce a long list of identifiable traits among Trump's MAGA footsoldiers. Altemeyer in particular has identified about a dozen such traits.

- They are highly ethnocentric, inclined to see the world as their in-group versus everyone else, and are prone to making zero-sum calculations about minority rights.
- They are extremely fearful of a dangerous world, and perceive threats in everything from masked anti-fascists to Disney World "groomers."
- They are extraordinarily self-righteous, often in as bellicose a fashion as possible.
- They are aggressive, both verbally and physically, and are not merely tolerant of violent rhetoric and behavior but prone to indulging in it themselves.
- They are not just extremely tolerant of bigoted prejudice against racial and ethnic minorities, non-heterosexuals, and women in general, but once again prone to such behavior as well.

- Their beliefs are a mass of contradictions, dependent on compartmentalized thinking.
- They reason poorly, and they are prone to projection.
- They are highly dogmatic.
- They are very dependent on social reinforcement of their beliefs.
- Because they severely limit their exposure to different people and ideas, they vastly overestimate the extent to which other people agree with them.
- They are prone to conspiracist thinking and a gullibility about "alternative facts."[31]

Authoritarianism as a worldview always creates a certain kind of cognitive dissonance, a feeling of unreality, because it runs smack into the complex nature of the modern world. Authoritarian personalities attempt to impose their simplified, black-and-white explanation of reality onto a factual reality that contradicts and undermines them at every turn—which is why Trump's version of reality appeals so deeply to them.

People with authoritarian personalities willingly slip into the conspiracist alternative universe because it helps soothe this dissonance, allowing its occupants to glide over inconvenient facts because they participate in a larger "truth." This universe, as a creation of right-wing authoritarians, has always played a key role: a refuge for people who reject factual reality that contravenes their cherished propaganda narratives, a place where they can convene and reassure one another in the facticity of their fabricated version of how the world works.

Conspiracism appeals to people with such personality traits—the people who tell pollsters they "don't recognize their country anymore" and are bewildered by the brown faces filling the cultural landscape in places where they never used to be. One study found conspiracy theories are compelling to "those with low self-worth, especially with regard to their sense of agency in the world at large." They long for America with lawns and all-white cul-de-sacs and are angry the world no longer works that way.

Conspiracy theories offer narratives that explain to the adherent why the country is no longer what they wish it to be, why it has that alien shape. And so in their minds the alternative universe comes to represent a deeper truth about their world, while repeatedly reinforcing their long-held prejudices, and enables them to ignore the real, factual (and often uncomfortable) nature of the changes the world is undergoing.

Simply put, it provides a clear, self-reinforcing answer to the source of their personal disempowerment. It also has the advantage of telling believers that they are the solo, go-it-alone action heroes in the movies of their own lives.

The deep irony in all this is that the overall effects of conspiracy theories are such that they are profoundly disempowering. Conspiracists disconnect from the rest of the world, whose occupants they either hold in paranoid suspicion or contempt, except the like-minded. Conspiracism creates a worldview in which the world is actually being run by secretive schemers intent on suppressing them, against whose immense power an ordinary individual is almost entirely impotent. Even their neighbors are suspect.[32]

There can even be outright cognitive effects, suggested by a variation on an old Upton Sinclair adage: "It is difficult to get a man to understand something, when the entire worldview around which his emotional life revolves depends on his not understanding it." Reality that's obvious to everyone else isn't to them, because their configuration of the world deliberately excludes any evidence that contravenes their adopted narrative. People who are "red-pilled," as the conspiracy-loving alt-righters have dubbed themselves, see themselves as utterly detached from their communities, fighting a desperate battle with only the help of their fellow conspiracists against truly dark and evil forces.[33]

Alex Jones constantly refers to his targets as "demonic." It's not just a bleak world; it's one in which people can become overwhelmed with feelings of hopelessness and rage. That's one of the primary reasons conspiracist beliefs are so often associated with horrific acts of terrorist violence: Anders Breivik's massacre of 69 teens in Norway in 2011, or Timothy McVeigh's Oklahoma City bomb that killed 168 in 1996, or Jared Loughner's murderous attack on a Democratic congresswoman in Tucson in 2011, or Dylann Roof's rampage at the Charleston church in 2015, or Robert Bowers's lethal synagogue attack in Pittsburgh in 2018, or Patrick Crusius's attack on Hispanic people at an El Paso Walmart in 2019.

All of these people, and their many other domestic-terrorist cohorts, acted out of a desperation fueled by anger over their sense of deep disempowerment—all of it a product of a belief in conspiracy theories. The violence committed by domestic terrorists serves the purposes of authoritarians in profound ways: it ratchets up the levels of fear in society generally, and a resort to the false security of authoritarianism is a common psychological response.

Here the role played by authoritarian leaders is key. Because rather than ease people's fears, as a normative democratic leader would do, authoritarians immediately reach for the panic button. Keeping the populace in a state of fearful hypervigilance is a cornerstone of their rule. Want to win elections? Hype up whatever threats you can concoct—refugees and immigrant caravans, inner-city crime, "Antifa," "critical race theory," or "grooming"— and claim that your enemies are the cause of these problems, and that only you can solve them.

Authoritarian leaders, as Altemeyer has explored, have a personality type quite distinct from their followers. It is called social dominance orientation (SDO), essentially a form of narcissism on steroids. A portrait of an SDO leader would look and act like Trump.

SDOs are far more interested in the personal acquisition of power than are right-wing authoritarians, who by nature are more inclined to march on someone else's behalf. They also have different reasoning capacities, and are far more calculating and manipulative.[34]

What they all have in common, more than anything else, is a dismissive view of equality. They believe inequality is the natural state of things, and any attempts to tamper with it are doomed to fail and screw everything up. Both SDOs and authoritarians believe that there is a natural hierarchy of the gifted and the less so. The difference is that SDOs tend to see themselves among the former, while authoritarians are more likely to view themselves among the latter, but harbor ambitions to achieve the former.

Given its innate preference for autocratic rule, authoritarianism is toxic for any kind of democratic society. The antidemocratic far right's express hostility to democracy and its institutions makes its rise as a political phenomenon a concern not just in the United States, but around the world.

The attacks on democracy come both from below—by Trump's violent and fanatical footsoldiers, people like the Proud Boys and the Oath Keepers—and from above, from the president and his administration, as well as his enablers in the Republican Party and in right-wing media. The attack on Jim Acosta and other reporters in November 2018 was a manifestation of that reality.

Tellingly, the question that Acosta was asking at the time Trump blew up was about the role his fearmongering about the immigrant caravan had in inspiring violence—notably the Pittsburgh synagogue shooting only twelve days before, when an angry anti-Semite who blamed Jews for the caravan gunned down worshipers at Shabbat morning services, killing eleven people and wounding six.

Trump wouldn't let Acosta ask his question. And he never confronted questions about his culpability in political violence, blowing up any press conference when asked. The technique worked for him, especially in keeping his bigoted white supporters well within the fold. Trump winked and nudged at people who committed acts of violence in his name since at least the 2016 campaign.

He bluffed his way through justifying their violence: The victims had it coming. In 2016, when two Boston men badly beat a homeless Latino man and urinated on him, claiming Trump inspired them, he in turn explained to reporters that some of his followers "are very passionate."[35]

When anyone asked him about his connection to recent terrorism or other political violence, he would retort that the media created the violence with "fake news." The logic was clear: if you were submissive to my rule, reported news as I like it, you wouldn't be facing this violence.

And no one agreed more with this logic than his followers. Altemeyer lucidly describes "the lethal union" of right-wing authoritarian followers with a social-dominance-oriented leader: that moment, he says, when "the two can then become locked in a cyclonic death spiral that can take a whole nation down with them."

———————

THE AUTHORITARIAN TIDAL WAVE that washed through Fox News after the November election and the insurrection also inundated the Republican Party. Members of Congress had multiple opportunities to repudiate Trump and Trumpist political violence over the weeks following January 6, but only a small fraction of Republicans did so—and were immediately punished for it.

When members returned to the chambers the evening after the insurrection, Republicans continued to play along with Trump's schemes. Six Republican senators still voted to reject the Electoral College ballots for Arizona, while Congressman Paul Gosar of Arizona led the failed attempt to reject the ballot in the House, and was joined by 120 members.[36]

The Democratic House immediately attempted to hold Trump accountable for the insurrection, voting on January 13 to impeach him a second time for inciting the mob to besiege the Capitol. Republicans treated the entire affair as purely a matter of partisan politics: Senator Lindsey Graham said the impeachment "will do more harm than good," and later tweeted: "It is past time for all of us to try to heal our country and move forward. Impeachment would be a major step backward."[37] Oklahoma senator James

Lankford said: "This is not a trial; this is political theater. You cannot remove someone from the office who is already out of office."[38]

After passing the House 232–197—with the support of ten Republicans, all of whom were shortly targeted for 2022 primary challenges by Trump himself—the impeachment failed in the Senate when the vote was 57–43 to convict, ten votes short of the constitutionally required two thirds.

It soon became clear why Republicans in Congress were so reluctant to acknowledge factual reality in public: if these Republicans dared admit that Biden fairly won the election and Trump incited a mob, they risked the insane wrath of the millions of GOP voters out there who had wholly swallowed all that false Trumpian propaganda.

That became evident among Republicans at the state and local levels in the weeks following January 6. Whenever Republicans made any gestures toward acknowledging either Biden's win or Trump's seditionist behavior, voters at the state and local level responded with outrage and threats.

"The evidence is overwhelming that local parties across the country, in blue states and red states, are radicalized and support extremely far outside the mainstream positions like, for example, ending our democratic experiment to install Donald Trump as president over the will of the people," Tim Miller, former political director of Republican Voters Against Trump, told *The Guardian*.[39]

"They believe in unhinged COVID denialism and QAnon and all these other conspiracies. It's endemic, not just a couple of state parties. It's the vast majority of state parties throughout the country."

One example is Oregon. The state's Republican Party issued a lengthy statement stuffed full of conspiracy theories and disinformation condemning the ten Republican members of Congress who voted to impeach Trump after the insurrection. It claimed, "there is growing evidence that the violence at the Capitol was a 'false flag' operation designed to discredit President Trump and his supporters." (Some twenty-three Republican members of the state House repudiated the statement, noting that "there is no credible evidence to support false flag claims," adding that such rumor-mongering had become a distraction.)[40]

Meanwhile in Wyoming, GOP activists opened a campaign to "recall" Congresswoman Liz Cheney after she joined the Republicans voting to impeach Trump, and they collected over fifty-five thousand signatures. Ten county-level parties in the state voted to censure Cheney, and rival candidates came out of the woodwork. The Wyoming Republican state party said "there has not been a time during our tenure when we have seen this type of an outcry from our fellow Republicans, with the anger and frustration being palpable in the comments we have received."[41] Trump selected a MAGA loyalist named Harriet Hageman for his endorsement. She ended up winning the August 2022 primary by 32 points.

The sentiments in Wyoming were deep and widespread. A Gillette woman named Shelley Horn started the Cheney recall petition, and told CNN: "You just can't go, 'Oh well, I need to vote with my conscience.' No! Vote for what your people put you in there to do. You're a Republican, you're supposed to back your party regardless."

The push to embrace Trumpism roiled other state Republican parties as well. In Wisconsin—where fifteen Republican lawmakers signed a letter to Vice President Mike Pence the day before the Washington, D.C., riot urging him to postpone the certification, and two Republican congressmen from the state, Scott Fitzgerald and Tom Tiffany, objected to the electoral votes—the party was divided into two camps.[42]

"The Republican Party right now is relatively divided, but it's not the traditional ideological divisions that used to be in place, as much as it's between the sane and insane wings of the party," *RightWisconsin* editor James Wigderson told Madison's *The Capital Times*. "I think that there's a chance of a real fracture coming."

Establishment Republicans such as former lieutenant governor Rebecca Kleefisch, however, defended the Trumpists for their paranoia and embrace of partisan disinformation: "That is the perspective they have, that is the view that they have and it's valid; you can't say someone's opinion of a subjective matter is invalid," she said. "I mean, what gives us the right to judge someone's opinion like that?"

In Michigan, where Republicans also embraced the Stop the Steal campaign prior to the insurrection, the impulse to maintain their embrace of Trumpism remained largely undiminished. The Allegan County Republican Party censured Congressman Fred Upton because he voted to impeach Trump. Upton shortly afterward announced he would not seek reelection.[43]

In Georgia, Republican Party officials were grimacing at the wounds being inflicted on their voter-appeal operations by the presence of QAnon-loving Congresswoman Marjorie Taylor Greene in the state's delegation, as well as in the media as her multiple conspiracist pronouncements—such as her approval of a follower's statement that House Speaker Nancy Pelosi be shot in the head, or her suggestion on Facebook that California wildfires were being caused by Jewish-owned lasers shooting incendiary beams from space—came increasingly to light.[44]

"If you have any common sense, you know she's an anchor on the party. She is weighing us down," said Gabriel Sterling, a Georgia Republican election administrator who criticized the baseless election conspiracy theories espoused by Trump and his supporters.

"Some people are saying maybe Nancy Pelosi will throw her out" of Congress, Sterling said. "The Democrats would never throw her out. They want her to be the definition of what a Republican is. They're gonna give her every opportunity to speak and be heard and look crazy—like what came out Wednesday, the Jewish space laser to start fires. I mean, I don't know how far down the rabbit hole you go."

The unhinged behavior and conspiracism, as well as the self-righteousness, persecution complex, and projection endemic to extremist conspiracism, became common and widespread, thanks in no small part to its open endorsement by leading members of the GOP. And trying to hold Republicans accountable for the ensuing violence became, in their warped cognitive world-views, only further evidence of a conspiracy against all conservatives. Shelley Horn, the Wyoming petitioner, blamed Cheney's impeachment vote for divid-ing the nation: "It's just sows more hate and division," Horn told the *Cowboy State Daily*, "and people are tired of it. Our country can't stand much more."[45]

FOR PEOPLE ON THE Trumpian side of the epistemological divide, the elec-tion of 2020 and the subsequent events of January 6 became core markers of their versions of reality: Trump had been cheated and was still the real president. January 6 wasn't an insurrection, it was righteous patriotic pro-test, and anyway it was Antifa that caused the violence, and besides the FBI had actually schemed up the whole thing as a way to imprison Trump supporters. Because Trump had told them so, they didn't believe they were lying when they repeated those lies.

Which is why so many Trump voters gobbled them up: over 70 percent of them ardently believe the first claim, and some 58 percent of whom lap up the "Antifa" lie as well.[46]

And as far as they're concerned, that's all that matters: They have a nar-rative to tell themselves and one another. Because that's really the only au-dience for their lies that matters to them. Who cares if the rest of the world knows it's hogwash?

Indeed, the two lies contradict each other, narratively speaking: If the election was stolen, why would Antifa want to invade the Capitol? And if it was "legitimate political discourse," as the Republican National Committee would describe it, then why would the FBI have tried to set people up in criminal acts? But logical consistency is meaningless in their alternative universe. What matters most is muddying the waters so they can evade con-sequences for their innate violence, mainly by resorting to the hoary rhe-torical manipulation of claiming that critics are "waving the bloody shirt."

The New York Times examined how the "Antifa did it" lie was generated and then spread. It began, as the story documented, even while the Capitol invasion was underway, thanks mainly to a bogus story about Antifa in *The Washington Times* that was corrected about twenty-four hours later—more than enough time for the lie to get on its horse and gallop around the world a couple of times with an assist from the usual suspects for right-wing disinformation: namely, the Gateway Pundit, Rush Limbaugh's radio show, and Laura Ingraham, along with helpers among Republican elected officials, notably Congressmen Matt Gaetz of Florida and Mo Brooks of Alabama, as well as Wisconsin senator Ron Johnson.[47]

While some backed away from the Antifa claims, others doubled down—notably Johnson, who asserted once again that Antifa was responsible for the violence during a Senate hearing. Johnson, reading from an account by J. Michael Waller in *The Federalist*, claimed the "great majority" of protesters had a "jovial, friendly, earnest demeanor." He blamed the deadly violence on "plainclothes militants, agent provocateurs, fake Trump protesters, and a disciplined uniformed column of attackers."

The "Antifa did it" theorists, including Congressman Louie Gohmert of Texas, claimed that an African American man they linked to Black Lives Matter, John Earle Sullivan of Utah, played a central role in the insurrection.

There was just one problem with this story: It had, once again, been thoroughly debunked. Sullivan, as *The Washington Post* reported in detail, is a man who initially attempted to organize BLM protests in Utah outside of the existing African American protest community.[48] In short order, a person was shot during one of his events, and then Proud Boys began showing up to support his Utah protests in numbers. Among BLM activists, he was widely regarded as a duplicitous "double agent." His last organized protest of the summer of 2020 was a pro–gun rights rally featuring large numbers of far-right militiamen, including Oath Keepers. When he entered the Capitol on January 6 and began shooting video inside, he was again in their company.

The *Times* story overlooked a central aspect of the narrative: The radical right actually began building it on social media well before the January 6 insurrection. First, conspiracy theorists began circulating rumors that Antifa would disguise themselves as Trump supporters for the January 6 rally, but would be identifiable by the backward MAGA hats they intended to wear.[49] Then Proud Boys began talking among themselves about arriving in disguise at the January 6 event dressed up in Antifa-style "black bloc" gear.[50]

The latter idea had, of course, real logistical flaws, since other Proud Boys might mistake the disguised participants for the real thing and assault them. The strategy the Proud Boys eventually settled on for January 6 was to eschew their usual black polos and red MAGA hats for ordinary street clothes, instead adopting orange armbands and orange wool beanies as their group identifier.

Many of those same Proud Boys and Oath Keepers then found themselves under arrest and awaiting trial for their roles in the insurrection. Most of them, in fact, expressed their indignation from prison at the attempt to give Antifa credit for what they believed was their good patriotic work.

"Don't you dare try to tell me that people are blaming this on Antifa and [Black Lives Matter]," wrote insurgent Jonathan Mellis on Facebook days after the event, prior to being charged with multiple crimes. "We proudly take responsibility for storming the Castle. Antifa and BLM or [sic] too pussy . . . We are fighting for election integrity. They heard us."[51]

Faced with this reality, Republicans in leadership positions—both in Congress and in the right-wing media ecosystem—in short order fell in line by embracing all the lies by just juggling them constantly and gaslighting the public relentlessly, reassuring them that they didn't see what they thought they saw on January 6: that wasn't a violent insurrection you watched happen in real time, it was just a super-boisterous protest.

That was the operative strategy by early May, in a House hearing on the insurrection, when a parade of GOP House members tried to convince the public that what it witnessed that day wasn't real. The hearing, titled "The Capitol Insurrection: Unexplained Delays and Unanswered Questions," featured testimony from former Trump officials—then-acting attorney general Jeffrey Rosen, and then-acting defense secretary Christopher Miller—involved in the slow response by security forces to intervene in the riot. Both men generally refused to directly answer any of the questions posed to them by Democrats, and mostly claimed they had done nothing wrong that day.[52]

But the hearing was dominated by Republicans who, like Charles Boyer telling Ingrid Bergman those gaslights weren't flickering, insisted that Democrats were making much ado out of nothing. The most audacious of the bunch was Congressman Andrew Clyde of Georgia, who opened the hearing's second half with a straight shot of alternative-universe ether:

> This hearing is called "The Capitol Insurrection." Let's be honest with the American people: It was not an insurrection, and we cannot call it that and be truthful. The Cambridge English dictionary defines an "insurrection" as, and I quote, "An organized attempt by a group of people to defeat their government and take control of their country, usually by violence." And then from the Century Dictionary, "The act of rising against civil authority, or governmental restraints, specifi-cally the armed resistance of a number of persons against the power of the state."
>
> As one of the members who stayed in the Capitol and on the House floor, who with other Republican colleagues, helped to barricade the door until almost 3 p.m. that day from the mob who tried to enter. I can tell you, the House was never breached, and it was not an insurrection.
>
> This is the truth: There was an undisciplined mob, there were some rioters and some who committed acts of vandalism, but let me be clear—there was no insurrection, and to call it an insurrection, in my opinion, is a boldfaced lie.

Other Republicans in the hearing piled on with similar deflections. Congressman Ralph Norman of South Carolina claimed the insurrectionists weren't really Trump supporters. Jody Hice, a congressman from Georgia, insisted that Trump was innocent of having incited the mob to insurrection by citing the sole line from his speech in which he told them to protest "peacefully and patriotically." Others, like Clay Higgins of Louisiana, compared the January 6 mob to the Black Lives Matter protesters who clashed with police in the summer of 2020, claiming that "19 people died" and "hundreds and hundreds were injured." Arizona's Gosar claimed that the Biden administration intended to use the insurrection to "unleash the national security state against law-abiding citizens—especially Trump voters."

No one mentioned that the protests were an attempt to prevent the peaceful transfer of power in a national election. Likewise, not a single Republican denounced Donald Trump's role in the events or even managed to acknowledge that the insurrection was inspired by the broad dissemination of Trump's claim that the election was stolen, and its broad support by a large number of congressional GOP members and right-wing pundits. That apparently didn't fit into their cognitive bandwidth.

THE PUNDIT WHO LED the gaslighting brigade that provided Republican officials with their talking points was Fox News's Tucker Carlson. By late January, Carlson and the writers for his nightly show had assembled a counternarrative to the standard January 6 storyline, one plausible mostly to right-wing conservatives: the whole thing is part of a liberal scheme to imprison and persecute white Trump supporters.

Carlson looked out at his audience and assured them that this meant them:

> Got that? Vote the wrong way and you are a jihadi. You thought you were an American citizen with rights and just a different view. But no, you're a jihadi. And we're going to treat you the way we did those

radicals after 9/11. The way we treated Bin Laden. Get in line, pal. This is a war on terror . . .

Keep in mind, they're talking about American citizens here. They're talking about you. But nobody seems to notice or care.[53]

He also claimed that Joe Biden had suspended the First Amendment and placed the nation under "some form of martial law":

What, you may be wondering, does a case like this mean for the First Amendment? Well, it means that it's effectively suspended. You can now be arrested for saying the wrong things. And at 7 a.m. this morning, one journalist actually was arrested for that. Almost no one tonight seems to be defending him. "He had bad thoughts! He deserves it!" They think it's OK. And that shouldn't surprise you. Because we're clearly living under some form of martial law at the moment.

This new version of democracy is a democracy where everyone fervently agrees with the people in power or else they go immediately to jail. [Notorious white nationalist] Doug Mackey's problem [arrested for conducting a scheme to defraud Black voters], it turns out, is that he doesn't properly understand what democracy is.

Carlson identified people like Mackey with ordinary conservatives:

You may have thought you were a decent American in good standing. Ten years ago, nobody in this country would have called your views extreme. They weren't extreme then. You don't think they're extreme now, you've always considered yourself a pretty moderate person—live your life and get along with others. Oh ho, that's not possible now—because the rules have changed. You are now a dangerous insurgent. You are no different from a bloodthirsty Pashtun in Helmand Province, or an ISIS terrorist in Erbil! You're part of a guerrilla insurgency.

This formed the essence of the gathering Republican response to any kind of effort to confront the right-wing extremism that fueled the January 6 insurrection: When you crack down on white supremacists and far-right domestic terrorists, you crack down on ordinary Republicans.

Carlson was not alone. Kentucky senator Rand Paul attacked Joe Biden's inauguration speech, in which he called for confronting domestic terrorism, as "thinly veiled innuendo" targeting Republicans. "Calling us white supremacists, calling us racists, calling us every name in the book," he said on Fox News.[54]

Carlson's reality-distortion field around January 6 kept shifting and growing. By mid-June, Carlson's narrative had metastasized into a full-blown Deep State conspiracy theory, straight out of something on *Infowars*.[55] According to Carlson, the FBI orchestrated the whole thing.

This conspiracy theory did originate with Alex Jones, who discussed it as a likelihood shortly after the event. It was propped up by reportage from the far-right website *Revolver News*, which has a long history of publishing and promoting disinformation. The reportage by editor Darren Beattie—a far-right propagandist best known for being fired as a Trump White House speechwriter after his ties to white nationalists were exposed—in fact revealed a "journalist" who had no grasp of how federal prosecutions or witness programs work. Carlson hosted Beattie on his nightly Fox program, claiming that the article demonstrated that "the FBI was organizing the riots of January 6." "It certainly suggests that possibility," said Beattie.[56]

Carlson told his audience:

> But strangely, some of the key people who participated on January 6 have not been charged. Look at the documents; the government calls those people unindicted co-conspirators. What does that mean? Well, it means that in potentially every single case they were FBI operatives. Really? In the Capitol on January 6?

However, as Aaron Blake of *The Washington Post* explained: "Legal experts say the government literally cannot name an undercover agent as an unindicted co-conspirator."[57]

"There are many reasons why an indictment would reference unindicted co-conspirators, but their status as FBI agents is not one of them," Jens David Ohlin, a criminal law professor at Cornell Law School, told Blake.

CNN's senior legal analyst Elie Honig agreed: "In fact, prosecutors use those generic labels for a variety of reasons, most commonly to refer to people who participated in the conspiracy but have not yet been publicly charged," Honig said.[58]

Carlson further emphasized his utter incomprehension (though probably deliberate) of the federal legal system when he went on to suggest that one of the unindicted coconspirators was actually an FBI operative—when in fact that person was the wife of one of the indicted insurrectionists, a woman who had entered a cooperative agreement with the government. In the alternative universe, simple facts simply don't matter.

Carlson, moreover, was undeterred. He doubled down the next evening on his broadcast, asserting bald-facedly: "The events of January 6 . . . were at least in part organized and carried out in secret by people connected to federal law enforcement." He also alleged that the government won't release Capitol surveillance footage of the riot because "people they know are on the tape."

Later that month he went off the paranoid deep end:

> The Biden administration is signaling a very real change to actual federal policy. The "War on Terror," now ongoing for 20 years, has pivoted in its aims. The War on Terror is now being waged against American citizens, opponents of the regime.
>
> We saw this on display on Jan. 6. We told you a couple of weeks ago, based on language in publicly available indictments, that the FBI clearly

had foreknowledge of the riot at the Capitol that day. The agents we spoke to this weekend confirmed that is true. Quote: "The FBI had sources in that crowd—confidential sources, snitches. That's 100% certain."[59]

In late October 2021, Carlson and his team created an independent "documentary" made available at Fox's pay streaming service titled "Patriot Purge." It posited, once again, that the Capitol insurrection actually was a "false flag" operation by the "Deep State" intended to ensnare and imprison American "patriots" simply for "disagreeing with Joe Biden."[60]

The film uses so many quick-moving flash cuts, particularly when showing footage of the Capitol siege, that watching it is both disorienting and headache-inducing, which may be the point: the camera only seems to slow down when Carlson or his guests are speaking, making them appear voices of calm and reason amid the videotaped chaos. Most of all, it is an exercise in fearmongering. "The left is hunting the right," a disembodied voice tells the audience, tracking them and "sticking them in the gulag, sticking them in Guantanamo Bay for American citizens."

In the documentary, Carlson tried to explore the core claims of his conspiracy theory about January 6 in depth, mainly by interviewing sources whose veracity is dubious at best. Among these was a primary proponent of the false flag claim, an ex–Army captain named Emily Rainey who was present in the pro-Trump rally that preceded the riot, and who told Carlson that she felt compelled to resign after her involvement came under scrutiny. Rainey, in fact, had already resigned her commission over an unrelated reprimand before she traveled to D.C. for the event.

Rainey touted her background in psychological operations, telling Carlson:

RAINEY: So if that was an insurrection, it was the most poorly conducted insurrection ever.

CARLSON: If it wasn't an insurrection, then what was it?

RAINEY: Special Operations uses the military deception tactic of a false flag abroad against the enemies of America. A false flag is any time you want to frame another group so that you can then take action against that group. It is my opinion that false flags have happened in this country. One of which may have been January 6.

The documentary's claims drew widespread rebukes for Carlson, who nonetheless continued to insist on his conspiracist narrative. It was even debunked on Fox News: A *Special Report with Bret Baier* segment reporting on the ongoing congressional investigation into the insurrection featured an interview with Marc Polymeropoulos, a former veteran CIA officer. He was flatly dismissive of the false-flag theory.[61]

"One of the things with false flag operations as well, is sometimes it's used by conspiracy theorists to actually hide the truth," Polymeropoulos said. "Pretty far-fetched—in no way was January 6 a false flag operation."

The whole point of conspiracy theories, particularly those fueled by eliminationist politics, is to create permission for their followers to act out violently. As Jason Stanley, the author of *How Fascism Works*, explained, Carlson's "documentary" followed this classic fascist blueprint:

> The message of the series is clear: a great wrong has been done. The government and media have engineered a false narrative directed in the first instance towards discrediting the patriots who seek to address it, and, ultimately, with the goal of hunting down and violently suppressing them. Our media's complicity is demonstrated by their differential coverages of the BLM protests, which are here portrayed as senseless violent riots, and the events of January 6 . . . It is impossible to accept this message in total without taking it to justify violent mass action against the current government, or something like a police and military coup.[62]

Carlson's narrative readily spread, picked up particularly among ostensibly mainstream conservative pundits who have embraced Trumpism—especially in the orbit of the right-wing Claremont Institute, a think tank
that has published screeds embracing neofascist politics in the name of defending the ex-president. A piece in the Hillsdale College organ *Imprimis*
by Roger Kimball, headlined "The January 6 Insurrection Hoax," agreed
with Carlson that it was merely "a political protest that 'got out of hand.'"
Kimball also asserted that the Big Lie is factual, and that "every honest
person knows that the 2020 election was tainted."[63]

Gaslighting narratives like this are not merely disinformation; rather,
they are attempts to persuade the public that it didn't see what it watched
unfold on January 6 in Washington, or later watched in full and frightening
detail in the multiple definitive video investigations by *The New York Times*
and other publications; that what it witnessed was just some good patriotic
folk who got justly irate at a stolen election, rather than the attempt by a
violent, armed mob to lynch members of Congress and prevent the peaceful transfer of power from a defeated president to his successor that we all
saw that day.

The intent is to get people to distrust their senses, to disbelieve factual
reality, to turn that reality on its head, thereby driving a wedge between the
true believers and the rest of the world, planted in reality. It is a recipe for
cultist authoritarianism—in this case, the Trumpist kind.

––––––––––

BY JULY 2021, RIGHT-WING media had already reached the peak phase of their
mind-bending efforts to help Republicans avoid accountability for the
January 6 insurrection. Violent perpetrators, in their rhetorical retelling,
were magically transformed into hapless victims, and their victims into
malicious evildoers. And nowhere was this more apparent than when it
came time for what should have been an automatic, pro forma next step:
creating a congressional investigation of the insurrection.

First, Republicans in the Senate refused to agree to a bicameral House-Senate commission to investigate the event after Senate minority leader Mitch McConnell protested against the "slanted and unbalanced" proposal that had emerged from the House.[64] Six Republicans still voted with Democrats to create the commission, but it wasn't enough to overcome McConnell's filibuster.

House Speaker Nancy Pelosi instead created a House commission to investigate the event, and invited GOP minority leader Kevin McCarthy to designate a slate of Republican members to participate. McCarthy offered up five members who primarily were interested in undermining the whole affair, including Jim Banks of Indiana and Jim Jordan of Ohio, both of whom had voted to overturn the Electoral College results immediately after the insurrection.

Jordan promptly demanded to know about Pelosi's supposed culpability for the Capitol siege, based on false reports that she had been in charge of the National Guard that day. Banks issued a statement inexplicably blaming the Biden administration, which was not in office at the time, for its response to the January 6 attack: "Make no mistake, Nancy Pelosi created this committee solely to malign conservatives and to justify the Left's authoritarian agenda," Banks said. "Even then, I will do everything possible to give the American people the facts about the lead up to January 6, the riot that day, and the responses from Capitol leadership and the Biden administration. I will not allow this committee to be turned into a forum for condemning millions of Americans because of their political beliefs."[65]

Pelosi told McCarthy that she wouldn't put obvious saboteurs like Jordan and Banks on the committee to preserve its integrity; he responded by withdrawing the entire slate of nominees. So she completed the committee by naming two Republicans—Liz Cheney and Adam Kinzinger, both outspoken Trump critics after the insurrection.[66]

This was the moment Republicans went into their proverbial "bloody shirt" mode, claiming that Democrats were only concerned with exploiting the insurrection for political advantage while victimizing the "ordinary pa-triotic Americans" who participated in it.

This has become a customary defense: claim that the perpetrators of violence are the real victims, and their targeted victims are the real per-petrators; bullies become the brutalized, and the brutalized the bullies. Historically speaking, one of the American right's favorite sleights of hand is to accuse their critics of "waving the bloody shirt" whenever real violence occurs: characterizing anyone daring to hold the perpetrators and their enablers accountable for that violence as grifters seeking to engage in cheap demagoguery for crass political purposes. The problem isn't the violence; the problem is holding the people who cause it accountable.[67]

It's a rhetorical twist perfected by the right during post–Civil War Reconstruction era—when Southern politicians used it to deride their Northern counterparts whenever the cruelties of the Ku Klux Klan and the Red Shirts were raised. (The phrase originated from an incident in which a Klan beating of a schoolteacher in the South stirred the ire of Northern Republicans, one of whom denounced the violence in Congress; a false legend arose that he had waved the schoolteacher's bloody shirt on the floor of the House, which then became a bigger scandal than the original violence.)[68] It's remained in constant use ever since: as a deflection against lynching crimes and "race riots" in the 1920s, and against the advances of civil rights in the 1950s and '60s. Rush Limbaugh indulged in it to claim that Bill Clinton blamed him for the Oklahoma City bombing in 1995, and the Fox News pundit class wielded it to accuse the Department of Homeland Security of "smearing veterans" in 2009 when it issued a bulletin warning of the spread of far-right extremism and its recruitment within the ranks of the military.[69]

Channeling her conservative forebears, Congresswoman Elise Stefanik from upstate New York joined Jim Jordan on Fox News, saying: "We need a broad-scoped commission that's focused on political violence. What the Pelosi sham commission is focused on is only January 6 and trying to shame over 70 million Americans who are standing up for constitutional and election integrity issues."[70]

Indeed, Stefanik, the House minority whip, spent the week defending the insurrectionists by attacking Democrats. She also had Pelosi in her sights: "The American people deserve to know the truth. That Nancy Pelosi bears responsibility, as speaker of the House, for the tragedy that occurred on January 6," Stefanik told a press conference. Cheney tartly observed that she "would be deeply ashamed of myself" for such remarks. Stefanik retorted that Cheney was "a Pelosi pawn."[71]

The final component of the "bloody shirt" narrative entails blaming the victims. After the opening hearing of the House January 6 commission, Fox contributor Julie Kelly tweeted out an attack on Michael Fanone, a Capitol police officer who was brutalized during the insurrection and testified before the panel, in which she made fun of him for crying. Kelly dismissed him as a "crisis actor," adding that "he has many tattoos."[72]

In a similar vein, right-wing pundit Matt Walsh sneered at Kinzinger for his tears during his remarks at the hearing: "Men should not cry in public. It is unmanly and dishonorable."[73]

But the focus of the demonization, as Stefanik's remarks suggested, was on Pelosi. Calling her "Nancy the Insurrectionist," Ingraham told her Fox News audience that Democrats were engaging in a plan to take total control of the nation's politics: "They're following Nancy Pelosi and her efforts to poison the well, to accuse Republicans of fascism and otherwise drive their opponents from public life."[74]

The presence of Cheney and Kinzinger on the commission—which kept unearthing embarrassing revelations about the role played by key members of Trump's inner circle in fomenting the insurrection—remained a burr under Republicans' saddles, who considered their participation a complete betrayal. It all came to a head in February 2022, when the Republican National Committee voted overwhelmingly to censure both of them.[75]

The language of the resolution showed no concern for that day's violence or the fact that a mob had besieged the US Congress—rather, its sole focus was on how Cheney and Kinziger had allegedly destroyed their party's chances in November's midterm elections.[76]

Cheney and Kinziger, the letter declared, "are participating in a Democrat-led persecution of ordinary citizens engaged in legitimate political discourse."

Later polling found that 54 percent of Americans disagreed with the RNC, saying they considered the January 6 attack on the Capitol illegitimate political discourse; only 21 percent thought it was legitimate. But 33 percent of Republicans thought it was legitimate, and only 38 percent thought it was not.[77]

AS THE SUMMER OF 2022 progressed, it became clear that, while Donald Trump was unquestionably the chief figurehead of the radical right's ongoing war on American democracy, he was not the general—the man who organizes the troops, feeds them the requisite propaganda, and deploys them strategically to undermine democratic institutions at every level. That role belonged to Michael Flynn, the QAnon-loving Army general who has long been part of Trump's inner circle.[78]

At one time, Flynn was a respected member of the Pentagon leadership, serving as director of the Defense Intelligence Agency under President Obama from 2012 to 2014, until he was forced into retirement. The public-facing reason for his dismissal was that he had become "abusive with staff, didn't listen, worked against policy, bad management, etc." Flynn reportedly exhibited a loose relationship with the truth, leading his subordinates to refer to Flynn's repeated dubious assertions as "Flynn facts."[79]

What generally went unmentioned was that his increasingly cozy relationship with Russia had raised alarms within the intelligence community.[80] During his tenure he gave a lecture on leadership at the Moscow headquarters of the GRU, the Russian military intelligence directorate—the first American official ever admitted entry to the building. He attempted to arrange a follow-up visit that was disallowed, and he also attempted to arrange a visit by high-ranking GRU officials to the United States, but that proposal also was scotched by his superiors.

At a London intelligence conference in February 2014, a longtime informant for the American intelligence community with long-running Republican credentials had a disturbing encounter with Flynn.[81] The general's close association with a Russian woman named Svetlana Lokhova—a Cambridge scholar with suspected ties to the GRU—so alarmed the informant that he passed along his concerns to American authorities that Flynn may have been compromised by Russian intelligence. Flynn later insisted that his only interpersonal contact with Lokhova was at the dinner and only lasted twenty minutes, but he also invited her to accompany him on his next trip to Moscow (which never materialized), and the two continued to correspond via email over an unclassified channel for several years afterward.[82]

After leaving the Army, Flynn created a consultancy in Washington that provided intelligence services for businesses and governments, including in Turkey. But his relationship with Russia remained close; in December 2015, Flynn delivered a speech at the ten-year anniversary celebration of Russia Today (RT), a state-controlled Russian international television network, in Moscow, for which he was paid $45,000. He sat next to Russian president Vladimir Putin at the banquet table.[83]

Trump hired Flynn as a national security adviser to his campaign in 2016; after Trump won the presidency, he promptly appointed Flynn director of national intelligence. Flynn's tenure was brief; caught lying to the FBI about his contacts with a Russian ambassador, Flynn was fired in February 2017. Flynn pleaded guilty to felony lying-to-the-FBI charges in December of that year, but he never served any prison time; his sentencing was the subject of constant deferrals, and the Justice Department under Trump's attorney general, William Barr, attempted to have the charges dismissed. Those efforts were denied by the federal courts.[84]

Trump eventually pardoned Flynn in late November 2020, after the election.[85] The pardon appears to have had the effect of unleashing Flynn as general of MAGA's endless insurrection. Almost immediately, Flynn became prominently involved in Stop the Steal events, speaking at the December 12 rally in Washington.[86] He also was a participant in the December 20 meeting with Trump at the White House to plan ways to prevent Joe Biden from assuming the presidency, including Flynn's suggestion that Trump use the military to seize ballot boxes.[87] Flynn, of course, was present on the Mall during the January 6 Stop the Steal events, but he did not join the mob on Capitol Hill. Later, though, he embarked on a speaking tour at QAnon and COVID-denialism events in the summer of 2021, which gradually morphed into the aforementioned MAGA election denialist gatherings: Flynn melded the two seamlessly, claiming that the COVID pandemic had actually been a Deep State conspiracy to distract the public from the theft of the election.

In September 2022, the Associated Press and PBS *Frontline* published a joint investigation into Flynn's leadership in the MAGA movement's drive to regain and permanently seize power in America, which exposed the breadth and depth of Flynn's work to unite evangelical Christians with QAnon-fueled Trumpist conspiracism using election denialism as their primary culture war fodder.[88] Flynn himself manifested the strategy he deployed—to elect MAGA politicians to office at every level, beginning with local institutions like city councils and school boards—by signing on as a local GOP committeeman and volunteer "poll watcher" in his Florida hometown.

The Associated Press/Frontline investigation found that Flynn, in addition to headlining revival-style roadshows, called ReAwaken America, featuring long rosters of right-wing figures who toured the country, had built a network of nonprofit groups, including one with fifty million dollars in projected spending. In the process, Flynn and his companies had earned hundreds of thousands of dollars for his efforts.

Flynn covered a broad range of culture war hot spots in his speeches, reeling off crowd-pleasing one-liners with heavy religious overtones. He often told audiences that America was in the midst of a "spiritual war" and listed a number of democratic institutions and principles as "the enemy."

His brand of Christian nationalism was moreover decidedly authoritarian. Speaking to a Texas audience on the ReAwaken America tour in November 2021, he explained that his idea of national unity involved everyone thinking and worshiping in exactly the same way.[89]

"If we are going to have one nation under God, which we must, we have to have one religion," Flynn said. "One nation under God and one religion under God, right? All of us, working together."

He claimed a nefarious "globalist" cabal created COVID-19 and told his audiences that there are seventy-five members of the Socialist Party in Congress. Flynn regularly tells audiences he doesn't trust the US government or government institutions that oversee the rule of law and claims Democrats are trying to destroy the country.

"The people that are in charge of our government right now, they are intentionally trying to destroy our country," he said at one rally. "These people, they're not incompetent. They're not stupid. They're evil!"[90]

Flynn also called the media "the number one enemy," claiming it has done a "horrible, horrible disservice to the country by just constantly lying and trying to deceive us." Public elementary schools, he claims, are teaching "filth" and "pornography." He called the left "our enemies" and said they are "godless" and "soulless."[91]

But the primary focus of these rallies was election denialism. At a rally in Utah's Salt Palace Convention Center, Flynn declared once again that Trump had won the 2020 election and said, "our government is corrupt." Flynn repeatedly told ReAwaken America audiences that Biden's presidency constituted "a moment of crisis" for America. He proclaimed the election system is "totally broken," and blamed both Democratic "socialists" and establishment "RINOs" (Republicans in Name Only).

The roadshows were only the most visible component of the election-denialist movement, which both was well-financed and broadly organized. Flynn had a number of prominent allies: Mike Lindell, the fanatically Trumpist CEO of MyPillow; right-wing provocateur Dinesh D'Souza, who produced a widely debunked pseudo-documentary titled *2000 Mules*, which purported to reveal widespread voter fraud but which fact-checkers consistently found was only a farrago of false claims that proved nothing; Overstock.com founder Patrick Byrne, another MAGA businessman who had been present, with Flynn, at the December 20, 2020, Oval Office meeting with Trump at which martial law was discussed; and a Texas-based organization called True the Vote, overseen by longtime right-wing operatives Catherine Engelbrecht and Gregg Phillips, who had made their bones by circulating conspiracist claims that "voter fraud" had given Hillary Clinton her popular-vote victory in 2016.[92]

True the Vote formed an alliance in the summer of 2022 with so-called "constitutional sheriffs" who had announced they intended to determine if various conspiracy theories about the 2020 vote—notably those claiming that Dominion Voting Systems machines had been "rigged," as well as D'Souza's bogus "mules" claims—were accurate.[93] Richard Mack, the founder of the far-right Constitutional Sheriffs and Peace Officers Association (CSPOA), announced that "we are asking for all local law enforcement agencies to work together to pursue investigations to determine the veracity of the *2000 Mules* information."[94]

In an interview with Lindell, Mack informed him that "the ultimate power is in the sheriff in every county, and he's the one, as my book says, the county sheriffs are America's last hope. And if we're going to restore liberty in America, it's going to be county by county, one good sheriff at a time, working with his citizens to reestablish our Constitution as the supreme law of the land. County by county."

In short order, Engelbrecht and Phillips showed up at a gathering organized by Mack in Nevada. Engelbrecht marveled to the audience about how the election denialists came to form a coalition with the CSPOA, regaling them with descriptions of how they had found that the FBI and state governments had stonewalled their efforts to open investigations into supposed ballot box stuffing by "mules" based on their "evidence."[95]

She told the audience that she had finally figured out how to surmount the problem when she was contacted by Mack and "constitutionalist" sheriff Mark Lamb of Pinal County, Arizona, and informed of their interest in the *2000 Mules* claims: "The lights went on: 'It's the sheriffs! That's who can do these investigations, that's who we can trust, that's who we can turn over information to.'"

Engelbrecht proclaimed that True the Vote would be partnering with CSPOA and another far-right law-enforcement group, Protect America Now, to get "eyes on those drop boxes in states where they still exist."

These allies and their tactics fell neatly in line with the explicit strategy outlined by Flynn, namely: go local. Flynn, who touted the adage that "local action has national impact," told audiences that "people at the county level have the ability to change this country." He explained that elected county commissioners could write more restrictive voting laws, and that elected sheriffs could enforce those laws—which happens to mesh neatly with the strategy of "constitutionalist sheriffs" and their Trumpist allies.

"We need to take this country back one town at a time, one county at a time, one state at a time, if that's what it takes," he told the crowd in Salt Lake City.[96]

"As long as I got a breath left in me, I am going to continue to push this message of local action and national impact," Flynn said another time. "And now I, now I wanna be able to tell people when they say, when somebody says, well, are you doing, what are you doing specifically? I'm gonna, I am now part of the Republican executive committee for the Sarasota GOP. And I also am volunteering to be a poll watcher in the upcoming elections, particularly in this county, in the state of Florida."[97]

The "poll watching" operations became a central focus of this local strategy as the fall elections drew nearer. Another Flynn operation financed by Byrne called the America Project created affiliate groups in at least nine states as part of its Operation Eagles Wings, designed to promote this tactic. Its Florida affiliate announced on Facebook that it was seeking "America First Poll Watchers," offering free training to interested groups. This training includes grassroots social activism, poll watching, and get-out-the-vote efforts. Promotional material for the sessions said it would teach participants to "expose weaknesses," "monitor and evaluate absentee voting," and conduct "investigative canvassing."[98]

In states around the nation, poll-watching operations were organized, often under the auspices of the Republican Party. In Pennsylvania, the Republican National Committee's director of election integrity, Andrea Raffle, told trainees that the party had increased the numbers of poll watchers it recruited from one thousand to six thousand. Activists from election-denialist groups began appearing at events with Republican officials, recruiting volunteers to help watch the polls.

There were a couple of halting attempts to organize poll watching during primary elections, notably in the Seattle area in July, and in Nevada's June vote. But the campaign began showing up during early voting in states like Arizona.

In Mesa, camo-clad poll watchers operating out of a pickup truck showed up armed with both guns and cameras, and made a point of aggressively photographing people dropping off their ballots. When people asked them what they were doing, they disingenuously answered: "Oh, just catching some Vitamin D."[99]

The group organizing the Mesa surveillance operations was a paramilitary Patriot group calling itself Lions of Liberty, affiliated with the Oath Keepers. The League of Women Voters filed a federal lawsuit against them, saying they were "scheming to baselessly accuse voters of being 'mules' and to 'dox' them (publicly reveal their personal information online)." That would result in "unjustifiably exposing voters to harm to not only their reputations, but also their safety," the lawsuit said. Lions of Liberty promptly announced they were shutting down the operation.[100]

PART III

A Hundred Little Insurrections

9

Concocting Enemies

THE AMERICAN RIGHT HAS a long history of creating grand bogeymen, erecting existential threats out of dubious strands of fact: Black rapists after the Civil War, anarchists and Communists in the 1920s and '50s, hippies in the '60s, the welfare mothers of the 1970s and '80s, sharia law in the 2000s. In the Trump era, the great menace to America became "Antifa," the anti-fascists who turned out in the streets to oppose white-nationalist organizing.[1]

Stop and think about it: As existential threats to America go, "Antifa" and its "dark shadows" did seem to come out of nowhere, didn't they? As recently as 2016, hardly any American could have even told you what the word meant, let alone pronounce it. (The latter is still a matter of debate: An-TEEF-uh or AN-ti-fuh? Your call.)

If there was one place the great "Antifa" bogeyman came from, it was the fevered imaginations of the white nationalists and far-right conspiracy theorists who demonized and distorted a leftist movement dedicated to opposing their ugly racial politics. They managed to conjure a frightening vision of scary and mysterious radicals whose "dark shadows" completely obscured the growth of violent white nationalism from public view. And it worked.

In reality, Antifa traces its origins to the leftist groups that organized in Europe in the 1920s and '30s, particularly in Germany and Italy, to oppose fascists in those countries. Its modern iterations began organizing in the early part of the twenty-first century, with the first local anti-fascist group, Rose City Antifa, forming in Portland in 2007. The movement remains deliberately decentralized with no official leadership.[2]

The essence of the movement (which in many ways grew out of the punk music scene) is the motto "We go where they go"—that is, they believe in confronting fascists in the public spaces where they appear and removing their materials. This is why doxing—the public exposure of the identities and even home addresses and phone numbers of far-right activists, who often work under cover of anonymity—is central to the anti-fascist mission, and is an aspect that goes little mentioned by its often hysterical critics on the right.[3]

There is no national "Antifa" organization—only small local cooperative groups, all of them officially leaderless—and no national "leaders," despite anti-Semitic conspiracy theorists' risibly false claims that George Soros is the man behind it all.

Most of all, its operating philosophy is not—contrary to the right's characterization of the movement—focused on creating violence, but rather on preventing it if possible, particularly violence against vulnerable minorities frequently targeted by right-wing extremists and hate groups. At the same time, unlike other leftist groups, it does not eschew the use of violence to defend those minorities from violence—which is why so many of its members get caught up in street brawls and are regularly seen engaging in violent acts. And it justifies some violent acts as preemptive.

The majority, but not all, of Antifa's violence is reactive—unlike that of the Proud Boys and other street brawling groups with whom they have been engaging, whose violence is almost entirely deliberate and provocative.

Those groups' entire reason for existence is to create violent scenes in liberal urban centers, all supposedly in defense of "Western civilization."

None of that, however, is apparent to media audiences who have been subjected over the past six years to a steady stream of reports from such outlets as Fox News—as well as right-wing pundits like the late Rush Limbaugh and Ben Shapiro—falsely depicting Antifa as a "Marxist" movement intent on destroying America and poised to invade middle America to burn down their way of life.

The "Antifa" bogeyman is a very recent addition to the American right's long history of manufacturing folk devils and moral panics. Throughout 2016, for instance, Fox News only mentioned the movement once—in reporting on the violent melee that erupted in Sacramento, California, during a march organized by the neo-Nazi Traditionalist Worker Party in June.[4] Fox, of course, blamed the anti-fascists for the brawl that produced stabbings and hospitalizations, despite multiple videos showing neo-Nazis starting at least some of the fights that broke out; in fact, both sides used extreme violence during the confrontation.[5]

Antifa only arrived on the right's radar in January 2017, when a bundle of conspiracy theorists tried to claim that they were leading the charge for a Communist attempt to prevent Trump from being sworn in as president on January 20, with Alex Jones of *Infowars* and "Health Ranger" Mike Adams leading the charge.[6]

They were joined by a wide array of conspiracist right wingers. The website of the Oath Keepers, as well as its Facebook page, churned out apocalyptic warnings in the week leading up to the inauguration: "Communists Intend to Overthrow the United States Before Inauguration Day"; "10,000 Men with Guns To Prevent Coup on Inauguration Day"; "In Just 10 Days, the Radical Left Will Attempt to Overthrow the U.S. Government."

At the *Infowars* conspiracy mill run by Jones, the theories were multifarious as well as frantic: "Anarchists Are Hoping to Turn Donald Trump's Inauguration on January 20th into One of the Biggest Riots in U.S. History";

"Will the CIA Assassinate Trump?"; "Alex Jones' Emergency Message to President Donald Trump to Deter Martial Law."

The hysteria was inspired by a series of protests planned for Washington, D.C., that week by a small anti-fascist group called Refuse Fascism, the offspring of a cultish far-left operator named Bob Avakian and his fringe Revolutionary Communist Party. Videos from these marches revealed that it was a small organization that managed to attract only a couple dozen protesters to march in Washington the weekend before the inauguration.

Adams, a longtime conspiracy theorist and onetime associate of Jones's Infowars, was one of the primary sources about the planned disruptions of the inauguration. (In 2013, just before the second inauguration of Barack Obama, Adams warned antigovernment "Patriots" that the president would soon be issuing a "mass of kill orders" for them.)

"What I am hearing is that there is an actual planned coup attempt," Jones told his audience in a video promoted by the Oath Keepers. He conflated the Refuse Fascism protests with the long-announced Women's March on Washington, scheduled the day after the inauguration and expected to attract two hundred thousand, saying that the "cover story" for the coup would be "the women's march, the labor union march, whatever it is."

"We WILL be there," a commenter named Marlene wrote on the Oath Keepers Facebook page. "And we will be prepared. We will not allow soros and the globalists to start a civil war where we fight against each other. But we are prepared for a full scale revolution against tyranny on OUR own terms at a later time. Most of these anti-American fascists are not even Americans. They represent the dregs of humanity Obama has brought into our country just for this purpose—all illegal all foreign and all who hate us because they hate themselves."

On the day of the inauguration, Oath Keepers and their cohorts were visibly present, vowing "to protect peaceable American patriots who are now being threatened with assault and other acts of violence by radical leftist groups."[7] As it happened, there was no violence and only a handful of arrests of protesters. But the rhetoric formed the template for the attacks on anti-fascist protesters heard for the next four years: Antifa, in their alternative universe, had become so vast, powerful, and insidious that it threatened to overthrow the American government through an overnight revolution that entailed the beheadings of white Christians.

OVER THE SPRING AND summer of 2017, anti-fascist activists were involved in a number of violent protests, notably in Berkeley, California; Olympia, Washington; and Portland, Oregon.[8] In September, Fox News created a video calling Antifa an "alt-left group" in late June, claiming that anti-fascists' goal was "political intimidation and chaos through the threat of violence."[9]

Coverage of Antifa became muted in right-wing media circles for the next couple of months—though Tucker Carlson's publication *The Daily Caller* became a reliable source of stories demonizing Antifa during this time. Headlines like "'Anti-Fascism' Group Bears Striking Resemblance to Actual Terrorists," "Revealed: The Antifa Plan to Get Liberals to Embrace Violence," and "Here's Why George Soros Is Siding with Fascists," became common there.

The Antifa-demonization narrative then erupted widely in the wake of the horrifying events of August 11–12, 2017, in Charlottesville, Virginia, at the lethal Unite the Right march event. Fox News crafted a popular red-meat narrative by beating a steady drumbeat declaring Antifa to be the far more dire threat to the nation than violent white nationalists. It ran prominent stories on a clash between far-right provocateurs who attempted to organize protest rallies in the Bay Area the weekend of August 26–27, claiming that anti-fascists had "attacked peaceful protesters."[10] (The reality, as usual, was much more complicated.[11]) It ran news stories attacking a Dartmouth professor who had the temerity to defend anti-fascists.[12]

The anti-anti-fascist backlash soon reached a fever pitch. An "open letter" at Fox to "the hatemongers" of "the violent extremist group Antifa" featured a bizarrely inverted version of the reality of what happened at Unite
the Right:

> In Charlottesville, you arrived on the scene with clubs and shields,
> prepared to commit violence. Instead, your sick plans were superseded
> by the monstrous behavior of neo-Nazis, Ku Klux Klan members and
> other right-wing extremists as lunatic as you are. But they don't have
> much of the liberal media working as agit-prop wings for them every
> day, like you do.[13]

A Steve Kurtz piece similarly attacking the movement claimed: "Antifa gets
to decide who the fascists are, and don't look now, but it's you."[14] And what
appeared to be a straight news piece described how a petition presented to
the White House urged the Trump administration to label Antifa a "terror
group," then added: "Antifa has earned this title due to its violent actions in
multiple cities and their influence in the killings of multiple police officers
throughout the United States."[15] (No police killings of any kind by members
of Antifa have been recorded to date.)

A similar opinion piece by Ned Ryun insisted that "Antifa is a domestic
terrorist organization" and demanded that Democrats denounce the movement.[16] Meanwhile, Tucker Carlson devoted a segment of his nightly Fox
show to discussing whether Antifa should be barred from gathering on
American college campuses.[17]

Rush Limbaugh weighed in after the Charlottesville events, claiming
Republicans who denounced the white nationalists afterward were being
weak by "conferring moral authority on militant leftist protesters," and
within a couple of weeks had shifted the narrative on its head, arguing
that "the Democrats' media and their Antifa pitbulls are the real threat
to America."[18]

"I'll tell you what this shows," Limbaugh said. "It shows the power of the fake news media to create a crisis out of literally nothing because there is no threat to America from white supremacists. The number of white supremacists, in relation to voters, wouldn't fill a bathtub."

TEN MONTHS AFTER TRUMP'S inauguration, right-wing conspiracists—once again led by Alex Jones and *Infowars*—briefly resurrected the same hysterical scenario from January, claiming that "Antifa" and associated satanists were planning to spark a violent civil war, with Trump's overthrow being the ultimate purpose—which was then carried credulously by mainstream right-wing media, notably Fox.[19]

The planned rallies were real: Refuse Fascism once again was advertising plans to hold anti-Trump rallies in a number of cities around the country on November 4. The organization bought a full-page ad in *The New York Times* and set up a website devoted to the event, which was never billed as anything other than an entirely peaceful protest.

Viewed through the prism of right-wing conspiracism, however, the rallies were quickly characterized as potentially violent actions intended to spark a "civil war" against the government. And in response, several self-described "patriots" threatened to create violence on their own.

"Honestly, I'm happy," one YouTuber told his audience. "Dude, we've been on the verge of the great war for what seems like forever and I'm just ready to get it going."[20]

Following a Refuse Fascism rally in Los Angeles in late September, *Infowars* reporter Paul Joseph Watson filed a piece headlined "Antifa Plans 'Civil War' to Overthrow Government," warning that "Antifa" groups had targeted November 4 as a day of nationwide civil unrest and violence, "part of a plot to start a 'civil war.'" (Marchers carried a banner predicting an electoral shift which read "November 4 It Begins.")

Soon the John Birch Society, one of the hoariest of conspiracy-theory mills, joined the fray; CEO Arthur Thompson posted a video warning Birchers about the looming "Antifa" violence and offering helpful tips about what they could do about it.

Jones had some fresh theories. He claimed that financier George Soros had poured eighteen billion dollars in resources into the operation, and that protests would be led by Women's March organizer Linda Sarsour, who he described as "the pro-sexual-mutilation Muslim."

Amateur conspiracy theorists joined in. Someone named Jordan Peltz who self-identified as a "deputy" (although he was seen wearing a badge from the "United States Warrant Service," a private company) posted a popular YouTube video (with over a million views) warning of "Antifa" plans: "They will start off by attacking police officers, first responders, anybody that's in uniform, they will then go after the citizens and the people and the government and all of that. So if you're white, you're a Trump supporter, you're a Nazi then, to them. And it will be open game on you."

According to another theory, the Department of Defense was planning secret exercises designed to support the mass "Antifa" uprising. As the theories multiplied, so did mockery of them on social media—which then gave birth to new permutations.

On Twitter, a satirical lefty shitposter mused sarcastically: "can't wait for Nov. 4th when millions of antifa supersoldiers will behead all white parents and small business owners in the town square." In short order, it became an article of faith that violent "Antifa" thugs were planning to behead all white Christian parents, the joke tweet becoming "evidence" broadcast widely on the popular right-wing blog Gateway Pundit and throughout right-wing anti-Antifa circles on social media and message boards.

The Oath Keepers, in the meantime, eagerly believed the attack was imminent, urging people to always remain armed and to insist on being permitted to bring their guns to church. Founder Stewart Rhodes told his followers to expect "a wave of left wing terrorism targeting conservatives, libertarians, Christians, police, military, veterans, etc (anyone the left considers on the right or part of the system). Expect it. Prepare yourselves in case this does lead to a full blown civil war."

This time, the Antifa panic spread to a broader audience, including Fox News, which carried a report claiming that "Antifa" planned to topple the "Trump regime": "Will the so-called 'Antifa apocalypse' come with a bang or a whimper?" a Fox News story asked in its lede.[21]

When November 4 arrived, *Infowars* reporters spread out across the country to report on the Refuse Fascism rallies, with a warning from Jones at the website: "Attention, devil worshipers. Attention meth heads. Attention Antifa scum. We're fully aware of the globalists funding your operation to push for a violent revolution in America."

However, they found that only a handful of protesters showed up for them, and that no violence or civil war was in the offing. Conspiracy theorists claimed victory. According to them, they had scared the conspirators off, even though most observers predicted the protests would be inconsequential.

No one noticed that the looming existential threat of the Evil Antifa Horde—which they already had declared beaten—really was nonexistent. But the mythical monster, the Enemy that the conspiracist Trumpian army of wannabe heroes needed, had been born.

FOX'S COVERAGE OF ANTIFA went through cycles, and its ebb and flow there as a story reflect its usefulness as a propaganda tool for attacking liberals and defending Trump. Fox initially promoted the story hardest as part of a pushback against concerns about the rise of white nationalism after Charlottesville—but none of that compares to the open floodgates accompanying the nationwide protests over police brutality.

In 2016, Fox had carried one anti-Antifa piece; but after the violence of mid-August 2017, it rushed out eighteen pieces, all attacking the movement, mostly in the month of September. The network then ran ten Antifa hit pieces between October and December.

The subject was comparatively deemphasized at Fox for 2018, with some twenty-one pieces in total—the majority of those appearing in August, around the time of the anniversary of the Unite the Right events. And for the start of 2019, the story seemed almost to vanish, with only six pieces running between January and late June.

However, the network began bashing Antifa again seriously after the June 30 assault by anti-fascists with a milkshake on Portland pseudo-journalist/provocateur Andy Ngo—regaling the public with ten pieces attacking Antifa over the short space of the next seven days. For the re-mainder of the year, the Antifa hit pieces became more persistent, with thirty-four such stories running through early November (and then going quiet entirely for the next two months).

Indeed, Antifa largely disappeared from Fox's news radar again for the first six months of 2020—but after the May 28 killing of George Floyd sparked nationwide protests against police brutality, the story came roar-ing back with a vengeance. Antifa, right-wing pundits unanimously pro-claimed, was almost solely responsible for violence during the protests.

These claims became common in the first week of the protests. Tucker Carlson's opening monologue on June 2 raised the spectral bogeyman of Antifa, warning that they were coming soon to your neighborhood, where "violent young men with guns will be in charge. They will make the rules, including the rules in your neighborhood. They will do what they want. You will do what they say. No one will stop them. You will not want to live here when that happens."[22]

Between May 31 and June 6, 2020, Fox News ran a total of forty hit pieces blaming Antifa for the protest violence. Between June 8 and early September came fifty-seven more pieces. The national narrative that emerged from all this coverage, and which became entrenched conventional wisdom not just among

Fox-watching conservatives but in rural and suburban America generally: Antifa and BLM had burned down American cities in the summer of 2020.[23]

None of that was true.

In reality, the vast majority of that summer's protests—over 95 percent of the 7,305 events in all fifty states that were recorded around the country—were peaceful, and Antifa was not a factor in any of those at which violence of some kind occurred; the more common source of violence involved street clashes between marchers protesting the Floyd murder (many of them under the banner of Black Lives Matter) and police deploying aggressive street crowd–control tactics. Police made arrests at only 5 percent of the events, while protesters or bystanders reported injuries at only 1.6 percent of them. And there was property damage at only 3.7 percent of them, with arson fires confined to a small handful of locations. Of the twenty-seven deaths associated with the protests, none were concretely linked to demonstrators. Several were killed by police.[24]

———————

IT'S UNLIKELY THAT MARTIN Gugino, the seventy-five-year-old activist who Donald Trump labeled an "Antifa provocateur" for the sin of being clobbered to the pavement on video by police in Buffalo, New York, during a George Floyd protest in June 2020, ever in fact identified as a member of an "Antifa" group.[25] Not that it mattered to Trump, who only wanted to demonize the poor man by casting him as an embodiment of the right's favorite bogeyman. But the message was constant and relentless.

It was a constant of his campaign speeches and on Twitter. In late May, he tweeted that "the United States of America will be designating ANTIFA as a Terrorist Organization"—a mostly empty threat, since there is no place in American law that would enable him to make such a designation, and doing so would have been unconstitutional.[26]

On *Fox and Friends* on June 4, the show's cohosts, aghast, warned that "Antifa is dropping off bricks and pickaxes to attack cops and take out buildings and stores," showing videos of blue plastic boxes filled with bricks and rocks.[27] In reality, the containers were from construction sites and were nowhere near any planned protests.[28] Similar tales of Molotov cocktails being delivered to protest sites turned out to revolve around a single incident in Las Vegas at which far-right Boogaloo Bois were responsible for making the incendiary devices—with the intent of blaming Antifa for the violence—though they never got the chance to use them.[29]

FBI officials, in fact, were firm in their insistence all summer that they had found no evidence of "Antifa" involvement in any of the violence at these rallies. Antifa was not involved in coordination, nor was anyone from the movement involved in planning violence.[30]

The climax of the Evil Antifa Threat narrative came in September when the Department of Homeland Security's acting chief, Chad Wolf, announced on Tucker Carlson's show that the Department of Justice planned on "targeting and investigating the head of these organizations, [and] the individuals that are paying for these individuals to move across the country."[31] Wolf's plan came on the heels of a viral video showing protesters heckling Sen. Rand Paul as he left the Republican National Convention in Washington, D.C., after which Paul demanded a similar investigation.

That same week Trump told Laura Ingraham that "people that are in the dark shadows" are "controlling the streets" of Democratic cities. And when Ingraham warned him that he sounded like he was promoting a conspiracy theory, he doubled down with a pitch-perfect rendition of the "evil Antifa thug" caricature central to the narrative attacking the movement.[32]

"We had somebody get on a plane from a certain city this weekend, and in the plane it was almost completely loaded with thugs wearing these dark uniforms, black uniforms, with gear and this and that," he claimed.

Likewise, and without evidence, Attorney General William Barr told CNN's Wolf Blitzer, "I've talked to every police chief in every city where there has been major violence and they all have identified Antifa as the ramrod for the violence. They are flying around the country. We know people who are flying around the country."[33]

All of this provided Trump's DHS with a convenient pretext to send an army of contracted goons into the city of Portland, Oregon, in the summer of 2020 to arrest citizens protesting against police brutality—summarily sweeping people off the street on the pretext of a kind of preventative arrest based on groundless speculation that they were "Antifa" conspiring to "burn down our cities," as Trump put it.[34]

The Floyd protests were an international phenomenon, spreading to thousands of cities and towns, occurring in all fifty states as well as in over sixty other countries.[35] Demonstrators turned out en masse to support those seeking justice for Floyd and the wider Black Lives Matter movement, and to stand up against police brutality.[36] Most of these protests lasted one or two days; however, in Portland, where police brutality issues had taken on an extraordinary edge, the protests became a daily affair—one that eventually surpassed one hundred consecutive days.[37]

By early July, most of the protests had become quiet and nonviolent, with only sporadic violence and vandalism, with the notable exception of an arson attack on the federal courthouse downtown—which is about the time that DHS agents began showing up, wearing anonymous military gear, arresting protesters on the streets and spiriting them away.[38]

It played out like a nightmare from a banana republic: Unmarked vans with federal officers drove around downtown Portland, coming to abrupt halts when a targeted protester was spotted, upon which the protestor was surrounded by heavily armed agents and swept into a van with no explanation why they were being arrested. The arrests were caught on video and shared on social media, and DHS acknowledged that these were their employees.

Acting Deputy Secretary Ken Cuccinelli told National Public Radio that it was done to keep officers safe and away from crowds and to move detainees to a "safe location for questioning."

"I fully expect that as long as people continue to be violent and to destroy property that we will attempt to identify those folks," he added.[39]

Over the course of the summer, between June 4 and August 31, DHS sent at least 755 officers—from agencies that ranged from the Federal Protective Service to US Customs and Border Protection, as well as US Immigration and Customs Enforcement, Secret Service, and US Department of Homeland Security's Office of Intelligence and Analysis—to Portland, tasked with protecting the city's downtown federal courthouse.

An internal DHS review later revealed that it was also an extraordinary exercise in authoritarian incompetence. It showed that senior DHS leadership pushed unfounded conspiracy theories about anti-fascists, encouraged the contractors they hired to violate protesters' constitutional rights, and made spurious connections, based on no real evidence, between protesters who engaged in criminal activity. It also revealed poor training and inadequate guidance, which contributed to the federal intelligence officers' lack of knowledge on legal restrictions for the collection of such information, and turned the entire operation into a massive mess.[40]

"The report was a stunning analysis of the incompetence and mismanagement and abuse of power during the summer of 2020," Oregon senator Ron Wyden, who released a redacted version of the document, told Oregon Public Broadcasting.[41]

It found that senior DHS leaders attempted to politicize intelligence in order to support Trump's claims that a massive "Antifa" conspiracy was behind the many anti-police protests around the nation, but particularly so in Portland. The same leaders pressured subordinates to illegally search phones, and, when legal staff objected, sought to cut them out of the discussion.[42]

An inexperienced team of open-source intelligence collectors, tasked with analyzing information obtained from public sources, also created dossiers on protesters and journalists—which they called "baseball cards"—despite having no clear connections to domestic terrorism or security threats.

The internal review found that out of the forty-eight reports provided, thirteen of them involved people accused of nonviolent offenses. One "baseball card" focused on a person who was arrested and accused of flying a drone and identified on social media as a journalist.

"The report documents shocking, coordinated efforts by our government to abuse its power and to invade liberty in violation of the Constitution," said Oregon federal public defender Lisa Hay. "In Portland, we were concerned that the government unconstitutionally collected information, including through the illegal search of protestors' cellphones last summer. This report confirms that was their intent."

Over the next few nights, they clashed with protesters in the area around the courthouse, using flash-bangs and munitions to disperse the crowds. One protester was shot in the forehead by an "impact weapon" round that caused him brain damage.[43] Another protester—a Navy veteran who was attempting to speak with the DHS officers—was brutally beaten with batons, breaking his hand.[44]

That was when the scene exploded. On the night of July 24, thousands of Portlanders took to the streets to protest the arrests. The protest was entirely peaceful—drum circles, groups of teachers and nurses, a marching band, a Wall of Moms contingent wearing yellow shirts—until the DHS officers began unleashing tear gas on the crowd.[45] A brigade of "fathers" arrived with leaf blowers and blew the gas back at the officers.[46]

The protests continued nightly. DHS officials called the protests "criminal violence perpetrated by anarchists targeting city and federal properties." It brought in reinforcements on July 28, even though many of these officers lacked proper training, and both Mayor Ted Wheeler and Governor Kate Brown—along with both of the state's senators—demanded the DHS police be withdrawn.[47] Eventually, they negotiated a phased withdrawal, and the DHS arrests ceased.[48]

It was quickly apparent that the right-wing attempt to make "Antifa" and Black Lives Matter into bogeymen responsible for the protest violence was utterly bogus. An Associated Press review of the arrest documents from the summer's protests showed that most of the people taken into custody were not left-wing radicals and had no ties to larger movements. It had already been clear for months that "Antifa" was not responsible for the violence—which in many instances appeared in fact to have been instigated by police pushing back on protesters.

The internal review at DHS revealed that the push for concocting intelligence about Antifa intended to fit this narrative came from the top. Though the names are redacted, it is safe to assume that Chad Wolf, the DHS unconfirmed "acting secretary," was particularly involved, since he made numerous public statements at the time that mirror the shape of the discussions within the agency.[49]

The review also found that Wolf and his immediate underlings pushed staffers to describe the protests as "Violent Antifa Anarchist Inspired" (VAAI) actions—an entirely new category that had no evidentiary support or background.

"You could see where this VAAI definition was coming from a mile away," a career analyst is quoted saying in the report. "He got tired of [Redacted Name] telling him they did not have the reporting and he was convinced it was ANTIFA so he was going to fix the problem by changing what the collectors were reporting."

An email was sent to DHS senior leaders "instructing them that henceforth, the violent opportunists in Portland were to be reported as VAAI, unless the intel 'show[ed] . . . something different.'"

The report says that the DHS leadership "did make other attempts to controvert the collection-analysis process," pointing particularly to the push for VAAI designations. One memo from the same leader posited that "we have overwhelming intelligence regarding the ideologies driving individuals toward violence," but the analysts responded with factual reality: "In fact, overwhelming intelligence regarding the motivations or affiliations of the violent protesters did not exist," the report says. "Indeed, the review team could not identify any intelligence that existed to support [Redacted Name]'s assertion."

The review also noted that Federal Protective Services officers requested assistance from DHS's Homeland Identities, Targeting, and Exploitation Center to search protesters' cell phones. The latter team found the searches were illegal, and resisted pressure from senior Homeland Security leaders to assist in the searches.

No matter; Republicans took the bogus narrative and functionally made it an official one widely believed across the country—namely, that "Antifa and BLM burned down cities across the nation"—and subsequently used it to justify the January 6 Capitol insurrection by claiming the summer 2020 violence was far worse and a greater threat to the nation.

The narrative also was primarily responsible for the failures by both DHS and other federal law-enforcement agencies, notably the FBI, to adequately take the very real and building threat of white-nationalist terrorism seriously. The result, in fact, unleashed a plague of far-right violence that reached a high-tide mark on January 6, but which has still not receded.[50]

THE ANTIFA HYSTERIA HIT its peak in July 2020: In rural towns across America, men with guns could be seen roaming the streets, looking out for the threat to their homes they were warned about on Facebook: hordes of ravening "Antifa" activists, loaded en masse onto buses and intent on wreaking havoc. Local sheriffs jumped on the bandwagon, too. Never mind that it was all a hoax.[51]

The hoaxes were primarily spread on Facebook, though some Twitter accounts relayed the fake information as well. A typical post followed the formula used in others: a claim to have "real information" about "Antifa" piling into buses from nearby urban centers with the intent of attacking defenseless small towns.

One such hoax circulated in the Midwest, citing the notorious conspiracy-theory operation *Natural News*, and claiming that "Antifa operatives are organizing a plan to bus large numbers of Antifa terrorists to the vicinity of Sparta, Illinois, where they will be directed to target rural white Americans by burning farm houses and killing livestock. The purpose of the attack, according to sources, is so that Antifa can send a message to white America that 'not even rural whites are safe' from the reach of Antifa, and that if their radical left-wing demands are not met, all of America will burn (not just the cities)."[52]

Rumors spread by the militia group Real Three Percenters of Idaho on Facebook claimed that anti-fascists were being bused into Boise and neighboring counties to ransack local businesses.[53]

In Sioux Falls, South Dakota, the local chamber of commerce spread the rumors, tweeting out: "We're being told that buses are en route from Fargo for today's march downtown. DT businesses—please bring in any furniture, signs, etc. that could possibly be thrown through windows. Let's keep our city safe and peaceful!"[54]

In Northern California, law-enforcement officials played a key role in spreading the rumors among police departments. The panic apparently originated with a law-enforcement official in Redding who, on June 1, shared screenshots with her staff of a couple of social media posts warning of approaching "Antifa buses." She asked them to check out the reports.[55]

One was an Instagram post: "BE AWARE," it read, "I have heard, from a reliable source, that ANTIFA buses with close to 200 people (domestic terrorists) are planning to infiltrate Redding and possibly cause distraction and destruction."

The other was a Facebook post featuring a grainy image of a van with "Black Lives Matter" written on the back. It claimed that busloads of protesters from Portland had stopped in Klamath Falls, Oregon, "but there was no rioting or burning as they decided to move on."

These posts were similar to others that were shared in a number of locales across the country, often spurring a similar response. Indeed, the scene in Klamath Falls had been spurred by similar hoax posts, as NBC News reported at the time.[56]

"I am not one to spread false information," one claimed. "There are two buses heading this way from Portland, full of ANTIFA members and loaded with bricks. Their intentions are to come to Klamath Falls, destroy it, and murder police officers. There have been rumors of the antifa going into residential areas to 'fuck up the white hoods.'"

That thread gained support with a screenshot message from Col. Jeff Edwards, commander of the Oregon Air National Guard's 173rd Fighter Wing, based in Klamath Falls, posted to one of the groups, reading: "Team Kingsley, for your safety I ask you to please avoid the downtown area this evening. We received an alert that there may be 2 busloads of ANTIFA protesters en route to Klamath Falls and arriving in downtown around 2030 tonight."

A spokesperson for the 173rd Fighter Wing confirmed that the message had come from Edwards, saying he had sent it "to the Citizen-Airmen of the 173d Fighter Wing for their situational awareness and safety." She noted that Edwards's message was shared with local law enforcement, and it spread from there.

The same day that Redding officials circulated the memo, NBC News reported that at least some of the rumors were started by the white-nationalist group Identity Evropa, posing on Twitter as "Antifa" and threatening to "move into the residential areas" of "white hoods" and "take what's ours."[57]

Among the law-enforcement officials contacted by Redding police was Elizabeth Barkley, then the California Highway Patrol (CHP) Northern Division chief. She asked colleagues to look into the stories and "notify our allied agencies in town." Shortly afterward, her request was shared with officers by another CHP official, who commented: "The thought is these buses are roaming—looking for events to attend (and possibly cause problems)."[58]

In short order, a CHP sergeant told a LISTSERV of commanders that "possible ANTIFA buses [are] heading to Redding," and that they "could be wandering around Northern Division." He added that the agency's tactical alert center had been notified and that an aerial search was underway: "Air Ops is currently up and trying to locate them on I-5 if possible."

In Humboldt County, Sheriff William Honsal not only spread the hoax widely, but insisted afterward that it was perfectly legitimate: "We did have reports—substantiated, law enforcement reports—that said antifa did have people in buses that were in southern Oregon and in the Central Valley," he said. "These aren't unsubstantiated stories. This is the reality, and we have to deal with that."

In Curry County, Oregon, Sheriff John Ward informed his constituents: "I don't know if the rumors are true or not just yet but I got information about 3 bus loads of ANTIFA protesters are making their way from Douglas County headed for Coquille then to Coos Bay."[59]

Some law-enforcement officers did try to squelch the false rumors. In Toms River, New Jersey, the sheriff and county prosecutor posted warnings on social media that the widely circulating rumors of "Antifa" planning to riot in "primarily white neighborhoods" were "not true."[60]

"I am spending an inordinate amount of time dispelling social media rumors and misinformation," said local prosecutor Bradley D. Billhimer.

Yet even despite those warnings, the outcome became predictable in an age where armed "Patriots" were eager for a "Boogaloo": businesses boarded up their windows, and militiamen began organizing street patrols through social media.

In Klamath Falls, the whole town was buzzing with anticipation of the incoming "Antifa buses." It became something of a game, shared on Facebook: An empty green bus at the community college was spotted. So was a white bus, with "Black Lives Matter" and peace signs painted on it, in the local Walmart parking lot. A U-Haul in front of T.J. Maxx somehow set off alarms.

"I saw some scattered SJWs and some in black at Albertsons," one woman posted.[61]

A handful of Klamath Falls "Patriots" took to the streets, weapons in hand. "As you can tell, we are ready," one such man said in a Facebook live stream. "Antifa members have threatened our town and said that they're going to burn everything and to kill white people, basically."

The person whose Instagram post was circulated by Redding law enforcement commented on the scene as well: "Word got out and the populace of the area showed up in town armed to the teeth. Never seen so many AR-15s."

They didn't find any Antifa buses in Klamath Falls. But in the coastal Washington state town of Forks, they thought they had. It actually was a family of four from Spokane, who had arrived in town with a full-length bus they had converted to a camper, intent on visiting the local rain forests (Forks also attracts a number of visitors because it is the setting of the popular *Twilight* series of vampire novels and movies). First, they paid a visit to a local sporting-goods shop in town to stock up on supplies. According to the sheriff's office, after getting their goods, the family found itself confronted in the parking lot by "seven or eight car loads of people," who "repeatedly asked them if they were 'ANTIFA' protesters."[62]

The family—composed of a husband and wife, their sixteen-year-old daughter, and the man's elderly mother—told their interrogators that they had nothing to do with the movement and were just there to camp. Thinking the matter was resolved, they nervously drove their bus past the groups and got onto Highway 101, then drove up the side road taking them toward the Sol Duc River. They found themselves being followed by about four vehicles from the parking lot, and told the sheriff later that they believed a couple of people in the vehicles had semiautomatic rifles. Eventually, they turned onto a logging road and pulled off to set up camp.

While parked there, they began to hear gunfire and the sound of chainsaws. So the family decided to pack up and head back, but now found that their way had been blocked by trees their pursuers had cut across the road. Fortunately, some local teenagers arrived from the other side and cut down the blockade, freeing the family, who promptly fled the area and called authorities. Apologetic deputies helped the family get its bus running again after a brief breakdown.

Local "patriots" were quite happy with themselves on social media afterward. A set of screenshots showed a picture of the trees blocking the road, captioned: "Protect your town! #ForksStrong." One of the replies: "This makes me happy. I love our locals and feel pretty damn safe." Another resident said: "U think they realized they [came] to the wrong place yet?" To which one replied: "I think they have a good idea now." He later added that "it's like the purge."[63]

In Coeur d'Alene, Idaho, dozens of people showed up on armed patrol, toting AR-15s and wearing body armor, at a downtown shopping strip mall. In a cell phone video shared on Facebook, one videographer said: "If you guys are thinking of coming to Coeur d'Alene, to riot or loot, you'd better think again. Because we ain't having it in our town . . . I guess there's a big rumor that people from Spokane are gonna come out here and act up. But that shit ain't gonna happen."[64]

A "prepper" YouTube personality added: "There's a lot of good guys with guns out here. I don't think they'll be setting foot in Idaho."

A similarly disturbing scene developed in Snohomish, an exurb about forty miles outside Seattle, where similar rumors grew so thick that a large contingent of heavily armed "Patriot" militiamen showed up on the streets of the town, ready and eager to defend local businesses from marauding anti-fascists. As the scene grew rowdier, Confederate flags began to show up. Proud Boys also made their presence known, flashing white-power "OK" hand signals and wearing body armor.

Snohomish County sheriff Adam Fortney nonetheless defended them afterward: after speaking with two groups of armed locals on opposite sides of the Snohomish River bridge, he pronounced them all later to the county council as being Snohomish parents and business owners, "not white nationalists, they were not extremists."[65]

And in Coos County, Oregon, following the rumor posted by the neighboring Curry County sheriff, hundreds of armed men turned out on the streets of the county seat, Coquille, determined to fend off the Antifa hordes. "When people tell us someone is coming to our hometown, after hearing threats and reading them online, I feel defensive and want to protect my home," one of the men told a local reporter.[66]

Police in Columbus, Ohio, targeted an old school bus called *Buttercup* used by a group of artists and decorated with the words "Black Lives Matter" and other slogans, suggesting to the conspiracists that it was being used to transport violent protesters. On Facebook and Twitter, Columbus police on June 1 posted a photo of it being pulled over and explained: "There was a suspicion of supplying riot equipment to rioters. Detectives followed up with a vehicle search today and found numerous items: bats, rocks, meat cleavers, axes, clubs, and other projectiles. Charges are pending as the investigation continues."[67]

No charges were ever filed, but the disinformation spread like wildfire. Angry Facebook commenters railed against Antifa rioters, claiming they were funded by George Soros. On Twitter, where CPD's post was retweeted nearly fourteen thousand times, others commented: "Here ya go doubters . . . this bus was bringing riot tools to protests in Columbus. Columbus police caught them. Good."

Florida senator Marco Rubio joined in the hoax, quote retweeting the CPD post with the comment: "Police in Ohio found a bus near protests filled with bats, rocks & other weapons. But I guess still 'no evidence' of an organized effort to inject violence & anarchy into the protests right?"[68]

On several occasions, the turnout of large groups of armed men was in response to actual protests of the killing of George Floyd by local activists, mostly Black Lives Matter groups and their liberal associates holding up signs and placards peacefully. And when that was the case, the presence of armed men served mainly to intimidate and threaten the protesters, who frequently were simply young local residents carrying no weapons.

This was the case in Medford, Oregon, as well as in Klamath Falls, where the intimidation was even more self-evident: The armed "defenders" carried "flags, baseball bats, hammers and axes. But mostly, they carried guns."[69]

Frederick Brigham, thirty-one, Klamath Falls resident and musician, told NBC News that the presence of the armed "defenders" was chilling: "It felt like walking through an enemy war camp," he said.

In Sandpoint, Idaho, a Black Lives Matter protest was met with a similar attempt at intimidation. That prompted the mayor of the town to post a protest of his own on Facebook: "None of the young protesters I spoke with felt any safer in the presence of these armed vigilantes," Shelby Rognstad wrote. "Rather, they felt scared, intimidated and in some cases harassed. None of the downtown business owners I have since spoken to felt any safer from the militant presence."[70]

The same dynamic played out later in August 2020, when similar hoax rumors on social media claimed that "Antifa arsonists" were secretly behind the wave of wildfires that were then ravaging the West Coast. Once again, rural areas were subjected to clusters of heavily armed men roaming their towns and even setting up vigilante checkpoints along roadways—all while being encouraged and enabled by local law-enforcement officers.[71]

A particularly popular set of posts, shared thousands of times on Facebook, originated from a hoax account called "Scarsdale NY Antifa," and claimed to be helping set the fires: "We and other chapters of Antifa around Oregon have collaborated to ignite fires around the state to draw attention to #ClimateEmergency," one post read. Others from the same account made similar claims.

The comments from people who believed the claims still proliferated on Facebook through Monday: "All evidence Antifa is behind Oregon and Washington state fires," read one. Another, after listing various reports of arson arrests, none of which have been connected to politics, concluded: "These are probably coordinated by Antifa or homegrown terrorists."

More disturbingly, small groups of armed vigilantes began popping up in short order in rural Oregon, primarily in Clackamas and Multnomah Counties, forming ad-hoc "citizen checkpoints" demanding drivers give them identification and interrogating them about their politics. Some of these chased journalists, including an Oregon Public Broadcasting reporter and a photographer on assignment, out of the areas.[72]

The Multnomah County Sheriff's Office tweeted out a statement explaining that such behavior is illegal: "Deputies have contacted several groups of residents in Corbett who have set up checkpoints and are stopping cars," it said. "While we understand their intent is to keep the community safe, it is never legal to block a public roadway or force other citizens to stop."

Clackamas County sheriff Craig Roberts similarly told CNN that he was concerned about the checkpoints: "The first thing I'd ask them to do is please stop that," said Roberts. "It is illegal to stop somebody at gunpoint."

However, Roberts's pleas were undermined by one of his own deputies, Mark Nikolai, who turned up in a pair of YouTube videos that went viral giving advice to the vigilantes on how to avoid prosecution for shooting anyone they suspect of being a looter—and moreover amplifying the claims that Antifa was targeting rural areas with arson and looting.

In the first video, Nikolai can be heard advising the checkpoint vigilantes to stay within the law, because "the courts don't give a shit about what you're trying to do." Later, he can be heard advising them how to prepare for a criminal case in the event they shot anyone: "You have to prove there was a serious physical injury or death, now you throw a fucking knife in their hand after you shoot them, that's on you," he said.

In the second video, Nikolai fills a reporter in on likely Antifa activities: "What I'm worried about is that there's people stashing stuff. It means they're going to go in preparation," he says. "I don't want to sound like a doomsdayer but it's getting serious. We need the public's help on this." Then he adds: "Antifa motherfuckers are out causing hell, and there's a lot of lives at stake and there's a lot of people's property at stake because these guys got some vendetta."

Nikolai was suspended shortly afterward.[73]

The "Antifa arsons" narrative soon bubbled up from the fever swamps of the far right into mainstream right-wing narrative, broadcast widely by key figures atop the media food chain: Donald Trump, Joe Rogan, Fox News, and leading Republican political candidates.

Trump retweeted an alt-right-flavored anti-Biden video suggesting he was ignoring Antifa arsonists threatening the suburbs. Rogan, a wildly popular podcast host, told his audience that "left-wing people" were responsible for the fires (and apologized for it the next day). Fox News appeared especially eager to blame Antifa for the wildfires as a way of denying the role of climate change. And in Washington state, where the fires hit hard, the Republican nominee in the governor's race joined in spreading the claims through a campaign video.[74]

ANTIFA WAS NOT THE only monster concocted largely out of whole cloth by the Trumpist right, of course. Chinese Communists, satanic occultists, George Soros and his fellow globalist overlords, cultural Marxists, Black Lives Matter radicals, migrant caravans, adrenochrome-harvesting pedophilia rings, "groomers" lurking in Disney cartoons—all had their turns as right-wing bogeymen during Trump's tenure and afterward.

The most notorious right-wing monster to emerge in the post-Trump-presidency environment was critical race theory (CRT), which seemed to have appeared out of nowhere as the latest great threat to America.[75] On Fox News, the issue was mentioned zero times in 2018; four times in 2019; seventy-seven times in 2020; and by November 2021, 626 times.[76] Despite the issue having received almost zero attention until 2021, Republican-controlled state legislatures in places like Idaho, Tennessee, Texas, and Oklahoma all passed laws outlawing its use in their public classrooms, while school boards around the country found themselves besieged by right-wing ideologues demanding it be excised from their curricula.[77]

The whole campaign against CRT, in fact, was primarily the work of a handful of astroturfing "dark money" right-wing organizations. The central figure in the campaign was a former right-wing think-tank pundit named Christopher Rufo, who had a history of promoting various kinds of spurious enemy concoctions in the Seattle area, where he was fond of spreading claims that homelessness was the product of a left-wing conspiracy.

Exactly what is critical race theory? It's an academic framework based on the idea—one well-grounded in factual history—that racial discrimination and inequality are built into the American systems of law and governance as well as its culture. Most of this framework emerged in the 1970s and afterward, with the first academic workshop on it occurring in 1989. For the most part, this framework is considered something of an academic niche, one that mostly comes into play in law schools and in political science.[78]

But thanks largely to the factually dubious rantings of a cadre of right-wing ideologues online and in the media, over the course of 2021 it came to be functionally synonymous with "cultural Marxism," another far-right bogeyman concocted as an existential threat to Western civilization. So the term was suddenly on the tongues of the throng of Republican propagandists appearing on right-wing media, and the legislators who then sponsored new laws prohibiting teachers from discussing CRT—none of whom in fact can actually describe what it is in real terms or provide factual examples.

One Republican lawmaker from Alabama named Chris Pringle was asked by a reporter to define the term. He said that CRT "basically teaches that certain children are inherently bad people because of the color of their skin, period." Who was teaching that? "Yeah, uh, well—I can assure you—I'll have to read a lot more."[79]

Pringle insisted that the threat was real, apparently because he had seen a video with a conspiracy theory: "These people, when they were doing the training programs—and the government—if you didn't buy into what they taught you a hundred percent, they sent you away to a reeducation camp." Say again? "The white male executives are sent to a three-day re-education camp, where they were told that their white male culture wasn't their—"

In fact, Pringle likely was regurgitating an anecdote Rufo had described to Tucker Carlson on Fox News—one involving corporate sensitivity training sessions—even if he couldn't quite get the story straight.[80]

What all the right-wing torch-bearers could tell you, though, was that CRT is some kind of attack on American capitalism and white people. One political action committee dedicated to backing anti-CRT school-board candidates, the 1776 Project PAC, claimed that CRT advocates are trying to remake the United States to reject capitalism and the nation's founding principles, and that CRT is "hostile to white people."

Another claimed: "I think CRT, and in particular the 1619 project, does in fact seek to make children feel guilt and even anguish, not because of anything they've done, but solely based on the color of their skin. I think that is a definite issue and a problem because I don't think anyone should feel guilty about the way God made them."[81]

"Let me be clear, there's no room in our classrooms for things like critical race theory," Florida governor Ron DeSantis said at a March news conference. "Teaching kids to hate their country and to hate each other is not worth one red cent of taxpayer money."[82]

Educators, at least, understood the score. The Texas chapter of the American Federation of Teachers noted in a late-May statement that anti-education rightists "want this to be a wedge issue" with the public: "The bill is part of a national movement by conservatives trying to sow a narrative of students being indoctrinated by teachers. Our members rightfully have expressed outrage against this insult of their professionalism to provide balanced conversations with students on controversial issues."[83]

Even some of the participants were surprisingly up front about the dynamic at work.

One lawyer for parents suing their child's school district over alleged CRT-fueled discrimination was frank with NBC News: "Some people are treating it like a gold rush," Jonathan O'Brien said. "This is a new area where people think they can either become famous or make money on the issue, and they're probably right."[84]

O'Brien, in fact, later joined a group of attorneys focused on CRT that was organized by Rufo, who is a senior fellow at the right-wing Manhattan Institute think tank.

In a March Twitter exchange with another CRT-hysteria promoter, James Lindsay, Rufo explicitly outlined their cynical marketing strategy to make their concocted bogeyman the repository of all things the public dislikes:

> We have successfully frozen their brand—"critical race theory"— into the public conversation and are steadily driving up negative perceptions. We will eventually turn it toxic, as we put all of the various cultural insanities under that brand category.
>
> The goal is to have the public read something crazy in the newspaper and immediately think "critical race theory." We have decodified the term and will recodify it to annex the entire range of cultural constructions that are unpopular with Americans.[85]

Rufo spent a number of years in Seattle as a fellow at the Discovery Institute, a creationist organization that specializes in promoting "intelligent design" as an education wedge issue.[86] It also has assiduously promoted the "cultural Marxism" threat, while Rufo's disquisitions on Marxism there have helped build the new branded narrative around critical race theory.[87]

Rufo also was a prominent figure in the right-wing narrative that "Seattle is dying" that circulated in right-wing media from 2019 to 2020, particularly in his attacks on what he called the "politics of ruinous compassion" and the "homeless-industrial complex," which he claims is a "billion-dollar industry."[88] Rufo ran for Seattle city council in 2019, but performed poorly in local polling and dropped out, claiming he and his family had been subjected to threats. (Rufo later tried to substantiate the claim by producing an email from an interlocutor who told him to "get bent.")[89]

But after drifting through a number of right-wing causes, Rufo—who moved out of Seattle to take up residence in rural Kitsap County, where he set up a studio for peddling his propaganda—the "critical race theory" brand clearly caught on for him.

"Rufo and his fellow travelers hold that sinister forces are at work whenever students are exposed to real American history," observed Alex Shephard at *The New Republic*. "It may seem good to educate yourself about racial injustices and the institutional structures that have propped them up for centuries, but that's just a cover for a more fanciful threat: the takeover of American institutions by a cabal of Marxist-Leninists and social justice warriors."[90]

Shephard also correctly identified the primary reason the controversy, such as it is, even exists—namely, because the American right is desperate to create some kind of enemy, any kind of enemy, as long as they can make it sound plausible:

> Much like their recent obsessions with "lab leak theory," conservatives' fixation with critical race theory can best be understood as a useful proxy villain filling the vacuum left by their failure to uncover a more substantive way of attacking Joe Biden during the first six months of his term—a vacuum that mainly exists because of the Republican Party's retreat from policy debates. The fact that critical race theory is always so hazily defined—and also so completely malevolent—makes it the perfect catch-all malefactor for a culture-war-obsessed right that's desperate to end conversations around corrupt policing and structural racism. It is everywhere and nowhere at once; a spectral threat forever lurking in the shadows that's just nonexistent enough to ensure that it can never be defeated.

And that is how concocted monsters have always worked for the American right.

10

Taking It to the Streets

THOSE "ANTIFA BUSES" AND "Antifa arsonists" rumors weren't simply hoaxes: they were also classic right-wing projection, accusing their enemies and targets of the same foul behavior that they themselves were both planning and currently undertaking. During the three years preceding the summer of 2020, busloads of right-wing thugs from rural and exurban areas had been organizing to descend on unsuspecting liberal urban centers—primarily Portland, Seattle, San Francisco, and New York—in order to engage in faux "protests" primarily intended to generate violence, for which they came eagerly prepared.[1]

There was a basic blueprint to these bused-in protests, as a *Washington Post* investigative piece found, focusing on the man who organized a late August 2020 Cruise for Trump rally in Portland: a nonresident of a liberal urban center—in this case, Alex Kuzmenko of Meridian, Idaho, an eight-hour drive away from Portland—organizes a protest ostensibly around the right-wing cause du jour, which then attracts a horde of other nonresidents, whose supposed purpose is to come tell people who live in those cities how terrible their politics are—but whose underlying purpose, betrayed by the weapons and defensive gear they bring along with an attitude of eagerness to punch "leftists," is to create opportunities for violence and then freely engage in it.[2]

In this instance, the August 29, 2020, event through downtown Portland—in which Trump supporters drove en masse down Interstate 5, through the center of the city, with banners waving: American flags, Trump banners, yellow "Don't Tread On Me" Gadsden flags—purportedly was organized to remain on the freeways through Portland and not enter the city's downtown. That didn't stop many, at the rally's end, from driving directly into downtown Portland, plowing their pickups through crowds on the streets and shooting paintball guns from their pickup beds at pedestrians on the sidewalks. Proud Boys who had been in the procession brawled on the streets with protesters, wielding paintball guns and baseball bats.

The ugliness culminated late that evening with the shooting of a far-right Trump supporter, Aaron Danielson, thirty-nine, by a self-described anti-fascist who later claimed he was acting in self-defense—shortly before he was shot dead by law-enforcement officers.[3] The shooting sparked broad calls among far-right activists to declare "civil war" against left-wing activists nationally.[4]

Alex Kuzmenko, the thirty-three-year-old Ukrainian immigrant from Meridian who put the rally together, insisted afterward that the rally had not been intended to go into Portland's downtown. He disavowed the Trump supporters who had done so, as well as the violence that followed.[5]

Kuzmenko was a political novice who first organized similar rallies in nearby Boise that summer, then decided to target Portland. He and his family members insisted that the intent was simply to show support for Trump: "Nobody's paying us to do any of this," said one brother. However, his rallies were soon being promoted by groups linked to the Russian American community and with likely ties to the Kremlin, notably the Facebook group Russian-Americans for Law and Order.[6]

Like similar pro-Trump rallies in the Portland area, both preceding and following, the August 29 event was primarily designed as far-right street theater whose entire purpose was to create a "violent left" bogeyman for media consumption—mainly through the presence of violence-seeking far-right activists. In the process, the lines between mainstream Republicans and the right-wing extremists was blurred, if not erased altogether.[7]

Alt-right provocateur Jack Posobiec—who has deep links to white nationalists and neo-Nazis, as well as a Twitter following of over a million—enthusiastically promoted the rally: "MAGA is heading into Portland," he wrote. Trump shared Posobiec's tweet the next morning, adding: "GREAT PATRIOTS!"[8]

The Kremlin-financed RT website tweeted out videos of the caravan's entry into Portland, including footage of armed men driving large pickups through clusters of pedestrians on the streets crossing with the light at an intersection. The text on the tweet read: "Portland rioters try to block pro-Trump caravan."[9]

"Oregonians tired of riots organized a mass car rally in support of Donald Trump," read the Russian caption on the video shared on Facebook by Russian-Americans for Law and Order.

ALEX KUZMENKO INSISTED THAT the caravan route was supposed to avoid downtown Portland, but that renegade elements—mostly members of the street-brawling Patriot Prayer, American Guard, and Proud Boys organizations—went anyway. Danielson was a member of the first group.[10]

Indeed, those three groups had been responsible for the vast majority of the far-right rallies organized around the nation for the previous three years leading up to the summer of 2020, particularly in the Pacific Northwest. These street-brawling groups—which themselves went through multiple upheavals due to the combustible nature of their respective memberships, frequently erupting in vicious infighting—would advertise each event's purpose as a protest against some political grievance or another, often handily capitalizing on issues being widely disseminated in such mainstream-right media as Fox News at the time.

The marches became causes unto themselves, such as when hundreds of out-of-town Proud Boys gathered in Portland in August 2019 and paraded through the town, sometimes with a full police escort—while more than a dozen counterprotesters were arrested by police.[11]

The right then began applying the same strategy in a variety of contexts, all responding to the various national upheavals that had befallen the American landscape in 2020:

Protests arising from anti-COVID-19 pandemic measures, mainly stay-at-home orders and business closures, brought out scores of armed "Patriots" angrily opposed to the supposed abrogation of their freedoms. The Boogaloo fanatics itching for a civil war who showed up to these protests formed an ominous presence.[12]

In Idaho, armed protesters managed to break into legislative chambers and disrupt proceedings while lawmakers were considering COVID-19-related policies.[13]

The anti-police-brutality protests that erupted nationwide after the murder of George Floyd also proved to be a rich opportunity for far-right intimidation tactics, primarily on behalf of police, featuring gun-toting militiamen clad in body armor.[14]

Perhaps most ominously, the Cruise for Trump and other pro-Trump rallies in Oregon featuring Proud Boys and other far-right extremists became more than mere attempts at intimidation—they evolved into massive conduits for the full absorption of extremist politics into the mainstream Republican Party. Indeed, whatever line existed between them seemingly vanished with a flourish of semiautomatic weapons and camo gear.[15]

———————

WHY WOULD A PACK of violent, street-brawling far-right thugs like the Proud Boys show up to demonstrate in a quiet little suburb like Gresham, Oregon?

The official, stated purpose of the demonstration in front of Gresham City Hall in August 2020 was to protest the presence of a Black Lives Matter (BLM) flag on the city's plaza flag display. But in reality, the Proud Boys showed up with their semiautomatic guns and Trump flags and MAGA hats to spread fear among the people who live in suburbs—not fear of valiant "Patriots" like themselves, of course, but of Black Lives Matter and the "violent left."[16]

The rally—dubbed a "flag waving" event to support police officers while simultaneously protesting the BLM flag—was organized by a Proud Boy activist from Texas named Alan Swinney, who made a habit of appearing at Portland area far-right protests, including the August 2019 Portland Proud Boys rally.

Swinney was a notable presence there, wielding a paintball gun to blast counterprotesters. He also was photographed brandishing a handgun and pointing it at protesters—which inspired an investigation by the Portland Police Bureau. (Swinney was eventually charged in 2021 with multiple counts of assault and convicted, then handed a ten-year prison sentence.)[17] He was accompanied by a full phalanx of Proud Boys, including Chandler Pappas, an Astoria, Oregon, resident who was a regular at Portland-area far-right rallies and who brandished his faux semiautomatic rifle (actually a paintball gun) at the Gresham crowd. At a similar protest in July 2020, one of the anti-BLM protesters had also brandished a gun.

The crowd of about one hundred protesters encountered a significantly larger crowd of counterprotesters there to defend the presence of the BLM flag—most of them local residents, unlike Swinney and his cohorts. These included a sizable contingent of the Wall of Moms bloc—which had attracted national attention at demonstrations in Portland over the previous months—wearing yellow T-shirts.

The pro-Trump side chanted "All Lives Matter!" and were drowned out by louder chants of "Black Lives Matter!" Some protesters began pushing and shoving, at which point a line of Gresham police officers moved in and separated the two sides for the remainder of the two-hour event.

If the anti-BLM protesters were hoping to get the flag taken down by Gresham officials, they failed: the city council voted to keep it in place.

However, that wasn't the purpose of these rallies. Neither was the rush to respond with a hysterical armed defense of small rural and suburban towns against the supposed imminent threat of hordes of black-clad leftists arriving in George Soros–funded "Antifa buses" really about protecting those towns.

Rather, these events served a twofold purpose: first, to threaten and intimidate pro–Black Lives Matter protesters; and second, to create violent and menacing images intended to persuade the people who live in these suburbs and elsewhere—people who are far removed from most of the events—that protests of any kind against police brutality promote "Antifa," "anarchism," and Marxism, collectively dubbed the "violent left." The threatening bogeyman then became an open pretext for any kind of violence the extremist right wanted to dish out.

This reached its apotheosis in Kenosha, Wisconsin.

WHILE FLOYD'S MURDER ON May 25, 2020—caught vividly on a video that went viral—had set the country and indeed the world aflame with protests against police brutality, Kenosha became the epicenter of these protests in August after a similar shooting caught on video: Jacob Blake, a twenty-nine-year-old Black man, was shot seven times in the back and side after he refused to cooperate during an arrest on August 23. Blake survived with egregious injuries, including being paralyzed from the waist down.[18]

Protests soon broke out in Kenosha. That night, protesters damaged police vehicles and set fire to a dump truck while the local courthouse was vandalized. About two hundred Wisconsin National Guardsmen were deployed after Kenosha County officials declared a state of emergency. The evening of Monday, August 24, the protesters set fires and looted businesses for a second night.

A militia group calling itself the Kenosha Guard had organized on Facebook, ostensibly to prevent violence at the protests. On Monday, it had published a post calling for "Armed Citizens to Protect Our Lives and Property," with text reading: "Any patriots willing to take up arms and defend our city tonight from the evil thugs? No doubt they are currently planning on the next part of the city to burn tonight."[19]

One of the people who responded was a seventeen-year-old from Antioch, Illinois—about a thirty-mile drive away—named Kyle Rittenhouse. Though unable to legally own an AR-15 in Wisconsin, he had convinced an adult friend in Kenosha to act as a proxy buyer for him, and he joined up with members of the Kenosha Guard (though he was not a member) on the streets the night of August 25, armed and ready for action.[20]

Rittenhouse was captured on video early in the evening with several militiamen as they appeared to be getting water bottles handed to them by Kenosha police. In that video, he says: "By the way, I'm Kyle."

The protests and fires continued that night throughout Kenosha, and he was one of multiple civilians armed with guns patrolling parts of the city. But he was the only one who shot three people, killing two of them.

Captured on multiple videos, the shootings began in the parking lot of a gas station/repair shop at about 11:45 p.m. Witnesses said the shooter, who was carrying a semiautomatic rifle and wearing a green T-shirt, got into a confrontation with a protester at whom he then fired multiple rounds. One of these apparently hit the protester in the head.

Video showed Rittenhouse surveying the body of the victim while talking on a cell phone and saying, "I just shot someone," then fleeing the scene.

Subsequent videos shot by other witnesses show a number of protesters following Rittenhouse, who at one point stumbled and fell to the street without having been contacted. As he tried to recover himself, three other protesters approached him and tried to take his gun away—one of them swinging his skateboard at him—at which point he opened fire on them as well. The man with the skateboard fell dead, shot in the chest. Another of his victims, shot in the arm, shouted for a medic.

Rittenhouse then got back on his feet and continued down the street until he encountered arriving police vehicles. Although he put his hands up, the police apparently ignored him, and he continued walking away.

Kenosha police later issued a statement that they had tentatively identified the gunman, and then announced that Rittenhouse had been charged with first-degree murder, and was being sought as a fugitive.

After the shooting, the Kenosha Guard's Facebook page featured a post reading: "We are unaware if the armed citizen was answering the Kenosha Guard Militia's call to arms. Just like the shooting of Jacob Blake, we need all the facts and evidence to come out before we make a judgement." The Kenosha Guard's Facebook page was subsequently taken down.

Several anti-fascist social media accounts noted that Rittenhouse had a history of associations with police, including enrolling in a local "police cadet" program. Rittenhouse's Facebook was also festooned with "Blue Lives Matter" material and logos.

On Monday, Kenosha County sheriff David Beth had publicly refused to deputize citizens to patrol the city's streets. After the shootings Tuesday, he reiterated that position.

"I've had people saying, 'Why don't you deputize citizens?'" he said. "This is why you don't deputize citizens with guns to protect Kenosha."[21]

———

IN SHORT ORDER, THE right-wing narrative was in clear disagreement with such sentiments: Praise for Rittenhouse's lethal act as "heroic" came welling up on social media, then on mainstream media, and then among Republican politicians. His defenders promptly constructed an image of a crowd of violent rioters threatening a frightened boy who was only moti-vated by patriotic values and a wish to defend himself. [22]

The ardent defense of Rittenhouse, that he acted purely in self-defense, became a foregone conclusion. Trump echoed this when he came to Kenosha for a rally.

"That was an interesting situation," he told the audience. "You saw the same tape as I saw. And he was trying to get away from them. I guess it looks like he fell and then they very violently attacked him. And it was something that we're looking at right now, and it's under investigation. But I guess he was in very big trouble. He would have been—probably would have been killed, but it's under investigation."[23]

The fulsome praise for Rittenhouse became an official GOP talking point, with consequences for the 2020 election.[24] In Waukesha County, Wisconsin, a gathering of Republicans gave his mother a standing ovation.[25] At Arizona State University in Tempe, a Republican student group held a fundraiser for his legal defense. Congressman Thomas Massie of Kentucky praised Rittenhouse: "He also exhibited incredible restraint and presence and situational awareness. He didn't empty a magazine into a crowd. There were people around him who could have caused him harm, but as soon as they showed any sign of retreat or nonaggression, he did not shoot them. He exhibited more restraint than a lot of the police videos I've seen."[26]

NBC News's Julia Ainsley reported that DHS officials were given talking points instructing them to support this narrative in their public comments, notably the claim that Rittenhouse "took his rifle to the scene of the riot-ing to help defend small business owners." Other talking points: "Kyle was seen being chased and attacked by rioters before allegedly shooting three of them, killing two." "Subsequent video has emerged reportedly showing that there were 'multiple gunmen' involved, which would lend more credence to the self-defense claims."[27]

The purpose of this factually dubious narrative was to reinforce a larger right-wing narrative about a supposed "violent left" composed of Black

Lives Matter and Antifa while erasing the reality of a growing army of violent right-wing thugs, including unaccountable bodies of militiamen, directing their heavily armed ire at these concocted enemies.

It was also grossly distorted. Rittenhouse's first victim, thirty-six-year-old Joseph Rosenbaum, was widely reviled on right-wing social media—including by pseudo-journalist Andy Ngo, who immediately broadcast his prison record and status as a sex offender.

However, Rosenbaum was not connected in any way to either Black Lives Matter or Antifa. In reality, he was a mentally ill man who had only been released two hours beforehand from the hospital on mental-health orders after a suicide attempt. No one has any clear idea why he wandered over to the protest and began harassing militia members, including Rittenhouse, and then followed him down the street, shouting.[28]

Nor did Rosenbaum hurl a Molotov cocktail at Rittenhouse, as the latter's defenders initially claimed. In fact, as their confrontation reached its climax, Rosenbaum had thrown a clear plastic bag containing a deodorant stick, underwear, and socks at Rittenhouse, missing him, and then reached for his gun in an apparent attempt to disarm him. Rittenhouse responded by shooting him three times, killing him.

The second victim, Anthony Huber, twenty-six, similarly had no connections to BLM or Antifa, and was attending only his second protest. When Rittenhouse stumbled and fell to the ground as he was fleeing the scene of the first shooting, Huber tried to disarm him by using his skateboard as a weapon, swinging at Rittenhouse's shoulder while reaching for the gun. However, Rittenhouse was able to recover first and shot him with a single lethal round to the chest.

The only victim who posed a lethal threat to Rittenhouse was the third man, twenty-six-year-old Gaige Grosskreutz, who had participated in multiple protests and was carrying both a medic's kit and a handgun—which he had out as he was approaching Rittenhouse while he was still on the ground and fending off Huber. Rittenhouse turned to Grosskreutz and shot him in the right arm.

Rittenhouse himself—whose online handle was @4doorsmorewhores—appears to have digested a steady diet of pro-Trump and pro-police "Blue Lives Matter" talking points about protesters. He also attended a Trump rally in Des Moines on January 30.[29]

There was nothing unusual about that; most of the American right has taken to parroting Trump's tweets and speeches blaming protest violence on "professional anarchists, violent mobs, arsonists, looters, criminals, rioters, Antifa, and others." He described Antifa as "leading instigators of this violence."

However, while many of Rittenhouse's defenders in the media were eager to proclaim him innocent by virtue of self-defense, the larger narrative that they spun out of the Kenosha shootings was chilling to anyone who believes in American democracy: Armed vigilantes not only are justified in opening fire on protesters, but more of them are needed wherever there is an anti-police protest. It was a green light for wanton murder.

This ranged from Ann Coulter's (later deleted) tweet—"I want him [Rittenhouse] for my president"—to Tucker Carlson's morally deranged explanation for the shootings:

> People in charge from the governor of Wisconsin on down refused to enforce the law. They stood back and they watched Kenosha burn.
>
> So are we really surprised that looting and arson accelerated to murder? How shocked are we that 17-year-olds with rifles decided they had to maintain order when no one else would?[30]

Carlson—who eventually worked out a deal to have a film crew accompany Rittenhouse during his trial—was not the only figure at Fox News to rush to Rittenhouse's defense: Sean Hannity's attorney solicited donations on his behalf.[31]

Alex Jones described the Kenosha protests as part of a "communist overthrow of the country," and Rittenhouse's shootings as an act of
self-preservation.[32]

White-nationalist Groyper figure Nick Fuentes tweeted: "Kyle
Rittenhouse did nothing wrong." A website dedicated to propagating
that meme immediately popped up online. White nationalist Cassandra
Fairbanks echoed it on her Twitter account.[33]

Fairbanks, who writes for *Gateway Pundit,* also retweeted an admirer's
post saying: "I don't give a fuck anymore. I gone full Cassandra. Kill all
the idiots violently terrorizing our towns. If the white suprematist [sic]
do it then they're more useful than elected officials." "Yeah," responded
Fairbanks, "I'm literally just sitting here like . . . maybe some people will
think twice about rioting tomorrow."

Predictably, a number of extremist groups took this narrative to heart. A
militia calling itself the North Carolina Constitutional Guard announced
a "call to action from all American organized militia groups" to demand
Rittenhouse's immediate release. Moreover, it said it was planning "an
armed march into the city of Kenosha, alongside other militia groups, in
demand for Kyle's immediate release and freedom."

The leader of a QAnon Save Our Children rally in Texas announced
that she was planning to attend the event fully armed and with body armor—posting a selfie photo dressed in the gear and brandishing a semiautomatic rifle.

A late-August study by Alexander Reid Ross of the Centre for Analysis of
the Radical Right found that, in the weeks following Floyd's murder, there
had been more than five hundred incidents in which right-wing counterprotesters had threatened and assaulted people protesting police brutality.
These include "64 cases of simple assault, 38 incidents of vigilantes driving
cars into demonstrators, and nine times shots were fired at protesters."[34]

"Going forward, we need to seriously reconsider the permissiveness
with which we are allowing armed paramilitaries to roam the streets of our

nation's towns and cities, as if this is normal," observed Steven Gardiner, an analyst at Political Research Associates. "There's nothing normal about this. We don't want to be living in a war zone."[35]

FOUR DAYS AFTER RITTENHOUSE killed two people in Kenosha, Aaron Danielson and Michael Reinoehl crossed paths in Portland.[36]

It happened at the end of Alex Kuzmenko's August 29 Cruise for Trump, after the parade of pickup trucks had cruised up and down Portland's grid, with men seated in the back end and passenger seats firing paintball guns at the crowds and at random pedestrians; among the people hit with a paintball was the *New York Times*'s regional bureau chief.[37] Sometimes the caravan's stream was broken by other drivers and by groups of counterprotesters, who would block their progress with their bodies. The night was a running nightmare of dangerous and potentially explosive confrontations.

"The shooting was not part of the event. It was not part of the cruise rally," Kuzmenko said in a video in which he suggested that Antifa had funneled people downtown.

As the evening wore on, a number of the Trump caravan participants parked their vehicles elsewhere and began making their way downtown to the area where Black Lives Matter demonstrators had been protesting for the previous ninety-three days, clearly intent on making trouble. Among them were Danielson, a thirty-nine-year-old member of Patriot Prayer from Portland, and his friend Chandler Pappas, the Proud Boy who had shown up toting an air gun in Gresham with Alan Swinney.[38]

Danielson and Pappas were heading up Southwest Third Avenue when they were spotted by Reinoehl, a forty-eight-year-old from nearby Clackamas who had been participating in the protests of the previous three months, providing security. He was carrying a pistol in his pocket. Surveillance video later showed that he had apparently spotted the two street brawlers as they all headed toward the demonstrations, ducked into a parking garage to let them pass, and then walked out into the street behind them, where another anti-fascist was walking.[39]

Reinoehl shouted: "Hey, we got some right here. We got a couple right here."

Danielson, who was carrying a metal baton, pulled out a can of bear spray and ran toward the men. Reinoehl's companion shouted: "He's macing you, he's pulling it out," as Danielson began spraying them.

Reinoehl pulled out his gun and fired twice. The first shot hit the can of mace in Danielson's hand, causing it to explode. The second shot hit Danielson in the chest and killed him.

While Chandler Pappas shouted for help and anti-fascist medics began trying to help Danielson, Reinoehl fled the scene. Danielson was declared dead by police when they arrived.

Reinoehl went on the lam, and for five days, no one seemed to know where he was. On Thursday, September 3, an interview with Reinoehl appeared on the *Vice News* website in which he insisted that he shot Danielson in self-defense, but that he did not trust the police and would not turn himself in.[40]

"I had no choice," he said. "I mean, I, I had a choice. I could have sat there and watched them kill a friend of mine of color. But I wasn't going to do that."

Reinoehl, who on social media described himself as "100% antifa," told the interviewer that he was coming to the defense of a friend of his who was surrounded by heavily armed men in trucks coming out of a parking garage when he found himself confronted by two men—Danielson and Pappas. He claimed one of them had a knife (though that may have been Danielson's baton) and they were using mace. "Had I stepped forward, he would have maced or stabbed me," Reinoehl said.

Hours after that interview was published, police tracked him down and, when he apparently fired a gun at the arresting federal marshals, shot and killed him.[41]

Reinoehl had taken refuge in the semirural Washington state village of Tanglewilde, an unincorporated area near Lacey, which is itself a suburb of Olympia, some 120 miles north of Portland. Portland police issued an arrest warrant on Thursday, and Reinoehl was found by officers emerging from an apartment in Tanglewilde at about seven in the evening.

According to witnesses at the scene, Reinoehl was stopped in his car by members of a task force dedicated to finding him. He got into a dispute with the officers, who then fired rounds into his vehicle. Reinoehl got out of the vehicle at that point, and officers then fired more shots and killed him. Police declined to say whether Reinoehl fired a weapon at them.

Police quickly became opaque about the event. No body cameras were used, no surveillance video available, and official stories about the shooting from authorities constantly changed.

Eventually, an investigation by *ProPublica* and Oregon Public Broadcasting into the case revealed a troubling portrait of how the shooting transpired: multiple witnesses said the police gave no warning, and that Reinoehl did not display a gun, suggesting that the forty-eight-year-old fugitive was not arrested so much as he was simply executed.[42]

A marshal claimed that Reinoehl had pointed a gun at him, but his only gun was found in his front pants pocket after he was shot, fully loaded.

One witness said the bullets from the fusillade the marshals unleashed—without any kind of warning or order to surrender—were flying around the apartment complex where the arrest happened. Children were present, and one father described running his two young children inside his home for safety. "There was no 'drop your weapon' or 'freeze' or 'police'—no warning at all," the man recalled.

Donald Trump himself may have played a role in the officers' apparent eagerness to kill Reinoehl. One hour before the fugitive was killed, Trump had tweeted:

Why aren't the Portland Police ARRESTING the cold blooded killer of Aaron "Jay" Danielson. Do your job, and do it fast. Everybody knows who this thug is. No wonder Portland is going to hell![43]

After Reinoehl had been killed, Trump commented approvingly on the outcome at a campaign rally in Greenville, North Carolina. He told the crowd, in fact, that there was no intention of arresting Reinoehl: "We sent in the U.S. Marshals, it took 15 minutes and it was over, 15 minutes and it was over . . . They knew who he was, they didn't want to arrest him, and 15 minutes that ended. And they call themselves peaceful protesters."[44]

Attorney General William Barr issued a statement on Justice Department letterhead that was equally bloodthirsty:

The tracking down of Reinoehl—a dangerous fugitive, admitted Antifa member, and suspected murderer—is a significant accomplishment in the ongoing effort to restore law and order to Portland and other cities. I applaud the outstanding cooperation among federal, state, and local law enforcement, particularly the fugitive task force team that located Reinoehl and prevented him from escaping justice. The streets of our cities are safer with this violent agitator removed, and the actions that led to his location are an unmistakable demonstration that the United States will be governed by law, not violent mobs.[45]

Trump subsequently told Maria Bartiromo of Fox News: "This guy was a violent criminal, and the U.S. Marshals killed him. And I'll tell you something—that's the way it has to be. There has to be retribution."[46]

THE TRUMP TRAINS, AS they called the caravan-style demonstrations that emerged that summer, originally were a sort of land-based variation on the "Trump flotilla" boat parades that first caught the media's attention in

2019, then became sensations in 2020, attracting huge numbers of boats at lakes and waterways around the country, first on Memorial Day and then the Fourth of July: garish displays of Trump worship and its attendant authoritarian version of "patriotism."[47]

The flotillas showcased bad boater behavior as captains, particularly those with big boats and big Trump banners, revved up huge waves that sank a number of other boaters. On Labor Day at Lake Travis, Texas, five boats ended up on the lake bottom. The owner of a ski boat on the Willamette River in Portland was capsized by a passing Trump flotilla.[48]

Trump was enamored of the flotillas, which his aides made sure he was shown videos about as a way to lift his spirits. "Are we polling the boaters yet?" he kept asking his aides. "Thank you to our beautiful boaters," he posted on Instagram. "I will never let you down."

The Trump Trains that began organizing during the summer of 2020 were in the same mold, but with a more working-class demographic than the wealthy boat owners who showed up for the flotillas. Moreover, as the Portland caravan demonstrated, their organizing energy was attracting the same crowd that came out to the far-right protest events of the previous three years: Proud Boys, Three Percenters, and Oath Keepers and other "Patriot" militiamen.[49]

They became a central nexus that summer for these extremists to commingle with mainstream Republicans, many of whom would show up at the rally organizing and departure site expecting just to be displaying their support for the incumbent president and soon found themselves swept up in moving displays of intimidation and nastiness, as happened in Portland. And once in it, many found themselves enjoying it.

When a couple of Trump Trains went rumbling down Interstate 5 in the Portland area again in early September, their destination was noteworthy: the state capitol building, fifty miles south in Salem.[50] About a hundred of them gathered there. Led by a faction of Proud Boys and Patriot Prayer supporters, the cruisers had broken away from the Cruise

Rally for Trump. The event began peacefully enough, but the speakers were notably unhinged. One woman in an "Oregon Women for Trump" shirt briefly reflected on "everything we're going through right now, the racial war, Black Lives Matter." The most unhinged speech, however, came from one speaker, who displayed the presence of QAnon fanatics in the crowd as he ranted:

> The God's honest truth is the pedophile agenda is being normalized, it is being pushed forward, and I think these Democrat leaders who allowed this to happen need to be shot dead in the streets!

The crowd applauded.

The same speaker was later recorded commenting on the presence of right-wing extremists: "Even if there is a couple of racists and Nazis amongst us, I don't even care, because they still love their country and they're fighting for their freedom," he said.

As the speakers were winding up, a crowd of right-wing rallygoers— many of them armed with guns and baseball bats—rushed a smaller group of Black Lives Matters counterdemonstrators, firing paint gun pellets at them. One man was caught by the group, punched and beaten with a bat, and then maced fully in the face.

A little while later, another couple of armed militiamen chased down and assaulted a counterprotester, but were quickly stopped by police, who arrested two men: Ty Parker, fifty-three, of Durango, Colorado, and Trenton Wolfskill, thirty-seven, of Eugene, Oregon, both on misdemeanor assault charges. The men were later released, police reported.

The event broke up shortly afterward, and there were no further incidents. But the violence revealed the large gap between the reality of far-right-wing aggression at these events and the perception of the causes of the violence among mainstream Trump supporters, who blamed everything on Black Lives Matter and Antifa.

There seemed to be no distinction between the extremists who both assaulted counterprotesters and made deranged speeches and the seemingly ordinary Trump supporters wearing red "Oregon Women for Trump" shirts who applauded them lustily. And maybe that was the point, too.

NOWHERE DID THE ANGRY, bellicose style common to the Patriot movement manifest itself within the mainstream Republican Party more intensely than in Texas late in the campaign: On October 30, a caravan of Donald Trump supporters driving dozens of mostly banner-festooned pickup trucks and SUVs deliberately ambushed a Biden-Harris campaign bus traveling to Austin and other parts of Texas. The Trump fans harassed them constantly en route and seemed to be trying to force them off the road.[51]

Videos show pro-Trump vehicles surrounding the bus on the freeway and slowing its progress as passengers and drivers shouted obscenities and various epithets; one witness claimed many of them were armed. At one point, a pickup driver veered into a campaign staff vehicle following the bus and smashed its fender, forcing it into another lane.

Neither Joe Biden nor Kamala Harris were aboard the bus, which was traveling from San Antonio to Austin on Interstate 35. The bus was part of a late Texas push for the Biden campaign, which organized several events in the state as part of a "Battle for the Soul of the Nation" tour featuring various Democratic candidates appearing with Harris. The pro-Trump vehicles surrounded it as it passed near New Braunfels en route to Austin, and remained with it until San Marcos, twenty miles down the road.[52]

A campaign staffer told reporters that the Trump supporters appeared to be trying to force the bus off the road. Police were called from the bus, and they reportedly helped the driver reach Austin safely. Once in Austin, however, a crowd of Trump supporters surrounded the bus and continued the harassment. Fearing the threats would escalate, Democrats canceled the event.

Nor was that the only canceled event. The Biden bus had also been scheduled to make a stop in Pflugerville to campaign with Texas House representative Sheryl Cole, who was waiting there. Cole tweeted that the Biden bus also had to cancel due to security reasons.

"Pro-Trump Protesters have escalated well beyond safe limits," she posted.

The Trump Trains' real utility, however, went well beyond intimidating Democrats. They became a prime vector for blurring the lines between far-right extremists such as the Proud Boys and ostensibly mainstream Republicans on a mass-politics level as the latter rushed to embrace the menacing tactics unleashed in Texas.

Led by Donald Trump himself, Republicans officially embraced their inner thugs: Trump praised the ambush by tweeting a video of the event on Saturday with the text, "I LOVE TEXAS!"[53]

The FBI acknowledged that it was investigating the incident, which was captured on multiple videos, including several posted on social media by Trump Train organizers and participants. Trump furiously denied that there was even an investigation—branding reportage on the matter as "false." The next day, responding to the FBI San Antonio tweet acknowledging the investigation—almost certainly because a congressman and two congressional candidates were aboard the bus—Trump tweeted:

> In my opinion, these patriots did nothing wrong. Instead, the FBI & Justice should be investigating the terrorists, anarchists, and agitators of ANTIFA, who run around burning down our Democrat run cities and hurting our people!

A few days later, he went even further, claiming that a CNN report on the investigation was wrong: "This story is FALSE. They did nothing wrong. But the ANTIFA Anarchists, Rioters and Looters, who have caused so much harm and destruction in Democrat run cities, are being seriously looked at!"

Trump also boasted about the caravan at campaign events. In Washington, Michigan, he told the audience: "Did you see the way our people were protecting his bus yesterday? Because they're nice. Saw his bus. They had hundreds of cars. Trump! Trump! Trump! And the American flag."

There was a series of other Trump Train events around the country over the weekend before the election, though none of the others targeted Democratic campaign vehicles for harassment. In New Jersey, a caravan of pro-Trump vehicles managed to briefly shut down Garden State Parkway, and also were able to shut down the Mario Cuomo Bridge in New York for a while.[54] In Indianapolis, a pro-Trump caravan circled the city on Interstate 465, essentially shutting down freeway traffic for hours and jamming streets downtown and elsewhere.[55] It was not clear how, as late-stage campaign strategies go, creating massive traffic problems was intended to sway voters into backing Trump.

None of the drivers involved in the Texas incident were condemned by any prominent Texas Republicans, nor by any Trump spokespeople. Instead, Texas GOP chairman Allen West issued a scathing statement Friday that presaged Trump's defense of the intimidation tactics—as well as indulging in anti-Semitic memes suggesting that George Soros finances anti-fascists:

> Three Trump supporters have been executed, one in Portland, one in Denver, and one Milwaukee. A leftist mob attempted to storm the house of the McCloskeys, threatened to burn their house down, rape Mrs. McCloskey, and then kill them both.
>
> Where is the liberal corporate media's concern about that real violence? Additionally, none of what your question implies is accurate. It is more fake news and propaganda.
>
> Prepare to lose . . . stop bothering me. Maybe Soros can cut y'all another check in 2022.[56]

Republicans on the national scene joined in. At a Florida Trump rally prior to his arrival, Senator Marco Rubio—who once decried Trump's indulgence in violent rhetoric—joined in the Trump Train parade: "I saw yesterday a video of these people in Texas," Rubio said. "Did you see it? All the cars on the road, we love what they did."[57]

One local Texas GOP official, Naomi Narvaiz, who apparently participated in the Trump Train, told *The Texas Tribune* that the event was simply about supporting Trump: "We decided we would jump on 35 to show support for our president," she said. "I didn't see anyone being overly aggressive."[58]

Yet on Twitter, Narvaiz struck a different tone: "We sent the @JoeBiden @KamalaHarris bus out of Hays! Your kind aren't welcome here!"

"We don't want any of the values or policies that the Democratic Party is embracing," she told the *Tribune*. "We don't want any of those in Texas."

Indeed, in a since-deleted video Trump Train organizer Randi Ceh posted on Facebook—one showing the collision between a white van driven by a campaign staffer following the bus closely and a black pro-Trump pickup that rammed it from the right and forced it into another lane— Ceh could be heard telling her audience: "Running them out of Texas. It is hilarious."

THE MENACING PRESENCE OF the Trump Trains remained the most active front of the Trump campaign through the election—and afterward, when he lost, they formed much of the foundation around which the resistance to his defeat revolved. Many of the Stop the Steal protests outside vote-counting centers in battleground states featured Trump Train–style displays and drew people who had participated in earlier rallies.[59]

They coalesced around the November 14 Million MAGA March, the first post-election pro-Trump protest in Washington, D.C. Billing it as "the largest Trump rally in U.S. history," the list of "prominent attendees" touted by organizers for the event was a virtual who's who of the white-nationalist far right, and leading far-right figures and groups organized and ardently promoted it, not least Alex Jones and his *Infowars* operation. The message of the whole event, in the words of Oath Keepers founder Stewart Rhodes: "We must refuse to EVER recognize this as a legitimate election, and refuse to recognize Biden as a legitimate winner, and refuse to ever recognize him as the president of the United States."[60]

The organizers incorporated the Trump Trains concept into the event by sponsoring and promoting a cross-country Million MAGA March caravan, which they claimed "will be driving through the entire country and arriving this weekend to protest the contested election." The route being promoted, however, only originated in Texas and drove through the South and up through Georgia and the Carolinas to reach Washington.

Like Rhodes and Oath Keepers, Jones and *Infowars* were especially active in promoting both the D.C. event and the accompanying cross-country Trump Caravan. Cohost Owen Shroyer held events at each stop. On his daily show, Jones proclaimed: "So don't worry, President Trump. The cavalry is coming." Biden's election—which he insists only occurred through fraud—was the final apocalyptic straw for Jones, who concluded: "We must not comply. This is the final assault. It's the takeover. And it's here." The turnout on November 14, however, was far short of the million attendees suggested by the name organizers had given the rally. Neutral observers estimated the crowd to number in the low tens of thousands. And while it was generally portrayed in the media as a mainstream Republican event, the rally was dominated by the presence of the far-right extremists who had organized it, and the rhetoric of the speakers—which was not just violently hyperbolic but often insurrectionary—reflected that.[61]

From the outset, the aggregation of white nationalists, street brawlers, "Patriot" militiamen, and conspiracy theorists who had organized and promoted the event on social media made their presence felt. Even before the midmorning event was scheduled to start, a block-long phalanx of several hundred thuggish Proud Boys marched through downtown Washington, chanting "Fuck Antifa" and "USA! USA!" as they made their way to Liberty Plaza near the White House, the event's main gathering point.

Trump had promoted the event in a tweet the day before, saying he found the rally "heartwarming," and that he "may even try to stop by and say hello." And indeed he did, cruising past the marchers in his limousine and waving to them from inside a rear passenger window, en route to a day on the golf course.

Throughout the event, far-right extremists of a variety of stripes announced their presence: White nationalists from Nick Fuentes's Groyper army led the march from the White House to the Congress and Supreme Court buildings, their blue "America First" banners held high. Oath Keepers and other militiamen, wearing body armor and prepared for battle—though unarmed, since Washington forbids open carry of guns within its city limits—joined eagerly.

The violence was not pronounced during the daytime at the event, despite some fighting that broke out between anti-Trump protesters and rally participants. However, after most of the rally had cleared away by evening, large clusters of Proud Boys and other violent pro-Trump brawlers took to the streets of downtown Washington and began punching, shoving, kicking, and stabbing protesters, even as Metro Police devoted most of their energy to restraining the anti-Trump bloc.

Some twenty people were arrested, including four people on gun charges. At least one person who was stabbed was hospitalized in serious condition.[62]

Trump used the violence as an opportunity to promote his narrative about the "violent left" on Twitter, tweeting about how "Antifa scum ran for the hills."

The reality on the streets bore little resemblance to Trump's narrative. Throughout the evening, Proud Boys and other pro-Trump brawlers could be seen deliberately attacking anyone who dared protest them. Eventually police would intervene, but they invariably directed their attention to the protesters, turning their backs on the Proud Boys, and seeming to protect them.

Some of the assaults broke out in the middle of intersections, where protesters sometimes gathered. At other times, gangs of pro-Trump rallygoers could be seen chasing individual protesters. Proud Boys knocked out a Black woman and left her laid out in the street.

One of the people stabbed amid the melees was journalist Talia Jane, who said someone came up behind her and stabbed her in the ear. Jane was also punched by a man who simply came up to her and knocked her down. She had her wound bandaged, and continued working throughout the night.

Other journalists experienced constant harassment from the rallygoers. MSNBC reporter Ellison Barber, at one point, was chased and followed by shouting MAGA fans: "The crowd here is chanting 'fake news, fake news,'" Barber told her audience. "Not fans of ours, as you can tell. Which that's fine as long as they give us a little space."

"It's hostile here, at least for us," she continued. "They're following us and chasing us as we walk further back."

The subsequent Stop the Steal rally in D.C. on December 12—organized around most of the same activists—went similarly: a long day of pro-Trump speeches denouncing the election results, calling them a globalist conspiracy and denouncing Democrats and Joe Biden as evil Communists, followed by an evening of Proud Boys violence on the streets of downtown Washington.[63]

They vandalized African American churches, tearing down their Black Lives Matter banners and burning them. The first vandalization occurred at Asbury United Methodist Church, one of the city's oldest African American churches. A group of Proud Boys tore down the church's large Black Lives Matter banner and carried it into the streets, parading it as a trophy.[64]

Eventually, a cluster of them set the banner aflame in the street, dousing it with liquid fuel. The men chanted, "Fuck Antifa!" and the white-nationalist dogwhistle, "Uhuru!" Among the men captured on video setting it alight was Proud Boys national chairman Enrique Tarrio, who was arrested for the act when he returned to Washington on January 4 to prepare for the big January 6 event.

For January 6, the Trump Train concept morphed into organized bus tours, featuring large luxury buses festooned with pro-Trump banners traveling across the country and picking up passengers in cities along the way, all headed for D.C. One such tour featuring pro-Trump figures Diamond and Silk held events in a variety of towns—such as Bowling Green, Kentucky; West Monroe, Louisiana; and Franklin, Tennessee—in order to drum up support for the march.[65]

Elsewhere, buses were organized to transport MAGA fanatics to the event. Wisconsin media reported on one such bus carrying at least forty-nine Trump supporters from the state, organized by a woman named Tamara Gasparick.

"We started the signup at 3:00, and it was literally going a person a minute," said Shannon Charles, who was assisting the effort. "At 3:14 we had 14 people, at 3:21 we had 21." She said a backup bus was organized on standby.

"We truly think that we won this election," Gasparick said. "All of the evidence is showing that."

They had all come for an insurrection. And they got one.

THE FALLOUT FROM JANUARY 6 temporarily sidelined all these forces, particularly as investigators arrested dozens of participants, including key national leaders like Joe Biggs and Ethan Nordean. For a few weeks, at least, their supporters fell silent, mostly claiming that someone else—particularly Antifa subversives—was secretly responsible for the chaos, until leading pundits like Tucker Carlson began defending them and claiming that the right was being persecuted by Democrats.

By early May, Proud Boys in the Pacific Northwest felt emboldened enough to finally sponsor a rally—this time in Salem, the Oregon state capital. Calling it a "Second Amendment" rally titled One Nation, One God, they neglected to obtain a permit, but set up a stage anyway and invited a roster of right-wing speakers, and then proceeded to boot out anyone they didn't like the looks of—including an elderly man out walking his dog.[66]

Promoted online as a "May Day 2A Rally," the event drew between one hundred and two hundred attendees, according to reporters. They were observed carrying semiautomatic pistols or rifles. And despite the lack of any authority to do so, they "closed" the public park to media and forced out anyone they believed didn't belong. The Proud Boys, acting as gun-bearing "security" for the rally at Salem's Riverfront Park, were able to close off access to anyone deemed undesirable, threatening both journalists and citizens with impunity. The only sign of law enforcement was a police helicopter hovering overhead.

Journalist Tim Gruver of The Center Square Oregon was threatened by Proud Boys and refused entrance to cover the event. "Riverfront is a public park," Gruver noted on Twitter. "Families are gathered right next door."

Oregon Proud Boys had deep connections to the January 6 insurrection; their members included two brothers who were arrested for their roles in the Capitol siege.[67] Moreover, their participation in the invasion of the Oregon State Capitol in Salem on December 21, 2020, was in many ways a powerful precursor of the January 6 event, especially in terms of the far right's antidemocratic strategies.[68]

The headline speaker for the May event was Rep. Mike Nearman, the Dalles-based state house member who was seen on video opening a door to allow insurrectionists into the building on December 21. Nearman was charged with two misdemeanors—official misconduct in the first degree and criminal trespass in the second degree—for that act.[69]

However, Nearman was a no-show. Instead, the best-known speaker was Jo Rae Perkins, the QAnon-loving Republican nominee for Oregon's US

Senate seat in 2020 (and later in 2022). Perkins called COVID-19 vaccines a "bioweapon," repeated false "stolen election" claims, and claimed the state is "going after your children."

"Let's take back Oregon, let's take back this country," she said.

A number of Salem residents remarked on the threatening and bullying behavior and the absence of a police presence on social media. "The Proud Boys are basically illegally taking over Riverfront park for the day and are forcefully ejecting people they don't like," tweeted one citizen. "They have weapons. Salem PD are doing nothing and have blocked me, a Salem resident, on this platform. This is not ok."

EVEN BEFORE THE TRIAL of Kyle Rittenhouse began, it had become a right-wing cause célèbre, his innocence as a matter of self-defense widely pronounced, both on right-wing social media and on establishment media like Fox News.[70]

The early court proceedings foreshadowed the outcome. Kenosha County Circuit Court judge Bruce Schroeder told prosecutors before trial that he would exclude evidence—including Rittenhouse's later mugging with Proud Boys at a tavern—that would involve any of the teenager's ideological beliefs. "This is not a political trial," he would later admonish prosecutors.[71]

He also informed attorneys in the case that they could not describe the three men Rittenhouse shot as "victims," but would permit defense attorneys to describe them as "looters," "rioters," or "arsonists," even though none of the three were ever accused of those crimes.[72]

Prosecutors struggled to assemble a coherent case, especially since they could neither discuss Rittenhouse's motives for being in Kenosha with a gun—which were entirely political—nor the Patriot militiamen whose ranks he had come to join, and in whose patrols he was participating. At every turn, it seemed, Schroeder puts his thumb on the scales of justice in the trial. In its second week alone the judge[73]:

- Called on the court to applaud a defense witness for being a veteran. Schroeder, noting that it was Veterans Day, asked if anyone in the court was a veteran; when witness John Black said he was, Schroeder called for the court to applaud him. Jurors joined in on the applause.[74]
- Rejected video of Rittenhouse shooting one of his victims, claiming that using Apple's zoom functions might distort the image. "iPads, which are made by Apple, have artificial intelligence in them that allow things to be viewed through three-dimensions and logarithms," defense attorneys insisted. "It uses artificial intelligence, or their logarithms, to create what they believe is happening. So this isn't actually enhanced video, this is Apple's iPad programming creating what it thinks is there, not what necessarily is there." Schroeder agreed.[75]
- Refused to permit prosecutors to ask defense witness Drew Hernandez, a pseudo-journalist who specializes in filming and posting misleadingly edited videos about anti-fascists and anti-police protesters, about his work for former Trump adviser Steve Bannon's Real America's Voice network. Hernandez also was present at the January 6 insurrection inside the Capitol, before which he had spoken at the Stop the Steal rally, telling the crowd: "We punch back, we fight back. Because we will not go down without a fight. We will not go down without bloodshed. If they want a second civil war, then they got one. I will fight to the very last breath." Schroeder ruled that the jury could not learn about his background because "this is not a political trial."[76]

So it was not a great surprise when, on November 19, 2021, the jury announced Rittenhouse's unanimous acquittal. Neither was it a surprise when the outcome was broadly celebrated on the right, particularly among the extremists who eagerly interpreted it as a green light, the narrative they needed to "get to use the guns."[77]

The bloodlust was palpable. Online trolls celebrated that "it's Open Season on pedo-commies" and boasted that the verdict means "there's nothing you can do about it." A neo-Nazi channel on Twitter urged readers to "let this win fuel your rage." A fan of pseudo-journalist Andy Ngo commented in a retweet: "Every one of these anarchist criminal thugs should be shot in the street like the worthless dogs they are."

Patriot-movement extremists saw the verdict as vindication for vigilantism and militia organizing. The Washougal Moms, a militia-friendly group from eastern Washington state, opined:

> Today the jury and legal system has reaffirmed our rights as citizens. The second amendment in all aspects, to form a well regulated militia, the right to bear arms in self defense, and against enemies both foreign and domestic!

Kurt Schlichter, a right-wing troll with over 380,000 followers, taunted MSNBC's Mehdi Hasan, who had expressed concern about the racial double standard that the verdict reflected, on Twitter.

> Your pain delights me. Kyle Rittenhouse killed two leftist catspaws and bisected the bicep of another and there's nothing you can do about it.

Other Proud Boys were more focused on their long-anticipated civil war. "There's still a chance for this country," wrote one. Another wrote: "The left wont stop until their bodies get stacked up like cord wood."

"Getting Rittenhoused" became a popular way of threatening leftists. After Andy Ngo posted a handful of tweets from leftists angry about the verdict, hundreds of his fans piled on, making threats of violence against them. "Someone will Rittenhouse them too," one responded. Another replied: "I came here to say that!"

The neo-Nazi group White Lives Matter had this advice for its white-supremacist followers:

Don't let this one victory lull you back to sleep. That's what they want. They know small "victories" can placate the angry masses more than anything else. Instead let this win fuel your rage. Never forget the simple fact that this clear-cut self-defense should never have gone to trial in the first place. Muslim, Hispanic, and African invaders have raped millions of our women, WHITE women. Their time of terrorizing our People with 0 consequences is coming to an end. The Rittenhouse verdict is a single tick in the scoreboard on our side. Our enemy doesn't have a scoreboard big enough for their victories. Fight harder, stronger, fiercer, and with the same remorse they have shown us. None. Get going, White man.

11

Those That Work Forces

HAD DARNELLA FRAZIER NOT been in downtown Minneapolis on May 25, 2020, and pulled out her cell phone to record the final moments of George Floyd's life as a police officer knelt blithely on his neck, his death probably would have gone unnoticed, relegated to the long list of American Black men who unaccountably die at the hands of police. But she was, and she did, and it changed the world.[1]

Millions of people saw Frazier's video after she posted it to Facebook, and it was both gut-wrenching and outrageous: Floyd's pleas for his mother as the life was forced out of his body, and the smug smirk on the face of Derek Chauvin, the Minneapolis cop kneeling on him. And nearly all of those millions—with certain exceptions—were outraged.

Organized protests began the next night in Minneapolis, and then spread to other cities: Los Angeles and Memphis on May 27, New York and Chicago the next day, and Seattle, Portland, and a dozen others the next day. Many of them went on for several days and even weeks.

Moreover, they quickly turned into riots as police aggressively confronted protesters, frequently assaulting them for their mere presence.

Journalists were often targeted for police violence, which included rubber bullets, gang tackling, and shoving people, including bystanders, to the ground. They sent an unmistakable message: police in America will target ordinary citizens who demand accountability for their actions and brutalize them into silence.[2]

It was, in fact, a demonstration of the very tactics used by police in city after city—certainly not just Minneapolis—that had driven so many people out into the streets to demonstrate their anger and insist on change in the first place. Black Lives Matter had become a vibrant movement over the preceding years because of the litany of protests demanding change after yet another callous and brutal police killing, from Ferguson, Missouri, to New York City to Los Angeles. It had built momentum over the preceding half-decade: Floyd's murder was the final spark.

Nowhere was that more the case than Portland, Oregon—which is why the police-brutality protests there continued for 104 days straight. The anger in Portland over police accountability had been building for years. And it turned the normally calm Northwest city into a national flashpoint in 2020.

The problem is decades old in Portland, but the watershed event for the community anger over fatal interactions with officers from the Portland Police Bureau (PPB) occurred in 2003, when an unarmed twenty-one-year-old Black woman named Kendra James was fatally shot during a traffic stop; afterward, police had pulled her from the car and handcuffed her, and left her unattended on the ground. She died by the time medical assistance arrived.[3]

There were community protests then, but they seemed to have little effect. Over the intervening seventeen years, Portland police shot and killed thirty-nine more people. They were disproportionately Black: while only 8 percent of the city's population is African American, they comprised 28 percent of the victims. More than sixty officers fired a gun in these forty incidents, but none were ever disciplined by PPB or indicted by a grand jury, although there were attempts to fire or suspend some of them.

In the four years leading up to the summer of 2020, however, the animus between Portland's left-leaning community and the police intensified with each invasion of the city by Joey Gibson's Patriot Prayer street brawlers and their accompanying Proud Boys and militiamen, because their handling of these factions was unmistakably biased: Anti-fascists were often arrested and sometimes brutalized by police, while the violence-seeking out-of-towners were rarely arrested and almost never prosecuted, despite engaging in genuinely frightening acts of violence. At times, police could be seen eagerly cooperating with far-right extremists and targeting leftists.

The George Floyd protests in Portland, which began on May 28, in short order became violent affairs. The next night, police fired tear gas to disperse the crowd that had assembled near the Multnomah County Justice Center, and protesters responded by rioting: smashing windows, sparking arsons, and vandalizing businesses. Police declared riots for three straight nights, and arrested about one hundred people.[4]

The nightly protests continued, with sporadic violence erupting: the crowd pushed down the fencing that had surrounded the justice center and was dispersed by tear gas again. Eventually, the protests settled into mostly peaceful events, though their ongoing presence disrupted business downtown, and there was still friction with police.

That friction, however, became explosive in early July when Donald Trump—intent on crushing the Antifa bogeyman he had built up—sent hundreds of Homeland Security agents to Portland and they began sweeping protesters off the streets in unmarked vans and arresting them, while others violently clashed with protesters at the fencing they had erected around the federal courthouse next door to the county's justice center. Even after Trump's Homeland Security forces backed down and eventually dispersed, the protests continued nightly in Portland, and the intermittent conflicts with city police continued.

To understand why, consider two incidents that occurred as the protests stretched into their eightieth day in mid-August, 2020.[5]

The first occurred on August 10, when Portland Police arrested a prominent Wall of Moms organizer named Demetria Hester at a protest outside police-union headquarters, which had been attacked the night before by activists who threw flaming debris inside the building, though the flames were quickly extinguished. Officers walked into a crowd of people and selected Hester, telling her: "You're under arrest." She was charged with interfering with a police officer and disorderly conduct.[6]

The next night, at a protest organized at Laurelhurst Park in northeast Portland, pipe bombs were hurled at protesters by shadowy figures who had shown up along its fringes; one of them detonated, but didn't harm anyone, and the other failed to go off and was eventually recovered by investigators. Police responded slowly to the scene and—despite having a wealth of information available online about the likely perpetrator—only announced they had opened an investigation into the case that ultimately went nowhere.[7]

A good deal became quickly known about the man believed to be at least one of the participants in the pipe bombing attempt, identified after video showed him fleeing the scene: Louis Garrick Fernbaugh, fifty-two, a retired Navy SEAL who claims to have been a contractor for the CIA, and most recently comanaged a private business in suburban Portland that specializes in providing tactical training and "threat assessments for schools, businesses, and other venues."

He was identified after a video shared on Instagram (and then on Twitter) showed protesters chasing darkly clad men out of the park following the blast. Another video, also shared on Twitter, showed one of the independent journalists at the park pursuing one of those men, who was carrying what appeared to be night vision goggles, apparently to the man's car, where he behaved threateningly toward the journalist.

The man recording the incident—Portland videographer Scott Keeler, who said he had observed the man in the park earlier walking away from the explosions—was using a flashlight, and first asked the man to stop as he walked up to him at a car the man appeared to be using. "Why are you throwing pipe bombs at people?" Keeler asked.

"Look man, I'm not the guy you wanna fuck with," the man responded. Keeler again queried him about the bombs, to which the man replied: "I don't know what you're talking about. But I'm not that guy you wanna fuck with. I'm fucking telling you."

Shortly after these videos were posted, several anti-fascists quickly identified the man as Fernbaugh. Fernbaugh deleted his Facebook account, but anti-fascist internet sleuths were able to find archived versions and created a record of his posts and comments gathered from various social media platforms.

For the most part, Fernbaugh's account was full of pro-Trump talking points—accusing Hillary Clinton of criminality, claiming that Robert Mueller's investigation of Trump was fraudulent, and so on—but his underlying far-right extremism lurked throughout, too. A couple of 2015 posts reproduced World War II–era anti-Semitic Nazi propaganda. Others included alt-right memes.

In a video rant he posted on Facebook, Fernbaugh claimed that "leftists" were responsible for "political terrorism" in the United States and was skeptical about the attempted mail bombings of liberal figures in October 2018. In the post's description, he wrote: "I'm surprised no one has slaughtered these sheep that have grown horns (ANTIFA)."

Fernbaugh claimed in another Facebook post warning of a coming civil war that "George Soros is known to have paid ANTIFA to instigate rioting and create chaos that has caused millions in damage across numerous cities, but especially Portland, OR." In a later comment on Facebook, Fernbaugh claimed to have "infiltrated ANTIFA" during a downtown Portland protest.

Most of the accounts associated with Fernbaugh were deleted shortly after he was identified. But at a Twitter account linked to his former business, he posted two comments, one a taunt and the other a threat: "ANTIFA had fireworks thrown at them and called the police. hahaha, yeah whatever," and "Training to shoot commies." The tweets were deleted shortly afterward.

PPB promptly announced that it was opening an investigation. However, a police spokesperson told reporters that investigators still had not heard from "someone who was actually there" that morning.

"Investigators would like to remind the public that PPB still needs in-person witnesses and/or potential victims to come forward. Detailed in-person witness accounts are crucial in moving this case forward. Those with knowledge who have spoken to the press are encouraged to contact investigators," PPB's statement read.

Police acknowledged that they had identified the man in the video, calling Fernbaugh a "person of interest" in the case, "and he still needs to be interviewed." The spokesperson said investigators had "attempted to contact him" but apparently failed, adding that officers "would encourage" him to contact PPB.

Two days later, PPB updated its statement, acknowledging that the FBI was assisting in the investigation and was conducting forensic analysis on the unexploded bomb:

> Portland Police Bureau investigators have been contacted by Mr. Fernbaugh by phone. Mr. Fernbaugh is represented by an attorney and is not making any statement at this time. Mr. Fernbaugh has not been cleared at this time and unless a witness, who was actually present, comes forward to investigators connecting him directly to the crime, he will not be arrested.[8]

When I inquired with PPB seven months later, the detective in charge of the investigation made clear that the case was going nowhere because of the lack of witnesses. "His presence on video is leaving the area approximately one half hour after the explosion," she wrote. "He is not observed on the video of the explosion. If there is not someone that can identify him present then there is no probable cause of his arrest."

SELECTIVE PASSIVITY BY PORTLAND police officers in the face of extremist violence featured prominently in the case of Demetria Hester as well.

When PPB sought her out for arrest on August 10, they targeted a respected community leader who had been the victim of a notorious hate crime in which a tepid and racist police response directly led to Jeremy Christian's horrific fatal assault on a Portland commuter train.

Hester met Christian on a Portland MAX commuter train late in the evening on May 25, 2017. When Christian boarded, he promptly announced that he was a Nazi and was looking to recruit others to join him. He shouted that he hated Jews, Mexicans, Japanese, and anyone who wasn't Christian.[9]

Hester—the only person of color on the train—spoke up and told Christian he needed to keep it down. What she didn't know was that the large, bellicose white man had, two weeks before, marched with a far-right group called Patriot Prayer, wrapped in an American flag—and had been kicked out for giving a Nazi salute and calling a counterprotester a "white nigger."

"Fuck you, bitch!" he screamed at her, adding that she had neither the right to speak nor to be on the train.

"I built this country!" he shouted. "You don't have a right to speak. You're Black. You don't have a right to be here. All you Muslims, Blacks, Jews, I will kill all of you."

As the train pulled into Hester's stop, she stood up to leave. Christian made clear he intended to get off and began shouting loudly at everyone on the train that he didn't care if anyone wanted to call the police because he wasn't scared.

"I will kill anyone who stands in my way because I have a right to do this," he told them. He looked at Hester and seethed: "Bitch, you're about to get it now."

As she stepped off the train, Christian lunged at her with a Gatorade bottle and smacked her above the right eye with it just as she whipped out her can of mace and gave him a faceful. It knocked him down on the platform. She staggered away and awaited police, who finally arrived about twenty minutes later. Hester said the officers treated her as a likely suspect, even though witnesses pointed out Christian—still washing pepper spray out of his eyes—standing feet away.

Christian wound up walking away from the scene and going home for the night. Police later blamed this on confusion regarding who the perpetrator was.

Hester later testified that, when she asked why Christian was being allowed to walk away, a PPB officer told her: "He said he didn't do it"—even though she and every witness who remained on the scene had told them he had.[10]

The next day, May 26, Christian boarded another MAX train—the Green Line, at Lloyd Center—during rush hour. This time he had a knife.

Unlike the night before, when he had harassed Hester, this train was full of people. But that didn't stop Christian. No sooner had he boarded than he spotted two young women of color—one of whom was wearing a hijab—and immediately stood in front of them, shouting about how they didn't belong in Portland. That Muslims should die, because they had been killing Christians for hundreds of years. That the girl in the hijab should go back to Saudi Arabia.

The girls got up and fled to the back of the train, seeking another seat. Christian followed them, still shouting.[11]

Three men, regular commuters who had been watching the scene unfold, stepped between Christian and the two women. One of them—Rick Best, fifty-three, a Portland city employee—stood closest to Christian and tried using reason: "I know you are a taxpayer, but this is not OK. You're scaring people." Christian kept shouting that it was about his free speech.

As they neared the next stop, Taliesen Myrddin Namkai-Meche, twenty-three, pleaded with Christian: "Please get off this train."

Another of the trio, Micah David-Cole Fletcher, twenty-one, recognized Christian from the alt-right march the month before, when he had marched with the counterprotesters and Christian had made a scene. He tried pushing himself between Christian and the women.

"You fucking touch me again and I'll kill you," Christian snarled at him. At that moment he lost his balance and fell back; when he came back up, he had a knife in his hand, and he plunged it into Best's neck, then turned to Namkai-Meche and Fletcher and did the same to each of them. Then he ran from the train and away from the Hollywood station. The two Muslim women fled the train, too, leaving their belongings behind.

Best bled out before help could arrive and was declared dead at the scene. Namkai-Meche, who told everyone who stopped to help that he loved them, died in the intensive care ward at the nearby hospital. Only Fletcher, who remained in the hospital for a month recovering from his wound, survived the attack.[12] During his ride to the police station, Jeremy Christian exulted in having stabbed the men to death, saying they should have heeded his warnings: "That's what liberalism gets you," he said.[13]

At his arraignment on murder and attempted murder charges—but, mysteriously, no hate-crime charges involving Hester's confrontation—two days later, Christian ranted behind the glass for the benefit of the press.

"Free speech or die, Portland!" He shouted. "You got no safe place. This is America! Get out if you don't like free speech!

After hearing the official charges being read, he shouted again: "Death to the enemies of America! Leave this country if you hate our freedom. Death to Antifa!

"You call it terrorism, I call it patriotism!"[14]

"FREE SPEECH" WAS, AS it happened, the radical right's battle cry nine days later, June 4, when Patriot Prayer—which denounced Christian and claimed he was never a member, pointing to his earlier ejection—held what would be the first of many right-wing rallies in downtown Portland over the next few years, ignoring the pleas of Portland mayor Ted Wheeler to postpone the event so soon after the MAX murders. The rally featured a number of notable alt-right and "Patriot" figures, including Proud Boys cofounder Kyle Chapman, Tim "Baked Alaska" Gionet, and Oath Keepers founder Stewart Rhodes.[15]

However, their modestly large turnout of several hundred supporters was dwarfed by the thousands of protesters—including groups from local unions, peace activists, and various leftist and anti-fascist organizations. For the bulk of the afternoon, the scene remained peaceful if contentious, with police generally keeping both sides separated.

But there was disturbing behavior by the police throughout. At one point, uniformed officers made an arrest of a man being detained by a "Patriot" militiaman, with his assistance.[16] Late in the afternoon, police became aggressive against the counterprotesters, kettling anti-fascist demonstrators who had marched downtown at the rally's end. Some fourteen people were arrested, all counterprotesters.[17]

The message was clear: Portland police were eager to protect the "free speech" rights of the assembled far-right extremists, yet had no compunction at all about trampling the free speech rights of the people who turned out to protest them. It was self-evident at the scene that the police had taken a side in the conflict—aligning themselves against ordinary Portland citizens and with the extremist out-of-towners whose questionable insistence that their "free speech" was under attack had just inspired a horrific hate crime.

This established what became a routine pattern over the next few years. Patriot Prayer and its leader, Joey Gibson, began organizing a seemingly endless series of "protests" in the Portland and Seattle areas that continued for the next two years and more, many of which produced clashes between protesters, counterprotesters, and police. At each of these events, arrests of leftist marchers became common, while only handfuls of arrests of the right-wing extremists involved in the violence occurred.

An early city review of police on the scene found they tended to believe that the Patriot Prayer protesters were "much more mainstream."[18] When journalists and activists raised the issue of apparent bias in the behavior of Portland police, both police and city officials denied that any such issue existed. When city commissioner Chloe Eudaly asked the bureau a series of questions about their behavior—including why the police bureau treated protesters who did not obey dispersal orders, but were not engaged in violence, as "fair game" for riot cops to shoot with exploding munitions and pepper spray; and whether police always ordered left-wing counterdemonstrators to disperse rather than issuing that order to right-wing groups—the police refused to answer.[19]

Reporters began digging into the seemingly amicable relationship between Patriot Prayer and PPB. In February 2019, journalists at *Willamette Week* and the *Portland Mercury* confirmed the activists' suspicions.[20] Text exchanges between Portland police officers and Joey Gibson, published in the two papers' reports, revealed a startling chumminess with the far-right activists and clear sympathy for their views. Even more disturbingly, the main officer involved, Lt. Jeff Niiya, appeared to have shared information about an ongoing investigation involving a key Patriot Prayer member, Tusitala "Tiny" Toese, with Gibson.

The revelations prompted an immediate uproar in Portland. Mayor Ted Wheeler vowed an investigation of police conduct in the case—to be led by Police Chief Danielle Outlaw. However, city commissioner Jo Ann Hardesty called for an independent investigation, in no small part because Outlaw's previous statements suggesting an anti-leftist bias—she once boasted on a right-wing talk radio show that her officers had "kicked their butts," referring to anti-fascist protesters—raised doubts about her fairness.[21]

"The incidents we hear about are not 'one-offs' but everyday examples of a broken policing system in Portland that must be addressed," Hardesty said. "I look forward to supporting actions of accountability. I ask that the Mayor and Police Chief Outlaw take swift action and I will also be here to demand justice if that call is not met."

In some instances, Niiya appeared to have been the source for misinformation that may have affected Patriot Prayer's violent behavior at rallies. Prior to the Portland rally that recruited far-right demonstrators from around the country on August 4, 2018, Gibson told his supporters that police intended to treat the event as "mutual combat," meaning they would not provide police protection for people engaged in violence.

"Mutual combat is a law that states that, it's something that happens in a lot of bars and stuff, if two guys go outside and they both agree to fight, kinda like training or whatever, no charges can be pressed, which I understand, I get that," Gibson explained incorrectly. "So basically if you want to be able to march in Portland, and the Portland citizens disagree with you, and they choose to use violence, you're going to have to defend yourself."

Some of Patriot Prayer's supporters interpreted all this as a kind of carte blanche for violence. "It means that if you show up to a fight that means your [sic] willing and there is no law broken," posted one of the group's coordinators on Facebook. "So either you stand up and take that dam [sic] green light you've been given or stay home and let it spill over to your own city." When the Southern Poverty Law Center inquired about the "mutual combat" narrative being bandied about before the event, Portland Police spokesman Christopher Burley sidestepped the question: "Crowd management events are complex incidents that require a balance of many different interests and factors," he said.

Unsurprisingly, Portland's internal investigation—the results of which were released in September 2019—exonerated Niiya and PPB.[22] Police Chief Danielle Outlaw told reporters that the city's Independent Police Review, a city auditing division, had ruled all the allegations "unfounded": "There was no evidence to prove any of the allegations considered," Outlaw said.

The audit did, however, point to poor training prior to the events. "This investigation found Lt. Niiya received no training or guidance regarding how he was expected to carry out his work as a liaison. Simply put, Lt. Niiya was left to figure it out on his own," the investigative report said. "As a result, Lt. Niiya has faced personal criticism, and damage to his professional reputation, in large part because the Police Bureau failed to clearly describe Lt. Niiya's job to him and failed to provide him training on how he should do it."

For the most part, the report found that Niiya had not violated department standards, suggesting that he had been as friendly with left-wing protesters as he was with those from the far right. Niiya eventually left PPB and moved to Boise, Idaho, to serve on its police force.

The right-wing protests and provocations continued. The ostensible causes for these protests were highly mutable and opportunistic, depending largely on whatever was the right-wing cause célèbre of the moment: if it wasn't "sanctuary city" status for immigrants, or Seattle's strict gun laws, or a March Against Sharia, the far-right protest organizers were always able to come up with a pretext.

The point of the events wasn't the controversy du jour: the point was the violence. As the ranks of the Patriot Prayer rally-goers filled with Proud Boys and other thuggish street-brawling elements, it became clear that the main reason most of the men—the vast majority of whom did not live in the city—out marching in Portland's streets were present was that they were eager to provoke violence with "Antifa" and the counterprotesters. And it frequently was very violent indeed, particularly a June 30, 2018, event dedicated to "cleaning the streets of Portland" of leftists.[23]

The culmination of all these protests was the August 17, 2019, Proud Boys march through downtown Portland, which drew hundreds of the street brawlers from around the nation, including Joe Biggs and Enrique

Tarrio—and yet was still badly outnumbered by thousands of anti-fascists and their supporters. There were relatively few confrontations between the Proud Boys and counterprotesters, largely because police maintained rigorous security around the marchers, and even provided personal escorts for some of them.[24]

However, police again behaved very differently toward the counterprotesters. They arrested thirteen of them, the majority under dubious circumstances, including a woman arrested for revving her motorbike in the vicinity of Proud Boys marchers. Another was a woman named Hannah Ahern, who was arrested for spitting on the street in front of officers: "I wanted to express my general disagreement with what was going on," she told the *Portland Mercury* later. "I felt compelled to show disgust."[25]

She was speaking for many Portlanders.

The right-wing protests became infrequent and sporadic after that, including a planned Ku Klux Klan rally at which no Klansmen actually showed up, though there was once again a large crowd of counterprotesters. When the COVID-19 pandemic and ensuing lockdown measures first hit in mid-March 2020, protests vanished altogether—until the murder of George Floyd.

DEMETRIA HESTER WAS A key witness in Jeremy Christian's trial in early 2020, detailing her ordeal for the jury at length. She was questioned by one of Christian's defense attorneys about the testimony she gave to legislators in June 2019 regarding a state senate bill to expand Oregon's hate-crime laws.[26]

"Why do you feel so strongly about speaking out about this?" Hester was asked.

"There are a lot of hate crimes in the world today and they need to be stopped," she replied.

Christian was convicted by unanimous verdict in February on multiple counts of first-degree murder and hate crimes for his threats against the two young women. At his sentencing in June, Hester again testified, and turned her moment on the stand into a condemnation of police inaction when dealing with far-right violence.

"I blame the system for creating and facilitating people like Jeremy, and then we the community have to deal with him," she said. "In my case, the white supremacist got special treatment from the police officer reacting, believing the assault was made against the assailant. He didn't believe me or the two Trimet supervisors." She ended by telling Christian to "rot in hell."[27]

Her comments set off Christian, who tore off his face mask and began screaming at her: "I should've killed you, bitch!" He was carried out of the courtroom. The judge sentenced Christian to life in prison with no chance of parole.[28]

Hester helped lead the Moms brigade at protests beginning in late July, in her capacity as leader of Moms United for Black Lives. Her tenure was interrupted on August 9 when police arrested her. However, the next day, Hester was released as the Multnomah County District Attorney's Office announced that it was dismissing the charges, saying it "was in the interest of justice upon reviewing the police reports in this matter."[29]

Hester spoke to a crowd of supporters outside the courthouse. "This is about our future, this is about peace," she said. "Our peace of mind to walk down the street and care for each other again. Peace to go to your neighbors and say, 'I love you. What do you need?'"

Hester's release, however, was only part of a larger official rebuke handed to PPB for its handling of protest-related arrests by the district attorney's office. The next day, it announced that it would not prosecute over five hundred cases involving charges brought by police related to the protests.[30]

"As prosecutors, we acknowledge the depth of emotion that motivates these demonstrations and support those who are civically engaged through peaceful protesting," the office said in a prepared statement. "We recognize that we will undermine public safety, not promote it, if we leverage the force

of our criminal justice system against peaceful protestors who are demanding to be heard."

The shift came about under the auspices of new management in the
office: District Attorney Mike Schmidt was elected the previous May on
an agenda promising sweeping reforms in the criminal justice system; he
garnered over 75 percent of the vote against an establishment candidate
who had been avidly supported by the Portland Police Association.[31] The
message in that outcome was unmistakable—but then fully ignored by the
police afterward.

There are many possible explanations for the obdurate culture of police
forces in places like Portland and Seattle that seemed to encourage outright
contempt for the citizens they are professedly serving and protecting. These
attitudes were summed up in a social media video capturing a protester's
conversation with a Seattle officer who drove onto a sidewalk full of protesters at high speed, after which he described with relish how the protesters on
the sidewalk scattered like "cockroaches."[32]

Some of the problems originate with the longtime drive by police forces
around the country to emphasize their "professionalization" during training—which also has the effect of conditioning police officers to see themselves as separate from the communities they serve.[33] Other problems
include the increasing trend of urban police officers living in suburban and
exurban places distantly removed culturally and otherwise from the communities they police—which is notably the case in both Portland (where
only 18 percent of police live inside the city) and Seattle.[34]

But the heart of the Portland situation—the invisibility of right-wing
extremist violence to police officers as a serious community threat—is one
that infects police forces throughout the nation.

As Hester, reflecting on how Christian's attack affected her, told Oregon
Public Broadcasting: "I couldn't believe we were in 2017 because I'm from
Memphis, Tennessee, where they do burn crosses, and they do drag you
out of your house—the KKK, which are the police. That Portland, Oregon,

allows people like Jeremy Joseph Christian to spew hate to everyone and to then back him up.[35]

"That's what pushed me, because the night of the incident, the police knew who he was, allowed him to do what he did, treated me like the assailant, wanted my ID, had no compassion. I asked him [the police officer] why he wasn't pursuing him, and he said 'He said he didn't do it.' Those types of things, being a victim and then having to be revictimized by the system."

"SOME OF THOSE THAT work forces are the same that burn crosses"—a line from the song "Killing in the Name" by Rage Against the Machine—is a common adage shared among leftist protest groups, reflecting their belief that police forces are riddled with closet white supremacists. Amid the seemingly endless violent mishandling of Black people by arresting officers, their nakedly preferential treatment of right-wing extremists, their vicious retaliation against marching citizens in too many street clashes, the suspicions became conventional wisdom in places like Portland—that not only are police officers sympathetic to white supremacists, but that too many cops may in fact be active hate-group members themselves.

A September 2020 report by the Brennan Center for Justice authored by a respected law-enforcement analyst and former FBI agent—titled *Hidden in Plain Sight: Racism, White Supremacy, and Far-Right Militancy in Law Enforcement*—confirmed that those suspicions were very well-founded.[36] The author of the report, Michael German, worked undercover on cases involving far-right extremists in the 1990s for the FBI, and since then has been involved in analyzing federal counterterrorism efforts for the ACLU and the Brennan Center.

German explained that "only a tiny percentage of law enforcement officials are likely to be active members of white supremacist groups." However, the evidence of "overt and explicit racism within law enforcement" is also well established:

Since 2000, law enforcement officials with alleged connections to white supremacist groups or far-right militant activities have been exposed in Alabama, California, Connecticut, Florida, Illinois, Louisiana, Michigan, Nebraska, Oklahoma, Oregon, Texas, Virginia, Washington, West Virginia, and elsewhere. Research organizations have uncovered hundreds of federal, state, and local law enforcement officials participating in racist, nativist, and sexist social media activity, which demonstrates that overt bias is far too common. These officers' racist activities are often known within their departments, but only result in disciplinary action or termination if they trigger public scandals.

The report went on to explore the utterly inadequate response within the ranks of law enforcement, or the officialdom charged with oversight of them, to known affiliations with white supremacist and militant groups by law-enforcement officers. He noted the FBI's 2015 counterterrorism policy "indicates not just that members of law enforcement might hold white supremacist views, but that FBI domestic terrorism investigations have often identified 'active links' between the subjects of these investigations and law enforcement officials."

The response to the exposure of those links is instructive: agents are instructed simply to use a website function that would screen potential subjects of investigation from knowledge of FBI scrutiny—and its only concern is that its agents be shielded from culpability for those active links.

This has been going on a long time, and is "hiding in plain sight," as German's report detailed. He identified three core problems:

- A lack of mitigation policies to protect communities against biased police officers;
- A failure by the Department of Justice to vigorously police law-enforcement misconduct, as is its duty;
- And that the behavior of police departments in protest situations

inflamed by police violence has only inflamed further violence, and reveals a deep bias within law-enforcement departments.

The latter, as German notes, directly undermines police safety, security, and lives, especially considering how often far-right militants have killed police officers: "The overlap between militia members and the Boogaloo movement—whose adherents have been arrested for manufacturing Molotov cocktails in preparation for an attack at a Black Lives Matter protest in Nevada, inciting a riot in South Carolina, and shooting, bombing, and killing police officers in California—highlights the threat that police engagement with these groups poses to their law enforcement partners."

German observed how blinkered our national culture—not just within law enforcement, but within the halls of officialdom and in the national media—has become about the real threat posed by white nationalists:

> If the government knew that al-Qaida or Isis had infiltrated American law enforcement agencies, it would undoubtedly initiate a nationwide effort to identify them and neutralize the threat they posed. Yet white supremacists and far-right militants have committed far more attacks and killed more people in the U.S. over the last 10 years than any foreign terrorist movement. The FBI regards them as the most lethal domestic terror threat. The need for national action is even more critical.

German testified before a Senate Judiciary Subcommittee hearing ostensibly directed at "protecting speech" from "anarchist violence" (chaired by a prevaricating Senator Ted Cruz), warning the senators: "We're all concerned about protest violence, but framing the issue as a problem of anarchist violence only spreads misinformation that puts law enforcement officers and the communities they serve at greater risk. It also distracts from the police accountability and anti-discrimination issues that millions of Black Lives Matter supporters come into the streets to support."[37]

Later in the hearing, he discussed how too many police departments—including those in Portland, where ongoing protests against police violence became a daily reality for most of 2020—rely on a model of protest control from the 1960s that has been long discredited and displaced with more temperate models that rely less on the use of force.

"It's very important to look at the research and develop our tactics for reducing police violence based on objective research, and not adopt tactics that were discredited decades ago," he said.

———————

THE JANUARY 6 INSURRECTION revealed just how deep the problem of extremist sympathies within the ranks of American police forces had become. The issue became self-evident when it shortly emerged that some thirty-one law-enforcement officers in twelve states were linked to the Capitol siege.[38]

The American policymakers who denounced the rise of far-right political violence in the insurrection's aftermath faced a real conundrum: How could law enforcement effectively curtail the illegal activities of right-wing extremists when so many officers are themselves participants in these movements?

The answer—which is that it could not—suggested that effectively confronting far-right extremism must begin with police reform, and particularly the task of weeding extremists out of our police forces. The public, after all, cannot expect agencies tasked with enforcing the laws that prohibit extremist violence to do so seriously when those same extremists permeate their ranks.

Police departments around the country began struggling with the enormity of the job. A *Los Angeles Times* report focusing on the efforts of Los Angeles police chief Michel Moore to confront extremism within the force he oversees suggested that weeding out extremist cops was nearly an intractable complication.[39]

The most difficult aspect of the problem for police is the extent to which far-right views have been normalized within the mainstream, and particularly within the ranks of police officers. The issue gets to the heart of a police culture that has become increasingly politicized by right-wing politics and is simultaneously hostile to accountability for its own behavior. When cops are also far-right extremists who engage in discriminatory policing, American police officials have a history of closing ranks and defending the status quo.

Moore voiced some of these cultural tensions when asked whether he would drum out officers who were found to be members of the Proud Boys. He at first suggested that the Proud Boys were part of a broad category of groups that included Black Lives Matter with which the public was still grappling. However, he clarified that he personally considers the Proud Boys an organization that "runs counter to this democracy," and does not believe that "there is any place for a law enforcement officer to be a member of such organizations or advocate for their existence."

Moore added that he was unaware of any Proud Boys or members of any other extremist group within the ranks of current LAPD officers, but was prepared to investigate any such claims, indicating he would fire anyone who "crosses the line" of what is acceptable.

LAPD officials were driven by the anti-police-brutality protests of 2020, Moore said, to examine how best to comb their ranks for extremists and weed them out, suggesting they were especially motivated by the realization that the presence of such police would seriously undermine efforts to rebuild trust within the city's diverse neighborhoods. Moore rejected any suggestion that extremism was prevalent among his officers, noting that the LAPD is a diverse department, both ethnically and politically.

Extremism within the ranks of law enforcement, however, is not just a community-relations problem. Much more broadly, it also affects what laws are enforced and how. And it has a direct impact on the broader national effort to push back the incoming tide of white-nationalist and other far-right extremist violence.

The primary problem with domestic terrorism in America is that our law-enforcement apparatus at every level—federal, state, and local—has failed to enforce the laws already on the books that provide them with more than enough authority and ability to confront it. The ongoing presence of officers sympathetic to the cause of domestic terrorists—and for whom, in fact, their radical extremism is invisible—is one of the major proximate causes of this failure.

It is already, for example, a federal crime to share bomb-making recipes on the internet. It's also a federal crime to advocate the assassinations of public officials or to otherwise threaten them with violence. Yet what began as a few angry voices on the fringes of the internet—and was thus easy for law-enforcement authorities to ignore—has grown into a massive flood in large part because these laws are only selectively and lightly enforced.[40]

In a paper for *Just Security*, Michael German explored why new laws are not necessary to confront the problem. As he explained, the problem for federal law enforcement has not been a lack of tools to deal with domestic terrorism, but an utter lack of prioritization of the issue by high-level officials.[41]

"While Justice Department officials have used notorious incidents of white supremacist violence to push for a new domestic terrorism statute, the Department itself continues to de-prioritize far-right violence and focus its most aggressive tactics instead against environmentalists, political protesters, and communities of color," he wrote. "It isn't hard to guess who would likely be targeted with new domestic terrorism laws."

The presence of ideologically sympathetic extremists within law enforcement also poses a security threat to any agency dealing with their criminal activities, particularly officers who keep any fascist affiliations secret and work to implement a far-right agenda from within the force.

"Police officers have access to sensitive information," explained associate Georgetown law professor Vida Johnson. "For example, they might know if they're looking into the Proud Boys or the Three Percenters or the Oath Keepers, so they can tip them off. That's one reason why careers in law enforcement are so appealing to people who hold far-right belief systems. They get this opportunity to not only police people of color, to control their goings and comings and how they live their lives, but also they get this inside information about whether [far-right groups] are in fact being investigated."[42]

American law enforcement has never systematically addressed the problem of extremism within its ranks, which historically speaking is not a new phenomenon at all, but has worsened dramatically in the past few decades. "It's clear that extremist groups on the right and white supremacists have been agents of chaos, of violence in our community, and the fact that police are just now interested in training on this, I find more than disturbing," Johnson told the *Los Angeles Times*.[43]

Johnson, in a 2019 academic paper titled "KKK in the PD: White Supremacist Police and What to Do About It," found that police departments across the country exhibited evidence of white supremacist ideology, citing "scandals in over 100 different police departments, in over 40 different states, in which individual police officers have sent overtly racist emails, texts or made racist comments via social media."[44]

She observed that it should be a cause for concern when officers become followers of QAnon or claim that COVID-19 is a hoax or espouse theories that Trump's reelection was fraudulently stolen from him.

"People who can't separate fact from fiction probably shouldn't be the ones enforcing laws with guns," Johnson said.

———————

IN OCTOBER 2021, HACKERS released a trove of internal data in the Oath Keepers organization—one that incidentally revealed the breadth and depth of the penetration into the ranks of law-enforcement authorities by such far-right extremists, and the stark reality that, if anything, it had worsened since the insurrection.[45]

Not only was there a surge in interest in joining the group after the January 6 violence, but the interest was pronounced among law-enforcement officers. A survey of the data by *USA Today* found more than two hundred people who signed up to join the group over the past decade who identified themselves as members of a police agency; of those, twenty-one are still serving today.

Despite the group's well-established role in the insurrection, hundreds of people either joined the Oath Keepers anew or renewed their membership afterward. These included people who cited their military ranks when they joined; among their numbers were combat veterans, national guardsmen, retired servicepeople, and members of the clergy. Others who joined were connected to the firearms industry or engaged in security contracting.[46]

"The Oath Keepers subscribe to anti-government conspiracy theories, so the fact that officers belong to an organization that believes in this type of stuff really calls into question their discretion and their ability to make sound judgments," domestic-terrorism analyst Daryl Johnson said.

The active law-enforcement officers identified on the membership list included Riverside County, California, sheriff Chad Bianco, who told *USA Today* he enrolled in 2014 with a single year's membership. Sheriff Bianco had long been aligned with far-right "constitutionalist" beliefs. He announced earlier in summer 2021 that he would refuse to enforce the state's COVID-19 mandates, proclaiming himself as "the last line of defense from tyrannical government overreach."

Another officer on the list—Maj. Eben Bratcher, operations chief with the Yuma County Sheriff's Office in Arizona—left a note for the Oath Keepers when he signed up: "We have 85 sworn officers and Border (of) Mexico on the South and California on the West. I've already introduced your web site to dozens of my Deputies." He told *USA Today* that he didn't recall writing that. He said he received newsletters from the group for "some time" but dropped out "due to the sheer volume of email I received."

A Ferndale, Washington, police officer, identified as Scott Langton, reportedly inquired with the Oath Keepers on February 4, saying: "I'm not looking to be on some Liberal hit list." Langton had been sued at least twice for allegedly committing civil rights and use-of-force abuses while in uniform; one suit was settled, the other remains active in federal court. He was placed on administrative leave after his attempts to join the Oath Keepers were revealed, but was eventually cleared of wrongdoing by an internal investigation and returned to the beat.[47]

A common misconception shared by most police officers is that they have a First Amendment right to say just about anything on social media or in public, Val Van Brocklin, a former federal prosecutor who trains police departments on using social media, told *USA Today*. But people in charge of enforcing the law are also expected to be nonpartisan and unbiased in that work, and spouting far-right extremism places a cloud over entire departments.

"The vast majority of cops in the country don't understand this," Van Brocklin said. "A public employer does not have to pay you for your insubordination or dishonorable conduct that sullies the badge and the uniform."

JOHN DONNELLY WAS THE living incarnation of these fears. For years, the residents of Woburn, Massachusetts—a suburb just north of Boston—knew him as a friendly local Irish American cop, president of a "back the blue" nonprofit that raised funds for law enforcement, as well as a firearms instructor for his father's gunmaking company. He was probably best known for the billboards bearing his likeness, touting his side job as an award-winning real estate agent.[48]

He was also an active neo-Nazi who participated in white-nationalist chat rooms under the nom de plume Johnny O'Malley. Under that guise, he helped organize the lethal Unite the Right rally in Charlottesville, Virginia, in August 2017, where he served as part of the bodyguard detail for notorious white nationalist Richard Spencer.

Donnelly's double life was exposed in October 2022 by *HuffPost* reporter Christopher Mathias (working with anti-fascist researchers at Ignite the Right), who was able to piece together a long trail of online and real-world clues to accurately identify the Woburn officer as "O'Malley." Mathias noted that Donnelly's record included a long history of racist and anti-Semitic posts on those forums. He was also a workout fanatic who liked to boast about wearing "Right Wing Death Squad" clothing to the gym.

In one thread, Donnelly commented: "Friendly reminder that if you don't lift today the kikes win."

Donnelly, thirty-three, acknowledged to his superiors at the Woburn police department that the article was accurate, and he was suspended pending an investigation; a few days later, he tendered his resignation. Woburn police chief Robert F. Rufo Jr. said Donnelly "violated multiple department policies through involvement in extremist groups."

Middlesex district attorney Marian Ryan announced an investigation into Donnelly's involvement with the rally, as well as a review of all cases in which he had been involved.

The New England Innocence Project, a civil rights group, called on further action. "Every case this officer touched should be dismissed, every conviction vacated," the group said in a statement on Twitter. "There is no integrity in a system that relies on his credibility, judgment, or fairness. Nothing he has said or done in the job can be sufficient to bring criminal consequences to someone else."

Donnelly's presence, as the New England Innocence Project noted, indicates that the problem runs deeper than a single officer.

"This white supremacist officer had partners, supervisors, and trainers," the group said. "If he made arrests, prosecutors and judges relied on his reports and testimony. Yet, NONE of these people recognized and exposed him; they enabled him to be in a position of power over our community."

12

Going Local

FOR THE FIRST FEW weeks after the January 6 insurrection, the Proud Boys largely vanished from the public radar. However, by May 2021, the neofascist street thugs began popping up all over—but operating on a purely local level, consistently hijacking causes and events organized by local activists and communities.[1]

That, in fact, was the primary post-insurrection strategy, suggested by Ethan Nordean in his pre-arrest Telegram chats: namely, to scale down their operations and spread their recruitment by focusing on local issues.[2] Within a matter of weeks, they began enacting it in places like Nashua, New Hampshire; Miami and Tampa, Florida; and Salem, Oregon.[3]

The strategy mostly entailed identifying local grievances that could provide opportunities for Proud Boys to involve themselves, and avoiding the large mass rallies of the previous four years.

Nordean's online chats with his fellow Proud Boys about how to proceed after January 6 laid out this strategy. "I'm gunna press on with some smart level headed non emotional guys and create a game plan for how to approach this year, we aren't gunna stop getting involved in the community, especially with the momentum we have," Nordean wrote.

The focus, Nordean said, would be: "Meet n greets with the public, raise money, community service, security for events etc . . . but we can work on an effective process so we look more organized and have properly vetted members who are representing the club."

This was consistent with Proud Boys' proclaimed self-image as just normal American guys, their belief right up to January 6 that the police were on their side, and their ongoing denials of being racist or extremist. The localized issues were often the same right-wing grievances being ginned up nightly on Fox News, as with critical race theory in New Hampshire schools. The common thread among the issues being hijacked by Proud Boys was that they were congenial to (if not fueled by) conspiracism, and primarily revolved around concocted enemies.

This was how they proceeded. In Miami, for instance, Proud Boys leader Enrique Tarrio turned up uninvited with several cohorts, offering "support" for a protest by the Cuban American community backing dissidents in Cuba.[4]

In Nashua, Proud Boys turned up at school board meetings, masked and wearing their uniform shirts, to protest "critical race theory" in local schools. Their presence riled local residents.

"Proud Boys come to our board meetings for what? For what? What is the purpose of them being here? Are they here for our children? I think not," said board member Gloria Timmons, who doubles as president of the Nashua chapter of the National Association for the Advancement of Colored People.[5]

They marched in a Fourth of July parade in Buhl, Idaho, and announced a "fundraising event for veterans" in Helena, Montana, that was promptly squelched.[6] They were among the protesters in Tallahassee who turned out to protest the detention of the January 6 insurrectionists.[7] All told, they turned up at about a dozen events around the country.[8]

One of the more insidious aspects of the Proud Boys' strategy was how it manipulated small-town environments to insinuate themselves within them, and, once there, how it divided and created turmoil within those communities where little existed previously. As a local account in *Mainer News* demonstrated, the Proud Boys' gradual takeover of a small old tavern in Portland, Maine, alienated and angered local residents, who blamed the tavern owner for permitting it.[9]

The owner, as the report explained, wasn't necessarily sympathetic to the Proud Boys, but really had little idea about their background. "Oh, they're not that bad," the man reportedly told his longtime bouncer, who quit over the situation.

"They're bad as the fuckin' Klan, Bobby!" the bouncer replied. He then pointed at a group of Proud Boys across the street, and added: "Yeah, I'm talking about you motherfuckers."

THE HYPERLOCAL STRATEGY DEPLOYED by the Proud Boys had one stark effect: It created explicit alliances with other far-right movements that typically had fallen outside of their sphere, particularly with Christian nationalists.

This manifested itself in early August 2021 in Portland, Oregon, when Proud Boys tangled with counterprotesters and anti-fascists in the city's downtown area.[10] This led to a number of ugly scenes with armed and armored men in masks pointing their rifles at journalists and onlookers.

The clashes originated on Saturday, August 7, when a far-right evangelical preacher and popular Christian rocker named Sean Feucht, using Proud Boys as "security," held a rally downtown at the city's waterfront park. Fuecht had been organizing anti–COVID measure protests on his West Coast tour. This naturally attracted counterprotesters and resulted in some fights and tossed fireworks; those conflicts later spread downtown, where a group of Proud Boys tangled with anti-fascists briefly. Then, on Sunday evening, even more Proud Boys prowled the downtown streets with weapons and roaring pickups, but the confrontations remained brief.

The weekend's violence was sparked by a warm-up act, when Canadian preacher Artur Pawlowski, another anti-masker, was setting up to speak to a small crowd on Saturday and the event was broken up by anti-fascists. The anti-fascists confronted several far-right brawlers, including Patriot Prayer's Joey Gibson, early in the dispute. They then began tossing the group's loudspeakers and public-address system into the nearby Willamette River. Portland police broke up the fracas.

Conflicts continued between counterprotesters and the security team during the rest of the Pawlowski presentation. Bang fireworks were tossed, reportedly into a group of children at one point. Afterward, the confrontations carried over into the streets of downtown Portland, and some of the Proud Boys could be seen strolling through carrying batons, baseball bats, and paintball rifles. A cluster of them encountered a band of anti-fascists, threatened to assault them, and were sprayed with mace, which scattered them. Many piled into the back of a pickup and fled.

"The Nazis came out and we drove them off again," anti-fascist Wade Varner told the *Portland Tribune*'s Zane Sparling. "I'm sitting here, totally unarmed, in a wheelchair, and this fucker shoots me in the face with a paintball."[11]

On Sunday, Feucht's rally again attracted a crowd of several hundred. Afterward, Feucht tweeted out thanks to his security squad with a photo of them (including Gibson), with a threatening text:

These are all ex-military, ex-police, private security & most importantly LOVERS OF JESUS & freedom. If you mess with them or our 1st amendment right to worship God—you'll meet Jesus one way or another.

The post-rally conflicts on Sunday, however, were more widespread and intense, thanks primarily to the presence of Proud Boys "security," who threatened and assaulted bystanders. One of the security teams was led by notorious Proud Boy brawler Tusitala "Tiny" Toese, who threatened protesters with various weapons, including batons and a two-by-four.

As evening descended, the fighting became more intense and more widespread. Oregon Public Broadcasting's Sergio Olmos recorded a number of the confrontations, which took place over the better part of an hour.[12] Anti-fascists lobbed fireworks at the Proud Boys while Toese egged them on by promising to hit them with a baseball bat. Large pickups drove aggressively through the protesters, seemingly intent on hitting some of them.

At one point, a man was seen toting what appeared to be a semiautomatic rifle around the streets of Portland (where open carry of firearms is illegal), walking past a crowded bar. He also was observed pointing it at a photojournalist who was following him, as well as at an unarmed Black protester who yelled at him.

The man reportedly turned himself in to police, who then ascertained that the man's rifle was in fact a nonlethal Airsoft pellet gun designed to imitate an AR-15 semiautomatic. He was released and continued to prowl downtown streets.

As Toese and his cohorts left Portland, they fired Roman candles directed at the protesters. The fireworks ricocheted off downtown buildings.

———————

THE STRATEGY OF TURNING Proud Boys out to support local right-wing protests, however, soon morphed along with the targets of these events. That's when they started showing up to threaten school boards. The threats and intimidation started out with letters and emails: Hundreds of them, many anonymous, sent to school-board members, threatening them over CRT, transgender bathroom use, and COVID-19 measures. And it happened nearly everywhere the spring, summer, and fall of 2021.

In Loudoun County, Virginia, the former chair of the local school board, Brenda Sheridan, received a flood of messages threatening her or the entire school board. One read: "Brenda, I am going to gut you like the fat fucking pig you are when I find you." That message, as well as another sent to her home, also threatened her children.[13]

Board members in Pennsbury School District in Bucks County, Pennsylvania, received racist and anti-Semitic emails sent from around the nation, attacking the district over its racial-diversity efforts. One said: "This why hitler threw you cunts in a gas chamber."[14]

An anonymous letter sent to the Dublin, Ohio, board president vowed that officials would "pay dearly" for supporting education programs on race, as well as COVID-19 mask mandates. "You have become our enemies and you will be removed one way or the other," it said.[15]

When Reuters contacted some of the people who sent these messages, they responded defiantly. One of them described himself as a "patriot" enraged by "leftist scum" and "Antifa," while another declared: "LGBTQ is an abomination." A third claimed that the Loudoun County race-sensitivity program tells children "that race will determine their outcomes in life," calling it "truly sick."

They began turning up at meetings, too. In Mendon, Illinois, a thirty-year-old man showed up at a school board meeting and assaulted a member of the board, for which he was arrested.[16] In Franklin, Tennessee, a mob that had protested mask mandates inside a board meeting, which was subsequently suspended because of their unruly behavior, followed the medical professionals who had spoken in favor of the mandate out to the parking lot and threatened them there.

"We know who you are. You can leave freely, but we will find you," one man said.[17]

The school board for Washoe County, Nevada, decided in April 2021 to suspend in-person meetings after right-wing protesters filled a large auditorium and lobbed insults and threats of violence. It decided to reopen meetings to the public again in May, this time in a small office capable of accommodating only a few speakers at a time.[18]

The right-wing activists were undeterred. Hundreds—most of whom did not even have children enrolled in the district—turned up to wait in the Reno sun until their names were called.

"This is an opportunity for what I feel like I've been screaming from the rooftops about," testified Karen England, executive director for the anti-LGBTQ Nevada Family Alliance, which had proposed placing body cameras on teachers to ensure they weren't teaching critical race theory.

Its June meeting lasted eleven hours. Speakers relentlessly attacked the board members, calling them Marxists, racists, Nazis, and child abusers.

It came as a shock to most of the members of the nation's local school boards when they suddenly found themselves under assault by these organized right-wing extremists turning up at their meetings to rant at them about "critical race theory" (which few of them had even heard of previously) and masking mandates.[19]

They had, in fact, become the primary targets of a nationwide far-right campaign to overwhelm such political entities with attacks over CRT, as well as COVID-19-related anti-vaccination/-masking agitation. In many cases, board members were targeted with recall campaigns and election challenges as the agitators worked to gain majority control of the boards. Those explicit takeover strategies happened to mesh neatly with the Proud Boys' emerging tactic of attaching themselves to local right-wing political events. As in Reno, many of these extremists, in fact, had no children enrolled in the school districts where they showed up to wreak chaos.[20]

Much of the organizing came from well-established right-wing groups. Tony Perkins of the Family Research Council—an anti-LGBTQ hate group—laid the strategy out for his followers in a fundraising letter, claiming that the school-board takeovers reflect a grassroots campaign:

In many of America's 13,800 school districts, grassroots efforts are beginning to nominate conservative, pro-family, pro-American candidates to run against left-wing incumbents. Some have launched recall campaigns to unseat school board members before the next election—before they can do any more to influence our impression-able children.

We need to grow these small and sometimes disorganized efforts into an army of activists ready to do battle on behalf of the family and America.

Most of the original organizing for the takeovers revolved around CRT. Most of those campaigns were closely affiliated with evangelical religious organizations, particularly those from the Christian nationalist wing of the far right—which had been forming alliances with the Proud Boys on other fronts as well. Their strategy included video training sessions: the Leadership Institute, a long-established evangelical political training center for right-wing activists, promoted a twenty-hour online course explaining how conservatives could seek election to their local school boards in order to "stop the teaching of Critical Race Theory before it destroys the fabric of our nation."

Similar organizations, such as Citizens for Renewing America, cropped up in other locales, offering tool kits for training activists in combating critical race theory. They described CRT as "identity politics" intended to destroy any "oppressive" institution—from traditional marriage to free markets to Christianity—while labeling "straight white people" the primary oppressors.[21]

Citizens for Renewing America is the brainchild of a former Trump ad-ministration official named Russ Vought, who as director of the Office of Management and Budget worked to implement the president's executive order banning funding for diversity training.

"The days of taxpayer-funded indoctrination trainings that sow division and racism are over," Vought tweeted in September 2020.

Vought's nonprofit became the behind-the-scenes leader in the battle over CRT being fought in churches and school boards around the country. Observers worried that the spate of school board interruptions by a few zealots would change the discussion about race and racial justice—any mention of either had suddenly become labeled as CRT, and any policies for addressing racial inequities rejected because of that label.

NBC News found at least 165 local and national organizations whose purpose is disrupting curricula involving race and gender. Moreover, it found that the fight over CRT was soon joined by similar right-wing forces organizing against COVID-19 health restrictions in schools, particularly mask and vaccine mandates: "Reinforced by conservative think tanks, law firms and activist parents, these groups have found allies in families frustrated over COVID-19 restrictions in schools and have weaponized the right's opposition to critical race theory, turning it into a political rallying point," NBC reported.[22]

While the campaigns often varied according to local conditions, they appeared to operate from an identical blueprint, sharing disruption, publicity, and mobilization strategies. The recipe was simple: swarm school board meetings, inundate districts with time-consuming public records requests, and file lawsuits and federal complaints alleging discrimination against white students or students declining to wear masks or take the vaccine.

The primary strategy involved targeting as many school board members as they could for removal. By September 2021, activists and parents had launched fifty recall efforts aimed at unseating 126 school board members, surpassing the record for a single year.[23] Most of these recalls started as objections to COVID-19 restrictions, but others included concerns about CRT.

Prominent GOP political figures rushed in to support the parent activists, believing these local battles would generate enthusiasm among conservative voters in 2022 and beyond. Former Trump adviser Steve Bannon observed on his podcast: "The path to save the nation is very simple—it's going to go through the school boards."[24]

The strategy closely resembled the 2009–11 Tea Party organizing—generating right-wing controversy over mainstream liberal issues, which then manifested as volatile localized and even nationalized protests. The current campaign's organizers even acknowledge the connection.

"It seems very Tea Party–ish to me," Dan Lennington, a lawyer with a Wisconsin organization offering free legal advice to parent groups pursuing or considering school board recalls, told the Associated Press. "These are ingredients for having an impact on future elections."[25]

Like the Tea Party, the school-board takeover groups were a form of "astroturf" organizing—activism made to look like grassroots efforts that in reality is manufactured by well-moneyed interests. "Outsiders are tapping into some genuine concerns, but the framing of the issues are largely regularized by national groups," Jeffrey Henig, a professor at Teachers College at Columbia University, told the AP.

In late September 2021, the National School Boards Association (NSBA)—an organization for local school boards—sent a letter to President Joe Biden asking the federal government to look into whether the incidents violated federal statutes on domestic terrorism and hate crimes.[26]

"America's public schools and its education leaders are under an immediate threat," the letter stated. It asked for "immediate assistance" due to "attacks against school board members and educators for approving policies for masks to protect the health and safety of students and school employees."

The US Department of Justice announced a week later that Attorney General Merrick Garland had directed the FBI and the US Attorneys' Offices to meet with local law-enforcement agencies to discuss how to address "harassment, intimidation, and threats of violence against school board members, teachers, and workers in our nation's public schools."[27]

Garland's memo explained that the Justice Department "will launch a series of additional efforts in the coming days designed to address the rise in criminal conduct directed toward school personnel."

The right-wing outrage machine immediately sprang into action. North Carolina congressman Madison Cawthorn, an ardently Trumpist Republican, declared on Twitter: "Parents who protest CRT and COVID restrictions in school board meetings are NOT domestic terrorists, they're patriots."[28]

Republican senator Josh Hawley of Missouri, who had notoriously given the gathering crowd of insurrectionists a thumbs-up sign on January 6, attacked Deputy Attorney General Lisa Monaco during a Senate Judiciary Committee hearing: "If this isn't a deliberate attempt to chill parents from showing up at school board meetings, for their elected school boards, I don't know what is," he declared.[29]

Having the FBI investigate any "intimidation" and "harassment" targeting school boards, Hawley told Monaco, was an attempt to "intimidate" and "silence" parents and "interfere with their rights as parents . . . and voters."

A letter from Republican senators—the same senators who also voted to block any investigation of the insurrection—declared: "Not wearing a mask in a public place may or may not be a violation of a local law, but at most it is a petty offense wholly unworthy of the federal government's attention."[30]

"Parents who are angry at school board members, and even verbally attack them on a personal level," the senators added, "are not necessarily making true threats."

This characterization of the situation did not even remotely reflect the reality on the ground. Particularly not when the Proud Boys joined the action.

The Orange County, North Carolina, school board meetings transformed in September when the Proud Boys and other white nationalist groups began showing up both at their sessions and at high school football games to protest the district's LGBTQ and pandemic-related policies.[31] Officials decided to hire extra security and pass a resolution opposing "incidents of hostile and racist behavior" because of the flood of threats and intimidation.

The resolution described how the right-wing activists had "shouted racist and homophobic slurs at students," and told of "emails from teachers and
students who describe how unsafe they feel being around the Proud Boys."

A local radio station quoted Orange County board chairwoman Hillary
MacKenzie describing a board session: "There were two men in Proud Boys
shirts and hats. One wore a stocking over his face, which completely obscured his entire face for the whole meeting. The other one told our board
during public comment that someone should tie rocks around our necks
and we should throw ourselves in a river."[32]

"They've been piggybacking on other people's events," Jared Holt, a
fellow at the Atlantic Council's Digital Forensic Research Lab, told *USA
Today*. "They go where they believe the culture war is being fought, because they see themselves as potentially violent enforcers in a broader
culture war."[33]

———————

THE ANTIDEMOCRATIC MOVEMENT'S STRATEGY of expanding their reach
through a focus on local politics and bringing their particular brand of
bellicose intimidation into play was also intended to have a secondary effect: namely, fueling the election of like-minded right-wing extremists to
local offices, particularly in rural areas.

It happened in places like the western Washington town of Eatonville,
where a Three Percent activist—a woman who homeschools her children,
refusing to enroll them in the district—was elected to the local school board.
The campaign was fueled by the larger embrace of extremist propaganda
in such rural areas, and demonstrated how it engenders an environment
of fear and threats directed at anyone who fails to do likewise, particularly
mainstream liberals.[34]

The Eatonville school board already had one notorious "Patriot" as a
member: Matt Marshall, the founder of Washington State Three Percenters,
which in 2019 claimed it had broken off affiliation with any national Three

Percent organization. Marshall's group nonetheless openly affiliated itself with Joey Gibson of the far-right street brawlers Patriot Prayer, and staunchly defended extremist ex-legislator Matt Shea at a January 2020 protest in Seattle.[35] Marshall later ran in the 2020 GOP primary against the state Republican house minority leader, J. T. Wilcox, over Shea's expulsion from the legislature, but lost badly.[36]

Marshall also was a staunch advocate of the far-right Boogaloo movement, appearing at anti-COVID-measure protests in Olympia wearing their trademark Hawaiian shirt and claiming on social media that the movement is nonviolent, despite its extensive track record of actual and planned murderous terrorism.[37] (In a comical event, Marshall's group was hoodwinked by prankster Sacha Baron Cohen into joining in on a racist singalong in Olympia.)[38] Its politics of intimidation came into play when Marshall publicized the names and private information of people who had reported businesses for COVID measure violations, resulting in a flood of threats and abuse.[39]

Most of all, Marshall's organization has been quietly spreading its brand of right-wing conspiracism around the region, turning up in communities like Whidbey Island and elsewhere.[40] This was part of Marshall's explicit strategy of rallying like-minded "Patriots" into local politics and community organizing, and his endorsement of far-right anti-vaccination activist Ashley Sova for the Eatonville school board in its 2021 election ended up propelling her into office alongside him.

By 2022, Marshall claimed that his organization could boast of members in dozens of official posts around Washington: a mayor, a county commissioner, and at least five school board seats. The Eatonville school board electee, Ashley Sova, was one of four Three Percent members who ran in local races that year. Three of them won.

A central feature of the spread of far-right politics is the intimidation directed at mainstream liberals and even Republicans who refuse to participate in their incoherent conspiracism: As with all authoritarian movements, aggression directed at anyone who fails to submit to their rule is a foundational component of their real-world behavior. And in the rural areas where their politics already dominate, they often have free rein to threaten their neighbors with impunity.[41]

The Washington Post's Hannah Allam interviewed people in Eatonville, and found that a number of longtime residents, mostly mainstream Democrats who had raised their families there, described how their community had transformed into something they no longer recognized: a place where neighbors asked them if they were "leftists." Where random drivers, seeing their Biden campaign yard signs, would stop and yell at them, "Get the fuck out of here!"

When that happened, their first response was defiance: "I was like, are you kidding me? At my home?" the husband told Allam. "I brought the .38 and sat it out there and then I thought, 'No, don't do that.'"

That was soon followed by fear: "We felt so threatened because we've lived here for so long," the wife said tearily. "We built our own house our own selves here. We raised our kids here."

The wife began researching not just Sova's far-right connections, but the spread of extremism in their community generally, and came to realize "just how many Three Percenters we have around us." In the end, she chose not to publicize her research on Sova because she had concluded that it would end up actually bolstering her candidacy: "We think it would've helped her," she said. "That's what the concern was."

Their fresh understanding not just of the breadth of "Patriot" beliefs in their rural community now, but its underlying menace, had induced them to try to keep low profiles: "Someone looking at it would think, 'Idiots, stand up for something. For Chrissake, democracy is on fire, kick some ass,'" the husband said. "But it's those little social, nuanced things where you see Matt Marshall with a crown of bullets, in his Boogaloo boys shirt, stomping around Olympia. And it does make you stop and think."

"The race was basically sabotaged by the national narrative," said the "PTA mom" who Sova defeated, Sarah Cole, adding her incredulity that parents would vote for a "Patriot" extremist whose children aren't even enrolled in public school: "I don't even know how to explain it except to say, in the face of the facts, they still chose to run with fears."

ALL AROUND THE TRUMP-LOVING rural sectors of the nation, daily life by the fall of 2021 had become filled with foreboding, intimidation, threats, and ugliness, all emanating from authoritarian right-wingers directing their aggression at anyone who failed to follow their dictates—and the intensity only seemed to be ratcheting upward.[42] Many observers, including historians, compared it to previous periods of societal strife in the United States, including the Civil War and the Civil Rights era.

"What's different about almost all those other events is that now, there's a partisan divide around the legitimacy of our political system," Owen Wasow, a Pomona College political scientist, told *The New York Times.* "The elite endorsement of political violence from factions of the Republican Party is distinct for me from what we saw in the 1960s. Then, you didn't have—from a president on down—politicians calling citizens to engage in violent resistance."

By the year's end, Proud Boys and militia "Patriots" were turning up with regularity to harass LGBTQ-friendly teens at libraries, mask-promoting school board members, and mall shops that required masks. White supremacists openly marched in rural capitals, threatening bystanders. On a single weekend in December, members of the racist group White Lives Matter held a rally in Helena, Montana, near the state capitol; Proud Boys turned up at a mall in suburban Oregon City, Oregon, to harass customers and shop clerks about requirements to wear masks; other Proud Boys turned up for a school board meeting in Washougal, Washington, to harass and threaten both school board members and other citizens; and in Post Falls, Idaho, militia "Patriots" showed up at the city library to harass students who turned out for an LGBTQ-friendly program.[43]

In some cases, such as the rally in Helena, no local pretense was even deemed necessary; White Lives Matter's Montana chapter originally planned its march to occur on the grounds of the state capitol as part of a nationwide WLM campaign for that day. It's unclear whether the marchers ever appeared at the capitol, but their demonstration, replete with a couple of large banners, appeared a short distance down one of the city's busiest boulevards for a while.

A local resident approached them with a cell phone and was aggressively confronted by masked neo-Nazis wearing skull masks; one of them carried a hammer. The men were flashing Nazi salutes and the white-nationalist "OK" sign, and demanded of the person with the cell phone: "You're white too! You should be standing with us! Why are you a traitor to your race?" Another one said: "You're not a white man!"

More often, however, the tactics involved using threatening speech at organized civic events or public spaces that for various reasons—usually involving pandemic-related restrictions or the nonsensical CRT bogeyman— attract right-wing activists. Proud Boys and Three Percenter militiamen in particular have been flexing their muscles in rural communities, especially since law enforcement in those precincts is generally sympathetic to them.

One Proud Boy showed up at a school board meeting in Washougal, a Portland-area exurb, and threatened both members of the school board as well as fellow audience members with retribution for their "cowardice" on CRT, sex education, and "the masks"—while himself hiding his identity behind one—as part of a threatening defense of the Proud Boys, which he called "the greatest brotherhood in the world." The man's speech was greeted with enthusiastic applause by the audience.

A few days later, a group of "Patriots" organizing under the name Free Oregon, led by a Proud Boy (and Republican legislative candidate) named Dan

Tooze, organized an anti-masking protest at the Clackamas town center mall in unincorporated Happy Valley, an exurban area east of Portland. The group parked their flag-festooned pickups in the parking lot of a sporting goods store and proceeded to stroll through the mall, harassing store clerks and mall security personnel who attempted to enforce the mall's mask requirements.

In late November 2021, a coalition of evangelical Christians and "Patriot" militiamen organized a protest in Post Falls outside the city library on the night it was hosting a program called Rainbow Squad, an LGBTQ-friendly reading-discussion program.[44]

Among the signs they carried, police body-camera footage showed, were slogans like "Flee From Sexual Immorality," "Obey God Not Men," "Sexual Immorality is an Abomination to God," and "The Solution is Jesus Christ."

On Facebook, a local Panhandle Patriots group, closely associated with the far-right American Redoubt movement organizing in the region, shared a post with its members calling out the library network's upcoming meeting and urging others to attend:

> The perversion that is becoming so pervasive in these libraries needs to be called out and CAST OUT.
>
> We need people to show up and speak out, demand the removal of pro-LGBT books like the following:
>
> [Links to such books as Auntie Uncle: Drag Queen Hero and Be Amazing: A History of Pride.][45]

A Post Falls native named Michelle White told the *Coeur d'Alene Press* that she and her two children had been participating for several months in Rainbow Squad events, saying she had always thought of the library as a "safe space" without judgment.

"These people are making it not a safe place for kids to gather by picketing and yelling at them as they go inside," she told the *Press*. "Creating an environment that is not safe is not OK."

Jessica Mahuron, the *North Idaho Pride Alliance* outreach coordinator, attended the November Rainbow Squad event and observed how the protesters' intention was to eliminate that safe space—and they succeeded.

"There were some people who felt intimidated from entering the building, others left because they were feeling so terrible, and for some, this is nothing new to them, so they stood strong," Mahuron said. "The program is supposed to provide a safe, inclusive space for fun and friendship. What they experienced coming into that meeting was the exact opposite."

That was clearly the intent. The pastor of the Family Worship Center in Hayden, Steven Hemming, claimed responsibility for the protest and responded to the coverage of it by defending it ardently, saying that "a lot of people present at the library that night are part of my congregation."

"In other parts of our country the exploitation and sexualization of our children has come to a place where it is a losing battle with things like 'drag queen story hour' and other agendas to make immorality a fashion campaign for our future generations and completely destroy the family unit that God intended to thrive and prosper with His blessing," he wrote.

He continued: "I, myself, and many, many others in our community are now aware of who we have on the library network board and who makes these decisions for our community. If the community does not want these things taking place in our libraries, then why are they happening?"

Katie Blank, chair of the Community Library Network board in Kootenai County, worried that the library would cease to be a safe space for all citizens.

"I think we have a very radical, conservative element in our community, and there's an element that wants people to live one certain way and not allow people free choice," she said. "That's of concern to me."

A November 2021 *New York Times* piece described the politics of menace that had inundated rural America, explaining that it had become an essential component of modern Republican politics—and how living under that cloud has exactly the powerful anti-democratic effect its users intend.[46]

Michigan congresswoman Debbie Dingell related how, after Tucker

Carlson denounced her on his Fox News show, she was threatened by men with assault weapons outside her home. She shared a small sample of what she said were hundreds of profanity-laden threats she received.

"They ought to try you for treason," one caller screamed in a lengthy, graphic voice mail message. "I hope your family dies in front of you. I pray to God that if you've got any children, they die in your face."

The threats are especially effective in shutting down democratic institutions and traditions. The *Times* described how Bradford Fitch, president of a firm that advises lawmakers on managing their offices, now recommends that none of them from either party conduct open public meetings because politics have become "too raw and radioactive."

"I don't think it's a good idea right now," Fitch said. "I hope we can get to a point where we can advise members of Congress that it's safe to have a town-hall meeting."

———

THE RADICAL RIGHT'S STRATEGY of targeting local politics proved so effective at driving ordinary civic-minded people away from democratic institutions and replacing them with conspiracist ideologues that it shortly became clear what democracy's defenders are all up against.[47]

In Shasta County, California, voters turned out longtime establishment Republicans after an aggressive campaign by "Patriot" movement ideologues. Militiaman Carlos Zapata—fond of threatening county supervisors that "it's not going to be peaceful much longer," and "good citizens are going to turn to real concerned and revolutionary citizens real soon"—led a successful recall against Supervisor Leonard Moty, a Republican and the former police chief of Redding.[48]

"In Shasta County, we're supposed to be red country up here, not blue country," Zapata said during the recall campaign. "Take your masks off. Quit muzzling yourself. Join us. Fight with us against what's going on in Sacramento."[49]

Zapata appeared as a guest on Alex Jones's *Infowars* program. He turned up on Fox News a few months later.

In the Michigan town of Grand Blanc—one of hundreds of ordinary rural towns across the country that suddenly faced this bewildering barrage from the far right—the environment became surreal, as Adam Harris explored in *The Atlantic*. The school board's monthly meetings—once the most mundane and boring of affairs, typical for communities everywhere—became battlegrounds for conspiracists, who packed the seats with people, took over the open-question sessions, and dominated the gatherings with talk about critical race theory and grooming.[50]

For Grand Blanc, the problem was aggravated by the presence of a QAnon-quoting extremist already on the board—one who suddenly claimed no connection to the conspiracist cult. "I'm a victim of cancel culture," said Amy Facchinello. "I think they're using the QAnon narrative to cancel conservatives . . . If you question their narrative, they label you a QAnon conspiracy theorist."

Local residents said it was less her belief in QAnon theories and more "the division and the chaos that she brings" that concerned them. Most of all, as Harris explained, it was driving away qualified people from public office because the threats and harassment simply made it untenable:

> With the increasing hostilities of the job, many school-board members have seen resignation or retirement as their only way forward. In Wisconsin, a board member resigned after receiving threats and seeing a car idling outside his house while his children were home; in Tennessee, members were called child abusers and harassed for supporting mask mandates. "My most recent time on the board has impacted who I am as a person and my inability to have peace and joy in my life," one school-board member in Indiana wrote in a resignation letter last year. "If the past two years have taught me anything, it is that life is precious and that time is short."

One such small town—Sequim, Washington, the retirement-oriented community where the QAnon-loving mayor and his bullyboys on the city council took over local politics—fought back, however, and succeeded.[51] After the mayor forced out the city's popular manager and began issuing dubious health directions during the COVID pandemic—and the subsequent coverage of Sequim's takeover by QAnon, which embarrassed many longtime locals—concerned residents organized the Sequim Good Governance League (SGGL), which lined up a slate of candidates to run in the fall 2021 elections.

It worked, as Sasha Abramsky reported for *The Nation*:

> When the votes were counted, they showed that the SGGL-backed candidates had ridden a wave of genuine popular fury against the faux populists aligned with [Mayor William] Armacost. In Sequim, the five SGGL candidates for city council—[Lowell] Rathbun, [Brandon] Janisse, Vicki Lowe, Kathy Downer, and Rachel Anderson—all got between 65 and 70 percent of the vote. Both hospital commissioners' positions in the county went to SGGL candidates, as did the fire commission and school district posts up for election last year.
>
> "Our community has spoken and they want a change," said Lowe, who had 68% of the vote against the incumbent. "Now we can take the focus back from everything else that doesn't have to do with Sequim City Council, and start talking about housing and sidewalks and how our recycling is really getting recycled," she added.[52]

Those kinds of results could point to a blueprint for pushing back against extremists at the local level, Devin Burghart of the Institute for Research and Education on Human Rights observed. He noted that the candidates' success began with repeatedly calling attention to their opponents' affiliations with QAnon, as well as their excessive devotion to nonlocal issues, and was sealed by their strategic and energetic combined organizing and door-knocking during the campaign.

"That combination is going to be a key for defeating far-right efforts to take over local government around the country," he said.

"It does have a national ramification," Bruce Cowan, a politically active Port Townsend, Washington, retiree, said. "Folks who don't believe in government—populists, people who don't have faith in the institutions of governance—shouldn't be in charge of the government. One of the things that happened in Sequim is that people were not engaged enough to see how important it was to find candidates for city council. Now they understand the importance."

The right's politics of menace and intimidation directed at local school boards also began to run into organized opposition, with encouraging results in places like Missouri and New Hampshire and mixed results in others like Wisconsin.

The key critical factor in all of them is simple: recognizing that you have a radical-right problem. Once communities can be persuaded out of denial about what they are up against, and what they are dealing with—namely, an organized onslaught against American democracy and pluralistic self-governance itself—and that the only effective answer is to out-organize them, then there is a very good chance of success.

POSTSCRIPT

The Echoes of History

BEFORE JANUARY 6, 2021, there had been only one other insurrection against the US federal government: the Whiskey Rebellion of 1794, a civilian revolt against Alexander Hamilton's excise tax on liquor—the first tax imposed by the new government, in 1792—by populist elements in Appalachia. After two years of open lawlessness in which tax collectors were tarred and feathered and whipped, and open agitation (including a convention) for armed rebellion occurred, a force of five hundred men descended on the home of the regional tax collector and set it aflame. In early August, rebels began to gather at Braddock's Field near Pittsburgh amid open talk of marching on the city and burning it to the ground.[1]

George Washington did not trifle with them. ("Laws," he told Hamilton, could not "be trampled with impunity" for if "a minority ... is to dictate to a majority, there is an end put at one stroke to republican government.") He ordered an armed force of 12,500 men, composed of four state militias, and personally reviewed and led them to Reading, Pennsylvania, with Hamilton serving as a civilian adviser.[2] Washington returned to Philadelphia (then the seat of government), while Hamilton remained. Under the command of

Revolutionary War hero Daniel Morgan, the force proceeded across western Pennsylvania, upon which the rebellion completely collapsed, and its leaders scattered into hiding. Some twenty-four men were indicted for high treason, but only two of them were ever convicted, and Washington pardoned them both.[3]

Washington's victory was popular at the time, but it also had a durable legacy: It established that the fledgling government had both the will and the ability to overwhelm violent resistance to its laws. It helped enable Washington's most powerful legacy to the nation: the peaceful transition of power that came two years later, when he stepped down as president and handed the keys to the nation to his successor, John Adams.

So there is no shortage of irony in the upside-down reality that the people who undertook the next historic insurrection against the federal government, on January 6, believed themselves the true legatees of the Founding Fathers. They called their rebellion "their 1776 moment," and the Gadsden flag—which dates to the Revolutionary War era—was everywhere outside and inside the Capitol.[4]

Yet what they were attempting was to interrupt and overturn, for the first time in the nation's history, the peaceful transfer of power between presidential administrations, following the express will of American voters. The predecessor to the Insurrection Act they were hoping Trump would invoke (the Militia Act of 1792) was in fact the law Washington had invoked to suppress insurrection like theirs in his time.

Right-wing talk-show host Rush Limbaugh—who, more than any other cultural figure, could lay claim, as the person who had fed seditionist rhetoric to them for three decades, to being the godfather of the insurrection—took to the airwaves the day afterward, comparing the rioters to the Founders. "We're supposed to be horrified by the protesters. There's a lot of people out there calling for the end of violence," he said. "A lot of conservatives, social media, who say that any violence or aggression at all is unacceptable regardless of the circumstances. I am glad Sam Adams, Thomas

Paine, the actual Tea Party guys, the men at Lexington and Concord, didn't feel that way." (He also suggested that the violence was actually the work of "Antifa and Democrat-sponsored instigators" in the Capitol and "a coup launched in the office of Barack Obama four years ago.")[5] Limbaugh died of cancer a little over a month later.[6]

Over the ensuing months, armed with an unbelievable wealth of video and other digital evidence—thanks to the insurrectionists' eagerness to record what they believed would be a historic event—the Department of Justice began arresting and charging hundreds of participants, compiling evidence as they did so, and searching out the identities of otherwise anonymous participants. A year later, federal agents had arrested and charged more than 725 defendants; half a year after that, the tally had climbed to over 840.[7]

DOJ officials called it "the most complex prosecution in history," and that wasn't an exaggeration; no other large prosecution in the nation's past could match it for sheer scale, not to mention the complicated layers of evidence and the seriousness of the charges.[8] While many of the indictees were charged with such lesser crimes as illegally entering the Capitol, and others faced more serious charges related to the assaults on Capitol police officers and vandalizing the Capitol, the most serious charges—seditionist conspiracy—were finally filed nearly a year afterward, against the cadres of Oath Keepers and Proud Boys who coordinated and spearheaded the violence.

Most of those trials, as of this writing, are still pending; the latter cases are expected to be heard in federal courtrooms sometime in 2023. A number of trials in the lesser cases have already been heard, with a spotless conviction record for prosecutors in all of them—including Stewart Rhodes's conviction for seditionist conspiracy in November 2022. By early 2023, some 465 of the more than 960 people charged in what the Justice Department calls "Capitol Breach" cases had entered guilty pleas.[9]

While most of the remaining indictees were released on bail while awaiting trial, a number of them facing the more serious charges remained behind bars, the large majority held in D.C.'s Correctional Treatment Facility, held collectively in a section of the jail. The prisoners have dubbed it the "Patriot Wing" of the facility. Every night at six, the men sing the national anthem together.[10]

Republican politicians and pundits, following Limbaugh's lead, came to their defense, labeling them "political prisoners." Five Trumpist members of Congress—Matt Gaetz of Florida, Marjorie Taylor Greene of Georgia, Louie Gohmert of Texas, and Paul Gosar and Andy Biggs of Arizona, all of whom (not coincidentally) had voted against accepting the Electoral College count on January 6—held a press conference outside of the Justice Department, denouncing the detention of the "political prisoners," on the same day that the House's January 6 committee opened its hearings. Gosar called on Amnesty International, Human Rights Watch, and the ACLU to investigate the treatment of Capitol rioters. [11]

Shortly afterward, three of them—Gaetz, Greene, and Gohmert—went to the D.C. detention center and demanded to be let in, but were turned away. "We're in totalitarian, Marxist territory here," Gohmert told reporters. "This is the way Third World people get treated."

Fox News's Tucker Carlson dabbled in this narrative frequently: "If you are holding people in solitary confinement in DC jails for non-violent crimes, at some point they become political prisoners," he said in a July 2021 segment. "I try not to use that phrase. You know, you don't want to hype anything or sensationalize. But at what point does it become a political prosecution?"[12] By the fall of 2022, this had become conventional Republican wisdom: It was not unusual to hear Republican candidates on the campaign trail describe the jailed insurrectionists as "political prisoners."

Most of the people facing charges, in fact, embraced their martyrdom. And their fellow Patriots and Republicans made clear that they had no intention of letting the prosecutions and the legal aftermath of the insurrection deter them from their goals.

One of the accused insurrectionists, a former police officer from Virginia named Thomas Robertson, was released by a judge to await trial on his multiple felony charges. Among the conditions of his release was an order to stay away from guns in the meantime. So upon returning home, he promptly went out and purchased thirty-four guns online and a large cache of ammunition, all of which he kept in the hands of a Roanoke gun broker. He also constructed a pipe bomb and a booby trap in his home, and kept an M4 carbine in his house.[13]

Before authorities had caught on and returned him to prison, he also boasted about his participation in the insurrection in online forums. When someone asked him about it on Gunbroker.com, he answered:

> I've said before. They are trying to teach us a lesson. They have. But its definitely not the intended lesson. I have learned that if you peacefully protest than [sic] you will be arrested, fired, be put on a no fly list, have your name smeared and address released by the FBI so every loon in the US can send you hate mail. I have learned very well that if you dip your toe into the Rubicon . . . cross it. Cross it hard and violent and play for all the marbles.[14]

———————

IT BECAME CLEAR DURING the midterm elections of 2022 that the Republican right's extremist fever had not broken on January 6, 2020, but indeed had deepened and worsened. The Republican Party continued to embrace the Trumpist politics of conspiracism, with hundreds of GOP candidates denying the viability of the 2020 election and spreading disinformation about the nation's election system.[15] The Trumpist faction also managed to place a slate of election denialists on the ballot for secretary of state in key battleground states around the country, echoing Trump's post-election strategy of targeting state-level electoral officials in hopes of overturning the vote count.[16]

Republicans triumphantly anticipated a "red tsunami" in November. Steve Bannon predicted "We're gonna win a 100-seat majority. We're taking a hundred seats and we're going to govern for a hundred years." But it largely evaporated on Election Day, with Democrats winning the U.S. Senate (but narrowly losing the House), as well as a number of key governor's races around the nation in which prominent election denialists like Arizona's Kari Lake lost. The insurrectionist right, predictably, had a meltdown: The lead headline at the far-right "Gateway Pundit" website read: "BLOOD MOON BLOODBATH... Democrats Steal Midterms, Communism Comes Home to America... Crime, Inflation, Record Gas Prices, War, Open Borders and Corruption WIN BIG." [17]

Afterwards, losing candidates like Lake continued to deny the legitimacy of the outcome, traveling to Trump's Mar-A-Lago estate to bolster the election-denial narrative.[18] Lake filed several lawsuits to overturn the count that promptly lost in court, but still vowed not to back down. "I promise you one thing: This fight to save our republic has just begun. I love you Arizona, and I love you America," she said.

In spite of the ability of Democrats to hold the line, there were nonetheless more than 180 Republican election denialists (a number of them incumbents) who won their elections to the House—meaning that more than a third of the members of Congress after 2022 will have questioned or denied the 2020 election.[19] This also means that a large majority of states will have at least one Republican representative who is an election denialist.[20]

While the insurrectionist right may have been briefly discouraged, it was never deterred. That was obvious a month later at the suit-and-tie gala for the New York Young Republicans Club, which had fully transformed into a white-nationalist affair—one still lusting for an uncivil war.[21]

"We want to cross the Rubicon. We want total war. We must be prepared to do battle in every arena. In the media. In the courtroom. At the ballot box. And in the streets," NYYRC president Gavin Wax declared.

"This is the only language the left understands. The language of pure and unadulterated power."

Any thought that the insurrectionist army that America saw assault democracy on January 6 was either behind bars or discredited should have been finally laid to rest during the eliminationism-themed "America Fest 2022" put on in December by Charlie Kirk's Turning Point USA, which drew thousands of MAGA true believers to Phoenix.[22]

Steve Bannon gave the wrap-up speech for the weeklong affair, and it was like the exhortations of a cheerleading executive, except for the subject. "Are we at war?" he demanded to know at the outset.[23]

After a feeble "Yes" from the audience, he repeated: "No! I wanna hear it! Are we at war?" "Yes!!!" the audience shouted.

"Are you prepared to take this to its ultimate conclusion and destroy the Deep State?" he demanded. "Yes!!!!" they replied. "Root and branch?" "Yeahhh!!!"

"This is what they fear," Bannon continued. "They fear not just an electorate that is informed, but an electorate that says, 'No longer are we just going to sit there and take it!'"

"You are an awakened army!" he bellowed. The crowd cheered.

Bannon anticipated how his exhortations would be reported. "Now what they're going to sit there and say is, 'Oh, he's getting them all worked, right? Getting them all worked up out there in Arizona'," he said, but nonetheless seemingly acknowledged that this kind of rhetoric historically inflames and inspires violence. "No. We're tougher, smarter, and we gotta be more cunning than they are. They're gonna try to bait you into everything. You have to be smarter than that, right?" He notably also didn't condemn violent actions.

"From this day forward, it's no more talk, it's just action, action, action!" he proclaimed.

When someone in the audience shouted, "Lock them up!" Bannon pointed and nodded. "Lock 'em up. Lock 'em up!" he agreed. "Lock 'em up and throw—" He held out the mic as the crowd chanted, "Lock them up!" then added: "And throw away the frickin' key!"

Bannon claimed that "they" stole both Trump's presidency by keeping him under a constant onslaught, and then his re-election. "Is there anybody in this audience that thinks Donald John Trump did not win the 2020 election?" "Noooo!!!" they shouted back.

"Trump won! You're damn right he won, and Trump won big," Bannon insisted. "Impeaching Joe Biden's too good for him! Then we gotta bring the criminal charges and send him to prison for treason and selling out this country!"

At the speech's conclusion, he wrapped his audience together:

> Are you a cadré now? Are you a vanguard? Are you a tip of a new revolutionary generation that's gonna save this country? Are you sure about that? [Yeah!] Is your task and purpose every day to take your country back? [Yeah!] Are there any days off? [No!] God bless you. There's no substitute for victory.

Keeping the insurrectionist army intact and enraged, in fact, has largely been Bannon's mission since the events of January 6 in which, as Trump's frequent consigliere, he played a central role. His podcast, "Pandemic War Room with Steve Bannon," has long been a steady platform for right-wing conspiracists and extremists of all stripes, from anti-vax hatemongers to election denialists to European white nationalists. Since the insurrection, the ongoing message has been: Be proud of what happened on January 6. Work to make it happen again.

As Tim Miller observed, "their effort to overthrow the government has been undeterred by the initial setback of Joe Biden being inaugurated. While Republican elites try to minimize the events of Jan. 6th, the War Room and their minions have continued to take the coup both literally and seriously. In their view the Biden 'regime' is illegitimate, and the regime's medical establishment has covered up nearly a half a million deaths from the COVID 'vaccines.'"[24]

This is why Congressman Jamie Raskin, the chief overseer of the House's January 6 committee investigation, emphasized that the panel's final report elucidated "the clear and continuing present danger of the forces that have been unleashed against us."

Raskin warned: "The political scientists tell us that the signs of an authoritarian political party are this: 1) they don't accept the results of democratic elections if they don't go their way; 2) they embrace political violence or refuse to disavow it [...]; and 3) they are organized around a charismatic or allegedly charismatic political figure."[25]

Indeed, the committee's final report notes that federal Circuit Judge Michael Luttig reached similar conclusions during his live hearing testimony: "I have written, as you said, Chairman Thompson, that, today, almost two years after that fateful day in January 2021, that, still, Donald Trump and his allies and supporters are a clear and present danger to American democracy."[26]

The report also observed: "If President Trump and the associates who assisted him in an effort to overturn the lawful outcome of the 2020 election are not ultimately held accountable under the law, their behavior may become a precedent and invitation to danger for future elections."

Stanford cybersecurity professor Herbert Lin sees what people like Bannon are doing—namely, creating a massive epistemic crisis not just for America but for the world—as the chief obstacle to defending democracy from the insurrectionist onslaught:

> We now live in an environment in which no conceivable evidence can persuade true believers to change their minds, and the resulting epistemic fractures translate into a once-unified nation sharply divided against itself. A worse national posture to meet the challenges of coming great-power competition could not be imagined.[27]

"Last year the faithful acted," observed Miller. "Today they are marshaling their forces and gathering their strength to do so again."

They'll only succeed, of course, if we keep our eyes closed to the continuing threat and fail to be prepared. Because as far as they're concerned, they are "at war." Only a fool would disbelieve them.

Endnotes

Preface: The Road to Sedition

1 See Brian Naylor, "Read Trump's Jan. 6 Speech, a Key Part of Impeachment Trial," National Public Radio, Feb. 10, 2021. Online: https://www.npr.org/2021/02/10/966396848/read-trumps-jan-6-speech-a-key-part-of-impeachment-trial.

2 See Josh Dawsey, "Trump Deflects Blame for Jan. 6 Silence, Says He Wanted to March to Capitol," *The Washington Post*, April 7, 2022. Online: https://www.washingtonpost.com/politics/2022/04/07/trump-interview-jan6.

3 See Sarah Repucci and Amy Slipowitz, "The Global Expansion of Authoritarian Rule," Freedom House, 2022. Online: https://freedomhouse.org/report/freedom-world/2022/global-expansion-authoritarian-rule.

4 See Yasmeen Serhan, "The EU Watches as Hungary Kills Democracy," *The Atlantic*, April 2, 2020. Online: https://www.theatlantic.com/international/archive/2020/04/europe-hungary-viktor-orban-coronavirus-covid19-democracy/609313. See also Sean Young, "Turkey's Democratic Decline: The End of Kemalish Turkey and the Rise of Authoritarianism," *The Boston Political Review*, Aug. 23, 2022. Online: https://www.bostonpoliticalreview.org/post/turkey-s-democratic-decline-the-end-of-kemalish-turkey-and-the-rise-of-authoritarianism.

5 See Debasish Roy Chowdhury, "Modi's India Is Where Global Democracy Dies," *The New York Times*, Aug. 24, 2022. Online: https://www.nytimes.com/2022/08/24/opinion/india-modi-democracy.html.

6 See John Feffer, "The Global Far Right Is Alive and Kicking," *The Nation*, Dec. 7, 2021. Online: https://www.thenation.com/article/world/global-right-germany. See also Steven Erlanger and Christina Anderson, "Rise of Far-Right Party in Sweden Was Both Expected and Shocking," *The New York Times*, Sept. 15, 2022. Online: https://www.nytimes.com/2022/09/15/world/europe/sweden-election-far-right.html. See also David Broder, "Italy's Drift to the Far Right Began Long Before the Rise of Giorgia Meloni," *The Guardian*, Sept. 26, 2022. Online: https://www.the-

guardian.com/commentisfree/2022/sep/26/italy-far-right-before-giorgia-meloni-berlusconi-brothers-of-italy.

7 See Ishaan Tharoor, "The Mainstreaming of the West's Far Right Is Complete," *The Washington Post*, Sept. 27, 2022. Online: https://www.washingtonpost.com/world/2022/09/27/mainstreaming-wests-far-right-is-complete.

8 See "Steve Bannon's (Lonely) European Vacation," *Intelligence Report*, Feb. 20, 2019. Online: splcenter.org/fighting-hate/intelligence-report/2019/steve-bannons-lonely-european-vacation. See also David Neiwert, "Steve Bannon Promotes 'Populist' Movement Down Under, Stirs Free-Speech Debate," *Hatewatch*, Sept. 14, 2018. Online: https://www.splcenter.org/hatewatch/2018/09/14/steve-bannon-promotes-populist-movement-down-under-stirs-free-speech-debate.

9 See Matt Bradley, "Europe's Far-Right Enjoys Backing from Russia's Putin," NBC News, Feb. 12, 2017. Online: https://www.nbcnews.com/news/world/europe-s-far-right-enjoys-backing-russia-s-putin-n718926.

10 See Jo Becker, "The Global Machine Behind the Rise of Far-Right Nationalism," *The New York Times*, Aug. 10, 2019. Online: https://www.nytimes.com/2019/08/10/world/europe/sweden-immigration-nationalism.html.

11 See Edward Wong, "Russia Secretly Gave $300 Million to Political Parties and Officials Worldwide, U.S. Says," *The New York Times*, Sept. 13, 2022. Online: https://www.nytimes.com/2022/09/13/us/politics/russia-election-interference.html.

12 See Luke O'Brien, "The Making of an American Nazi," *The Atlantic*, Dec. 2017. Online: https://www.theatlantic.com/magazine/archive/2017/12/the-making-of-an-american-nazi/544119/.

13 See Casey Michel, "How Russia Became the Leader of the Global Christian Right," *Politico*, Feb. 9, 2017. Online: https://www.politico.com/magazine/story/2017/02/how-russia-became-a-leader-of-the-worldwide-christian-right-214755.

14 See David Neiwert, "Russia's Gay-Bashing Politics Look Like a Descent Into Fascism," *Crooks and Liars*, Sept. 17, 2013. Online: https://crooksandliars.com/david-neiwert/russias-gay-bashing-politics-look-de.

15 See Nick Penzenstadler, Brad Heath, and Jessica Guynn, "We Read Every One of the 3,517 Facebook Ads Bought by Russians. Here's What We Found," *USA Today*, May 11, 2018. Online: https://www.usatoday.com/story/news/2018/05/11/what-we-found-facebook-ads-russians-accused-election-meddling/602319002.

16 See David Neiwert, "Racially Incendiary Russian Ads Apparently Had Their Intended Effect," *Hatewatch*, June 6, 2018. Online: https://www.splcenter.org/hatewatch/2018/06/06/racially-incendiary-russian-ads-apparently-had-their-intended-effect.

17 See David Neiwert, "Russian Neofascists and Their Presence in Putin's Invading Army Expose His Lies About Ukraine," *Daily Kos*, April 14, 2022. Online: https://www.dailykos.com/stories/2022/4/14/2092019/-Russian-neofascists-and-their-presence-in-Putin-s-invading-army-expose-his-lies-about-Ukraine.

18 See William Etchikson, "Viktor Orbán's Anti-Semitism Problem," *Politico*, May 13, 2019. Online: https://www.politico.eu/article/viktor-orban-anti-semitism-problem-hungary-jews.

19 See Kevin Liptak and Betsy Klein, "Biden Criticizes 'Semi-Fascism' Underpinning the 'Extreme MAGA Philosophy' in Fiery Return to the Campaign Trail," CNN, Aug. 25, 2022. Online: https://www.cnn.com/2022/08/25/politics/joe-biden-mid-

term-speech-abortion/index.html. See also Paul Farhi, "As Biden Warned About Democracy's Collapse, TV Networks Aired Reruns," *The Washington Post*, Sept. 2, 2022. Online: https://www.washingtonpost.com/media/2022/09/02/biden-speech-network-coverage-independence-hall.

20 See Federico Finchelstein, "Biden Called Trumpism 'Semi-Fascism.' The Term Makes Sense, Historically," *The Washington Post*, Sept. 1, 2022. Online: https://www.washingtonpost.com/made-by-history/2022/09/01/biden-called-trumpism-semi-fascism-term-makes-sense-historically.

21 See Robert O. Paxton, *The Anatomy of Fascism* (New York: Vintage Press, 2005), p. 218.

22 See Henry Olsen, "No, MAGA Republicans Do Not Support 'Semi-Fascism,'" *The Washington Post*, Aug. 26, 2022. Online: https://www.washingtonpost.com/opinions/2022/08/26/semi-fascism-biden-maga-gop.

23 See, e.g., Sean Hannity's *Deliver Us from Evil: Defeating Terrorism, Despotism, and Liberalism* (New York: William Morrow, 2005) and Michael Savage's *Liberalism Is a Mental Disorder* (New York: Thomas Nelson, 2010). See also Liam Stack, "He Calls Hillary Clinton a 'Demon.' Who Is Alex Jones?" *The New York Times*, Oct. 13, 2016. Online: https://www.nytimes.com/2016/10/14/us/politics/alex-jones.html. Video of Jones raging about Clinton and Barack Obama as demons available at https://youtu.be/mGZMYJVZsH0.

24 See Ira Katznelson, "What America Taught the Nazis," *The Atlantic*, November 2017. Online: https://www.theatlantic.com/magazine/archive/2017/11/what-america-taught-the-nazis/540630. See also Timothy Snyder, "Hitler's American Dream," Slate, March 28, 2017. Online: https://slate.com/news-and-politics/2017/03/nazi-germanys-american-dream-hitler-modeled-his-concept-of-racial-struggle-and-global-campaign-after-americas-conquest-of-native-americans.html.

25 See Paxton, *Anatomy*, p. 49.

26 Probably the best account of the Ruby Ridge tragedy is Jess Walter's *Every Knee Shall Bow: The Truth & Tragedy of Ruby Ridge & The Randy Weaver Family* (New York: HarperCollins, 1995).

27 See Hatewatch Staff, "Update: 1,094 Bias-Related Incidents in the Month Following the Election," *Hatewatch*, Dec. 16, 2016. Online: https://www.splcenter.org/hatewatch/2016/12/16/update-1094-bias-related-incidents-month-following-election. See also "Hate Crimes Increase in the US Since Trump's Election," *Politics Today*, July 22, 2019. Online: https://politicstoday.org/hate-crimes-increase-in-the-us-since-trumps-election. See also Griffin Sims Edwards and Stephen Rushin, "The Effect of President Trump's Election on Hate Crimes," SSRN, Jan. 18, 2018. Online: https://papers.ssrn.com/sol3/papers.cfm?abstract_id=3102652.

28 See David Neiwert, "The Hokoana Trial: Inside the 'Antifa' Shooting Incident the Media Don't Want to Talk About," *Daily Kos*, Sept. 28, 2019. Online: https://www.dailykos.com/stories/2019/9/28/1888326/-The-Hokoana-trial-Inside-the-Antifa-shooting-incident-the-media-don-t-want-to-talk-about.

29 See, e.g., David Neiwert, "Pro-Trump Rally Expected to Bring Chaos, Violence to D.C. Streets While Congress Certifies Election," *Daily Kos*, Jan. 4, 2021. Online: https://www.dailykos.com/stories/2021/1/4/2005924/-Pro-Trump-rally-expected-to-bring-chaos-violence-to-D-C-streets-while-Congress-certifies-election.   Also: David Neiwert, "Clash with Police at Washington's BLM Plaza Previews Trump Supporters' Violent Plans for March Today," *Daily Kos*, Jan. 6, 2021 (10:53 a.m.).

Chapter 1: An Uncivil War

1   See Jesse McKinley, Alex Traub, and Troy Closson, "10 People Are Killed and 3 Are
    Wounded in a Mass Shooting at a Buffalo Grocery Store," *The New York Times*, May
    14, 2022. Online: https://www.nytimes.com/live/2022/05/14/nyregion/buffalo-shoot-
    ing/at-least-10-people-are-killed-in-a-mass-shooting-at-a-buffalo-grocery-store-a-
    local-official-says.

2   See David Neiwert, "Buffalo Shooter's Manifesto Reveals How He Was a Product
    of Republicans' 'Replacement Theory,'" *Daily Kos*, May 15, 2022. Online: https://
    www.dailykos.com/stories/2022/5/15/2098173/-Buffalo-shooting-only-the-lat-
    est-attack-in-the-radical-right-s-insurgent-war-on-American-democracy.

3   See David Neiwert, "How the 'Cultural Marxism' Hoax Began, and Why It's
    Spreading into the Mainstream," *Daily Kos*, Jan. 23, 2019. Online: https://www.
    dailykos.com/stories/2019/1/23/1828527/-How-the-cultural-Marxism-hoax-
    began-and-why-it-s-spreading-into-the-mainstream.

4   See Vice Staff, "How the 'Great Replacement' Myth Inspired a Wave of Racist Terror
    Attacks," *Vice News*, July 11, 2022. Online: https://www.vice.com/en/article/v7vezb/
    great-replacement-theory-decade-of-hate. See also David Neiwert, "Domestic Ter-
    ror in the Age of Trump," *Reveal News*, July 9, 2020. Online: https://revealnews.org/
    article/domestic-terror-in-the-age-of-trump.

5   See Jacob Davey and Julia Ebner, "'The Great Replacement': The Violent Conse-
    quences of Mainstreamed Extremism," Institute for Strategic Dialogue, July 7, 2019.
    Online: https://www.isdglobal.org/isd-publications/the-great-replacement-the-vio-
    lent-consequences-of-mainstreamed-extremism.

6   See Robert A. Pape, "Why We Cannot Afford to Ignore the American Insurrec-
    tionist Movement," *Chicago Project on Security and Threats*, Aug. 6, 2021. Online:
    https://cpost.uchicago.edu/publications/why_we_cannot_afford_to_ignore_the_
    american_insurrectionist_movement.

7   See David Neiwert, "Fox News Waves 'Bloody Shirt' Trope to Gaslight Critics
    about Culpability for Buffalo Terrorism," *Daily Kos*, May 17, 2022. Online: https://
    www.dailykos.com/stories/2022/5/17/2098596/-Tucker-and-Co-insist-problem-
    isn-t-white-nationalist-terrorism-it-s-people-blaming-them-for-it.

8   See David Neiwert, "Tucker Completes Fox's Descent into White-Nationalist
    Propaganda with 'Great Replacement' Rant," *Daily Kos*, Sept. 23, 2021. Online:
    https://www.dailykos.com/stories/2021/9/23/2053989/-Tucker-completes-Fox-s-
    descent-into-white-nationalist-propaganda-with-great-replacement-rant. See also
    David Neiwert, "After Carlson Spouts White Nationalist 'Replacement Theory,'
    ADL Chief Says: 'Tucker Must Go,'" *Daily Kos*, April 21, 2021. Online: https://
    www.dailykos.com/stories/2021/4/9/2025163/-After-Carlson-spouts-white-natio-
    nalist-replacement-theory-ADL-chief-says-Tucker-must-go.

9   See Madeline Peltz, "Tucker Carlson's Descent into White Supremacy: A Timeline,"
    Media Matters for America, Oct. 28, 2018. Online: https://www.mediamatters.
    org/tucker-carlson/tucker-carlsons-descent-white-supremacy-timeline. See also
    Madeline Peltz, "Unearthed Audio Shows Tucker Carlson Using White National-
    ist Rhetoric and Making Racist Remarks," *Media Matters for America*, March 11,
    2019. Online: https://www.mediamatters.org/tucker-carlson/unearthed-audio-
    shows-tucker-carlson-using-white-nationalist-rhetoric-and-making.

10 See John Kerr and Alazar Moges, "Tucker Carlson Is Using His Fox News Show to Mainstream White Nationalism," *Media Matters for America*, April 9, 2018. Online: https://www.mediamatters.org/tucker-carlson/tucker-carlson-using-his-fox-news-show-mainstream-white-nationalism. See also Erik Wemple, "Tucker Carlson Easily Snookers Trump on South Africa," *The Washington Post*, Aug. 23, 2018. Online: https://www.washingtonpost.com/blogs/erik-wemple/wp/2018/08/23/tucker-carlson-easily-snookers-trump-on-south-africa. See also Daniel Mortiz-Rabson, "White Nationalist Website VDare Thanks Fox News Host Tucker Carlson for Support," *Newsweek*, Feb. 27, 2019. Online: https://www.newsweek.com/white-nationalist-website-thanks-fox-news-host-tucker-carlson-1346578.

11 See Will Carless and Aaron Sankin, "The Hate Report: What White Nationalists Think about Tucker Carlson," *Reveal*, Dec. 7, 2018. Online: https://revealnews.org/blog/the-hate-report-what-white-nationalists-think-about-tucker-carlson. See also Ezra Klein, "Why White Supremacists Kove Tucker Carlson," Vox [video], Dec. 19, 2018. Online: https://www.facebook.com/watch/?v=334888754010616. See also Matt Stieb, "Ex-White Nationalist Says Tucker Carlson Hits Far-Right Messaging 'Better Than They Have,'" *New York Magazine*, April 1, 2019. Online: https://nymag.com/intelligencer/2019/04/ex-white-nationalist-says-they-get-tips-from-tucker-carlson.html.

12 See David Neiwert, "Tucker Carlson Leads a Whitewash Parade for White Nationalism: Calling It Out Stirs Up Hate, He Says," *Daily Kos*, April 15, 2019. Online: https://www.dailykos.com/stories/2019/4/15/1850353/-Tucker-Carlson-leads-a-whitewash-parade-for-white-nationalism-Calling-it-out-stirs-up-hate-he-says.

13 See David Neiwert, "Tucker's Gaslighting Campaign Is About More Than Just Justifying the Jan. 6 Capitol Onsurrection," *Daily Kos*, Nov. 4, 2021. Online: https://www.dailykos.com/stories/2021/11/4/2062386/-Tucker-s-gaslighting-campaign-is-about-more-than-just-justifying-the-Jan-6-Capitol-insurrection.

14 See David Neiwert, "'Waving the Bloody Shirt': Conservatives Resort To a Time-Worn Tactic to Gaslight the Public," *Daily Kos*, Feb. 25, 2021. Online: https://www.dailykos.com/stories/2021/2/25/2018098/-Republicans-embrace-old-wave-the-bloody-shirt-trope-to-gaslight-the-public-on-Jan-6-violence.

15 See Jonathan Greenblatt, "ADL Letter to Fox News Condemns Tucker Carlson's Impassioned Defense of 'Great Replacement Theory,'" Anti-Defamation League, April 9, 2021. Online: https://www.adl.org/news/media-watch/adl-letter-to-fox-news-condemns-tucker-carlsons-impassioned-defense-of-great.

16 See Bill Keveny, "Tucker Carlson doubles down on voter 'replacement' comments after ADL calls for his firing," *USA Today*, April 12, 2021. Online: https://www.usatoday.com/story/entertainment/tv/2021/04/12/fox-backs-tucker-carlson-and-rejects-adl-call-his-firing/7197805002/.

17 See David Neiwert, "Fox executives think Tucker's 'replacement theory' talk was just fine as white nationalists exult," *Daily Kos*, April 15, 2021. Online: https://www.dailykos.com/stories/2021/4/15/2026094/-White-nationalists-celebrate-as-Tucker-Carlson-doubles-down-on-pitching-replacement-theory.

18 See David Neiwert, "Patriot Front Discovers Coeur d'Alene Not the Best Place to Bring Fascist Violence to Pride Events," *Daily Kos*, June 13, 2022. Online: https://www.dailykos.com/stories/2022/6/13/2103960/-Police-arrest-31-Patriot-Front-marchers-from-around-the-country-outside-Idaho-Pride-gathering.

19 See David Neiwert, "'They Are Trying to Take Your Children': Far-Right Idaho 'Patriots' Plan to Confront Pride Gathering," *Daily Kos*, May 2, 2022. Online: https://www.dailykos.com/stories/2022/5/2/2095345/-Spouting-groomer-rhetoric-Patriot-bikers-plan-to-confront-Pride-rally-next-month-in-Idaho.

20 See Leah Sotille, "The Chaos Agents," *The New York Times Magazine*, Aug. 19, 2020. Online: https://www.nytimes.com/interactive/2020/08/19/magazine/boogaloo.html.

21 See David Neiwert, "'Antifa Buses!' Panicked Armed Men Hit Small-Town Streets Across America to Fend Off Imagined Hordes," *Daily Kos*, June 9, 2020. Online: https://www.dailykos.com/stories/2020/6/9/1951844/--Antifa-buses-Panicked-armed-men-hit-small-town-streets-across-America-to-fend-off-imagined-hordes.

22 See David Neiwert, "Far-Right Idaho 'Patriots' Change Name of Anti-Pride Event, but Not Their Threatening Rhetoric," *Daily Kos*, May 12, 2022. Online: https://www.dailykos.com/stories/2022/5/12/2097670/-Far-right-Idaho-Patriots-change-name-of-anti-Pride-event-but-not-their-threatening-rhetoric.

23 See David Neiwert, "'Patriot Front' Marchers Wave Their Fascist Banners Down Capitol Mall as Radical Right Returns," *Daily Kos*, Jan. 29, 2021. Online: https://www.dailykos.com/stories/2021/1/29/2012760/--Patriot-Front-fascists-mark-far-right-s-return-to-Washington-with-march-down-Capitol-Mall.

24 See Flint McColgan, "Boston Mayor Condemns 'White Supremacist' March Through City; Civil Rights Probe Launched," *Boston Herald*, July 2, 2022. Online: https://www.bostonherald.com/2022/07/02/white-supremacist-group-the-patriot-front-reportedly-marching-through-boston.

25 See Aja Romano, "The Right's Moral Panic over 'Grooming' Invokes Age-Old Homophobia," *Vox*, April 21, 2022. Online: https://www.vox.com/culture/23025505/leftist-groomers-homophobia-satanic-panic-explained.

26 See David Neiwert, "'Groomer' Rhetoric's Toxic Spread on Social Media Revolves Around 10 Key Far-Right Influencers," *Daily Kos*, Aug. 11, 2022. Online: https://www.dailykos.com/stories/2022/8/11/2115986/--Groomer-rhetoric-s-toxic-spread-on-social-media-revolves-around-10-key-far-right-influencers.

27 See Danny Cevallos, "No, Sen. Hawley, Ketanji Brown Jackson Isn't Soft on Child Pornography," NBC News, March 25, 2022. Online: https://www.nbcnews.com/think/opinion/supreme-court-nominee-ketanji-brown-jackson-isn-t-soft-child-ncna1293073.

28 See Philip Bump, "The New Red Scare: The Right Leans Into Pedophilia Accusations," *The Washington Post*, April 5, 2022. Online: https://www.washingtonpost.com/politics/2022/04/05/new-red-scare-right-leans-into-pedophilia-accusations.

29 See David Gilbert, "'She Needs to Be Executed': The Far-Right Is Doxxing School Officials They Think Are 'Groomers'," *Vice*, April 13, 2022. Online: https://www.vice.com/en/article/jgm3xx/far-right-groomers-doxxing-school-officials.

30 See David Neiwert, "'Shoot Them in the Back of the Head': Evangelical Preachers Ratchet Up Anti-LGBTQ Hate Rhetoric," *Daily Kos*, June 9, 2022. Online: https://www.dailykos.com/stories/2022/6/9/2103264/--Shoot-them-in-the-back-of-the-head-Evangelical-preachers-ratchet-up-anti-LGBTQ-hate-rhetoric.

31 See David Neiwert, "Far Right Trains Its Eliminationist Sights on LGBTQ Community with Deluge of Threatening Rhetoric," *Daily Kos*, May 27, 2022. Online: https://www.dailykos.com/stories/2022/5/27/2100782/-Far-right-trains-its-eliminationist-sights-on-LGBTQ-community-with-deluge-of-threatening-rhetoric.

32 See David Neiwert, "Once Again, a Gay-Hating Evangelical Threatens Neighbors, Pride Parade, Bringing Police Response," *Daily Kos*, June 21, 2022. Online: https://www.dailykos.com/stories/2022/6/21/2105485/-Arrest-of-Whidbey-Island-man-only-the-latest-incident-of-far-right-inspired-anti-LGBTQ-threats.

33 See David Neiwert, "White-Nationalist APU Provocateurs Intimidate Family-Friendly Pride Event at Dallas Gay Bar," *Daily Kos*, June 6, 2022. Online: https://www.dailykos.com/stories/2022/6/6/2102618/-Neofascists-show-up-to-protest-menace-kid-friendly-Pride-week-drag-show-at-Dallas-gay-bar.

34 See Ben Lorber, "'The Forgotten Gamers of America'," *Political Research Associates*, July 21, 2021. Online: https://politicalresearch.org/2021/07/20/forgotten-gamers-america. See also ADL Staff, "AFPAC III: The Groyper Army Seeks to Normalize White Nationalism," Anti-Defamation League, Feb. 25, 2022. Online: https://www.adl.org/blog/afpac-iii-the-groyper-army-seeks-to-normalize-white-nationalism.

35 See Kathryn Joyce and Ben Lorber, "Self-Described 'Christian Fascist' Movement is Trying to Sabotage LGBTQ Pride Month," *Political Research Associates*, June 14, 2022. Online: https://politicalresearch.org/2022/06/14/self-described-christian-fascist-movement-trying-sabotage-lgbtq-pride-month.

36 See David Neiwert, "Proud Boys Ginned Up on 'Groomer' Rhetoric Bring Their Menacing Ways to LGBTQ Pride Events," *Daily Kos*, June 23, 2022. Online: https://www.dailykos.com/stories/2022/6/23/2105911/-Proud-Boys-ginned-up-on-groomer-rhetoric-bring-their-menacing-ways-to-LGBTQ-Pride-events.

37 See Vandana Ravikumar, "Proud Boys Storm Reading Event Hosted by Drag Queen at California Library, Deputies Say," *Sacramento Bee*, June 13, 2022. Online: https://www.sacbee.com/news/nation-world/national/article262475427.html.

38 See Kathryn Joyce, "Lone Star Hate: Right-Wing Activists in Texas Drive a New Wave of Anti-LGBTQ Bigotry," *Salon*, June 22, 2022. Online: https://www.salon.com/2022/06/22/lone-star-hate-right-wing-activists-in-texas-drive-a-new-wave-of-anti-lgbtq-bigotry.

39 See Jamey Cross, "Children's LGBTQ Pride Event at Library Disrupted by Demonstrators, Police Respond," *Wilmington Star News*, June 22, 2022. Online: https://www.msn.com/en-us/news/us/children-s-lgbtq-pride-event-at-library-disrupted-by-demonstrators-police-respond/ar-AAYKjKR.

40 See Marek Mazurek, "Members of Proud Boys Hate Group Disrupt LGBTQ-Themed Event at Tutt Branch of Library," *South Bend Tribune*, June 29, 2022. Online: https://www.southbendtribune.com/story/news/2022/06/29/proud-boys-library-disrupt-lgbtq-event-south-bend/7770036001.

41 See, "Extremists Target LGBTQ+ Community During Pride Month," Center on Extremism, Anti-Defamation League, June 15, 2022. Online: https://www.adl.org/resources/blog/extremists-target-lgbtq-community-during-pride-month.

42 See Joyce, "Lone Star Hate."

43 See Ikran Dahir, "A Drag Queen Was Interrupted by a Right-Wing Group During a Library's Story Hour, and Police Are Investigating," *BuzzFeed News*, June 12, 2022. Online: https://www.buzzfeednews.com/article/ikrd/proud-boys-drag-queen-story-hour-alameda.

44 See Fortesa Latifi, "Bay Area Drag Queen Speaks Out Against Far-Right Extremists," *Teen Vogue*, June 14, 2022. Online: https://www.teenvogue.com/story/drag-brunch-story-time-kyle-chu.

45 See David Neiwert, "As Republicans Increasingly Embrace Far-Right Radicalization, a Crisis of Democracy Looms Large," *Daily Kos*, Feb. 10, 2021. Online: https://www.dailykos.com/stories/2021/2/10/2015248/-Far-right-radicalization-has-transformed-the-Republican-Party-into-an-anti-democratic-entity.

46 See Cassie Miller, "SPLC Poll Finds Substantial Support for 'Great Replacement' Theory and Other Hard-Right Ideas," *Hatewatch*, June 1, 2022. Online: https://www.splcenter.org/news/2022/06/01/poll-finds-support-great-replacement-hard-right-ideas.

47 See David Neiwert, "Decline in Hate-Group Numbers Disguises How Deeply Extremism Has Spread Within the GOP," *Daily Kos*, March 9, 2022. Online: https://www.dailykos.com/stories/2022/3/9/2084970/-SPLC-report-on-hate-in-2021-finds-decline-in-group-numbers-as-extremism-spread-to-mainstream.

Chapter 2: "When Do We Get to Use the Guns?"

1 See David Neiwert, "TPUSA Audience Member at Idaho Event Wants to Know How Long 'Before We Kill These People,'" *Daily Kos*, Oct. 27, 2022. Online: https://www.dailykos.com/stories/2021/10/27/2060573/--When-do-we-get-to-use-the-guns-TPUSA-audience-member-asks-Charlie-Kirk-at-Idaho-event.

2 See David Neiwert, "Black 'American' Flags at Right-Wing Protests, on Front Porches Cow 'No Quarter' Against Liberals," *Daily Kos*, Oct. 13, 2021. Online: https://www.dailykos.com/stories/2021/10/13/2057922/-Black-American-flags-at-right-wing-protests-on-front-porches-vow-no-quarter-against-liberals.

3 See David Neiwert, "In the Year Since Jan. 6, America's Radical Right Has Hardened into an Anti-Democratic Insurgency," *Daily Kos*, Jan. 5, 2022. Online: https://www.dailykos.com/stories/2022/1/5/2072917/-In-the-year-since-Jan-6-America-s-radical-right-has-hardened-into-an-anti-democratic-insurgency.

4 See Heidi Beirich, "One Year Later: U.S. Democracy in Peril as Far-Right Extremism Spreads Globally," Global Project Against Hate and Extremism, Jan. 4, 2022. Online: https://globalextremism.org/post/one-year-later-u-s-democracy-in-peril-as-far-right-extremism-spreads-globally.

5 See David Neiwert, "The 'Tea Party' Nexus: Mainstream Conservatives Empowering Far-Right Extremists Who Want a New Civil War," *Crooks and Liars*, Aug. 11, 2009. Online: https://crooksandliars.com/david-neiwert/tea-party-nexus-mainstream-conservat.

6 See David Neiwert, "Glenn Beck Plots Out Our Dystopian Future, Run by Militias," *Crooks and Liars*, Feb. 28, 2009. Online: https://crooksandliars.com/david-neiwert/glenn-beck-plots-out-our-dystopian-f.

7 See David Neiwert, "'Oath Keepers' Leader Arrested for Child Rape; Cops Find Stolen Grenade Launcher in His House," *Crooks and Liars*, Jan. 21, 2010. Online: https://crooksandliars.com/david-neiwert/tea-party-leader-arrested-rape.

8 See David Neiwert, "'Doomsday Prepper' arrested on gun charges in Washington state," *Hatewatch*, Jan. 21, 2014. Online: https://www.splcenter.org/hatewatch/2014/01/21/doomsday-prepper-arrested-gun-charges-washington-state.

9 See David Neiwert, "Conspiracy Theories Fan Fears of Race War, with Alex Jones Leading the Parade," *Hatewatch*, Dec. 4, 2014. Online: https://www.splcenter.org/hatewatch/2014/12/04/conspiracy-theories-fan-fears-race-war-alex-jones-leading-parade.

10 See David Neiwert, "West Virginia Klan Leader Claims Returning Military Will Help Them Train for 'the Upcoming Battle,'" *Hatewatch*, June 13, 2014. Online: https://www.splcenter.org/hatewatch/2014/06/13/west-virginia-klan-leader-claims-returning-military-will-help-them-train-upcoming-battle.

11 See David Neiwert, "Savage's New Book Not About Averting, but Fomenting Civil War," *Hatewatch*, Nov. 5, 2014. Online: https://www.splcenter.org/hatewatch/2014/11/05/savage%E2%80%99s-new-book-not-about-averting-fomenting-civil-war.

12 See David Neiwert, "Back at the Bundy Ranch, It's Oath Keepers vs. Militiamen as Wild Rumors Fly," *Hatewatch*, April 30, 2014. Online: https://www.splcenter.org/hatewatch/2014/04/30/back-bundy-ranch-its-oath-keepers-vs-militiamen-wild-rumors-fly.

13 See David Zucchino, "A Militia Gets Battle Ready for a 'Gun-Grabbing' Clinton Presidency," *The New York Times*, Nov. 4, 2016. Online: https://www.nytimes.com/2016/11/05/us/a-militia-gets-battle-ready-for-a-gun-grabbing-clinton-presidency.html.

14 See David Neiwert, "Right Wing Civility: A Collection," YouTube (video), Feb. 25, 2019. Online: https://youtu.be/goMfm4bmEj4 (at 12:10).

15 See Lynn Buhl, "'I Am Dreaming of a Way to Kill Almost Every Last Person on Earth': A Self-Proclaimed White Nationalist Planned a Mass Terrorist Attack, the Government Says," *The Washington Post*, Feb. 20, 2019. Online: https://www.washingtonpost.com/local/public-safety/self-proclaimed-white-nationalist-planned-mass-terror-attack-government-says-i-am-dreaming-of-a-way-to-kill-almost-every-last-person-on-earth/2019/02/20/61daf6b8-3544-11e9-af5b-b51b7ff322e9_story.html.

16 See David Neiwert, "Christopher Hasson Is Just the Latest Sign of America's Rising Far-Right Domestic Terrorist Tide," *Daily Kos*, Feb. 21, 2019. Online: https://www.dailykos.com/stories/2019/2/21/1836747/-Christopher-Hasson-is-just-the-latest-sign-of-the-rising-American-far-right-domestic-terrorist-tide.

17 See Cody Fenwick, "Laura Ingraham Guest Claims the United States Is 'In a Civil War'—and Americans Should 'Buy Guns,'" *Salon*, Feb. 22, 2019. Online: https://www.salon.com/2019/02/22/laura-ingraham-guest-claims-the-united-states-is-in-a-civil-war-and-americans-should-buy-guns_partner.

18 See Nicole Goodkind, "Former Trump Adviser Roger Stone Is Ready for Civil War," *Newsweek*, June 13, 2018. Online: https://www.newsweek.com/2018/06/22/trump-adviser-roger-stone-ready-civil-war-973354.html.

19 See Brian Tashman, "Jim Bakker: We Will Have a Civil War if Trump Is Impeached," *Right Wing Watch*, May 31, 2017. Online: https://www.rightwingwatch.org/post/jim-bakker-we-will-have-a-civil-war-if-trump-is-impeached.

20 See Kurt Schlichter, "Why Democrats Would Lose the Second Civil War, Too," *Townhall*, March 12, 2018. Online: https://townhall.com/columnists/kurtschlichter/2018/03/12/why-democrats-would-lose-the-second-civil-war-too-n2459833.

21 See Mitch Smith, "Kansas Trio Convicted in Plot to Bomb Somali Immigrants," *The New York Times*, April 18, 2018. Online: https://www.nytimes.com/2018/04/18/us/kansas-militia-somali-trial-verdict.html.

22 See David Neiwert, "Thanks to Impeachment, 'Civil War' Talk Is on the Tip of All the Far-Right Wingnuts' Tongues," *Daily Kos*, Dec. 26, 2019. Online: https://www.dailykos.com/stories/2019/12/26/1907050/-Thanks-to-impeachment-civil-war-talk-is-on-the-tip-of-all-the-far-right-wingnuts-tongues.

23 Criminal Complaint, United States District Court for the Eastern District of Virginia, *United States v. Elena Alekseevna Khusyaynova*, Case No. 1:18-MJ-464, Sept. 28, 2018. Online: https://www.justice.gov/usao-edva/press-release/file/1102591/download.

24 See Robert Bridge, "Democrats' Push to Impeach Trump Is Just the Latest Chapter of US Civil War 2.0," *RT*, Dec. 18, 2019. Online: https://www.rt.com/op-ed/476183-impeachment-vote-trump-democrats.

25 See ADL Staff, "The Boogaloo: Extremists' New Slang Term for a Coming Civil War," Anti-Defamation League, Nov. 26, 2019. Online: https://www.adl.org/blog/the-boogaloo-extremists-new-slang-term-for-a-coming-civil-war.

26 See David Neiwert, "'Boogaloo' Civil War Talk Takes on a Life of Its Own as Far-Right Extremists Coalesce," *Daily Kos*, Feb. 25, 2020. Online: https://www.dailykos.com/stories/2020/2/25/1921786/--Boogaloo-civil-war-talk-takes-on-a-life-of-its-own-as-far-right-extremists-coalesce.

27 See Brandy Zadrozny, "What Is the 'Boogaloo'? How Online Calls for a Violent Uprising Are Hitting the Mainstream," NBC News, Feb. 19, 2020. Online: https://www.nbcnews.com/tech/social-media/what-boogaloo-how-online-calls-violent-uprising-are-getting-organized-n1138461.

28 See David Neiwert, "Beyond Monday's Gun-Laden March in Richmond, Militias' Plans for a 'Civil War' Look to Go National," *Daily Kos*, Jan. 19, 2020. Online: https://www.dailykos.com/stories/2020/1/19/1912573/-Beyond-Monday-s-gun-laden-march-in-Richmond-militias-plans-for-a-civil-war-look-to-go-national.

29 See David Neiwert, "As the Far-Right Prepares for a 'Boogaloo,' Virginia Governor Declares Emergency," *Daily Kos*, Jan. 16, 2020. Online: https://www.dailykos.com/stories/2020/1/16/1911814/-As-the-far-right-prepares-for-a-Boogaloo-Virginia-governor-declares-emergency.

30 See "Today's Guests: Stewart Rhodes and Sheriff Richard Mack," *The Power Hour*, Jan. 8, 2020. Online: https://thepowerhour.com/todays-guests-stewart-rhodes-sheriff-richard-mack-james-mccanney.

31 See David Neiwert, "Conspiracy Theories, Wxtremism Have Infected the Public During Pandemic as Exposure Rises," *Daily Kos*, Feb. 15, 2021. Online: https://www.dailykos.com/stories/2021/2/15/2016288/-Far-right-extremism-has-gained-traction-during-COVID-19-pandemic-thanks-to-online-radicalization. See also "White Supremacy Search Trends in the United States," Moonshot, June 2021. Online: https://moonshotteam.com/resource/white-supremacy-search-trends-in-the-united-states.

32 See David Neiwert, "On Facebook, QAnon Conspiracism Is Reaching a Global Critical Mass Amid the Pandemic," *Daily Kos*, Aug. 11, 2020. Online: https://www.dailykos.com/stories/2020/8/11/1968531/-QAnon-s-crazy-quilt-conspiracy-universe-has-grown-to-immense-size-during-the-pandemic.

33 See "Extremists Are Using Facebook to Organize for Civil War Amid Coronavirus," Tech Transparency Project, April 22, 2020. Online: https://www.techtransparencyproject.org/articles/extremists-are-using-facebook-to-organize-for-civil-war-amid-coronavirus.

34 See David Neiwert, "The Far Right Wants to Make Its Shared 'Boogaloo' Fantasy of Violent Civil War a Reality," *Daily Kos*, April 28, 2020. Online: https://www.dailykos.com/stories/2020/4/28/1940542/-The-far-right-wants-to-make-its-shared-Boogaloo-fantasy-of-violent-civil-war-a-reality.

35 See David Neiwert, "Michigan Militiamen Successfully Threaten Legislators over COVID-19 Lockdown Orders," *Daily Kos*, May 1, 2020. Online: https://www.dailykos.com/stories/2020/5/1/1941901/-Michigan-militiamen-successfully-threaten-legislators-over-COVID-19-lockdown-orders.

36 See David Neiwert, "Anti-Lockdown Protesters Are Just the Authoritarian Foot Soldiers Trump Ordered," *Daily Kos*, April 21, 2020. Online: https://www.dailykos.com/stories/2020/4/21/1939036/-Anti-lockdown-protesters-are-just-the-authoritarian-footsoldiers-Trump-ordered.

37 See Alex Goldenberg and Joel Finkelstein, "Cyber Swarming, Memetic Warfare and Viral Insurgency: How Domestic Militants Organize on Memes to Incite Violent Insurrection and Terror Against Government and Law Enforcement," Network Contagion Research Institute, Feb. 7, 2020. Online: https://networkcontagion.us/reports/cyber-swarming-memetic-warfare-and-viral-insurgency-how-domestic-militants-organize-on-memes-to-incite-violent-insurrection-and-terror-against-government-and-law-enforcement.

38 See David Neiwert, "Bay Area 'Boogaloo Bois' Charged with Ambush of Federal Officers at Anti-Police Protest," *Daily Kos*, June 17, 2020. Online: https://www.dailykos.com/stories/2020/6/17/1953901/-Bay-Area-Boogaloo-Bois-charged-with-ambush-of-federal-officers-at-anti-police-protest.

39 See David Neiwert, "'Boogaloo Boi' Eager for Civil War Arrested for Shooting 2 Deputies, Linked to Protest Killings," *Daily Kos*, June 12, 2020. Online: https://www.dailykos.com/stories/2020/6/12/1952757/--Boogaloo-Boi-eager-for-civil-war-arrested-for-shooting-2-deputies-linked-to-protest-killings.

40 See David Neiwert, "'Boogaloo Boi' Killer Was an Active Member of a Secretive Terrorist Militia Group Planning Violence," *Daily Kos*, June 7, 2021. Online: https://www.dailykos.com/stories/2020/6/12/1952757/--Boogaloo-Boi-eager-for-civil-war-arrested-for-shooting-2-deputies-linked-to-protest-killings.

41 See Gisela Pérez de Acha, Kathryn Hurd, and Ellie Lightfoot, "'I Felt Hate More Than Anything': How an Active Duty Airman Tried to Start a Civil War," *ProPublica*, April 13, 2021. Online: https://www.propublica.org/article/i-felt-hate-more-than-anything-how-an-active-duty-airman-tried-to-start-a-civil-war.

42 See David Neiwert, "Turning reality on its head, Cruz claims right-wing 'Boogaloo' killer was 'antifa'," *Daily Kos*, August 6, 2020. Online: https://www.dailykos.com/stories/2020/8/6/1967309/-Ted-Cruz-lies-outrageously-at-Senate-hearing-blames-far-right-terror-on-antifa. See also David Neiwert, "By portraying Oakland cop killer as 'leftist,' Pence joins GOP chorus erasing far-right violence," *Daily Kos*, August 27, 2020. Online: https://www.dailykos.com/stories/2020/8/27/1972816/-Pence-s-acceptance-speech-models-how-Republicans-have-erased-lethal-far-right-violence.

43 See David Neiwert, "'Boogaloo Boi' Arrest for Attack on Minneapolis Station Confirms Far-Right Role in Protest Violence," *Daily Kos*, Oct. 23, 2020. Online: https://www.dailykos.com/stories/2020/10/23/1989023/--Boogaloo-Boi-arrest-for-attack-on-Minneapolis-station-confirms-far-right-role-in-protest-violence.

44 See Zoe Jackson, "2 'Boogaloo Bois' Charged with Conspiring with Terrorist Organization," *Star Tribune*, Sept. 4, 2020. Online: https://www.startribune.com/2-boogaloo-bois-charged-with-conspiring-with-terrorist-organization/572321772.

45 See David Neiwert, "'Boogaloo Bois' Arrested En Route to Las Vegas Protest with Arsenal of Molotov Cocktails," *Daily Kos*, June 4, 2020. Online: https://www.dailykos.

com/stories/2020/6/4/1950514/-Feds-arrest-trio-of-Boogaloo-Bois-planning-to-lob-Molotov-cocktails-at-Vegas-protest-crowd.

46 See Emmanuel Felton, "A Self-Proclaimed 'Boogaloo Boy' Was Arrested After Allegedly Livestreaming His Hunt to Kill a Police Officer," *BuzzFeed News*, April 22, 2020. Online: https://www.buzzfeednews.com/article/emmanuelfelton/boogaloo-boy-arrested-texarkana-swenson.

47 See David Neiwert, "Unhinged Lockdown Protester in Colorado Attracts FBI's Interest, so They Find a Cache of Pipe Bombs," *Daily Kos*, May 6, 2020. Online: https://www.dailykos.com/stories/2020/5/6/1942843/-When-FBI-agents-checked-out-Colorado-lockdown-protester-they-found-cache-of-pipe-bombs-in-his-home.

48 See David Neiwert, "FBI Arrests an Ohio 'Boogaloo Boi' for Plotting Ambush of Police Officers at National Park," *Daily Kos*, May 13, 2020. Online: https://www.dailykos.com/stories/2020/5/13/1944847/-FBI-arrests-an-Ohio-Boogaloo-Boi-for-plotting-ambush-of-police-officers-at-national-park.

49 See David Neiwert, "Don't Be Fooled: 'Boogaloo' May Attract All Kinds of Fans, but It's a Violent Far-Right Movement," *Daily Kos*, July 14, 2020. Online: https://www.dailykos.com/stories/2020/7/14/1960787/-Don-t-be-fooled-Boogaloo-may-attract-all-kinds-of-fans-but-it-s-a-violent-far-right-movement.

50 See Mike Baker, "One Person Dead in Portland After Clashes Between Trump Supporters and Protesters," *The New York Times*, Aug. 30, 2020. Online: https://www.nytimes.com/2020/08/30/us/portland-trump-rally-shooting.html.

51 See David Neiwert, "'Civil War Is Here, Right Now': 'Patriots' Urge Trump to Empower Militias to Fight Antifa in Streets," *Daily Kos*, Aug. 31, 2020. Online: https://www.dailykos.com/stories/2020/8/31/1974015/-Oath-Keepers-to-Trump-Send-out-the-militias-to-stop-antifascists-Marxist-takeover-of-America.

52 See David Neiwert, "Report on Killing of Portland Antifa Shooter by Federal Officers Suggests It Was Never an Arrest," *Daily Kos*, Oct. 14, 2020. Online: https://www.dailykos.com/stories/2020/10/15/1986658/-Report-on-killing-of-Portland-antifa-shooter-by-federal-officers-suggests-it-was-never-an-arrest.

53 See Mark Sumner, "Oath Keepers Plead 'not guilty' to Charges of Seditious Conspiracy, as Founder Asks for Release," *Daily Kos*, Jan. 25, 2002. Online: https://www.dailykos.com/stories/2022/1/25/2076721/-Oath-Keepers-plead-not-guilty-to-charges-of-seditious-conspiracy-as-founder-asks-for-release.

54 See David Neiwert, "'Million MAGA March' Saturday Will Commingle White Nationalists, Conspiracists, Trump Fans," *Daily Kos*, Nov. 11, 2020. Online: https://www.dailykos.com/stories/2020/11/11/1995112/--Million-MAGA-March-Saturday-will-commingle-white-nationalists-conspiracists-Trump-fans.

55 See Devlin Barrett and Spencer Hsu, "How Trump's Flirtation with an Anti-Insurrection Law Inspired Jan. 6 Insurrection," *The Washington Post*, Jan. 23, 2022. Online: https://www.washingtonpost.com/national-security/stewart-rhodes-insurrection-act-trump/2022/01/23/fa009626-7c47-11ec-bf02-f9e24ccef149_story.html.

56 See Ryan J. Reilly, "A Sampling of Jan. 6 Defendant Ryan Nichols' Political Discourse," *Twitter*, Feb. 4, 2022. Online: https://twitter.com/ryanjreilly/status/1489747752020066307.

Chapter 3: Over the Rubicon

1 See Eric Hananoki, "A Comprehensive Guide To Alex Jones: Conspiracy Theorist And Trump 'Valuable Asset'," Media Matters, Decwember 1, 2016. Online: https://www.mediamatters.org/donald-trump/comprehensive-guide-alex-jones-conspiracy-theorist-and-trump-valuable-asset.

2 See Alana Abramson, "How Donald Trump Perpetuated the 'Birther' Movement for Years," ABC News, Sept. 26, 2016. Online: https://abcnews.go.com/Politics/donald-trump-perpetuated-birther-movement-years/story?id=42138176.

3 See Philip Bump, "President Trump loves conspiracy theories. Has he ever been right?," *The Washington Post*, November 26, 2019. Online: https://www.washingtonpost.com/politics/2019/11/26/president-trump-loves-conspiracy-theories-has-he-ever-been-right/.

4 See Justin Wise, "Trump suggests that it could get 'very bad' if military, police, biker supporters play 'tough'," *The Hill*, March 14, 2019. Online: https://thehill.com/homenews/administration/434110-trump-suggests-that-things-could-get-very-bad-if-military-police/.

5 See David Neiwert, "Militiamen and nascent neo-Nazi terrorists jump to attention when Trump tweets about 'civil war'," *Daily Kos*, October 4, 2019. Online: https://www.dailykos.com/stories/2019/10/4/1889899/-Militiamen-and-nascent-neo-Nazi-terrorists-jump-to-attention-when-Trump-tweets-about-civil-war.

6 See Dan Berry and Sheera Frenkel, "'Be There. Will Be Wild!': Trump All but Circled the Date," *The New York Times*, January 6, 2021. Online: https://www.nytimes.com/2021/01/06/us/politics/capitol-mob-trump-supporters.html.

7 See Alex Newhouse, "Far-right activists on social media telegraphed violence weeks in advance of the attack on the US Capitol," *The Conversation*, January 8, 2021. Online: https://theconversation.com/far-right-activists-on-social-media-telegraphed-violence-weeks-in-advance-of-the-attack-on-the-us-capitol-152861.

8 See Jerry Lambe, "'Wait for the 6th When We Are All in DC to Insurrection': New Communications Indicate Coordination Between Oath Keepers, Proud Boys, and Three-Percenters," *Law and Crime*, March 24, 2021. Online: https://lawandcrime.com/u-s-capitol-siege/wait-for-the-6th-when-we-are-all-in-dc-to-insurrection-new-communications-indicate-coordination-between-oath-keepers-proud-boys-and-three-percenters/.

9 See Robert Evans, "How the Insurgent and MAGA Right are Being Welded Together on the Streets of Washington D.C.," *Bellingcat*, January 5, 2021. Online: https://www.bellingcat.com/news/americas/2021/01/05/how-the-insurgent-and-maga-right-are-being-welded-together-on-the-streets-of-washington-d-c/.

10 See Tess Owen, "I asked these guys if civil war is what they wanted," Twitter, January 6, 2021. Online: https://twitter.com/misstessowen/status/1346932836704653314.

11 See Aleszu Bajak, Jessica Guynn, and Mitchell Thorson, "When Trump started his speech before the Capitol riot, talk on Parler turned to civil war," *USA Today*, February 1, 2021. Online: https://www.usatoday.com/in-depth/news/2021/02/01/civil-war-during-trumps-pre-riot-speech-parler-talk-grew-darker/4297165001/.

12 See William M. Arkin, "Exclusive: Classified Documents Reveal the Number of January 6 Protestors," *Newsweek*, December 23, 2021. Online: https://www.newsweek.com/exclusive-classified-documents-reveal-number-january-6-protestors-1661296.

13 See Carter Walker, "Militia, 'patriots' met in Lancaster County 3 days before Jan. 6 Capitol attack; here's a look at why," *LNP Online*, January 9, 2022. Online:

https://lancasteronline.com/news/politics/militia-patriots-met-in-lancaster-coun-ty-3-days-before-jan-6-capitol-attack-heres-a/article_b4bbf2fe-6ff4-11ec-bfb9-9f5de5499e37.html.

14   See Erin Mansfield, "Prosecutors: Oath Keepers leader stood outside Capitol on Jan. 6 as members stormed inside," *USA Today*, March 9, 2021. Online: https://www.usatoday.com/story/news/2021/03/09/prosecutors-oath-keepers-leader-messaged-members-outside-capitol/6931224002/.

15   See Aram Rostam, "Exclusive: FBI probes pre-Capitol riot meeting of far-right groups," Reuters, February 8, 2022. Online: https://www.reuters.com/world/us/exclusive-fbi-probes-pre-capitol-riot-meeting-far-right-groups-2022-02-08/.

16   See Alan Feuer, "Another Far-Right Group Is Scrutinized About Its Efforts to Aid Trump," *The New York Times*, January 3, 2022. Online: https://www.nytimes.com/2022/01/03/us/politics/first-amendment-praetorian-trump-jan-6.html.

17   See William Breddeman and Will Sommer, "The Far-Right Paramilitary Wannabes Feeding Mike Flynn's Conspiracy Machine," *The Daily Beast,* June 11, 2021. Online: https://www.thedailybeast.com/1st-amendment-praetorian-the-far-right-paramili-tary-wannabes-feeding-mike-flynns-conspiracy-machine.

18   See Ryan J. Reilly, "'Quick Reaction Forces' And The Lingering Mysteries Of The Plot Against The Capitol," *Huffpost,* January 8, 2022. Online: https://www.huffpost.com/entry/quick-reaction-forces-qrf-oath-keepers-capitol-attack_n_61f2d986e4b02de5f51634bd.

19   See Christiaan Triebert, Ben Decker, Derek Watkins, Arielle Ray and Stella Coo-per, "First They Guarded Roger Stone. Then They Joined the Capitol Attack," *The New York Times*, February 14, 2021. Online: https://www.nytimes.com/interac-tive/2021/02/14/us/roger-stone-capitol-riot.html.

20   See "'A bloody and desperate fight:' U.S. prosecutors release Oath Keepers' com-munications," Reuters, January 13, 2022. Online: https://www.reuters.com/world/us/a-bloody-desperate-fight-us-prosecutors-release-oath-keepers-communica-tions-2022-01-13/. See also U.S. Department of Justice, "Superseding Indictment," June 22, 2022. Online: https://www.justice.gov/usao-dc/case-multi-defendant/file/1514876/download.

21   See U.S. Department of Justice, "Superseding Indictment," June 22, 2022. Online: https://www.justice.gov/usao-dc/case-multi-defendant/file/1514876/download.

22   See U.S. Department of Justice, "Second Superseding Indictment," June 6, 2022. Online: https://www.justice.gov/usao-dc/case-multi-defendant/file/1510981/down-load.

23   See U.S. Department of Justice, "Indictment," February 26, 2021. Online: https://www.justice.gov/usao-dc/case-multi-defendant/file/1371356/download.

24   See Will Cleveland, "Dominic Pezzola and other NY Proud Boys kept in contact at Capitol riot, feds allege," *Rochester Democrat and Chronicle*, July 1, 2021. On-line: https://www.democratandchronicle.com/story/news/2021/07/01/dominic-pe-zzola-matthew-greene-william-pepe-other-proud-boys-contact-capitol-riot-feds-allege/7814190002/.

25   See Luke Mogelson, "Among the Insurrectionists," *The New Yorker*, January 21, 2021. Online: https://www.newyorker.com/magazine/2021/01/25/among-the-insur-rectionists.

26   See U.S. Department of Justice, "Statement of Facts," Gabriel Agustin Garcia, Janu-ary 16, 2021. Online: https://www.justice.gov/opa/page/file/1356776/download.

27 See Judy Thomas, "Olathe Proud Boy describes Capitol riot in phone calls," *Kansas City Star*, June 11, 2021. Online: https://www.kansascity.com/news/local/article252046703.html.

28 See Washington Post staff, "Identifying far-right symbols that appeared at the U.S. Capitol riot," *The Washington Post*, January 15, 2021. Online: https://www.washingtonpost.com/nation/interactive/2021/far-right-symbols-capitol-riot/.

29 See Malachi Barrett, "Far-right activist who encouraged U.S. Capitol occupation also organized 'stop the steal' rally in Michigan," *Michigan Live*, January 7, 2021. Online: https://www.mlive.com/politics/2021/01/far-right-activist-who-encouraged-us-capitol-occupation-also-organized-stop-the-steal-rally-in-michigan.html.

30 See David Neiwert, "Clash with police at Washington's BLM plaza previews Trump supporters' violent plans for march today," *Daily Kos*, January 6, 2021. Online: https://www.dailykos.com/stories/2021/1/6/2006324/-MAGA-marchers-ginned-up-on-violent-rhetoric-give-Washington-preview-of-today-s-election-protests. See also, "After pre-rally, pro-Trump marchers take to streets, clash with police," YouTube video, January 6, 2021. Online: https://youtu.be/MpuksuzOS3Y.

31 See David Neiwert, "White nationalist Fuentes gets subpoena from Jan. 6 committee, but he's preparing for mockery," *Daily Kos*, January 30, 2022. Online: https://www.dailykos.com/stories/2022/1/20/2075882/-Jan-6-Committee-subpoenas-notorious-white-nationalist-Fuentes-but-there-s-a-danger-within.

32 See Luke Mogelson, "Among the Insurrectionists," *The New Yorker*, January 21, 2021. Online: https://www.newyorker.com/magazine/2021/01/25/among-the-insurrectionists.

33 See David Neiwert, "Neo-Nazi accelerationist linked to theft of Pelosi's laptop makes a liar out of Tucker Carlson," *Daily Kos*, February 26, 2021. Online: https://www.dailykos.com/stories/2021/2/26/2018288/-White-supremacists-at-Capitol-siege-Woman-linked-to-Pelosi-s-laptop-theft-just-the-latest-example.

34 See U.S. Department of Justice, "Statement of Facts," Anthime Gionet, January 7, 2021. Online: https://www.justice.gov/opa/page/file/1355771/download.

35 See Zachary Petrizzo, "Nick Fuentes tells followers who took part in Capitol riot to destroy their cellphones," *Daily Dot*, June 30, 2021. Online: https://www.dailydot.com/debug/nick-fuentes-capitol-riot-cellphones/.

36 See Zachary Petrizzo, "White nationalist 'groyper' leader doubles down on Jan. 6 Capitol riot, calling it 'awesome'," *Salon*, June 30, 2021. Online: https://www.salon.com/2021/06/30/white-nationalist-groyper-leader-doubles-down-on-jan-6-capitol-riot-calling-it-awesome/.

37 See Jonathan Capehart, "Former white nationalist Derek Black puts the Jan. 6 insurrection into perspective," *The Washington Post* (podcast), January 26, 2021. Online: https://www.washingtonpost.com/podcasts/capehart/former-white-nationalist-derek-black-puts-the-jan-6-insurrection-into-perspective/.

38 See "Eli Saslow and Derek Black: Leaving the KKK and White Supremacy," YouTube (The Daily Show), January 11, 2021. Online: https://www.youtube.com/watch?v=0eD-TKZlbMk.

39 See Alexander Zaitchik, "Meet Alex Jones," *Rolliing Stone*, March 2, 2011. Online: https://www.rollingstone.com/culture/culture-news/meet-alex-jones-175845/.

40 See Roger Parloff, "The Conspirators: The Proud Boys and Oath Keepers on Jan. 6," *Lawfare*, January 6, 2022. Online: https://www.lawfareblog.com/conspirators-proud-boys-and-oath-keepers-jan-6.

41 See David Neiwert, "Epik's hosting services provide connection for Jones' Infowars and Fuentes' white nationalists," *Daily Kos*, November 16, 2021. Online:
https://www.dailykos.com/stories/2021/11/16/2064684/-Epik-s-hosting-services-
provide-connection-for-Jones-Infowars-and-Fuentes-white-nationalists. See also
David Neiwert, "Alex Jones tried to play obstruction games with Sandy Hook
'hoax' lawsuits, but judge pulls plug," *Daily Kos*, October 1, 2021. Online: https://
www.dailykos.com/stories/2021/10/1/2055577/-Judgement-Day-looms-for-Alex-
Jones-after-judge-issues-default-judgement-in-Sandy-Hook-lawsuits.

42 See Frontline, "What Conspiracy Theorist Alex Jones Said in the Lead Up to the
Capitol Riot," *Frontline* (Pubic Bradcasting Service), January 12, 2021. Online:
https://www.pbs.org/wgbh/frontline/article/what-conspiracy-theorist-alex-jones-
said-in-the-lead-up-to-the-capitol-riot/.

43 See Lexi Lonas, "Trump donor, Alex Jones played key role in Jan. 6 rally: report," *The
Hill*, January 30, 2021. Online: https://thehill.com/homenews/news/536615-trump-
donor-alex-jones-played-key-role-in-jan-6-rally-report/.

44 See Timothy Johnson, "Infowars' Alex Jones funded and fomented the mob," Media Matters, January 11, 2021. Online: https://www.mediamatters.org/alex-jones/
infowars-alex-jones-funded-and-fomented-mob.

45 See "From a January 5, 2021, video posted to Infowars streaming platform Banned.
video," Media Matters (video), January 11, 2021. Online: https://www.mediamatters.
org/media/3922181.

46 See Frontline, "What Conspiracy Theorist Alex Jones Said in the Lead Up to the
Capitol Riot," *Frontline* (Pubic Bradcasting Service), January 12, 2021. Online:
https://www.pbs.org/wgbh/frontline/article/what-conspiracy-theorist-alex-jones-
said-in-the-lead-up-to-the-capitol-riot/.

47 See U.S. Department of Justice, "Affidavit in Support of Criminal Complaint and
Arrest Warrant," April 8, 2021. Online: https://www.justice.gov/usao-dc/case-
multi-defendant/file/1386671/download.

48 See Jonathan Edwards, "Infowars host Owen Shroyer wanted a 'new revolution' on
Jan. 6, feds say. Now he's charged in the Capitol riot," *The Washington Post*, August
23, 2021. Online: https://www.washingtonpost.com/nation/2021/08/23/infowars-
host-capitol-riot-charges/. See also Shawna M. Reading, "San Marcos man, Infowars
staffer, arrested in connection to Capitol riot," KVUE-TV, April 14, 201. Online:
https://www.kvue.com/article/news/local/capitol-riot-arrest-san-marcos-austin-
samuel-christopher-montoya/269-73b3876a-cc1a-48df-9bd2-26f069406245.

49 See Peter Jamison, Hannah Natanson, John Woodrow Cox and Alex Horton, "'The
storm is here': Ashli Babbitt's journey from capital 'guardian' to invader," *The Washington Post*, January 10, 2021. Online: https://www.washingtonpost.com/dc-md-
va/2021/01/09/ashli-babbitt-capitol-shooting-trump-qanon/.

50 See Shayan Sardarizadeh, "Here are some social media posts by influential QAnon
believers with huge followings tonight," Twitter, January 6, 2021. Online: https://
twitter.com/Shayan86/status/1347039515286892545.

51 See Rachel E. Greenspan, "The QAnon conspiracy theory and a stew of misinformation fueled the insurrection at the Capitol," *Insider*, January 7, 2021. Online: https://
www.insider.com/capitol-riots-qanon-protest-conspiracy-theory-washington-dc-
protests-2021-1.

52 See Ben Collins, "QAnon's Dominion voter fraud conspiracy theory reaches the
president," NBC News, November 13, 2020. Online: https://www.nbcnews.com/

tech/tech-news/q-fades-qanon-s-dominion-voter-fraud-conspiracy-theory-reaches-n1247780.

53 See Alex Newhouse, "Far-right activists on social media telegraphed violence weeks in advance of the attack on the US Capitol," *The Conversation*, January 8, 2021. Online: https://theconversation.com/far-right-activists-on-social-media-telegraphed-violence-weeks-in-advance-of-the-attack-on-the-us-capitol-152861.

54 See Jane Lytvynenko and Molly Hensely-Clancy, "The Rioters Who Took Over The Capitol Have Been Planning Online In The Open For Weeks," *Buzzfeed News*, January 6, 2021. Online: https://www.buzzfeednews.com/article/janelytvynenko/trump-rioters-planned-online.

55 See Peter Jamison, Hannah Natanson, John Woodrow Cox and Alex Horton, "'The storm is here': Ashli Babbitt's journey from capital 'guardian' to invader," *The Washington Post*, January 10, 2021. Online: https://www.washingtonpost.com/dc-md-va/2021/01/09/ashli-babbitt-capitol-shooting-trump-qanon/.

56 See Drew Harwell, Isaac Stanley-Becker, Razzan Nakhlawi and Craig Timberg, "QAnon reshaped Trump's party and radicalized believers. The Capitol siege may just be the start," *The Washington Post*, January 13, 2021. Online: https://www.washingtonpost.com/technology/2021/01/13/qanon-capitol-siege-trump/.

57 See "QAnon backer from Iowa was among first to breach Capitol, FBI says," Associated Press, January 13, 2021. Online: https://www.latimes.com/world-nation/story/2021-01-13/iowa-qanon-backer-among-first-breach-capitol-riot. See also U.S. Department of Justice, "Statement of Facts," Douglas Jensen, January 8, 2021. Online: https://www.justice.gov/opa/page/file/1353376/download.

58 See Justin Vallejo, "QAnon Shaman: How Jacob Chansley went from storming the Capitol to turning against 'first love' Donald Trump," *The Independent*, November 17, 2021. Online: https://www.independent.co.uk/news/world/americas/qanon-shaman-capitol-riot-sentencing-b1958223.html.

59 See Jack Jenkins, "The insurrectionists' Senate floor prayer highlights a curious Trumpian ecumenism," *Religion News Service*, February 25, 2021. Online: https://religionnews.com/2021/02/25/the-insurrectionists-senate-floor-prayer-highlights-a-curious-trumpian-ecumenism/.

60 See Tom Jackman, "'QAnon shaman' sentenced to 41 months for role in Capitol riot," *The Washington Post*, November 17, 2021. Online: https://www.washingtonpost.com/local/legal-issues/jacob-chansley-qanon-shaman-sentence/2021/11/17/59d9ce26-47b1-11ec-95dc-5f2a96e00fa3_story.html.

61 See "'This is really happening': Times reporters discuss their experience outside the Capitol on Jan. 6," *The New York Times*, January 6, 2021. Online: https://www.nytimes.com/2022/01/06/us/politics/jan-6-capitol-journalists.html.

62 See "Day of Rage: How Trump Supporters Took the U.S. Capitol" (video), *The New York Times*, June 30, 2021. Online: https://www.nytimes.com/video/us/politics/100000007606996/capitol-riot-trump-supporters.html.

63 See Tom Porter, "QAnon supporters believed marching on the Capitol could trigger 'The Storm,' an event where they hope Trump's foes will be punished in mass executions," *Business Insider*, January 7, 2021. Online: https://www.businessinsider.in/politics/world/news/qanon-supporters-believed-marching-on-the-capitol-could-trigger-the-storm-an-event-where-they-hope-trumps-foes-will-be-punished-in-mass-executions/articleshow/80157755.cms.

64 See Tom Jackman, "'QAnon shaman' sentenced to 41 months for role in Capitol riot," *The Washington Post,* November 17, 2021. Online: https://www.washingtonpost.com/local/legal-issues/jacob-chansley-qanon-shaman-sentence/2021/11/17/59d9ce26-47b1-11ec-95dc-5f2a96e00fa3_story.html.

65 See Rob Kuznia, Curt Devine, Nelli Black and Drew Griffin, "Stop the Steal's massive disinformation campaign connected to Roger Stone," CNN, November 14, 2020. Online: https://www.cnn.com/2020/11/13/business/stop-the-steal-disinformation-campaign-invs/index.html.

66 See Matt Labash, "Roger Stone, Political Animal," *The Weekly Standard*, November 5, 2007. Online: https://www.washingtonexaminer.com/weekly-standard/roger-stone-political-animal-15381. See also Michael E. Miller, "'It's insanity!': How the 'Brooks Brothers Riot' killed the 2000 recount in Miami," *The Washington Post*, November 15, 2018. Online: https://www.washingtonpost.com/history/2018/11/15/its-insanity-how-brooks-brothers-riot-killed-recount-miami/. See also Robert Costa, "Trump ends relationship with longtime political adviser Roger Stone," *The Washington Post*, August 8, 2015. Online: https://www.washingtonpost.com/news/post-politics/wp/2015/08/08/trump-ends-relationship-with-longtime-political-adviser-roger-stone/.

67 See Peter Baker, Maggie Haberman and Sharon LaFraniere, "Trump Commutes Sentence of Roger Stone in Case He Long Denounced," *The New York Times*, July 10, 2020. Online: https://www.nytimes.com/2020/07/10/us/politics/trump-roger-stone-clemency.html. See also Doha Madani, "Trump pardons Roger Stone, Paul Manafort, Charles Kushner and others," NBC News, December 23, 2020. Online: https://www.nbcnews.com/politics/politics-news/trump-pardons-roger-stone-paul-manafort-charles-kushner-others-n1252307.

68 See Lamar White Jr., "Theater of the Absurd: How A Louisiana Extremist Helped the Trump Campaign Manufacture Outrage," *Bayou Brief*, November 8, 2020. Online: https://www.bayoubrief.com/2020/11/08/theater-of-the-absurd-how-a-louisiana-extremist-helped-the-trump-campaign-manufacture-outrage/.

69 See Michael Edison Hayden, "Far Right Resurrects Roger Stone's #StopTheSteal During Vote Count," *Hatewatch* (SPLC), November 6, 2020. Online: https://www.splcenter.org/hatewatch/2020/11/06/far-right-resurrects-roger-stones-stopthesteal-during-vote-count.

70 See Charles Homans, "How 'Stop the Steal' Captured the American Right," *The New York Times*, July 19, 2022. Online: https://www.nytimes.com/2022/07/19/magazine/stop-the-steal.html.

71 See Rob Kuznia, Curt Devine, Nelli Black and Drew Griffin, "Stop the Steal's massive disinformation campaign connected to Roger Stone," CNN, Noivember 14, 2020. Online: https://www.cnn.com/2020/11/13/business/stop-the-steal-disinformation-campaign-invs/index.html.

72 See "Facebook: From Election to Insurrection," Avaaz, March 18, 2021. Online: https://secure.avaaz.org/campaign/en/facebook_election_insurrection/.

73 See Atlantic Council DFR Lab, "#StopTheSteal: Timeline of Social Media and Extremist Activities Leading to 1/6 Insurrection," *Just Security*, February 10, 2021. Online: https://www.justsecurity.org/74622/stopthesteal-timeline-of-social-media-and-extremist-activities-leading-to-1-6-insurrection/.

74 See Michael Edison Hayden, "Law Firm Tied to Far-Right Fringe Registers Stop the Steal LLC in Alabama," *Hatewatch* (SPLC), December 18, 2020. Online: https://

www.splcenter.org/hatewatch/2020/12/18/law-firm-tied-far-right-fringe-registers-stop-steal-llc-alabama.

75 See David Neiwert, "Michelle Malkin chooses the white nationalist side in the internecine 'Groyper War,' gets fired," *Daily Kos*, November 18, 2019. Online: https://www.dailykos.com/stories/2019/11/18/1900398/-Michelle-Malkin-chooses-the-white-nationalist-side-in-the-internecine-Groyper-War-gets-fired. See also David Neiwert, "Here's Malkin at the 2020 America First PAC convention of Groypers," Twitter, March 30, 2022. Online: https://twitter.com/david-neiwert/status/1509237741967458305.

76 See Olivia Little, "'Stop The Steal' organizer bragged about a phone call with 'people from the White House' weeks before the insurrection," Media Matters, January 28, 2021. Online: https://www.mediamatters.org/january-6-insurrection/stop-steal-organizer-bragged-about-phone-call-people-white-house-weeks.

77 See Atlantic Council DFR Lab, "#StopTheSteal: Timeline of Social Media and Extremist Activities Leading to 1/6 Insurrection," *Just Security*, February 10, 2021. Online: https://www.justsecurity.org/74622/stopthesteal-timeline-of-social-media-and-extremist-activities-leading-to-1-6-insurrection/.

78 See Casey Tolan, "Former Trump campaign staffers worked on National Mall rally the day of the Capitol riot," CNN, January 19, 2021. Online: https://www.cnn.com/2021/01/19/politics/capitol-riot-permits-trump-campaign-invs/index.html.

79 See David Neiwert, "Trail from Oath Keepers to Trump via Roger Stone comes into view with sedition guilty plea," *Daily Kos*, March 3, 2022. Online: https://www.dailykos.com/stories/2022/3/3/2083716/-Trail-from-Oath-Keepers-to-Trump-via-Roger-Stone-comes-into-view-with-sedition-guilty-plea.

80 See Valerie Wirtschafter and Chris Meserole, "Prominent political podcasters played key role in spreading the 'Big Lie'," *TechStream* (Brookings), January 4, 2022. Online: https://www.brookings.edu/techstream/prominent-political-podcasters-played-key-role-in-spreading-the-big-lie/.

81 See Harper Neidig, "Bannon predicted 'all hell is going to break loose tomorrow' after Jan. 5 call with Trump," *The Hill*, July 12, 2022. Online: https://thehill.com/homenews/house/3556166-bannon-predicted-all-hell-is-going-to-break-loose-tomorrow-after-jan-5-call-with-trump/.

82 See David Gilbert, "Steve Bannon Urged Facebook Followers to 'Take Action' on Eve of Capitol Riot," *Vice*, January 15, 2021. Online: https://www.vice.com/en/article/n7vqgb/steve-bannon-urged-facebook-followers-to-take-action-on-eve-of-capitol-riot.

83 See Kat Lonsdorf, Courtney Dorning, Amy Isackson, Mary Louise Kelly, and Ailsa Chang, "A timeline of how the Jan. 6 attack unfolded — including who said what and when," National Public Radio, June 9, 2022. Online: https://www.npr.org/2022/01/05/1069977469/a-timeline-of-how-the-jan-6-attack-unfolded-including-who-said-what-and-when.

84 See Jason Stanley, "Movie at the Ellipse: A Study in Fascist Propaganda," *Just Security*, February 4, 2021. Online: https://www.justsecurity.org/74504/movie-at-the-ellipse-a-study-in-fascist-propaganda/.

85 See "'Let's have trial by combat' over election—Giuliani" (video), Reuters, January 6, 2021. Online: https://www.reuters.com/video/watch/idOVDU2NS9R.

86 See Micheal Kranish, "Mo Brooks urged a Jan. 6 crowd to 'fight.' Now his actions long before the insurrection face new scrutiny," *The Washington Post*, January 10,

2022. Online: https://www.washingtonpost.com/politics/2022/01/10/mo-brooks-jan6-eric-swalwell-lawsuit-insurrection/.

87   See "Cawthorn speaks at Trump rally before violent mob attacked Capitol" (video), *News & Observer*, January 12, 2021. Online: https://www.newsobserver.com/news/politics-government/national-politics/article248444495.html.

88   See Hunter Walker, "EXCLUSIVE: Jan. 6 Protest Organizers Say They Participated in 'Dozens' of Planning Meetings With Members of Congress and White House Staff," *Rolling Stone*, October 24, 2021. Online: https://www.rollingstone.com/politics/politics-news/exclusive-jan-6-organizers-met-congress-white-house-1245289/.

89   See Casey Tolan, Curt Devine, Drew Griffin and Scott Bronstein, "GOP lawmakers' fiery language under more scrutiny after deadly Capitol riot," CNN, January 13, 2021. Online: https://www.cnn.com/2021/01/12/politics/gop-lawmakers-fiery-language-under-scrutiny-invs/index.html.

90   See Paul Gosar, "Biden should concede," Twitter, January 6, 2021. Online: https://twitter.com/DrPaulGosar/status/1346865455571599363.

91   See Teo Armus, "A 'Stop the Steal' organizer, now banned by Twitter, said three GOP lawmakers helped plan his D.C. rally," *The Washington Post*, January 13, 2021. Online: https://www.washingtonpost.com/nation/2021/01/13/ali-alexander-capitol-biggs-gosar/.

92   See Katie Benner, Catie Edmondson, Luke Broadwater and Alan Feuer, "Meadows and the Band of Loyalists: How They Fought to Keep Trump in Power," *The New York Times*, December 15, 2021. Online: https://www.nytimes.com/2021/12/15/us/politics/trump-meadows-republicans-congress-jan-6.html.

93   See Paul Gosar, "Great meeting today with @realDonaldTrump," Twitter, December 21, 2020. Online: https://twitter.com/DrPaulGosar/status/1341256607636705281.

94   See Josh Hawley, "Somebody has to stand up," Twitter, December 30, 2020. Online: https://twitter.com/HawleyMO/status/1344505790854553602.

95   See Alex Shephard, "Trump Blew Up Ted Cruz's Cynical Plan to Contest the Election," *The New Republic*, January 5, 2021. Online: https://newrepublic.com/article/160778/trump-blew-ted-cruzs-cynical-plan-contest-election.

96   See Dominic Montanaro, "Timeline: How One Of The Darkest Days In American History Unfolded," National Public Radio, January 7, 2021. Online: https://www.npr.org/2021/01/07/954384999/timeline-how-one-of-the-darkest-days-in-american-history-unfolded.

97   See "Day of Rage: How Trump Supporters Took the U.S. Capitol" (video), *The New York Times,* June 30, 2021. Online: https://www.nytimes.com/video/us/politics/100000007606996/capitol-riot-trump-supporters.html.

98   See David A. Graham, "The Paperwork Coup," *The Atlantic*, December 15, 2021. Online: https://www.theatlantic.com/ideas/archive/2021/12/trumps-coup-before-january-6/620998/.

99   See Michael S. Schmidt and Maggie Haberman, "The Lawyer Behind the Memo on How Trump Could Stay in Office," *The New York Times*, October 2, 2021. Online: https://www.nytimes.com/2021/10/02/us/politics/john-eastman-trump-memo.html.

100 See Luke Broadwater and Alan Feuer, "Jan. 6 Panel and State Officials Seek Answers on Fake Trump Electors," *The New York Times*, January 21, 2022. Online: https://www.nytimes.com/2022/01/21/us/politics/jan-6-fake-trump-electors.html.

101 See Tim Dickinson, "Trump Adviser Worried He's Not Getting Enough Credit for Trying to Ruin American Democracy," *Rolling Stone*, December 28, 2021. Online: https://www.rollingstone.com/politics/politics-news/jan6-peter-navarro-ted-cruz-green-bay-sweep-1276742/.

102 See Michael S. Schmidt and Maggie Haberman, "The Lawyer Behind the Memo on How Trump Could Stay in Office," *The New York Times*, October 2, 2021. Online: https://www.nytimes.com/2021/10/02/us/politics/john-eastman-trump-memo.html.

103 See Michael S. Schmidt and Maggie Haberman, "Trump Aides Prepared Insurrection Act Order During Debate Over Protests," *The New York Times*, June 25, 2021. Online: https://www.nytimes.com/2021/06/25/us/politics/trump-insurrection-act-protests.html.

104 See "Tom Cotton: Send In the Troops," *The New York Times*, June 3, 2020. Online: https://www.nytimes.com/2020/06/03/opinion/tom-cotton-protests-military.html.

105 See Devlin Barrett and Spencer S. Hsu, "How Trump's flirtation with an anti-insurrection law inspired Jan. 6 insurrection," *The Washington Post*, January 23, 2022. Online: https://www.washingtonpost.com/national-security/stewart-rhodes-insurrection-act-trump/2022/01/23/fa009626-7c47-11ec-bf02-f9e24ccef149_story.html.

106 See Will Bunch, "Is the 'smoking gun' in Trump's Jan. 6 attempted coup hiding in plain sight?", *The Philadelphia Inquirer*, January 3, 2022. Online: https://www.inquirer.com/opinion/trump-january-6-letter-insurrection-act-20220103.html.

107 See Betsy Woodruff Swan, "Read the never-issued Trump order that would have seized voting machines," *Politico*, January 21, 2022. Online: https://www.politico.com/news/2022/01/21/read-the-never-issued-trump-order-that-would-have-seized-voting-machines-527572.

108 See David E. Sanger and Eric Schmitt, "Trump Stacks the Pentagon and Intel Agencies With Loyalists. To What End?," *The New York Times*, November 11, 2020. Online: https://www.nytimes.com/2020/11/11/us/politics/trump-pentagon-intelligence-iran.html.

109 See "Emma Brown, Jon Swaine, Jacqueline Alemany, Josh Dawsey and Tom Hamburger, "Election denier who circulated Jan. 6 PowerPoint says he met with Meadows at White House," *The Washington Post*, December 11, 2021. Online: https://www.washingtonpost.com/investigations/phil-waldron-mark-meadows-powerpoint/2021/12/11/4ea67938-59df-11ec-9a18-a506cf3aa31d_story.html.

110 See Susan B. Glasser, ""You're Gonna Have a Fucking War": Mark Milley's Fight to Stop Trump from Striking Iran," *The New Yorker*, July 15, 2021. Online: https://www.newyorker.com/news/letter-from-bidens-washington/youre-gonna-have-a-fucking-war-mark-milleys-fight-to-stop-trump-from-striking-iran.

111 See Dan Lamothe, "The time to question election results has passed, all living former defense secretaries say," *The Washington Post*, January 3, 2021. Online: https://www.washingtonpost.com/national-security/former-defense-secretaries-rebuke-trump-election/2021/01/03/1c708f64-4de5-11eb-b2e8-3339e73d9da2_story.html.

112 See Mary Papenfuss, "As D.C. Clashes Erupt, Trump Sics Police On 'Antifa Scum' In Stunningly Vicious Tweet," *Huffpost*, November 15, 2020. Online: https://www.huffpost.com/entry/trump-antifa-proud-boys-violence-tweet_n_5fb0b47ac5b68baab0fce6e7.

113 See David Neiwert, "Proud Boys torch their claims to nonviolence with hate crime attacks on Black churches in D.C.," *Daily Kos*, December 17, 2020. Online: https://

www.dailykos.com/stories/2020/12/17/2002658/--Reminiscent-of-cross-burnings-Proud-Boys-torch-pretense-along-with-D-C-churches-BLM-signs.

114 See Sean Boynton, "Trump moves to label Antifa a terrorist organization, bar members from entering U.S.," *Global News*, January 5, 2021. Online: https://globalnews.ca/news/7557777/trump-antifa-immigration/.

115 See Michael M. Grynbaum, Davey Alba and Reid J. Epstein, "How Pro-Trump Forces Pushed a Lie About Antifa at the Capitol Riot," *The New York Times*, March 1, 2021. Online: https://www.nytimes.com/2021/03/01/us/politics/antifa-conspiracy-capitol-riot.html.

116 See Olivier Knox, "The Meadows texts and the weird PowerPoint take Jan. 6 inside the White House," *The Washington Post*, December 14, 2021. Online: https://www.washingtonpost.com/politics/2021/12/14/meadows-texts-weird-powerpoint-take-jan-6-inside-white-house/.

117 See Jeremy Barr, "Fox News hosts urged Meadows to have Trump stop Jan. 6 violence, texts show," *The Washington Post*, December 13, 2021. Online: https://www.washingtonpost.com/media/2021/12/13/fox-ingraham-hannity-kilmeade-jan-6-trump-texts/.

118 See Louis Jacobson, "What happened during the Jan. 6 call between Donald Trump and Kevin McCarthy?," *Politifact*, April 26, 2021. Online: https://www.politifact.com/article/2021/apr/26/what-happened-during-jan-6-call-between-donald-tru/.

119 See Charles R. Davis and Lauren Frias, "A timeline of how Trump incited his followers to storm the Capitol and attempt a coup," *Business Insider*, January 6, 2021. Online: https://www.businessinsider.com/how-trump-in-final-weeks-incited-his-followers-to-storm-the-capitol-2021-1.

120 See Ryan Lucas, "Where the Jan. 6 insurrection investigation stands, one year later," National Public Radio, January 6, 2022. Online: https://www.npr.org/2022/01/06/1070736018/jan-6-anniversary-investigation-cases-defendants-justice.

121 See Jie Jenny Zou and Erin B. Logan, "Key facts to know about the Jan. 6 insurrection," *The Los Angeles Times*, January 5, 2022. Online: https://www.latimes.com/politics/story/2022-01-05/by-the-numbers-jan-6-anniversary.

122 See Tim Elfrink, "He wore a QAnon shirt while chasing police on Jan. 6. Now he says he was deceived by 'a pack of lies,'" *The Washington Post*, June 8, 2021. Online: https://www.washingtonpost.com/nation/2021/06/08/douglas-jensen-qanon-conspiracy/.

123 See Ashley Cole, "St. Louis attorney's statement on client not being pardoned in Capitol riot," KSDK-TV, January 20, 2021. Online: https://www.ksdk.com/article/news/local/st-louis-attorneys-statement-on-client-not-being-pardoned-in-capitol-riot/63-32553345-a5f3-4a13-9196-b4251643df56.

124 See David Neiwert, "Bitter about being abandoned by Trump, Proud Boys' chats reveal preparations for 'absolute war,'" *Daily Kos*, May 18, 2021. Online: https://www.dailykos.com/stories/2021/5/18/2031008/-Bitter-about-being-abandoned-by-Trump-Proud-Boys-chats-reveal-preparations-for-absolute-war.

Chapter 4: Patriots of the Seditionist Kind

1 See J.D. Vance, "The prosecution of Rittenhouse is a disgrace," Twitter, November 10, 2021. Online: https://twitter.com/JDVance1/status/1458483554556514304.

2 See David Neiwert, "Tucker's gaslighting campaign is about more than just justifying the Jan. 6 Capitol insurrection," *Daily Kos*, November 4, 2021. Online: https://

www.dailykos.com/stories/2021/11/4/2062386/-Tucker-s-gaslighting-campaign-is-about-more-than-just-justifying-the-Jan-6-Capitol-insurrection.

3 See Tess Owen, "Capitol Rioters in Jail's 'Patriot Wing' Have Their Own Rituals and a Growing Fan Base," *Vice*, October 21, 2021. Online: https://www.vice.com/en/article/akvwjp/january-6-rioters-jailed-together-forming-rituals-fanbase.

4 See George Thomas, "'America Is a Republic, Not a Democracy' Is a Dangerous—And Wrong—Argument," *The Atlantic*, November 22, 2020. Online: https://www.theatlantic.com/ideas/archive/2020/11/yes-constitution-democracy/616949/.

5 See Robert Welch, "Republics and Democracies," *The New American*, May 14, 2013: Online: https://thenewamerican.com/republics-and-democracies/.

6 See Joshua Keating, "The Real Reason Why Republicans Keep Saying 'We're a Republic, Not a Democracy'," *Slate*, October 13, 2020. Online: https://slate.com/news-and-politics/2020/10/republic-democracy-mike-lee-astra-taylor.html.

7 See Zack Beauchamp, "Sen. Mike Lee's tweets against 'democracy,' explained," *Vox*, October 8, 2020. Online: https://www.vox.com/policy-and-politics/21507713/mike-lee-democracy-republic-trump-2020.

8 See "'Patriot' Movement," Anti-Defamation League, June 26, 2017. Online: https://www.adl.org/resources/glossary-term/patriot-movement.

9 See James Aho, *The Politics of Righteousness: Idaho Christian Patriotism* (Seattle: University of Washington Press, 1995). Online: https://books.google.com/books/about/The_Politics_of_Righteousness.html.

10 See J.M. Berger, "The Strategy of Violent White Supremacy Is Evolving," *The Atlantic*, August 7, 2019. Online: https://www.theatlantic.com/ideas/archive/2019/08/the-new-strategy-of-violent-white-supremacy/595648/.

11 See David Neiwert, *In God's Country: The Patriot Movement and the Pacific Northwest* (Pullman: Washington State University Press, 1999).

12 See Alexander Zaitchik, "Meet Alex Jones," *Rolliing Stone*, March 2, 2011. Online: https://www.rollingstone.com/culture/culture-news/meet-alex-jones-175845/.

13 See David Neiwert, "The Minutemen's Demise," Type Investigations, July 23, 2012. Online: https://www.typeinvestigations.org/investigation/2012/07/23/minutemens-demise/.

14 See David Neiwert, "Chris Simcox's Fall From Minuteman Heights Ends in 19 1/2-Year Sentence For Molesting Girls," *Hatewatch* (SPLC), July 13, 2016. Online: https://www.splcenter.org/hatewatch/2016/07/13/chris-simcoxs-fall-minuteman-heights-ends-19-12-year-sentence-molesting-girls.

15 See Mark Potok, "The Patriot Movement Explodes," *Hatewatch* (SPLC), March 1, 2012. Online: https://www.splcenter.org/fighting-hate/intelligence-report/2012/patriot-movement-explodes.

16 See David Neiwert, "The Tea Party's Armed Extremists," Type Investigations, November 22, 2010. Online: https://www.typeinvestigations.org/investigation/2010/11/22/tea-partys-armed-extremists/.

17 See Rob Walker, "The Shifting Symbolism of the Gadsden Flag," *The New Yorker*, October 2, 2016. Online: https://www.newyorker.com/news/news-desk/the-shifting-symbolism-of-the-gadsden-flag.

18 See Hatewatch Staff, "War in the West: The Bundy Ranch Standoff and the American Radical Right," *Hatewatch* (SPLC), July 10, 2014. Online: https://www.splcenter.org/20140709/war-west-bundy-ranch-standoff-and-american-radical-right.

19 See Mark Potok, "Alleged Las Vegass Cop Killers in 'Patriot' Movement, Warned of 'Sacrifices'," *Hatewatch* (SPLC), June 9, 2014. Online: https://www.splcenter.org/hatewatch/2014/06/09/alleged-las-vegas-cop-killers-'patriot'-movement-warned-'sacrifices'.

20 See Paul Bruski, "Yellow Gadsden flag, prominent in Capitol takeover, carries a long and shifting history," *The Conversation*, January 6, 2021. Online: https://the-conversation.com/yellow-gadsden-flag-prominent-in-capitol-takeover-carries-a-long-and-shifting-history-145142. See also Dan MacGuill, "Did Woman Who Died at Capitol Riot Carry a 'Don't Tread on Me' Flag?," *Snopes*, January 12, 2021. Online: https://www.snopes.com/fact-check/rosanne-boyland-trampled-flag/. See also "Capitol rioters' causes of death released; Capitol officer's still 'pending'," Fox 5 News, April 7, 2021. Online: https://www.fox5dc.com/news/capitol-rioters-cause-of-death-information-released-capitol-officers-cause-of-death-pending.

21 See Washington Post Photo Staff, "Cleaning up the damage and destruction at the U.S. Capitol," *The Washington Post*, January 8, 2021. Online: https://www.washingtonpost.com/graphics/photography/2021/01/07/photos-aftermath-capitol-riot/.

22 "Oath Keepers," Southern Poverty Law Center "Antigovernment Extremist Group" Profile. Online: https://www.splcenter.org/fighting-hate/extremist-files/group/oath-keepers.

23 See Sam Jackson, *Oath Keepers: Patriotism and the Edge of Violence in a Right-Wing Government Group* (New York: Columbia University Press, 2020), pp. 142-148.

24 See Alan Maimon, "Oath Keepers pledges to prevent dictatorship in United States," *Las Vegas Review-Journal*, October 18, 2019. Online: https://www.reviewjournal.com/news/oath-keepers-pledges-to-prevent-dictatorship-in-united-states/.

25 See David Neiwert, "Will Ex-military 'Patriots' Form A More Dangerous Kind Of Militias?," *Crooks and Liars*, March 5, 2009. Online: https://crooksandliars.com/david-neiwert/willl-ex-military-patriots-form-more.

26 See David Neiwert, "'Oath Keepers' Leader Arrested For Child Rape; Cops Find Stolen Grenade Launcher In His House," *Crooks and Liars*, January 21, 2010. Online: https://crooksandliars.com/david-neiwert/tea-party-leader-arrested-rape.

27 See David Neiwert, "After Dyer's Rape Arrest, 'Oath Keepers' Disavow Any Association With Onetime Key Figure," *Crooks and Liars,* January 21, 2010. Online: https://crooksandliars.com/david-neiwert/after-dyers-rape-arrest-oath-keepers.

28 See David Neiwert, "Tasha Adams, Stewart Rhodes' ex-wife, spills tea over his paranoid and abusive career in extremism," *Daily Kos*, February 1, 2022. Online: https://www.dailykos.com/stories/2022/2/1/2077991/-Tasha-Adams-Stewart-Rhodes-ex-wife-spills-tea-over-his-paranoid-and-abusive-career-in-extremism.

29 See "Examining Extremism: The Oath Keepers," Center for Strategic Studies, June 17, 2021. Online: https://www.csis.org/blogs/examining-extremism/examining-extremism-oath-keepers.

30 See Eric McQueen, "Examining Extremism: The Oath Keepers," Center for Strategic Studies, June 17, 2021. Online: https://www.csis.org/blogs/examining-extremism/examining-extremism-oath-keepers

31 See Justine Sharrock, "Oath Keepers and the Age of Treason," *Mother Jones*, March/April 2010. Online: https://www.motherjones.com/politics/2010/02/oath-keepers/.

32 See David Neiwert, "Antigovernment 'Patriots' Gather Near Scene of Nevada Rancher's Dispute Over Cattle Grazing Rights," *Hatewatch* (SPLC), April 10, 2014.

Online: https://www.splcenter.org/hatewatch/2014/04/10/antigovernment-patriots-gather-near-scene-nevada-ranchers-dispute-over-cattle-grazing.

33 See Hatewatch Staff, "War in the West: The Bundy Ranch Standoff and the American Radical Right," *Hatewatch* (SPLC), July 10, 2014. Online: https://www.splcenter.org/20140709/war-west-bundy-ranch-standoff-and-american-radical-right.

34 See David Neiwert, "Militiamen and Oath Keepers Drew Weapons, Threatened to Kill Each Other," *Hatewatch* (SPLC), May 2, 2014. Online: https://www.splcenter.org/hatewatch/2014/05/02/militiamen-and-oath-keepers-drew-weapons-threatened-kill-each-other.

35 See David Neiwert, "Antigovernment 'Patriots' Show Up at Military Recruiting Centers Nationwide to 'Protect the Protectors,'" *Hatewatch* (SPLC), August 4, 2015. Online: https://www.splcenter.org/hatewatch/2015/08/04/antigovernment-'patriots'-show-military-recruiting-centers-nationwide-'protect-protecters'.

36 See David Neiwert, "Oath Keepers Descend Upon Oregon With Dreams of Confrontation Over Mining Dispute," *Hatewatch* (SPLC), April 23, 2015. Online: https://www.splcenter.org/hatewatch/2015/04/23/oath-keepers-descend-upon-oregon-dreams-armed-confrontation-over-mining-dispute.

37 See David Neiwert, "'Patriots' Declare Victory for Oregon Mine After Judge Issues Stay for BLM Enforcement," *Hatewatch* (SPLC), May 26, 2015. Online: https://www.splcenter.org/hatewatch/2015/05/26/'patriots'-declare-victory-oregon-mine-after-judge-issues-stay-blm-enforcement.

38 See "Interview With Spencer Sunshine On The Oregon Militia Occupation," *It's Going Down*, January 11, 2016. Online: https://itsgoingdown.org/interview-spencer-sunshine-oregon-militia-occupation/.

39 See "Appendix: Response to the Malheur Occupation," from "Up in Arms: A Guide to Oregon's Patriot Movement," Rural Organizing Project, October 2016. Online: https://rop.org/uia/section-i/appendix-response-malheur-occupation/.

40 See David Neiwert, "The right-wing Oregon occupiers have a martyr now, and that should worry everyone," *The Washington Post*, February 10, 2016. Online: https://www.washingtonpost.com/posteverything/wp/2016/02/10/the-right-wing-oregon-occupiers-have-a-martyr-now-and-that-should-worry-everyone/.

41 See Bill Morlin, "Four Arrests at Oregon Refuge End 41-Day Standoff," *Hatewatch* (SPLC), February 11, 2016. Online: https://www.splcenter.org/hatewatch/2016/02/11/four-arrests-oregon-refuge-end-41-day-standoff.

42 See Jessica Garrison, Ken Bensinger, and Slavador Hernandez, "Person One," *BuzzFeed News*, March 4, 2021. Online: https://www.buzzfeednews.com/article/jessicagarrison/stewart-rhodes-oath-keepers-early-history-conflicts.

43 See "Racism & Identity in the Patriot Movement," from "Up in Arms: A Guide to Oregon's Patriot Movement," Rural Organizing Project, October 2016. Online: https://rop.org/uia/section-i/the-patriot-movement-historically-nationally/racism-identity-movement/.

44 See "Racism & Identity in the Patriot Movement," from "Up in Arms: A Guide to Oregon's Patriot Movement," Rural Organizing Project, October 2016. Online: https://rop.org/uia/section-i/the-patriot-movement-historically-nationally/racism-identity-movement/.

45 See Angelo Fichera and Saranac Hale Spencer, "Trump's Long History With Conspiracy Theories," FactCheck.org, October 20, 2020. Online: https://www.factcheck.org/2020/10/trumps-long-history-with-conspiracy-theories/.

46 See David Neiwert, "Donald Trump Claims To Be The Ideal Tea Party Candidate: 'I Represent A Lot Of The Ingredients Of The Tea Party'," *Crooks and Liars*, April 7, 2011. Online: https://crooksandliars.com/david-neiwert/donald-trump-claims-be-ideal-tea-par.

47 See David Neiwert, "Oath Keepers as travesty: 'Patriot' group's Trump-loving authoritarianism may affect election," *Daily Kos*, October 6, 2020. Online: https://www.dailykos.com/stories/2020/10/6/1984210/-Oath-Keepers-as-travesty-Patriot-group-s-Trump-loving-authoritarianism-may-affect-election.

48 See David Neiwert, "Do the far-right Oath Keepers have an official role with the Trump-Pence campaign?," *Daily Kos*, October 11, 2019. Online: https://www.dailykos.com/stories/2019/10/11/1891802/-Do-the-far-right-Oath-Keepers-have-an-official-role-with-the-Trump-Pence-campaign.

49 See David Neiwert, "Militiamen and nascent neo-Nazi terrorists jump to attention when Trump tweets about 'civil war'," *Daily Kos*, October 4, 2019. Online: https://www.dailykos.com/stories/2019/10/4/1889899/-Militiamen-and-nascent-neo-Nazi-terrorists-jump-to-attention-when-Trump-tweets-about-civil-war.

50 See Ryan Lenz, "The Oath Keepers didn't show up for their own protest of Maxine Waters," *Hatewatch* (SPLC), July 20, 2018. Online: https://www.splcenter.org/hatewatch/2018/07/20/oath-keepers-didnt-show-their-own-protest-maxine-waters.

51 See Amelia Templeton, "Militia Leader Warns Against Attending Portland Rally, Citing Legal Risks And White Nationalist Presence," Oregon Public Broadcasting, August 16, 2019. Online: https://www.opb.org/news/article/oath-keepers-militia-leader-portland-oregon-rally-warning/.

52 See David Neiwert, "Oath Keepers announce national 'Spartan' training program aimed at 'violent left'," *Hatewatch* (SPLC), August 23, 2018. Online: https://www.splcenter.org/hatewatch/2018/08/23/oath-keepers-announce-national-'spartan'-training-program-aimed-'violent-left'.

53 See David Neiwert, "'Civil war is here, right now': 'Patriots' urge Trump to empower militias to fight antifa in streets," *Daily Kos*, August 31, 2020. Online: https://www.dailykos.com/stories/2020/8/31/1974015/-Oath-Keepers-to-Trump-Send-out-the-militias-to-stop-antifascists-Marxist-takeover-of-America.

54 See David Neiwert, "Oath Keepers not only played key role in insurrection, they may have had some official help," *Daily Kos*, February 22, 2021. Online: https://www.dailykos.com/stories/2021/2/22/2017579/-As-Oath-Keepers-key-role-In-Jan-6-Capitol-siege-grows-clear-ties-to-law-enforcement-loom-larger.

55 See Jennifer Valentino-DeVries, Denise Lu, Eleanor Lutz and Alex Leeds Matthews, "A Small Group of Militants' Outsize Role in the Capitol Attack," *The New York Times*, February 21, 2021. Online: https://www.nytimes.com/interactive/2021/02/21/us/capitol-riot-attack-militants.html.

56 See U.S. Department of Justice, "Criminal Complaint," February 12, 2021. Online: https://www.justice.gov/file/1369066/download.

57 See Spencer S. Hsu and Aaron C. Davis, "Oath Keepers founder Stewart Rhodes was in direct contact with rioters before and during Capitol breach, U.S. alleges," *The Washington Post*, March 9, 2021. Online: https://www.washingtonpost.com/local/legal-issues/stewart-rhodes-oathkeepers-capitol-riot/2021/03/09/2c3d7fd8-808a-11eb-9ca6-54e187ee4939_story.html.

58 See David Neiwert, "Rhodes' speech at phony 'border crisis' rally shows how disinformation spreads on the right," *Daily Kos*, April 1, 2021. Online: https://www.dailykos.

com/stories/2021/4/1/2023982/-Indictment-looming-for-Jan-6-role-Oath-Keepers-chief-still-spreads-disinformation-at-the-border.

59 See David Neiwert, "Jan. 6 siege comes home to roost for Oath Keepers' Rhodes with 'seditious conspiracy' charge," *Daily Kos*, January 13, 2022. Online: https://www.dailykos.com/stories/2022/1/13/2074491/-Jan-6-siege-comes-home-to-roost-for-Oath-Keepers-Rhodes-with-seditious-conspiracy-charge.

60 See Spencer S. Hsu, Rachel Weiner and Tom Jackman, "U.S.: Oath Keepers, Rhodes attacked 'bedrock of democracy' on Jan. 6," *The Washington Post*, October 3, 2022. Online: https://www.washingtonpost.com/dc-md-va/2022/10/03/oath-keepers-trial-openings-rhodes/.

61 See Jason Wilson, "Stewart Rhodes Found Guilty of Seditious Conspiracy," *Hatewatch* (Southern Poverty Law Center), November 30, 2022. Online: https://www.splcenter.org/hatewatch/2022/11/30/stewart-rhodes-found-guilty-seditious-conspiracy.

62 See James Brooks, "At Alaska trial, Oath Keepers founder says group was acting in 'counter-revolution'," *Alaska Beacon*, December 20, 2022. Online: https://alaska-beacon.com/2022/12/20/at-alaska-trial-oath-keepers-founder-says-group-was-acting-in-counter-revolution/. See also Liz Ruskin, "Oath Keeper founder Stewart Rhodes testifies in Alaska Rep. Eastman's defense," Alaska Public Media, December 19, 2022. Online: https://alaskapublic.org/2022/12/19/oath-keeper-founder-stewart-rhodes-testifies-in-alaska-rep-eastmans-defense/.

Chapter 5: Proud of Your Boys

1 See David Neiwert, "Portland far-right rally once again quickly turns violent as march becomes a riot," *Hatewatch* (SPLC), July 3, 2018. Online: https://www.splcenter.org/hatewatch/2018/07/03/portland-far-right-rally-once-again-quickly-turns-violent-march-becomes-riot.

2 See Hatewatch Staff, "Facebook's fight club: how the Proud Boys use the social media platform to vet their fighters," *Hatewatch* (SPLC), August 2, 2018. Online: https://www.splcenter.org/hatewatch/2018/08/02/facebooks-fight-club-how-proud-boys-use-social-media-platform-vet-their-fighters.

3 See Cassie Miller, "Why are the Proud Boys so violent? Ask Gavin McInnes," *Hatewatch* (SPLC), October 18, 2018. Online: https://www.splcenter.org/hatewatch/2018/10/18/why-are-proud-boys-so-violent-ask-gavin-mcinnes.

4 See "RUFIO PANMAN Patriot Who Knocked Out Masked, ANTIFA Commie Thug Joins Infowars LIVE" (video), YouTube, July 7, 2018. Online: https://www.youtube.com/watch?v=2orRPKbRl4M.

5 See David Neiwert, "We know Ethan Nordean is a public menace," Twitter, January 26, 2021. Online: https://twitter.com/DavidNeiwert/status/1354266157126012929.

6 See Richard Read, "He led the Proud Boys in the Capitol riot and shamed his town," *Los Angeles Times*, May 16, 2021. Online: https://www.latimes.com/world-nation/story/2021-05-16/proud-boys-father-nordean.

7 See Andy Campbell, *We Are Proud Boys: How a Right-Wing Street Gang Ushered In a New Era of American Extremism* (New York: Hatchette Books, 2022), pp. 13-38.

8 See Vanessa Grigoriadis, "The Edge of Hip: Vice, the Brand," *The New York Times*, September 28, 2003. Online: https://www.nytimes.com/2003/09/28/style/the-edge-of-hip-vice-the-brand.html.

9 See Gavin McInnes, "Transphobia is Perfectly Natural," *Thought Catalog*, August 2014. Online: https://www.doc-developpement-durable.org/file/programmes-de-sensibilisations/transphobie/transphobia-is-perfectly-natural_Gender%20Identity%20Watch.pdf.

10 See "Proud Boys," Southern Poverty Law Center "Hate Group" profile. Online: https://www.splcenter.org/fighting-hate/extremist-files/group/proud-boys.

11 See Gavin McInnes, "Introducing the Proud Boys," *Taki's Magazine*, Septmber 15, 2016. Online: https://www.takimag.com/article/introducing_the_proud_boys_gavin_mcinnes/.

12 See David Neiwert, "How the 'cultural Marxism' hoax began, and why it's spreading into the mainstream," *Daily Kos*, January 23, 2019. Online: https://www.dailykos.com/stories/2019/1/23/1828527/-How-the-cultural-Marxism-hoax-began-and-why-it-s-spreading-into-the-mainstream.

13 See Martin Jay, "Dialectic of Counter-Enlightenment: The Frankfurt School as Scapegoat of the Lunatic Fringe," *Salmagundi Magazine*, December 22, 2011. Online: https://web.archive.org/web/20111124045123/http:/cms.skidmore.edu/salmagundi/backissues/168-169/martin-jay-frankfurt-school-as-scapegoat.cfm.

14 See Claudio Corradetti, "The Frankfurt School and Critical Theory," Internet Encylopedia of Philosophy. Online: https://iep.utm.edu/critical-theory-frankfurt-school/.

15 See Patrick Buchanan, *The Death of the West: How Dying Populations and Immigrant Invasions Imperil Our Country and Civilization* (New York: St. Martin's Griffin, 2001), pp. 80-81.

16 See Anti-Defamation League, "14 Words," in "Hate on Display" database. Online: https://www.adl.org/resources/hate-symbol/14-words.

17 See Vic Berger, "Let's not forget," Twitter, November 4, 2019. Online: https://twitter.com/VicBergerIV/status/1191403799144849408.

18 See Cassie Miller, "McInnes, Molyneux, and 4chan: Investigating pathways to the alt-right," *Hatewatch* (SPLC), April 19, 2018. Online: https://www.splcenter.org/20180419/mcinnes-molyneux-and-4chan-investigating-pathways-alt-right.

19 See "Proud Boys," Southern Poverty Law Center "Hate Group" profile. Online: https://www.splcenter.org/fighting-hate/extremist-files/group/proud-boys.

20 See Zoë Beery, "How Fred Perry Polos Came to Symbolize Hate," *The Outline*, June 20, 2017. Online: https://theoutline.com/post/1760/fred-perry-polo-skinheads.

21 See Cassie Miller, "Why are the Proud Boys so violent? Ask Gavin McInnes," *Hatewatch* (SPLC), October 18, 2018. Online: https://www.splcenter.org/hatewatch/2018/10/18/why-are-proud-boys-so-violent-ask-gavin-mcinnes.

22 See Joseph Bernstein, "Here's How Breitbart And Milo Smuggled White Nationalism Into The Mainstream," *BuzzFeed News*, October 25, 2017. Online: https://www.buzzfeednews.com/article/josephbernstein/heres-how-breitbart-and-milo-smuggled-white-nationalism.

23 See David Neiwert, "Alt-Right Event in Seattle Devolves Into Chaos and Violence Outside, Truth-Twisting Inside," *Hatewatch* (SPLC), January 23, 2017. Online: https://www.splcenter.org/hatewatch/2017/01/23/alt-right-event-seattle-devolves-chaos-and-violence-outside-truth-twisting-inside. See also David Neiwert, "The Hokoana trial: Inside the 'Antifa' shooting incident the media don't want to talk about," *Daily Kos*, September 28, 2019. Online: https://www.dailykos.com/

stories/2019/9/28/1888326/-The-Hokoana-trial-Inside-the-Antifa-shooting-incident-the-media-don-t-want-to-talk-about.

24 See Anonymous Contributor, "Beating Milo: How Berkeley Defeated The Alt-Right's Biggest Troll," *It's Going Down*, February 7, 2017. Online: https://itsgoingdown.org/beating-milo-how-berkeley-defeated-alt-rights-biggest-troll/.

25 See Jeremy Peters, "Milo Yiannopoulos Resigns From Breitbart News After Pedophilia Comments," *The New York Times*, February 21, 2017. Online: https://www.nytimes.com/2017/02/21/business/milo-yiannopoulos-resigns-from-breitbart-news-after-pedophilia-comments.html.

26 See Amy B. Wang, "Pro-Trump rally in Berkeley turns violent as protesters clash with the president's supporters," *The Washington Post*, March 5, 2017. Online: https://www.washingtonpost.com/news/post-nation/wp/2017/03/05/pro-trump-rally-in-berkeley-turns-violent-as-protesters-clash-with-the-presidents-supporters/.

27 See David Neiwert, "Far Right Descends On Berkeley For 'Free Speech' And Planned Violence," *Hatewatch* (SPLC), April 17, 2017. Online: https://www.splcenter.org/hatewatch/2017/04/17/far-right-descends-berkeley-free-speech-and-planned-violence.

28 See Bill Morlin, "New 'Fight Club' Ready for Street Violence," *Hatewatch (SPLC), April 25, 2017.*

29 See David Neiwert, "Joey Gibson's rotating cast of followers has a history of violent extremists and white nationalists," *Daily Kos*, October 1, 2019. Online: https://www.dailykos.com/stories/2019/10/1/1889194/-Joey-Gibson-s-rotating-cast-of-followers-has-a-history-of-violent-extremists-and-white-nationalists.

30 See Andy Mattarese and Lauren Dake, "Joey Gibson aims to 'liberate conservatives' via his Patriot Prayer group," *The Daily Columbian*, July 2, 2017. Online: https://www.columbian.com/news/2017/jul/02/joey-gibson-aims-to-liberate-conservatives-via-his-patriot-prayer-group/.

31 See "Portland pro-Trump rally organizer: 'I can't control everybody'," CBS News, May 31, 2017. Online: https://www.cbsnews.com/news/portland-train-stabbing-suspect-jeremy-christian-free-speech-organizer-joey-gibson/.

32 See Jason Wilson, "Portland knife attack: tension high as 'free speech rally' set for weekend," *The Guardian*, May 29, 2017. Online: https://www.theguardian.com/us-news/2017/may/28/portland-knife-attack-free-speech-rally--sunday.

33 See David Neiwert, "Defiant Alt-Right 'Patriots' Encounter Portland's Simmering Anger After Train Killings," *Hatewatch* (SPLC), June 6, 2017. Online: https://www.splcenter.org/hatewatch/2017/06/06/defiant-alt-right-patriots-encounter-portlands-simmering-anger-after-train-killings.

34 See David Neiwert, "Joey Gibson's rotating cast of followers has a history of violent extremists and white nationalists," *Daily Kos*, October 1, 2019. Online: https://www.dailykos.com/stories/2019/10/1/1889194/-Joey-Gibson-s-rotating-cast-of-followers-has-a-history-of-violent-extremists-and-white-nationalists.

35 See Hatewatch Staff, "Live-Blog: ACT for America's "March Against Sharia" Rallies," *Hatewatch* (SPLC), June 10, 2017. Online: https://www.splcenter.org/hatewatch/2017/06/10/live-blog-act-americas-march-against-sharia-rallies.

36 See David Neiwert, "Evergreen State Protest By 'Patriot' Group Dwarfed By Angry Response," *Hatewatch* (SPLC), June 16, 2017. Online: https://www.splcenter.org/hatewatch/2017/06/16/evergreen-state-protest-patriot-group-dwarfed-angry-response.

37 See David Neiwert, "'Patriot' Rally Trolls Portland's Left for Violence, But Only Smatterings Occur," *Hatewatch* (SPLC), August 8, 2017. Online: https://www.splcenter.org/hatewatch/2017/08/07/patriot-rally-trolls-portlands-left-violence-only-smatterings-occur.

38 See Hatewatch Staff, "Alleged Charlottesville Driver Who Killed One Rallied With Alt-Right Vanguard America Group," *Hatewatch* (SPLC), August 13, 2017. Online: https://www.splcenter.org/hatewatch/2017/08/12/alleged-charlottesville-driver-who-killed-one-rallied-alt-right-vanguard-america-group. See also Richard Fausset and Alan Feuer, "Far-Right Groups Surge Into National View in Charlottesville," *The New York Times*, August 13, 2017. Online: https://www.nytimes.com/2017/08/13/us/far-right-groups-blaze-into-national-view-in-charlottesville.html.

39 See "Proud Boys," Southern Poverty Law Center "Hate Group" profile. Online: https://www.splcenter.org/fighting-hate/extremist-files/group/proud-boys.

40 See David Neiwert, "Seattle 'Patriot Prayer' Rally Takes a Twist As Leader Gibson Denounces Supremacists," *Hatewatch* (SPLC), August 15, 2017. Online: https://www.splcenter.org/hatewatch/2017/08/15/seattle-patriot-prayer-rally-takes-twist-leader-gibson-denounces-supremacists.

41 See David Neiwert, "Bay Area Weekend Rallies Turn South For 'Patriot Prayer,' End In Violence," *Hatewatch* (SPLC), August 29, 2017. Online: https://www.splcenter.org/hatewatch/2017/08/29/bay-area-weekend-rallies-turn-south-%E2%80%98patriot-prayer%E2%80%99-ends-violence.

42 See David Neiwert, "'Patriot Prayer' rally again heavily outnumbered, again ends with violence, close call," *Hatewatch* (SPLC), September 12, 2017. Online: https://www.splcenter.org/hatewatch/2017/09/12/patriot-prayer-rally-again-heavily-outnumbered-again-ends-violence-close-call.

43 See David Neiwert, "Patriot Prayer whips up anger in Seattle, but not much of a crowd," *Hatewatch* (SPLC), February 12, 2018. Online: https://www.splcenter.org/hatewatch/2018/02/12/patriot-prayer-whips-anger-seattle-not-much-crowd.

44 See Shane Dixon Kavanaugh, "Dueling demonstrations set for Portland days after protest ordinance fails," *The Oregonian,* November 15, 2018. Online: https://www.oregonlive.com/portland/2018/11/dueling_demonstrations_set_for.html.

45 See David Neiwert, "Portland far-right rally once again quickly turns violent as march becomes a riot," *Hatewatch* (SPLC), July 3, 2018. Online: https://www.splcenter.org/hatewatch/2018/07/03/portland-far-right-rally-once-again-quickly-turns-violent-march-becomes-riot. See also Elise Herron, "Opposing Groups Plan to Disrupt Portland City Council Meeting With Demands About Police Response to the ICE Occupation," *Willamette Week*, June 26, 2018. Online: https://www.wweek.com/news/2018/06/26/opposing-groups-plan-to-disrupt-portland-city-council-meeting-with-demands-about-police-response-to-the-ice-occupation/.

46 See David Neiwert, "Portland far-right 'Patriot' street brawlers in disarray as Proud Boys part ways amid violent talk," *Daily Kos*, February 11, 2019. Online: https://www.dailykos.com/stories/2019/2/11/1833783/-Portland-far-right-Patriot-street-brawlers-in-disarray-as-Proud-Boys-part-ways-amid-violent-talk.

47 See Ryan Hernandez, "What do the videos show of the brawl at Cider Riot? Take a look," *The Oregonian*, Auguat 15, 2019. Online: https://www.oregonlive.com/news/g66l-2019/08/4691c664a91003/what-do-the-videos-show-of-the-brawl-at-cider-riot-take-a-look.html.

48 See David Neiwert, "Gibson eyes new career for Patriot Prayer pushing 'constitutionalist' ideas to local officials," *Daily Kos*, February 21, 2019. Online: https://www.dailykos.com/stories/2019/2/21/1836534/-Gibson-eyes-new-career-for-Patriot-Prayer-pushing-constitutionalist-ideas-to-local-officials.

49 See David Neiwert, "Oregon log-truck drivers jam Salem to protest cap-and-trade bill, with militiamen joining along," *Daily Kos*, June 28, 2019. Online: https://www.dailykos.com/stories/2019/6/28/1867903/-Oregon-log-truck-drivers-jam-Salem-to-protest-cap-and-trade-bill-with-militiamen-joining-along.

50 See David Neiwert, "Far-right 'Patriots' lining up to defend Matt Shea, their man in the Washington Legislature," *Daily Kos*, January 11, 2020. Online: https://www.dailykos.com/stories/2020/1/11/1910065/-Far-right-Patriots-lining-up-to-defend-Matt-Shea-their-man-in-the-Washington-Legislature.

51 See David Neiwert, "'Patriot' Rally Trolls Portland's Left for Violence, But Only Smatterings Occur," *Hatewatch* (SPLC), August 8, 2017. Online: https://www.splcenter.org/hatewatch/2017/08/07/patriot-rally-trolls-portlands-left-violence-only-smatterings-occur.

52 See Brett Barrouquere, "In unusual alliance, Infowars, Joey Gibson teaming up for 'street army' teams," *Hatewatch* (SPLC), August 31, 2018. Online: https://www.splcenter.org/hatewatch/2018/08/31/unusual-alliance-infowars-joey-gibson-teaming-%E2%80%98street-army%E2%80%99-teams. See also Mikael Thalen, "MSNBC faces backlash after 'softball' interview with Patriot Prayer," *Daily Dot, August 31, 2020.*

53 See David Neiwert, "Far-right street brawlers just can't escape their violent, hateful, and bigoted roots," *Daily Kos*, May 27, 2019. Online: https://www.dailykos.com/stories/2019/5/27/1859465/-Far-right-street-brawlers-just-can-t-escape-their-violent-hateful-and-bigoted-roots.

54 See David Neiwert, "Portland far-right 'Patriot' street brawlers in disarray as Proud Boys part ways amid violent talk," *Daily Kos*, February 11, 2019. Online: https://www.dailykos.com/stories/2019/2/11/1833783/-Portland-far-right-Patriot-street-brawlers-in-disarray-as-Proud-Boys-part-ways-amid-violent-talk.

55 See Christopher Mathias, "Forgot to post this earlier," Twitter, August 4, 2018. Online: https://twitter.com/letsgomathias/status/1025969475344982017.

56 See David Neiwert, "Radio host Larson platforms a far-right veteran's plan to murder antifascists in their homes," *Daily Kos*, September 19, 2019. Online: https://www.dailykos.com/stories/2019/9/19/1886568/-Radio-host-Larson-platforms-a-far-right-veteran-s-plan-to-murder-antifascists-in-their-homes.

57 See Hatewatch Staff, "Facebook's fight club: how the Proud Boys use the social media platform to vet their fighters," *Hatewatch* (SPLC), August 2, 2018. Online: https://www.splcenter.org/hatewatch/2018/08/02/facebooks-fight-club-how-proud-boys-use-social-media-platform-vet-their-fighters.

58 See Heidi Beirich and Susy Buchanan, "2017: The Year in Hate and Extremism," *Hatewatch* (SPLC), February 11, 2018. Online: https://www.splcenter.org/fighting-hate/intelligence-report/2018/2017-year-hate-and-extremism.

59 See Jason Wilson, "Who are the Proud Boys, 'western chauvinists' involved in political violence?," *The Guardian*, July 14, 2018. Online: https://www.theguardian.com/world/2018/jul/14/proud-boys-far-right-portland-oregon.

60 See Cassie Miller, "Why are the Proud Boys so violent? Ask Gavin McInnes," *Hatewatch* (SPLC), October 18, 2018. Online: https://www.splcenter.org/hatewatch/2018/10/18/why-are-proud-boys-so-violent-ask-gavin-mcinnes.

61 See Colin Moynihan, "Two Members of Proud Boys Convicted in Brawl Near Republican Club," *The New York Times*, August 19, 2019. Online: https://www.nytimes.com/2019/08/19/nyregion/proud-boys-verdict-trial.html.

62 See Jason Wilson, "FBI now classifies far-right Proud Boys as 'extremist group', documents say," *The Guardian*, November 19, 2018. Online: https://www.theguardian.com/world/2018/nov/19/proud-boys-fbi-classification-extremist-group-white-nationalism-report.

63 See Jason Wilson, "Proud Boys founder Gavin McInnes quits 'extremist' far-right group," *The Guardian*, November 22, 2018. Online: https://www.theguardian.com/world/2018/nov/22/proud-boys-founder-gavin-mcinnes-quits-far-right-group.

64 See Jorge L. Ortiz, "'We're doing our job': Southern Poverty Law Center sued by Proud Boys founder Gavin McInnes," *USA Today*, February 5, 2019. Online: https://www.usatoday.com/story/news/2019/02/05/proud-boys-founder-gavin-mcinnes-sues-southern-poverty-law-center-over-hate-group-label/2783956002/.

65 See David Neiwert, "Proud Boys' ex-attorney used his comrades to spy on man he wanted to kill, police say," *Daily Kos*, April 19, 2019. Online: https://www.dailykos.com/stories/2020/4/19/1938272/-Proud-Boys-ex-attorney-used-his-comrades-to-spy-on-man-he-wanted-to-kill-police-say.

66 See Anonymous Contributor, "Who Are The New Proud Boy Elders?," *It's Going Down*, December 13, 2018. Online: https://itsgoingdown.org/who-are-the-new-proud-boy-elders/.

67 See David D. Kirkpatrck and Alan Feuer, "Police Shrugged Off the Proud Boys, Until They Attacked the Capitol," *The New York Times*, March 14, 2021. Online: https://www.nytimes.com/2021/03/14/us/proud-boys-law-enforcement.html.

68 See David Neiwert, "Portland protesters targeted by pipe bombs at city park, and activists identify a suspect," *Daily Kos*, Auguat 11, 2020. Online: https://www.dailykos.com/stories/2020/8/11/1968248/-Pipe-bombs-targeting-Portland-protesters-appear-to-be-the-latest-twist-in-far-right-tactics.

69 See David Neiwert, "Portland Police's chummy handling of far-right extremists creates a well-earned uproar," *Daily Kos*, February 18, 2019. Online: https://www.dailykos.com/stories/2019/2/18/1835528/-Portland-Police-s-chummy-handling-of-far-right-extremists-creates-a-well-earned-uproar.

70 See David Neiwert, "Proud Boys plan to terrorize Portland behind phony rubric of rally protesting far-left terrorism," *Daily Kos*, August 12, 2019. Online: https://www.dailykos.com/stories/2019/8/12/1878401/-Proud-Boys-plan-to-terrorize-Portland-behind-phony-rubric-of-rally-protesting-far-left-terrorism.

71 See David Neiwert, "Proud Boys' would-be violent march on Portland turns and heads the other direction," *Daily Kos*, August 18, 2019. Online: https://www.dailykos.com/stories/2019/8/18/1879837/-Proud-Boys-would-be-violent-march-on-Portland-turns-and-heads-the-other-direction.

72 See David Neiwert, "Proud Boys leader Joe Biggs fed FBI agents information on antifa, was cozy with Oregon cops," *Daily Kos*, March 31, 2021. Online: https://www.dailykos.com/stories/2021/3/31/2023785/-Proud-Boys-leader-Joe-Biggs-fed-FBI-agents-information-on-antifa-was-cozy-with-Oregon-cops.

73 See David Neiwert, "Proud Boys again bring violence to Portland, and police again stand by and do nothing," *Daily Kos*, August 24, 2020. Online: https://www.dailykos.com/stories/2020/8/24/1972004/-Proud-Boys-again-bring-violence-to-Portland-and-police-again-stand-by-and-do-nothing.

74 See David Neiwert, "Proud Boys torch their claims to nonviolence with hate crime attacks on Black churches in D.C.," *Daily Kos*, December 17, 2020. Online: https://www.dailykos.com/stories/2020/12/17/2002658/--Reminiscent-of-cross-burnings-Proud-Boys-torch-pretense-along-with-D-C-churches-BLM-signs.

75 See Vivik Saxena, "Pro-Trump protesters furiously turn on cops for protecting Antifa," *BizPacReview*, January 3, 2021. Online: https://www.bizpacreview.com/2021/01/03/pro-trump-protesters-furiously-turn-on-cops-for-protecting-antifa-1012158/.

76 See Ford Fischer, "Just tell them we're antifa and they'll give us a handjob!", Twitter, Jan. 2, 2021. Online: https://twitter.com/FordFischer/status/1345415294685224963.

77 See Tess Owen, "Proud Boys and Hardcore Trump Supporters Are Turning Their Backs on Cops," *Vice*, January 5, 2021. Online: https://www.vice.com/en/article/88avmx/proud-boys-and-hardcore-trump-supporters-are-turning-their-backs-on-cops.

78 See Robert O. Paxton, *The Anatomy of Fascism* (New York: Alfred A. Knopf, 2004), p. 41.

79 See especially Roger Griffin, *The Nature of Fascism* (London: Routledge, 1991), which defines fascism generically as "palingenetic ultranationalist populism," pp. 12-15.

80 See Stanley Payne, *Fascism: Comparison and Definition* (University of Wisconsin Press, 1983), p. 18.

81 See Umberto Eco, "Ur-Fascism," *The New York Review of Books*, June 22, 1995. Online: https://www.nybooks.com/articles/1995/06/22/ur-fascism/.

82 See David Neiwert, "Bitter about being abandoned by Trump, Proud Boys' chats reveal preparations for 'absolute war'," *Daily Kos*, May 18, 2021. Online: https://www.dailykos.com/stories/2021/5/18/2031008/-Bitter-about-being-abandoned-by-Trump-Proud-Boys-chats-reveal-preparations-for-absolute-war.

83 See David Neiwert, "Proud Boys come creeping back out of the woodwork, one hijacked local event at a time," *Daily Kos*, July 30, 2021. Online: https://www.dailykos.com/stories/2021/7/30/2043006/-Post-insurrection-strategy-for-Proud-Boys-manifests-Aim-for-local-controversies-hijack-them.

84 See David Neiwert, "Police go missing as Proud Boys shut down public park in Oregon for armed far-right rally," *Daily Kos*, May 3, 2021. Online: https://www.dailykos.com/stories/2021/5/3/2028797/-Proud-Boys-mark-their-public-return-with-a-threatening-Oregon-rally-and-no-police-presence.

85 See "Riot declared during fight between Proud Boys, antifa in Oregon City, police say," KGW-TV, June 18, 2021. Online: https://www.kgw.com/article/news/local/riot-declared-during-fight-between-proud-boys-antifa-in-oregon-city/283-d042e7c8-845c-49ef-9578-68ddeea040d8.

86 See Zac Ezzone, "Far right group participates in Buhl Sagebrush Days parade," *Magic Valley News*, July 11, 2021. Online: https://magicvalley.com/news/local/govt-and-politics/far-right-group-participates-in-buhl-sagebrush-days-parade/article_45c46c10-a41b-5056-b74e-0436ff88d032.html. See also Laura Cassels, Danielle J. Brown and Isaac Morgan, "Proud Boys, other groups, rally at FL's Old Capitol to demand release of 'patriots' from Jan. 6 insurrection," *Florida Phoenix*, July 10, 2021. Online: https://floridaphoenix.com/2021/07/10/proud-boys-other-groups-rally-at-fl-capitol-to-demand-release-of-patriots-from-jan-6-insurrection/. See also "Two arrested during brawl between Proud Boys, counter-protesters in Salem, po-

lice say," KGW-TV, July 14, 2021. Online: https://www.kgw.com/article/news/crime/two-arrested-during-brawl-proud-boys-salem-oregon/283-36a46d7b-5c5e-409b-aa49-244fdfe8baa1. See also Thomas Kika, "Los Angeles Police Declare Unlawful Assembly as Proud Boys Protest Wi Spa's Transgender Policy," *Newsweek*, July 17, 2021. Online: https://www.newsweek.com/los-angeles-police-declare-unlawful-assembly-proud-boys-protest-wi-spas-transgender-policy-1610751. See also Allan Stellar, "Proud Boys make appearance in Red Bluff," *Red Bluff (CA) Daily News*, July 19, 2021. Online: https://www.redbluffdailynews.com/2021/07/19/proud-boys-make-appearance-in-red-bluff/. See also "Proud Boys marched through downtown Tampa flashing 'white power' symbols last weekend," *Creative Loafing*, July 24, 2021. Online: https://www.cltampa.com/tampa/proud-boys-marched-through-downtown-tampa-flashing-white-power-symbols-last-weekend/Slideshow/12386908.

87 See Paul Jurgens, "Proud Boys withdraw from sponsoring street dance in Scotland," KFGO-AM, July 20, 2021. Online: https://kfgo.com/2021/07/20/proud-boys-withdraw-from-sponsoring-street-dance-in-scotland/. See also Phil Drake, "Proud Boys poker run to benefit veterans canceled," *Independent-Record*, July 14, 2021. Online: https://helenair.com/news/local/proud-boys-poker-run-to-benefit-veterans-canceled/article_12eebb7e-6b61-51ca-aa9b-678511144e3d.html.

Chapter 6: White Fright

1 See Hatewatch Staff, "Meet 'Patriot Front': Neo-Nazi network aims to blur lines with militiamen, the alt-right," *Hatewatch* (SPLC), December 12, 2017. Online: https://www.splcenter.org/hatewatch/2017/12/11/meet-patriot-front-neo-nazi-network-aims-blur-lines-militiamen-alt-right.

2 See Kevin McCarty, "Flyers with white nationalist propaganda found plastered around Gig Harbor," KIRO-TV, November 11, 2017. Online: https://www.kiro7.com/news/local/flyers-with-white-nationalist-propaganda-found-plastered-around-gig-harbor/649452887/.

3 See Sarah Posner and David Neiwert, "How Trump Took Hate Groups Mainstream," *Mother Jones*, October 14, 2016. Online: https://www.motherjones.com/politics/2016/10/donald-trump-hate-groups-neo-nazi-white-supremacist-racism/.

4 See Daniel Lombroso and Yoni Appelbaum, "'Hail Trump!': White Nationalists Salute the President-Elect," *The Atlantic*, December 21, 2016. Online: https://www.theatlantic.com/politics/archive/2016/11/richard-spencer-speech-npi/508379/.

5 See Hatewatch Staff, "Andrew Anglin brags about "indoctrinating" children into Nazi ideology," *Hatewatch* (SPLC), January 28, 2018. Online: https://www.splcenter.org/hatewatch/2018/01/18/andrew-anglin-brags-about-indoctrinating-children-nazi-ideology.

6 See David Neiwert, "A deluge of 'red-pilled' rage: Young white men are being radicalized online and acting out violently," *Daily Kos*, January 29, 2019. Online: https://www.dailykos.com/stories/2019/1/29/1830633/-A-deluge-of-red-pilled-rage-Young-white-men-are-being-radicalized-online-and-acting-out-violently.

7 See J.M. Berger, "Nazis vs. ISIS on Twitter: A Comparative Study of White Nationalist and ISIS Online Social Media Networks," GW Program on Extremism, September 2016. Online: https://extremism.gwu.edu/sites/g/files/zaxdzs2191/f/downloads/Nazis%20v.%20ISIS.pdf.

8   See David Neiwert, "Far Right Descends On Berkeley For 'Free Speech' And Planned Violence," *Hatewatch* (SPLC), April 17, 2017. Online: https://www.splcenter.org/hatewatch/2017/04/17/far-right-descends-berkeley-free-speech-and-planned-violence.

9   See Frances Dinkelspiel, "White nationalist group came to Berkeley in 2017 with intent to cause violence, documents contend," *Berkeleyside*, November 1, 2018. Online: https://www.berkeleyside.org/2018/11/01/white-nationalist-group-came-to-berkeley-in-2017-with-intent-to-cause-violence-documents-contend.

10 See A.C. Thompson, Ali Winston and Darwin Bondgraham, "Racist, Violent, Unpunished: A White Hate Group's Campaign of Menace," *ProPublica*, October 19, 2017. Online: https://www.propublica.org/article/white-hate-group-campaign-of-menace-rise-above-movement.

11 See David Neiwert, "Sentencing memo provides a revealing glimpse inside a neo-Nazi street-brawling gang," *Daily Kos*, July 23, 2019. Online: https://www.dailykos.com/stories/2019/7/23/1873810/-Sentencing-memo-provides-a-revealing-glimpse-inside-a-neo-Nazi-street-brawling-gang.

12 See especially "Documenting Hate: Charlottesville," *Frontline/ProPublica*, August 7, 2018. Online: https://www.pbs.org/wgbh/frontline/documentary/documenting-hate-charlottesville/.

13 See David Neiwert, "Sentencing memo provides a revealing glimpse inside a neo-Nazi street-brawling gang," *Daily Kos*, July 23, 2019. Online: https://www.dailykos.com/stories/2019/7/23/1873810/-Sentencing-memo-provides-a-revealing-glimpse-inside-a-neo-Nazi-street-brawling-gang.

14 See Hatewatch Staff, "Alleged Charlottesville Driver Who Killed One Rallied With Alt-Right Vanguard America Group," *Hatewatch* (SPLC), August 13, 2017. Online: https://www.splcenter.org/hatewatch/2017/08/12/alleged-charlottesville-driver-who-killed-one-rallied-alt-right-vanguard-america-group.

15 See Tim Marcin, "Noted Racist Richard Spencer Apparently Yelled Racist Slurs After Racist Rally," *Vice*, November 4, 2019. Online: https://www.vice.com/en/article/8xw3a4/shocker-noted-racist-richard-spencer-apparently-yelled-racist-slurs-after-racist-rally.

16 See David Neiwert, "Lawsuit over injuries at Charlottesville delivers a finishing blow to Spencer's alt-right think tank," *Daily Kos*, May 6, 2021. Online: https://*www.dailykos.com/stories/2021/5/6/2029275/-Lawsuit-over-injuries-at-Charlottesville-delivers-a-finishing-blow-to-Spencer-s-alt-right-think-tank.

17 See "Four Local Members of White Supremacy Group Face Federal Charges in Attacks at Political Rallies across California," U.S. Attorney's Office, Central District of Columbia press release, October 24, 2018. Online: https://www.justice.gov/usao-cdca/pr/four-local-members-white-supremacy-group-face-federal-charges-attacks-political-rallies.

18 See Adam Goldman and Ali Winston, "F.B.I. Arrests White Nationalist Leader Who Fled the Country for Central America," *The New York Times*, October 24, 2018. Online: https://www.nytimes.com/2018/10/24/us/fbi-white-nationalist-robert-paul-rundo-rise-above.html.

19 See Julia Sclafani, "Judge dismisses federal charges against 3 members of H.B.-based white power group," *Los Angeles Times*, June 4, 2019. Online: https://www.latimes.com/socal/daily-pilot/news/tn-dpt-me-hb-ram-charges-dropped-20190604-story.html.

20 See "Riot charges reinstated against California white supremacist," Fox10, March 5, 2021. Online: https://www.fox10phoenix.com/news/riot-charges-reinstated-against-california-white-supremacist.

21 See U.S. Court of Appeals for the Ninth Circuit ruling, *U.S. v. Rundo et. al.*, November 17, 2020. Online: https://www.documentcloud.org/documents/20499474-9th-circuit-rundo-et-al-decision.

22 See Tess Owen, "A White Supremacist Is Organizing Fight Clubs Across the US," *Vice*, September 27, 2021. Online: https://www.vice.com/en/article/y3d8qj/robert-rundo-white-supremacist-organizing-fight-clubs-across-the-us.

23 See "Patriot Front," Southern Poverty Law Center Extremist Group profile. Online: https://www.splcenter.org/fighting-hate/extremist-files/group/patriot-front.

24 See Hatewatch Staff, "Meet 'Patriot Front': Neo-Nazi network aims to blur lines with militiamen, the alt-right," *Hatewatch* (SPLC), December 12, 2017. Online: https://www.splcenter.org/hatewatch/2017/12/11/meet-patriot-front-neo-nazi-network-aims-blur-lines-militiamen-alt-right.

25 See David Neiwert, "Founder of fascist 'Patriot Front' group arrested in Texas for plastering stickers at courthouse," *Daily Kos*, August 4, 2020. Online: https://www.dailykos.com/stories/2020/8/4/1966538/-Founder-of-fascist-Patriot-Front-group-arrested-in-Texas-for-plastering-stickers-at-courthouse.

26 See Annemarie Mannion, "Area teen rallied in Charlottesville, got death threats, now planning move to 'solidly red' Alabama," *Chicago Tribune*, August 18, 2017. Online: https://www.chicagotribune.com/suburbs/western-springs/ct-dlg-lt-grad-death-threats-tl-0824-20170818-story.html.

27 See "Right Side Broadcasting, The 'Unofficial Version Of Trump TV,' Forced To Apologize For Contributor's Call To 'Kill The Globalists' At CNN," Media Matters, April 24, 2017. Online: https://www.mediamatters.org/cnn/right-side-broadcasting-unofficial-version-trump-tv-forced-apologize-contributors-call-kill.

28 See Kristin Toussaint, "Right-wing BU teen won't return to Boston after attending Charlottesville rally," *Metro*, August 16, 2017. Online: https://www.metro.us/right-wing-bu-teen-wont-return-to-boston-after-attending-charlottesville-rally/.

29 See Roy S. Johnson, "Alt-right's Nicholas Fuentes no longer affiliated with Right Side Broadcasting," *AL.com*, August 30, 2017. Online: https://www.al.com/news/2017/08/alt-rights_nicholas_fuentes_no.html.

30 See "James Orien Allsup," Southern Poverty Law Center Extremist Profile. Online: https://www.splcenter.org/fighting-hate/extremist-files/individual/james-orien-allsup.

31 See "Groyper Army and 'America First'," Anti-Defamation League profile, March 17, 2020. Online: adl.org/resources/backgrounder/groyper-army-and-america-first.

32 See David Neiwert, "'Groyper' general wishes for 'dictatorship,' wants to 'force the people to believe what we believe'," *Daily Kos*, November 11, 2022. Online: https://www.dailykos.com/stories/2022/11/11/2135415/--Groyper-general-wishes-for-dictatorship-wants-to-force-the-people-to-believe-what-we-believe.

33 See Ben Lorber, "'We Have To Push the Envelope'," *Political Research Associates*, January 5, 2022. Online: https://politicalresearch.org/2022/01/05/we-have-push-envelope.

34 See David Neiwert, "Alt-right trolls make life miserable for Charlie Kirk and his Turning Point USA 'Culture War' tour," *Daily Kos*, November 1, 2019. Online:

https://www.dailykos.com/stories/2019/11/1/1896408/-Alt-right-trolls-make-life-miserable-for-Charlie-Kirk-and-his-Turning-Point-USA-Culture-War-tour.

35 See Brendan Joel Kelly, "Turning Point USA's blooming romance with the alt-right," *Hatewatch* (SPLC), February 6, 2018. Online: https://www.splcenter.org/hate-watch/2018/02/16/turning-point-usas-blooming-romance-alt-right.

36 See Jane Mayer, "A Conservative Nonprofit That Seeks to Transform College Campuses Faces Allegations of Racial Bias and Illegal Campaign Activity," *The New Yorker,* December 21, 2017. Online: https://www.newyorker.com/news/news-desk/a-conservative-nonprofit-that-seeks-to-transform-college-campuses-faces-allegations-of-racial-bias-and-illegal-campaign-activity.

37 See Jane Coaston, "Why alt-right trolls shouted down Donald Trump Jr.," *Vox*, November 11, 2019. Online: https://www.vox.com/policy-and-poli-tics/2019/11/11/20948317/alt-right-donald-trump-jr-conservative-tpusa-yaf-rac-ism-antisemitism.

38 See Katie Shepherd, "Donald Trump Jr. went to UCLA to decry 'triggered' liberals. He was heckled off the stage by the far right," *The Washington Post*, December 11, 2019. Online: https://www.washingtonpost.com/nation/2019/11/11/donald-trump-jr-book-talk-ucla-derailed-by-far-right-protesters/.

39 See Ben Collins, "Pro-Trump conservatives are getting trolled in real life by a far-right group," NBC News, November 12, 2019. Online: https://www.nbcnews.com/tech/tech-news/pro-trump-conservatives-are-getting-trolled-real-life-far-right-n1080986.

40 See David Neiwert, "Alt-right trolls make life miserable for Charlie Kirk and his Turning Point USA 'Culture War' tour," *Daily Kos*, November 1, 2019. Online: https://www.dailykos.com/stories/2019/11/1/1896408/-Alt-right-trolls-make-life-miserable-for-Charlie-Kirk-and-his-Turning-Point-USA-Culture-War-tour.

41 See David Neiwert, "Michelle Malkin chooses the white nationalist side in the internecine 'Groyper War,' gets fired," *Daily Kos*, November 18, 2019. Online: https://www.dailykos.com/stories/2019/11/18/1900398/-Michelle-Malkin-chooses-the-white-nationalist-side-in-the-internecine-Groyper-War-gets-fired.

42 See David Neiwert, "Here's Malkin at the 2020 America First PAC convention of Groypers," Twitter, March 30, 2022. Online: https://twitter.com/davidneiwert/sta-tus/1509237741967458305.

43 See Guy Benson, "'Groyper' leader on segregation," Twitter, November 17, 2019. On-line: https://twitter.com/guypbenson/status/1196223196384632832.

44 See David Neiwert, "Epik's hosting services provide connection for Jones' Infowars and Fuentes' white nationalists," *Daily Kos*, November 16, 2021. Online: https://www.dailykos.com/stories/2021/11/16/2064684/-Epik-s-hosting-services-pro-vide-connection-for-Jones-Infowars-and-Fuentes-white-nationalists.

45 See David Neiwert, "How the 'Trump Effect' will live on: Openly fascist 'Patriot Front' haters gear up for next phase," *Daily Kos*, October 29, 2020. Online: https://www.dailykos.com/stories/2020/10/29/1990722/-How-the-Trump-Effect-will-live-on-Openly-fascist-Patriot-Front-haters-gear-up-for-next-phase.

46 See David Neiwert, "White nationalists flaunt their traction within Republican Party at annual gathering in Florida," *Daily Kos*, February 28, 2022. Online: https://www.dailykos.com/stories/2022/2/28/2083065/-White-nationalists-flaunt-their-traction-within-Republican-Party-at-annual-gathering-in-Florida.

47 See "Extremists and Mainstream Trump Supporters Gather for 'Million MAGA March'," Anti-Defamation League, November 15, 2020. Online: https://www.adl.org/resources/blog/extremists-and-mainstream-trump-supporters-gather-million-maga-march.

48 See David Neiwert, "'Million MAGA March' draws thousands of extremists to D.C. claiming Trump won the election," *Daily Kos*, November 14, 2020. Online: https://www.dailykos.com/stories/2020/11/14/1995811/--Million-MAGA-March-draws-thousands-of-extremists-to-D-C-claiming-Trump-won-the-election.

49 See Ryan J. Reilly and Zoë Richards, "Members of far-right group America First charged in connection with Jan. 6 riot," NBC News, September 20, 2022. Online: https://www.nbcnews.com/politics/justice-department/members-far-right-group-america-first-charged-connection-jan-6-riot-rcna48664.

50 See Robert A. Pape, "American Face of Insurrection: Analysis of Individuals Charged for Storming the US Capitol on January 6, 2021," Chicago Project on Security and Threats (Univerity of Chicago), January 5, 2022. Online: https://d3qi0qp55mx5f5.cloudfront.net/cpost/i/docs/Pape_-_American_Face_of_Insurrection_(2022-01-05).pdf.

51 See David Neiwert, "White nationalist Fuentes gets subpoena from Jan. 6 committee, but he's preparing for mockery," *Daily Kos*, January 20, 2022. Online: https://www.dailykos.com/stories/2022/1/20/2075882/-Jan-6-Committee-subpoenas-notorious-white-nationalist-Fuentes-but-there-s-a-danger-within.

52 See David Neiwert, "'Patriot Front' marchers wave their fascist banners down Capitol Mall as radical right returns," *Daily Kos*, January 29, 2021. Online: https://www.dailykos.com/stories/2021/1/29/2012760/--Patriot-Front-fascists-mark-far-right-s-return-to-Washington-with-march-down-Capitol-Mall.

53 See Jane Lytvenenko, "The White Extremist Group Patriot Front Is Preparing For A World After Donald Trump," *BuzzFeed News*, October 27, 2020. Online: https://www.buzzfeednews.com/article/janelytvynenko/patriot-front-preparing-after-trump.

54 See Chris Schiano and Dan Feidt, "Patriot Front Fascist Leak Exposes Nationwide Racist Campaigns," *Unicorn Riot*, January 21, 2022. Online: https://unicornriot.ninja/2022/patriot-front-fascist-leak-exposes-nationwide-racist-campaigns/.

55 See Megan Squire, Jeff Tischauser and Michael Edison Hayden, "One in Five Patriot Front Applicants Claim Military Ties," *Hatewatch* (SPLC), February 1, 2022. Online: https://www.splcenter.org/hatewatch/2022/02/01/one-five-patriot-front-applicants-claim-military-ties.

56 See David Neiwert, "Data leak gives an inside look at neofascist Patriot Front: Clownish operations with military edge," *Daily Kos*, February 2, 2022. Online: https://www.dailykos.com/stories/2022/2/2/2078346/-Data-leak-gives-an-inside-look-at-neofascist-Patriot-Front-clownish-operations-with-military-edge.

57 See Caroline Kitchener, Ellie Silverman and Michelle Boorstein, "Antiabortion activists brave cold, pandemic fears to rally for what they hope is the end of Roe v. Wade," *The Washington Post*, January 21, 2022. Online: https://www.washingtonpost.com/dc-md-va/2022/01/21/march-for-life-dc-anti-abortion/.

58 See Chris Schiano and Dan Feidt, "Patriot Front Fascist Leak Exposes Nationwide Racist Campaigns," *Unicorn Riot*, January 21, 2022. Online: https://unicornriot.ninja/2022/patriot-front-fascist-leak-exposes-nationwide-racist-campaigns/.

59 See David Neiwert, "As white nationalists, Jan. 6 extremists embrace Christian nationalism, even darker forces revive," *Daily Kos*, January 27, 2022. Online: https://www.dailykos.com/stories/2022/1/27/2077246/-As-white-nationalists-Jan-6-extremists-embrace-Christian-nationalism-even-darker-forces-revive.

60 See Jack Jenkins, "How the Capitol attacks helped spread Christian nationalism in the extreme right," *The Washington Post*, January 26, 2022. Online: https://www.washingtonpost.com/religion/2022/01/26/christian-nationalism-jan-6-extreme-right/.

61 See Katherine Stewart, "Christian Nationalism Is One of Trump's Most Powerful Weapons," *The New York Times*, January 6, 2022. Online: https://www.nytimes.com/2022/01/06/opinion/jan-6-christian-nationalism.html.

62 See Gregory A. Smith, Michael Rotolo, and Patricia Tevington, "45% of Americans Say U.S. Should Be a 'Christian Nation'," Pew Research Center, October 27, 2022. Online: https://www.pewresearch.org/religion/2022/10/27/45-of-americans-say-u-s-should-be-a-christian-nation/.

Chapter 7: Alt-America with a Q

1 See David Neiwert, "Trump's radical-right tango: Embrace them one day, distance the next, empower them constantly," *Daily Kos*, October 1, 2020. Online: https://www.dailykos.com/stories/2020/10/1/1982564/-Trump-s-radical-right-tango-Embrace-them-one-day-distance-the-next-empower-them-constantly.

2 See Brie Stimson, "Trump blasts ballots when asked about election aftermath: 'The ballots are a disaster'," *Fox News*, September 24, 2020. Online: https://www.foxnews.com/politics/trump-pressed-on-peaceful-transfer-of-power-have-to-see-what-happens.

3 See David Neiwert, "Conspiracy meta-theory 'The Storm' pushes the 'alternative' envelope yet again," *Hatewatch* (SPLC), January 17, 2018. Online: https://www.splcenter.org/hatewatch/2018/01/17/conspiracy-meta-theory-storm-pushes-alternative-envelope-yet-again.

4 See David Neiwert, "'Pizzagate' Theories Inspire D.C. Gunman, But Still Have Defenders in Powerful Places," *Hatewatch* (SPLC), December 8, 2016. Online: https://www.splcenter.org/hatewatch/2016/12/06/'pizzagate'-theories-inspire-dc-gunman-still-have-defenders-powerful-places.

5 See Hatewatch Staff, "What You Need To Know About QAnon," *Hatewatch* (SPLC), October 27, 2020. Online: https://www.splcenter.org/hatewatch/2020/10/27/what-you-need-know-about-qanon.

6 See Brendan Joel Kelly and Hatewatch Staff, "QAnon Conspiracy Increasingly Popular with Antigovernment Extremists," *Hatewatch* (SPLC), April 23, 2019. Online: https://www.splcenter.org/hatewatch/2019/04/23/qanon-conspiracy-increasingly-popular-antigovernment-extremists.

7 See Alex Kaplan, "Trump has repeatedly amplified QAnon Twitter accounts. The FBI has linked the conspiracy theory to domestic terror," Media Matters, Augut 8, 2019. Online: https://www.mediamatters.org/twitter/fbi-calls-qanon-domestic-terror-threat-trump-has-amplified-qanon-supporters-twitter-more-20.

8 See Zeke Miller, Jill Colvin, and Amanda Seitz, "Trump praises QAnon conspiracists, appreciates support," Associated Press, August 19, 2020. Online: https://apnews.

com/article/election-2020-ap-top-news-religion-racial-injustice-535e145ee67dd-757660157be39d05d3f.

9   See David Neiwert, "Fancy footwork fails to disguise Trump's continuing far-right conspiracist tango at town hall," *Daily Kos*, October 16, 2020. Online: https://www.dailykos.com/stories/2020/10/16/1986951/-Trump-tangoes-with-the-far-right-at-Town-Hall-First-a-distancing-step-then-a-warm-embrace.

10 See David Neiwert, "Republicans are being eaten from within by the QAnon cult, and no one can stop it," *Daily Kos*, July 16, 2020. Online: https://www.dailykos.com/stories/2020/7/16/1961352/-The-creep-of-the-QAnon-cult-threatens-to-consume-what-s-left-of-the-Republican-Party.

11 See Michael Flynn, "#TakeTheOath," Twitter, July 4, 2020. Online: https://twitter.com/GenFlynn/status/1279590652200849409.

12 See Jack Brewster, "Eric Trump Promotes QAnon Conspiracy On Instagram While Plugging Tulsa Rally," *Forbes*, July 20, 2020. Online: https://www.forbes.com/sites/jackbrewster/2020/06/20/eric-trump-promotes-qanon-conspiracy-on-instagram-while-plugging-tulsa-rally/?sh=7c50d9b31988.

13 See Eric Hananoki, "OAN's White House correspondent: QAnon is anonymous 'for a very good reason" and "people need to respect that'," Media Matters, July 15, 2020. Online: https://www.mediamatters.org/one-america-news-network/oans-chanel-rion-made-pro-qanon-remarks-qanon-program.

14 See Matthew Rosenberg and Jennifer Steinhauer, "The QAnon Candidates Are Here. Trump Has Paved Their Way," *The New York Times*, July 14, 2020. Online: https://www.nytimes.com/2020/07/14/us/politics/qanon-politicians-candidates.html. See also Eric Hananoki, "GOP organizations in Florida and Georgia have been promoting QAnon on Facebook," Media Matters, June 18, 2020. Online: https://www.mediamatters.org/qanon-conspiracy-theory/gop-organizations-florida-and-georgia-have-been-promoting-qanon-facebook.

15 See Jana Winter, "Exclusive: FBI document warns conspiracy theories are a new domestic terrorism threat," *Yahoo! News*, August 1, 2019. Online: https://news.yahoo.com/fbi-documents-conspiracy-theories-terrorism-160000507.html.

16 See David Neiwert, "QAnon-loving Senate candidate wants martial law declared in Oregon to combat 'antifa'," *Daily Kos*, June 5, 2020. Online: https://www.dailykos.com/stories/2020/6/5/1950834/-QAnon-loving-Senate-candidate-wants-martial-law-declared-in-Oregon-to-combat-antifa.

17 See Alex Kaplan, "Here are the QAnon supporters running for Congress in 2020," Media Matters, January 7, 2020. Online: https://www.mediamatters.org/qanon-conspiracy-theory/here-are-qanon-supporters-running-congress-2020.

18 See Tina Nguyen, "Trump isn't secretly winking at QAnon. He's retweeting its followers," *Politico*, July 12, 2020. Online: https://www.politico.com/news/2020/07/12/trump-tweeting-qanon-followers-357238.

19 See Matt Keeley, "Oregon GOP Senate Candidate Recites QAnon 'Oath of Office' on Video," *Newsweek*, June 27, 2020. Online: https://www.newsweek.com/oregon-gop-senate-candidate-recites-qanon-oath-office-video-1513896.

20 See Shayan Sardarizadeh, "The meteoric rise of #TakeTheOath," Twitter, July 6, 2020. Online: https://twitter.com/Shayan86/status/1280287853394776064.

21 See Jerry Dunleavy, "Michael Flynn recites oath of office using slogan associated with QAnon," *Washington Examiner*, July 5, 2020. Online: https://www.washing-

tonexaminer.com/news/michael-flynn-recites-oath-of-office-using-slogan-associ-ated-with-qanon.

22 See Marshall Cohen, "Michael Flynn posts video featuring QAnon slogans," CNN, July 7, 2020. Online: https://www.cnn.com/2020/07/07/politics/michael-flynn-qa-non-video/index.html.

23 See William Mansell, "Man pleads guilty to terrorism charge after blocking Hoover Dam bridge with armored truck," ABC News, February 12, 2020. Online: https://abcnews.go.com/US/man-pleads-guilty-terrorism-charge-blocking-bridge-ar-mored/story?id=68955385.

24 See Jana Winter, "Exclusive: FBI document warns conspiracy theories are a new do-mestic terrorism threat," *Yahoo! News*, August 1, 2019. Online: https://news.yahoo.com/fbi-documents-conspiracy-theories-terrorism-160000507.html.

25 See Ali Watkins, "Accused of Killing a Gambino Mob Boss, He's Presenting a Novel Defense," *The New York Times,* December 6, 2019. Online: https://www.nytimes.com/2019/12/06/nyregion/gambino-shooting-anthony-comello-qanon.html.

26 See Michael Scheuer, "Those who do not believe QANON will be mighty surprised," *Michael Scheuer/Non-Intervention,* December 7, 2019. Online: http://www.non-intervention2.com/2019/12/07/those-who-do-not-believe-qanon-will-be-mighty-surprised/.

27 See Michael Scheuer, "A republican citizenry's greatest, last-resort duty is to kill those seeking to impose tyranny," *Non-Intervention.com*, July 4, 2018. Online: https://ar-chive.vn/20180716071311/http:/non-intervention.com/3238/a-republican-citizen-rys-greatest-last-resort-duty-is-to-kill-those-seeking-to-impose-tyranny/#selec-tion-159.0-159.94.

28 See Dan Goldberg, "'It's going to disappear': Trump's changing tone on coronavi-rus," *Politico*, March 17, 2020. Online: https://www.politico.com/news/2020/03/17/how-trump-shifted-his-tone-on-coronavirus-134246.

29 See "Remarks by President Trump in Address to the Nation," Trump White House, March 11, 2020. Online: https://trumpwhitehouse.archives.gov/briefings-state-ments/remarks-president-trump-address-nation/.

30 See Chris Cilizza, "Here's Donald Trump's angry response when asked what he would tell scared Americans," CNN, March 20, 2020. Online: https://www.cnn.com/2020/03/20/politics/peter-alexander-donald-trump-coronavirus/index.html.

31 See Daniel Wolfe and Daniel Dale, "'It's going to disappear': A timeline of Trump's claims that Covid-19 will vanish," CNN, October 31, 2020. Online: https://edition.cnn.com/interactive/2020/10/politics/covid-disappearing-trump-comment-tracker/.

32 See Annie Karni and Katie Thomas, "Trump Says He's Taking Hydroxychloroquine, Prompting Warning From Health Experts," *The New York Times*, May 18, 2020. Online: https://www.nytimes.com/2020/05/18/us/politics/trump-hydroxychloro-quine-covid-coronavirus.html.

33 See Jason Wilson, "Disinformation and blame: how America's far right is capitalizing on coronavirus," *The Guardian*, March 19, 2020. Online: https://www.theguardian.com/world/2020/mar/19/america-far-right-coronavirus-outbreak-trump-alex-jones.

34 See Laura Newberry, "GOP candidate for L.A. congressional district tweets coro-navirus conspiracy theory," *The Los Angeles Times*, March 1, 2020. Online: https://www.latimes.com/california/story/2020-03-01/gop-candidate-for-l-a-congressio-nal-district-tweets-coronavirus-conspiracy-theory.

35   See Alex Kaplan, "QAnon conspiracy theory post about the coronavirus is spreading on social media," Media Matters, March 24, 2020. Online: https://www.mediamatters.org/coronavirus-covid-19/qanon-conspiracy-theory-post-about-coronavirus-spreading-social-media.

36   See Meagan Flynn, "Engineer intentionally crashes train near hospital ship Mercy, believing in weird coronavirus conspiracy, feds say," The Los Angeles Times, April 2, 2020. Online: https://www.washingtonpost.com/nation/2020/04/02/train-derails-usns-mercy-coronavirus/.

37   See David Neiwert, "Coronavirus conspiracy theorists are too nuts even for a zombie-apocalypse movie scenario," Daily Kos, April 3, 2020. Online: https://www.dailykos.com/stories/2020/4/3/1933811/-Coronavirus-conspiracy-theorists-are-too-nuts-even-for-a-zombie-apocalypse-movie-scenario.

38   See "Fox News contributor: I'm seeing videos on Twitter of empty hospital parking lots," Media Matters, March 30, 2020. Online: https://www.mediamatters.org/coronavirus-covid-19/fox-news-contributor-i-am-seeing-videos-twitter-empty-hospital-parking-lots.

39   See David Neiwert, "Coronavirus conspiracy theorists set 5G towers afire, believing they're the cause of the pandemic," Daily Kos, April 16, 2020. Online: https://www.dailykos.com/stories/2020/4/16/1937569/-Coronavirus-conspiracy-theorists-set-5G-towers-afire-believing-they-re-the-cause-of-the-pandemic.

40   See Laura Bradley, "Celebrities Are Spreading a Wacky Coronavirus 5G Conspiracy and They Need to Stop," The Daily Beast, April 6, 2020. Online: https://www.thedailybeast.com/celebrities-are-spreading-a-wacky-coronavirus-5g-conspiracy-and-they-need-to-stop-4.

41   See William Bradley, "Sussex radio station breaches Ofcom rules after broadcasting coronavirus and 5G link," Kent Live, April, 3, 2020. Online: https://www.kentlive.news/news/sussex-news/sussex-radio-station-breaches-ofcom-4015328.

42   See Jim Waterson, "Eamonn Holmes responds to complaints over handling of Covid-19 5G claims," The Guardian, April 14, 2020. Online: https://www.theguardian.com/technology/2020/apr/14/eamonn-holmes-responds-to-complaints-over-handling-of-covid-19-5g-claims.

43   See Verity Sulway and Dan Bloom, "Government urges Ofcom probe of LondonLive over David Icke coronavirus conspiracy," The Mirror (UK), April 9, 2020. Online: https://www.mirror.co.uk/tv/tv-news/government-urges-ofcom-probe-london-live-21838630.

44   See Jim Waterson, "Broadband engineers threatened due to 5G coronavirus conspiracies," The Guardian, April 3, 2020. Online: https://www.theguardian.com/technology/2020/apr/03/broadband-engineers-threatened-due-to-5g-coronavirus-conspiracies.

45   See John Timmer, "Celebs share rumors linking 5G to coronavirus, nutjobs burn cell towers," Ars Technica, April 12, 2020. Online: https://arstechnica.com/science/2020/04/in-the-uk-pandemic-panic-has-people-burning-cell-phone-towers/.

46   See "Dutch telecommunications towers damaged by 5G protestors: Telegraaf," Reuters, April 11, 2020. Online: https://www.reuters.com/article/us-netherlands-5g-sabotage/dutch-telecommunications-towers-damaged-by-5g-protestors-telegraaf-idUSKCN21T09P.

47 See Nii Ntreh, "Why are powerful pastors pushing the coronavirus and 5G tech conspiracy in Africa?," *Face2FaceAfrica*, April 10, 2020. Online: https://face2faceafrica.com/article/why-are-powerful-pastors-pushing-the-coronavirus-and-5g-tech-conspiracy-in-africa.

48 See Mark Sweney and Jim Waterson, "Arsonists attack phone mast serving NHS Nightingale hospital," *The Guardian*, April 14, 2020. Online: https://www.theguardian.com/technology/2020/apr/14/arsonists-attack-phone-mast-serving-nhs-nightingale-hospital.

49 See Tom Warren, "Why the 5G coronavirus conspiracy theories don't make sense," April 9, 2020. Online: https://www.theverge.com/2020/4/9/21214750/5g-coronavirus-conspiracy-theories-radio-waves-virus-internet.

50 See William J. Broad, "Your 5G Phone Won't Hurt You. But Russia Wants You to Think Otherwise," *The New York Times*, May 12, 2019. Online: https://www.nytimes.com/2019/05/12/science/5g-phone-safety-health-russia.html.

51 See "EEAS Special Report Update: Short Assessment of Narratives and Disinformation Around the COVID-19 Pandemic," April 1, 2020. Online: https://euvsdisinfo.eu/eeas-special-report-update-short-assessment-of-narratives-and-disinformation-around-the-covid-19-pandemic/.

52 See James Temperton, "How the 5G coronavirus conspiracy theory tore through the internet," *Wired*, April 6, 2020. Online: https://www.wired.co.uk/article/5g-coronavirus-conspiracy-theory.

53 See Tom Kertschner, "Fact-checking viral video alleging some New York hospitals are 'murdering' COVID-19 patients," *Politifact*, May 14, 2020. Online: https://www.politifact.com/article/2020/may/14/fact-checking-viral-video-alleging-some-new-york-h/.

54 See David Neiwert, "Unhinged pandemic denialist arrested in attempt to steal copter, attack hospital to 'free' patients," *Daily Kos*, May 21, 2020. Online: https://www.dailykos.com/stories/2020/5/21/1946786/-Unhinged-pandemic-denialist-arrested-in-attempt-to-steal-copter-attack-hospital-to-free-patient.

55 See Cole Waterman, "Michigan man gets probation for trying to steal Coast Guard helicopter to 'free' COVID patients," *MLive*, May 2, 2022. Online: https://www.mlive.com/news/saginaw-bay-city/2022/05/michigan-man-gets-probation-for-trying-to-steal-coast-guard-helicopter-to-free-covid-patients.html.

56 See David Neiwert, "Fringe right closes down Michigan capital with 'gridlock' protest against coronavirus measures," *Daily Kos*, April 16, 2020. Online: https://www.dailykos.com/stories/2020/4/16/1937852/-Fringe-right-closes-down-Michigan-capital-with-gridlock-protest-against-coronavirus-measures.

57 See David Neiwert, "Michigan militiamen successfully threaten legislators over COVID-19 lockdown orders," *Daily Kos*, May 1, 2020. Online: https://www.dailykos.com/stories/2020/5/1/1941901/-Michigan-militiamen-successfully-threaten-legislators-over-COVID-19-lockdown-orders.

58 See David Neiwert, "Idaho legislators bow down before extremists invading Statehouse to protest pandemic measures," *Daily Kos*, August 25, 2020. Online: https://www.dailykos.com/stories/2020/8/25/1972206/-Extremists-storm-Idaho-Statehouse-to-protest-COVID-19-measures-but-Republicans-are-cool-with-that.

59 See David Neiwert, "Terrorism experts fear outbreak of violence by pro-Trump 'Boogaloo' fans around 2020 election," *Daily Kos*, July 3, 2020. Online: https://

www.dailykos.com/stories/2020/7/3/1957327/-Terrorism-experts-fear-outbreak-of-violence-by-pro-Trump-Boogaloo-fans-around-2020-election.

60 See David Neiwert, "Anti-lockdown protesters are just the authoritarian foot sol-diers Trump ordered," *Daily Kos*, April 21, 2020. Online: https://www.dailykos.com/stories/2020/4/21/1939036/-Anti-lockdown-protesters-are-just-the-authoritarian-footsoldiers-Trump-ordered.

61 See Joseph O'Sullivan and David Gutman, "Demonstrators rally in Olympia against Washington's coronavirus stay-at-home order," *The Seattle Times*, April 19, 2020. Online: https://www.seattletimes.com/seattle-news/politics/demonstra-tors-rally-in-olympia-against-washingtons-coronavirus-stay-home-order/.

62 See Bruce Golding, "Hundreds of protesters defy coronavirus lockdown or-ders in Pennsylvania," *The New York Post*, April 20, 2020. Online: https://nypost.com/2020/04/20/hundreds-of-protesters-defy-lockdown-orders-in-pennsylvania/.

63 See James Walker, "Alex Jones Shakes Hands With Protesters at Texas Rally to Reopen State Against Stay-at-Home Orders," *Newsweek*, April 20, 2020. Online: https://www.newsweek.com/alex-jones-shakes-hands-protesters-texas-rally-stay-home-order-1498862.

64 See Jackie Salo, "Kentucky sees highest spike in coronavirus cases after lockdown protests," *The New York Post*, April 20, 2020. Online: https://nypost.com/2020/04/20/kentucky-sees-highest-spike-in-coronavirus-cases-after-protests/

65 See Linda Givetash, "Coronavirus: Trump says some governors 'have gone too far' on lockdown measures," NBC News, April 20, 2020. Online: https://www.nbcnews.com/news/world/coronavirus-trump-says-some-governors-have-gone-too-far-lockdown-n1187596.

66 See Aaron Rupar, "@Yamiche: Are you concerned downplaying the virus maybe got some people sick?," Twitter, April 20, 2020. Online: https://twitter.com/atrupar/sta-tus/1252373770670469122.

67 See David Neiwert, "QAnon's biggest prediction has failed, but don't expect the conspiracy-fueled cult to go away," *Daily Kos*, November 10, 2020. Online: https://www.dailykos.com/stories/2020/11/10/1994811/-QAnon-s-biggest-prediction-has-failed-but-don-t-expect-the-conspiracy-fueled-cult-to-go-away.

68 See Kevin Roose, "Shocked by Trump's Loss, QAnon Struggles to Keep the Faith," *The New York Times*, November 10, 2020. Online: https://www.nytimes.com/2020/11/10/technology/qanon-election-trump.html.

69 See Justin Ling, "As QAnon Copes With Trump's Likely Loss, They Wonder Where Q Is," *Foreign Policy*, November 6, 2020. Online: https://foreignpolicy.com/2020/11/06/qanon-coping-trump-likely-loss-where-is-q/.

70 See Drew Harwell and Craig Timberg, "'My faith is shaken': The QAnon conspira-cy theory faces a post-Trump identity crisis," *The Washington Post*, November 10, 2020. Online: https://www.washingtonpost.com/technology/2020/11/10/qanon-identity-crisis/.

71 See David Gilbert, "QAnon Is Here to Stay—Even Though Trump Lost," *Vice*, No-vember 9, 2020. Online: https://www.vice.com/en/article/7k9v4g/qanon-is-here-to-stayeven-though-trump-lost.

72 See Mike Rothschild, "Another day of 'Trump actually won a landslide and is only pretending he lost to expose the deep state'," Twitter, November 8, 2020. Online: https://twitter.com/rothschildmd/status/1325507756476882944.

73 See David Gilbert, "QAnon Is Here to Stay—Even Though Trump Lost," *Vice*, November 9, 2020. Online: https://www.vice.com/en/article/7k9v4g/qanon-is-here-to-stayeven-though-trump-lost.

74 See Drew Harwell and Craig Timberg, "'My faith is shaken': The QAnon conspiracy theory faces a post-Trump identity crisis," *The Washington Post*, November 10, 2020. Online: https://www.washingtonpost.com/technology/2020/11/10/qanon-identity-crisis/.

75 See David Neiwert, "Pro-Trump mobs fueled by conspiracy theories try to disrupt voting counts in contested states," *Daily Kos*, November 5, 2020. Online: https://www.dailykos.com/stories/2020/11/5/1993087/-Pro-Trump-mobs-fueled-by-conspiracy-theories-try-to-disrupt-voting-counts-in-contested-states.

76 See Hannah Knowles, Emma Brown and Meryl Kornfield, Election officials in Arizona rebut claims that ballots marked with Sharpies were disqualified," *The Washington Post*, November 4, 2020. Online: https://www.washingtonpost.com/politics/2020/11/04/sharpie-votes-arizona/.

77 See Darcie Moran, Omar Abdel-Baqui, Chanel Stitt, and Kristen Jordan Shamus, "Rival protests shout 'count every vote,' 'stop the count' in metro Detroit," *Detroit Free Press*, November 4, 2020. Online: https://www.freep.com/story/news/local/michigan/detroit/2020/11/04/rival-protesters-cry-count-every-vote-stop-count/6165558002/.

78 See "Dueling protests held outside convention center amid Trump campaign's push to halt vote counting," Fox29-TV, November 6, 2020. Online: https://www.fox29.com/news/dueling-protests-held-outside-convention-center-amid-trump-campaigns-push-to-halt-vote-counting.

79 See Dan Berry and Sheera Frankel, "'Be There. Will Be Wild!': Trump All but Circled the Date," *The New York Times*, January 6, 2021. Online: https://www.nytimes.com/2021/01/06/us/politics/capitol-mob-trump-supporters.html.

80 See David Neiwert, "Prosecutors' focus on one Trump tweet that inspired Jan. 6 insurrection hints at his culpability," *Daily Kos*, March 29, 2022. Online: https://www.dailykos.com/stories/2022/3/29/2088940/-Trump-s-Will-be-wild-tweet-for-Jan-6-was-call-to-action-for-wannabe-soldiers-in-an-uncivil-war.

81 See Dan Berry and Sheera Frankel, "'Be There. Will Be Wild!': Trump All but Circled the Date," *The New York Times*, January 6, 2021. Online: https://www.nytimes.com/2021/01/06/us/politics/capitol-mob-trump-supporters.html.

82 See David Neiwert, "'There will be blood': Fresh indictment shows trio of Californians eager for violence at Capitol," *Daily Kos*, November 30, 2021. Online: https://www.dailykos.com/stories/2021/11/30/2066905/--There-will-be-blood-Fresh-indictment-shows-trio-of-Californians-eager-for-violence-at-Capitol.

83 See Marcy Wheeler, "Gina Bisignano: If a Plea Deal Falls on the Docket and No One Hears It ..." *Emptywheel*, November 8, 2021. Online: https://www.emptywheel.net/2021/11/08/if-a-plea-deal-happens-and-no-one-knows-do-people-still-wail-that-the-january-6-investigation-is-accomplishing-nothing/.

84 See "Karen Goes On Homophobic Rant During L.A. Protest," *TMZ*, December 1, 2020. Online: https://www.tmz.com/2020/12/01/woman-homophobic-rant-protesting-covid-lockdown-los-angeles/.

85 See Sky Palma, "'Hateful moron': Trump supporter's business faces the internet's wrath after her anti-gay tirade goes viral," *Raw Story*, December 1, 2020. Online:

https://www.rawstory.com/2020/12/hateful-moron-trump-supporters-business-faces-the-internets-wrath-after-her-anti-gay-tirade-goes-viral/.

86   See U.S. Department of Justice, "Indictment," Daniel Joseph Rodriguez et. al., November 29, 2021. Online: http://cdn.cnn.com/cnn/2021/images/11/29/indictment.pdf.

87   See Sky Palma, "Capitol rioter busted after friend accidentally uses his real name on InfoWars call-in show," *Salon*, November 30, 2021. Online: https://www.salon.com/2021/11/30/capitol-rioter-busted-after-friend-accidentally-uses-his-real-name-on-infowars-call-in-show_partner/.

88   See U.S. Department of Justice, "Statement of Facts," January 16, 2021. Online: https://www.justice.gov/opa/page/file/1356556/download.

89   See Annie Grayer and Oliver Darcy, "Alex Jones met with 1/6 committee and says he pleaded the Fifth 'almost 100 times'," CNN, January 25, 2022. Online: https://www.cnn.com/2022/01/25/politics/alex-jones-january-6-plead-fifth/index.html.

90   See Ewan Palmer, "Alex Jones Says January 6 Committee 'Worse' Than McCarthyism Following Subpoena," *Newsweek*, November 23, 2021. Online: https://www.newsweek.com/alex-jones-subpoena-january-6-capitol-1652321.

91   See "Alex Jones turns on QAnon just days after leading QAnon through the streets of Washington D.C.," Facebook (video), January 14, 2021. Online: https://fb.watch/h-8rX26w8o/

92   See Susan Svrluga, "First, they lost their children. Then the conspiracy theories started. Now, the parents of Newtown are fighting back," *The Washington Post*, July 8, 2019. Online: https://www.washingtonpost.com/local/education/first-they-lost-their-children-then-the-conspiracies-started-now-the-parents-of-newtown-are-fighting-back/2019/07/08/f167b880-9cef-11e9-9ed4-c9089972ad5a_story.html.

93   See Chuck Lindell, "Texas Supreme Court: Alex Jones, InfoWars can be sued by Sandy Hook parents," *Austin American-Statesman,* January 22, 2021. Online: https://www.statesman.com/story/news/2021/01/22/alex-jones-sandy-hook-parents-texas-supreme-court/6670360002/.

94   See Frontline, "This Sandy Hook Father Lives In Hiding Because of Conspiracy Theories Fueled By Alex Jones," *PBS Frontline*, July 28, 2020. Online: https://www.pbs.org/wgbh/frontline/article/this-sandy-hook-father-lives-in-hiding-because-of-conspiracy-theories-fueled-by-alex-jones/.

95   See David Neiwert, "Alex Jones tried to play obstruction games with Sandy Hook 'hoax' lawsuits, but judge pulls plug," *Daily Kos*, October 1, 2021. Online: https://www.dailykos.com/stories/2021/10/1/2055577/-Judgement-Day-looms-for-Alex-Jones-after-judge-issues-default-judgement-in-Sandy-Hook-lawsuits.

96   See Jack Queen, "Jury awards $45.2 million in punitive damages in Alex Jones Sandy Hook trial," Reuters, August 6, 2022. Online: https://www.reuters.com/business/media-telecom/jury-alex-jones-defamation-case-begin-deliberations-punitive-damages-2022-08-05/.

97   See David Neiwert, "Alex Jones mocks $1 billion Sandy Hook verdict, but his fellow conspiracy theorists freak out," *Daily Kos*, October 14, 2022. Online: https://www.dailykos.com/stories/2022/10/14/2129035/-Alex-Jones-mocks-1-billion-Sandy-Hook-verdict-but-his-fellow-conspiracy-theorists-freak-out.

98   See Emily S. Rueb, "Sandy Hook Father Is Awarded $450,000 in Defamation Case," *The New York Times*, October 19, 2016. Online: https://www.nytimes.com/2019/10/16/us/sandy-hook-defamation.html.

99   See Karma Allen, "Sandy Hook shooting 'conspiracy theorist' arrested after tormenting families of victims: Police," ABC News, January 27, 2020. Online: https://abcnews.go.com/US/sandy-hook-shooting-conspiracy-theorist-arrested-tormenting-families/story?id=68570486.

100 See Derek Hawkins, "Sandy Hook hoaxer gets prison time for threatening 6-year-old victim's father," *The Washington Post*, June 8, 2017. Online: https://www.washingtonpost.com/news/morning-mix/wp/2017/06/08/sandy-hook-hoaxer-gets-prison-time-for-threatening-6-year-old-victims-father/.

101 See Zoe Tillman, "Infowars Host Owen Shroyer Has Been Charged In The Jan. 6 Riots," *BuzzFeed News*, August 20, 2021. Online: https://www.buzzfeednews.com/article/zoetillman/infowars-owen-shroyer-capitol-riot.

102 See Ewan Palmer, "Alex Jones Says January 6 Committee 'Worse' Than McCarthyism Following Subpoena," *Newsweek*, November 23, 2021. Online: https://www.newsweek.com/alex-jones-subpoena-january-6-capitol-1652321.

103 See David Neiwert, "The creep of QAnon: A small Puget Sound town feels the political effects of authoritarian cult," *Daily Kos*, January 27, 2021. Online: https://www.dailykos.com/stories/2021/1/27/2012401/-The-creep-of-QAnon-A-small-Puget-Sound-town-feels-the-political-effects-of-authoritarian-cult.

104 See Will Sommer, "Mayor Aims to Turn Small Town Into QAnon, USA," *The Daily Beast*, January 26, 2021. Online: https://www.thedailybeast.com/mayor-aims-to-turn-small-town-into-qanon-usa.

105 See Eric Wilkinson, "'He doesn't represent us': Group wants Sequim mayor ousted after QAnon conspiracy comments," KING-5 TV, September 17, 2020. Online: https://www.king5.com/article/news/local/sequim-mayor-william-armacost-qanon-conspiracy/281-4642ddc8-678f-4cc0-9398-d9b67246557c.

106 See William Armacost, "Letter to the editor," *Sequim Gazette*, August 19, 2020. Online: https://www.sequimgazette.com/letters/letters-to-the-editor-aug-19-2020/.

107 See Matthew Nash, "Support for city manager," *Peninsula Daily News*, January 25, 2021. Online: https://www.peninsuladailynews.com/news/support-for-city-manager/.

108 See David Neiwert, "Far-right radicalization interwoven with COVID conspiracist organizing as it spreads globally," *Daily Kos*, November 29, 2021. Online: https://www.dailykos.com/stories/2021/11/29/2066701/-Far-right-radicalization-interwoven-with-COVID-conspiracist-organizing-as-it-spreads-globally.

109 See Miles Parks, "Few Facts, Millions Of Clicks: Fearmongering Vaccine Stories Go Viral Online," National Public Radio, March 25, 2021. Online: https://www.npr.org/2021/03/25/980035707/lying-through-truth-misleading-facts-fuel-vaccine-misinformation.

110 See Michael Hiltzik, "Column: Following FDA approval of Pfizer's shot, the anti-vaccine movement cooks up new conspiracy theory," *The Los Angeles Times*, September 1, 2021. Online: https://www.latimes.com/business/story/2021-09-01/hiltzik-fda-approves-pfizer-anti-vax-conspiracy-theory.

111 See Nick Robins-Early, "How the Far-Right Is Radicalizing Anti-Vaxxers," *Vice*, November 29, 2021. Online: https://www.vice.com/en/article/88ggqa/how-the-far-right-is-radicalizing-anti-vaxxers.

112 See David Neiwert, "Neo-fascist attack in Rome shows how the far-right 'mini-insurrection' strategy is now global," *Daily Kos*, October 11, 2021. Online: https://www.dailykos.com/stories/2021/10/11/2057505/-Neo-fascist-attack-in-Rome-shows-how-the-far-right-mini-insurrection-strategy-is-now-global.

113 See Sebastian Leber, "Anti-Semitism online: Attila Hildmann blames Jews—and defends Hitler," *Tagespiel*, June 19, 2020. Online: https://www.tagesspiegel.de/gesellschaft/attila-hildmann-gibt-juden-die-schuld--und-verteidigt-hitler-4175905.html.

114 See Nick Robins-Early, "How the Far-Right Is Radicalizing Anti-Vaxxers," *Vice*, November 29, 2021. Online: https://www.vice.com/en/article/88ggqa/how-the-far-right-is-radicalizing-anti-vaxxers.

115 See David Neiwert, "Joined by array of far-right extremists, anti-vaxxers' D.C. march completes their transformation," *Daily Kos*, January 24, 2022. Online: https://www.dailykos.com/stories/2022/1/24/2076573/-Anti-mandates-march-in-D-C-manifests-how-anti-vaxxers-have-morphed-into-a-far-right-movement.

116 See Katie Mettler, Lizzie Johnson, Justin Wm. Moyer, Jessica Contrera, Emily Davies, Ellie Silverman, Peter Hermann and Peter Jamison, "Anti-vaccine activists march in D.C.—a city that mandates coronavirus vaccination—to protest mandates," *The Washington Post*, January 24, 2022. Online: https://www.washingtonpost.com/dc-md-va/2022/01/23/dc-anti-vaccine-rally-mandates-protest/.

117 See David Neiwert, "Violence emanating from far-right anti-vaccine/anti-mask contingent keeps ratcheting higher," *Daily Kos*, September 22, 2021. Online: https://www.dailykos.com/stories/2021/9/22/2053846/-Violence-emanating-from-far-right-anti-vaccine-anti-mask-contingent-keeps-ratcheting-higher.

118 See David Neiwert, "Montana 'Red Pill Festival' manifests how far-right conspiracism is mainstreamed in rural U.S.," *Daily Kos,* July 26, 2021. Online: https://www.dailykos.com/stories/2021/7/26/2042148/-Montana-Red-Pill-Festival-manifests-how-far-right-conspiracism-is-mainstreamed-in-rural-U-S.

Chapter 8: When Extremism Goes Mainstream

1 See Molly Ball, "The Final Humiliation of Reince Priebus," *The Atlantic*, July 30, 2017. Online: https://www.theatlantic.com/politics/archive/2017/07/the-final-humiliation-of-reince-priebus/535368/.

2 See Dylan Mathews, "Report: Reince Priebus literally got kicked out of the presidential motorcade," *Vox,* July 28, 2017. Online: https://www.vox.com/2017/7/28/16060352/reince-priebus-motorcade-air-force-one-departure.

3 See Philip Bump, "No senator ever voted to remove a president of his party from office. Until Mitt Romney," *The Washington Post*, Febraru 5, 2020. Online: https://www.washingtonpost.com/politics/2020/02/05/no-senator-ever-voted-remove-president-his-party-office-until-mitt-romney/.

4 See Bryan Schott, "How Utah Sen. Mike Lee tried to make the scheme to overturn Trump's election loss fit the Constitution," *The Salt Lake Tribune*, January 4, 2023. Online: https://www.sltrib.com/news/politics/2023/01/04/how-utah-sen-mike-lee-tried-make/.

5 See Sam Levine and Spencer Mestel, "'Just like propaganda': the three men enabling Trump's voter fraud lies," *The Guardian*, October 26, 2020. Online: https://www.theguardian.com/us-news/2020/oct/26/us-election-voter-fraud-mail-in-ballots.

6 See Maggie Haberman and Stephanie Saul, "Trump Encourages People in North Carolina to Vote Twice, Which Is Illegal," *The New York Times*, September 2, 2020. Online: https://www.nytimes.com/2020/09/02/us/politics/trump-people-vote-twice.html.

7 See Colby Itkowitz, "Trump won't commit to a 'peaceful transfer of power' if he loses," *The Washington Post*, September 23, 2020. Online: https://www.washington-

post.com/politics/trump-transfer-of-power/2020/09/23/be6954d0-fdf0-11ea-b555-4d71a9254f4b_story.html.

8   See Jane Timm, "Fact check: Echoing Trump, Barr misleads on voter fraud to attack expanded vote-by-mail," NBC News, September 9, 2020. Online: https://www.nbc-news.com/politics/2020-election/fact-check-echoing-trump-barr-misleads-voter-fraud-attack-expanded-n1240144.

9   See David Neiwert, "Brief moment of integrity so enraged Fox News' fans, they gave it a final shove into the abyss," *Daily Kos*, June 9, 2021. Online: https://www.dailykos.com/stories/2021/6/9/2034509/--We-went-crazy-How-Fox-News-was-finally-pushed-into-the-journalistic-abyss-by-its-audience.

10   See Brian Stelter, "'We turned so far right we went crazy:' How Fox News was radicalized by its own viewers," CNN, June 8, 2021. Online: https://www.cnn.com/2021/06/08/media/fox-news-hoax-paperback-book/index.html.

11   See Alex Gabbatt, "'Walked a fine line': how Fox News found itself in an existential crisis," *The Guardian*, November 15, 2020. Online: https://www.theguardian.com/media/2020/nov/15/fox-news-trump-criticism-supporters.

12   See Sarah Ellison, "Trump campaign was livid when Fox News called Arizona for Biden — and tensions boiled over on-air," *The Washington Post*, November 4, 2020. Online: https://www.washingtonpost.com/lifestyle/style/fox-news-election-night-arizona/2020/11/04/194f9968-1e71-11eb-90dd-abd0f7086a91_story.html.

13   See Lois Beckett, "'Fox News sucks!': Trump supporters decry channel as it declares Biden wins," *The Guardian*, November 6, 2020. Online: https://www.theguardian.com/media/2020/nov/05/fox-news-sucks-trump-supporters.

14   See Jeremy Barr, "Newsmax hopes conservative anger at Fox News and a few Trump tweets can boost the much smaller network," *The Washington Post*, November 10, 2020. Online: https://www.washingtonpost.com/media/2020/11/10/newsmax-fox-news-trump-tweets/.

15   See Alex Gabbatt, "'Walked a fine line': how Fox News found itself in an existential crisis," *The Guardian*, November 15, 2020. Online: https://www.theguardian.com/media/2020/nov/15/fox-news-trump-criticism-supporters.

16   See Matt Gertz, "Fox News is a loaded gun aimed at American democracy," Media Matters, May 14, 2021. Online: https://www.mediamatters.org/fox-news/fox-news-loaded-gun-aimed-american-democracy.

17   See David Neiwert, "Tucker Carlson transmits rising eco-fascist themes about immigrants in attacks on border policies," *Daily Kos*, March 22, 2021. Online: https://www.dailykos.com/stories/2021/3/22/2022359/-Tucker-Carlson-transmits-rising-ecofascist-themes-about-immigrants-in-attacks-on-border-policies.   See also David Neiwert, "Conservatives increasingly seeing fascism as a preferred alternative to liberal democratic rule," *Daily Kos*, March 30, 2021. Online: https://www.dailykos.com/stories/2021/3/30/2023717/-Blaming-the-left-red-pilled-conservatives-ready-to-give-up-on-democracy-and-embrace-fascism.   See also David Neiwert, "Tucker gives the Republican response to white nationalists: Gaslight, lie, and identify with them," *Daily Kos*, January 28, 2021. Online: https://www.dailykos.com/stories/2021/1/28/2012598/-Tucker-gives-the-Republican-response-to-white-nationalists-Gaslight-lie-and-identify-with-them. See also David Neiwert, "After Carlson spouts white nationalist 'replacement theory,' ADL chief says: 'Tucker must go'," *Daily Kos*, April 9, 2021. Online: https://www.dailykos.com/

stories/2021/4/9/2025163/-After-Carlson-spouts-white-nationalist-replacement-theory-ADL-chief-says-Tucker-must-go.

18 See "Remarks by President Biden Commemorating the 100th Anniversary of the Tulsa Race Massacre" (Greenwood Cultural Center, Tulsa, Oklahoma), Biden White House, June 1, 2021. Online: https://www.whitehouse.gov/briefing-room/speeches-remarks/2021/06/02/remarks-by-president-biden-commemorating-the-100th-an-niversary-of-the-tulsa-race-massacre/.

19 See Nikki McCann Ramirez, "Tucker Carlson falsely claims Joe Biden called white Republican men 'more dangerous than ISIS'," Twitter, June 1, 2021. Online: https://twitter.com/NikkiMcR/status/1399881458001580032.

20 See Nikki McCann Ramirez, "After self-reporting last night, Tucker once again defends white supremacists," Twitter, June 2, 2021. Online: https://twitter.com/NikkiMcR/status/1400249995715022851. See also David Neiwert, "Domestic terror in the age of Trump," Reveal News (Center for Investigative Reporting), July 9, 2020. Online: https://revealnews.org/article/domestic-terror-in-the-age-of-trump/.

21 See Matt Gertz, "Lachlan Murdoch gave Tucker Carlson the green light to spread 'replacement theory,' and he took it," Media Matters, June 8, 2021. Online: https://www.mediamatters.org/fox-news/lachlan-murdoch-gave-tucker-carlson-green-light-spread-replacement-theory-and-he-took-it.

22 See Media Matters staff, "As a Republican leader claims no one is questioning the election, Tucker Carlson and Mollie Hemingway cast doubt on the election," Media Matters, May 12, 2021. Online: https://www.mediamatters.org/fox-news/republican-leader-claims-no-one-questioning-election-tucker-carlson-and-mollie-hemingway.

23 See Alex Gabbatt, "'Walked a fine line': how Fox News found itself in an existential crisis," The Guardian, November 15, 2020. Online: https://www.theguardian.com/media/2020/nov/15/fox-news-trump-criticism-supporters.

24 See Peter Baker and Linda Qiu, "Inside What Even an Ally Calls Trump's 'Reality Distortion Field'," The New York Times, October 31, 2018. Online: https://www.nytimes.com/2018/10/31/us/politics/fact-check-trump-distortion-campaign.html.

25 See Devan Cole, "Scaramucci says Trump is a 'liar'," CNN, October 24, 2018. Online: https://www.cnn.com/2018/10/24/politics/anthony-scaramucci-donald-trump-liar-cnntv/index.html.

26 See Michael M. Grynbaum, "'You Are a Rude, Terrible Person': After Midterms, Trump Renews His Attacks on the Press," The New York Times, November 7, 2018. Online: https://www.nytimes.com/2018/11/07/business/media/trump-press-conference-media.html.

27 See especially Robert Altemeyer, The Authoritarians (Manitoba: Cherry Hill Publishing, 2007) and Marc J. Hetherington and Jonathan Weiler, Authoritarianism and Polarization in American Politics (Cambridge: Cambridge University Press, 2007).

28 See Michelle Gelfand, "Authoritarian leaders thrive on fear. We need to help people feel safe," The Guardian, January 2, 2020. Online: https://www.theguardian.com/commentisfree/2020/jan/02/authoritarian-leaders-people-safe-voters

29 See Amanda Taub, "The rise of American authoritarianism," Vox, March 1, 2016. Online: https://www.vox.com/2016/3/1/11127424/trump-authoritarianism.

30 See Robert R. McCrae, "Conceptions and Correlates of Openness to Experience," in *Handbook of Personality Psychology* (Academic Press, 1997), pp. 825-847. Online: https://www.sciencedirect.com/science/article/pii/B9780121346454500329.

31 See John W. Dean and Bob Altemeyer, *Authoritarian Nightmare: The Ongoing Nightmare of Trump's Followers* (New York: Melville House, 2021), pp. 150-174.

32 See David Neiwert, *Red Pill, Blue Pill: How to Counteract the Conspiracy Theories That Are Killing Us* (Lanham, MD: Prometheus Books, 2020), pp. 95-112.

33 See Thea Buckley, "Why Do Some People Believe in Conspiracy Theories?," *Scientific American*, July 1, 2015. Online: https://www.scientificamerican.com/article/why-do-some-people-believe-in-conspiracy-theories/.

34 See F. Pratto, J. Sidanius, L.M. Stallworth, and B.F. Malle, "Social dominance orientation: A personality variable predicting social and political attitudes," *Journal of Personality and Social Psychology*, 67(4), 741–763 (1974). Online: https://doi.org/10.1037/0022-3514.67.4.741.

35 See Russell Berman, "A Trump-Inspired Hate Crime in Boston," *The Atlantic*, August 20, 2015. Online: https://www.theatlantic.com/politics/archive/2015/08/a-trump-inspired-hate-crime-in-boston/401906/.

36 See Barbara Sprunt, "Here Are The Republicans Who Objected To The Electoral College Count," National Public Radio, January 7, 2021. Online: https://www.npr.org/sections/insurrection-at-the-capitol/2021/01/07/954380156/here-are-the-republicans-who-objected-to-the-electoral-college-count.

37 See Alexx Altman-Devilbiss, "Sen. Graham says 2nd impeachment 'will do far more harm than good'," WPDE-TV, January 12, 2021. Online: https://wpde.com/news/local/sen-graham-says-2nd-impeachment-will-do-far-more-harm-than-good.

38 See James Lankford, "Lankford Issues Statement on Impending Impeachment Trial in the Senate," Senate office press release, January 26, 2021. Online: https://www.lankford.senate.gov/news/press-releases/lankford-issues-statement-on-impending-impeachment-trial-in-the-senate.

39 See David Smith, "'It's endemic': state-level Republican groups lead party's drift to extremism," *The Guardian*, January 31, 2021. Online: https://www.theguardian.com/us-news/2021/jan/30/republicans-radical-extreme-state-parties.

40 See Lee Moran, "Oregon GOP Embraces Capitol Riot 'False Flag' Conspiracy Theory," *Huffpost*, January 27, 2021. Online: https://www.huffpost.com/entry/oregon-gop-donald-trump-capitol-riot_n_60113f4ac5b6c5586aa534a7.

41 See Alex Rogers, Lucy Kafanov and Jason Kravarik, "Matt Gaetz rails against Liz Cheney in Wyoming," CNN, January 29, 2021. Online: https://www.cnn.com/2021/01/28/politics/gaetz-cheney-rally-cheyenne-republican-reaction/index.html.

42 See Brianna Riley, "Wisconsin Republicans grapple with state of party post-Trump," *The Capital Times*, February 1, 2021. Online: https://captimes.com/news/local/govt-and-politics/wisconsin-republicans-grapple-with-state-of-party-post-trump/article_a7ea2bba-6769-5696-ba46-e3e3786db76b.html.

43 See Cheyna Roth, Jake Neher, "Michigan GOP at a Crossroads," WDET-FM, January 25, 2021. Online: https://wdet.org/2021/01/25/Michigan-GOP-at-a-Crossroads/.

44 See Marc Caputo, "'She is weighing us down': Georgia GOP cringes at Marjorie Taylor Greene spectacle," *Politico*, January 31, 2021. Online: https://www.politico.com/news/2021/01/31/marjorie-taylor-greene-georgia-gop-cringes-464170.

45   See Jennifer Kocher, "CNN Visits Gillette Woman Who Started Liz Cheney Recall Petition," *Cowboy State Daily*, January 28, 2021. Online: https://cowboystatedaily.com/2021/01/28/cnn-visits-gillette-woman-who-started-liz-cheney-recall-petition/.

46   See David Neiwert, "Republicans brazenly lie to cover their tracks from Jan. 6 insurrection because it actually works," *Daily Kos*, March 1, 2021. Online: https://www.dailykos.com/stories/2021/3/1/2018801/-Republicans-brazenly-lie-to-cover-their-tracks-from-Jan-6-insurrection-because-it-actually-works. See also Susan Page and Sarah Elbeshbishi, "Exclusive: Defeated and impeached, Trump still commands the loyalty of the GOP's voters," *USA Today*, February 21, 2021. Online: https://www.usatoday.com/story/news/politics/2021/02/21/exclusive-trump-party-he-still-holds-loyalty-gop-voters/6765406002/.

47   See Michael M. Grynbaum, Davey Alba and Reid J. Epstein, "How Pro-Trump Forces Pushed a Lie About Antifa at the Capitol Riot," *The New York Times*, March 1, 2021. Online: https://www.nytimes.com/2021/03/01/us/politics/antifa-conspiracy-capitol-riot.html.

48   See Tom Jackman, Marissa J. Lang and Jon Swaine, "Man who shot video of fatal Capitol shooting is arrested, remains focus of political storm," *The Washington Post*, January 16, 2021. Online: https://www.washingtonpost.com/nation/2021/01/16/sullivan-video-arrested/.

49   See Meg Anderson, "Antifa Didn't Storm The Capitol. Just Ask The Rioters," National Public Radio, March 2, 2021. Online: https://www.npr.org/2021/03/02/972564176/antifa-didnt-storm-the-capitol-just-ask-the-rioters.

50   See Joshua Zitser, "Far-right group Proud Boys claim they will attend January 6 DC rally 'incognito' and wear all-black to blend in with antifa protesters," *Business Insider*, January 3, 2021. Online: https://www.businessinsider.com/proud-boys-attend-january-6-dc-rally-incognito-all-black-2021-1.

51   See Marshall Cohen, "Trump supporters who breached the Capitol: 'It was not Antifa'," CNN, February 27, 2021. Online: https://www.cnn.com/2021/02/27/politics/capitol-attack-trump-supporters-not-antifa/index.html.

52   See David Neiwert, "Republicans double down on gaslighting narrative in House hearing: 'It was not an insurrection'," *Daily Kos*, May 12, 2021. Online: https://www.dailykos.com/stories/2021/5/12/2030221/-Republicans-double-down-on-gaslighting-narrative-in-House-hearing-It-was-not-an-insurrection.

53   See David Neiwert, "Tucker gives the Republican response to white nationalists: Gaslight, lie, and identify with them," *Daily Kos*, January 28, 2021. Online: https://www.dailykos.com/stories/2021/1/28/2012598/-Tucker-gives-the-Republican-response-to-white-nationalists-Gaslight-lie-and-identify-with-them.

54   See Nathalie Baptiste, "Biden Pledged to Fight White Supremacy. Prominent Conservatives Felt Personally Attacked," *Mother Jones*, January 22, 2021. Online: https://www.motherjones.com/politics/2021/01/biden-pledged-to-fight-white-supremacy-prominent-conservatives-felt-personally-attacked/.

55   See David Neiwert, "Tucker's gaslighting campaign is about more than just justifying the Jan. 6 Capitol insurrection," *Daily Kos*, November 24, 2021. Online: https://www.dailykos.com/stories/2021/11/4/2062386/-Tucker-s-gaslighting-campaign-is-about-more-than-just-justifying-the-Jan-6-Capitol-insurrection.

56   See David Neiwert, "Pre-insurrection intel revelations raise questions—just not the ones Tucker and Co. want to ask," *Daily Kos*, June 22, 2021. Online: https://

www.dailykos.com/stories/2021/6/22/2036638/-Pre-insurrection-intel-revela-tions-raise-questions-just-not-the-ones-Tucker-and-Co-want-to-ask.

57 See Aaron Blake, "Tucker Carlson's wild, baseless theory blaming the FBI for orga-nizing the Jan. 6 Capitol riot," *The Washington Post*, June 16, 2021. Online: https://www.washingtonpost.com/politics/2021/06/16/tucker-carlsons-tinfoil-hat-theory-blaming-fbi-jan-6/.

58 See Marshall Cohen, "Fact-check: Fox News and Republican lawmakers push new false flag conspiracy that FBI orchestrated US Capitol attack," CNN, June 17, 2021. Online: https://www.cnn.com/2021/06/17/politics/tucker-carlson-capitol-insurrec-tion-conspiracy/index.html.

59 See David Neiwert, "Carlson piles lie upon lie claiming white supremacist ter-ror is no threat, but NSA is spying on him," *Daily Kos*, June 30, 2021. Online: https://www.dailykos.com/stories/2021/6/30/2037826/-Carlson-piles-lie-upon-lie-claiming-white-supremacist-terror-is-no-threat-but-NSA-is-spying-on-him.

60 See David Neiwert, "Tucker's gaslighting campaign is about more than just justify-ing the Jan. 6 Capitol insurrection," *Daily Kos*, November 24, 2021. Online: https://www.dailykos.com/stories/2021/11/4/2062386/-Tucker-s-gaslighting-campaign-is-about-more-than-just-justifying-the-Jan-6-Capitol-insurrection.

61 See Stephen Battaglio, "Fox Nation streams Tucker Carlson doc pushing conspir-acy theory that government agents spurred insurrection," *The Los Angeles Times*, November 1, 2021. Online: https://www.latimes.com/entertainment-arts/business/story/2021-11-01/tucker-carlson-documentary-suggest-jan-6-insurrection-was-manipulated-by-the-government.

62 See Jason Stanley, "Tucker Carlson's 'Patriot Purge' Is Too Crazy to Believe — and Too Dangerous to Ignore," *Rolling Stone*, November 2, 2021. Online: https://www.rollingstone.com/politics/political-commentary/tucker-carlson-fox-news-january-6-fascism-1251277/.

63 See Roger Kimball, "The January 6 Insurrection Hoax," *Imprimis* (Hillsdale Col-lege), September 2021. Online: https://imprimis.hillsdale.edu/january-6-insur-rection-hoax/.

64 "How Mitch McConnell killed the US Capitol attack commission," *The Guardian*, May 29, 2021. Online: https://www.theguardian.com/us-news/2021/may/29/mitch-mcconnell-us-capitol-attack-commission-senate-republicans.

65 See "McCarthy Taps Banks to Lead Republicans on Jan. 6 Committee," press release, U.S. Congressman Jim Banks, July 19, 2021. Online: https://banks.house.gov/news/documentsingle.aspx?DocumentID=1921.

66 See Annie Grayer and Jeremy Herb, "McCarthy pulls his 5 GOP members from 1/6 committee after Pelosi rejects 2 of his picks," CNN, July 21, 2021. Online: https://www.cnn.com/2021/07/21/politics/nancy-pelosi-rejects-republicans-from-commit-tee/index.html.

67 See David Neiwert, "'Waving the bloody shirt': Conservatives resort to a time-worn tactic to gaslight the public," *Daily Kos*, February 25, 2021. Online: https://www.dailykos.com/stories/2021/2/25/2018098/-Republicans-embrace-old-wave-the-bloody-shirt-trope-to-gaslight-the-public-on-Jan-6-violence.

68 See Stephen Budiansky, *The Bloody Shirt: Terror After Appomatox* (New York: Penguin Books, 2008). See also Stephen Budiansky, "'The Bloody Shirt'," *The New York Times*, Janury 30, 2008. Online: https://www.nytimes.com/2008/01/30/books/chapters/1st-chapter-the-bloody-shirt.html.

69   See Brett Murphy, Will Carless, Marisa Kwiatkowski, and Tricia L. Nadolny, "A 2009 warning about right-wing extremism was engulfed by politics. There are signs it's happening again," *USA Today*, January 25, 2021. Online: https://www.usatoday.com/story/news/investigations/2021/01/25/twelve-years-before-capitol-riot-warning-right-wing-extremism-buried/6658284002/?gnt-cfr=1.

70   See "'Hannity' on updated mask guidance, immigration," Fox News (transcript), July 28, 2021. Online: https://www.foxnews.com/transcript/hannity-on-updated-mask-guidance-immigration.

71   See Nicholas Fandos, "Republicans are blaming Nancy Pelosi for the Jan. 6 attack. Their claims don't add up," *The New York Times*, July 27, 2021. Online: https://www.nytimes.com/2021/07/27/us/insurrection-pelosi-claims-fact-check.html. See also Savannah Rychick, "Elise Stefanik Calls Liz Cheney a 'Pelosi Pawn'," *Independent Journal Review*, July 28, 2021. Online: https://ijr.com/elise-stefanik-calls-liz-cheney-pelosi-pawn/.

72   See John Whitehouse, "Frequent Fox News guest calls officer testifying to January 6 commission a crisis actor," Media Matters, July 27, 2021. Online: https://www.mediamatters.org/january-6-insurrection/frequent-fox-news-guest-calls-officer-testifying-january-6-commission-crisis.

73   See David Neiwert, "'Bloody shirt' gaslighting hits fruition as Republicans valorize insurrectionists, attack accusers," *Daily Kos*, July 29, 2021. Online: https://www.dailykos.com/stories/2021/7/29/2042815/--Bloody-shirt-gaslighting-hits-fruition-as-Republicans-valorize-insurrectionists-attack-accusers.

74   See Fox News Staff, "Ingraham: Nancy Pelosi exploits January 6 in a ruthless power grab," Fox News, July 22, 2021. Online: https://www.foxnews.com/media/ingraham-nancy-pelosi-exploits-january-6-in-a-ruthless-power-grab.

75   See Sam Metz, "GOP censures Cheney, Kinzinger as it assails Jan. 6 probe," Associated Press, February 4, 2022. Online: https://apnews.com/article/donald-trump-salt-lake-city-election-2020-campaign-2016-liz-cheney-cca6eba133e2edee-7987cac10e86d5c7.

76   See "Read the Republican Censure of Cheney and Kinzinger," *The New York Times*, February 4, 2022. Online: https://www.nytimes.com/interactive/2022/02/04/us/rnc-resolution-censure-cheney-kinziger.html.

77   See Eli Yockley, "Most Voters Reject Jan. 6 as Legitimate Discourse, but Republicans Are Divided," *Morning Consult*, February 16, 2022. Online: https://morningconsult.com/2022/02/16/voters-reject-jan-6-legitimate-discourse-but-republicans-divided/.

78   See David Neiwert, "Trump's loyal general, Michael Flynn, 'at the center' of the insurrectionist war on democracy," *Daily Kos*, September 13, 2022. Online: https://www.dailykos.com/stories/2022/9/13/2122716/-In-the-right-s-war-on-democracy-Michael-Flynn-is-the-general-marshaling-Trump-s-MAGA-army.

79   See Matthew Rosenberg and Maggie Haberman, "Michael Flynn, Anti-Islamist Ex-General, Offered Security Post, Trump Aide Says," *The New York Times*, November 17, 2016. Online: https://www.nytimes.com/2016/11/18/us/politics/michael-flynn-national-security-adviser-donald-trump.html.

80   See Luke Harding, Stephanie Kirchgaessner and Nick Hopkins, "Michael Flynn: new evidence spy chiefs had concerns about Russian ties," *The Guardian*, March 31, 2017. Online: https://www.theguardian.com/us-news/2017/mar/31/michael-flynn-new-evidence-spy-chiefs-had-concerns-about-russian-ties.

81 See By Adam Goldman, Mark Mazzetti and Matthew Rosenberg, "F.B.I. Used In-
    formant to Investigate Russia Ties to Campaign, Not to Spy, as Trump Claims," *The
    New York Times*, May 18, 2018. Online: https://www.nytimes.com/2018/05/18/us/
    politics/trump-fbi-informant-russia-investigation.html.

82 See Luke Harding, Stephanie Kirchgaessner and Nick Hopkins, "Michael Flynn:
    new evidence spy chiefs had concerns about Russian ties," *The Guardian*, March 31,
    2017. Online: https://www.theguardian.com/us-news/2017/mar/31/michael-flynn-
    new-evidence-spy-chiefs-had-concerns-about-russian-ties.

83 See Emmarie Huetteman and Matthew Rosenberg, "Pentagon Inquiry Seeks to
    Learn if Flynn Hid Foreign Payment," *The New York Times*, April 27, 2017. Online:
    https://www.nytimes.com/2017/04/27/us/politics/michael-flynn-trump-investiga-
    tion-defense-department.html.

84 See Katelyn Polantz, "Appeals court denies Michael Flynn and Justice Depart-
    ment's effort to end his case," CNN, August 31, 2020. Online: https://www.cnn.
    com/2020/08/31/politics/michael-flynn-court-case/index.html.

85 See Eric Tucker, "Trump pardons Flynn despite guilty plea in Russia probe," Associ-
    ated Press, Niovember 26, 2020. Online: https://apnews.com/article/donald-trump-
    pardon-michael-flynn-russia-aeef585b08ba6f2c763c8c37bfd678ed.

86 See Nathalie Baptiste, "Newly Pardoned Michael Flynn Was a Crowd Favorite
    Among the Extremists at Trump's Latest Rally," *Mother Jones*, December 12, 2020.
    Online: https://www.motherjones.com/politics/2020/12/march-for-trump-dc-mi-
    chael-flynn/.

87 See Robert Draper, "Michael Flynn Is Still at War," *The New York Times*, February
    4, 2022. Online: https://www.nytimes.com/2022/02/04/magazine/michael-flynn-
    2020-election.html.

88 See Michelle R. Smith, "Michael Flynn: From government insider to holy warrior,"
    Associated Press/PBS Frontline, September 7, 2022. Online: https://apnews.com/ar-
    ticle/michael-flynn-christian-nationalism-investigation-50fa5dcff7f99cf93409fcd-
    6c1357bee.

89 See Bob Smietana, "Michael Flynn calls for 'one religion' at event that is a who's
    who of the new Christian right," *The Washington Post*, November 19, 2021. Online:
    https://www.washingtonpost.com/religion/2021/11/19/michael-flynn-alex-jones-
    feucht/.

90 See Simon Montlake, "Disgraced general to far-right hero: Michael Flynn rides the
    next wave," *Christian Science Monitor*, April 28, 2022. Online: https://www.csmoni-
    tor.com/USA/Politics/2022/0428/Disgraced-general-to-far-right-hero-Michael-
    Flynn-rides-the-next-wave.

91 See Michelle R. Smith, "Michael Flynn: From government insider to holy warrior,"
    Associated Press/PBS Frontline, September 7, 2022. Online: https://apnews.com/ar-
    ticle/michael-flynn-christian-nationalism-investigation-50fa5dcff7f99cf93409fcd-
    6c1357bee.

92 See David Neiwert, "The army of Trumpists gathering at megachurch rallies
    build around myth of stolen election," *Daily Kos*, April 25, 2022. Online: https://
    www.dailykos.com/stories/2022/4/26/2094096/-Trumpists-coalesce-at-mega-
    church-rallies-to-create-their-own-brand-of-a-far-right-extremism.

93 See David Neiwert, "'Constitutional sheriffs' want to be able to seize Dominion
    voting machines for 'investigation'," *Daily Kos*, June 24, 2022. Online: https://

www.dailykos.com/stories/2022/6/24/2106150/--Constitutional-sheriffs-want-to-be-able-to-seize-Dominion-voting-machines-for-investigation.

94   See David Neiwert, "Trumpists team up with far-right 'constitutional sheriffs' to promote plan to seize voting machines," *Daily Kos*, July 14, 2022. Online: https://www.dailykos.com/stories/2022/7/14/2110352/-Trumpists-team-up-with-far-right-constitutional-sheriffs-to-promote-plan-to-seize-voting-machines.

95   See David Neiwert, "Drop-box surveillance, central to CSPOA-Trumpist strategy, already happening in Seattle area," *Daily Kos*, July 20, 2022. Online: https://www.dailykos.com/stories/2022/7/20/2111546/-Drop-box-surveillance-central-to-CSPOA-Trumpist-strategy-already-happening-in-Seattle-area.

96   See Michelle R. Smith, "Michael Flynn: From government insider to holy warrior," Associated Press/PBS Frontline, September 7, 2022. Online: https://apnews.com/article/michael-flynn-christian-nationalism-investigation-50fa5dcff7f99cf93409fcd-6c1357bee.

97   See Michael Daly, "Even by Florida GOP Standards, This Is Lunacy," *The Daily Beast*, September 13, 2022. Online: https://www.thedailybeast.com/making-michael-flynn-a-sarasota-poll-watcher-is-lunacy.

98   See Peter Stone, "'It's a sham': fears over Trump loyalists' 'election integrity' drive," *The Guardian*, July 7, 2022. Online: https://www.theguardian.com/us-news/2022/jul/07/sham-fears-over-trump-loyalists-election-integrity-drive.

99   See Nicole Grigg, "'VITAMIN D': 'we're just out here getting some Vitamin D'," Twitter, October 19, 2022. https://twitter.com/nicolesgrigg/status/1582904476393820160.

100 See Brahm Resnick, "Ballot box watchers in Arizona face lawsuits by voting-rights advocates," 12News.com, October 25, 2022. Online: https://www.12news.com/article/news/politics/elections/decision/ballot-box-watchers-arizona-face-lawsuits-voting-rights-advocates/75-dc2fd978-09ea-47c4-9c2b-c3ae54a73ca3.

Chapter 9: Concocting Enemies

1   See David Neiwert, "The right's eliminationist narrative about antifa was borne of conspiracism and lives in it now," *Daily Kos*, September 2, 2020. Online: https://www.dailykos.com/stories/2020/9/2/1974558/-The-Fox-bred-Antifa-threat-narrative-began-as-a-far-right-conspiracy-theory-that-went-mainstream.

2   See Nicholas Bogel-Burroughs and Sandra E. Garcia, "What Is Antifa, the Movement Trump Wants to Declare a Terror Group?," *The New York Times*, Septmber 28, 2020. Online: https://www.nytimes.com/article/what-antifa-trump.html.

3   Seed Mark Bray, *ANTIFA: The Antifascist Handbook* (Brooklyn: Melville House, 2017.) See also Donald D. Denton, "ANTIFA: The Anti-Fascist Handbook and From Fascism to Populism in History" (review), *Terrorism and Political Violence*, January 8, 2021, Vol. 33, No. 1, 205-208. Online: https://www.tandfonline.com/doi/abs/10.1080/09546553.2021.1864970?journalCode=ftpv20.

4   See William La Jeunesse, "Several people stabbed during Neo-Nazi event in Sacramento," Fox News, June 27, 2016. Online: https://www.foxnews.com/us/several-people-stabbed-during-neo-nazi-event-in-sacramento.

5   See "The Hate Group Behind the Sacramento White Supremacist Rally," Anti-Defamation League, June 28, 2016. Online: https://web.archive.org/web/20160817211615/http://blog.adl.org/extremism/the-hate-group-behind-the-sacramento-white-supremacist-rally.

6 See David Neiwert, "'Communist Takeover' Paranoia Gets a Final Resuscitation for Trump's Inauguration," *Hatewatch* (SPLC), January 17, 2017. Online: https://www.splcenter.org/hatewatch/2017/01/17/'98communist-takeover'-paranoia-gets-final-resuscitation-trump's-inauguration.

7 See Hatewatch Staff, "Oath Keepers On Guard at Inauguration of President Donald Trump," *Hatewatch* (SPLC), January 20, 2017. Online: https://www.splcenter.org/hatewatch/2017/01/20/oath-keepers-guard-inauguration-president-donald-trump.

8 See David Neiwert, "Far Right Descends On Berkeley For 'Free Speech' And Planned Violence," *Hatewatch* (SPLC), April 17, 2017. Online: https://www.splcenter.org/hatewatch/2017/04/17/far-right-descends-berkeley-free-speech-and-planned-violence. See also David Neiwert, "Evergreen State Protest By 'Patriot' Group Dwarfed By Angry Response," *Hatewatch* (SPLC), June 16, 2017. Online: https://www.splcenter.org/hatewatch/2017/06/16/evergreen-state-protest-patriot-group-dwarfed-angry-response. See also David Neiwert, "Defiant Alt-Right 'Patriots' Encounter Portland's Simmering Anger After Train Killings," *Hatewatch* (SPLC), June 6, 2017. Online: https://www.splcenter.org/hatewatch/2017/06/06/defiant-alt-right-patriots-encounter-portlands-simmering-anger-after-train-killings.

9 See "Antifa: What is the alt-left group?," Fox News, September 7, 2017. Online: https://www.foxnews.com/video/5477586753001#sp=show-clips.

10 See "5 assaulted at Berkeley protests as black-clad anarchists storm rightwing rally," Fox News, Septrember 25, 2017. Online: https://www.foxnews.com/us/5-assaulted-at-berkeley-protests-as-black-clad-anarchists-storm-rightwing-rally.

11 See David Neiwert, "Bay Area Weekend Rallies Turn South For 'Patriot Prayer,' Ends In Violence," *Hatewatch* (SPLC), August 29, 2017.

12 See Katherine Lam, "Dartmouth faculty supports professor's comments justifying Antifa violence," Fox News, September 25, 2017. Online: https://www.foxnews.com/us/dartmouth-faculty-supports-professors-comments-justifying-antifa-violence.

13 See Ray Starmann, "An open letter to the hatemongers of Antifa," Fox News, September 19, 2017. Online: https://www.foxnews.com/opinion/an-open-letter-to-the-hatemongers-of-antifa.

14 See Steve Kurtz, "What I learned from the Antifa handbook: For starters, you won't believe who is defined as a 'fascist'," Fox News, September 18, 2017. Online: https://www.foxnews.com/opinion/what-i-learned-from-the-antifa-handbook-for-starters-you-wont-believe-who-is-defined-as-a-fascist.

15 See "Petition urging terror label for Antifa gets enough signatures for White House response," Fox News, September 25, 2017. Online: https://www.foxnews.com/politics/petition-urging-terror-label-for-antifa-gets-enough-signatures-for-white-house-response.

16 See Ned Ryun, "Antifa is a domestic terrorist organization and must be denounced by Democrats," Fox News, September 18, 2017. Online: https://www.foxnews.com/opinion/antifa-is-a-domestic-terrorist-organization-and-must-be-denounced-by-democrats.

17 See Tucker Carlson, "Should Antifa groups be barred from gathering?," Fox News (Tucker Carlson Tonight video), September 12, 2007. Online: https://www.foxnews.com/video/5560198797001.

18 See Rush Limbaugh, "The Democrats, Media and their Antifa Pit Bulls Are the Real Threat to America," *The Rush Limbaugh Show*, August 31, 2017. Online: https://

www.rushlimbaugh.com/daily/2017/08/31/the-democrats-media-and-their-antifa-pitbulls-are-the-real-threat-to-america/.

19 See David Neiwert, "Far-right conspiracists stir up hysteria about nonexistent 'civil war' plot by 'antifa'," *Hatewatch* (SPLC), November 14, 2017. Online: https://www.splcenter.org/hatewatch/2017/11/13/far-right-conspiracists-stir-hysteria-about-nonexistent-civil-war-plot-antifa.

20 See Kyle Swenson, "The antifa apocalypse is coming this weekend, if you believe the hype," *The Washington Post*, November 1, 2017. Online: https://www.washingtonpost.com/news/morning-mix/wp/2017/11/01/the-antifa-apocalypse-is-coming-this-weekend-if-you-believe-the-hype/.

21 See Caleb Parke, "Antifa apocalypse? Anarchist group's plan to overthrow Trump 'regime' starts Saturday," Fox News, November 3, 2017. Online: https://www.foxnews.com/us/antifa-apocalypse-anarchist-groups-plan-to-overthrow-trump-regime-starts-saturday.

22 See Media Matters staff, "Tucker Carlson: "Violent young men with guns will be in charge. They will make the rules, including the rules in your neighborhood," Media Matters, June 2, 2020. Online: https://www.mediamatters.org/tucker-carlson/tucker-carlson-violent-young-men-guns-will-be-charge-they-will-make-rules-including.

23 See David Neiwert, "Far-right conspiracists stir up hysteria about nonexistent 'civil war' plot by 'antifa'," *Hatewatch* (SPLC), November 14, 2017. Online: https://www.splcenter.org/hatewatch/2017/11/13/far-right-conspiracists-stir-hysteria-about-nonexistent-civil-war-plot-antifa.

24 See Erica Chenowerth and Jeremy Pressman, "This summer's Black Lives Matter protesters were overwhelmingly peaceful, our research finds," *The Washington Post*, October 16, 2020. Online: https://www.washingtonpost.com/politics/2020/10/16/this-summers-black-lives-matter-protesters-were-overwhelming-peaceful-our-research-finds/. See also Philip Bump, "Few of the deaths linked to recent protests are known to have been caused by demonstrators," *The Washington Post*, August 26, 2020. Online: https://www.washingtonpost.com/politics/2020/08/26/almost-none-deaths-linked-recent-protests-are-known-have-been-committed-by-protesters/.

25 See Mark Sumner, "White House doubles down on Trump's ugly attack on 75-year-old peace activist injured by police," *Daily Kos*, June 10, 2020. Online: https://www.dailykos.com/stories/2020/6/10/1952043/-White-House-doubles-down-on-Trump-s-ugly-attack-on-75-year-old-peace-activist-injured-by-police.

26 See Evan Perez and Jason Hoffman, "Trump tweets Antifa will be labeled a terrorist organization but experts believe that's unconstitutional," CNN, May 31, 2020. Online: https://www.cnn.com/2020/05/31/politics/trump-antifa-protests/index.html.

27 See Eric Kleefeld, "Fox & Friends spreads a debunked conspiracy theory about 'bricks and pickaxes' near protest sites," Media Matters, August 4, 2020. Online: https://www.mediamatters.org/crime-and-criminal-justice/fox-friends-spreads-debunked-conspiracy-theory-about-bricks-and-pickaxes.

28 See Anna Merlan, "NYPD Claims 'Looters' Put Bricks at a Brooklyn Corner Miles From Any Protest," *Vice*, June 30, 2020. Online: https://www.vice.com/en/article/889g8a/nypd-claims-looters-put-bricks-at-a-brooklyn-corner-miles-from-any-protest.

29 See David Neiwert, "'Boogaloo Bois' arrested en route to Las Vegas protest with arsenal of Molotov cocktails," *Daily Kos*, June 4, 2020. Online: https://www.dailykos.com/stories/2020/6/4/1950514/-Feds-arrest-trio-of-Boogaloo-Bois-planning-to-lob-Molotov-cocktails-at-Vegas-protest-crowd.

30 See Ken Klippenstein, "The FBI Finds 'No Intel Indicating Antifa Involvement' in Sunday's Violence," *The Nation*, June 1, 2020. Online: https://www.thenation.com/article/activism/antifa-trump-fbi/.

31 See Yael Halon, "DOJ 'targeting and investigating' leaders, funders of far-left groups and rioters, Wolf tells Tucker," Fox News, August 31, 2020. Online: https://www.foxnews.com/politics/chad-wolf-doj-investigating-far-left-rioters.

32 See Katie Shepherd, "Trump blames people in 'dark shadows' for protest violence, cites mysterious plane full of 'thugs' in black," *The Washington Post*, September 1, 2020. Online: https://www.washingtonpost.com/nation/2020/09/01/trump-laura-ingraham-conspiracy-theory/.

33 See Jan Wolfe, "U.S. Attorney General Barr says antifa 'flying around' U.S. to incite violence," Reuters, September 22, 2020. Online: https://www.reuters.com/article/us-global-race-barr-police/u-s-attorney-general-barr-says-antifa-flying-around-u-s-to-incite-violence-idUSKBN25T3AI.

34 See David Neiwert, "Internal review shows Trump's DHS concocted bogus intelligence blaming antifa for violence," *Daily Kos*, October 7, 2021. Online: https://www.dailykos.com/stories/2021/10/7/2056752/-Portland-invasion-by-Trump-s-DHS-goons-was-an-incompetent-shambles-internal-review-finds.

35 See Derrick Bryson Taylor, "George Floyd Protests: A Timeline," *The New York Times*, November 5, 2021. Online: https://www.nytimes.com/article/george-floyd-protests-timeline.html.

36 See Jason Silverstein, "The global impact of George Floyd: How Black Lives Matter protests shaped movements around the world," CBS News, June 4, 2021. Online: https://www.cbsnews.com/news/george-floyd-black-lives-matter-impact/.

37 See Gillian Flaccus, "Portland's grim reality: 100 days of protests, many violent," Associated Press, September 4, 2020. Online: https://apnews.com/article/virus-outbreak-ap-top-news-race-and-ethnicity-id-state-wire-or-state-wire-b57315d97dd2146c4a89b4636faa7b70.

38 See Mark Sumner, "DHS actions in Portland are making things worse, by design," *Daily Kos*, July 22, 2020. Online: https://www.dailykos.com/stories/2020/7/22/1962859/-DHS-forces-in-Portland-drive-increase-in-violence-as-they-proactively-grab-people-off-the-streets.

39 See Richard Read, "Federal agents in Portland continue crackdown; protesters and local leaders shout, 'Go home'," *The Los Angeles Times*, July 18, 2020. Online: https://www.latimes.com/world-nation/story/2020-07-18/portland-protests-federal-agents.

40 See David Neiwert, "Internal review shows Trump's DHS concocted bogus intelligence blaming antifa for violence," *Daily Kos*, October 7, 2021. Online: https://www.dailykos.com/stories/2021/10/7/2056752/-Portland-invasion-by-Trump-s-DHS-goons-was-an-incompetent-shambles-internal-review-finds.

41 See Julie Sabatier, "A conversation with Oregon Sen. Ron Wyden," Oregon Public Broadcasting, October 5, 2021. Online: https://www.opb.org/article/2021/10/05/a-conversation-with-oregon-sen-ron-wyden/.

42 See Department of Homeland Security, "Report on DHS Administrative Review into I&A Open Source Collection and Dissemination Activities During Civil Unrest," January 6, 2021. Online: https://www.documentcloud.org/documents/21074152-dhs-intelligence-internal-review-report-20210930.

43 See Ryan Nguyen, "Police shoot Portland protester in head with impact weapon, causing severe injuries," *The Oregonian*, July 12, 2020. Online: https://www.oregonlive.com/news/2020/07/police-shoot-portland-protester-in-head-with-impact-weapon-causing-severe-injuries.html.

44 See John Ismay, "A Navy Veteran Had a Question for the Feds in Portland. They Beat Him in Response," *The New York Times*, July 20, 2020. Online: https://www.nytimes.com/2020/07/20/us/portland-protests-navy-christopher-david.html.

45 See Alex Hardgrave, "'Standing next to our sisters': Shared experiences with Portland's Wall of Moms," *The Oregonian*, July 27, 2020. Online: https://www.oregonlive.com/portland/2020/07/the-people-behind-portlands-wall-of-moms.html.

46 See Karina Brown, "Feds Use Tear Gas on Thousands of Portland Protesters," *Courthouse News*, July 25, 2020. Online: https://www.courthousenews.com/feds-use-tear-gas-on-thousands-of-portland-protesters/.

47 See Sergio Olmos, Mike Baker and Zolan Kanno-Youngs, "Federal Officers Deployed in Portland Didn't Have Proper Training, D.H.S. Memo Said," *The New York Times*, July 18, 2020. Online: https://www.nytimes.com/2020/07/18/us/portland-protests.html.

48 See Melissa Quinn, "Federal agents in downtown Portland to begin leaving, Oregon governor announces," CBS News, July 30, 2020. Online: https://www.cbsnews.com/news/federal-agents-portland-phased-withdrawal-leaving/.

49 See Department of Homeland Security, "Report on DHS Administrative Review into I&A Open Source Collection and Dissemination Activities During Civil Unrest," January 6, 2021. Online: https://www.documentcloud.org/documents/21074152-dhs-intelligence-internal-review-report-20210930.

50 See David Neiwert, "Whistleblower reveals how Trump has unleashed another plague: white-supremacist terrorism," *Daily Kos*, September 12, 2020. Online: https://www.dailykos.com/stories/2020/9/12/1976976/-Whistleblower-reveals-how-Trump-has-unleashed-another-plague-white-supremacist-terrorism.

51 See David Neiwert, "'Antifa buses!' Panicked armed men hit small-town streets across America to fend off imagined hordes," *Daily Kos*, June 9, 2020. Online: https://www.dailykos.com/stories/2020/6/9/1951844/--Antifa-buses-Panicked-armed-men-hit-small-town-streets-across-America-to-fend-off-imagined-hordes.

52 See Mike Adams, "BREAKING: Antifa terrorists to be bused to Sparta, Illinois with orders to burn farm houses and kill livestock in rural 'white' areas," *Natural News*, June 3, 2020. Online: https://naturalnews.com/2020-06-03-antifa-terrorists-sparta-illinois-burn-farmhouses-kill-livestock.html.

53 See Nicole Blanchard and Ruth Brown, "Police: No, antifa not sending 'a plane load of their people' to Idaho to incite riots," *The Idaho Statesman*, June 2, 2020. Online: https://www.idahostatesman.com/news/local/article243180241.html.

54 See Joe Sneve, "Sioux Falls Police chief: Rumors of out-of-state agitators being bused in appear to be 'false flag'," *Sioux Falls Argus Leader*, June 1, 2020. Online: https://www.argusleader.com/story/news/2020/06/01/sioux-falls-police-chief-fargo-busses-protests/5310672002/.

55 See David Neiwert, "Police officials' amplification of 'antifa bus' hoax rumors in summer 2020 bodes ill for future," *Daily Kos,* January 17, 2022. Online: https://m.dailykos.com/stories/2022/1/17/2074517/-Police-officials-amplification-of-antifa-bus-hoax-rumors-in-summer-2020-bodes-ill-for-future.

56   See Brandy Zadrozny and Ben Collins, "In Klamath Falls, Oregon, victory declared over antifa, which never showed up," NBC News, June 6, 2020. Online: https://www.nbcnews.com/tech/social-media/klamath-falls-oregon-victory-declared-over-antifa-which-never-showed-n1226681.

57   See Ben Collins, Brandy Zadrozny and Emmanuelle Saliba, "White nationalist group posing as antifa called for violence on Twitter," NBC News, June 1, 2020. Online: https://www.nbcnews.com/tech/security/twitter-takes-down-washington-protest-disinformation-bot-behavior-n1221456.

58   See David Neiwert, "Police officials' amplification of 'antifa bus' hoax rumors in summer 2020 bodes ill for future," Daily Kos, January 17, 2022. Online: https://m.dailykos.com/stories/2022/1/17/2074517/-Police-officials-amplification-of-antifa-bus-hoax-rumors-in-summer-2020-bodes-ill-for-future.

59   See Christian Giardinelli, "'Not a call to arms,' Curry County Sheriff explains Facebook post on rumored 'Antifa bus'," KTVL-TV, June 3, 2020. Online: https://ktvl.com/news/local/not-a-call-to-arms-curry-county-sheriff-explains-facebook-post-on-rumored-antifa-bus.

60   See Karen Wall, "Fake Online Posts Sow Fear, Anxiety In NJ Amid Unrest," Patch (Toms River, NJ), June 5, 2020. Online: https://patch.com/new-jersey/tomsriver/fake-online-posts-sow-fear-anxiety-nj-amid-unrest.

61   See Brandy Zadrozny and Ben Collins, "In Klamath Falls, Oregon, victory declared over antifa, which never showed up," NBC News, June 6, 2020. Online: https://www.nbcnews.com/tech/social-media/klamath-falls-oregon-victory-declared-over-antifa-which-never-showed-n1226681.

62   See "Family reportedly harassed in Forks after being accused of being members of Antifa," Peninsula Daily News, June 6, 2020. Online: https://www.peninsuladailynews.com/crime/family-harassed-in-forks-after-being-accused-of-being-members-of-antifa/.

63   See Caroline Warnock, "Family Harassed & Accused of Being Antifa by Residents in Forks, Wash," Heavy, June 5, 2020. Online: https://heavy.com/news/2020/06/forks-washington-campers-harassed/.

64   See Jason Wilson, "Rightwing vigilantes on armed patrol after fake rumours of antifa threat," The Guardian, June 6, 2020. Online: https://www.theguardian.com/us-news/2020/jun/06/rightwing-vigilante-armed-antifa-protests.

65   See Caleb Hutton and Ian Davis-Leonard, "100 armed vigilantes rouse fear, soul-searching in Snohomish," The Daily Herald (Everett, WA), June 8, 2020. Online: https://www.heraldnet.com/news/100-armed-vigilantes-rouse-fear-soul-searching-in-snohomish/.

66   See Jillian Ward, "Hundreds turn out to stop rumored riot," The Western World (Bandon, OR), June 3, 2020. Online: https://theworldlink.com/news/local/hundreds-turn-out-to-stop-rumored-riot/article_b58d6386-a59b-11ea-90f0-7f3504c58c5d.html.

67   See John Oliphint, "False rumors, police and mayoral tweets targeted bus named Buttercup amid protests," The Columbus Dispatch, June 16, 2020. Online: https://www.dispatch.com/story/special/2020/06/16/false-rumors-police-and-mayoral-tweets-targeted-bus-named-buttercup-amid-protests/42142157/.

68   See Marco Rubio, "Police in Ohio," Twitter, June 1, 2020. Online: https://twitter.com/marcorubio/status/1267615757548113920.

69   See Shelby Reilly and Christina Giradinelli, "Protest against the killing of George Floyd continues into the night in downtown Medford," KTVL-TV, June 1, 2020. On-

line: https://ktvl.com/news/local/hundreds-gather-in-medford-to-protest-death-of-george-floyd.

70 See Kip Hill and Chad Sokol, "Armed presence in North Idaho towns questioned by some politicians, business owners," *The Spokesman-Review,* June 5, 2020. Online: https://www.spokesman.com/stories/2020/jun/04/armed-presence-in-north-idaho-downtowns-questioned/.

71 See David Neiwert, "'Antifa arson' hoax rumors spread faster than wildfires in besieged West Coast rural areas," *Daily Kos,* September 10, 2020. Online: https://www.dailykos.com/stories/2020/9/10/1976604/--Antifa-arson-hoax-rumors-spread-faster-than-wildfires-in-besieged-West-Coast-rural-areas.

72 See David Neiwert, "Armed vigilantes set up rural checkpoints in Oregon as 'antifa fires' hoax inflames social media," *Daily Kos,* September 14, 2020. Online: https://www.dailykos.com/stories/2020/9/14/1977463/-Armed-vigilantes-set-up-rural-checkpoints-in-Oregon-as-antifa-fires-hoax-inflames-social-media.

73 See K. Rambo, "Clackamas County deputy placed on leave after video captures him blaming antifa for putting 'lives at stake' in wildfires," *The Oregonian,* September 14, 2020. Online: https://www.oregonlive.com/news/2020/09/clackamas-county-deputy-placed-on-leave-after-video-captures-him-blaming-antifa-for-putting-lives-at-stake-in-wildfires.html.

74 See David Neiwert, "'Antifa arsonists' hoax gets a boost from Trump, Rogan, Fox and others into the mainstream," *Daily Kos,* September 18, 2020. Online: https://www.dailykos.com/stories/2020/9/18/1978583/--Antifa-arsonists-hoax-gets-a-boost-from-Trump-Rogan-Fox-and-others-into-the-mainstream.

75 See David Neiwert, "What's the 'critical race theory' uproar really about? The right-wing need to fabricate enemies," *Daily Kos,* June 17, 2021. Online: https://www.dailykos.com/stories/2021/6/17/2035824/-What-s-the-critical-race-theory-uproar-really-about-The-right-wing-need-to-fabricate-enemies.

76 See Matt Grossman, "Fox News mentions of 'critical race theory'," Twitter, June 14, 2021. Online: https://twitter.com/MattGrossmann/status/1404641163492171782. See also Lis Power, "Fox News' obsession with critical race theory, by the numbers," Media Matters, June 15, 2021. Online: https://www.mediamatters.org/fox-news/fox-news-obsession-critical-race-theory-numbers.

77 See Sarah Schwartz, "Map: Where Critical Race Theory Is Under Attack," *Education Week, June 11, 2021.* Online: https://www.edweek.org/policy-politics/map-where-critical-race-theory-is-under-attack/2021/06. See also Tyler Kingkade, Brandy Zadrozny, and Ben Collins, "Critical race theory battle invades school boards—with help from conservative groups," NBC News, June 15, 2021. Online: https://www.nbcnews.com/news/us-news/critical-race-theory-invades-school-boards-help-conservative-groups-n1270794.

78 See Marisa Iati, "What is critical race theory, and why do Republicans want to ban it in schools?," *The Washington Post,* May 29, 2021. Online: https://www.washington-post.com/education/2021/05/29/critical-race-theory-bans-schools/.

79 See Laura Clawson, "Reporter asks Republican lawmaker to define critical race theory. The result is what you'd expect," *Daily Kos,* June 15, 2021. Online: https://www.dailykos.com/stories/2021/6/15/2035402/-Republican-demonization-of-critical-race-theory-would-be-hilarious-if-it-wasn-t-so-dangerous.

80 See "Lockheed Martin is forcing a 'neo-racist' reeducation camp on employees, subsidized by taxpayers: Chris Rufo," Fox News, May 26, 2021. Online: https://www.

foxnews.com/media/lockheed-martin-forcing-neo-racist-reeducation-camp-subsidized-taxpayers-chris-rufo.

81 See Abby Liorico, "Explaining critical race theory and why it's causing a stir in schools across the country," KSDK-TV, May 3, 2021. Online: https://www.ksdk.com/article/news/education/explaining-critical-race-theory-causing-stir-schools-across-country/63-75fe7982-8613-4555-b519-d1a7a85be20e.

82 See Jon Greenberg and Amy Sherman, "What is critical race theory, and why are conservatives blocking it?," *Politifact*, May 24, 2021. Online: https://www.politifact.com/article/2021/may/24/what-critical-race-theory-and-why-are-conservative/.

83 See Kate McGee, "Texas "critical race theory" bill limiting teaching of current events signed into law," *The Texas Tribune*, June 15, 2021. Online: https://www.texastribune.org/2021/06/15/abbott-critical-race-theory-law/.

84 See Tyler Kingkade, Brandy Zadrozny, and Ben Collins, "Critical race theory battle invades school boards — with help from conservative groups," NBC News, June 15, 2021. Online: https://www.nbcnews.com/news/us-news/critical-race-theory-invades-school-boards-help-conservative-groups-n1270794.

85 See Christopher Rufo, "The goal is to have the public read," Twitter, March 15, 2021. Online: https://web.archive.org/web/20210609235759/https://twitter.com/realchrisrufo/status/1371541044592996352.

86 See "The Wedge Document," Discovery Institute, published 1998. Online: https://ncse.ngo/wedge-document.

87 See "Marxism," Discovery Institute topic. Online: https://www.discovery.org/t/marxism/. See also Scott S. Powell, "Cultural Marxism and Universal Misery," Discovery Institute, September 21, 2020. Online: https://www.discovery.org/v/cultural-marxism-and-universal-misery/. See also Christopher Rufo, "What You Need To Know About Critical Race Theory," Discovery Institute, September 23, 2020. Online: https://www.discovery.org/v/what-you-need-to-know-about-critical-race-theory/.

88 See Christopher Rufo, "The Politics of Ruinous Compassion," Discovery Institute, October 16, 2018. Online: https://www.discovery.org/a/20243/. See also Ross Reynolds, "'Homelessness is now a billion-dollar industry,' says this Seattle conservative," KUOW-FM, March 12, 2019. Online: https://www.kuow.org/stories/chris-rufo-thinks-seattle-must-rethink-its-approach-to-solving-homelessness.

89 See Katie Herzog, "Former City Council Candidate Chris Rufo Presents His Evidence of Online Harassment," *The Stranger*, November 16, 2018. Online: https://www.thestranger.com/articles/2018/11/16/35689714/former-city-council-candidate-chris-rufo-presents-his-evidence-of-online-harassment.

90 See Alex Shephard, "The Specter of Critical Race Theory Is Rotting Republicans' Brains," *The New Republic*, June 16, 2021. Online: https://newrepublic.com/article/162737/critical-race-theory-conservative-scam.

Chapter 10: Taking It to the Streets

1 See David Neiwert, "Street brawlers as strategy: Far-right invasions of liberal urban areas prove adaptable, successful," *Daily Kos*, September 22, 2020. Online: https://www.dailykos.com/stories/2020/9/22/1979777/-Street-brawlers-as-strategy-Far-right-invasions-of-liberal-urban-areas-prove-adaptable-successful.

2 See Isaac Stanley-Becker, Joshua Partlow and Carissa Wolf, "Luxury cars, MAGA flags and Facebook invites: How an unknown Idaho family organized the Port-

land rally that turned deadly," *The Washington Post*, September 21, 2020. Online: https://www.washingtonpost.com/politics/idaho-family-portland-trump-rally/2020/09/21/246ef878-f2e5-11ea-b796-2dd09962649c_story.html.

3   See Faiz Siddiqui and Isaac Stanley-Becker, "One person shot dead in Portland following clashes between pro-Trump supporters, counterprotesters," *The Washington Post*, August 30, 2020. Online: https://www.washingtonpost.com/nation/2020/08/29/blm-activists-counterprotesters-clash-portland-leading-arrests/. See also David Neiwert, "Police track down man suspected of Portland protest shooting, kill him in hail of gunfire," *Daily Kos*, September 4, 2020. Online: https://www.dailykos.com/stories/2020/9/4/1974937/-Police-track-down-man-suspected-of-Portland-protest-shooting-kill-him-in-hail-of-gunfire.

4   See David Neiwert, "'Civil war is here, right now': 'Patriots' urge Trump to empower militias to fight antifa in streets," *Daily Kos*, August 31, 2020. Online: https://www.dailykos.com/stories/2020/8/31/1974015/-Oath-Keepers-to-Trump-Send-out-the-militias-to-stop-antifascists-Marxist-takeover-of-America.

5   See Isaac Stanley-Becker, Joshua Partlow and Carissa Wolf, "Luxury cars, MAGA flags and Facebook invites: How an unknown Idaho family organized the Portland rally that turned deadly," *The Washington Post*, September 21, 2020. Online: https://www.washingtonpost.com/politics/idaho-family-portland-trump-rally/2020/09/21/246ef878-f2e5-11ea-b796-2dd09962649c_story.html.

6   See Igor Ostanin, "Russian-State-Linked Figures Promoted Portland 'Cruise Rally' & Fake News Site Inciting New American Civil War," *Byline Times*, September 5, 2020. Online: https://bylinetimes.com/2020/09/05/russian-state-linked-figures-promoted-portland-cruise-rally-and-fake-news-site-inciting-new-american-civil-war/.

7   See David Neiwert, "Trump caravan in Oregon deliberately blurs lines between mainstream GOP and extremist right," *Daily Kos*, September 8, 2020. Online: https://www.dailykos.com/stories/2020/9/8/1975970/-Trump-caravan-in-Oregon-deliberately-blurs-lines-between-mainstream-GOP-and-extremist-right.

8   See David Nakamura, Matt Viser and Robert Klemko, "'Great Patriots!': Trump lavishes praise on supporters amid deadly clashes with social justice protesters," *The Washington Post*, August 30, 2020. Online: https://www.washingtonpost.com/politics/trump-biden-kenosha-portland/2020/08/30/42f50c50-ead5-11ea-ab4e-581edb849379_story.html.

9   See RT, "#Portland rioters try to block pro-Trump 'caravan'," Twitter, August 30, 2020. Online: https://twitter.com/rt_com/status/1300123618198855681.

10   See Isaac Stanley-Becker, Joshua Partlow and Carissa Wolf, "Luxury cars, MAGA flags and Facebook invites: How an unknown Idaho family organized the Portland rally that turned deadly," *The Washington Post*, September 21, 2020. Online: https://www.washingtonpost.com/politics/idaho-family-portland-trump-rally/2020/09/21/246ef878-f2e5-11ea-b796-2dd09962649c_story.html.

11   See David Neiwert, "Proud Boys' would-be violent march on Portland turns and heads the other direction," *Daily Kos*, August 18, 2019. Online: https://www.dailykos.com/stories/2019/8/18/1879837/-Proud-Boys-would-be-violent-march-on-Portland-turns-and-heads-the-other-direction.

12   See David Neiwert, "Always paranoid, 'Patriot' militiamen push back against coronavirus social isolation measures," *Daily Kos*, March 31, 2020. Online: https://www.dailykos.com/stories/2020/3/31/1932782/-Always-paranoid-Patriot-militiamen-push-back-against-coronavirus-social-isolation-measures.

13 See David Neiwert, "Far-right Idaho legislators' session whips up extremists' sound and fury over COVID-19 orders," *Daily Kos*, June 25, 2020. Online: https://www.dailykos.com/stories/2020/6/25/1955902/-Far-right-Idaho-legislators-session-whips-up-extremists-sound-and-fury-over-COVID-19-orders.

14 See David Neiwert, "Militiamen's reactionary presence at protests threatens democracy, and police appear on their side," *Daily Kos*, July 29, 2020. Online: https://www.dailykos.com/stories/2020/7/29/1964969/-Militiamen-s-reactionary-presence-at-protests-threatens-democracy-and-police-appear-on-their-side.

15 See David Neiwert, "Trump caravan in Oregon deliberately blurs lines between mainstream GOP and extremist right," *Daily Kos*, September 8, 2020. Online: https://www.dailykos.com/stories/2020/9/8/1975970/-Trump-caravan-in-Oregon-deliberately-blurs-lines-between-mainstream-GOP-and-extremist-right.

16 See David Neiwert, "Far-right street theater is all about creating a 'violent left' bogeyman for mass consumption," *Daily Kos*, August 27, 2020. Online: https://www.dailykos.com/stories/2020/8/27/1972883/-Far-right-street-theater-is-all-about-creating-a-violent-left-bogeyman-for-mass-consumption.

17 See Maxine Bernstein, "Judge sends self-proclaimed Proud Boy Alan Swinney to prison for 10 years, citing his lack of remorse," *The Oregonian*, December 14, 2021. Online: https://www.oregonlive.com/crime/2021/12/judge-sends-self-proclaimed-proud-boy-alan-swinney-to-prison-for-10-years-citing-his-lack-of-remorse.html.

18 See Christian Morales, "What We Know About the Shooting of Jacob Blake," *The New York Times*, November 16, 2021. Online: https://www.nytimes.com/article/jacob-blake-shooting-kenosha.html.

19 See Russell Brandon, "Facebook takes down 'call to arms' event after two shot dead in Kenosha," *The Verge*, August 26, 2020. Online: https://www.theverge.com/2020/8/26/21402571/kenosha-guard-shooting-facebook-deplatforming-militia-violence.

20 See David Neiwert, "Teenage militiaman fatally shoots two Kenosha protesters, is charged with first-degree murder," *Daily Kos*, August 26, 2020. Online: https://www.dailykos.com/stories/2020/8/26/1972478/-Armed-militiaman-shoots-protesters-two-fatally-during-Kenosha-protests-over-police-shooting.

21 See Julie Bosman and Sarah Mervosh, "Justice Dept. to Open Investigation Into Kenosha Shooting," *The New York Times*, Augut 26, 2020. Online: https://www.nytimes.com/2020/08/26/us/kenosha-shooting-protests-jacob-blake.html.

22 See David Neiwert, "Green-lighting murder: Tide of right-wing support for Kenosha protest killings will encourage more," *Dailly Kos*, August 28, 2020. Online: https://www.dailykos.com/stories/2020/8/28/1973189/-Green-lighting-murder-Tide-of-right-wing-support-for-Kenosha-protest-killings-will-encourage-more.

23 See Bill Glauber, Sophie Carson, and Molly Beck, "Trump mischaracterizes Kenosha protest shooting, defends Rittenhouse on eve of visit to city roiled by unrest, violence," *Milwaukee Journal-Sentinel*, August 31, 2020. Online: https://www.jsonline.com/story/news/politics/elections/2020/08/31/trump-doesnt-condemn-rittenhouse-mischaracterizes-kenosha-shooting-visit-wisconsin/5679100002/.

24 See Connor Perrett, "Kyle Rittenhouse's mom reportedly received a 'standing ovation' from the crowd at a Republican event in Wisconsin," *Insider*, September 26, 2020. Online: https://www.insider.com/wendy-kyle-rittenhouse-standing-ovation-at-gop-event-2020-9.

25 See Alaa Elassar, "A Republican student group at Arizona State University is raising money for the legal defense of the Kenosha shooting suspect," CNN, August 31, 2020. Online: https://www.cnn.com/2020/08/31/us/kenosha-arizona-state-university-kyle-rittenhouse-donations-trnd/index.html.

26 See Brooke Seipel, "GOP lawmaker praises Kyle Rittenhouse's 'restraint' for not emptying magazine during shooting," *The Hill*, September 4, 2020. Online: https://thehill.com/homenews/news/515181-gop-lawmaker-praises-kyle-rittenhouses-restraint-for-not-emptying-magazine/.

27 See Julia Ainsley, "Internal document shows Trump officials were told to make comments sympathetic to Kyle Rittenhouse," NBC News, October 1, 2020. Online: https://www.nbcnews.com/politics/national-security/internal-document-shows-trump-officials-were-told-make-comments-sympathetic-n1241581.

28 See Robert Klemko and Greg Jaffe, "A mentally ill man, a heavily armed teenager and the night Kenosha burned," *The Washington Post*, October 3, 2020. Online: https://www.washingtonpost.com/nation/2020/10/03/kenosha-shooting-victims/.

29 See Aldous J. Pennyfarthing, "Kenosha shooter was photographed sitting in front row of Trump rally in January," *Daily Kos*, August 26, 2020. Online: https://www.dailykos.com/stories/2020/8/26/1972595/-Kenosha-shooter-was-photographed-sitting-in-front-row-of-Trump-rally.

30 See Media Matters staff, "Tucker Carlson: 'How shocked are we that 17-year-olds with rifles decided they had to maintain order when no one else would?'," Media Matters, August 26, 2020. Online: https://www.mediamatters.org/tucker-carlson/tucker-carlson-how-shocked-are-we-17-year-olds-rifles-decided-they-had-maintain.

31 See Madeline Peltz, "Sean Hannity's lawyer is apparently soliciting donations for the Kenosha gunman," Media Matters, August 27, 2020. Online: https://www.mediamatters.org/sean-hannity/sean-hannitys-lawyer-apparently-soliciting-donations-kenosha-gunman.

32 See Olivia Little, Rhea Bhatnagar, and Pam Vogel, "Right-wing media hype vigilante violence after gunman shoots and kills protesters in Kenosha," Media Matters, August 26, 2020. Online: https://www.mediamatters.org/black-lives-matter/right-wing-media-hype-vigilante-violence-after-gunman-shoots-and-kills.

33 See David Neiwert, "Green-lighting murder: Tide of right-wing support for Kenosha protest killings will encourage more," *Dailly Kos*, August 28, 2020. Online: https://www.dailykos.com/stories/2020/8/28/1973189/-Green-lighting-murder-Tide-of-right-wing-support-for-Kenosha-protest-killings-will-encourage-more.

34 See Tobi Thomas, Adam Gabbatt and Caelainn Barr, "Nearly 1,000 instances of police brutality recorded in US anti-racism protests," *The Guardian*, October 29, 2020. Online: https://www.theguardian.com/us-news/2020/oct/29/us-police-brutality-protest. See also Mara Hvistendahl and Alleen Brown, "Armed Vigilantes Antagonizing Protesters Have Received a Warm Reception From Police," *The Intercept*, June 19, 2020. Online: https://theintercept.com/2020/06/19/militia-vigilantes-police-brutality-protests/.

35 See Christopher Mathias, "White Vigilantes Have Always Had A Friend In Police," *Huffpost*, August 28, 2020. Online: https://www.huffpost.com/entry/white-vigilantes-kenosha_n_5f4822bcc5b6cf66b2b5103e.

36 See Evan Hill, Stella Cooper, Drew Jordan and Dmitriy Khavin, "How the Fatal Shooting at a Portland Protest Unfolded," *The New York Times*, August 31, 2020.

Online: https://www.nytimes.com/2020/08/31/video/portland-protests-shooting-investigation.html.

37　See Sergio Olmos, Jonathan Levinson, Bradley W. Parks, and Kimberly Freda, "Person shot and killed during pro-Trump car caravan through downtown Portland," Oregon Public Broadcasting, August 29, 2020. Online: https://www.opb.org/article/2020/08/30/portland-trump-cruise-rally-protest-rogue-river-pendleton/. See also "New York Times bureau chief hit with paintball while covering pro-Trump rally in Portland," *Press Freedom Tracker*, August 29, 2020. Online: https://pressfreedomtracker.us/all-incidents/two-journalists-hit-with-projectiles-while-covering-a-pro-trump-caravan-in-portland/.

38　See Conrad Wilson, "When the political divide turned deadly in Portland," Oregon Public Broadcasting, November 2, 2020. Online: https://www.opb.org/article/2020/11/02/when-the-political-divide-turned-deadly-in-portland/.

39　See Evan Hill, Stella Cooper, Drew Jordan and Dmitriy Khavin, "How the Fatal Shooting at a Portland Protest Unfolded," *The New York Times*, Auguat 31, 2020. Online: https://www.nytimes.com/2020/08/31/video/portland-protests-shooting-investigation.html.

40　See Vice News, "Man Linked to Killing at a Portland Protest Says He Acted in Self-Defense," *Vice*, September 3, 2020. Online: https://www.vice.com/en/article/v7g8vb/man-linked-to-killing-at-a-portland-protest-says-he-acted-in-self-defense.

41　See David Neiwert, "Police track down man suspected of Portland protest shooting, kill him in hail of gunfire," *Daily Kos*, September 4, 2020. Online: https://www.dailykos.com/stories/2020/9/4/1974937/-Police-track-down-man-suspected-of-Portland-protest-shooting-kill-him-in-hail-of-gunfire.

42　See Bryan Denson and Conrad Wilson, "New Eyewitness Accounts: Feds Didn't Identify Themselves Before Opening Fire on Portland Antifa Suspect," *ProPublica*, October 13, 2020. Online: https://www.propublica.org/article/new-eyewitness-accounts-feds-didnt-identify-themselves-before-opening-fire-on-portland-antifa-suspect.

43　See Donald Trump, "Why aren't the Portland Police ARRESTING the cold blooded killer of Aaron 'Jay' Danielson," Twitter, September 3, 2020. Online: https://twitter.com/realDonaldTrump/status/1301726907298385921,

44　See Acyn, "Trump: We sent in the US Marshals, took 15 minutes and it was over," Twitter, October 15, 2020. Online: https://twitter.com/Acyn/status/1316801262277455872.

45　See "Statement by Attorney General William P. Barr on the Tracking Down of Fugitive Michael Forest Reinoehl," Department of Justice press release, September 4, 2020. Online: https://www.justice.gov/opa/pr/statement-attorney-general-william-p-barr-tracking-down-fugitive-michael-forest-reinoehl.

46　See Jason Hanna and Josh Campbell, "Trump gloats about US Marshals' killing of Portland 'antifa' suspect," CNN, October 15, 2020. Online: https://www.cnn.com/2020/10/15/politics/trump-fugitive-shooting/index.html.

47　See Asawin Suebsaeng, "Team Trump Frantically Plots New Ways to Make Him Feel Good About Himself," *The Daily Beast*, July 16, 2020. Online: https://www.thedailybeast.com/team-trump-frantically-plots-new-ways-to-make-him-feel-good-about-himself.

48　See Jose Pagliery and Asawin Suebsaeng, "Trump Boat Parades Left Untold Destruction in Their Wake," *The Daily Beast*, July 4, 2021. Online: https://www.thedailybeast.com/donald-trump-boat-parades-left-untold-destruction-in-their-wake.

49 See David Neiwert, "Street brawlers as strategy: Far-right invasions of liberal urban areas prove adaptable, successful," *Daily Kos*, September 22, 2020. Online: https://www.dailykos.com/stories/2020/9/22/1979777/-Street-brawlers-as-strategy-Far-right-invasions-of-liberal-urban-areas-prove-adaptable-successful.

50 See David Neiwert, "Trump caravan in Oregon deliberately blurs lines between mainstream GOP and extremist right," *Daily Kos*, September 8, 2020. Online: https://www.dailykos.com/stories/2020/9/8/1975970/-Trump-caravan-in-Oregon-deliberately-blurs-lines-between-mainstream-GOP-and-extremist-right.

51 See David Neiwert, "Texas 'Trump Train' of flag-bearing pickups ambushes, harasses Biden-Harris campaign bus," *Daily Kos*, October 31, 2020. Online: https://www.dailykos.com/stories/2020/10/31/1991393/-Caravan-of-pro-Trump-vehicles-harasses-Biden-Harris-campaign-bus-in-Texas-freeway-ambush.

52 See David Neiwert, "As Texas 'Trump Train' terrorized Biden campaign bus, some police refused to provide escort," *Daily Kos*, November 1, 2021. Online: https://www.dailykos.com/stories/2021/11/1/2061550/-As-Texas-Trump-Train-terrorized-Biden-campaign-bus-some-police-refused-to-provide-escort.

53 See David Neiwert, "Election by intimidation: Texas bus ambush by 'Trump Train' embraced eagerly by Republicans," *Daily Kos*, November 2, 2020. Online: https://www.dailykos.com/stories/2020/11/2/1991980/-Election-by-intimidation-Texas-bus-ambush-by-Trump-Train-embraced-eagerly-by-Republicans.

54 See Gustavo Martínez Contreras, Amanda Oglesby, and Erik Larsen, "Garden State Parkway, Lakewood play host to Trump 'MAGA Drag' car rallies in NJ," *Asbury Park Press*, November 2, 2020. Online: https://www.app.com/story/news/politics/2020/11/01/support-trump-rolls-strong-lakewood-across-garden-state-parkway/6114257002/.

55 See Brooke Kemp, "Pro-Trump caravan rally around I-465 impacts traffic, State Police official says," *Indianapolis Star*, November 1, 2020. Online: https://www.indystar.com/story/news/local/2020/11/01/pro-trump-caravan-rally-circles-465-indianapolis-and-impacts-traffic/6117219002/.

56 See "Statement Regarding 'Biden Bus' Incident," Republican Party of Texas, press release, October 31, 2020. Online: https://texasgop.org/statement-biden-bus-incident/.

57 See "'We Love What They Did': Florida Sen. Marco Rubio Supports Pro-Trump Caravan That Swarmed Biden Bus," CBS News, November 3, 2020. Online: https://www.cbsnews.com/miami/news/florida-senator-marco-rubio-supports-pro-trump-caravan-swarmed-biden-bus-texas/.

58 See Kate McGee, Jeremy Schwartz, and Abby Livingston, "Biden camp cancels multiple Texas events after a 'Trump Train' surrounded a campaign bus," *The Texas Tribune*, October 31, 2020. Online: https://www.texastribune.org/2020/10/31/biden-trump-texas-bus/.

59 See David Neiwert, "Trump's dead-enders organize capitol-steps rallies around the nation populated with extremists," *Daily Kos*, November 9, 2020. Online: https://www.dailykos.com/stories/2020/11/9/1994542/-Trump-s-dead-enders-organize-capitol-steps-rallies-around-the-nation-populated-with-extremists.

60 See David Neiwert, " 'Million MAGA March' Saturday will commingle white nationalists, conspiracists, Trump fans," *Daily Kos*, November 11, 2020. Online: https://www.dailykos.com/stories/2020/11/11/1995112/--Million-MAGA-March-Saturday-will-commingle-white-nationalists-conspiracists-Trump-fans.

61 See David Neiwert, "'Million MAGA March' draws thousands of extremists to D.C. claiming Trump won the election," *Daily Kos*, November 14, 2020. Online: https://www.dailykos.com/stories/2020/11/14/1995811/--Million-MAGA-March-draws-thousands-of-extremists-to-D-C-claiming-Trump-won-the-election.

62 See David Neiwert, "Violence breaks out after nightfall in D.c. as MAGA marchers bring thug tactics to the capital," *Daily Kos*, November 15, 2020. Online: https://www.dailykos.com/stories/2020/11/15/1996002/-After-nightfall-MAGA-marchers-bring-far-right-s-street-brawling-tactics-to-the-nation-s-capital.

63 See Lauren Sue, "DC cops accused of standing idle during 'springtime for Proud Boys and White Supremacy'," *Daily Kos*, December 13, 2020. Online: https://www.dailykos.com/stories/2020/12/13/2001697/--Stop-guys-stop-please-stop-DC-Cops-meet-Proud-Boys-violent-rampage-with-polite-request.

64 See David Neiwert, "Proud Boys torch their claims to nonviolence with hate crime attacks on Black churches in D.C.," *Daily Kos*, December 17, 2020. Online: https://www.dailykos.com/stories/2020/12/17/2002658/--Reminiscent-of-cross-burnings-Proud-Boys-torch-pretense-along-with-D-C-churches-BLM-signs.

65 See David Neiwert, "Pro-Trump rally expected to bring chaos, violence to D.C. streets while Congress certifies election," *Daily Kos*, January 4, 2021. Online: https://www.dailykos.com/stories/2021/1/4/2005924/-Pro-Trump-rally-expected-to-bring-chaos-violence-to-D-C-streets-while-Congress-certifies-election.

66 See David Neiwert, "Police go missing as Proud Boys shut down public park in Oregon for armed far-right rally," *Daily Kos*, May 3, 2021. Online: https://www.dailykos.com/stories/2021/5/3/2028797/-Proud-Boys-mark-their-public-return-with-a-threatening-Oregon-rally-and-no-police-presence.

67 See Spencer S. Hsu and Emily Davies, "Two more tied to Proud Boys hit with conspiracy charges in Jan. 6 Capitol breach," *The Washington Post*, March 26, 2021. Online: https://www.washingtonpost.com/local/legal-issues/proud-boys-brothers-charged/2021/03/26/e70b66bc-8e64-11eb-a730-1b4ed9656258_story.html.

68 See Claire Withycombe and Virginia Barreda, "4 arrests made after protesters attempt to enter Oregon State Capitol during session," *Salem Statesman-Journal*, Dedcember 21, 2020. Online: https://www.statesmanjournal.com/story/news/politics/2020/12/21/protesters-gather-oregon-legislature-starts-special-session/3993102001/.

69 See Tim Gruver, "Oregon lawmaker charged with two misdemeanors for role in invasion of state capitol," *The Center Square Oregon*, May 1, 2021. Online: https://www.thecentersquare.com/oregon/oregon-lawmaker-charged-with-two-misdemeanors-for-role-in-invasion-of-state-capitol/article_275672c0-aa3a-11eb-9f00-b7898e30cd64.html.

70 See Justine Coleman, "Fox News host says Kyle Rittenhouse was 'innocent,' 'demonized'," *The Hill*, September 23, 2020. Online: https://thehill.com/homenews/media/517854-fox-news-host-says-kyle-rittenhouse-was-innocent-demonized/.

71 See Robert Mackey, "Rittenhouse Trial Judge Blocks Prosecutor From Asking If Far-Right Videographer Is Biased," *The Intercept*, November 11, 2021. Online: https://theintercept.com/2021/11/11/rittenhouse-trial-judge-blocks-prosecutor-asking-far-right-videographer-biased/.

72 See Erik Ortiz, "Rittenhouse judge in spotlight after disallowing word 'victims' in courtroom," NBC News, October 27, 2021. Online: https://www.nbcnews.com/

news/us-news/rittenhouse-judge-spotlight-after-disallowing-word-victims-court-room-n1282559.

73 See David Neiwert, "As judge puts thumb on scales of justice, Rittenhouse's likely acquittal creates recipe for violence," *Daily Kos*, November 12, 2021. Online: https://www.dailykos.com/stories/2021/11/12/2064025/-Rittenhouse-s-inevitable-ac-quittal-will-be-green-light-for-far-right-extremists-itching-for-violence.

74 See Nicholas Bogel-Burroughs, "At the Kyle Rittenhouse trial this morning," Twitter, November 11, 2021. Online: https://twitter.com/NickAtNews/sta-tus/1458820790007308300.

75 See Sean Hollister, "Judge buys Rittenhouse lawyer's inane argument that Apple's pinch-to-zoom manipulates footage," *The Verge*, November 10, 2021. Online: https://www.theverge.com/2021/11/10/22775580/kyle-rittenhouse-trial-judge-apple-ai-pinch-to-zoom-footage-manipulation-claim.

76 See Ron Filipowski, "Here, we learn on cross-examination in the Rittenhouse tri-al," Twitter, November 11, 2021. Online: https://twitter.com/RonFilipkowski/sta-tus/1458886930205192192.

77 See David Neiwert, "Rittenhouse verdict celebrated on right-wing social media as green light for killing protesters," *Daily Kos*, November 20, 2021. Online: https://www.dailykos.com/stories/2021/11/20/2065434/-Rittenhouse-verdict-celebrated-on-right-wing-social-media-as-green-light-for-killing-protesters.

Chapter 11: Those That Work Forces

1 See Brittany Shammas, Timothy Bella, Katie Mettler and Dalton Bennett, "Four Minneapolis officers are fired after video shows one kneeling on neck of black man who later died," *The Washington Post*, May 26, 2020. Online: https://www.washing-tonpost.com/nation/2020/05/26/minneapolis-police-death-custody-fbi/.

2 See Kim Barker, Mike Baker, and Ali Watkins, "In City After City, Police Mishan-dled Black Lives Matter Protests," *The New York Times*, March 20, 2021. Online: https://www.nytimes.com/2021/03/20/us/protests-policing-george-floyd.html.

3 See Noelle Crombie and Shane Dixon Kavanaugh, "Shots fired: Deadly Portland police encounters reveal troubling patterns," *The Oregonian*, August 15, 2020. On-line: https://www.oregonlive.com/portland/2020/08/shots-fired-deadly-portland-police-encounters-reveal-troubling-patterns.html.

4 See "Nearly 100 arrested during 4 days of Portland protests, DA's office says," KATU-TV, June 2, 2020. Online: https://katu.com/news/local/nearly-100-arrested-during-4-days-of-portland-protests-das-office-says.

5 See David Neiwert, "Contrasting cases reveal why Portland's citizens no longer be-lieve their police will protect them," *Daily Kos*, August 16, 2020. Online: https://www.dailykos.com/stories/2020/8/16/1969837/-80-days-of-protest-Two-dispa-rate-cases-illustrate-the-chasm-between-Portland-and-its-police-force.

6 See Katie Shepherd, "Portland police arrest a hate crime survivor and Wall of Moms organizer in crackdown," *The Washington Post*, August 10, 2020. Online: https://www.washingtonpost.com/nation/2020/08/10/portland-demetria-hester-arrest/.

7 See David Neiwert, "Portland protesters targeted by pipe bombs at city park, and activists identify a suspect," *Daily Kos*, August 11, 2020. Online: https://www.dailykos.com/stories/2020/8/11/1968248/-Pipe-bombs-targeting-Portland-protesters-appear-to-be-the-latest-twist-in-far-right-tactics.

8 See "Update: PPB Needs Help From In-Person Witnesses in Regard to Explosive Device," Portland Police Bureau news release, August 18, 2020. Online: https://flashalert.net/id/portlandpolice/136808.

9 See Conrad Wilson and Amelia Templeton, "Portland Woman Attacked Day Before Fatal MAX Stabbings Says Police, TriMet Failed Her," Oregon Public Broadcasting, August 18, 2017. Online: https://www.opb.org/news/article/jeremy-christian-demetria-hester-max-train-attack-portland-police/. See also Maxine Bernstein, "Woman criticizes TriMet, Portland police response on day before MAX stabbing," *The Oregonian*, August 18, 2017. Online: https://www.oregonlive.com/portland/2017/08/max_attack_victim_criticizes_t.html.

10 See Allison Frost, Dave Miller, and Samantha Matsumoto, "Portland activist Demetria Hester on Moms United for Black Lives and the revolution," Oregon Public Broadcasting, August 12, 2020. Online: https://www.opb.org/article/2020/08/12/portland-activist-demetria-hester-on-moms-united-for-black-lives-and-the-revolution/.

11 See Amy B. Wang, "'Final act of bravery': Men who were fatally stabbed trying to stop anti-Muslim rants identified," *The Washington Post*, May 27, 2017. Online: https://www.washingtonpost.com/news/post-nation/wp/2017/05/27/man-fatally-stabs-2-on-portland-ore-train-after-they-interrupted-his-anti-muslim-rants-police-say/.

12 See Maxine Bernstein, "Portland MAX hero's last words: 'Tell everyone on this train I love them'," *The Oregonian*, May 29, 2017. Online: https://www.oregonlive.com/portland/2017/05/max_heros_last_words_tell_ever.htm.

13 See Ralph Ellis, Eliott C. McLaughlin and Madison Park, "Portland stabbing suspect yells in court: Free speech or die," CNN, May 31, 207. Online: https://www.cnn.com/2017/05/30/us/portland-train-teenager-stabbing-arraignment/.

14 See Terray Sylvester, "Suspect in fatal Portland attack yells about 'free speech' at hearing," Reuters, May 30, 2017. Online: https://www.reuters.com/article/us-usa-muslims-portland-idUSKBN18Q11F.

15 See David Neiwert, "Defiant Alt-Right 'Patriots' Encounter Portland's Simmering Anger After Train Killings," *Hatewatch* (SPLC), June 6, 2017. Online: https://www.splcenter.org/hatewatch/2017/06/06/defiant-alt-right-patriots-encounter-portlands-simmering-anger-after-train-killings.

16 See Jason Wilson, "Member of Portland militia-style group helps police arrest anti-fascist protester," *The Guardian*, June 8, 2017. Online: https://www.theguardian.com/us-news/2017/jun/08/portland-alt-right-rally-militia-member-police-arrest.

17 See Brad Schmidt, "Dueling Portland rallies end without major violence, but police intervene," *The Oregonian*, June 5, 2017. Online: https://www.oregonlive.com/portland/2017/06/dueling_portland_rallies_end_w.html.

18 See Katie Shepherd, "Portland Police Saw Right-Wing Protesters as "Much More Mainstream" Than Leftist Ones," *Willamette Week*, June 27, 2018. Online: https://www.wweek.com/news/courts/2018/06/27/portland-police-saw-right-wing-protesters-as-much-more-mainstream-than-leftist-ones/.

19 See Katie Shepherd, "Commissioner Chloe Eudaly Asked Portland Police A Series of Questions About Past Protests. They Declined to Answer Most of Them," *Willamette Week*, November 8, 2018. Online: https://www.wweek.com/news/courts/2018/11/08/commissioner-chloe-eudaly-asked-portland-police-a-series-of-questions-about-past-protests-they-declined-to-answer-most-of-them/.

20 See Katie Shepherd, "Texts Between Portland Police and Patriot Prayer Ringleader Joey Gibson Show Warm Exchange," *Willamette Week*, February 14, 2019. Online:

https://www.wweek.com/news/courts/2019/02/14/texts-between-portland-police-and-patriot-prayer-ringleader-joey-gibson-show-warm-exchange/. See also Alex Zielinski, "Texts Show Protective Relationship Between Portland Cops and Patriot Prayer," *The Portland Mercury*, February 14, 2019. Online: https://www.portland-mercury.com/news/2019/02/14/25885836/texts-show-protective-relationship-between-portland-cops-and-patriot-prayer.

21 See David Neiwert, "Portland Police's chummy handling of far-right extremists creates a well-earned uproar," *Daily Kos*, February 18, 2019. Online: https://www.dailykos.com/stories/2019/2/18/1835528/-Portland-Police-s-chummy-handling-of-far-right-extremists-creates-a-well-earned-uproar.

22 See David Neiwert, "To no one's surprise, Portland internal investigation exonerates Patriots' liaison officer," *Daily Kos*, September 13, 2019. Online: https://www.dailykos.com/stories/2019/9/13/1885204/-To-no-one-s-surprise-Portland-internal-investigation-exonerates-Patriots-liaison-officer.

23 See David Neiwert, "Portland far-right rally once again quickly turns violent as march becomes a riot," *Hatewatch* (SPLC), July 3, 2018. Online: https://www.splcenter.org/hatewatch/2018/07/03/portland-far-right-rally-once-again-quickly-turns-violent-march-becomes-riot.

24 See David Neiwert, "Proud Boys' would-be violent march on Portland turns and heads the other direction," *Daily Kos*, August 18, 2019. Online: https://www.dailykos.com/stories/2019/8/18/1879837/-Proud-Boys-would-be-violent-march-on-Portland-turns-and-heads-the-other-direction.

25 See Alex Zielinski, "Hall Monitor: Seeing Red," *The Portland Mercury*, September 26, 2019. Online: https://www.portlandmercury.com/news/2019/09/26/27205184/hall-monitor-seeing-red.

26 See Meerah Powell, "Woman Assaulted Day Prior To MAX Train Killings Testifies In Trial," Oregon Public Broadcasting, January 31, 2020. Online: https://www.opb.org/news/article/portland-oregon-max-train-killings-jeremy-christian-trial-day-4/.

27 See Meerah Powell, "Portland MAX Stabbing Victims Call Out Racist System During Sentencing Hearing," Oregon Public Broadcasting, June 23, 2020. Online: https://www.opb.org/news/article/jeremy-christian-sentencing-hearing-victim-impact-statements-portland-oregon/.

28 See Aime Green, "Judge sentences MAX train murderer Jeremy Christian to 'true life': He should never be released from prison," *The Oregonian*, June 24, 2020. Online: https://www.oregonlive.com/news/2020/06/live-updates-max-train-murderer-jeremy-christian-will-be-sentenced-after-more-victims-testify.html. See also *The Oregonian* video, "Jeremy Christian threatens to kill victim during outburst at sentencing," YouTube, June 24, 2020. Online: https://www.youtube.com/watch?v=Cw1DrzcQBHA.

29 See Jayati Ramakrishnan, "Demetria Hester urges protesters to 'do your part' as charges dismissed after arrest," *The Oregonian*, August 10, 2020. Online: https://www.oregonlive.com/pacific-northwest-news/2020/08/demetria-hester-urges-protesters-to-do-your-part-as-charges-dismissed-after-arrest.html.

30 See Maxine Bernstein, "Hundreds of Portland protesters will see their criminal cases dropped as DA announces plan to 'recognize the right to speak'," *The Oregonian*, August 11, 2020. Online: https://www.oregonlive.com/crime/2020/08/hundreds-of-portland-protesters-will-see-their-criminal-cases-dropped-as-da-announces-plan-to-recognize-the-right-to-speak.html.

31 See Tess Riski, "Reform Candidate Mike Schmidt Wins Multnomah County District Attorney Race," *Willamette Week*, May 19, 2020. Online: https://www.wweek.com/news/2020/05/19/reform-candidate-mike-schmidt-wins-multnomah-county-district-attorney-race/.

32 See Spek, "Huge follow-up on the car attack committed by Seattle Police a few nights ago," Twitter, August 15, 2020. Online: https://twitter.com/spekulation/status/1294725350576939008.

33 See Bureau of Justice Assistance, "Understanding Community Policing: A Framework for Action," U.S. Department of Justice Monograph, August 1994. Online: https://www.ojp.gov/pdffiles/commp.pdf. See also Robert C. Ankony, "Community Alienation and Its Impact on Police," National Criminal Justice Reference Service, Octobere 1999. Online: https://www.ojp.gov/ncjrs/virtual-library/abstracts/community-alienation-and-its-impact-police.

34 See John Eligon and Kay Nolan, "When Police Don't Live in the City They Serve," *The New York Times*, August 18, 2016. Online: https://www.nytimes.com/2016/08/19/us/when-police-dont-live-in-the-city-they-serve.html.

35 See Allison Frost, Dave Miller, and Samantha Matsumoto, "Portland activist Demetria Hester on Moms United for Black Lives and the revolution," Oregon Public Broadcasting, August 12, 2020. Online: https://www.opb.org/article/2020/08/12/portland-activist-demetria-hester-on-moms-united-for-black-lives-and-the-revolution/.

36 See Michael German, "Hidden in Plain Sight: Racism, White Supremacy, and Far-Right Militancy in Law Enforcement," Brennan Center for Justice, August 27, 2020. Online: https://www.brennancenter.org/our-work/research-reports/hidden-plain-sight-racism-white-supremacy-and-far-right-militancy-law.

37 See David Neiwert, "'Those that work forces' are too often connected to the racist far right, report finds," *Daily Kos*, September 3, 2020. Online: https://www.dailykos.com/stories/2020/9/3/1974810/--Those-that-work-forces-are-too-often-connected-to-the-racist-far-right-report-finds.

38 See David Neiwert, "Police officials grapple with post-Jan. 6 reality: Extremism in their own ranks is problem No. 1," *Daily Kos*, February 19, 2021. Online: https://www.dailykos.com/stories/2021/2/19/2017057/-Police-officials-grapple-with-post-Jan-6-reality-Extremism-in-their-own-ranks-is-problem-No-1.

39 See Kevin Rector and Richard Winton, "Law enforcement confronts an old threat: far-right extremism in the ranks. 'Swift action must be taken'," *The Los Angeles Times*, February 17, 2021. Online: https://www.latimes.com/california/story/2021-02-17/lapd-other-police-agencies-struggle-with-where-to-draw-the-line-with-political-extremism-in-their-ranks.

40 See Moustafa Bayoumi, "No, We Do Not Need New Anti-Terrorism Laws to Combat Right-Wing Extremists," *The Nation*, January 11, 2021. Online: https://www.the-nation.com/article/politics/capitol-domestic-terrorism/.

41 See Michael German, "Why New Laws Aren't Needed to Take Domestic Terrorism More Seriously," *Just Security*, December 14, 2018. Online: https://www.justsecurity.org/61876/laws-needed-domestic-terrorism/.

42 See Samantha Michaels, "A Road Map for Getting Rid of Racist Cops," *Mother Jones*, January 28, 2021. Online: https://www.motherjones.com/crime-justice/2021/01/a-road-map-for-getting-rid-of-racist-cops/.

43 See Kevin Rector and Richard Winton, "Law enforcement confronts an old threat: far-right extremism in the ranks. 'Swift action must be taken'," *The Los Angeles Times*,

February 17, 2021. Online: https://www.latimes.com/california/story/2021-02-17/lapd-other-police-agencies-struggle-with-where-to-draw-the-line-with-political-extremism-in-their-ranks.

44   See Vida B. Johnson, "KKK in the PD: White Supremacist Police and What to Do About It," *Lewis & Clark Law Review*, Vol. 23:1, April 1, 2019. Online: https://perma.cc/94GX-VP9P.

45   See David Neiwert, "Deeper examination of Oath Keepers' member data finds hundreds of law enforcement officers," *Daily Kos*, September 7, 2022. Online: https://www.dailykos.com/stories/2022/9/7/2121426/-Deeper-examination-of-Oath-Keepers-member-data-finds-hundreds-of-law-enforcement-officers.

46   See Will Carless, Grace Hauck, and Erin Mansfield, "Hack exposes law enforcement officers who signed up to join anti-government Oath Keepers," *USA Today*, October 2, 2021. Online: https://www.usatoday.com/story/news/nation/2021/10/02/oath-keepers-hack-exposes-law-enforcement-officers-across-us/5949281001/.

47   See Ken Bensinger, Jessica Garrison, and Christopher Miller, "Hacked Oath Keepers Records Show Active Members Of Law Enforcement And The Military Tried To Join The Group After Jan. 6," *BuzzFeed News*, October 1, 2021. Online: https://www.buzzfeednews.com/article/kenbensinger/oath-keepers-hacked-emails.

48   See Christopher Mathias, "He Marched At The Nazi Rally In Charlottesville. Then He Went Back To Being A Cop," *Huffpost*, October 13, 2022. Online: https://www.huffpost.com/entry/john-donnelly-police-officer-charlottesville-white-suprema-cist-woburn-massachusetts_n_634856a1e4b08e0e60812d63.

Chapter 12: Going Local

1   See David Neiwert, "Proud Boys come creeping back out of the woodwork, one hijacked local event at a time," *Daily Kos*, July 30, 2021. Online: https://www.dailykos.com/stories/2021/7/30/2043006/-Post-insurrection-strategy-for-Proud-Boys-manifests-Aim-for-local-controversies-hijack-them.

2   See David Neiwert, "Bitter about being abandoned by Trump, Proud Boys' chats reveal preparations for 'absolute war'," *Daily Kos*, May 18, 2021. Online: https://www.dailykos.com/stories/2021/5/18/2031008/-Bitter-about-being-abandoned-by-Trump-Proud-Boys-chats-reveal-preparations-for-absolute-war.

3   See Tess Owen, "Proud Boys Crashed School Board Meetings to Protest Critical Race Theory," *Vice*, July 29, 2021. Online: https://www.vice.com/en/article/dyvk7a/masked-proud-boys-show-up-at-a-school-board-meeting-to-protest-critical-race-theory.

4   See Joshua Ceballos, "Video: Miami Police Chief Clashes With Proud Boys Member at Cuba Protest," *Miami New Times*, July 14, 2021. Online: https://www.miaminew-times.com/news/at-sos-cuba-protest-miami-police-chief-butts-heads-with-proud-boys-12526624.

5   See Kimberly Houghton, "Nashua school officials voice concerns over Proud Boy presence," *New Hampshire Union-Leader*, July 28, 2021. Online: https://www.union-leader.com/news/local/nashua-school-officials-voice-concerns-over-proud-boy-presence/article_232c9519-849f-5d4c-a4a8-c587d86fe6a4.html.

6   See Zac Ezzone, "Far-right group Participates in Buhl Sagebrush Days parade," *Magic Valley News*, July 11, 2021. Online: https://magicvalley.com/news/local/

govt-and-politics/far-right-group-participates-in-buhl-sagebrush-days-parade/
article_45c46c10-a41b-5056-b74e-0436ff88d032.html.

7 See Joshua Ceballos, "Video: Miami Police Chief Clashes With Proud Boys Member
at Cuba Protest," *Miami New Times*, July 14, 2021. Online: https://www.miaminew-
times.com/news/at-sos-cuba-protest-miami-police-chief-butts-heads-with-proud-
boys-12526624. See also Laura Cassels, Danielle J. Brown and Isaac Morgan, "Proud
Boys, other groups, rally at FL's Old Capitol to demand release of "patriots" from
Jan. 6 insurrection," *Florida Phoenix*, July 10, 2021. Online: https://floridaphoenix.
com/2021/07/10/proud-boys-other-groups-rally-at-fl-capitol-to-demand-release-
of-patriots-from-jan-6-insurrection/.

8 See David Neiwert, "Proud Boys come creeping back out of the woodwork,
one hijacked local event at a time," *Daily Kos*, July 30, 2021. Online: https://
www.dailykos.com/stories/2021/7/30/2043006/-Post-insurrection-strategy-for-
Proud-Boys-manifests-Aim-for-local-controversies-hijack-them.

9 See Chris Busby, "Proud Boys in Maine Meeting at Portland Dive Bar," *The Mainer
News*, July 20, 2021. Online: https://mainernews.com/proud-boys-in-maine-meet-
ing-at-portland-dive-bar/.

10 See David Neiwert, "Downtown Portland again plagued by invasion of Proud Boys
attached to 'Christian' anti-maskers," *Daily Kos*, August 9, 2021. Online: https://
www.dailykos.com/stories/2021/8/9/2044764/-Proud-Boys-follow-their-new-
script-by-using-Portland-anti-mask-rallies-to-crank-up-fresh-violence.

11 See Zane Sparling, "Left-, right-wing groups clash at rally in downtown Portland,"
The Portland Tribune, August 7, 2021. Online: https://www.portlandtribune.com/
news/left--right-wing-groups-clash-at-rally-in-downtown-portland/article_
b00860c5-887a-580d-9788-5d6c4122fd04.html.

12 See Sergio Olmos, "A man walking around downtown with an AR-15 with a sup-
pressor aims his weapon at journalist," Twitter, August 9, 2021. Online: https://twit-
ter.com/MrOlmos/status/1424638472858443776.

13 See Gabriella Borter, Joseph Ax, and Joseph Tantani, "School boards get death
threats amid rage over race, gender, mask policies," Reuters, February 15, 2022. Online: https://www.reuters.com/investigates/special-report/usa-education-threats/.

14 See David Badash, "'We will kill' your mother 'but first we will kill you!': Hundreds of threats of violence sent to school board members," *Raw Story*, February
16, 2022. Online: https://www.rawstory.com/we-will-your-mother-but-first-we-
will-you-hundreds-of-threats-of-violence-sent-to-school-board-members/.

15 See Gabriella Borter, Joseph Ax, and Joseph Tantani, "School boards get death
threats amid rage over race, gender, mask policies," Reuters, February 15, 2022. Online: https://www.reuters.com/investigates/special-report/usa-education-threats/.

16 See "Mendon man arrested following disturbance at school board meeting," *The
Herald-Whig*, September 2, 2021. Online: https://www.whig.com/news/illinois-
news/mendon-man-arrested-following-disturbance-at-school-board-meeting/ar-
ticle_c3f877ee-0c29-11ec-9275-1b143d1c3783.html.

17 See Aaron Rupar, "Anti-mask hysterics at Tennessee school board meeting show
how basic public health is now polarizing," *Vox*, August 11, 2021. Online: https://
www.vox.com/2021/8/11/22620254/williamson-county-school-board-meeting-
franklin-tennessee-mask-mandate.

18 See Tyler Kingkade, Brandy Zadrozny, and Ben Collins, "Critical race theory battle
invades school boards—with help from conservative groups," NBC News, June 15,

2021. Online: https://www.nbcnews.com/news/us-news/critical-race-theory-in-vades-school-boards-help-conservative-groups-n1270794.

19 See David Neiwert, "When Proud Boys show up at local school protests, they're following a larger far-right blueprint," *Daily Kos*, September 9, 2021. Online: https://www.dailykos.com/stories/2021/9/9/2051322/-School-boards-have-become-the-latest-target-in-far-right-s-Proud-Boys-led-assault-on-democracy.

20 See Peter Montgomery, "The Right-Wing Political Machine Is Out to Take Over School Boards by Fanning Fears of Critical Race Theory," *Right Wing Watch*, August 6, 2021. Online: https://www.rightwingwatch.org/post/the-right-wing-political-machine-is-out-to-take-over-school-boards-by-fanning-fears-of-critical-race-theory/.

21 See Eric Griffey, "Conservative groups are training activists to swarm school board meetings," *Spectrum Local News*, July 22, 2021. Online: https://spectrumlocalnews.com/tx/south-texas-el-paso/politics/2021/07/21/conservative-groups-are-training-activists-to-swarm-school-board-meetings-.

22 See Tyler Kingkade, Brandy Zadrozny, and Ben Collins, "Critical race theory battle invades school boards — with help from conservative groups," NBC News, June 15, 2021. Online: https://www.nbcnews.com/news/us-news/critical-race-theory-invades-school-boards-help-conservative-groups-n1270794.

23 See "School board recalls," Ballotopedia. Online: https://ballotpedia.org/School_board_recalls.

24 See Jonathan Zimmerman, "Why the Culture Wars in Schools Are Worse Than Ever Before," *Politico*, September 19, 2021. Online: https://www.politico.com/news/magazine/2021/09/19/history-culture-wars-schools-america-divided-512614.

25 See Thomas Beaumont and Stephen Groves, "Tea party 2.0? Conservatives get organized in school battles," Associated Press, August 31, 2021. Online: https://apnews.com/article/business-health-coronavirus-pandemic-3157002e9d011e5283f55886b-1c7078a.

26 See National School Boards Association letter to President, September 29, 2021. Online: https://www.documentcloud.org/documents/21094557-national-school-boards-association-letter-to-biden.

27 See "Justice Department Addresses Violent Threats Against School Officials and Teachers," U.S. Department of Justice press release, October 4, 2021. Online: https://www.justice.gov/opa/pr/justice-department-addresses-violent-threats-against-school-officials-and-teachers.

28 See David N. Bass, "Republicans denounce task force for chiding parents over school board meetings," *The Carolina Journal*, October 14, 2021. Online: https://www.carolinajournal.com/republicans-denounce-task-force-for-chiding-parents-over-school-board-meetings/.

29 See Caroline Downey, "Hawley Calls for Merrick Garland to Resign over FBI School-Board Memo," *National Review*, October 23, 2021. Online: https://www.nationalreview.com/news/hawley-calls-for-merrick-garland-to-resign-over-fbi-school-board-memo/.

30 See Arianna Figueroa, "GOP lawmakers push back against federal probe into threats against school board members," *Virginia Mercury*, October 8, 2021. Online: https://www.virginiamercury.com/2021/10/08/gop-lawmakers-push-back-against-federal-probe-into-threats-against-school-board-members/.

31 See Jeff Bryant, "The Proud Boys Are Coming for Public Schools," *The Progressive*, October 19, 2021. Online: https://progressive.org/public-schools-advocate/proud-boys-coming-public-schools-bryant-211019/.

32 See Elle Kehres, "Proud Boys' Presence Leads to Metal Detectors, Deputies at School Board Meetings," Chapelbro.com, October 12, 2021. Online: https://chapelboro.com/news/pre-k-12-education/proud-boys-presence-leads-to-metal-detectors-deputies-at-school-board-meetings.

33 See Will Carless, "With Trump in the rearview mirror, Proud Boys offer muscle at rallies against vaccine mandates, masks," *USA Today*, September 8, 2021. Online: https://www.usatoday.com/story/news/nation/2021/09/08/proud-boys-join-protests-against-covid-vaccine-mandates-masks/5703785001/.

34 See David Neiwert, "A rural school board election manifests far-right strategy to spread their politics of intimidation," *Daily Kos*, January 10, 2022. Online: https://www.dailykos.com/stories/2022/1/10/2073893/-A-rural-school-board-election-manifests-far-right-strategy-to-spread-their-politics-of-intimidation.

35 See David Neiwert, "Far-right 'Patriots' lining up to defend Matt Shea, their man in the Washington Legislature," *Daily Kos*, January 11, 2020. Online: https://www.dailykos.com/stories/2020/1/11/1910065/-Far-right-Patriots-lining-up-to-defend-Matt-Shea-their-man-in-the-Washington-Legislature.

36 See "Matthew Marshall," Ballotopedia. Online: https://ballotpedia.org/Matthew_Marshall.

37 See David Neiwert, "The far right wants to make its shared 'Boogaloo' fantasy of violent civil war a reality," *Daily Kos*, April 28, 2020. Online: https://www.dailykos.com/stories/2020/4/28/1940542/-The-far-right-wants-to-make-its-shared-Boogaloo-fantasy-of-violent-civil-war-a-reality.

38 See David Neiwert, "Far-right protest rally gets pranked by Sacha Baron Cohen performing a racist singalong," *Daily Kos*, June 29, 2020. Online: https://www.dailykos.com/stories/2020/6/29/1956966/-Far-right-protest-rally-gets-pranked-by-Sacha-Baron-Cohen-performing-a-racist-singalong.

39 See David Neiwert, "Washington's far right exposes names, info of lockdown informants, and a flood of threats follow," *Daily Kos*, May 11, 2020. Online: https://www.dailykos.com/stories/2020/5/11/1944309/-Washington-s-far-right-exposes-names-info-of-lockdown-informants-and-a-flood-of-threats-follow.

40 See David Neiwert, "Three Percent takeover of Whidbey Island Grange shows how proto-fascist forces creep into mainstream," *Daily Kos*, December 14, 2020. Online: https://www.dailykos.com/stories/2020/12/14/2001995/-III-er-takeover-of-Whidbey-Island-Grange-shows-how-proto-fascist-forces-creep-into-mainstream.

41 See Hannah Allam, "A rural Washington school board race shows how far-right extremists are shifting to local power," *The Washington Post*, January 8, 2022. Online: https://www.washingtonpost.com/national-security/2022/01/08/far-right-school-boards/.

42 See Lisa Lerer and Astead W. Herndon, "Menace Enters the Republican Mainstream," *The New York Times*, November 16, 2021. Online: https://www.nytimes.com/2021/11/12/us/politics/republican-violent-rhetoric.html.

43 See David Neiwert, "For mainstream liberals in rural America, daily life involves dealing with far-right intimidation," *Daily Kos*, December 20, 2021. Online: https://www.dailykos.com/stories/2021/12/20/2070366/-In-rural-precincts-right-wing-extremists-wage-a-campaign-of-intimidation-against-the-mainstream.

44 See Madison Hardy, "Protesters target teen library patrons," *The Coeur d'Alene Press*, December 1, 2021. Online: https://cdapress.com/news/2021/dec/01/not-all-sunshine-and-rainbows/.

45 See Amber B. Dodd, "After teens going to an LGBTQ library group were met with protesters in North Idaho, a debate has erupted about the region's political climate," *The Spokesman-Review*, December 16, 2021. Online: https://www.spokesman.com/stories/2021/dec/16/after-teens-going-to-an-lgbtq-library-group-were-m/.

46 See Lisa Lerer and Astead W. Herndon, "Menace Enters the Republican Mainstream," *The New York Times*, November 16, 2021. Online: https://www.nytimes.com/2021/11/12/us/politics/republican-violent-rhetoric.html.

47 See Adam Harris, "School Boards Are No Match for America's Political Dysfunction," *The Atlantic*, April 27, 2022. Online: https://www.theatlantic.com/politics/archive/2022/04/parents-partisan-school-board-meeting-covid/629669/.

48 See Rebekah Sager, "California recall race bellwether of far-right militia groups pivoting from fringe to local politics," *Daily Kos*, February 3, 2022. Online: https://www.dailykos.com/stories/2022/2/3/2078234/-Milita-groups-pivot-targeting-school-boards-county-seats-A-bellwether-of-more-extremism-to-come.

49 See Scot Shafer, "A Militia-Led Recall Is Targeting a Shasta County Supervisor—Who's a Republican," KQED-FM, January 28, 2022. Online: https://www.kqed.org/news/11902718/militia-led-recall-targets-republican-supervisor-in-shasta-county.

50 See Adam Harris, "School Boards Are No Match for America's Political Dysfunction," *The Atlantic*, April 27, 2022. Online: https://www.theatlantic.com/politics/archive/2022/04/parents-partisan-school-board-meeting-covid/629669/.

51 See David Neiwert, "The creep of QAnon: A small Puget Sound town feels the political effects of authoritarian cult," *Daily Kos*, January 27, 2021. Online: https://www.dailykos.com/stories/2021/1/27/2012401/-The-creep-of-QAnon-A-small-Puget-Sound-town-feels-the-political-effects-of-authoritarian-cult.

52 See Sasha Abramsky, "The Town That QAnon Nearly Swallowed," *The Nation*, February 21, 2022. Online: https://www.thenation.com/article/politics/sequim-qanon/.

Postscript: The Echoes of History

1 See Thomas P. Slaughter, *The Whiskey Rebellion: Frontier Epilogue to the American Revolution* (Oxford: Oxford University Press, 1998). Online sample: https://books.google.com/books?id=jEsrDwAAQBAJ. See also: Wythe Holt, "The Whiskey Rebellion of 1794: A Democratic Working-Class Insurrection," University of Georgia, January 6, 2004 (presented on January 23, 2004 at the "Georgia Workshop in Early American History and Culture"). Online: https://web.archive.org/web/20110925091324/http://www.uga.edu/colonialseminar/whiskeyrebellion-6.pdf.

2 See Ron Chernow, *Alexander Hamilton* (New York: Penguin Books, 2004), pp. 718-19.

3 See Thomas J. Craughwell and M. William Phelps, *Failures of the Presidents: From the Whiskey Rebellion and War of 1812 to the Bay of Pigs and War in Iraq.* (Beverly, MA: Fair Winds Press, 2008). p. 22

4 See Franita Tolson, "Op-Ed: Why the mob thought attacking the Capitol was their '1776 moment'," *The Los Angeles Times*, Jan. 21, 2021. Online: https://www.latimes.com/opinion/story/2021-01-21/insurrection-capitol-attack-patriotism-1776.

5 See Blake Montgomery, "Rush Limbaugh Likens Capitol Rioters to Founding Fathers," *The Daily Beast*, January 7, 2021. Online: https://www.thedailybeast.com/

rush-limbaugh-likens-capitol-rioters-to-founding-fathers-dismisses-concerns-over-pro-trump-violence.

6 See Robert D. McFadden and Michael M. Grynbaum, "Rush Limbaugh Dies at 70; Turned Talk Radio Into a Right-Wing Attack Machine," *The New York Times*, February 17, 2021. Online: https://www.nytimes.com/2021/02/17/business/media/rush-limbaugh-dead.html.

7 See "One Year Since the Jan. 6 Attack on the Capitol," U.S. Department of Justice press release, January 6, 2022. Online: https://www.justice.gov/usao-dc/one-year-jan-6-attack-capitol.

8 See Kyle Cheney and Josh Gerstein, "Prosecutors seek a slowdown in Capitol attack cases, calling probe the 'most complex' in history," *Politico*, March 12, 2021. Online: https://www.politico.com/news/2021/03/12/prosecutors-capitol-riot-investigation-475505.

9 See "Capitol Breach Cases," U.S. Department of Justice database. Online: https://www.justice.gov/usao-dc/capitol-breach-cases.

10 See Tess Owen, "Capitol Rioters in Jail's 'Patriot Wing' Have Their Own Rituals and a Growing Fan Base," *Vice*, October 21, 2021. Online: https://www.vice.com/en/article/akvwjp/january-6-rioters-jailed-together-forming-rituals-fanbase.

11 See Tess Owen, "How the GOP Is Turning Capitol Rioters Into 'Political Prisoners'," *Vice*, August 2, 2021. Online: https://www.vice.com/en/article/g5gkkb/how-the-gop-is-turning-capitol-rioters-into-political-prisoners.

12 See Media Matters staff, "Tucker Carlson calls jailed insurrectionists 'political prisoners'," Media Matters, July 8, 2021. Online: https://www.mediamatters.org/fox-news/tucker-carlson-calls-jailed-insurrectionists-political-prisoners.

13 See Andrea Salcedo, "A former police officer arrested after the Jan. 6 riot was told to stay away from guns. He bought 34, feds say," *The Washington Post*, July 2, 2021. Online: https://www.washingtonpost.com/nation/2021/07/02/thomas-robertson-cop-arsenal-weapons-capitolriot/.

14 See Spencer S. Hsu, "Former Va. officer convicted on all counts in the 2nd Jan. 6 jury trial," *The Washingtion Post*, April 11, 2022. Online: https://www.washingtonpost.com/dc-md-va/2022/04/11/robertson-jan6-guilty-trial/.

15 See Karen Yourish, Danielle Ivory, Aaron Byrd, Weiyi Cai, Nick Corasaniti, Meg Felling, Rumsey Taylor and Jonathan Weisman, "Over 370 Republican Candidates Have Cast Doubt on the 2020 Election," *The New York Times*, October 13, 2022. Online: https://www.nytimes.com/interactive/2022/10/13/us/politics/republican-candidates-2020-election-misinformation.html.

16 See David Neiwert, "Election denialists could wreak havoc by electing secretaries of state in key battleground states," *Daily Kos*, October 10, 2022. Online: https://www.dailykos.com/stories/2022/10/10/2128157/-Election-denialists-could-wreak-havoc-by-electing-secretaries-of-state-in-key-battleground-states,

17 See David Neiwert, "Right-wing pundits, poohbahs reach for the Copium after their 'red tsunami' fails to materialize," *Daily Kos*, November 9, 2022. Online: https://www.dailykos.com/stories/2022/11/9/2134913/-Right-wing-pundits-poohbahs-reach-for-the-Copium-after-their-red-tsunami-fails-to-materialize.

18 See David Neiwert, "Kari Lake refuses to 'back down' in Arizona, then promptly heads to Mar-a-Lago to court Trump," *Daily Kos*, November 18, 2022. Online: https://m.dailykos.com/stories/2022/11/18/2137137/-Kari-Lake-s-refusal-to-concede-Arizona-loss-may-j.

19 See Karen Yourish, Danielle Ivory, Weiyi Cai and Ashley Wu, "See Which 2020 Election Deniers and Skeptics Won and Lost in the Midterm Elections," *The New York Times*, November 10, 2022. Online: https://www.nytimes.com/interactive/2022/11/09/us/politics/election-misinformation-midterms-results.html.

20 See David Neiwert, "Midterms held back the election denialists, but they gained a foothold and they're not going away," *Daily Kos*, November 16, 2022. Online: https://www.dailykos.com/stories/2022/11/16/2136645/-Midterms-held-back-the-election-denialists-but-they-gained-a-foothold-and-they-re-not-going-away.

21 See Hannah Gais and Michael Edison Hayden, "White Nationalists, Other Republicans Brace for 'Total War'," *Hatewatch* (SPLC), December 11, 2022.

22 See David Neiwert, "Lindsay leads anti-LGBTQ hate parade at TPUSA's annual gathering, with large supporting cast," *Daily Kos*, December 20, 2022. Online: https://www.dailykos.com/stories/2022/12/20/2143019/-TPUSA-s-big-confab-brings-Republicans-far-right-extremists-together-to-spew-anti-LGBTQ-hate.

23 See David Neiwert, "'Are we at war?' Bannon exhorts TPUSA's 'awakened army' to 'take this to its ultimate conclusion'," *Daily Kos*, December 23, 2022. Online: https://www.dailykos.com/stories/2022/12/23/2143504/--Are-we-at-war-Bannon-exhorts-TPUSA-s-awakened-army-to-take-this-to-its-ultimate-conclusion.

24 See Tim Miller, "I Spent Insurrection Week Listening to Steve Bannon," *The Bulwark*, January 10, 2022. Online: https://www.thebulwark.com/i-spent-insurrection-week-listening-to-steve-bannon/.

25 See Bruce DePuyt, "Jan. 6 report will lay out the 'continuing' danger facing the U.S., Raskin says," *Maryland Matters*, December 9, 2022. Online: https://www.maryland-matters.org/2022/12/09/jan-6-report-will-lay-out-the-continuing-danger-facing-the-u-s-raskin-says/.

26 See *Final Report: Select Committee to Investigate the January 6th Attack on the United States Capitol*, December 2022. Online: https://int.nyt.com/data/documenttools/january-6-committee-final-report/2095325cbebd8378/full.pdf.

27 See Melissa Morgan, "The Legacy of January 6," Stanford FSI News, January 5, 2022. Online: https://fsi.stanford.edu/news/legacies-january-6,

Bibliography

Aho, James. *The Politics of Righteousness: Idaho Christian Patriotism.* Seattle: University of Washington Press, 1990.

Aho, James. *This Thing of Darkness: A Sociology of the Enemy.* Seattle: University of Washington Press, 1994.

Altemeyer, Robert. *The Authoritarians.* Winnipeg: University of Manitoba Press, 2004.

Ben-Giat, Ruth. *Strongmen: Mussolini to the Present.* New York: W.W. Norton and Company, 2020.

Campbell, Andy. *We Are Proud Boys: How a Right-Wing Streety Gang Ushered in a New Era of American Extremism.* New York: Hatchette Books, 2022.

Griffin, Roger. *The Nature of Fascism.* New York: Routledge, 1993.

Griffin, Roger. *Fascism (Key Concepts in Political Theory).* London: Polity, 2018.

Hetherington, Marc J., and Weiler, Jonathan D. *Authoritarianism and Polarization in American Politics.* New York: Cambridge University Press, 2009.

Hermansson, Patrik; Lawrence, David; Mulhall, Joe; and Murdoch, Simon. *The International Alt-Right: Fascism for the 21st Century?* New York: Routledge, 2020.

Jackson, Sam. *Oath Keepers: Patriotism and the Edge of Violence in a Right-Wing Antigovernment Group.* New York: Columbia University Press, 2020.

Johnson, Daryl. *Right-Wing Resurgence: How a Domestic Terrorism Threat is Being Ignored.* Lanham, MD: Rowman and Littlefield, 2012.

Lavin, Talia. *Culture Warlords: My Journey Into the Dark Web of White Supremacy.* New York: Hatchette Books, 2020.

Levitas, Daniel. *The Terrorist Next Door: The Militia Movement and the Radical Right.* New York: Thomas Dunne Books, 2002.

Merlan, Anna. *Republic of Lies: American Conspiracy Theorists and Their*

Surprising Rise to Power. New York: Henry Holt and Co., 2019.

Paxton, Robert O. *The Anatomy of Fascism.* New York: Alfred A. Knopf, 2004.

Reid, Shannon E., and Valasik, Matthew. *Alt-Right Gangs: A Hazy Shade of White.* Berkeley: University of California Press, 2020.

Rothschild, Mike. *The Storm is Upon Us: How QAnon Became a Movement, Cult, and Conspiracy Theory of Everything.* Brooklyn: Melville House, 2021.

Sargent, Greg. *An Uncivil War: Taking Back Our Democracy in an Age of Trumpian Disinformation and Thunderdome Politics.* New York, Custom House, 2018.

Stewart, Katherine. *The Power Worshippers: Inside the Dangerous Rise of Religious Nationalism.* New York: Bloomsbury, 2019.

Wendling, Mike. *Alt-Right: From 4chan to the White House.* London: Pluto Press, 2018.

Zeskind, Leonard. *Blood and Politics: The History of the White Nationalist Movement From the Margins to the Mainstream.* New York: Farrar, Straus and Giroux, 2009.

Acknowledgements

FOR A JOURNALIST WHO writes daily about the rise of right-wing extremism in America, assembling a sprawling and wide-ranging project like this can be something akin to a large jigsaw puzzle: Each day's reportage is like a single piece of the puzzle, so creating a comprehensive picture of the problem—especially when so many of the storylines intersect—entails figuring out how to get them all to fit together into a coherent whole, one that makes the larger picture and all of its details equally clear, so that everyday readers can better understand the depth and scope of the threat to American democracy the insurrectionist right represents.

So much of *The Age of Insurrection* is built from the pieces of my reportage over the past six years, woven into a whole quilt that, I hope, is greater than the sum of its parts. Readers already familiar with my work may recognize some its passages from my reports for the progressive news site *Daily Kos* and, before that, the Southern Poverty Law Center's *Hatewatch* site. Nonetheless, it also contains fresh details I've not previously reported, and moreover offers a cohesive narrative—a whole portrait, as it were, rather than just an assemblage of piecemeal work.

Thus, the people who to whom I am most indebted for making this book possible are my editors and colleagues: At *Daily Kos,* managing editor Barb Morrill has helped keep me focused on the subject and guided my reportage along the way, while a number of colleagues have provided essential journalistic (and collegial) support, including Joan McCarter, Laura Clawson, Brandi Buchman, Mark Sumner, Michael "Hunter" Lazarro, Kerry Eleveld, and Walter Einenkel. At *Hatewatch,* then-managing editor Susy Buchanan was my indispensable guide, while I owe a lasting debt to my colleagues there: Heidi Beirich, Ryan Lenz, Laurie Wood, Josh Glasstetter, Mark Potok, Nick Martin, Evelyn Schlatter, and Alex Amend.

I especially owe a lifelong debt to my late SPLC colleague Bill Morlin, who left us unexpectedly last year. Bill was the model of a gumshoe reporter who worked the beat and was unfailingly rigorous about facts and details, but also never lost sight of the far-right forest growing around us during his decades at the Spokane *Spokesman-Review.* He was already something of a legend when I first met him in 1996 while covering the Montana Freemen standoff out in windswept Jordan, but I was honored to have Bill as a mentor in the ensuing years, and then to have eight years working together as the SPLC's Northwest contingent. This book's attention to detail and fealty to factuality are, I hope, reflective of Bill's mentorship.

I'm also indebted to the Southern Poverty Law Center's current staff of researchers and reporters, who keep forging ahead with fresh revelations and insights and are doing the hard work of shining a light on global extremism, especially Cassie Miller, Michael Edison Hayden, Hannah Gais, Jeff Tischauser, Megan Squire, and Creede Newton. I owe a particularly deep debt to the SPLC's Jason Wilson, who often had my back (as I had his) while we both were covering Proud Boys events that often devolved into street violence in the Pacific Northwest.

Likewise, I have leaned heavily over the years on the work of the Anti-Defamation League's team of researchers, including Senior Research Fellow Mark Pitcavage; Oren Segal, vice president of the Center on Extremism; and the center's inestimable staff. Another invaluable resource for two decades has been Brian Levin, director of the Center for Hate and Extremism at California State University-San Bernardino. Eric Ward, executive director of the Western States Center in Portland, is also a longtime friend and colleague in research, and his staff at the WSC has also provided invaluable input, particularly Stephen Piggott (also a former SPLC colleague) and Lindsay Schubiner. Likewise, I have long been indebted to the research of Devin Burghart and Chuck Tanner of the Institute for Research and Education on Human Rights.

A number of academic and activist researchers have also provided key insights and resources for my work over the years, including three based in the Portland area: Alexander Reid Ross, Spencer Sunshine, and Shane Burley. I'm also continually indebted to the research of Carolyn Orr Bueno of the University of Maryland; Jared Holt of the Center for Strategic Dialogue; Ruth Ben-Ghiat of New York University; Dr. Cynthia Miller-Idriss of American University's Polarization and Extremism Research Lab; Kate Starbird of the University of Washington; Alex Newhouse, deputy director of the Center on Terrorism, Extremism, and Counterterrorism; Samantha Kutner of the Advancing Research on Conflict (ARC) Consortium; Ben Lorber, senior research analyst for Political Research Associates; Juliet Jeske of Decoding Fox News. I've also found a number of antifascist researchers to be reliable (and amiable) resources, including Molly Conger of Charlottesville, Virginia; Abner Häuge of Left Coast Right Watch; Redoubt Anitfascists; Alissa Azar of Portland; and a number of others whose preference is for anonymity.

I'm especially grateful to the new generation of younger journalists who are making coverage of right-wing extremism the dedicated beat it needs to be (or at least incorporating it regularly into their work), as with any phenomenon that poisons the national well and threatens democracy. People like Leah Sottile of High Country News; Tess Owen of Vice; Andy Campbell and Christopher Mathias of Huffpost; Talia Lavin of *The New Yorker*; Will Sommer and Kelly Weill of *The Daily Beast*; Will Carless of *USA Today*; Robert Evans of *Bellingcat*; and Brandy Zadrozny and Ben Collins of NBC News. They've helped inspire this aging newshound by opening up fresh vistas of coverage—all too necessary in an era of metastasizing extremism.

And despite losing Bill, there are a still a few old newshounds out there working this beat from time to time, and their contributions are important: Marcy Wheeler, freelancing at emptywheel.com; Will Bunch of *The Philadelphia Inquirer*; and my longtime friend, Hal Bernton of *The Seattle Times*.

Last but not least, I couldn't have made it through this project without the loving support of my family—my wife of 33 years, Lisa Dowling, and my son Devin—and my growing circle of friends on our semi-remote island. You all know who you are.